UNIVERSITY CASEBOOK SERIES®

TRANSNATIONAL BUSINESS PROBLEMS

SIXTH EDITION

DETLEV F. VAGTS
Late Bemis Professor of Law
Harvard University

WILLIAM S. DODGE
Martin Luther King, Jr. Professor of Law and
John D. Ayer Chair of Business Law
University of California, Davis
School of Law

HANNAH L. BUXBAUM
John E. Schiller Chair in Legal Ethics
Indiana University
Maurer School of Law

HAROLD HONGJU KOH
Sterling Professor of International Law and
Former Dean of the Law School
Yale University

FOUNDATION
PRESS

University Casebook Series is a trademark registered in the U.S. Patent and Trademark Office.

© 1986, 1998, 2003 FOUNDATION PRESS
© 2008 By THOMSON REUTERS/FOUNDATION PRESS
© 2014 LEG, Inc. d/b/a West Academic
© 2019 LEG, Inc. d/b/a West Academic
     444 Cedar Street, Suite 700
     St. Paul, MN 55101
     1-877-888-1330

Printed in the United States of America

ISBN: 978-1-68328-652-3

PREFACE

Designing a coursebook for International Business Transactions presents a series of challenges. The field is broad and complex, potentially including almost any legal materials anywhere in the world. Within that universe, editors must choose, hoping that the selection gives the student a feel for the environments within which transnational business practice occurs and a fair sampling of issues that may arise. The materials included in this volume are intended to be representative, not comprehensive, and we have tried not to include more than might reasonably be covered in a one semester course. Teachers will come to these materials with different experiences and different approaches. Some will have dealt with licensing of copyrights in Africa, others with construction contracts in the Middle East. Some will have had an experience heavily involved with tax questions, others with antitrust or securities law. The structure of this book will readily permit them to substitute or add materials from their own experiences while relying on what is offered here for those matters beyond the range of their special expertise.

An ideal approach to transnational business problems would start with a basic knowledge of transnational law. One should not consider the details of making an investment in reliance on a bilateral investment treaty before one has a basic understanding of treaty law, both as an agreement between states subject to international law rules and as a source of law that will be applied directly to the investor. Similarly, the general international rules about expropriation must be understood before evaluating the risks of a specific transaction. Such a basic understanding could be derived from the course (and coursebook) Transnational Legal Problems, currently in its fourth edition, out of which this book grew. Alternatively, it could be derived from a different course in international or transnational law. We have tried to edit the sixth edition of this book so that it can be used independent of any prior background in transnational law, at some sacrifice of depth. Chapter III is designed to provide a modest background if that is needed.

Part One, the reader will note, is devoted to some rather general aspects of the environments within which international business transactions take place. Part Two takes up a series of hypothetical, but fairly typical, proposed transactions. In most cases we have tried to give a focus to the problem by presenting a sample document. It is our judgment that such documents bring a transaction's legal issues into focus in a way that cannot be matched by more abstract presentation. As any practitioner knows, forms are dangerous, particularly when they are used with faith rather than skepticism. That is particularly true of the forms in this volume, which have been designed for teaching purposes and contain provisions that may be problematic under the laws of one or more jurisdictions. Cases and other materials have been heavily edited, with omissions indicated by ellipses. Footnotes have generally been omitted; those retained have been renumbered. The materials generally reflect developments through December 2018.

WILLIAM S. DODGE

HANNAH L. BUXBAUM

HAROLD HONGJU KOH

Davis, California
Bloomington, Indiana
New Haven, Connecticut
January 2019

ACKNOWLEDGMENTS

The names of those to whom this book is in one way or another indebted are indeed legion. They include students in our classes from year to year who have pointed to issues and offered reactions. They also include colleagues who answered questions and suggested new directions for research. Our largest debt is to our friend and co-author Detlev F. Vagts, who shepherded this book through its first four editions and passed away in 2013. Detlev was an exemplary colleague and an international lawyer, scholar, and teacher of the first rank. Since this volume grew out of earlier editions of Transnational Legal Problems edited with Henry J. Steiner, it also owes much to him and to all those who contributed to the first three editions of that book in one way or another. And we acknowledge a debt to Milton Katz and Kingman Brewster, Jr., whose book The Law of International Transactions and Relations preceded the first edition of Transnational Legal Problems. Together, Professors Katz, Brewster, Steiner, and Vagts pioneered a transnational approach to law and business that we have tried to carry forward, individually and jointly. We can only hope to repay our intellectual debt to them by continuing their work.

With respect to the present edition, we are grateful for the comments, suggestions, and assistance of Susan Franck, Jessica Gillotte, Marc Korman, Xandra Kramer, Daniela Cuellar Muller, Julian Nyarko, Mark Schneider, and Fernando Fernandes Xavier among others. Last, but certainly not least, we would like to thank our families.

We gratefully acknowledge the permission extended by the following authors, publishers, and organizations to reprint excerpts from the sources indicated in parentheses after their names: American Law Institute (excerpts from the Restatement (Second) of Conflict of Laws (1971), the Restatement (Third) of Foreign Relations Law (1987), the Restatement (Fourth) of Foreign Relations Law (2018), and the Uniform Commercial Code); American Society of International Law (excerpts from the American Journal of International Law and International Legal Materials); Foreign Affairs (excerpt from Spar, The Spotlight and the Bottom Line, 77 For. Aff. 7 (Mar.–Apr. 1998)); International Chamber of Commerce (excerpts from Incoterms 2010 and the Uniform Customs and Practices for Documentary Credits (2007)); Oxford University Press (excerpt from Muchlinski, Multinational Enterprises and the Law (2d ed. 2007)); Armin Rosencranz (excerpts from Rosencranz, Divan & Noble, Environmental Law and Policy in India (1991)).

WILLIAM S. DODGE
HANNAH L. BUXBAUM
HAROLD HONGJU KOH

v

SUMMARY OF CONTENTS

TABLE OF CONTENTS

PART TWO. PROBLEM EXERCISES
IN TRANSNATIONAL BUSINESS

TABLE OF CASES

The principal cases are in bold type.

UNIVERSITY CASEBOOK SERIES®

TRANSNATIONAL BUSINESS PROBLEMS

SIXTH EDITION

PART ONE

THE ENVIRONMENTS OF TRANSNATIONAL BUSINESS

Part One introduces the student to the environments within which transnational business operations take place. It is preliminary to a more narrowly focused examination of concrete business transactions, which is the subject of Part Two.

In Chapter I, we look at the rules that govern and restrict the practice of law by lawyers in one state with respect to matters having significant contacts with other states. We then turn in Chapter II to consider various options for the resolution of transnational disputes, including domestic courts and international arbitration.

A brief introduction to transnational law is afforded in Chapter III, although a substantial number of students using this book will have already taken a course in Public International Law or Transnational Law. It does seem necessary that one approach this casebook with some awareness of treaties, customary international law, and the extraterritorial reach of domestic legal systems.

Chapter IV introduces the topic of corporate social responsibility. It begins with anticorruption efforts, focusing on the U.S. Foreign Corrupt Practices Act. It then describes the organization of multinational enterprises (MNEs) and some of the mechanisms for influencing their behavior, including voluntary codes of conduct and litigation in domestic courts.

CHAPTER I

TRANSNATIONAL LAWYERING

Lawyers who handle transnational business dealings operate in various contexts. Some are lawyers in large global law firms—often formed by mergers of multiple firms—that have offices in dozens of different countries and employ thousands of attorneys. Others serve in more localized firms, which may be large or small in size. There are some international boutiques, in the United States and in other countries, that specialize in serving the legal needs of foreigners. But quite a lot of transnational work falls into the hands of lawyers who have never before done any significant work of that type. The phenomenon of "globalization," however one defines it, has increased the incidence of transnational issues in all sorts of legal practice. Indeed, it is fair to say that every American lawyer practicing today should have at least a basic understanding of the transnational aspects of lawyering.

This chapter attempts to orient the student to the rules that govern international lawyers, both in the United States and abroad. Part A discusses the legal profession from a comparative perspective, noting certain aspects of the training and practice of lawyers that vary across legal systems. Part B introduces the rules that govern the cross-border practice of law, focusing on the American Bar Association's Model Rules of Professional Conduct. Part C turns to some specific ethical norms, describing the extent to which they may differ from country to country and highlighting the conflicts such differences present.

A. THE LAWYER'S ROLE IN DIFFERENT LEGAL SYSTEMS

Probably the first step in understanding the legal profession in any given country is to know the terms by which its members are designated and what those terms mean, particularly when the foreign profession is subdivided into different categories. In the United States, for example, the term "attorney at law" describes lawyers engaged in litigation as well as those engaged in transactional practice; in the United Kingdom, by contrast, "barrister" is used to describe the former, and "solicitor" the latter.

In the United States, "notary" refers to non-lawyers who serve the limited role of verifying the identity of persons executing documents. In Germany, France, Mexico and other civil law systems, however, the counterpart terms (*Notar*, *Notaire*, or *Notario*) stand for members of a profession whose educational qualifications may be the same as or fully equivalent to those of persons designated as lawyers or attorneys, but who serve special functions in certain types of transactions. (The confusion is such that California has forbidden notaries within its jurisdiction from advertising themselves as "*notarios*" because of the false impressions they were creating among Latino immigrants. Cal. Gov't Code § 8219.5.) Consider by way of contrast with the U.S. notary the following paragraphs about the German *Notar*:

> German civil law notaries play a key role in real estate law, the law of mortgages, the law of contracts, corporate law as well as family and succession law. Within the German system of "preventive justice" the civil law notaries' function is complementary to the role of a judge. The intervention of a notary is required by law in cases of important transactions with long-term effects and a particular economic or personal significance for the parties concerned. Such cases are, among others, the sale of land, the establishment of a mortgage, the incorporation of a limited liability company (GmbH) or a public limited company (Aktiengesellschaft), certain corporate share deals or asset deals and matrimonial property agreements.

> Civil law notaries act as independent, impartial and objective advisers to all parties to a transaction. They examine the intentions of the parties, draft the contracts and instruments necessary to carry out the intended transaction and ensure that the contractual provisions are in full compliance with the law. Civil law notaries also verify that the parties have full (mental and legal) capacity to enter into the intended agreement and that they have fully understood the legal implications of their commitment. Otherwise, the civil law notary is required by law to refuse his participation. The idea underlying this system is to establish a preventive legal control in order to avoid costly and time-consuming litigation about the validity and the meaning of contractual provisions in the aftermath of a transaction.[1]

When one has identified the classes of lawyers within the relevant jurisdiction, one should go on to ask some further questions about the profession there:

(1) What are the structures of the profession as a whole and of the groupings within the profession that in fact do the legal work? In some cases the bar is quite tightly organized and exerts a substantial amount of supervision over the activities of its members. It may for example be quite rigorous about terminating the status of members whose financial integrity has been proved lacking. It may insist on post-graduate training programs and attempt to maintain standards of professional expertise. Or it may do none of these things. Within the profession, there may be rampant individualism or collegial organization. Both poles are represented in the British professions. The largest firms of solicitors in London are indistinguishable in size and degree of specialization from their American counterparts. On the other hand, barristers were

---

[1]   www.bundesnotarkammer.de/en/admission.php.

traditionally expected to practice strictly as individuals, their collaboration with other barristers being limited to the sharing of modest support facilities. Elsewhere custom or rules have stood in the way of the growth of large firms on the American model.

(2) Rules and practices about entry to the legal profession tell us a good deal about its composition. Law schools differ substantially from the American model. In most civil law nations, law school is part of the university, and students enter the study of law coming at 18 or 19 years of age straight out of the *liceo, lycée,* or *Gymnasium,* which are roughly equivalent to high school. At least in the first years the classes are apt to be huge (some law schools enroll, at least nominally, some 15,000 students) and are conducted almost entirely by lecture. Later on the numbers may dwindle as students drop out or shift to other programs. There may be smaller classes and seminars. In the German system, academic study is capped by a period as clerk or *Referendar* during which the aspirant lawyer works for a judge and a lawyer or a government bureaucrat. There may be a general bar exam conducted not by the school but, as in the United States, by a government examining body. Thus the minimum guarantees of aptitude afforded by simple admission to the bar are seldom very reliable and in some cases are non-existent.

(3) Much attention has been devoted to the question of the number of lawyers in different societies, both in absolute terms and in relation to the population as a whole. It is not at all clear what relevance such figures have to the concerns of a lawyer trying to work on a specific task in a foreign country, although one may make some inference about the role of lawyers in that society from such statistics. Indeed the impetus behind these studies came largely from the political side, from proponents of the view that America is over-lawyered to the extent that its industrial competitiveness is diminished by the excessive costs of legal services, in particular of litigation. More careful studies show that the contrast between the number of lawyers in the United States and other countries has been much exaggerated and that there is a tendency of countries to move nearer the American proportions as they become more prosperous and industrialized.

B. THE RULES OF TRANSNATIONAL LEGAL PRACTICE

Characteristically lawyers are members of a bar that possesses a monopoly on the practice of law in a particular jurisdiction—which may be a national jurisdiction, or, as in the United States, a political sub-unit such as a state. How far that monopoly extends differs from jurisdiction to jurisdiction. Some countries have been quite open to the presence of foreign lawyers within their borders—for instance, permitting foreign firms to open offices where they practice domestic law (as long as the individual lawyers engaged in that practice have local qualifications), or permitting foreign firms to create partnerships that employ local lawyers. There may be certain restrictions on the spheres of activity open to foreigners; the right to appear in court, for example, is one that is commonly reserved to locals. And some countries have kept their borders completely closed to foreign lawyers. This has long been in the case in India. In general, then, the fact that one belongs to the bar of one jurisdiction does not automatically entitle one to practice in another. This situation of course presents enormous obstacles both to the individual lawyers and to the law firms engaged in transnational practice.

In recent years, the pace of liberalization in the market for legal services has accelerated. This is due in part to the General Agreement on Trade in Services (GATS), a multilateral treaty that grew out of the treaty creating the World Trade Organization. WTO members (as of January 2019, over 160 countries) have committed to liberalizing trade in services, and many have taken steps specifically intended to facilitate trade in legal services across borders. Germany, for instance, permits a limited practice for lawyers from all countries that are members of the World Trade Organization. *Bundesrechtsanwaltsordnung* §§ 206–209. The desire to remove barriers to trade in services within particular regions has also been a contributing factor. For example, a European Union directive mandates that each member state adopt rules liberalizing the regulation of lawyers from other EU members.[2] In each member state, lawyers from other European states may practice (subject to restrictions as to courtroom work) under their home country title, and may give advice "on the law of [the] home Member State, on Community law, on international law and on the law of the host Member State." Thus a Spanish *abogado* can work in Germany using that title. After three years in the country, a foreign lawyer may drop that title. And, of course, the possibility of reciprocal access to foreign markets motivates some countries to open their own.

Within the United States, several steps have been taken to loosen restrictions on practice by foreign lawyers. First, some states now allow foreign lawyers to sit for their bar examinations without completing a full three-year course of study in the United States. They may require candidates to have completed a one-year LL.M. program at a U.S. law school, but may also accept candidates who have met other specified requirements. By way of this path, many foreign lawyers have become fully licensed to practice law within the United States. Second, in most states, foreign lawyers may alternatively be licensed to practice as "foreign legal consultants" without taking a bar examination. New York adopted the first such rule in 1974. N.Y. Court of Appeals Rules Part 521. Under this rule, such a legal consultant may give advice about her own country's law and may even advise clients on New York and U.S. law if based upon advice from a regular member of the New York Bar. Legal consultants are subject to discipline by the New York Bar in the same

---

[2]   Directive 98/5/EC of the European Parliament and of the Council of 16 February 1998 to facilitate practice of the profession of lawyer on a permanent basis in a Member State other than that in which the qualification was obtained, 1998 O.J. (L 77) 36.

manner as other attorneys. Although the ABA has approved a Model Rule for the Licensing of Foreign Legal Consultants, state laws vary widely. Third, foreign lawyers may be permitted to perform work in a particular jurisdiction on a temporary basis. For instance, it has long been customary to allow members of other bars to appear by leave of the court, *pro hac vice*, in a particular lawsuit. It has also been generally regarded as legitimate for lawyers who are not licensed in a particular state to represent a party in an international arbitration being held there.[3] And more recently, a number of states have adopted a temporary practice rule (also known as "fly in, fly out," or FIFO) aimed at transactional lawyers. These states permit not only lawyers from other U.S. states (as in the ABA's Model Rule 5.5(c), below) but also foreign lawyers to render legal services of limited scope, provided that they meet certain requirements and do not establish permanent offices in the state. These rules typically authorize services that are performed for a client in the lawyer's home country, are related to a matter arising in that country, or are governed by foreign or international law.[4]

Nevertheless, plenty of gray areas remain regarding the latitude of lawyers to serve clients in other jurisdictions. Presumably a lawyer could consult with a client in state X by telephone from an office in state Y—or by writing a letter, email, or fax. What about taking a trip to the client's state to consult more personally face to face? In El Gemayel v. Seaman, 533 N.E.2d 245 (N.Y. 1988), a Lebanese lawyer who made phone calls to a New York client and traveled once to New York in connection with child custody proceedings in Lebanon was held not to have illegally practiced in New York since his contacts were "incidental and innocuous" and so he was allowed to collect his fee. On the other hand, Birbrower, Montalbano, Condon & Frank, P.C. v. Superior Court, 949 P.2d 1 (Cal. 1998), cert. denied, 525 U.S. 920 (1998), held that a New York firm had unlawfully practiced law in California in connection with a software marketing agreement by sending lawyers to California to confer with officers of the client, to interview possible arbitrators, to negotiate with the opposing party and, after initiating arbitration, to settle the matter.

ABA Model Rule of Professional Conduct 5.5 addresses the practice of law across jurisdictional boundaries:

RULE 5.5 Unauthorized Practice of Law;
Multijurisdictional Practice of Law

(a) A lawyer shall not practice law in a jurisdiction in violation of the regulation of the legal profession in that jurisdiction, or assist another in doing so.

---

[3] Following this trend, California amended its law in 2018 to permit foreign lawyers to appear in international arbitrations there without local counsel. See Cal. Civ. Pro. Code § 1297.185–.189.

[4] See, e.g., Colorado Rules Governing Admission to the Practice of Law in Colorado, Rule 205.2, Temporary Practice by Foreign Attorney.

(b) A lawyer who is not admitted to practice in this jurisdiction shall not:

(1) except as authorized by these Rules or other law, establish an office or other systematic and continuous presence in this jurisdiction for the practice of law; or

(2) hold out to the public or otherwise represent that the lawyer is admitted to practice law in this jurisdiction.

(c) A lawyer admitted in another United States jurisdiction, and not disbarred or suspended from practice in any jurisdiction, may provide legal services on a temporary basis in this jurisdiction that:

(1) are undertaken in association with a lawyer who is admitted to practice in this jurisdiction and who actively participates in the matter;

(2) are in or reasonably related to a pending or potential proceeding before a tribunal in this or another jurisdiction, if the lawyer, or a person the lawyer is assisting, is authorized by law or order to appear in such proceeding or reasonably expects to be so authorized;

(3) are in or reasonably related to a pending or potential arbitration, mediation, or other alternative resolution proceeding in this or another jurisdiction, if the services arise out of or are reasonably related to the lawyer's practice in a jurisdiction in which the lawyer is admitted to practice and are not services for which the forum requires pro hac vice admission; or

(4) are not within paragraphs (c)(2) or (c)(3) and arise out of or are reasonably related to the lawyer's practice in a jurisdiction in which the lawyer is admitted to practice.

(d) A lawyer admitted in another United States jurisdiction or in a foreign jurisdiction, and not disbarred or suspended from practice in any jurisdiction or the equivalent thereof, or a person otherwise lawfully practicing as an in-house counsel under the laws of a foreign jurisdiction, may provide legal services through an office or other systematic and continuous presence in this jurisdiction that:

(1) are provided to the lawyer's employer or its organizational affiliates; are not services for which the forum requires pro hac vice admission; and when performed by a foreign lawyer and requires advice on the law of this or another U.S. jurisdiction or of the United States, such advice shall be based upon the advice of a lawyer who is duly licensed and authorized by the jurisdiction to provide such advice; or

(2) are services that the lawyer is authorized by federal or other law or rule to provide in this jurisdiction.

(e) For purposes of paragraph (d):

(1) the foreign lawyer must be a member in good standing of a recognized legal profession in a foreign jurisdiction, the members of which are admitted to practice as lawyers or counselors at law or the equivalent, and subject to effective regulation and discipline by a duly constituted professional body or a public authority; or,

(2) the person otherwise lawfully practicing as an in-house counsel under the laws of a foreign jurisdiction must be authorized to practice under this rule by, in the exercise of its discretion, [the highest court of this jurisdiction].

Rule 5.5(d) originally extended only to lawyers licensed in another U.S. jurisdiction. In 2009, the American Bar Association created the Commission on Ethics 20/20 to review the system of lawyer regulation in light of both technological advances and the increasing globalization of law practice. The Commission found that the increase in foreign companies with substantial operations in the United States (as well as the increase in U.S. companies with substantial foreign operations) had led to increased employment of foreign in-house lawyers within the United States. In light of that trend, it proposed revising Rule 5.5(d) to authorize limited practice by foreign in-house counsel. The ABA approved those revisions, as reflected in the provisions set forth above. It also approved revisions to the Model Rule on Pro Hac Vice Admission in order to allow state courts and agencies, at their discretion, to grant limited and temporary practice authority to foreign lawyers.

The rules discussed above assume that practice is territorial—that its legitimacy depends on where the lawyer is physically at the time. But law is also located in intellectual space; that is, a lawyer works with rules that belong to a particular national or state legal system. Does one have to be a lawyer qualified in that system in order to give an opinion about it or draft a contract subject to it? ABA Model Rule 1.1 states: "A lawyer shall provide competent representation to a client. Competent representation requires the legal knowledge, skill, thoroughness and preparation reasonably necessary for the representation." Failing to provide competent representation may subject a lawyer not only to discipline by the state bar but also to liability for malpractice. Consider the following comment from Degen v. Steinbrink, 202 App. Div. 477, 195 N.Y.S. 810, aff'd mem., 236 N.Y. 669, 142 N.E. 328 (1923):

When a lawyer undertakes to prepare papers to be filed in a state foreign to his place of practice, it is his duty, if he has not knowledge of the statutes, to inform himself, for, like any artisan, by undertaking the work, he represents that he is capable of performing it in a skillful manner. Not to do so, and to prepare documents that have no legal potency, by reason of their lack of compliance with simple statutory requirements, is such a negligent discharge of his duty to his client as should render him liable for loss sustained by reason of such negligence.

Of course, American lawyers do quite regularly give their views on the laws of other states. For example, New York lawyers advise their clients about the ramifications of Delaware corporation law all the time. But crossing a national frontier may raise additional concerns. One observes the consequence of such concerns in the form of opinions by American lawyers who disclaim coverage of issues arising under foreign law or who state that as to the law of X they rely on the opinion of local counsel from X. Sometimes such opinions state that reliance on the opinion of X is reasonable, that is, they assert that X was chosen after a reasonable investigation. In some cases, the principal opinion states that the writer made an independent investigation of the law of X and sees no reason to doubt that X lawyer's opinion. It is often the case that the drafting of a legal opinion on foreign law by foreign local counsel is a collaborative effort between that lawyer and U.S. counsel, as the opinion must be relevant and effective within the framework of the specific transaction and of U.S. law. It may be advisable to set out and emphasize the issues that particularly worry the U.S. lawyer.

Cooperation between U.S. and foreign lawyers characteristically involves translation issues. The translation of legal concepts and principles can be more complicated and create more pitfalls than the already difficult task of linguistic translation. (For instance, you could understand why someone unfamiliar with U.S. law might assume that "judicial notice" referred to "notice given by a judge" rather than the ability of a judge to "take notice" of certain facts under the Federal Rules of Evidence.) Experienced transnational lawyers are very sensitive to those problems, and the major multinational law firms generally have rules requiring everything written that goes out of the office to be read by somebody who is a native speaker of the language involved. Given these complexities, legal agreements that are translated into additional languages may specify that one version is the binding one, or they may say that both languages are equally authentic, which accentuates the controversy if there is in fact a significant difference in the meaning of the texts.

C. THE ETHICAL RULES GOVERNING TRANSNATIONAL LAWYERS

The rules governing the legal profession differ in significant ways from one country to another. Many of these differences have to do with the degree to which the bar has been willing to accept business-like practices that are taken for granted in the American profession. For example, although the Supreme Court of the United States ruled years ago that the First Amendment protects advertising by lawyers, permission to advertise one's services has been granted very slowly and reluctantly in most other countries. Likewise, rules on fees are very different. In many countries, fees are set by the authorities regulating the bar rather than by negotiation between lawyer and client. Such rules can generally be set aside by explicit agreement, but an unwary American can be exposed to exorbitant charges.[5] Not infrequently those rules, because of their emphasis on the amount of money at issue, can produce a large fee for very little work. On the other side of the coin, many countries do not permit lawyers to recover contingency fees, viewing them as contrary to public policy.

More generally, while almost all systems of legal ethics agree on certain fundamental norms, the application of those norms in practice can vary enormously. For example, preparing a witness for trial or arbitration is considered part of an American lawyer's obligation to represent a client diligently, while in countries like Germany it is viewed as witness tampering and may subject a lawyer to criminal penalties. To take another example, consider confidentiality. Everywhere lawyers are expected to keep confidential the information that their clients give them. They are also typically protected by a privilege against having to reveal communications with their clients. But the contours of that privilege can vary from country to country. For instance, what if a lawyer is aware that a client intends to commit an act of financial fraud by making false representations to somebody with whom the client is negotiating? U.S. states have taken different positions, but at least some permit or require the lawyer to reveal that fact. Some foreign codes of conduct, by contrast, make no exception to the duty of confidentiality for fraud, or limit the exception to fraud upon the court.

The following case explores another aspect of confidentiality under EU law, revealing significant differences between that law and the norms governing confidentiality in the United States.

AM & S Europe v. Commission of the European Communities

Court of Justice of the European Communities, Case No. 155779, May 18, 1982
[1982] E.C.R. 1575

[Australian Mining & Smelting Europe Limited (AM & S) was a company incorporated in the United Kingdom. On February 10, 1978, the Commission of the European Communities initiated an investigation of AM & S for possible infringement of competition rules under Articles 85 and 86 of the Treaty of Rome (which today are Articles 101 and 102 of the Treaty on the Functioning of the European Union). Pursuant to its investigative authority under Article 14 of Council Regulation No. 17, the Commission requested that AM & S supply it with specified documents. AM & S sent certain documents to the Commission but refused to submit others, claiming that the confidentiality of written communications between lawyer and client was protected under Community law. In a

---

[5]   See Ackermann v. Levine, 788 F.2d 830 (2d Cir. 1986).

decision pursuant to Article 14 of Regulation No. 17, the Commission required AM & S to submit those documents for which legal privilege was claimed. After unsuccessful negotiation between AM & S and the Commission, AM & S initiated proceedings before the European Court under Article 173 of the Treaty to have the Commission's decision declared void.]

* * *

The application is based on the submission that in all the Member States written communications between lawyer and client are protected by virtue of a principle common to all those States, although the scope of that protection and the means of securing it vary from one country to another. According to the applicant, it follows from that principle which, in its view, also applies "within possible limits" in Community law, that the Commission may not when undertaking an investigation pursuant to Article 14(3) of Regulation No. 17 of the Council of 6 February 1962 (OJ, English Special Edition 1959–1962, p. 87), claim production, at least in their entirety, of written communications between lawyer and client if the undertaking claims protection and takes "reasonable steps to satisfy the Commission that the protection is properly claimed" on the ground that the documents in question are in fact covered by legal privilege.

* * *

(b) Applicability of the protection of confidentiality in Community law

. . . [Competition] rules do not exclude the possibility of recognizing, subject to certain conditions, that certain business records are of a confidential nature. Community law, which derives from not only the economic but also the legal interpenetration of the Member States, must take into account the principles and concepts common to the laws of those States concerning the observance of confidentiality, in particular, as regards certain communications between lawyer and client. That confidentiality serves the requirements, the importance of which is recognized in all of the Member States, that any person must be able, without constraint, to consult a lawyer whose profession entails the giving of independent legal advice to all those in need of it.

As far as the protection of written communications between lawyer and client is concerned, it is apparent from the legal systems of the Member States that, although the principle of such protection is generally recognized, its scope and the criteria for applying it vary, as has, indeed, been conceded both by the applicant and by the parties who have intervened in support of its conclusions.

Whilst in some of the Member States the protection against disclosure afforded to written communications between lawyer and client is based principally on a recognition of the very nature of the legal profession, inasmuch as it contributes towards the maintenance of the rule of law, in other Member States the same protection is justified by the more specific requirement (which, moreover, is also recognized in the first-mentioned States) that the rights of the defence must be respected.

Apart from these differences, however, there are to be found in the national laws of the Member States common criteria inasmuch as those laws protect, in similar circumstances, the confidentiality of written communications between lawyer and client provided that, on the one hand, such communications are made for the purposes and in the interests of the client's rights of defence and, on the other hand, they emanate from independent lawyers, that is to say, lawyers who are not bound to the client by a relationship of employment.

Viewed in that context Regulation No 17 must be interpreted as protecting, in its turn, the confidentiality of written communications between lawyer and client subject to those two conditions, and thus incorporating such elements of that protection as are common to the laws of the Member States.

As far as the first of those two conditions is concerned, in Regulation No 17 itself, in particular in the eleventh recital in its preamble and in the provisions contained in Article 19, care is taken to ensure that the rights of the defence may be exercised to the full, and the protection of the confidentiality of written communications between lawyer and client is an essential corollary to those rights. In those circumstances, such protection must, if it is to be effective, be recognized as covering all written communications exchanged after the initiation of the administrative procedure under Regulation No 17 which may lead to a decision on the application of Articles 85 and 86 of the Treaty or to a decision imposing a pecuniary sanction on the undertaking. It must also be possible to extend it to earlier written communications which have a relationship to the subject-matter of that procedure.

As regards the second condition, it should be stated that the requirement as to the position and status as an independent lawyer, which must be fulfilled by the legal adviser from whom the written communications which may be protected emanate, is based on a conception of the lawyer's role as collaborating in the administration of justice by the courts and as being required to provide, in full independence, and in the overriding interests of that cause, such legal assistance as the client needs. The counterpart of that protection lies in the rules of professional ethics and discipline which are laid down and enforced in the general interest by institutions endowed with the requisite powers for that purpose. Such a conception reflects the legal traditions common to the Member States and is also to be found in legal order of the Community, as is demonstrated by Article 17 of the Protocols on the Statutes of the Court of Justice of the EEC and the EAEC, and also by Article 20 of the Protocol on the Statute of the Court of Justice of the ECSC.

Having regard to the principles of the Treaty concerning freedom of establishment and the freedom to provide services the protection thus afforded by Community law, in particular in the context of Regulation No 17, to written communications between lawyer and client must apply without distinction to any lawyer entitled to practise his profession in one of the Member States, regardless of the Member State in which the client lives.

Such protection may not be extended beyond those limits, which are determined by the scope of the common rules on the exercise of the legal profession as laid down in Council Directive 77/249/EEC of 22 March 1977 (OJ L 78, p. 17), which is based in its turn on the mutual recognition by all the Member States of the national legal concepts of each of them on this subject.

In view of all these factors it must therefore be concluded that although Regulation No 17, and in particular Article 14 thereof, interpreted in the light of its wording, structure and aims, and having regard to the laws of the Member States, empowers the Commission to require, in the course of an investigation within the meaning of that article, production of the business documents the disclosure of which it considers necessary, including written communications between lawyer and client, for proceedings in respect of any infringements of Articles 85 and 86 of the Treaty, that power is, however, subject to a restriction imposed by the need to protect confidentiality, on the conditions defined above, and provided that the communications in question are exchanged between an independent lawyer, that is to say one who is not bound to his client by a relationship of employment, and his client.

* * *

(d)   The confidential nature of the documents at issue

It is apparent from the documents which the applicant lodged at the Court on 9 March 1981 that almost all the communications which they include were made or are connected with legal opinions which were given towards the end of 1972 and during the first half of 1973.

It appears that the communications in question were drawn up during the period preceding, and immediately following, the accession of the United Kingdom to the Community, and that they are principally concerned with how far it might be possible to avoid conflict between the applicant and the Community authorities on the applicant's position, in particular with regard to the Community provisions on competition. In spite of the time which elapsed between the said communications and the initiation of a procedure, those circumstances are sufficient to justify considering the communications as falling within the context of the rights of the defence and the lawyer's specific duties in that connection. They must therefore be protected from disclosure.

In view of that relationship and in the light of the foregoing considerations the written communications at issue must accordingly be considered, in so far as they emanate from an independent lawyer entitled to practice his profession in a Member State, as confidential and on that ground beyond the Commission's power of investigation under Article 14 of Regulation No 17.

Having regard to the particular nature of those communications Article 1(b) of the contested decision must be declared void in so far as it requires the applicant to produce the documents mentioned in the appendix to its letter to the Commission of 26 March 1979 and listed in the schedule of documents lodged at the Court on 9 March 1981 under numbers 1(a) and (b), 4(a) to (f), 5 and 7.

———————

Under AM & S, written communications between lawyer and client are privileged if two conditions are met: first, the communications are made in the interests of the client's rights of defense; and second, the lawyer in question may not be bound to the client by an employment relationship. In 2010, the European Court of Justice revisited the latter condition. In Akzo Nobel Chemicals v. Commission, Case C-550/07 P, it affirmed the holding in AM & S, stating that

> [T]he concept of the independence of lawyers is determined not only positively, that is by reference to professional ethical obligations, but also negatively, by the absence of any employment relationship. An in-house lawyer, despite his enrolment with a Bar or Law Society and the professional ethical obligations to which he is, as a result, subject, does not enjoy the same degree of independence from his employer as a lawyer working in an external law firm does in relation to his client. Consequently, an in-house lawyer is less able to deal effectively with any conflicts between his professional obligations and the aims of his client. . . . [Further,] he occupies the position of an employee which, by its very nature, does not allow him to ignore the commercial strategies pursued by his employer, and thereby affects his ability to exercise professional independence.

Regulation No. 17, referred to in the European Court of Justice's decision, was replaced as of May 1, 2004 by Council Regulation No. 1/2003, 2003 O.J. (L 1) 1. The new regulation does not change the scope of the privilege discussed in AM & S (a point confirmed in the Akzo decision), but it does for the first time allow the sharing of information between the Commission and national competition authorities and among national competition authorities. The new regulation thus creates the possibility that information gathered under a lower standard of privilege might be used by a competition authority that is ordinarily subject to a higher standard of privilege.

The consequences of differences such as these can be problematic—particularly if an attorney is subject to discipline for following one of two conflicting rules.

In the United States, Model Rule 8.5 deals with such issues in both the interstate and international contexts:

RULE 8.5 Disciplinary Authority; Choice of Law

(a) *Disciplinary Authority.* A lawyer admitted to practice in this jurisdiction is subject to the disciplinary authority of this jurisdiction, regardless of where the lawyer's conduct occurs. A lawyer not admitted in this jurisdiction is also subject to the disciplinary authority of this jurisdiction if the lawyer provides or offers to provide any legal services in this jurisdiction. A lawyer may be subject to the disciplinary authority of both this jurisdiction and another jurisdiction for the same conduct.

(b) *Choice of Law.* In any exercise of the disciplinary authority of this jurisdiction, the rules of professional conduct to be applied shall be as follows:

(1) for conduct in connection with a matter pending before a tribunal, the rules of the jurisdiction in which the tribunal sits, unless the rules of the tribunal provide otherwise; and

(2) for any other conduct, the rules of the jurisdiction in which the lawyer's conduct occurred, or, if the predominant effect of the conduct is in a different jurisdiction, the rules of that jurisdiction shall be applied to the conduct. A lawyer shall not be subject to discipline if the lawyer's conduct conforms to the rules of a jurisdiction in which the lawyer reasonably believes the predominant effect of the lawyer's conduct will occur.

Of course, when a lawyer's work touches multiple jurisdictions, determining where that work has its "predominant effect" can be difficult. In 2013, the ABA approved new language in Comment [5] to this rule, intended to reduce ambiguity in the particular context of conflicts of interest. It promotes the use of choice-of-law agreements between lawyers and their clients selecting the law governing such conflicts. Comment [7] states that the choice of law provision in Rule 8.5 applies to lawyers engaged in transnational as well as domestic practice, "unless international law, treaties or other agreements between competent regulatory authorities in the affected jurisdictions provide otherwise."

For interstate conflicts, this provision should ensure that any particular conduct by a lawyer is subject to just one set of rules, at least if all American jurisdictions adopt Model Rule 8.5. For international conflicts, however, achieving the same goal depends on whether the conflicts rule applied by a foreign disciplinary body would choose the same substantive rules of professional conduct as Model Rule 8.5.

QUESTIONS

(1) Do any of the reasons given for the attorney-client privilege cease to apply if the attorney is a member of a system other than that asked to give the privilege? Are there other arguments relating to the transnational legal process that could be invoked for or against such a grant? Given the AM & S ruling, how would an American multinational's general counsel restructure the means through which the firm obtains legal services?

(2) What type of relationship would be possible between a lawyer qualified only under the laws of Germany and a law firm in a U.S. state? Could such a person be a partner? Would it be necessary or appropriate to indicate those facts in some special way?

(3) What seem to be the inherent advantages of the international law firm in providing legal services with respect to transnational problems? Could they be achieved in other ways, as by a network of separate firms?

Additional reading: For an encyclopedic survey of legal professions see Transnational Legal Practice (D. Campbell ed. 1982). On transnational legal practice generally, see The Internationalization of the Practice of Law (Drolshammer & Pfeifer eds. 2001); Silver, Regulatory Mismatch in the International Market for Legal Services, 23 Nw. J. Int'l L. & Bus. 487 (2003); Brand, Uni-State Lawyers and Multinational Practice: Dealing with International, Transnational, and Foreign Law, 34 Vand. J. Transnat'l L. 1135 (2001). On the professional responsibility of transnational lawyers, see Lutz, The Regulation of the Transnational Legal Profession in the United States, 50 Int'l Law. 445 (2017); Terry, The Impact of Global Developments on U.S. Legal Ethics During the Past Thirty Years, 30 Geo. J. Legal Ethics 365 (2017); Rogers, Fit and Function in Legal Ethics: Developing a Code of Conduct for International Arbitration, 23 Mich. J. Int'l L. 341 (2002); Vagts, Professional Responsibility in Transborder Practice: Conflict and Resolution, 13 Geo. J. Legal Ethics 677 (2000).

CHAPTER II

INTERNATIONAL DISPUTE RESOLUTION

This Chapter discusses the essential factors that bear on choosing a way to resolve disputes. Although this volume focuses primarily on the work of the transactional lawyer, some background in dispute resolution is necessary. Disputes are a normal part of business. Effective planning for such disputes can not only provide greater legal certainty but also save one's client a good deal of money. International contracts usually do—and always should—contain both a choice of forum clause (either a choice of court clause or an arbitration clause) and a choice of law clause. Choice of law is discussed in Problem 1. See infra pp. 152–161. This chapter focuses on the choice of a forum to resolve disputes.

From a U.S. perspective, there are three basic alternatives for dispute resolution: U.S. courts, foreign courts, and international commercial arbitration. The reader is likely to be familiar with many of the basic issues concerning litigation in U.S. courts, but even here the transnational context introduces complexities. How, for example, is the judgment to be enforced if the defendant has no assets in the United States? How can a party discover the evidence necessary to prove its case if that evidence is located abroad? The answers to such questions may, in turn, affect one's view as to which forum for dispute resolution is most appropriate for any particular transaction.

A. LITIGATION IN NATIONAL COURTS

The parties to an international contract may agree in advance to submit their disputes to courts of a particular jurisdiction, and most legal systems will respect that choice. See infra pp. 22–32.

Given an unfettered choice, most American parties would prefer to litigate in the United States. It is natural to have an instinctive dread of venturing into strange territory. Sometimes that feeling survives more careful study; some foreign courts are chaotic or biased against Americans. For example, an American firm was able to persuade a U.S. court that a Liberian judgment against it should not be enforced because the courts had been badly affected by civil strife there and corruption was rampant.[1] In addition, for certain kinds of litigation, such as products liability cases or similar mass tort actions, the advantages to bringing suit in the United States are so great that foreign plaintiffs frequently

---

[1] Bridgeway Corp. v. Citibank, 45 F.Supp.2d 276 (S.D.N.Y. 1999), aff'd, 201 F.3d 134 (2d Cir. 2000). Compare S.C. Chimexim S.A. v. Velco Enterprises Ltd., 36 F.Supp.2d 206 (S.D.N.Y. 1999) (post-Communist Romanian courts pass the test—barely).

seek the shelter of an American court. In this regard, consider the oft-quoted remarks by a distinguished British judge, Lord Denning:

> As a moth is drawn to the light, so is a litigant drawn to the United States. If he can only get his case into their courts, he stands to win a fortune. At no cost to himself; and at no risk of having to pay anything to the other side. The lawyers there will conduct the case "on spec" as we say, or on a "contingency fee" as they say. The lawyers will charge the litigant nothing for their services but instead they will take 40 percent of the damages, if they win the case in court, or out of court on a settlement. If they lose, the litigant will have nothing to pay to the other side. The courts in the United States have no such costs deterrent as we have. There is also in the United States a right to trial by jury. These are prone to award fabulous damages. They are notoriously sympathetic and know that the lawyers will take their 40 percent before the plaintiff gets anything. All this means that the defendant can be readily forced into a settlement. The plaintiff holds all the cards.[2]

On the other hand, reflection may suggest that filing an action in a commercial court of a European country may produce an outcome largely free from bias that is cheaper and faster than action in the United States. For one thing, there will be no need to bring another proceeding to enforce the U.S. judgment in defendant's home jurisdiction as there would be if the action were brought here.

To exercise intelligently whatever choices a party may have about where to litigate, it is necessary to have at least a basic understanding of some of the key differences between U.S. and foreign courts:

(1) Almost nowhere outside of the United States are you likely to encounter a jury in a civil case. Trial will be before a judge or in some cases a panel of judges. A civil law judge is likely to be like a civil servant, having started a judicial career right after law school; it is rare for one to have had a protracted career at the bar as is typical of American and British judges. Several consequences follow. The outcome will be more predictable because the judgments and opinions of a seasoned judge will be available for comparison. Questions of evidence will be downplayed; the purpose of the hearsay rule, for example, is to prevent a jury from being influenced by unreliable evidence that an experienced professional judge would ignore in any case. A trial before a judge, unlike a jury trial, can be discontinuous. It is typical for a judge to tell the parties that the hearing is adjourned and that by the next hearing date they should present evidence and arguments as to a new point that has emerged in

---

[2] Smith Kline & French Laboratories v. Bloch, [1983] 1 W.L.R. 730, 733–734 (C.A. 1982). Lord Denning seems to have overstated the amount of a typical contingency fee. In individual cases, the benchmark is generally one-third. In class action settlements, the percentage is often significantly lower. See Fitzpatrick, An Empirical Study of Class Action Settlements and Their Fee Awards, 7 J. Empirical Legal Stud. 811, 830–831 (2010); Eisenberg & Miller, Attorney Fees in Class Action Settlements: An Empirical Study, 1 J. Empirical Legal Stud. 27, 35–36 (2004).

the process. It also follows that there is less room for dramatic lawyering when no jury intrudes.

(2) Judicial backlogs are commonplace throughout the world but they differ widely from country to country and at various places within them. A lawyer seeking recovery for a client who needs the money will have to take this into account.

(3) The process of proving a case is different in a civil law system. Typically it will not be possible to follow the common American tactic of pleading a case against the defendant on the basis of instinct and inference and then relying on discovery to back it up. The plaintiff will be expected to present, along with the complaint, the major items of evidence on which it relies. There may be some rules that counteract this by shifting the burden of proof, but this approach makes it harder to succeed with a product liability complaint, for instance, than in the United States. After the initial complaint the process of developing the facts is much more in the hands of the judge than is the case in our courts. As a result there is nothing that much resembles what we know as discovery. Indeed the rules of the foreign court may prohibit a lawyer from interviewing witnesses so as to prevent him from "improving" the testimony that the judge will take.

(4) Appeals are more likely to include a more or less de novo review of the factual determinations of the trial judge, since no jury was involved. Appeals may involve several stages and can consume quite a lot of time.

(5) The costs of litigation are assigned quite differently in most legal systems than in the United States. In this country it is the norm that each party to the litigation bears the costs of its lawyers' work. This is often referred to as "the American rule," in contrast to the "British rule." The latter rule provides that the prevailing party is reimbursed for the lawyers' fees it expended. It turns out that it would be accurate to replace the term "the British rule" with "the almost everywhere but the United States rule." Almost all legal systems feel that it is incomplete justice to leave a prevailing party poorer by the costs it had to incur to vindicate its rights.

(6) Historically, other countries have not recognized the class action, at least not in as far-reaching a way as the U.S. federal and (most) state systems have. Thus it has not been worthwhile in many countries to bring an action on behalf of, for example, a group of consumers injured in similar ways by a defective product. This situation is beginning to change, as many countries have adopted, or are considering the adoption of, more robust group litigation procedures. The European Commission, for example, has proposed guidelines that would require European countries to develop class action mechanisms in the areas of antitrust and consumer protection. Some differences still persist: for instance, most other countries do not permit contingency fees in the American mode, regarding them as contrary to public policy. They may, on the other hand, permit third-party funding of litigation expenses or other mechanisms designed to facilitate collective action. These differences are of less significance in the commercial matters on which this book concentrates than in tort litigation.

Additional reading: Chase, Hershkoff, Silberman, Sorabji, Stürner, Taniguchi & Varano, Civil Litigation in Comparative Context (2d ed. 2017).

1. INTERNATIONAL JURISDICTION IN U.S. COURTS

Will a United States court take jurisdiction over the case? In a standard intra-American situation, one can be sure that some such court will. One possibility is the place where the particular cause of action arose—where the contract alleged to be breached was to be performed, or where the asserted tortious injury took place. When a court exercises jurisdiction with respect to claims arising out of a defendant's contacts with the forum, the court is said to be exercising "specific jurisdiction" over the defendant.

Other bases allow a court to exercise "general jurisdiction" over claims that do not arise out of a defendant's contacts with the forum. The most widely accepted basis internationally is residence or domicile of the defendant. (The equivalent for a corporate defendant is its state of incorporation, or the state in which it has its principal place of business.) It is thought that a defendant cannot complain if tracked to the home where it can defend most conveniently. Controversially, U.S. courts used to exercise general jurisdiction based upon the defendant's "continuous and systematic" contacts with the forum (so-called "doing business" jurisdiction). But the U.S. Supreme Court has now limited this basis for general jurisdiction to places where the defendants' contacts are "so 'continuous and systematic' as to render them essentially at home" in the forum. Daimler AG v. Bauman, 571 U.S. 117, 127, 134 S.Ct. 746, 754, 187 L.Ed.2d 624 (2014). For a corporation, these will generally only be the places where it is incorporated and where it has its principal place of business. Id. at 137; 134 S.Ct. at 760. Another jurisdictional basis that many other countries consider exorbitant is transient jurisdiction based upon service of process while the defendant is temporarily present in the forum (sometimes called "tag jurisdiction"). Other countries' disapproval obviously does not prevent a U.S. court from relying on a particular basis of jurisdiction, but it may affect the enforceability of the court's judgment abroad. A common ground for refusing enforcement of a judgment is that the court rendering the judgment lacked jurisdiction over the defendant. See infra pp. 36–40.

In the context of this course, a particularly important basis of jurisdiction is consent. When the two parties are roughly equal commercial entities, the policy considerations in favor of allowing them to choose a forum by contract are strong. The leading U.S. case on the enforceability of such clauses is set forth below.

M/S Bremen v. Zapata Off-Shore Company

Supreme Court of the United States, 1972
407 U.S. 1, 92 S.Ct. 1907, 32 L.Ed.2d 513

■ MR. CHIEF JUSTICE BURGER delivered the opinion of the Court.

We granted certiorari to review a judgment of the United States Court of Appeals for the Fifth Circuit declining to enforce a forum selection clause governing disputes arising under an international towage contract between petitioner and respondent. The Circuits have differed in their approach to such clauses. For the reasons stated hereafter, we vacate the judgment of the Court of Appeals.

In November 1967, respondent Zapata, a Houston-based American corporation, contracted with petitioner Unterweser, a German corporation, to tow Zapata's ocean-going, self-elevating drilling rig Chaparral from Louisiana to a point off Ravenna, Italy, in the Adriatic Sea where Zapata had agreed to drill certain wells.

Zapata had solicited bids for the towage, and several companies including Unterweser had responded. Unterweser was the low bidder and Zapata requested it to submit a contract, which it did. The contract submitted by Unterweser contained the following provision which is at issue in this case:

"Any dispute arising must be treated before the London Court of Justice."

In addition the contract contained two clauses purporting to exculpate Unterweser from liability for damages to the towed barge.

After reviewing the contract and making several changes, but without any alteration in the forum-selection or exculpatory clauses, a Zapata vice president executed the contract and forwarded it to Unterweser in Germany, where Unterweser accepted the changes and the contract became effective.

On January 5, 1968, Unterweser's deep sea tug *Bremen* departed Venice, Louisiana, with the Chaparral in tow bound for Italy. On January 9, while the flotilla was in international waters in the middle of the Gulf of Mexico, a severe storm arose. The sharp roll of the Chaparral in Gulf waters caused its elevator legs, which had been raised for the voyage, to break off and fall into the sea, seriously damaging the Chaparral. In this emergency situation Zapata instructed the *Bremen* to tow its damaged rig to Tampa, Florida, the nearest port of refuge.

On January 12, Zapata, ignoring its contract promise to litigate "any dispute arising" in the English courts, commenced a suit in admiralty in the United States District Court at Tampa, seeking $3,500,000 damages against Unterweser *in personam* and the *Bremen in rem* alleging negligent towage and breach of contract. Unterweser responded by invoking the forum clause of the towage contract, and moved to dismiss for lack of jurisdiction or on *forum non conveniens* grounds, or in the alternative to stay the action pending submission of the dispute to the London Court of Justice. Shortly thereafter, in February, before the District Court had ruled on its motion to stay or dismiss the United States action, Unterweser commenced an action against Zapata seeking damages for breach of the towage contract in the High Court of Justice in London, as the contract provided. Zapata appeared in that court to contest jurisdiction, but its challenge was rejected, the English courts holding that the contractual forum provision conferred jurisdiction.

In the meantime, Unterweser was faced with a dilemma in the pending action in the United States court at Tampa. The six-month period for filing action to limit its liability to Zapata and other potential claimants was about to expire, but the United States District Court in Tampa had not yet ruled on Unterweser's motion to dismiss or stay Zapata's action. On July 2, 1968, confronted with difficult alternatives, Unterweser filed an action to limit its liability in the District Court in Tampa. That court entered the customary injunction against proceedings outside the limitation court, and Zapata refiled its initial claim in the limitation action.

It was only at this juncture, on July 29, after the six-month period for filing the limitation action had run, that the District Court denied Unterweser's January motion to dismiss or stay Zapata's initial action. . . .

Thereafter, on January 21, 1969, the District Court denied another motion by Unterweser to stay the limitation action pending determination of the controversy in the High Court of Justice in London and granted Zapata's motion to restrain Unterweser from litigating further in the London court. . . .

On appeal, a divided panel of the Court of Appeals affirmed, and on rehearing *en banc* the panel opinion was adopted, with six of the 14 *en banc* judges dissenting. As had the District Court, the majority holding rested on the *Carbon Black* decision, concluding that "at the very least" that case stood for the proposition that a forum selection clause "will not be enforced unless the selected state would provide a more convenient forum than the state in which suit is brought." From that premise the Court of Appeals proceeded to conclude that, apart from the forum selection clause, the District Court did not abuse its discretion in refusing to decline jurisdiction on the basis of *forum non conveniens*. It noted that (1) the flotilla never "escaped the Fifth Circuit's mare nostrum, and the casualty occurred in close proximity to the district court"; (2) a considerable number of potential witnesses, including Zapata crewmen resided in the Gulf Coast area; (3) preparation for the voyage and inspection and repair work had been performed in the Gulf area; (4) the testimony of the *Bremen* crew was available by way of deposition; (5) England had no interest in or contact with the controversy other than the forum selection clause. The Court of Appeals majority further noted that Zapata was a United States citizen and "the discretion of the district

court to remand the case to a foreign forum was consequently limited"—
especially since it appeared likely that the English courts would enforce
the exculpatory clauses.[3] In the Court of Appeals' view, enforcement of
such clauses would be contrary to public policy in American courts under
Bisso v. Inland Waterways Corp., 349 U.S. 85, 75 S.Ct. 629, 99 L.Ed. 911
(1955), and Dixilyn Drilling Corp. v. Crescent Towing & Salvage Co., 372
U.S. 697, 83 S.Ct. 967, 10 L.Ed.2d 78 (1963). Therefore, "the district court
was entitled to consider that remanding Zapata to a foreign forum, with
little or no practical contact with the controversy, could raise a bar to
recovery by a United States citizen which its own convenient courts
would not countenance."

We hold, with the six dissenting members of the Court of Appeals,
that far too little weight and effect was given to the forum clause in
resolving this controversy. For at least two decades we have witnessed
an expansion of overseas commercial activities by business enterprises
based in the United States. The barrier of distance that once tended to
confine a business concern to a modest territory no longer does so. Here
we see an American company with special expertise contracting with a
foreign company to tow a complex machine thousands of miles across seas
and oceans. The expansion of American business and industry will hardly
be encouraged if, notwithstanding solemn contracts, we insist on a
parochial concept that all disputes must be resolved under our laws and
in our courts. Absent a contract forum, the considerations relied on by
the Court of Appeals would be persuasive reasons for holding an
American forum convenient in the traditional sense, but in an era of
expanding world trade and commerce, the absolute aspects of the
doctrine of the *Carbon Black* case have little place and would be a heavy
hand indeed on the future development of international commercial
dealings by Americans. We cannot have trade and commerce in world
markets and international waters exclusively on our terms, governed by
our laws and resolved in our courts.

Forum selection clauses have historically not been favored by
American courts. Many courts, federal and state, have declined to enforce
such clauses on the ground that they were "contrary to public policy," or
that their effect was to "oust the jurisdiction" of the court. Although this
view apparently still has considerable acceptance, other courts are
tending to adopt a more hospitable attitude toward forum-selection
clauses. This view, advanced in the well-reasoned dissenting opinion in
the instant case, is that such clauses are prima facie valid and should be
enforced unless enforcement is shown by the resisting party to be

---

[3]   The record contains an undisputed affidavit of a British solicitor stating an opinion that
the exculpatory clauses of the contract would be held "prima facie valid and enforceable" against
Zapata in any action maintained in England in which Zapata alleged that defaults or errors in
Unterweser's tow caused the casualty and damage to Chaparral.

In addition, it is not disputed that while the limitation fund in the District Court in Tampa
amounts to $1,390,000, the limitation fund in England would be only slightly in excess of
$80,000 under English law.

"unreasonable" under the circumstances. We believe this is the correct doctrine to be followed by federal district courts sitting in admiralty. It is merely the other side of the proposition recognized by this Court in National Equipment Rental, Ltd. v. Szukhent, 375 U.S. 311, 84 S.Ct. 411, 11 L.Ed.2d 354 (1964), holding that in federal courts a party may validly consent to be sued in a jurisdiction where he cannot be found for service of process through contractual designation of an "agent" for receipt of process in that jurisdiction. . . . This approach is substantially that followed in other common-law countries including England. It is the view advanced by noted scholars and that adopted by the Restatement of the Conflict of Laws. It accords with ancient concepts of freedom of contract and reflects an appreciation of the expanding horizons of American contractors who seek business in all parts of the world. Not surprisingly foreign businessmen prefer, as do we, to have disputes resolved in their own courts, but if that choice is not available, then a neutral forum with expertise in the subject matter. Plainly the courts of England meet the standards of neutrality and long experience in admiralty litigation. The choice of that forum was made in an arms-length negotiation by experienced and sophisticated businessmen and absent some compelling and countervailing reason it should be honored by the parties and enforced by the courts.

The argument that such clauses are improper because they tend to "oust" a court of jurisdiction is hardly more than a vestigial legal fiction. It appears to rest at core on historical judicial resistance to any attempt to reduce the power and business of a particular court and has little place in an era when all courts are overloaded and when businesses once essentially local now operate in world markets. It reflects something of a provincial attitude regarding the fairness of other tribunals. No one seriously contends in this case that the forum-selection clause "ousted" the District Court of jurisdiction over Zapata's action. The threshold question is whether that court should have exercised its jurisdiction to do more than give effect to the legitimate expectations of the parties manifested in their freely negotiated agreement, by specifically enforcing the forum clause.

There are compelling reasons why a freely negotiated private international agreement, unaffected by fraud, undue influence, or overweening bargaining power,[4] such as that involved here, should be

---

[4] The record here refutes any notion of overweening bargaining power. Judge Wisdom in the Court of Appeals noted:

"Zapata has neither presented evidence of nor alleged fraud or undue bargaining power in the agreement. Unterweser was only one of several companies bidding on the project. No evidence contradicts its Managing Director's affidavit that it specified English courts 'in an effort to meet Zapata Off-Shore Company half way.' Zapata's Vice President has declared by affidavit that no specific negotiations concerning the forum clause took place. But this was not simply a form contract with boilerplate language that Zapata had no power to alter. The towing of an oil rig across the Atlantic was a new business. Zapata did make alterations to the contract submitted by Unterweser. The forum clause could hardly be ignored. . . ."

given full effect. In this case, for example, we are concerned with a far from routine transaction between companies of two different nations contemplating the tow of an extremely costly piece of equipment from Louisiana across the Gulf of Mexico, and the Atlantic Ocean, through the Mediterranean Sea to its final destination in the Adriatic Sea. In the course of its voyage, it was to traverse the waters of many jurisdictions. The Chaparral could have been damaged at any point along the route, and there were countless possible ports of refuge. That the accident occurred in the Gulf of Mexico and the barge was towed to Tampa in an emergency were mere fortuities. It cannot be doubted for a moment that the parties sought to provide for a neutral forum for the resolution of any disputes arising during the tow. Manifestly much uncertainty and possibly great inconvenience to both parties could arise if a suit could be maintained in any jurisdiction in which an accident might occur or if jurisdiction were left to any place where the *Bremen* or Unterweser might happen to be found.[5] . . .

Thus, in the light of present day commercial realities and expanding international trade we conclude that the forum clause should control absent a strong showing that it should be set aside. Although their opinions are not altogether explicit, it seems reasonably clear that the District Court and the Court of Appeals placed the burden on Unterweser to show that London would be a more convenient forum than Tampa, although the contract expressly resolved that issue. The correct approach would have been to enforce the forum clause specifically unless Zapata could clearly show that enforcement would be unreasonable and unjust, or that the clause was invalid for such reasons as fraud or overreaching. Accordingly, the case must be remanded for reconsideration.

We note, however, that there is nothing in the record presently before us that would support a refusal to enforce the forum clause. The Court of Appeals suggested that enforcement would be contrary to the public policy of the forum under Bisso v. Inland Waterways Corp., 349 U.S. 85, 75 S.Ct. 629, 99 L.Ed. 911 (1955), because of the prospect that the English courts would enforce the clauses of the towage contract purporting to exculpate Unterweser from liability for damages to the Chaparral. A contractual choice of forum clause should be held unenforceable if enforcement would contravene a strong public policy of the forum in which suit is brought, whether declared by statute or by judicial decision. See, e.g., Boyd v. Grand Trunk W.R.R., 338 U.S. 263, 70 S.Ct. 26, 94 L.Ed. 55 (1949). It is clear, however, that whatever the proper reach of the policy expressed in *Bisso,* it does not reach this case. *Bisso*

---

[5]   At the very least, the clause was an effort to eliminate all uncertainty as to the nature, location, and outlook of the forum in which these companies of differing nationalities might find themselves. Moreover, while the contract here did not specifically provide that the substantive law of England should be applied, it is the general rule in English courts that the parties are assumed, absent contrary indication, to have designated the forum with the view that it should apply its own law. . . . It is therefore reasonable to conclude that the forum clause was also an effort to obtain certainty as to the applicable substantive law.

rested on considerations with respect to the towage business strictly in American waters, and those considerations are not controlling in an international commercial agreement. . . .

Courts have also suggested that a forum clause, even though it is freely bargained for and contravenes no important public policy of the forum, may nevertheless be "unreasonable" and unenforceable if the chosen forum is *seriously* inconvenient for the trial of the action. Of course, where it can be said with reasonable assurance that at the time they entered the contract, the parties to a freely negotiated private international commercial agreement contemplated the claimed inconvenience, it is difficult to see why any such claim of inconvenience should be heard to render the forum clause unenforceable. We are not here dealing with an agreement between two Americans to resolve their essentially local disputes in a remote alien forum. In such a case, the serious inconvenience of the contractual forum to one or both of the parties might carry greater weight in determining the reasonableness of the forum clause. The remoteness of the forum might suggest that the agreement was an adhesive one, or that the parties did not have the particular controversy in mind when they made their agreement, yet even there the party claiming should bear a heavy burden of proof. Similarly, selection of a remote forum to apply differing foreign law to an essentially American controversy might contravene an important public policy of the forum. For example, so long as *Bisso* governs American courts with respect to the towage business in American waters, it would quite arguably be improper to permit an American tower to avoid that policy by providing a foreign forum for resolution of his disputes with an American towee.

This case, however, involves a freely negotiated international commercial transaction between a German and an American corporation for towage of a vessel from the Gulf of Mexico to the Adriatic Sea. As noted, selection of a London forum was clearly a reasonable effort to bring vital certainty to this international transaction and to provide a neutral forum experienced and capable in the resolution of admiralty litigation. Whatever "inconvenience" Zapata would suffer by being forced to litigate in the contractual forum as it agreed to do was clearly foreseeable at the time of contracting. In such circumstances it should be incumbent on the party seeking to escape his contract to show that trial in the contractual forum will be so gravely difficult and inconvenient that he will for all practical purposes be deprived of his day in court. Absent that there is no basis for concluding that it would be unfair, unjust, or unreasonable to hold that party to his bargain.

In the course of his ruling on Unterweser's second motion to stay the proceedings in Tampa, the District Court did make a conclusionary finding that the balance of convenience was "strongly" in favor of litigation in Tampa. However, as previously noted, in making that finding the court erroneously placed the burden of proof on Unterweser to show that the balance of convenience was strongly in its favor. Moreover, the finding falls far short of a conclusion that Zapata would be effectively deprived of its day in court should it be forced to litigate in London. Indeed, it cannot even be assumed that it would be placed to the expense of transporting its witnesses to London. It is not unusual for important issues in international admiralty cases to be dealt with by deposition. Both the District Court and the Court of Appeals majority appeared satisfied that Unterweser could receive a fair hearing in Tampa by using deposition testimony of its witnesses from distant places, and there is no reason to conclude that Zapata could not use deposition testimony to equal advantage if forced to litigate in London as it bound itself to do. Nevertheless, to allow Zapata opportunity to carry its heavy burden of showing not only that the balance of convenience is strongly in favor of trial in Tampa (that is, that it will be far more inconvenient for Zapata to litigate in London than it will be for Unterweser to litigate in Tampa), but also that a London trial will be so manifestly and gravely inconvenient to Zapata that it will be effectively deprived of a meaningful day in court, we remand for further proceedings.

* * *

[Justice Douglas, dissenting, stressed that the "substantive rights" of respondent, an American citizen, would be adversely affected if respondent were remitted to the English court. The exculpatory clauses would not be enforceable in the United States but, according to evidence in the record, would be enforceable in England.]

The Zapata ruling was expanded in Carnival Cruise Lines, Inc. v. Shute, 499 U.S. 585, 111 S.Ct. 1522, 113 L.Ed.2d 622 (1991). There the objection to the forum selection clause was raised not by a sophisticated international corporation but by two residents of Seattle, Washington, one of whom was injured on a cruise aboard defendant's ship that sailed from Los Angeles, California. The Supreme Court held that they were bound by a fine print clause in their ticket which provided that any disputes were to be litigated in Florida where defendant had its headquarters. More recently there has been a series of cases involving the efficacy of clauses binding participants in Lloyd's insurance syndicates, known as "names," to litigate matters in London. The courts of appeal have upheld their validity. See, e.g., Lipcon v. Underwriters at Lloyd's, London, 148 F.3d 1285 (11th Cir. 1998), cert. denied, 525 U.S. 1093, 119 S.Ct. 851, 142 L.Ed.2d 704 (1999).

In Zapata, the High Court of Justice accepted jurisdiction based on the choice-of-forum clause despite the lack of any contacts with the United Kingdom. In the European Union, under the Brussels I Regulation (Recast), an agreement choosing the courts of an EU Member State is enforceable even if none of the parties is domiciled in an EU Member State. See Regulation (EU) No. 1215/2012 of the European

Parliament and of the Council on Jurisdiction and the Recognition and Enforcement of Judgments in Civil and Commercial Matters (Recast), art. 25, 2012 O.J. (L 351) 1.

New York General Obligations Law § 5–1402 expressly provides for the enforcement of clauses choosing New York courts in contracts for at least $1 million, if the parties have also chosen New York law to govern their obligations, despite the absence of other contacts with New York. California has a similar provision. Cal. Code Civ. Proc. § 410.40. The Supreme Court of Florida, on the other hand, has held that a forum-selection clause cannot be the sole basis for personal jurisdiction. C.R. McRae v. J.D./M.D. Inc., 511 So. 2d 540 (Fla. 1987). Although the Florida legislature subsequently amended its laws in a way that superficially resembles New York's and California's, the amended law does not allow the parties to choose Florida law unless their contract bears "a substantial or reasonable relation to this state" or every party is domiciled in the United States. Fla. Stat. ch. 685.101(2). Without an effective choice of Florida law, the choice of Florida courts is ineffective. Id. ch. 685.102.

Of course, the question of personal jurisdiction arises in foreign courts, too. As a general matter, they also will permit suit at the defendant's home base; they are apt to characterize that link as one of nationality rather than of residence. Foreign courts also recognize the idea of suit at a place connected with the cause of action, although foreign "long arms" tend to be shorter than their American counterparts. German courts, for example, would take jurisdiction over a tort if the action complained of took place in Germany, but would regard it as overreaching to take jurisdiction where consequences of an action transpired in Germany but the action itself took place in another country. A characteristic case that would differentiate the U.S. and German positions would be an automobile accident in one country that allegedly was due to a design or production failure in the other. Some countries have jurisdictional bases that strike the American observer as overreaching—the French Civil Code provision that asserts jurisdiction because the *plaintiff* is French, for example.

In 2005, the Hague Conference on Private International Law produced a Convention on Choice of Court Agreements, 44 I.L.M. 1294 (2005). The Convention applies "to exclusive choice of court agreements concluded in civil or commercial matters." Its key provisions are as follows:

Article 5. Jurisdiction of the chosen court

(1) The court or courts of a Contracting State designated in an exclusive choice of court agreement shall have jurisdiction to decide a dispute to which the agreement applies, unless the agreement is null and void under the law of that State.

(2) A court that has jurisdiction under paragraph 1 shall not decline to exercise jurisdiction on the ground that the dispute should be decided in a court of another State. [. . .]

Article 6. Obligations of a court not chosen

A court of a Contracting State other than that of the chosen court shall suspend or dismiss proceedings to which an exclusive choice of court agreement applies unless—

a) the agreement is null and void under the law of the State of the chosen court;

b) a party lacked the capacity to conclude the agreement under the law of the State of the court seised;

c) giving effect to the agreement would lead to a manifest injustice or would be manifestly contrary to the public policy of the State of the court seised;

d) for exceptional reasons beyond the control of the parties, the agreement cannot reasonably be performed; or

e) the chosen court has decided not to hear the case.

The Convention also requires other state-parties to recognize and enforce judgments rendered by a court designated in an exclusive choice of court agreement. The Convention entered into force in 2015 and currently applies to the members of the European Union, Mexico, Montenegro, and Singapore. The United Kingdom has ratified the Convention separately to take effect if and when it leaves the EU. China, Ukraine, and the United States have signed the treaty but have not ratified it.

QUESTIONS

(1) Assume that you are counsel for a British firm that has had a falling out with an American corporation for which it was the European distributor. The agreement says nothing about choice-of-forum, arbitration or choice-of-law. There are plausible bases for jurisdiction in both a British and an American forum. The issues involved would include antitrust questions, allegations about the failure of the U.S. party to deliver goods in conformity with good commercial practice, and issues about the patent protection for the products in question. Which forum seems more desirable? Which would be more economical? Make up a list of the issues of British law that would need to be put to London counsel.

(2) Does Zapata provide a comprehensive list of the factors that you would regard as relevant to determining whether a clause is (un)fair or (un)reasonable?

(3) What impact should Zapata have on state courts (or on federal courts in diversity cases) that consider international choice-of-forum clauses in ordinary contract cases?

(4) What defects can you identify in the dispute resolution provisions of the contract between Zapata and Unterweser? How would you redraft those provisions to remove the defects?

Additional reading: Born, International Arbitration and Forum Selection Agreements: Drafting and Enforcing (5th ed. 2016).

2. PROCEDURAL PROBLEMS IN INTERNATIONAL LITIGATION

Other countries have rules concerning service of process and discovery of evidence that may be quite different from those with which an American lawyer is familiar. To address some of these procedural differences, the United States has joined several treaties concerning judicial assistance. Prominent among these are two conventions negotiated under the auspices of the Hague Conference on Private International Law: the 1967 Convention on the Service Abroad of Judicial or Extrajudicial Documents in Civil or Commercial Matters (Hague Service Convention), 20 U.S.T. 1361, T.I.A.S. No. 6638, and the 1972 Convention on the Taking of Evidence Abroad in Civil or Commercial Matters (Hague Evidence Convention), 23 U.S.T. 2555, T.I.A.S. No. 7444.

Because service of process is considered a judicial function in many countries, the use of private process servers, familiar in the United States, is often forbidden. The Hague Service Convention was designed to shield other countries from methods of service they found objectionable and to provide a reliable means of service. In addition to the United States, 73 countries are parties to the Hague Service Convention as of 2019. The Convention requires each state-party to designate a Central Authority to which documents may be forwarded for service in that country. The Convention also allows each country to object to other methods of service, such as service by mail or service by diplomatic or consular agents (unless the document is to be served upon a national of the country in which the document originated). Germany, for example, has objected to each of these alternatives. Article 1 of the Convention makes it applicable "in all cases, in civil or commercial matters, where there is occasion to transmit a judicial or extrajudicial document for service abroad." The interpretation of this provision has been a matter of controversy. The United States Supreme Court held in Volkswagenwerk Aktiengesellschaft v. Schlunk, 486 U.S. 694, 108 S.Ct. 2104, 100 L.Ed.2d 722 (1988), that whether there is occasion to transmit a document for service abroad depends upon the domestic law of the forum state. Because Illinois law allowed a foreign corporation's domestic subsidiary to be used as an involuntary agent for service of process, the Supreme Court held that service was complete upon service of the subsidiary, that there was no occasion to transmit the document for service abroad, and that the foreign parent could not complain that it had not been served in accordance with the Convention.

Obtaining evidence also poses particular challenges in the transnational context. Some of those challenges arise from differing views of fact gathering and of proof. American lawyers are used to broader pretrial discovery than is common in other countries, both with respect to documentary evidence and with respect to the pretrial testimony of witnesses through depositions. In the United States, discovery is largely managed by the parties, and judicial intervention is usually infrequent. In some other countries, by contrast, the judge is regarded as having the basic responsibility for developing the relevant facts and ferreting out the truth from witnesses. The United States tends to emphasize the oral presentation of evidence by direct witnesses, often accompanied by stress on cross-examination as a key to the ascertainment of truth. Some other systems tend to give primary weight to written evidence and regard it as the best guarantee of accuracy.

The Hague Evidence Convention, to which the United States and 60 other countries are parties as of 2019, was designed to accommodate differences among national systems while facilitating the gathering of evidence. It requires each state-party to designate a Central Authority to receive Letters of Request from the judicial authorities of other state-parties. The Central Authority transmits a request to the proper authority within its own country for carrying the request out. If a witness does not appear voluntarily, the requested country is to use whatever compulsion would be available in domestic proceedings. Discovery under the Hague Evidence Convention is not as broad as under U.S. discovery rules, in particular because Article 23 of the Convention allows state-parties to declare that they "will not execute Letters of Request issued for the purpose of obtaining pre-trial discovery of documents as known in Common Law countries." Most other states have entered such declarations.

The question naturally arose whether the Evidence Convention should be the exclusive means of gathering evidence located in other state-parties, or whether U.S. courts could continue to employ the Federal Rules of Civil Procedure to compel discovery from foreign parties to the litigation and from non-parties abroad who are U.S. citizens or residents. In Société Nationale Industrielle Aérospatiale v. United States District Court for the Southern District of Iowa, 482 U.S. 522, 107 S.Ct. 2542, 96 L.Ed.2d 461 (1987), the United States Supreme Court took the latter view. The case originated in a complaint by the pilot and a passenger in an aircraft manufactured by defendant in France that crashed in Iowa, injuring plaintiffs. Plaintiffs filed a request for the production of documents under Rule 34, a set of interrogatories under Rule 33, and requests for admission under Rule 36. Defendants filed a motion for a protective order asserting that the discovery involved materials in France and that the only way to obtain them was through the procedures of the Hague Convention. The lower courts ruled that the Hague procedures were not meant to be exclusive, at least with respect to evidence in the possession of a party to the litigation. The Supreme Court agreed; it said "we conclude accordingly that the Hague Convention did not deprive the District Court of the jurisdiction it otherwise possessed to order a foreign national party before it to produce evidence physically located within a signatory nation." It found no plain statement within the Convention of an intention to deprive the U.S. courts of their power to order discovery: "A rule of exclusivity would subordinate the court's supervision of even the most routine of these pretrial proceedings to the actions, or, equally, to the inactions of foreign judicial authorities."

The result has been that a party seeking to uncover evidence abroad will usually employ the Federal Rules of Civil Procedure if it can, even if the evidence is located in a state-party to the Evidence Convention. Federal Rule of Civil Procedure 32(a)(3)(B) permits the use at trial of a deposition of a witness who "is out of the United States." Documentary evidence located abroad may be sought under Rule 34. A foreign party to the litigation who fails to comply with a U.S. court's discovery orders is subject to sanctions under Rule 37, just as a domestic party would be. Rule 45 and 28 U.S.C. § 1783 additionally allow a U.S. court to issue subpoenas to American nationals or residents abroad, even though they are not parties to the litigation, requiring them to testify or to produce documents. Resort to the Hague Evidence Convention to gather evidence for use in U.S. courts is thus limited, for the most part, to evidence from foreign non-parties.

Of course the discovery of evidence abroad may be blocked by rules of privilege. The laws of all countries protect some types of records and some witnesses against disclosure even in litigation, thus putting other interests above that of the search for truth. The interests recognized as being so significant vary from country to country; they may affect official secrets, professional (e.g., lawyers', doctors', accountants', or journalists') and clerical confidences; and may even protect private commercial and economic interests, such as customers' interests in secrecy of bank records. Article 11 of the Hague Evidence Convention allows a witness to claim a privilege under either the law of the state requesting evidence or the state in which the evidence is sought.

The conflict between U.S. discovery rules and foreign privileges reached the United States Supreme Court in Société Internationale Pour Participations Industrielles et Commerciales, S.A. v. Rogers, 357 U.S. 197, 78 S.Ct. 1087, 2 L.Ed.2d 1255 (1958). A Swiss company was seeking to recover the stock of General Aniline Film Company, an American chemical firm that had been seized in 1941 on the ground that it really belonged to a German firm, that is, to an "enemy." During the litigation, the U.S. government demanded records relevant to the relationship between Interhandel and the German firm in the hands of a Swiss bank. Interhandel asserted that the bank could not surrender those papers because they were privileged under Swiss law. The Supreme Court concluded that the demand for the papers was justified, but that the remedy of dismissing Interhandel's complaint was too drastic a sanction because failure to comply with the District Court's order had been due to inability, and not to wilfulness, bad faith, or any fault of Interhandel. It said that at trial, however, the District Court could draw inferences unfavorable to the Swiss corporation arising from gaps in the record and noted that in a trial on the merits the absence of the records might make it hard to dispel doubts created by the government's case.

The gathering of evidence for litigation in foreign courts obviously proceeds under foreign rules of discovery, but U.S. discovery rules may also be invoked sometimes to assist in foreign proceedings. 28 U.S.C. § 1782 permits a U.S. district court to order a person within its district to give testimony or produce documents "for use in a proceeding in a foreign or international tribunal . . . upon the application of any interested person." In Intel Corp. v. Advanced Micro Devices, Inc., 542 U.S. 241, 124 S.Ct. 2466, 159 L.Ed.2d 355 (2004), the United States Supreme Court held that the European Commission was a foreign or international tribunal when investigating an antitrust complaint and that the company filing the complaint was an interested person, who could invoke § 1782, even if it was not formally a party to the proceeding. The Supreme Court further rejected any requirement that the evidence sought under § 1782 be discoverable under foreign law. Nevertheless, the Court noted that a district court has discretion whether to grant a request for discovery under § 1782 and should consider whether the witness is a party to the foreign proceeding, the receptivity of the foreign tribunal to the evidence, whether the request appears to be an attempt to avoid foreign proof-gathering restrictions, and whether the request is unduly burdensome. Applying these factors to Advanced Micro Devices' request on remand, the District Court denied the request in full.

Is Section 1782 available to parties using arbitration? Courts have held that an arbitral tribunal established pursuant to bilateral investment treaties also qualifies as an "international tribunal" for purposes of § 1782. In re Chevron Corp., 633 F.3d 153, 161 (3d Cir. 2011). But courts have divided on whether tribunals in international commercial arbitration qualify. See Restatement (Fourth) of Foreign Relations Law § 426 reporters note 3 (2018) (collecting cases).

QUESTIONS

(1) Suppose that in a lawsuit in the United States concerning performance under a licensing agreement your client, the licensor, wishes to obtain certain data in the possession of the licensee about the way in which production operations were conducted in the licensee's plant. What means are available for obtaining that information? Which seem tactically preferable?

(2) Suppose that you represent a foreign party defendant in a lawsuit in the United States in the same case as that in Question (1). It

36   International Dispute Resolution   Chapter II

is suggested that the local government would be willing to issue a protective order preventing the disclosure of that information on the ground of national security. What should you say to your client about the risks and benefits of such a move?

(3) Suppose that you wish to obtain data in the same lawsuit from a non-party resident in the United Kingdom. How do you go about minimizing the risk that a British court will refuse to carry out the letter of request on the ground that it constitutes a fishing expedition?

(4) Do your readings about discovery processes in judicial systems contribute to your sense that arbitration is (or is not) the preferable device for commercial parties?

Additional reading: Restatement (Fourth) of Foreign Relations Law §§ 423 (service of process) & 426 (discovery of evidence); Born & Rutledge, International Civil Litigation in United States Courts Ch. 10– 11 (6th ed. 2018).

3. The Enforcement of Judgments Internationally

Most plaintiffs are interested not only in winning a judgment but in enforcing that judgment against the defendant's assets. Of course, there are limits even in stateside transactions. The other side may be judgment-proof. Or the judgment debtor may be successful in evading pursuit and in hiding assets. The problem is much more severe internationally, however. The full faith and credit clause of the U.S. Constitution stops at the water's edge. See Aetna Life Ins. Co. v. Tremblay, 223 U.S. 185, 190 (1912).

Other countries have concluded treaties that provide for the reciprocal enforcement of one another's court judgments. The best known is the Brussels Convention, 1990 O.J. (C 189) 1, originally concluded by the members of the European Economic Community in 1968, which has now been superceded for all EU members but Denmark by the so-called Brussels I Regulation (Recast). See Regulation (EU) No. 1215/2012 of the European Parliament and of the Council on Jurisdiction and the Recognition and Enforcement of Judgments in Civil and Commercial Matters (Recast), 2012 O.J. (L 351) 1. The United States, however, is currently party to no treaty providing for the recognition and enforcement of foreign judgments. Attempts at the Hague Conference on Private International Law to negotiate a broad judgments convention that the United States would join failed, although subsequent negotiations produced the narrower Convention on Choice of Court Agreements discussed above. If widely adopted, that Convention would establish a counterpart for court judgments to the New York Convention governing international arbitral agreements and awards. See infra pp. 41–44.

In the absence of a treaty, the enforceability of a U.S. judgment abroad depends on the local law of the jurisdiction where enforcement is sought. Consider the following provision from Germany's Code of Civil Procedure (*ZPO*):

§ 328   [Recognition of Foreign Judgments]

1.   Recognition of a foreign judgment is excluded:

(1)   If the courts of the state to which the foreign court belongs do not have jurisdiction according to German law;

(2)   If the defendant who did not participate in the foreign proceeding and who raises that defense was not properly served with the document initiating the proceedings, or was not served in sufficient time to enable him to defend himself;

(3)   If the judgment is inconsistent with a domestic judgment or with a prior foreign judgment entitled to recognition, or if the proceeding on which the judgment is based is inconsistent with a prior proceeding that earlier became pending here;

(4)   If recognition of the judgment would lead to a result manifestly incompatible with the fundamental principles of German law, in particular if recognition would be incompatible with basic [constitutional] rights;

(5)   If reciprocity is not assured.

* * *

Note that under paragraph 1(1), the jurisdiction of the foreign court is judged by German standards, so that a U.S. judgment based on transient jurisdiction would not be enforceable in Germany. Invoking paragraph 1(4)'s public policy exception, German courts have in the past refused to enforce U.S. judgments for punitive damages. Finally, note that paragraph 1(5) requires reciprocity for most kinds of judgments, that is, that the foreign court would enforce a German judgment.

In Hilton v. Guyot, 159 U.S. 113, 16 S.Ct. 139, 40 L.Ed. 95 (1895), the United States Supreme Court also imposed a reciprocity requirement for some kinds of foreign judgments. Hilton, however, had surprisingly little influence on the U.S. law of judgments. In the era before Erie Railroad Co. v. Tompkins, 304 U.S. 64, 58 S.Ct. 817, 82 L.Ed. 1188 (1938), Hilton was not binding on state courts, many of which declined to follow it. Since Erie, it has been assumed that the enforceability of foreign judgments is a question of state law, and that federal courts sitting in diversity must follow the rules of the state in which they sit. See Restatement (Fourth) of Foreign Relations Law § 481 cmt. a (2018). Thirty-four U.S. states and the District of Columbia have adopted one of two uniform acts providing for the recognition and enforcement of foreign judgments. Eleven states[6] have adopted the 1962 Uniform Foreign

---

6   Alaska, Connecticut, Florida, Maine, Maryland, Massachusetts, Missouri, New Jersey, New York, Ohio, and Pennsylvania.

Money-Judgments Recognition Act. Twenty-three states[7] and the District of Columbia have adopted the updated 2005 Uniform Foreign-Country Money Judgments Recognition Act, which provides in part as follows:

§ 4. Standards for Recognition of Foreign-Country Judgment.

(a)   Except as otherwise provided in subsections (b) and (c), a court of this state shall recognize a foreign-country judgment to which this [act] applies.

(b)   A court of this state may not recognize a foreign-country judgment if:

(1)   the judgment was rendered under a judicial system that does not provide impartial tribunals or procedures compatible with the requirements of due process of law;

(2)   the foreign court did not have personal jurisdiction over the defendant; or

(3)   the foreign court did not have jurisdiction over the subject matter.

(c)   A court of this state need not recognize a foreign-country judgment if:

(1)   the defendant in the proceeding in the foreign court did not receive notice of the proceeding in sufficient time to enable the defendant to defend;

(2)   the judgment was obtained by fraud that deprived the losing party of an adequate opportunity to present its case;

(3)   the judgment or the [cause of action] [claim for relief] on which the judgment is based is repugnant to the public policy of this state or of the United States;

(4)   the judgment conflicts with another final and conclusive judgment;

(5)   the proceeding in the foreign court was contrary to an agreement between the parties under which the dispute in question was to be determined otherwise than by proceedings in that foreign court;

(6)   in the case of jurisdiction based only on personal service, the foreign court was a seriously inconvenient forum for the trial of the action;

---

[7]   Alabama, Arizona, California, Colorado, Delaware, Georgia, Hawaii, Idaho, Illinois, Indiana, Iowa, Michigan, Minnesota, Montana, Nevada, New Mexico, North Carolina, North Dakota, Oklahoma, Oregon, Texas, Virginia, and Washington.

(7)   the judgment was rendered in circumstances that raise substantial doubt about the integrity of the rendering court with respect to the judgment; or

(8)   the specific proceeding in the foreign court leading to the judgment was not compatible with the requirements of due process of law.

(d)   A party resisting recognition of a foreign-country judgment has the burden of establishing that a ground for nonrecognition stated in subsection (b) or (c) exists.

§ 5. Personal Jurisdiction.

(a)   A foreign-country judgment may not be refused recognition for lack of personal jurisdiction if:

(1)   the defendant was served with process personally in the foreign country;

(2)   the defendant voluntarily appeared in the proceeding, other than for the purpose of protecting property seized or threatened with seizure in the proceeding or of contesting the jurisdiction of the court over the defendant;

(3)   the defendant, before the commencement of the proceeding, had agreed to submit to the jurisdiction of the foreign court with respect to the subject matter involved;

(4)   the defendant was domiciled in the foreign country when the proceeding was instituted or was a corporation or other form of business organization that had its principal place of business in, or was organized under the laws of, the foreign country;

(5)   the defendant had a business office in the foreign country and the proceeding in the foreign court involved a [cause of action] [claim for relief] arising out of business done by the defendant through that office in the foreign country; or

(6)   the defendant operated a motor vehicle or airplane in the foreign country and the proceeding involved a [cause of action] [claim for relief] arising out of that operation.

(b)   The list of bases for personal jurisdiction in subsection (a) is not exclusive. The courts of this state may recognize bases of personal jurisdiction other than those listed in subsection (a) as sufficient to support a foreign-country judgment.

Note that § 4 of the Uniform Act does not list lack of reciprocity as a basis for denying enforcement of a foreign judgment, although five states (Florida, Maine, Massachusetts, Ohio, and Texas) have added reciprocity as either a mandatory or a discretionary basis for non-enforcement. By contrast, a draft federal statute approved by the American Law Institute in 2006—which would provide uniform federal rules for the enforcement

of foreign judgments in federal and state courts—would require
reciprocity as a condition for enforcement.

QUESTIONS

(1) Should the enforcement of foreign judgments in the United
States be governed by state or federal law?

(2) Should reciprocity be a condition to the enforcement of foreign
judgments?

B. ARBITRATION

After this review of the problems surrounding international
litigation, it is hardly surprising that lawyers guiding clients into
international transactions routinely recommend arbitration and draft a
contract provision for it. The advantages they expect from this are
various. First, they count on the fact that the awards of arbitrators,
unlike judgments of courts, enjoy the protection of a widely adopted
multilateral treaty, the so-called New York Convention analyzed below.

Second, they hope that arbitration will prove speedy, cheap,
informal, and confidential. Such hopes are sometimes disappointed. A
determined and evasive opponent can introduce a variety of delays into
the process—for instance, by going to court to contest the validity of the
contract clause calling for arbitration, by challenging arbitrators as
biased, or by resisting enforcement of the resulting award. Arbitrating
can also be expensive. States pay for judges, but the costs of arbitrators
and those who administer the process must be borne by the parties. The
leading arbitrators generally receive more in compensation for their
services than judges earn by way of salaries, and there have been
complaints about the fees charged by major arbitration centers. In any
case, expensive counsel must spend time away from home, usually in
expensive hotels located in cities where the cost of living may be even
higher than in New York. Nor should one assume that arbitration will
always be confidential. Generally, such confidentiality requires the
agreement of both of the parties, and may be lost at the enforcement
stage if resort must be had to a national court.

Third, the parties hope to find a neutral ground since neither wishes
to litigate in the other's home courts. They must, however, recognize that
careful planning may be necessary since arbitrators can have their own
particular perspectives, and there is generally no substantive review of
or appeal from arbitrators' awards. Arbitral tribunals may also have
some difficulties in compelling testimony or the production of documents
from non-parties because they are not vested with all of the powers
possessed by national courts.

In drafting an arbitration clause, the parties should first decide
between institutional and *ad hoc* arbitration. With institutional
arbitration, an arbitral institution provides assistance in running the

arbitral proceedings in exchange for a fee, which may be helpful for parties with little experience in international disputes. Commonly used institutions include the International Chamber of Commerce, the London Court of International Arbitration, the International Centre for Dispute Resolution (which is the international division of the American Arbitration Association), the Hong Kong International Arbitration Centre, the Singapore International Arbitration Centre, and the Stockholm Chamber of Commerce. Each of these institutions has a set of rules for conducting arbitrations as well as for appointing arbitrators if one of the parties defaults. With *ad hoc* arbitration, no institution is involved and the burden of running the arbitral proceedings falls entirely on the parties. The rules most commonly used in *ad hoc* arbitrations are the UNCITRAL Arbitration Rules developed by the United Nations Commission on International Trade Law. If the parties choose *ad hoc* arbitration, they will have to designate an appointing authority to appoint arbitrators if one of the parties defaults.

Arbitral institutions each have a model arbitration clause that the parties can use as a starting point for drafting. The arbitration clause must identify the kinds of disputes that are subject to arbitration, for example "all disputes relating to" the contract, "all disputes arising out of" the contract, or "all disputes arising out of" particular portions of the contract. It is worth noting that the more limitations the parties place on the scope of arbitration, the more they invite arguments about whether a particular dispute falls within the clause. The parties should also choose the place—or "seat"—of arbitration. The courts at the seat of arbitration may provide oversight of the arbitral process, and they have the authority to review the arbitral award and to set it aside on any ground provided for in the arbitration law of the seat. Generally, the place of arbitration should be in a country that is party to the New York Convention. See infra pp. 41–44. The parties should also specify the number of arbitrators, the method of selecting them, and the language in which the arbitration will be conducted. It is most common to have either one or three arbitrators. When there are three, each of the parties will choose one, and the third will be selected jointly by the parties or by their arbitrators. If no agreement is possible, the arbitral institution or other appointing authority will choose the third arbitrator. While one arbitrator is cheaper than three, parties often feel more comfortable having at least one member of the tribunal they know will be sympathetic.

1. THE TREATY STRUCTURE OF INTERNATIONAL ARBITRATION

The effectiveness of international commercial arbitration depends critically on the regime established by the United Nations Convention on the Recognition and Enforcement of Foreign Arbitral Awards, commonly known as the New York Convention. The Convention, concluded in 1958, now counts 159 nations as parties, including the United States and most other leading commercial countries. The New York Convention imposes on its signatories two fundamental obligations: (1) to enforce agreements to arbitrate; (2) to recognize resulting awards and enforce them through proceedings not substantially more burdensome than those applicable to domestic awards.

Article II of the Convention contains the obligation to enforce agreements to arbitrate:

Article II

1.   Each Contracting State shall recognize an agreement in writing under which the parties undertake to submit to arbitration all or any differences which have arisen or which may arise between them in respect of a defined legal relationship, whether contractual or not, concerning a subject matter capable of settlement by arbitration.

2.   The term "agreement in writing" shall include an arbitral clause in a contract or an arbitration agreement, signed by the parties or contained in an exchange of letters or telegrams.

3.   The court of a Contracting State, when seized of an action in a matter in respect of which the parties have made an agreement within the meaning of this article, shall, at the request of one of the parties, refer the parties to arbitration unless it finds that the said agreement is null and void, inoperative or incapable of being performed.

Whether a subject matter is "capable of settlement by arbitration" and whether an agreement to arbitration is "null and void, inoperative or incapable of being performed" are questions the Convention leaves for the determination of its signatories and their courts. The first of these was at issue in the Mitsubishi case, excerpted below. See infra pp. 44–52.

To come within the scope of the Convention, an arbitral award must be made outside the territory of the enforcing state or must not be considered as "domestic" by the law of that state. The Convention permits a signatory to limit its application to awards rendered in other signatory countries and to awards in disputes that are considered "commercial." The United States has made both declarations. Article III requires the signatories to recognize and enforce arbitral awards. Article V, however, contains a narrow list of exceptions to this duty:

Article V

1.   Recognition and enforcement of the award may be refused, at the request of the party against whom it is invoked, only if that party furnishes to the competent authority where the recognition and enforcement is sought, proof that:

(a)   The parties to the agreement referred to in article II were, under the law applicable to them, under some incapacity, or the said agreement is not valid under the law to which the parties have subjected it or, failing any indication thereon, under the law of the country where the award was made; or

(b)   The party against whom the award is invoked was not given proper notice of the appointment of the arbitrator or of the arbitration proceedings or was otherwise unable to present his case; or

(c)   The award deals with a difference not contemplated by or not falling within the terms of the submission to arbitration, or it contains decisions on matters beyond the scope of the submission to arbitration, provided that, if the decisions on matters submitted to arbitration can be separated from those not so submitted, that part of the award which contains decisions on matters submitted to arbitration may be recognized and enforced; or

(d)   The composition of the arbitral authority or the arbitral procedure was not in accordance with the agreement of the parties, or, failing such agreement, was not in accordance with the law of the country where the arbitration took place; or

(e)   The award has not yet become binding on the parties, or has been set aside or suspended by a competent authority of the country in which, or under the law of which, that award was made.

2.   Recognition and enforcement of an arbitral award may also be refused if the competent authority in the country where recognition and enforcement is sought finds that:

(a)   The subject matter of the difference is not capable of settlement by arbitration under the law of that country; or

(b)   The recognition or enforcement of the award would be contrary to the public policy of that country.

The extent to which these defenses are exclusive is discussed below in the Toys "R" Us case. See infra pp. 53–61.

The Convention contains a "federalism clause," obligating a signatory's national government to put the treaty into effect as far as is within its own powers and, for the balance, to recommend action to its constituent states. Congress passed Chapter 2 of the Federal Arbitration Act to implement the Convention. Section 201 provides generally for the enforcement of the Convention. Section 202 limits the Act's applicability to awards arising out of "commercial relationships" and, in the case of dealings between citizens of the United States, to those arising out of a relationship that "involves property located abroad, envisages performance or enforcement abroad, or has some other reasonable relation with one or more foreign states." Section 203 vests jurisdiction over Convention cases in the federal courts without requiring an independent basis for federal jurisdiction. Under the Act, federal courts can also order arbitration as specified in the agreement even if the place agreed upon is outside the United States.

2.   ENFORCING THE AGREEMENT TO ARBITRATE

Article II of the New York Convention requires the courts of state-parties to the Convention to enforce agreements to arbitrate by staying or dismissing judicial proceedings regarding a dispute that is subject to the agreement. But a court need not enforce an agreement to arbitrate if it finds that the agreement is "null and void, inoperative or incapable of being performed." The grounds for finding an arbitration agreement "null and void" include fraud, duress, mistake, illegality, and unconscionability. But the U.S. Supreme Court has held that a party resisting enforcement of the agreement on one of these grounds must challenge the validity of the arbitration clause itself, not simply the validity of the contract as a whole. Prima Paint Corp. v. Flood & Conklin Mfg. Co., 388 U.S. 395, 403–404, 87 S.Ct. 1801, 1806, 18 L.Ed.2d 1270 (1967). Arguments that the contract as a whole is invalid must be considered by the arbitrators in the first instance. Buckeye Check Cashing, Inc. v. Cardegna, 546 U.S. 440, 446, 126 S. Ct. 1204, 1209, 163 L. Ed. 2d 1038 (2006).

Additionally, a court need not enforce an agreement to arbitrate if the subject matter of the dispute is non-arbitrable or, in the words of the New York Convention, if the subject matter is not "capable of settlement by arbitration." The Supreme Court addressed the question of arbitrability in Mitsubishi Motors, which remains the leading case.

Mitsubishi Motors Corporation v. Soler Chrysler-Plymouth, Inc.

Supreme Court of the United States, 1985
473 U.S. 614, 105 S.Ct. 3346, 87 L.Ed.2d 444

[In 1979 Soler Chrysler-Plymouth Inc. (Soler) entered into a distributorship agreement with Chrysler International S.A. (CISA), a Swiss subsidiary of Chrysler Corporation, to sell Plymouth passenger cars in a region of Puerto Rico. Paragraph 26 of that agreement authorized Chrysler to have Soler's orders filled by any Chrysler affiliate. At the same time CISA, Soler, and Mitsubishi Motors Corporation (Mitsubishi), a joint venture of CISA and Mitsubishi Heavy Industries, Inc., entered into a Sales Agreement referring to Paragraph 26. Paragraph VI of the Sales Agreement contained the following arbitration clause:

ARBITRATION OF CERTAIN MATTERS

All disputes, controversies or differences which may arise between MMC and BUYER out of or in relation to Articles I-B through V of this Agreement or for the breach thereof, shall be finally settled by arbitration in Japan in accordance with the rules and regulations of the Japan Commercial Arbitration Association.

After a number of years of satisfactory operation under the agreements, business slackened and disputes arose between Soler and Mitsubishi. Mitsubishi filed a request in Tokyo for arbitration under the agreement and brought an action in the U.S. District Court in Puerto Rico to compel arbitration. Soler denied the allegations and asserted causes of action under the Sherman Act, the Automobile Dealers Day in Court Act and Puerto Rican statutes. The District Court ordered arbitration on all issues except some that were not appealed. The Court of Appeals reversed that part of the order which submitted Soler's antitrust claims to arbitration. The Supreme Court granted certiorari and reversed. In an opinion by Justice Blackmun it found the antitrust claims were intended by the parties to be arbitrable and that this result was not precluded by the statute.]

* * *

We now turn to consider whether Soler's antitrust claims are nonarbitrable even though it has agreed to arbitrate them. In holding that they are not, the Court of Appeals followed the decision of the Second Circuit in *American Safety Equipment Corp. v. J.P. Maguire & Co.,* 391 F.2d 821 (1968). Notwithstanding the absence of any explicit support for such an exception in either the Sherman Act or the Federal Arbitration Act, the Second Circuit there reasoned that "the pervasive public interest in enforcement of the antitrust laws, and the nature of the claims that arise in such cases, combine to make ... antitrust claims ... inappropriate for arbitration." *Id.,* at 827–828. We find it unnecessary to assess the legitimacy of the *American Safety* doctrine as applied to agreements to arbitrate arising from domestic transactions. As in *Scherk v. Alberto-Culver Co.,* 417 U.S. 506, 94 S.Ct. 2449, 41 L.Ed.2d 270 (1974), we conclude that concerns of international comity, respect for the capacities of foreign and transnational tribunals, and sensitivity to the need of the international commercial system for predictability in the resolution of disputes require that we enforce the parties' agreement, even assuming that a contrary result would be forthcoming in a domestic context.

* * *

At the outset, we confess to some skepticism of certain aspects of the *American Safety* doctrine. As distilled by the First Circuit, 723 F.2d, at 162, the doctrine comprises four ingredients. First, private parties play a pivotal role in aiding governmental enforcement of the antitrust laws by means of the private action for treble damages. Second, "the strong possibility that contracts which generate antitrust disputes may be contracts of adhesion militates against automatic forum determination by contract." Third, antitrust issues, prone to complication, require sophisticated legal and economic analysis, and thus are "ill-adapted to strengths of the arbitral process, *i.e.,* expedition, minimal requirements of written rationale, simplicity, resort to basic concepts of common sense and simple equity." Finally, just as "issues of war and peace are too important to be vested in the generals, . . . decisions as to antitrust regulation of business are too important to be lodged in arbitrators chosen from the business community—particularly those from a foreign community that has had no experience with or exposure to our law and values." See *American Safety,* 391 F.2d, at 826–827.

Initially, we find the second concern unjustified. The mere appearance of an antitrust dispute does not alone warrant invalidation of the selected forum on the undemonstrated assumption that the arbitration clause is tainted. A party resisting arbitration of course may attack directly the validity of the agreement to arbitrate. . . .

Next, potential complexity should not suffice to ward off arbitration. We might well have some doubt that even the courts following *American Safety* subscribe fully to the view that antitrust matters are inherently insusceptible to resolution by arbitration, as these same courts have agreed that an undertaking to arbitrate antitrust claims entered into *after* the dispute arises is acceptable. . . . Moreover, it is often a judgment that streamlined proceedings and expeditious results will best serve their needs that causes parties to agree to arbitrate their disputes; it is typically a desire to keep the effort and expense required to resolve a dispute within manageable bounds that prompts them mutually to forgo access to judicial remedies. In sum, the factor of potential complexity alone does not persuade us that an arbitral tribunal could not properly handle an antitrust matter.

For similar reasons, we also reject the proposition that an arbitration panel will pose too great a danger of innate hostility to the constraints on business conduct that antitrust law imposes. International arbitrators frequently are drawn from the legal as well as the business community; where the dispute has an important legal component, the parties and the arbitral body with whose assistance they have agreed to settle their dispute can be expected to select arbitrators accordingly.[8] We decline to indulge the presumption that the parties and

---

[8]   See W. Craig, W. Park & J. Paulsson, supra, § 12.03, p. 28; Sanders, Commentary on UNCITRAL Arbitration Rules § 15.1, in II Yearbook Commercial Arbitration, supra, at 203.

We are advised by Mitsubishi and *amicus* International Chamber of Commerce, without contradiction by Soler, that the arbitration panel selected to hear the parties' claims here is composed of three Japanese lawyers, one a former law school dean, another a former judge, and the third a practicing attorney with American legal training who has written on Japanese antitrust law. Brief for Petitioner 26; Brief for International Chamber of Commerce as *Amicus Curiae* 16, n. 28.

arbitral body conducting a proceeding will be unable or unwilling to retain competent, conscientious, and impartial arbitrators.

We are left, then, with the core of the *American Safety* doctrine—the fundamental importance to American democratic capitalism of the regime of the antitrust laws. . . .

The importance of the private damages remedy, however, does not compel the conclusion that it may not be sought outside an American court. Notwithstanding its important incidental policing function, the treble-damages cause of action conferred on private parties by § 4 of the Clayton Act, 15 U.S.C. § 15, and pursued by Soler here by way of its third counterclaim, seeks primarily to enable an injured competitor to gain compensation for that injury. . . . And, of course, the antitrust cause of action remains at all times under the control of the individual litigant: no citizen is under an obligation to bring an antitrust suit, see *Illinois Brick Co. v. Illinois*, 431 U.S. 720, 746, 97 S.Ct. 2061, 2074, 52 L.Ed.2d 707 (1977), and the private antitrust plaintiff needs no executive or judicial approval before settling one. It follows that, at least where the international cast of a transaction would otherwise add an element of uncertainty to dispute resolution, the prospective litigant may provide in advance for a mutually agreeable procedure whereby he would seek his antitrust recovery as well as settle other controversies.

There is no reason to assume at the outset of the dispute that international arbitration will not provide an adequate mechanism. To be sure, the international arbitral tribunal owes no prior allegiance to the legal norms of particular states; hence, it has no direct obligation to vindicate their statutory dictates. The tribunal, however, is bound to effectuate the intentions of the parties. Where the parties have agreed that the arbitral body is to decide a defined set of claims which includes, as in these cases, those arising from the application of American antitrust law, the tribunal therefore should be bound to decide that dispute in accord with the national law giving rise to the claim. Cf. *Wilko v. Swan*, 346 U.S., at 433–434, 74 S.Ct., at 185–186.[9] And so long as the

---

The Court of Appeals was concerned that international arbitrators would lack "experience with or exposure to our law and values." 723 F.2d, at 162. The obstacles confronted by the arbitration panel in this case, however, should be no greater than those confronted by any judicial or arbitral tribunal required to determine foreign law. See, *e.g.*, Fed. Rule Civ. Proc. 44.1. Moreover, while our attachment to the antitrust laws may be stronger than most, many other countries, including Japan, have similar bodies of competition law. See, *e.g.*, 1, The Law of Transnational Business Transactions, ch. 9 (Banks, Antitrust Aspects of International Business Operations), § 9.03[7] (V. Nanda ed. 1984); H. Iyori & A. Uesugi, The Antimonopoly Laws of Japan (1983).

[9] In addition to the clause providing for arbitration before the Japan Commercial Arbitration Association, the Sales Agreement includes a choice-of-law clause which reads: "This Agreement is made in, and will be governed by and construed in all respects according to the laws of the Swiss Confederation as if entirely performed therein." App. 56. The United States raises the possibility that the arbitral panel will read this provision not simply to govern interpretation of the contract terms, but wholly to displace American law even where it otherwise would apply. Brief for United States as *Amicus Curiae* 20. The International Chamber of Commerce opines that it is "[c]onceivabl[e], although we believe it unlikely, [that] the arbitrators could consider Soler's affirmative claim of anticompetitive conduct by CISA and

prospective litigant effectively may vindicate its statutory cause of action in the arbitral forum, the statute will continue to serve both its remedial and deterrent function.

Having permitted the arbitration to go forward, the national courts of the United States will have the opportunity at the award enforcement stage to ensure that the legitimate interest in the enforcement of the antitrust laws has been addressed. The Convention reserves to each signatory country the right to refuse enforcement of an award where the "recognition or enforcement of the award would be contrary to the public policy of that country." Art. V(2)(b), 21 U.S.T., at 2520; see *Scherk,* 417 U.S., at 519, n. 14, 94 S.Ct., at 2457, n. 14. While the efficacy of the arbitral process requires that substantive review at the award enforcement stage remain minimal, it would not require intrusive inquiry to ascertain that the tribunal took cognizance of the antitrust claims and actually decided them.

As international trade has expanded in recent decades, so too has the use of international arbitration to resolve disputes arising in the course of that trade. The controversies that international arbitral institutions are called upon to resolve have increased in diversity as well as in complexity. Yet the potential of these tribunals for efficient disposition of legal disagreements arising from commercial relations has not yet been tested. If they are to take a central place in the international legal order, national courts will need to "shake off the old judicial hostility to arbitration," *Kulukundis Shipping Co. v. Amtorg Trading Corp.*, 126 F.2d 978, 985 (C.A.2 1942), and also their customary and understandable unwillingness to cede jurisdiction of a claim arising under domestic-law to a foreign or transnational tribunal. To this extent, at least, it will be necessary for national courts to subordinate domestic notions of arbitrability to the international policy favoring commercial arbitration. See *Scherk, supra.*[10]

Mitsubishi to fall within the purview of this choice-of-law provision, with the result that it would be decided under Swiss law rather than the U.S. Sherman Act." Brief for International Chamber of Commerce as *Amicus Curiae* 25. At oral argument, however, counsel for Mitsubishi conceded that American law applied to the antitrust claims and represented that the claims had been submitted to the arbitration panel in Japan on that basis. Tr. of Oral Arg. 18. The record confirms that before the decision of the Court of Appeals the arbitral panel had taken these claims under submission. See District Court Order of May 25, 1984, pp. 2–3.

We therefore have no occasion to speculate on this matter at this stage in the proceedings, when Mitsubishi seeks to enforce the agreement to arbitrate, not to enforce an award. Nor need we consider now the effect of an arbitral tribunal's failure to take cognizance of the statutory cause of action on the claimant's capacity to reinitiate suit in federal court. We merely note that in the event the choice-of-forum and choice-of-law clauses operated in tandem as a prospective waiver of a party's right to pursue statutory remedies for antitrust violations, we would have little hesitation in condemning the agreement as against public policy. . . .

[10] We do not quarrel with the Court of Appeals' conclusion that Art. II(1) of the Convention, which requires the recognition of agreements to arbitrate that involve "subject matter capable of settlement by arbitration," contemplates exceptions to arbitrability grounded in domestic law. . . . And it appears that before acceding to the Convention the Senate was advised by a State Department memorandum that the Convention provided for such exceptions. See S.Exec.Doc. E, 90th Cong., 2d Sess., 19 (1968).

* * *

[A dissenting opinion by Justice Stevens, joined by Justice Brennan and, in large part, by Justice Marshall found that there was no intention to arbitrate the antitrust claims. It pointed out that the clause applied only to two-party disputes between Soler and Mitsubishi and that this antitrust claim involved Chrysler as well. It also noted that the clause covered only a few articles of the Agreement, none of which was directly involved in the antitrust allegations. Portions of the dissent addressing the public policy issue follow.]

* * *

The Court has repeatedly held that a decision by Congress to create a special statutory remedy renders a private agreement to arbitrate a federal statutory claim unenforceable. . . .

To make this point it is appropriate to recall some of our past appraisals of the importance of this federal policy and then to identify some of the specific remedies Congress has designed to implement it. It was Chief Justice Hughes who characterized the Sherman Antitrust Act as "a charter of freedom" that may fairly be compared to a constitutional provision. See *Appalachian Coals, Inc. v. United States*, 288 U.S. 344, 359–360, 53 S.Ct. 471, 473–474, 77 L.Ed. 825 (1933). In *United States v. Philadelphia National Bank*, 374 U.S. 321, 371, 83 S.Ct. 1715, 1745, 10 L.Ed.2d 915 (1963), the Court referred to the extraordinary "magnitude" of the value choices made by Congress in enacting the Sherman Act. More recently, the Court described the weighty public interests underlying the basic philosophy of the statute:

> "Antitrust laws in general, and the Sherman Act in particular, are the Magna Carta of free enterprise. They are as important to the preservation of economic freedom and our free-enterprise system as the Bill of Rights is to the protection of our fundamental personal freedoms. And the freedom guaranteed each and every business, no matter how small, is the freedom to compete—to assert with vigor, imagination, devotion, and ingenuity whatever economic muscle it can muster. Implicit in such freedom is the notion that it cannot be foreclosed with respect to one sector of the economy because certain private citizens or groups believe that such foreclosure might promote

---

In acceding to the Convention the Senate restricted its applicability to commercial matters, in accord with Art. I(3). See 21 U.S.T., at 2519, 2560. Yet in implementing the Convention by amendment to the Federal Arbitration Act, Congress did not specify any matters it intended to exclude from its scope. See Act of July 31, 1970, Pub.L. 91–368, 84 Stat. 692, codified at 9 U.S.C. §§ 201–208. . . . The utility of the Convention in promoting the process of international commercial arbitration depends upon the willingness of national courts to let go of matters they normally would think of as their own. Doubtless, Congress may specify categories of claims it wishes to reserve for decision by our own courts without contravening this Nation's obligations under the Convention. But we decline to subvert the spirit of the United States' accession to the Convention by recognizing subject-matter exceptions where Congress has not expressly directed the courts to do so.

greater competition in a more important sector of the economy."
United States v. Topco Associates, Inc., 405 U.S. 596, 610, 92
S.Ct. 1126, 1135, 31 L.Ed.2d 515 (1972).

* * *

The Court assumes for the purposes of its decision that the antitrust
issues would not be arbitrable if this were a purely domestic dispute, . . .
but holds that the international character of the controversy makes it
arbitrable. The holding rests on vague concerns for the international
implications of its decision and a misguided application of *Scherk v.
Alberto-Culver*, 417 U.S. 506, 94 S.Ct. 2449, 41 L.Ed.2d 270 (1974).

International Obligations of the United States

Before relying on its own notions of what international comity
requires, it is surprising that the Court does not determine the specific
commitments that the United States has made to enforce private
agreements to arbitrate disputes arising under public law. As the Court
acknowledges, the only treaty relevant here is the Convention on the
Recognition and Enforcement of Foreign Arbitral Awards. 21 U.S.T.
2517, T.I.A.S. No. 6997. The Convention was adopted in 1958 at a
multilateral conference sponsored by the United Nations. This Nation
did not sign the proposed convention at that time; displaying its
characteristic caution before entering into international compacts, the
United States did not accede to it until twelve years later.

As the Court acknowledged in *Scherk v. Alberto-Culver Co.*, 417 U.S.,
at 520, n. 15, 94 S.Ct., at 2457, n. 15, the principal purpose of the
Convention "was to encourage the recognition and enforcement of
commercial arbitration agreements in international contracts and to
unify the standards by which agreements to arbitrate are observed and
arbitral awards are enforced in the signatory countries." However, the
United States, as *amicus curiae,* advises the Court that the Convention
"clearly contemplates" that signatory nations will enforce domestic laws
prohibiting the arbitration of certain subject matters. Brief for the United
States as *Amicus Curiae* 28. This interpretation of the Convention was
adopted by the Court of Appeals, 723 F.2d, at 162–166, and the Court
declines to reject it, *ante*, at 3360, n. 21. The construction is beyond doubt.

Article II(3) of the Convention provides that the court of a
Contracting State, "when seized of an action in a matter in respect of
which the parties have made an agreement within the meaning of this
article, shall, at the request of one of the parties, refer the parties to
arbitration." This obligation does not arise, however, (i) if the agreement
"is null and void, inoperative or incapable of being performed," Art. II(3),
or (ii) if the dispute does not concern "a subject matter capable of
settlement by arbitration," Art. II(1). The former qualification principally
applies to matters of fraud, mistake, and duress in the inducement, or
problems of procedural fairness and feasibility. 723 F.2d, at 164. The
latter clause plainly suggests the possibility that some subject matters

are not capable of arbitration under the domestic laws of the signatory nations, and that agreements to arbitrate such disputes need not be enforced.

This construction is confirmed by the provisions of the Convention which provide for the enforcement of international arbitration awards. Article III provides that each "Contracting State shall recognize arbitral awards as binding and enforce them." However, if an arbitration award is "contrary to the public policy of [a] country" called upon to enforce it, or if it concerns a subject matter which is "not capable of settlement by arbitration under the law of that country," the convention does not require that it be enforced. Art. V(2)(a) and (b). Thus, reading articles II and V together, the Convention provides that agreements to arbitrate disputes which are nonarbitrable under domestic law need not be honored, nor awards rendered under them enforced.

This construction is also supported by the legislative history of the Senate's advice and consent to the Convention. In presenting the Convention for the Senate's consideration the President offered the following interpretation of Article II(1):

> "The requirement that the agreement apply to a matter capable of settlement by arbitration is necessary in order to take proper account of laws in force in many countries which prohibit the submission of certain questions to arbitration. In some States of the United States, for example, disputes affecting the title to real property are not arbitrable." S. Exec. Doc. E, at 19.

The Senate's consent to the Convention presumably was made in light of this interpretation, and thus it is to be afforded considerable weight. *Sumitomo Shoji America, Inc. v. Avagliano*, 457 U.S. 176, 184–185, 102 S.Ct. 2374, 2379–2380, 72 L.Ed.2d 765 (1982).

International Comity

It is clear then that the international obligations of the United States permit us to honor Congress' commitment to the exclusive resolution of antitrust disputes in the federal courts. The Court today refuses to do so offering only vague concerns for comity among nations. The courts of other nations, on the other hand, have applied the exception provided in the Convention, and refused to enforce agreements to arbitrate specific subject matters of concern to them.[11]

It may be that the subject matter exception to the Convention ought to be reserved—as a matter of domestic law—for matters of the greatest public interest which involve concerns that are shared by other nations.

---

[11] For example, the Cour de Cassation in Belgium has held that disputes arising under a Belgian statute limiting the unilateral termination of exclusive distributorships are not arbitrable under the Convention in that country, *Audi-NSU Auto Union A.G. v. S.A. Adelin Petit & Cie.* (1979), in 5 Y.B. Commercial Arbitration 257, 259, and the Corte di Cassazione in Italy has held that labor disputes are not arbitrable under the Convention in that country, *Compagnia Generale Construzioni v. Piersanti*, [1980] Foro Italiano I 190, in 6 Y.B. Commercial Arbitration 229, 230.

The Sherman Act's commitment to free competitive markets is among our most important civil policies. Supra, at 3366–3370. This commitment, shared by other nations which are signatory to the Convention,[12] is hardly the sort of parochial concern that we should decline to enforce in the interest of international comity. Indeed, the branch of Government entrusted with the conduct of political relations with foreign governments has informed us that the "United States' determination that federal antitrust claims are nonarbitrable under the Convention . . . is not likely to result in either surprise or recrimination on the part of other signatories to the Convention." Brief for the United States as *Amicus Curiae* 30.

* * *

The Court's repeated incantation of the high ideals of "international arbitration" creates the impression that this case involves the fate of an institution designed to implement a formula for world peace. But just as it is improper to subordinate the public interest in enforcement of antitrust policy to the private interest in resolving commercial disputes, so is it equally unwise to allow a vision of world unity to distort the importance of the selection of the proper forum for resolving this dispute. Like any other mechanism for resolving controversies, international arbitration will only succeed if it is realistically limited to tasks it is capable of performing well—the prompt and inexpensive resolution of essentially contractual disputes between commercial partners. As for matters involving the political passions and the fundamental interests of nations, even the multilateral convention adopted under the auspices of the United Nations recognizes that private international arbitration is incapable of achieving satisfactory results.

In my opinion, the elected representatives of the American people would not have us dispatch an American citizen to a foreign land in search of an uncertain remedy for the violation of a public right that is protected by the Sherman Act. This is especially so when there has been no genuine bargaining over the terms of the submission, and the arbitration remedy provided has not even the most elementary guarantees of fair process. Consideration of a fully developed record by a jury, instructed in the law by a federal judge, and subject to appellate review, is a surer guide to the competitive character of a commercial practice than the practically unreviewable judgment of a private arbitrator.

* * *

---

[12] For example, the Federal Republic of Germany has a vigorous antitrust program, and prohibits the enforcement of pre-dispute agreements to arbitrate such claims under some circumstances. See Act Against Restraints of Competition § 91(1), in Organisation for Economic Co-operation and Development, Guide to Legislation on Restrictive Business Practices, Part D, 49 (1980). See also 2 G. Delaume, Transnational Contracts § 13.06, at 31 and n. 3 (1982).

3. ENFORCING ARBITRAL AWARDS

Once an arbitral tribunal has rendered an award, the losing party may seek limited review by a national court. Article V of the New York Convention contemplates review by two different court systems. First, Article V(1)(e) mentions the possibility that the award could be "set aside or suspended by a competent authority of the country in which, or under the law of which, that award was made." Courts in the United States generally have declined to recognize and enforce awards that have been set aside by a court having jurisdiction to do so. See, e.g., TermoRio S.A., E.S.P. v. Electranta S.P., 487 F.3d 928, 936 (D.C. Cir. 2007). But see Chromalloy Aeroservices v. Arab Republic of Egypt, 939 F.Supp. 907 (D.D.C. 1996) (enforcing award set aside by Egyptian courts).

Second, Article V allows review by the courts of the place where enforcement is sought to determine if one of the New York Convention's enumerated grounds for refusing recognition and enforcement exists. The case that follows considers whether the grounds for setting aside an award in the courts of the seat of arbitration may be broader than the grounds set forth in the New York Convention.

Yusuf Ahmed Alghanim & Sons, W.L.L. v. Toys "R" Us, Inc.

United States Court of Appeals for the Second Circuit, 1997
126 F.3d 15

■ MINER, CIRCUIT JUDGE.

* * *

BACKGROUND

In November of 1982, respondent-appellant Toys "R" Us, Inc. (collectively with respondent-appellant TRU (HK) Limited, "Toys 'R' Us") and petitioner-appellee Yusuf Ahmed Alghanim & Sons, W.L.L. ("Alghanim"), a privately owned Kuwaiti business, entered into a License and Technical Assistance Agreement (the "agreement") and a Supply Agreement. Through the agreement, Toys "R" Us granted Alghanim a limited right to open Toys "R" Us stores and use its trademarks in Kuwait and 13 other countries located in and around the Middle East (the "territory"). Toys "R" Us further agreed to supply Alghanim with its technology, expertise and assistance in the toy business.

From 1982 to the December 1993 commencement of the arbitration giving rise to this appeal, Alghanim opened four toy stores, all in Kuwait. According to Toys "R" Us, the first such store, opened in 1983, resembled a Toys "R" Us store in the United States, but the other three, two of which were opened in 1985 and one in 1988, were small storefronts with only limited merchandise. It is uncontested that Alghanim's stores lost some $6.65 million over the 11-year period from 1982 to 1993, and turned a profit only in one year of this period.

* * *

On July 20, 1992, Toys "R" Us purported to exercise its right to terminate the agreement, sending Alghanim a notice of non-renewal stating that the agreement would terminate on January 31, 1993. . . .

* * *

Through the balance of 1992 and 1993, the parties unsuccessfully attempted to renegotiate the agreement or devise a new arrangement. In September of 1993, the parties discussed Alghanim's willingness to relinquish its rights under the agreement. In one discussion, Amin Kadrie, Alghanim's chief operating officer and the head of its toy business, offered to "release the business right now" if Toys "R" Us would "give us $2 million for the losses we've incurred [in] trying to develop this business." (J.A. 457.) Toys "R" Us declined, offering instead to buy Alghanim's inventory at Alghanim's cost. The parties could not agree upon a reconciliation.

At the end of 1993, Toys "R" Us contracted with Al-Futtaim Sons Co., LLC ("Al-Futtaim") for the post-Alghanim rights to open Toys "R" Us stores in five of the countries under the agreement, including Kuwait, and with ATA Development Co. ("ATA") for the post-Alghanim rights to open Toys "R" Us stores in Saudi Arabia. These two companies initially offered $30 million for the rights, and eventually paid a total of $22.5 million.

On December 20, 1993, Toys "R" Us invoked the dispute-resolution mechanism in the agreement, initiating an arbitration before the American Arbitration Association. Toys "R" Us sought a declaration that the agreement was terminated on December 31, 1993. Alghanim responded by counterclaiming for breach of contract.

* * *

On July 11, 1996, the arbitrator awarded Alghanim $46.44 million for lost profits under the agreement, plus 9 percent interest to accrue from December 31, 1994. The arbitrator's findings and legal conclusions were set forth in a 47-page opinion.

Alghanim petitioned the district court to confirm the award under the Convention on the Recognition and Enforcement of Foreign Arbitral Awards of June 10, 1958 ("Convention"), 21 U.S.T. 2517, 330 U.N.T.S. 38, *reprinted at* 9 U.S.C. § 201. Toys "R" Us cross-moved to vacate or modify the award under the Federal Arbitration Act ("FAA"), 9 U.S.C. § 1 *et seq.,* arguing that the award was clearly irrational, in manifest disregard of the law, and in manifest disregard of the terms of the agreement. . . .

DISCUSSION

I.   *Availability of the FAA's Grounds for Relief*
     in Confirmation Under the Convention

* * *

A.   *Applicability of the Convention*

Neither party seriously disputes the applicability of the Convention to this case and it is clear to us that the Convention does apply. The Convention provides that it will

> apply to the recognition and enforcement of arbitral awards made in the territory of a State other than the State where the recognition and enforcement of such awards are sought, and arising out of differences between persons, whether physical or legal. It shall also apply to arbitral awards *not considered as domestic awards* in the State where their recognition and enforcement are sought.

Convention art. I(1) (emphasis added). The Convention does not define nondomestic awards. *See Bergesen v. Joseph Muller Corp.*, 710 F.2d 928, 932 (2d Cir.1983). However, 9 U.S.C. § 202, one of the provisions implementing the Convention, provides that

> [a]n agreement or award arising out of such a relationship which is entirely between citizens of the United States shall be deemed not to fall under the Convention unless that relationship involves property located abroad, envisages performance or enforcement abroad, or has some other reasonable relation with one or more foreign states.

In *Bergesen,* we held "that awards 'not considered as domestic' denotes awards which are subject to the Convention not because made abroad, but because made within the legal framework of another country, e.g., pronounced in accordance with foreign law or involving parties domiciled or having their principal place of business outside the enforcing jurisdiction." 710 F.2d at 932 (quoting 9 U.S.C. § 201). . . .

The Convention's applicability in this case is clear. The dispute giving rise to this appeal involved two nondomestic parties and one United States corporation, and principally involved conduct and contract performance in the Middle East. Thus, we consider the arbitral award leading to this action a non-domestic award and thus within the scope of the Convention.

B.   *Authority Under the Convention to Set Aside*
     An Award Under Domestic Arbitral Law

Toys "R" Us argues that the district court properly found that it had the authority under the Convention to apply the FAA's implied grounds for setting aside the award. We agree.

Under the Convention, the district court's role in reviewing a foreign arbitral award is strictly limited: "The court shall confirm the award unless it finds one of the grounds for refusal or deferral of recognition or enforcement of the award specified in the said Convention." 9 U.S.C. § 207. . . . Under Article V of the Convention, the grounds for refusing to recognize or enforce an arbitral award are [the Court quotes Article V, supra pp. 42–43]. . . . These seven grounds are the only grounds explicitly provided under the Convention.

In determining the availability of the FAA's implied grounds for setting aside, the text of the Convention leaves us with two questions: (1) whether, in addition to the Convention's express grounds for refusal, other grounds can be read into the Convention by implication, much as American courts have read implied grounds for relief into the FAA, and (2) whether, under Article V(1)(e), the courts of the United States are authorized to apply United States procedural arbitral law, i.e., the FAA, to nondomestic awards rendered in the United States. We answer the first question in the negative and the second in the affirmative.

1. Availability Under the Convention of Implied Grounds for Refusal

We have held that the FAA and the Convention have "overlapping coverage" to the extent that they do not conflict. *Bergesen,* 710 F.2d at 934. . . . However, by that same token, to the extent that the Convention prescribes the exclusive grounds for relief from an award under the Convention, that application of the FAA's implied grounds would be in conflict, and is thus precluded. . . .

In *Parsons & Whittemore Overseas Co. v. Societe Generale de L'Industrie du Papier (Rakta),* 508 F.2d 969 (2d Cir.1974), we declined to decide whether the implied defense of "manifest disregard" applies under the Convention, having decided that even if it did, appellant's claim would fail. *See id.* at 977. Nonetheless, we noted that "[b]oth the legislative history of Article V and the statute enacted to implement the United States' accession to the Convention are strong authority for treating as exclusive the bases set forth in the Convention for vacating an award." *Id.* (citation and footnote omitted).

There is now considerable caselaw holding that, in an action to confirm an award rendered in, or under the law of, a foreign jurisdiction, the grounds for relief enumerated in Article V of the Convention are the only grounds available for setting aside an arbitral award. . . . This conclusion is consistent with the Convention's pro-enforcement bias. . . . We join these courts in declining to read into the Convention the FAA's implied defenses to confirmation of an arbitral award.

2. Nondomestic Award Rendered in the United States

Although Article V provides the exclusive grounds for refusing confirmation under the Convention, one of those exclusive grounds is where "[t]he award . . . has been set aside or suspended by a competent authority of the country in which, or under the law of which, that award was made." Convention art. V(1)(e). Those courts holding that implied defenses were inapplicable under the Convention did so in the context of petitions to confirm awards rendered abroad. These courts were not presented with the question whether Article V(1)(e) authorizes an action to set aside an arbitral award under the domestic law of the state in which, or under which, the award was rendered. We, however, are faced head-on with that question in the case before us, because the arbitral award in this case was rendered in the United States, and both confirmation and vacatur were then sought in the United States.

We read Article V(1)(e) of the Convention to allow a court in the country under whose law the arbitration was conducted to apply domestic arbitral law, in this case the FAA, to a motion to set aside or vacate that arbitral award. . . .

* * *

This interpretation of Article V(1)(e) also finds support in the scholarly work of commentators on the Convention and in the judicial decisions of our sister signatories to the Convention. . . . The defense in Article V(1)(e)

> incorporates the entire body of review rights in the issuing jurisdiction. . . . If the scope of judicial review in the rendering state extends beyond the other six defenses allowed under the New York Convention, the losing party's opportunity to avoid enforcement is automatically enhanced: The losing party can first attempt to derail the award on appeal on grounds that would not be permitted elsewhere during enforcement proceedings.

Daniel M. Kolkey, *Attacking Arbitral Awards: Rights of Appeal and Review in International Arbitrations,* 22 Int'l Law. 693, 694 (1988).

* * *

There is no indication in the Convention of any intention to deprive the rendering state of its supervisory authority over an arbitral award, including its authority to set aside that award under domestic law. The Convention succeeded and replaced the Convention on the Execution of Foreign Arbitral Awards ("Geneva Convention"), Sept. 26, 1927, 92 L.N.T.S. 301. The primary defect of the Geneva Convention was that it required an award first to be recognized in the rendering state before it could be enforced abroad, *see* Geneva Convention arts. 1(d), 4(2), 92 L.N.T.S. at 305, 306, the so-called requirement of "double *exequatur.*" . . .

The Convention eliminated this problem by eradicating the requirement that a court in the rendering state recognize an award before it could be taken and enforced abroad. . . .

Nonetheless, under the Convention, the power and authority of the local courts of the rendering state remain of paramount importance. . . . Another commentator explained:

> Significantly, [Article V(1)(e)] fails to specify the grounds upon which the rendering State may set aside or suspend the award. While it would have provided greater reliability to the enforcement of awards under the Convention had the available grounds been defined in some way, such action would have constituted meddling with national procedure for handling domestic awards, a subject beyond the competence of the Conference.

Leonard V. Quigley, *Accession by the United States to the United Nations Convention on the Recognition and Enforcement of Foreign Arbitral Awards,* 70 Yale L.J. 1049, 1070 (1961). From the plain language and history of the Convention, it is thus apparent that a party may seek to vacate or set aside an award in the state in which, or under the law of which, the award is rendered. Moreover, the language and history of the Convention make it clear that such a motion is to be governed by domestic law of the rendering state, despite the fact that the award is nondomestic within the meaning of the Convention as we have interpreted it in *Bergesen,* 710 F.2d at 932.

In sum, we conclude that the Convention mandates very different regimes for the review of arbitral awards (1) in the state in which, or under the law of which, the award was made, and (2) in other states where recognition and enforcement are sought. The Convention specifically contemplates that the state in which, or under the law of which, the award is made, will be free to set aside or modify an award in accordance with its domestic arbitral law and its full panoply of express and implied grounds for relief. *See* Convention art. V(1)(e). However, the Convention is equally clear that when an action for enforcement is brought in a foreign state, the state may refuse to enforce the award only on the grounds explicitly set forth in Article V of the Convention.

II.   *Application of FAA Grounds for Relief*

Having determined that the FAA does govern Toys "R" Us's cross-motion to vacate, our application of the FAA's implied grounds for vacatur is swift. . . .

"[T]he confirmation of an arbitration award is a summary proceeding that merely makes what is already a final arbitration award a judgment of the court." *Florasynth, Inc. v. Pickholz,* 750 F.2d 171, 176 (2d Cir.1984). The review of arbitration awards is "very limited . . . in order to avoid undermining the twin goals of arbitration, namely, settling disputes efficiently and avoiding long and expensive litigation." *Folkways Music Publishers, Inc. v. Weiss,* 989 F.2d 108, 111 (2d Cir.1993). Accordingly, "the showing required to avoid summary confirmance is high." *Ottley v. Schwartzberg,* 819 F.2d 373, 376 (2d Cir.1987).

More particularly, "[t]his court has generally refused to second guess an arbitrator's resolution of a contract dispute." *John T. Brady & Co. v. Form-Eze Sys., Inc.*, 623 F.2d 261, 264 (2d Cir.1980). As we have explained: "An arbitrator's decision is entitled to substantial deference, and the arbitrator need only explicate his reasoning under the contract 'in terms that offer even a barely colorable justification for the outcome reached' in order to withstand judicial scrutiny." *In re Marine Pollution Serv., Inc.*, 857 F.2d 91, 94 (2d Cir.1988) (quoting *Andros Compania*, 579 F.2d at 704).

However, awards may be vacated, *see* 9 U.S.C. § 10, or modified, *see id.* § 11, in the limited circumstances where the arbitrator's award is in manifest disregard of the terms of the agreement, *see Leed Architectural Prods., Inc. v. United Steelworkers, Local 6674*, 916 F.2d 63, 65–66 (2d Cir.1990), or where the award is in "manifest disregard of the law," *Fahnestock & Co. v. Waltman*, 935 F.2d 512, 515–16 (2d Cir.1991); *Merrill Lynch, Pierce, Fenner & Smith, Inc. v. Bobker*, 808 F.2d 930, 933–34 (2d Cir.1986). We find that neither of these implied grounds is met in the present case.

A.   *Manifest Disregard of the Law*

Toys "R" Us argues that the arbitrator manifestly disregarded New York law on lost profits awards for breach of contract by returning a speculative award. This contention is without merit. "[M]ere error in the law or failure on the part of the arbitrator[ ] to understand or apply the law" is not sufficient to establish manifest disregard of the law. *Fahnestock*, 935 F.2d at 516 (quotations omitted). For an award to be in "manifest disregard of the law,"

> [t]he error must have been obvious and capable of being readily and instantly perceived by the average person qualified to serve as an arbitrator. Moreover, the term "disregard" implies that the arbitrator appreciates the existence of a clearly governing legal principle but decides to ignore or pay no attention to it.

Merrill Lynch, 808 F.2d at 933.

In the instant case, the arbitrator was well aware of and carefully applied New York's law on lost profits. The arbitrator specifically addressed *Kenford Co. v. County of Erie*, 67 N.Y.2d 257, 502 N.Y.S.2d 131, 493 N.E.2d 234 (1986), which contains New York's law on the subject and upon which Toys "R" Us relied in its arguments, and concluded:

> I do not think the Kenford case rules out damages in this case. Kenford disallowed damages based on future profits from concessions in a domed stadium that was never built. . . . In this case [Alghanim], which is forced into the estimating posture because of [Toys "R" Us's] breach, bases its damages not on its own experience but on [Toys "R" Us's]. [Toys "R" Us] has hundreds of toy stores worldwide. Since it has been found that the Agreements require [Toys "R" Us] to provide a wide variety

of services, similar to what it provides its own toy stores, I find that [Alghanim's] method of estimating damages is reasonable and believable, and provides a sound basis on which to fashion the award.

(J.A. 557.) We find no manifest disregard of the law in this analysis.

* * *

The fact that Alghanim lost $6.65 million over ten years does not make the arbitrator's award of future lost profits of $46 million "completely irrational." Past losses do not necessarily negate any expectation of future profits. . . .

As to the purported $2 million buyout offer, no witness has testified that the $2 million figure was an estimate of the value of Alghanim's toy business. Kadrie, the primary Alghanim officer involved with the toy business, testified that, in his understanding, settlement with Toys "R" Us would serve to provide Alghanim "some relief on the cost of liquidating [its] inventory." (J.A. 405–06.) Accordingly, Alghanim argues that $2 million was the value Alghanim placed on its inventory at the time. Furthermore, according to a Toys "R" Us executive, Kadrie, in making this offer, expressly stated that the $2 million was to recoup losses Alghanim had incurred in trying to develop the business. Therefore, there is no proof that this figure was Alghanim's, or anyone else's, estimation of the value of the business. Thus, the arbitrator did not manifestly disregard lost profits law in refusing to treat the $2 million figure as a buyout offer.

* * *

B.   Manifest Disregard of the Agreement

Toys "R" Us also argues that the district court erred in refusing to vacate the award because the arbitrator manifestly disregarded the terms of the agreement. In particular, Toys "R" Us disputes the arbitrator's interpretation of four contract terms: (1) the termination provision; (2) the conforming stores provision; (3) the non-assignment provision; and (4) the deletion provision. We find no error.

Interpretation of these contract terms is within the province of the arbitrator and will not be overruled simply because we disagree with that interpretation. *See United Steelworkers v. Enterprise Wheel & Car Corp.*, 363 U.S. 593, 599, 80 S.Ct. 1358, 1362, 4 L.Ed.2d 1424 (1960). . . .

As to each of these contract provisions, Toys "R" Us merely takes issue with the arbitrator's well-reasoned interpretations of those provisions, and simply offers its own contrary interpretations. Toys "R" Us does not advance a convincing argument that the arbitrator manifestly disregarded the agreement. We will not overturn the arbitrator's award merely because we do not concur with the arbitrator's reading of the agreement. For the reasons stated by the district court, we

find the arbitrator's interpretation of the contractual provisions
supportable.

———————

Toys "R" Us concludes that "manifest disregard" is not available as
a defense under the Arbitration Convention, on the basis that the
grounds for relief enumerated in Article V of that Convention are
exclusive. Like many courts before it, however, it accepts manifest
disregard as an implied ground for vacatur under the FAA. In 2008, the
U.S. Supreme Court rejected this position, holding that Sections 10 and
11 of that Act provide the exclusive grounds for vacatur and modification.
Hall Street Associates, L.L.C., v. Mattel, Inc., 552 U.S. 576 (2008).
However, the Court left room for the argument that manifest disregard
had developed not as an independent ground for relief, but as a
"shorthand" either for particular enumerated grounds in the FAA or for
all of them collectively. Many subsequent cases grappled with this
ambiguity, and several lower courts subscribed to the opinion that
manifest disregard survived the Hall Street decision as a "judicial gloss"
on the enumerated grounds for vacatur. Interestingly, in a 2010 decision,
the Supreme Court declined to clarify its own intent as to this point.
Stolt-Nielsen S.A. v. AnimalFeeds International Corp., 559 U.S. 662
(2010).

QUESTIONS

(1) If a court concluded that the party seeking to enforce the
arbitration clause was vastly more powerful than the other side, and that
the particular arbitral proceedings chosen would prejudice the other
side's chances of obtaining a fair hearing, must it enforce arbitration?

(2) Representing a party in a situation like that of the distributor
in Mitsubishi v. Soler, how would you assess your chances of persuading
an arbitrator that the manufacturer had violated the Sherman Act—in
comparison with a U.S. judge or jury? Does the case hold out any hope
that you could raise the issue in U.S. courts again if you failed to prevail
before the arbitrators?

(3) In a proceeding by Mitsubishi to enforce the award, would the
analysis in Toys "R" Us have permitted Soler to argue that the arbitrators
had ignored or misinterpreted U.S. antitrust laws? Should the standard
for enforcing an arbitral award in the face of claims of public policy be
the same as (or higher or lower than) that applied to a foreign court
judgment?

Additional reading: IBA Guidelines for Drafting International
Arbitration Clauses (2010); Debevoise International Arbitration Clause
Handbook (2018); Craig, Park & Paulsson on International Chamber of
Commerce Arbitration (2019); Lew, Mistelis & Kröll, Comparative
International Commercial Arbitration (2003); Redfern, Hunter, Blackaby
& Partasides, Redfern and Hunter on International Arbitration (6th ed.

2015). For a comparison of arbitration and litigation, see Vagts, Dispute-Resolution Mechanisms in International Business, 203 Hague Recueil des Cours 13 (1987).

CHAPTER III

A BASIC INTRODUCTION TO TRANSNATIONAL LAW

International business transactions occur within a web of legal frameworks. Some are national, like the legal systems of the parties' countries, while others are international, like the systems created by various treaties or the rules of customary international law. Yet the division between national and international should not be overstated. In fact, as we shall see, international law penetrates and influences national systems in a variety of ways, while national laws and practices also shape international law. To avoid misleading distinctions, Professor Philip Jessup (later a judge on the International Court of Justice) proposed the phrase "transnational law." Jessup defined this phrase "to include all law which regulates actions or events that transcend national frontiers. Both public and private international law are included, as are other rules which do not wholly fit into such standard categories."[1]

In the best of all possible intellectual worlds, the student of international business transactions would already have acquired a familiarity with international law and its relation to domestic legal systems in a course like Public International Law or Transnational Law. But realism and experience suggest that this is not always the case. This chapter therefore provides a brief introduction to some of the concepts an international business lawyer must understand. We begin with a brief discussion of terminology and of the relationship between international and national law. This is followed by sections on the two principal types of international law: customary international law and treaties. A final section examines the extraterritorial reach of national legal systems and the rules of international law that may constrain them.

A. A SKETCH OF TRANSNATIONAL LAW

At the outset, one confronts a bewildering array of terms: "transnational law," "the law of nations," "international law," "public international law," "private international law," "customary international law," "general principles of law," "conventions," "treaties," "executive agreements." Confusion may be heightened by the fact that such terms overlap and are not always used consistently.

"International law" is a relatively modern term. Coined by Jeremy Bentham in 1789, it entered into common usage only in the nineteenth century. An older term, used at the time the United States was founded, was "the law of nations." Article I, section 8 of the U.S. Constitution gives

---

[1] Jessup, Transnational Law 2 (1956).

Congress the power "[t]o define and punish. . . . Offenses against the Law of Nations," while the Alien Tort Statute, 28 U.S.C. § 1350, first passed as part of the Judiciary Act of 1789, gives the federal district courts jurisdiction over "any civil action by an alien for a tort only, committed in violation of the law of nations or a treaty of the United States." In the eighteenth century, the law of nations covered not only rules that applied between states but also maritime law, the law merchant, and the conflict of laws. Today, some of these topics have been domesticated, while new rules of international law have emerged in areas like human rights.

One may begin to understand what is meant by "international law" today by considering the directions given to the International Court of Justice by Article 38 of its Statute:

> 1. The Court, whose function is to decide in accordance with international law such disputes as are submitted to it, shall apply;

>> (a) international conventions, whether general or particular, establishing rules expressly recognized by the contesting states;

>> (b) international custom, as evidence of a general practice accepted as law;

>> (c) the general principles of law recognized by civilized nations;

>> (d) subject to the provisions of Article 59, judicial decisions and the teachings of the most highly qualified publicists of the various nations, as subsidiary means for the determination of rules of law.

"International conventions" refers to agreements between two or more countries, also commonly called "treaties." Within the United States' legal system, "treaties" refer to those agreements made with the concurrence of two-thirds of the Senate, as provided in Article II, section 2 of the U.S. Constitution. The Japan-U.S. Friendship Commerce and Navigation Treaty and the United Nations Convention on Contracts for the International Sale of Goods (CISG) are two examples we shall encounter later. However, U.S. practice also recognizes international conventions known as "executive agreements," which do not go through the Article II process but are nevertheless binding on the United States as a matter of international law. The General Agreement on Tariffs and Trade (GATT) and the North American Free Trade Agreement (NAFTA) are important examples.

Next on this list comes "international custom," also called "customary international law." "Customary international law results from a general and consistent practice of states followed by them from a sense of legal obligation." Restatement (Third) of Foreign Relations Law § 102(2) (1987). One may think of customary international law as unwritten law, in the sense that nations consent to it not through express agreements but tacitly through practice, though of course there is no shortage of written works expounding on the rules of customary international law. For the international business lawyer, two particularly important examples of custom are the rules governing the expropriation of foreign owned property and the rules limiting "prescriptive jurisdiction"—that is, the authority of nations to make rules for particular persons or conduct, sometimes outside of their own borders.

The best evidence of customary international law is the actual practice of states. It is often convenient, however, to refer to secondary sources that have collected and examined the primary evidence, such as the writings of scholars—"publicists" in the words of Article 38(1)(d)— and the decisions of international courts and tribunals. This has long been the U.S. practice. See United States v. Smith, 18 U.S. 153, 160–161, 5 L.Ed. 57 (1820) ("What the law of nations . . . is, may be ascertained by consulting the works of jurists, writing professedly on public law; or by the general usage and practice of nations; or by judicial decisions recognizing and enforcing that law."). Note that, in keeping with the civil law tradition, international law has no formal system of precedent, and Article 59 of the ICJ Statute accordingly states "The decision of the Court has no binding force except between the parties and in respect of that particular case." Nevertheless the opinions of the International Court of Justice and of other international tribunals are persuasive evidence of customary international law and are typically given great weight.

Customary international law must be distinguished from the "general principles of law," to which Article 38(1)(c) refers. The idea of "general principles" refers to practices by states with respect to their internal law, as distinguished from custom, which is behavior vis-à-vis other states. International tribunals have largely referred to general principles of law in relation to such issues as estoppel and other procedural matters. If national courts would estop a complainant in a given case, an international court might do likewise.

Customary international law and treaties are grouped together under the heading of "public international law." But there is also "private international law," a phrase that is used in two distinct ways. Outside the United States, it generally refers to the rules for resolving private disputes having a significant relationship to more than one jurisdiction, what Americans call the "conflict of laws." Although historically part of the "law of nations," these rules are largely rules of domestic law today. Traditionally, private international law is divided into three parts. First, it deals with the question when a court can take adjudicative jurisdiction over a party or property identified as "foreign." Second, it deals with the extent to which the judgment of a court in Country A is entitled to recognition or enforcement by the courts of Country B. Third, it deals with the choice of law question—what rules of law are to be applied in resolving a transborder dispute? If the case is being tried in Country A's courts, should that court apply its own law (the forum's) or the law applicable where the contract was made or is to be performed? We have encountered the first two questions in Chapter I, see supra pp. 22–40, and we shall examine the third in Problem 1, see infra pp. 152–161. "Private international law" is sometimes used in a different sense, however, to refer to the substantive rules of domestic law that govern private transactions across borders.

"Transnational law," in Jessup's definition, includes all of the above. The law that "regulates actions or events that transcend national frontiers" obviously includes a good deal of domestic law—from the law of contracts to antitrust law. It also includes domestic rules for mediating among national systems, that is, the rules of conflicts or of "private international law" narrowly defined. Finally, it includes rules of "public international law," found in treaties and in customary international law, that may limit the ways in which national governments may regulate or that may treat directly some topics usually governed by domestic law (for example, the CISG's rules of substantive contract law).

The abilities to navigate among different systems of law and to understand the ways in which they penetrate and influence each other are among the most difficult and important skills of an international lawyer. Nations often use their domestic experience as the basis for drafting treaties. Domestic legal systems serve as the basis for "general principles of law," and domestic practice (if followed out of a sense of international legal obligation) may contribute to the development of customary international law.

But international law also penetrates to the domestic level. International law is sometimes applied directly as a rule of decision to decide cases in U.S. courts. Under Article III of the U.S. Constitution the jurisdiction of the federal courts may extend to cases arising under treaties, and the Supremacy Clause of Article VI provides that treaties are part of the "supreme Law of the Land" binding on the judges in every state. Federal and state courts have interpreted and applied self-executing treaties like Friendship Commerce and Navigation Treaties and the CISG in a great many cases, some of which are excerpted below. See infra pp. 85–89, 169–173.

U.S. courts have also long applied rules of customary international law. At the turn of the twentieth century, the United States Supreme Court wrote: "International law is part of our law, and must be ascertained and administered by the courts of justice of appropriate jurisdiction as often as questions of right depending upon it are duly presented for their determination." The Paquete Habana, 175 U.S. 677, 700, 20 S.Ct. 290, 299, 44 L.Ed. 320 (1900). The Paquete Habana involved the right of American naval personnel to sell as lawful wartime prizes two Spanish fishing vessels they had captured in the course of the Spanish-American War. The Court investigated the practices of all the states then possessing navies and concluded that a custom of not seizing fishing vessels was in force. More recently, federal courts have applied customary international law rules prohibiting human rights abuses in cases brought under the Alien Tort Statute (ATS), a jurisdiction the Supreme Court confirmed in Sosa v. Alvarez-Machain, 542 U.S. 692, 124 S.Ct. 2739, 159 L.Ed.2d 718 (2004). ATS suits against corporations have met with limited success. In Kiobel v. Royal Dutch Petroleum Co., 133 S.Ct. 1659, 185 L.Ed.2d 671 (2013), the Supreme Court limited the implied cause of action under the ATS to cases that "touch and concern" the United States. In Jesner v. Arab Bank, PLC, 138 S.Ct. 1386, 200 L.Ed.2d 612 (2018), the Supreme Court held that the ATS cause of action does not extend to suits against foreign corporations. Occasionally, customary international law rules on expropriation have been applied directly by U.S. courts, see Banco Nacional de Cuba v. Chase Manhattan Bank, 658 F.2d 875 (2d Cir. 1981), though as we shall see there are substantial barriers to such suits. See infra pp. 70–81.

Customary international law and treaties also have an indirect influence on U.S. domestic law through the so-called Charming Betsy canon. Chief Justice Marshall wrote in Murray v. Schooner Charming Betsy, 6 U.S. (2 Cranch) 64, 118, 2 L.Ed. 208 (1804), that "an act of Congress ought never to be construed to violate the law of nations if any other possible construction remains." A more recent application of the rule is Lauritzen v. Larsen, 345 U.S. 571, 73 S.Ct. 921, 97 L.Ed. 1254 (1953). There the Jones Act purported to apply to "any seaman who shall suffer personal injury in the course of his employment." Noting that this language would extend to "a hand on a Chinese junk, never outside Chinese waters," the Court decided to apply the Jones Act "only to areas and transactions in which American law would be considered operative under prevalent doctrines of international law." Section 114 of the Restatement (Third) of Foreign Relations Law states the presumption this way: "Where fairly possible, a United States statute is to be construed so as not to conflict with international law or with an international agreement of the United States."

What if it is not fairly possible to construe a statute not to conflict with international law? Since the late nineteenth century it has been established that Congress has authority to supersede a treaty or a rule of customary international law as domestic law. See Head Money Cases, 112 U.S. 580, 5 S.Ct. 247, 28 L.Ed. 798 (1884). Instances of a treaty superseding an earlier statute are quite unusual, but do exist. See Cook v. United States, 288 U.S. 102, 53 S.Ct. 305, 77 L.Ed. 641 (1933). This "later-in-time" rule does not apply to state law; treaties prevail over inconsistent state law regardless of timing by virtue of the Constitution's Supremacy Clause. It is also worth noting that the later-in-time rule operates only on the level of domestic law. "That a rule of international law or of an international agreement is superseded as domestic law does not relieve the United States of its international obligation or of the consequences of a violation of that obligation." Restatement (Third) of Foreign Relations Law § 115(1)(b) (1987).

Other countries treat the relationship between international and national law differently from the United States. In the United Kingdom, treaties (with very limited exceptions) are not binding as domestic law until incorporated by an act of Parliament. In the Netherlands, the question whether a statute or treaty prevails in the case of inconsistency is settled by Article 94 of the Constitution, which provides that a statute shall not be applicable if it conflicts with a treaty. In Germany, the same is true with respect to customary international law. Article 25 of the *Grundgesetz*, or Basic Law, provides: "The general rules of international law form part of federal law. They take precedence over domestic law and create rights and duties directly for the inhabitants of the federal territory."

Additional reading: Jessup, Transnational Law (1956). On the Charming Betsy canon, see Bradley, The *Charming Betsy* Canon and Separation of Powers: Rethinking the Interpretive Role of International Law, 86 Geo. LJ. 479 (1998). On the later-in-time rule, see Vagts, The United States and Its Treaties: Observance and Breach, 95 Am. J. Int'l L. 313 (2001); Dodge, Customary International Law, Congress and the Courts: Origins of the Later-in-Time Rule, in Making Transnational Law Work in the Global Economy: Essays in Honour of Detlev Vagts (Bekker, Dolzer & Waibel eds., 2010). A very compact starter is Burgenthal & Murphy, Public International Law in a Nutshell (6th ed. 2019). The most comprehensive modern English-language treatises are Oppenheim's International Law (9th ed. Jennings & Watts 1992) and James Crawford, Brownlie's Principles of Public International Law (8th ed. 2012). For a history of international law in U.S. courts, see International Law in the U.S. Supreme Court: Continuity and Change (Sloss, Ramsey & Dodge eds., 2011).

B. CUSTOMARY INTERNATIONAL LAW

Customary international law is generally thought to have two elements: "general practice" (the material element) and "acceptance as law" (the psychological element), sometimes given the Latin tag *opinio juris sive necessitatis* or simply *opinio juris*. See Draft Conclusions on the Identification of Customary International Law, in Report of the International Law Commission, Seventieth Session, A/73/10, Conclusion 2 (2018) ("To determine the existence and content of a rule of customary international law, it is necessary to ascertain whether there is a general practice that is accepted as law (*opinio juris*)."); Restatement (Third) of Foreign Relations Law § 102(2) ("Customary international law results from a general and consistent practice of states followed by them from a sense of legal obligation.").

Each part of the idea carries complications. What constitutes state practice? A recent project by the International Law Commission (ILC) on the Identification of Customary International Law concludes: "Practice may take a wide range of forms. It includes both physical and verbal acts.

It may, under certain circumstances, include inaction." Draft Conclusions on the Identification of Customary International Law, Conclusion 6(1). State practice may include executive conduct, legislative and administrative acts, and the decisions of national courts. It may also include purely verbal acts, such as diplomatic correspondence, official statements, and protests by one state addressed to another. Deliberate inaction may sometimes constitute state practice, for example, abstaining from instituting criminal proceedings.

How general must state practice be? It is rare that one could find examples of state practice on a given issue from each of the 196 or so members of the family of nations. The ILC concludes that the relevant practice must be "widespread and representative, as well as consistent." Draft Conclusions on the Identification of Customary International Law, Conclusion 8(1); see also North Sea Continental Shelf (Germ. v. Den.; Germ. v. Neth.), 1969 I.C.J. 3, ¶ 74 (Feb. 20) (state practice "should have been both extensive and virtually uniform"). One must consider which states have had an opportunity to apply the alleged rule, how often opportunities to apply the rule have arisen, and whether states whose interests are especially affected have followed the rule. In determining the customary international law rules on maritime boundaries, for example, it makes little sense to look to the practice of land-locked states. See North Sea Continental Shelf, 1969 I.C.J. at ¶ 73. Absolute consistency is also not required. The ICJ "deems it sufficient that the conduct of States should, in general, be consistent with such rules." Military and Paramilitary Activities in and against Nicaragua (Nicar. v. U.S.), 1986 I.C.J. 14, ¶ 186 (June 26). In some instances, conduct inconsistent with a rule may even confirm the rule if a state "defends its conduct by appealing to exceptions or justifications contained within the rule itself." Id. As the Restatement (Third) summarized: "A practice can be general even if it is not universally followed; there is no precise formula to indicate how widespread a practice must be, but it should reflect wide acceptance of the states particularly involved in the relevant activity." Restatement (Third) of Foreign Relations Law § 102 cmt. b (1987).

And how can one tell that a practice has been accepted as law? The ILC reads the requirement of *opinio juris* to mean "that the practice in question must be undertaken with a sense of legal right or obligation." Draft Conclusions on the Identification of Customary International Law, Conclusion 9(1); see also North Sea Continental Shelf, 1969 I.C.J. at ¶ 77 ("Not only must the acts concerned amount to a settled practice, but they must also be such, or be carried out in such a way, as to be evidence of a belief that this practice is rendered obligatory by the existence of a rule of law requiring it."). Evidence of *opinio juris* is often found in statements—for example, diplomatic correspondence, debates in multilateral settings, pleadings before courts and tribunals, published opinions of government legal advisers, statements in national legislation, and the decisions of national courts. But it may also be inferred from action, and even from inaction "provided that States were in a position to react and the circumstances called for some reaction." Draft Conclusions on the Identification of Customary International Law, Conclusion 10(3). The requirement of *opinio juris* serves to distinguish practice that demonstrates a rule of law from practice that does not. Customary international law does not require a red carpet for visiting heads of state, for example, because the practice is not treated as legally obligatory even though it is general and consistent. See North Sea Continental Shelf, 1969 I.C.J. at ¶ 77 ("There are many international acts, e.g., in the field of ceremonial and protocol, which are performed almost invariably, but which are motivated only by considerations of courtesy, convenience or tradition, and not by any sense of legal duty.").

Customary international law rules concerning the expropriation of foreign investments have been central to international business lawyers. Expropriation is the taking of an investment by a government, either directly through a formal transfer of ownership or indirectly through actions that effectively deprive the investor of the benefits of ownership. See infra pp. 467–470. In recent years, rules governing expropriation have been incorporated in International Investment Agreements (IIAs), which are discussed in Problem 7. See infra pp. 470–482. Such treaties have also allowed investors to bring expropriation claims directly against host governments before panels of arbitrators. Before the system of IIAs developed, however foreign investors sometimes attempted to bring their expropriation claims under customary international law in U.S. courts. One such attempt reached the U.S. Supreme Court in the Sabbatino case, excerpted below. Sabbatino has much to say about the strengths of different branches of government in dealing with international claims. Sabbatino also raised the act of state doctrine as a substantial (though not impenetrable) barrier to bringing expropriation claims under customary international law in U.S. courts.

Banco Nacional de Cuba v. Sabbatino

Supreme Court of the United States, 1964
376 U.S. 398, 84 S.Ct. 923, 11 L.Ed.2d 804

[In February and July 1960, an American company Farr, Whitlock & Co. contracted to buy sugar from a subsidiary of Compania Azucarera Vertientes-Camaguey de Cuba (C.A.V.), a Cuban company principally owned by American investors. In August, Cuba expropriated C.A.V., and to obtain the release of the sugar Farr Whitlock entered new contracts with an instrumentality of the Cuban government. Both C.A.V. and Cuba subsequently claimed the right to payment for the sugar. Banco Nacional de Cuba brought suit for the proceeds in U.S. district court, which held that the expropriation violated customary international law because it was retaliatory, discriminatory, and failed to provide adequate compensation. The Second Circuit affirmed. The Supreme Court granted certiorari and reversed. After concluding that Cuba's status as an unfriendly power did not bar it from suing in U.S. courts, Justice Harlan turned to the act of state doctrine.]

IV.

The classic American statement of the act of state doctrine . . . is found in Underhill v. Hernandez, 168 U.S. 250, p. 252, 18 S.Ct. 83, at p. 84, 42 L.Ed. 456, where Chief Justice Fuller said for a unanimous Court:

> "Every sovereign state is bound to respect the independence of every other sovereign state, and the courts of one country will not sit in judgment on the acts of the government of another, done within its own territory. Redress of grievances by reason of such acts must be obtained through the means open to be availed of by sovereign powers as between themselves."

Following this precept the Court in that case refused to inquire into acts of Hernandez, a revolutionary Venezuelan military commander whose government had been later recognized by the United States, which were made the basis of a damage action in this country by Underhill, an American citizen, who claimed that he had had unlawfully assaulted, coerced, and detained in Venezuela by Hernandez.

None of this Court's subsequent cases in which the act of state doctrine was directly or peripherally involved manifest any retreat from Underhill. See American Banana Co. v. United Fruit Co., 213 U.S. 347, 29 S.Ct. 511, 53 L.Ed. 826; Oetjen v. Central Leather Co., 246 U.S. 297, 38 S.Ct. 309, 62 L.Ed. 726; Ricaud v. American Metal Co., 246 U.S. 304, 38 S.Ct. 312, 62 L.Ed. 733; Shapleigh v. Mier, 299 U.S. 468, 57 S.Ct. 261, 81 L.Ed. 355; United States v. Belmont, 301 U.S. 324, 57 S.Ct. 758, 81 L.Ed. 1134; United States v. Pink, 315 U.S. 203, 62 S.Ct. 552, 86 L.Ed. 796. On the contrary in two of these cases, Oetjen and Ricaud, the doctrine as announced in Underhill was reaffirmed in unequivocal terms.

* * *

In deciding the present case the Court of Appeals relied in part upon an exception to the unqualified teachings of Underhill, Oetjen, and Ricaud which that court had earlier indicated. In Bernstein v. Van Heyghen Freres Societe Anonyme, 2 Cir., 163 F.2d 246, suit was brought to recover from an assignee property allegedly taken, in effect, by the Nazi Government because plaintiff was Jewish. Recognizing the odious nature of this act of state, the court, through Judge Learned Hand, nonetheless refused to consider it invalid on that ground. Rather, it looked to see if the Executive had acted in any manner that would indicate that United States Courts should refuse to give effect to such a foreign decree. Finding no such evidence, the court sustained dismissal of the complaint. In a later case involving similar facts the same court again assumed examination of the German acts improper, Bernstein v. N.V. Nederlandsche-Amerikaansche Stoomvaart-Maatschappij, 2 Cir., 173 F.2d 71, but, quite evidently following the implications of Judge

Hand's opinion in the earlier case, amended its mandate to permit evidence of alleged invalidity, 2 Cir., 210 F.2d 375, subsequent to receipt by plaintiff's attorney of a letter from the Acting Legal Adviser to the State Department written for the purpose of relieving the court from any constraint upon the exercise of its jurisdiction to pass on that question.

This Court has never had occasion to pass upon the so-called Bernstein exception, nor need it do so now. For whatever ambiguity may be thought to exist in the two letters from State Department officials on which the Court of Appeals relied, 307 F.2d at 858, is now removed by the position which the Executive has taken in this Court on the act of state claim; respondents do not indeed contest the view that these letters were intended to reflect no more than the Department's then wish not to make any statement bearing on this litigation.

The outcome of this case, therefore, turns upon whether any of the contentions urged by respondents against the application of the act of state doctrine in the premises is acceptable: (1) that the doctrine does not apply to acts of state which violate international law, as is claimed to be the case here; (2) that the doctrine is inapplicable unless the Executive specifically interposes it in a particular case; and (3) that, in any event, the doctrine may not be invoked by a foreign government plaintiff in our courts.

V.

Preliminarily, we discuss the foundations on which we deem the act of state doctrine to rest, and more particularly the question of whether state or federal law governs its application in a federal diversity case.

We do not believe that this doctrine is compelled either by the inherent nature of sovereign authority, as some of the earlier decision seem to imply, see Underhill, supra; American Banana, supra; Oetjen, supra, 246 U.S. at 303, 38 S.Ct. at 311, 62 L.Ed. 726, or by some principle of international law. If a transaction takes place in one jurisdiction and the forum is in another, the forum does not by dismissing an action or by applying its own law purport to divest the first jurisdiction of its territorial sovereignty; it merely declines to adjudicate or makes applicable its own law to parties or property before it. The refusal of one country to enforce the penal laws of another is a typical example of an instance when a court will not entertain a cause of action arising in another jurisdiction. While historic notions of sovereign authority do bear upon the wisdom of employing the act of state doctrine, they do not dictate its existence.

That international law does not require application of the doctrine is evidenced by the practice of nations. Most of the countries rendering decisions on the subject fail to follow the rule rigidly. No international arbitral or judicial decision discovered suggests that international law prescribes recognition of sovereign acts of foreign governments, see 1 Oppenheim's International Law, § 115aa (Lauterpacht, 8th ed. 1955), and apparently no claim has ever been raised before an international tribunal that failure to apply the act of state doctrine constitutes a breach of international obligation. If international law does not prescribe use of the doctrine, neither does it forbid application of the rule even if it is claimed that the act of state in question violated international law. The traditional view of international law is that it establishes substantive principles for determining whether one country has wronged another. Because of its peculiar nation-to-nation character the usual method for an individual to seek relief is to exhaust local remedies and then repair to the executive authorities of his own state to persuade them to champion his claim in diplomacy or before an international tribunal. See United States v. Diekelman, 92 U.S. 520, 524, 23 L.Ed. 742. Although it is, of course, true that United States courts apply international law as a part of our own in appropriate circumstances, Ware v. Hylton, 3 Dall. 199, 281, 1 L.Ed. 568; The Nereide, 9 Cranch 388, 423, 3 L.Ed. 769; The Paquete Habana, 175 U.S. 677, 700, 20 S.Ct. 290, 299, 44 L.Ed. 320, the public law of nations can hardly dictate to a country which is in theory wronged how to treat that wrong within its domestic borders.

Despite the broad statement in Oetjen that "The conduct of the foreign relations of our government is committed by the Constitution to the executive and legislative . . . departments," 246 U.S. at 302, 38 S.Ct. at 311, 62 L.Ed. 726, it cannot of course be thought that "every case or controversy which touches foreign relations lies beyond judicial cognizance." Baker v. Carr, 369 U.S. 186, 211, 82 S.Ct. 691, 707, 7 L.Ed.2d 663. The text of the Constitution does not require the act of state doctrine; it does not irrevocably remove from the judiciary the capacity to review the validity of foreign acts of state.

The act of state doctrine does, however, have "constitutional" underpinnings. It arises out of the basic relationships between branches of government in a system of separation of powers. It concerns the competency of dissimilar institutions to make and implement particular kinds of decisions in the area of international relations. The doctrine as formulated in past decisions expresses the strong sense of the Judicial Branch that its engagement in the task of passing on the validity of foreign acts of state may hinder rather than further this country's pursuit of goals both for itself and for the community of nations as a whole in the international sphere. Many commentators disagree with this view; they have striven by means of distinguishing and limiting past decisions and by advancing various considerations of policy to stimulate a narrowing of the apparent scope of the rule. Whatever considerations are thought to predominate, it is plain that the problems involved are uniquely federal in nature. If federal authority, in this instance this Court, orders the field of judicial competence in this area for the federal courts, and the state courts are left free to formulate their own rules, the purposes behind the doctrine could be as effectively undermined as if there had been no federal pronouncement on the subject.

We could perhaps in this diversity action avoid the question of deciding whether federal or state law is applicable to this aspect of the litigation. New York has enunciated the act of state doctrine in terms that echo those of federal decisions decided during the reign of Swift v. Tyson, 16 Pet. 1, 10 L.Ed. 865. . . . Thus our conclusions might well be the same whether we dealt with this problem as one of state law, see Erie R. Co. v. Tompkins, 304 U.S. 64, 58 S.Ct. 817, 82 L.Ed. 1188; Klaxon Co. v. Stentor Elec. Mfg. Co., 313 U.S. 487, 61 S.Ct. 1020, 85 L.Ed. 1477; Griffin v. McCoach, 313 U.S. 498, 61 S.Ct. 1023, 85 L.Ed. 1481, or federal law.

However, we are constrained to make it clear that an issue concerned with a basic choice regarding the competence and function of the Judiciary and the National Executive in ordering our relationships with other members of the international community must be treated exclusively as an aspect of federal law. It seems fair to assume that the Court did not have rules like the act of state doctrine in mind when it decided Erie R. Co. v. Tompkins. Soon thereafter, Professor Philip C. Jessup, now a judge of the International Court of Justice, recognized the potential dangers were Erie extended to legal problems affecting international relations.[2] He cautioned that rules of international law should not be left to divergent and perhaps parochial state interpretations. His basic rationale is equally applicable to the act of state doctrine.

* * *

VI.

If the act of state doctrine is a principle of decision binding on federal and state courts alike but compelled by neither international law nor the Constitution, its continuing vitality depends on its capacity to reflect the proper distribution of functions between the judicial and political branches of the Government on matters bearing upon foreign affairs. It should be apparent that the greater the degree of codification or consensus concerning a particular area of international law, the more appropriate it is for the judiciary to render decisions regarding it, since the courts can then focus on the application of an agreed principle to circumstances of fact rather than on the sensitive task of establishing a principle not inconsistent with the national interest or with international justice. It is also evident that some aspects of international law touch much more sharply on national nerves than do others; the less important the implications of an issue are for our foreign relations, the weaker the justification for exclusivity in the political branches. The balance of relevant considerations may also be shifted if the government which perpetrated the challenged act of state is no longer in existence, as in the Bernstein case, for the political interest of this country may, as a result,

---

[2] The Doctrine of Erie Railroad v. Tompkins Applied to International Law, 33 Am.J.Int'l L. 740 (1939).

be measurably altered. Therefore, rather than laying down or reaffirming an inflexible and all-encompassing rule in this case, we decide only that the Judicial Branch will not examine the validity of a taking of property within its own territory by a foreign sovereign government, extant and recognized by this country at the time of suit, in the absence of a treaty or other unambiguous agreement regarding controlling legal principles, even if the complaint alleges that the taking violates customary international law.

There are few if any issues in international law today on which opinion seems to be so divided as the limitations on a state's power to expropriate the property of aliens.[3] There is, of course, authority, in international judicial[4] and arbitral[5] decisions, in the expressions of national governments,[6] and among commentators[7] for the view that a taking is improper under international law if it is not for a public purpose, is discriminatory, or is without provision for prompt, adequate, and effective compensation. However, Communist countries, although they have in fact provided a degree of compensation after diplomatic efforts, commonly recognize no obligation on the part of the taking country.[8] Certain representatives of the newly independent and underdeveloped countries have questioned whether rules of state responsibility toward aliens can bind nations that have not consented to them[9] and it is argued that the traditionally articulated standards

---

[3] Compare, e.g., Friedman, Expropriation in International Law 206–211 (1953); Dawson and Weston, "Prompt, Adequate and Effective": A Universal Standard of Compensation? 30 Fordham L.Rev. 727 (1962), with Note from Secretary of State Hull to Mexican Ambassador, August 22, 1938, V Foreign Relations of the United States 685 (1938); Doman, Postwar Nationalization of Foreign Property in Europe, 48 Col.L.Rev. 1125, 1127 (1948). We do not, of course, mean to say that there is no international standard in this area; we conclude only that the matter is not meet for adjudication by domestic tribunals.

[4] See Oscar Chinn Case, P.C.I.J., ser. A/B, No. 63, at 87 (1934); Chorzow Factory Case, P.C.I.J., ser. A., No. 17, at 46, 47 (1928).

[5] See, e.g., Norwegian Shipowners' Case (Norway/United States) (Perm.Ct.Arb.) (1922), 1 U.N.Rep.Int'l Arb.Awards 307, 334, 339 (1948), Hague Court Reports, 2d Series, 39, 69, 74 (1932); Marguerite de Joly de Sabla, American and Panamanian General Claims Arbitration 379, 447, 6 U.N.Rep.Int'l Arb.Awards 358, 366 (1955).

[6] See, e.g., Dispatch from Lord Palmerston to British Envoy at Athens, Aug. 7, 1846, 39 British and Foreign State Papers 1849–1850, 431–432. Note from Secretary of State Hull to Mexican Ambassador, July 21, 1938, V Foreign Relations of the United States 674 (1938); Note to the Cuban Government, July 16, 1960, 43 Dept. State Bull 171 (1960).

[7] See, e.g., McNair, The Seizure of Property and Enterprises in Indonesia, 6 Netherlands Int'l L.Rev. 218, 243–253 (1959); Restatement, Foreign Relations Law of the United States (Proposed Official Draft 1962), §§ 190–195.

[8] See Doman, supra, note 26, at 1143–1158; Fleming, States, Contracts and Progress, 62–63 (1960); Bystricky, Notes on Certain International Legal Problems Relating to Socialist Nationalisation, in International Assn. of Democratic Lawyers, Proceedings of the Commission on Private International Law, Sixth Congress (1956), 15.

[9] See Anand, Role of the "New" Asian-African Countries in the Present International Legal Order, 56 Am.J.Int'l L. 383 (1962); Roy, Is the Law of Responsibility of States for Injuries to Aliens a Part of Universal International Law? 55 Am.J.Int'l L. 863 (1961).

governing expropriation of property reflect "imperialist" interests and are inappropriate to the circumstances of emergent states.[10]

The disagreement as to relevant international law standards reflects an even more basic divergence between the national interests of capital importing and capital exporting nations and between the social ideologies of those countries that favor state control of a considerable portion of the means of production and those that adhere to a free enterprise system. It is difficult to imagine the courts of this country embarking on adjudication in an area which touches more sensitively the practical and ideological goals of the various members of the community of nations.[11]

When we consider the prospect of the courts characterizing foreign expropriations, however justifiably, as invalid under international law and ineffective to pass title, the wisdom of the precedents is confirmed. While each of the leading cases in this Court may be argued to be distinguishable in its facts from this one—Underhill because sovereign immunity provided an independent ground and Oetjen, Ricaud, and Shapleigh because there was actually no violation of international law—the plain implication of all these opinions, and the import of express statements in Oetjen, 246 U.S. at 304, 38 S.Ct. at 311, 62 L.Ed. 726, and Shapleigh, 299 U.S. at 471, 57 S.Ct. at 262, 81 L.Ed. 355, is that the act of state doctrine is applicable even if international law has been violated. In Ricaud, the one case of the three most plausibly involving an international law violation, the possibility of an exception to the act of state doctrine was not discussed. Some commentators have concluded that it was not brought to the Court's attention, but Justice Clarke delivered both the Oetjen and Ricaud opinions, on the same day, so we can assume that principles stated in the former were applicable to the latter case.

The possible adverse consequences of a conclusion to the contrary of that implicit in these cases in highlighted by contrasting the practices of the political branch with the limitations of the judicial process in matters of this kind. Following an expropriation of any significance, the Executive engages in diplomacy aimed to assure that United States citizens who are harmed are compensated fairly. Representing all claimants of this country, it will often be able, either by bilateral or multilateral talks, by submission to the United Nations, or by the employment of economic and political sanctions, to achieve some degree of general redress. Judicial determinations of invalidity of title can, on the other hand, have only an occasional impact, since they depend on the fortuitous circumstance of the property in question being brought into this country. Such decisions would, if the acts involved were declared invalid, often be likely to give

---

[10] See 1957 Yb.U.N.Int'l L.Comm'n (Vol. 1) 155, 158 (statements of Mr. Padilla Nervo (Mexico) and Mr. Pal (India)).

[11] There are, of course, areas of international law in which consensus as to standards is greater and which do not represent a battleground for conflicting ideologies. This decision in no way intimates that the courts of this country are broadly foreclosed from considering questions of international law.

offense to the expropriating country; since the concept of territorial sovereignty is so deep seated, any state may resent the refusal of the courts of another sovereign to accord validity to acts within its territorial borders. Piecemeal dispositions of this sort involving the probability of affront to another state could seriously interfere with negotiations being carried on by the Executive Branch and might prevent or render less favorable the terms of an agreement that could otherwise be reached. Relations with third countries which have engaged in similar expropriations would not be immune from effect.

The dangers of such adjudication are present regardless of whether the State Department has, as it did in this case, asserted that the relevant act violated international law. If the Executive Branch has undertaken negotiations with an expropriating country, but has refrained from claims of violation of the law of nations, a determination to that effect by a court might be regarded as a serious insult, while a finding of compliance with international law would greatly strengthen the bargaining hand of the other state with consequent detriment to American interests.

Even if the State Department has proclaimed the impropriety of the expropriation, the stamp of approval of its view by a judicial tribunal, however, impartial, might increase any affront and the judicial decision might occur at a time, almost always well after the taking, when such an impact would be contrary to our national interest. Considerably more serious and far-reaching consequences would flow from a judicial finding that international law standards had been met if that determination flew in the face of a State Department proclamation to the contrary. When articulating principles of international law in its relations with other states, the Executive Branch speaks not only as an interpreter of generally accepted and traditional rules, as would the courts, but also as an advocate of standards it believes desirable for the community of nations and protective of national concerns. In short, whatever way the matter is cut, the possibility of conflict between the Judicial and Executive Branches could hardly be avoided.

Respondents contend that, even if there is not agreement regarding general standards for determining the validity of expropriations, the alleged combination of retaliation, discrimination, and inadequate compensation makes it patently clear that this particular expropriation was in violation of international law. If this view is accurate, it would still be unwise for the courts so to determine. Such a decision now would require the drawing of more difficult lines in subsequent cases and these would involve the possibility of conflict with the Executive view. Even if the courts avoided this course, either by presuming the validity of an act of state whenever the international law standard was thought unclear or by following the State Department declaration in such a situation, the very expression of judicial uncertainty might provide embarrassment to the Executive Branch.

* * *

It is suggested that if the act of state doctrine is applicable to violations of international law, it should only be so when the Executive Branch expressly stipulates that it does not wish the courts to pass on the question of validity. See Association of the Bar of the City of New York, Committee on International Law, A Reconsideration of the Act of State Doctrine in United States Courts (1959). We should be slow to reject the representations of the Government that such a reversal of the Bernstein principle would work serious inroads on the maximum effectiveness of United States diplomacy. Often the State Department will wish to refrain from taking an official position, particularly at a moment that would be dictated by the development of private litigation but might be inopportune diplomatically. Adverse domestic consequences might flow from an official stand which could be assuaged, if at all, only by revealing matters best kept secret. Of course, a relevant consideration for the State Department would be the position contemplated in the court to hear the case. It is highly questionable whether the examination of validity by the judiciary should depend on an educated guess by the Executive as to probable result and, at any rate, should a prediction be wrong, the Executive might be embarrassed in its dealings with other countries. We do not now pass on the Bernstein exception, but even if it were deemed valid, its suggested extension is unwarranted.

However offensive to the public policy of this country and its constituent States an expropriation of this kind may be, we conclude that both the national interest and progress toward the goal of establishing the rule of law among nations are best served by maintaining intact the act of state doctrine in this realm of its application.

* * *

[Justice White filed a dissenting opinion, in which he argued that U.S. courts are obligated to decide cases in accordance with applicable law, and that customary international law is part of the law U.S. courts are bound to administer. Rather than a blanket presumption of nonreview, he would have required the State Department to determine if adjudication would interfere with U.S. foreign relations.]

Almost immediately, Congress acted to reverse the decision in Sabbatino. It adopted the Second Hickenlooper or Sabbatino Amendment, 22 U.S.C. § 2370(e)(2), which ultimately became a permanent part of the Foreign Assistance Act:

Notwithstanding any other provision of law, no court in the United States shall decline on the ground of the federal act of state doctrine to make a determination on the merits giving effect to the principles of international law in a case in which a claim of title or other right to property is asserted by any party including a foreign state (or a party claiming through such state) based upon (or traced through) a confiscation or other taking after January 1, 1959, by an act of that state in violation of the principles of international law, including the principles of compensation and the other standards set out in this subsection: *Provided*, That this subparagraph shall not be applicable (1) in any case in which an act of a foreign state is not contrary to international law or with respect to a claim of title or other right to property acquired pursuant to an irrevocable letter of credit of not more than 180 days duration issued in good faith prior to the time of the confiscation or other taking, or (2) in any case with respect to which the President determines that application of the act of state doctrine is required in that particular case by the foreign policy interests of the United States and a suggestion to this effect is filed on his behalf in that case with the court.

The reference to principles of compensation set out in this subsection is to the original Hickenlooper Amendment, 22 U.S.C. § 2370(e)(1), which calls for "speedy compensation for such property in convertible foreign exchange, equivalent to the full value thereof, as required by international law."

On remand, the Second Circuit upheld the constitutionality of the Second Hickenlooper Amendment in Banco Nacional de Cuba v. Farr, 383 F.2d 166, 180–183 (2d Cir. 1967), cert. denied, 390 U.S. 956, 88 S.Ct. 1038, 19 L.Ed.2d 1151 (1968). In a subsequent case, the Second Circuit interpreted the Amendment as limited to cases where the claimant's specific property was found in the United States. Banco Nacional de Cuba v. First National City Bank of New York, 431 F.2d 394, 399–402 (2d Cir. 1970), reversed on other grounds, First National City Bank v. Banco Nacional de Cuba, 406 U.S. 759, 92 S.Ct. 1808, 32 L.Ed.2d 466 (1972). But the D.C. Circuit has disagreed. Ramirez de Arellano v. Weinberger, 745 F.2d 1500, 1541 n.180 (D.C. Cir. 1984), rev'd on other grounds, 471 U.S. 1113 (1985). Under the Second Circuit's interpretation, the act of state doctrine as amended would not bar C.A.V.'s suit for the proceeds of sugar Cuba had expropriated because those proceeds were located in the United States, but it would still bar C.A.V. from bringing suit for the expropriation of its property located in Cuba.

Other potential exceptions to the act of state doctrine are inherent in its holding: "we decide only that the Judicial Branch will not examine the validity of a taking of property within its own territory by a foreign sovereign government, extant and recognized by this country at the time of suit, in the absence of a treaty or other unambiguous agreement regarding controlling legal principles, even if the complaint alleges that the taking violates customary international law." Lower courts have held that the act of state doctrine does not bar U.S. courts from questioning a foreign state's expropriation of property *outside* its own territory. See, e.g., Agudas Chasidei Chabad of U.S. v. Russian Federation, 528 F.3d

934, 951–952 (D.C. Cir. 2008). They have also recognized a "treaty exception," in cases where an international agreement provides controlling legal principles for a court to apply. See, e.g., Kalamazoo Spice Extraction Co. v. Provisional Military Government of Socialist Ethiopia, 729 F.2d 422, 425–427 (6th Cir. 1984).

Sabbatino mentioned, but did not pass upon, another exception to the act of state doctrine—the so-called Bernstein exception. In Bernstein v. N.V. Nederlandsche-Amerikaansche Stoomvaart-Maatschappij, 210 F.2d 375 (2d Cir. 1954), the Second Circuit gave effect to a letter from the State Department waiving the act of state doctrine and allowed claims for expropriation to go forward that it had previously held the act of state doctrine to bar. The exception came before the Supreme Court again in First National City Bank of New York v. Banco Nacional de Cuba, 406 U.S. 759, 92 S.Ct. 1808, 32 L.Ed.2d 466 (1972). A three-justice plurality relied upon the State Department's Bernstein letter in holding that the act of state doctrine did not apply. Six members of the court, two concurring in the judgment and the four dissenters, disapproved the exception but in separate opinions. So the Bernstein exception lives on.

The Supreme Court again splintered badly in Alfred Dunhill of London, Inc. v. Republic of Cuba, 425 U.S. 682, 96 S.Ct. 1854, 48 L.Ed.2d 301 (1976), with four justices suggesting a "commercial activities" exception to the act of state doctrine, four justices rejecting such an exception, and one finding it unnecessary to reach the question because the mere repudiation of a debt did not rise to the level of an act of state. A number of lower courts have rejected a "commercial activities" exception to the act of state doctrine. See Spectrum Stores, Inc. v. Citgo Petroleum Corp., 632 F.3d 938, 954 n.16 (5th Cir. 2011); Honduras Aircraft Registry, Ltd. v. Honduras, 129 F.3d 543, 550 (11th Cir. 1997); Int'l Ass'n of Machinists & Aerospace Workers v. OPEC, 649 F.2d 1354, 1360 (9th Cir.1981). But they have sometimes allowed suits based on commercial acts to proceed on the ground that the acts "cannot fairly be characterized as public or official acts of a sovereign government." McKesson Corp. v. Islamic Republic of Iran, 672 F.3d 1066, 1074 (D.C. Cir. 2012).

The Supreme Court significantly narrowed the potential scope of the act of state doctrine in W.S. Kirkpatrick & Co. v. Environmental Tectonics Corp., 493 U.S. 400, 110 S.Ct. 701, 107 L.Ed.2d 816 (1990). Kirkpatrick and its CEO had pleaded guilty to violating the Foreign Corrupt Practices Act (FCPA) by bribing Nigerian officials to win a construction contract. Environmental Tectonics, a losing bidder, then brought a civil RICO action with mail and wire fraud as the predicate acts. Kirkpatrick argued that the act of state doctrine should bar suits that would cause embarrassment to foreign governments and interfere with U.S. foreign relations. The United States, as amicus curiae, agreed though disagreeing with Kirkpatrick that this was such a suit. Writing for a unanimous Court, however, Justice Scalia rejected this argument.

"The act of state doctrine is not some vague doctrine of abstention but a *principle of decision* binding on federal and state courts alike.' " Id. at 406, 110 S.Ct. at 705 (quoting Banco Nacional de Cuba v. Sabbatino, 376 U.S. 398, 406, 84 S.Ct. 923, 11 L.Ed.2d 804 (1964) (emphasis added)). He explained that the act of state doctrine applies only when a "suit requires the Court to declare invalid, and thus ineffective as 'a rule of decision for the courts of this country,' the official act of a foreign sovereign." Id. at 405, 110 S.Ct. at 704 (quoting Ricaud v. American Metal Co., 246 U.S. 304, 310, 38 S.Ct. 312, 314, 62 L.Ed. 733 (1918)). Although the facts necessary to support Environmental Tectonics's claim might also show that Nigeria's award of the construction contract was unlawful, the court would not have to decide that question to decide the case. Justice Scalia concluded:

> The short of the matter is this: Courts in the United States have the power, and ordinarily the obligation, to decide cases and controversies properly presented to them. The act of state doctrine does not establish an exception for cases and controversies that may embarrass foreign governments, but merely requires that, in the process of deciding, the acts of foreign sovereigns taken within their own jurisdictions shall be deemed valid. That doctrine has no application to the present case because the validity of no foreign sovereign act is at issue.

Id. at 409–410, 110 S.Ct. at 707.

In sum, while the act of state is often a bar to bringing to expropriation claims in U.S. courts, sometimes an exception will allow the case to go forward. When an expropriation claim is brought against a foreign government or one of its agencies or instrumentalities, issues of foreign sovereign immunity also arise. In 1976, Congress codified the U.S. rules on foreign sovereign immunity in the Foreign Sovereign Immunities Act (FSIA), which is discussed further in Problem 8. See infra pp. 522–527. The FSIA contains an expropriation exception, permitting suits "in which rights in property taken in violation of international law are in issue" to be brought in U.S. courts. 28 U.S.C. § 1605(a)(3).

QUESTIONS

(1) According to Sabbatino, what is the foundation of the act of state doctrine? In the international arena, what activities are courts good at and what activities is the executive branch good at? What scope does Sabbatino leave for U.S. courts to decide issues of customary international law?

(2) Justice Harlan writes: "There are few if any issues in international law today on which opinion seems to be so divided as the limitations on a state's power to expropriate the property of aliens." Supra p. 75. How does he reach that conclusion? Is doing so consistent

with the view that courts should not undercut the negotiating position of the executive branch?

Additional reading: International Law Commission, Reports on Identification of Customary International Law, A/CN.4/663, A/CN.4/672, A/CN.4/682, A/CN.4/695, A./CN.4/717 (2013–18); International Law Association, London Statement of Principles Applicable to the Formation of General Customary International Law (2000); Crawford, Brownlie's Principles of Public International Law 23–34 (8th ed. 2012); Roberts, Traditional and Modern Approaches to Customary International Law: A Reconciliation, 95 Am. J. Int'l L. 757 (2001); Dickinson, Changing Concepts and the Doctrine of Incorporation, 26 Am. J. Int'l L. 239 (1932); Dodge, Customary International Law in the Supreme Court, 1946–2000, in International Law in the U.S. Supreme Court: Continuity and Change (Sloss, Ramsey & Dodge 2011).

C. THE LAW OF TREATIES

The likelihood of a private lawyer being concerned with a question of treaty law is much higher than with respect to customary rules. In the absence of international institutions with legislative functions, the treaty is effectively the only way in which rules can be generated to keep up with the variety and complexity of transnational economic activity. There is, of necessity, an international law underlying that treaty structure. That body of rules, now codified in the Vienna Convention on the Law of Treaties,[12] addresses such questions as the objections to the validity of a treaty on grounds such as fraud, mistake, or coercion, the rights of states not parties to a treaty, the effect on rights under a treaty of subsequent unforeseen events, the rights of the state parties to a treaty to denounce it, and so forth. These are questions that private lawyers are almost certain not to encounter in practice. The question whether, for example, the United States is no longer bound by a treaty because of changed circumstances (*rebus sic stantibus* is the international law phrase) cannot be raised by a private party but only by authority of the President. See Restatement (Fourth) of Foreign Relations Law § 313 (2018).

What is important for the private practitioner is the way in which a treaty becomes embedded in the law of the United States—or of a foreign country. First of all, one has to absorb a distinction that has been important in U.S. practice, although it has no counterpart in other countries. That is the distinction between treaties and executive agreements. From the point of view of foreign legal systems there is no distinction between the two—they all are commonly referred to as treaties. In the United States, we are familiar with the treaty in the sense of an agreement that after being negotiated by the President comes into

---

[12] 1155 U.N.T.S. 331. The United States has never ratified the Convention, but has stated that it regards the Convention as codifying the customary rules on treaties. See Restatement (Fourth) of Foreign Relations Law, Part III, Introductory Note and § 301, Reporters' Note 1 (2018).

effect after receiving the consent of two thirds of the Senate. Alongside the "treaty" in the sense of Article II of the Constitution has come to flourish the executive agreement. In fact, in numerical terms, the executive agreement is now by far the commoner way of dealing with an international problem. The category "executive agreement" in turn is divided into three subcategories. There is the legislative-executive agreement in which Congress, acting through a simple majority of both its houses, authorizes the President to enter into an agreement or agreements or else approves it after the President has acted. There is the sole executive agreement in which the President acts on the basis of powers given that office directly by the Constitution—usually commander-in-chief powers. Finally, there are a few cases in which a treaty contains authorization for the President to fill in details. There have been few cases in which either of the latter two types of agreements have affected private rights. But there are many cases in which private rights are affected by legislative-executive agreements. Most conspicuous in this regard have been agreements on trade, such as the North American Free Trade Agreement (NAFTA) and the Uruguay Round agreements revising the General Agreement on Tariffs and Trade (GATT), both of which were approved by Congress as legislative-executive agreement. The fact that NAFTA did not pass the Senate by a two-thirds majority reawakened interest in the question whether legislative-executive agreements are constitutional.[13] The U.S. Court of Appeals for the Eleventh Circuit held that this was a nonjusticiable political question. Made in the USA Foundation v. United States, 242 F.3d 1300 (11th Cir.), cert. denied 534 U.S. 1039, 122 S.Ct. 613, 151 L.Ed.2d 536 (2001).

Then one confronts the question of the internal effect of a treaty or an executive agreement, which includes the extent to which a private person can rely on it as a party in a court proceeding. The U.S. Constitution in Article VI says quite simply that treaties, like statutes, "shall be the supreme Law of the Land; and the Judges in every State shall be bound thereby, any Thing in the Constitution or Laws of any State to the Contrary notwithstanding." Despite that straightforward assertion, the U.S. Supreme Court has held since Foster v. Neilson, 27 U.S. 253, 7 L.Ed. 415 (1829), that some treaties (or portions thereof) are non-self-executing and cannot be enforced in court until implementing legislation has been enacted. The Supreme Court reaffirmed that principle in Medellín v. Texas, 552 U.S. 491, 128 S.Ct. 1346, 170 L.Ed.2d 190 (2008), holding that Article 94 of the U.N. Charter—under which each Member of the United Nations "undertakes to comply" with decisions of the ICJ—was not self-executing and that ICJ decisions were therefore not enforceable in U.S. courts without an act of Congress. On the other hand, the Court noted that a number of Friendship, Commerce,

---

[13] See Tribe, Taking Text and Structure Seriously: Reflections on Free-Form Method in Constitutional Interpretation, 108 Harv. L. Rev. 1221 (1995); Ackerman & Golove, Is NAFTA Constitutional? 108 Harv. L. Rev. 799 (1995).

and Navigation Treaties are self-executing. "Our cases simply require courts to decide whether a treaty's terms reflect a determination by the President who negotiated it and the Senate that confirmed it that the treaty has domestic effect." Id. at 521, 128 S.Ct. at 1365–1366. Since Medellín, the Senate has adopted a practice of declaring whether a treaty is self-executing in its resolution of advice and consent. See, e.g., Extradition Treaties with the European Union, S. Exec. Rep. No. 110–12, at 9–10 (2008); see generally Restatement (Fourth) of Foreign Relations Law § 310 (2018).

Sometimes the statute executing a treaty is a long and detailed separate piece of legislation, as in the case of the statute bringing into effect the United Nations Convention on the Recognition and Enforcement of Foreign Arbitral Awards (9 U.S.C. §§ 201–208). Sometimes it is terse and sweeping, as in the case of § 894(a)(1) of the Internal Revenue Code that makes effective a large array of different income tax treaties by simply saying that "the provisions of this title shall be applied . . . with due regard to any treaty obligation of the United States." Other provisions of law executing treaties are buried in statutes of a more general character. For example, the United States conformed its rules on patents to the TRIPS Agreement by amending the Patent Law, 35 U.S.C. § 154, to provide that the life of a patent is 20 years from the date of filing rather than 17 years from the date of grant.

Occasionally, Congress specifies that what otherwise might be self-executing provisions of an international agreement cannot be enforced in court by private parties. NAFTA Article 1102, for example, provides for national treatment of foreign investors from Canada and Mexico. Congress, however, provided in NAFTA's implementing legislation that "[n]o person other than the United States . . . shall have any cause of action or defense" under NAFTA or may challenge any action or inaction of the United States, a state, or a subdivision of a state "on the ground that such action or inaction is inconsistent with" NAFTA. 19 U.S.C. § 3312(c). Cf. Asakura v. City of Seattle, 265 U.S. 332, 44 S.Ct. 515, 68 L.Ed. 1041 (1924) (holding that national-treatment provision in U.S. treaty with Japan "operates of itself without the aid of any legislation"). The Senate has tried to achieve the same result with respect to Bilateral Investment Treaties after Medellín by giving its advice and consent subject to the declaration that only certain provisions are self-executing and that none confers a private right of action. See Investment Treaty with Rwanda, Treaty Doc. 110–23, at 13 (2010).

In actual practice the question that is most likely to involve the private practitioner is that of interpretation. What does the treaty in question mean? Article 31(1) of the Vienna Convention on the Law of Treaties (VCLT) provides: "A treaty shall be interpreted in good faith in accordance with the ordinary meaning to be given to the terms of the treaty in their context and in the light of its object and purpose." The Vienna Convention also directs those interpreting a treaty to take into account any subsequent agreement between the parties regarding its interpretation, any subsequent practice of the parties establishing their agreement regarding its interpretation, and any relevant rules of international law applicable between the parties. VCLT Art. 31(3). Article 32 of the Vienna Convention permits resort to the negotiating history of a treaty, which is generally referred to by its French name— *travaux préparatoires*. Although the U.S. Supreme Court rarely cites the Vienna Convention's rules on interpretation, its approach to treaty interpretation has generally been consistent with those rules. See Restatement (Fourth) of Foreign Relations Law § 306 Reporters' Note 3 (2018). Thus, the Court has said: "In interpreting treaties, we begin with the text of the treaty and the context in which the written words are used." Water Splash, Inc. v. Menon, 137 S.Ct. 1504, 1508–1509, 197 L.Ed.2d 826 (2017) (quotation marks and citation omitted). The Court has also invoked a treaty's "objects and purposes," Abbott v. Abbott, 560 U.S. 1, 20, 130 S.Ct. 1983, 1995 (2010), the "views of other contracting states," id. at 16, 130 S.Ct. at 1993, and the "drafting history," Water Splash, 137 S.Ct. at 1511.

An additional U.S. principle of interpretation that finds no counterpart in the Vienna Convention is that "the Executive Branch's interpretation of a treaty is entitled to great weight." Abbott, 560 U.S. at 15, 130 S.Ct. at 1993 (quotation marks and citation omitted). The Supreme Court has sometimes rejected the executive branch's interpretation of a treaty. See, e.g., Hamdan v. Rumsfeld, 548 U.S. 557, 629–631, 126 S.Ct. 2749, 2794, 165 L.Ed.2d 723 (2006) (rejecting the executive's interpretation of Common Article 3 of the Geneva Conventions based on the article's language and negotiating history). U.S. courts are particularly likely to accept the executive branch's interpretation when it is longstanding and accords with other rules of treaty interpretation. See, e.g., Water Splash, 137 S. Ct. at 1512. Section 306(6) of the Restatement (Fourth) of Foreign Relations summarizes this principle as follows: "Courts in the United States have final authority to interpret a treaty for purposes of applying it as law in the United States. In doing so, they ordinarily give great weight to an interpretation by the executive branch."

The following case illustrates a number of questions of the methodology of treaty interpretation in a context that significantly affected business interests.

Sumitomo Shoji America, Inc. v. Avagliano

Supreme Court of the United States, 1982
457 U.S. 176, 102 S.Ct. 2374, 72 L.Ed.2d 765

[Plaintiffs were past and present secretarial employees of Sumitomo Shoji America, Inc. (Sumitomo), a New York corporation and wholly owned subsidiary of Sumitomo Shoji Kabushiki Kaisha, a Japanese company. All of the plaintiffs were United States citizens, except for one who was a citizen of Japan. They brought a class action claiming that Sumitomo's alleged practice of hiring only male Japanese citizens to fill executive, managerial and sales positions violated *inter alia* Title VII of the Civil Rights Act of 1964, which makes it unlawful "to fail or refuse to hire or to discharge any individual, or otherwise to discriminate against any individual . . . because of such individual's race, color, religion, sex, or national origin." Sumitomo argued that its employment practices were protected under the 1953 Treaty of Friendship Commerce and Navigation between the United States and Japan. After stating the facts, Chief Justice Burger continued.]

* * *

Interpretation of the Friendship, Commerce and Navigation Treaty between Japan and the United States must, of course, begin with the language of the Treaty itself. The clear import of treaty language controls unless "application of the words of the treaty according to their obvious meaning effects a result inconsistent with the intent or expectations of its signatories." Maximov v. United States, 373 U.S. 49, 54, 83 S.Ct. 1054, 1057, 10 L.Ed.2d 184 (1963). See also The Amiable Isabella, 6 Wheat. (19 U.S.) 1, 72, 5 L.Ed. 191 (1821).

Article VIII(1) of the Treaty provides in pertinent part:

"*[C]ompanies of either Party* shall be permitted to engage, within the territories of the other party, accountants and other technical experts, executive personnel, attorneys, agents and other specialists of their choice." (Emphasis added.)[14]

Clearly Article VIII(1) only applies to companies of one of the Treaty countries operating in the other country. Sumitomo contends that it is a company of Japan, and that Article VIII(1) of the Treaty grants it very broad discretion to fill its executive, managerial and sales positions exclusively with male Japanese citizens.

Article VIII(1) does not define any of its terms; the definitional section of the Treaty is contained in Article XXII. Article XXII(3) provides:

"As used in the present Treaty, the term 'companies' means corporations, partnerships, companies, and other associations, whether or not with limited liability and whether or not for

---

[14] Similar provisions are contained in the Friendship, Commerce and Navigation Treaties between the United States and other countries. . . .

These provisions were apparently included at the insistence of the United States; in fact, other countries, including Japan, unsuccessfully fought for their deletion. . . .

According to Herman Walker, Jr., who at the time of the drafting of the Treaty served as Adviser on Commercial Treaties at the State Department, Article VIII(1) and the comparable provisions of other treaties were intended to avoid the effect of strict percentile limitations on the employment of Americans abroad and "to prevent the imposition of ultranationalistic policies with respect to essential executive and technical personnel." Walker, Provisions on Companies in United States Commercial Treaties, 50 Am. J. Int'l L. 373, 386 (1956); Walker, Treaties for the Encouragement and Protection of Foreign Investment; Present United States Practice, 5 Am. J. Comp. L. 229, 234 (1956). . . .

pecuniary profit. Companies constituted under the applicable laws and regulations within the territories of either Party *shall be deemed companies thereof* and shall have their juridical status recognized within the territories of the other Party." (Emphasis added.)

Sumitomo is "constituted under the applicable laws and regulations" of New York; based on Article XXII(3), it is a company of the United States, not a company of Japan. As a company of the United States operating in the United States, under the literal language of Article XXII(3) of the Treaty, Sumitomo cannot invoke the rights provided in Article VIII(1), which are available only to companies of Japan operating in the United States and to companies of the United States operating in Japan.

The Governments of Japan and the United States support this interpretation of the Treaty. Both the Ministry of Foreign Affairs of Japan and the United States Department of State agree that a United States corporation, even when wholly owned by a Japanese company, is not a company of Japan under the Treaty and is therefore not covered by Article VIII(1). The Ministry of Foreign Affairs stated its position to the American Embassy in Tokyo with reference to this case:

> "The Ministry of Foreign Affairs, as the Office of [the Government of Japan] responsible for the interpretation of the [Friendship, Commerce and Navigation] Treaty, reiterates its view concerning the application of Article 8, Paragraph 1 of the Treaty: For the purpose of the Treaty, companies constituted under the applicable laws . . . of either Party shall be deemed companies thereof and therefore, a subsidiary of a Japanese company incorporated under the law of New York is not covered by Article 8 Paragraph 1 when it operates in the United States."

The United States Department of State also maintains that Article VIII(1) rights do not apply to locally incorporated subsidiaries. Although not conclusive, the meaning attributed to treaty provisions by the government agencies charged with their negotiating and enforcement is entitled to great weight. Kolovrat v. Oregon, 366 U.S. 187, 194, 81 S.Ct. 922, 926, 6 L.Ed.2d 218 (1961).

Our role is limited to giving effect to the intent of the Treaty parties. When the parties to a treaty both agree as to the meaning of a treaty provision, and that interpretation follows from the clear treaty language, we must, absent extraordinarily strong contrary evidence, defer to that interpretation.

III

Sumitomo maintains that although the literal language of the Treaty supports the contrary interpretation, the intent of Japan and the United States was to cover subsidiaries regardless of their place of incorporation. We disagree.

Contrary to the view of the Court of Appeals and the claims of Sumitomo, adherence to the language of the Treaty would not "overlook the purpose of the Treaty." 638 F.2d at 556. The Friendship, Commerce and Navigation Treaty between Japan and the United States is but one of a series of similar commercial agreements negotiated after World War II. The primary purpose of the corporation provisions of the Treaties was to give corporations of each signatory legal status in the territory of the other party, and to allow them to conduct business in the other country on a comparable basis with domestic firms. Although the United States negotiated commercial treaties as early as 1778, and thereafter throughout the 19th and 20th centuries, these early commercial treaties were primarily concerned with the trade and shipping rights of individuals. Until the 20th century, international commerce was much more an individual than a corporate affair.

As corporate involvement in international trade expanded in this century, old commercial treaties became outmoded. Because "corporation[s] can have no legal existence out of the boundaries of the sovereignty by which [they are] created," Bank of Augusta v. Earle, 13 Peters (38 U.S.) 519, 588, 10 L.Ed. 274 (1839), it became necessary to negotiate new treaties granting corporations legal status and the right to function abroad. A series of treaties negotiated before World War II gave corporations legal status and access to foreign courts, but it was not until the postwar Friendship, Commerce and Navigation Treaties that United States corporations gained the right to conduct business in other countries. The purpose of the treaties was not to give foreign corporations greater rights than domestic companies, but instead to assure them the right to conduct business on an equal basis without suffering discrimination based on their alienage.

The treaties accomplished their purpose by granting foreign corporations "national treatment" in most respects and by allowing foreign individuals and companies to form locally-incorporated subsidiaries. These local subsidiaries are considered for purpose of the Treaty to be companies of the country in which they are incorporated; they are entitled to the rights, and subject to the responsibilities of other domestic corporations. By treating these subsidiaries as domestic companies, the purpose of the Treaty provisions—to assure that corporations of one treaty party have the right to conduct business within the territory of the other party without suffering discrimination as an alien entity—is fully met.

Nor can we agree with the Court of Appeals view that literal interpretation of the Treaty would create a "crazy-quilt pattern" in which the rights of branches of Japanese companies operating directly in the United States would be greatly superior to the right of locally incorporated subsidiaries of Japanese companies. 638 F.2d at 556. The Court of Appeals maintained that if such subsidiaries were not considered companies of Japan under the Treaty, they, unlike branch offices of Japanese corporations, would be denied access to the legal system, would be left unprotected against unlawful entry and molestation, and would be unable to dispose of property, obtain patents, engage in importation and exportation, or make payments, remittances and transfers of funds. 638 F.2d at 556. That this is not the case is obvious; the subsidiaries, as companies of the United States, would enjoy all of those rights and more. The only significant advantage branches may have over subsidiaries is that conferred by Article VIII(1).

IV

We are persuaded, as both signatories agree, that under the literal language of Article XXII(3) of the Treaty, Sumitomo is a company of the United States; we discern no reason to depart from the plain meaning of the Treaty language. Accordingly, we hold that Sumitomo is not a company of Japan and is thus not covered by Article VIII(1) of the Treaty.[15] The judgment of the Court of Appeals is vacated, and the case is remanded for further proceedings consistent with this opinion.

In 1987, Sumitomo settled this action, at a reported cost of $2.8 million including pay increases for class members and educational expenses to prepare them for promotion. See BNA Corporate Counsel Report, Jan. 21, 1987, p. 5.

Despite the broad "of their choice" language of the Japan-U.S. FCN treaty and similar treaties with other countries, Court of Appeals decisions after Sumitomo have tended to read such provisions to allow only discrimination based on citizenship, which Title VII and state antidiscrimination laws generally do not prohibit. The U.S. State Department has argued in favor of this interpretation. Courts adopting it have relied upon the apparent purpose of these provisions to avoid foreign laws requiring American companies to hire a certain percentage of host country nationals and upon representations made to the Senate during ratification. See, e.g., Wickes v. Olympic Airways, 745 F.2d 363 (6th Cir. 1984); MacNamara v. Korean Airlines, 863 F.2d 1135 (3d Cir. 1988), cert. denied, 493 U.S. 944, 110 S.Ct. 349, 107 L.Ed.2d 337 (1989); Ventress v. Japan Airlines, 486 F.3d 1111 (9th Cir. 2007). More recent U.S. treaties have focused specifically on prohibiting requirements to

---

[15] We express no view as to whether Japanese citizenship may be a bona fide occupational qualification for certain positions at Sumitomo or as to whether a business necessity defense may be available. There can be little doubt that some positions in a Japanese controlled company doing business in the United States call for great familiarity with not only the language of Japan, but also the culture, customs, and business practices of that country. However, the Court of Appeals found the evidentiary record insufficient to determine whether Japanese citizenship was a bona fide occupational qualification for any of Sumitomo's positions within the reach of Article VIII(1). Nor did it discuss the bona fide occupational qualification exception in relation to respondents' sex discrimination claim or the possibility of a business necessity defense. Whether Sumitomo can support its assertion of a bona fide occupational qualification or a business necessity defense is not before us. . . .

We also express no view as to whether Sumitomo may assert any Article VIII(1) rights of its parent.

"appoint to senior management positions individuals of any particular nationality." NAFTA Art. 1107(1); see also 2012 U.S. Model Bilateral Investment Treaty Art. 9(1).

Limiting the employment rights granted by these treaties to citizenship discrimination has reduced the potential for conflict with Title VII, since the Supreme Court has held that Title VII does not prohibit discrimination on the basis of citizenship. See Espinoza v. Farah Manufacturing Co., 414 U.S. 86, 94 S.Ct. 334, 38 L.Ed.2d 287 (1973). On the other hand, Title VII does prohibit discrimination of the basis of "national origin" and would reach citizenship discrimination "whenever it has the purpose or effect of discriminating on the basis of national origin." Id. at 92, 94 S.Ct. at 338. Faced with this possible conflict, the Courts of Appeals have tended to resolve it in favor of the treaties. See MacNamara, 863 F.2d at 1147–1148; Fortino v. Quasar Co., 950 F.2d 389, 392–393 (7th Cir. 1991).

Sumitomo's final footnote left open the question whether an American subsidiary might assert the treaty rights of its foreign parent. Some Courts of Appeals have answered this question in the affirmative, at least where the foreign parent "dictated the subsidiary's discriminatory conduct," Fortino, 950 F.2d at 393, or "made all the allegedly discriminatory decisions." Papila v. Uniden America Corp., 51 F.3d 54 (5th Cir.), cert. denied, 516 U.S. 868, 116 S.Ct. 187, 133 L.Ed.2d 124 (1995). But another court has pointed out that this turns Sumitomo "on its head," since "[t]he parent company will *always* have the power to control the management of its subsidiary." "It will be a rare case in which the subsidiary cannot produce evidence that its foreign parent 'dictated' the employment decision in question." Kirmse v. Hotel Nikko of San Francisco, Inc., 51 Cal. App. 4th 311, 319–320, 59 Cal. Rptr. 2d 96, 101 (Cal. Ct. App. 1996).

Can an employee's race, color, religion, sex, or national origin ever constitute a bona fide occupational qualification (BFOQ)? Sumitomo also left this question open in its final footnote. In Kern v. Dynalectron Corp., 577 F. Supp. 1196 (N.D. Tex. 1983), the court held that conversion to Islam was a BFOQ for helicopter pilots flying to Mecca because Saudi law prohibited non-Muslims from entering Mecca.

QUESTIONS

(1) Upon what factors does the Sumitomo Court rely to interpret the treaty? How does it weigh them to the extent they may be inconsistent? Looking to those same factors, have the Courts of Appeals been correct to hold that the protection afforded by such treaties is limited to citizenship discrimination?

(2) Does the distinction between the treatment of branches and subsidiaries make sense in this context? When, if ever, should a subsidiary be allowed to assert the treaty rights of its foreign parent?

(3) Assume that an American branch of a Japanese company discriminates on the basis of citizenship and is alleged to have thereby violated Title VII's prohibition against national-origin discrimination. How should a court resolve the conflict between the treaty and Title VII? How should a court resolve a conflict between the treaty and state law prohibiting discrimination on the basis of national origin or citizenship?

Additional reading: Ackerman & Golove, Is NAFTA Constitutional? 108 Harv. L. Rev. 799 (1995); Sloss, Executing Foster v. Neilson: The Two-Step Approach to Analyzing Self-Executing Treaties, 53 Harv. Int'l L.J. 135 (2012); Vázquez, The Four Doctrines of Self-Executing Treaties, 89 Am. J. Int'l L. 695 (1995); Vagts, Treaty Interpretation and the New American Ways of Law Reading, 4 Eur. J. Int. L. 472 (1993).

D. THE EXTRATERRITORIAL APPLICATION OF NATIONAL LAW

Nations are often legitimately concerned with conduct outside their borders. They may wish to regulate certain conduct by their nationals abroad, for example, or conduct by foreign parties that has effects within their borders. Such regulation is often characterized as "extraterritorial."

This section begins with an overview of the customary international law rules governing prescriptive jurisdiction. It then discusses three principles of statutory interpretation that courts in the United States use to determine the geographic scope of federal laws: (1) the presumption against extraterritoriality; (2) the principle of reasonableness; and (3) the *Charming Betsy* canon of interpreting statutes not to violate international law. This section concludes with an example involving antidiscrimination law, which the Supreme Court interpreted not to apply extraterritorially, only to be overridden by Congress.

1. PRESCRIPTIVE JURISDICTION UNDER CUSTOMARY INTERNATIONAL LAW

The customary international law rules most relevant to international business lawyers are those on expropriation, discussed in Problem 7, see infra pp. 467–470, and those governing jurisdiction to prescribe, discussed here. Scholars do not always agree on how different exercises of jurisdiction should be categorized or on how the customary international law requirements of state practice and *opinio juris* should be applied. The discussion here generally follows the recently completed Restatement (Fourth) of Foreign Relations Law (2018). The Restatement (Fourth) is not binding authority, but it reflects the best judgment of the American Law Institute on questions of jurisdiction under customary international law today.

Jurisdiction refers to the authority of a nation to make, apply, or compel compliance with law. The authority to make law is known as jurisdiction to prescribe. Legislatures exercise prescriptive jurisdiction when they pass statutes; administrative agencies exercise prescriptive jurisdiction when they issue regulations; and courts exercise prescriptive jurisdiction when they make common law. The authority to apply law is known as jurisdiction to adjudicate and is generally exercised by courts. A court may exercise adjudicative jurisdiction to determine the rights of the parties under its own law or under the law of another nation. The authority to compel compliance with law is known as jurisdiction to enforce. It is usually exercised by a nation's law enforcement officers, but often at the direction of its courts. Examples include the arrest of a person and the seizure of property. See Restatement (Fourth) of Foreign Relations Law § 401 (2018).

Customary international law imposes different limits on different kinds of jurisdiction. Jurisdiction to enforce has long been understood to be strictly territorial. See S.S. "Lotus" (Fr. v. Turk.), 1927 P.C.I.J. (ser. A) No. 10, at 18 (Sept. 7) ("[T]he first and foremost restriction imposed by international law upon a State is that—failing the existence of a permissive rule to the contrary—it may not exercise its power in any form in the territory of another State."). One nation may not arrest a person or seize property located in the territory of another state without the other state's consent. See Restatement (Fourth) of Foreign Relations Law § 432 (2018). Jurisdiction to adjudicate is generally not limited by customary international law, with the exception of various forms of immunity. See id. § 422 Reporters' Note 1.

For jurisdiction to prescribe, customary international law requires a "genuine connection" between a nation and the subject being regulated. Id. § 407. There are six traditional bases of prescriptive jurisdiction that meet this requirement: (1) Territorial jurisdiction permits a nation to prescribe law with respect to persons, property, and conduct within its territory. See id. § 408. (2) Effects jurisdiction permits a nation to prescribe law with respect to conduct that has a substantial effect within its territory. See id. § 409. (3) Active-personality (or nationality) jurisdiction permits a nation to prescribe law with respect to the conduct, interests, status, and relations of its own nationals outside its territory. See id. § 410. (4) Passive-personality jurisdiction permits a nation to prescribe law with respect to certain conduct outside its territory that harms its nationals, such as terrorism. See id. § 411. (5) Protective jurisdiction permits a nation to prescribe law with respect to certain conduct outside its territory by persons who are not its nationals that is directed against the security of the state or against a limited class of other fundamental state interests, such as espionage and counterfeiting. See id. § 412. (6) Universal jurisdiction permits a nation to prescribe law with respect to certain offenses of universal concern, such as genocide, crimes against humanity, war crimes, certain acts of terrorism, piracy, the slave trade, and torture, even if no specific connection exists between the state and the persons or conduct being regulated. See id. § 413. In short, customary international law allows "extraterritorial" regulation on a number of different bases.

For international business transactions, the most important bases of prescriptive jurisdiction are territory, effects, and nationality. The application of Title VII to foreign companies in the United States is an example of territorial jurisdiction. See supra pp. 85–90. The application of U.S. antitrust law to foreign anticompetitive conduct that causes injury in the United States is an example of effects jurisdiction. See infra p. 235. And the taxation of U.S. companies on their worldwide income is an example of nationality jurisdiction. See infra p. 314.

Sometimes, more than one nation will have concurrent jurisdiction to make law with respect to the same person or conduct. If a German company concludes an agreement in the United Kingdom to fix the prices of goods sold to the United States, Germany will have jurisdiction to prescribe based on nationality, the United Kingdom will have jurisdiction to prescribe based on territory, and the United States will have jurisdiction to prescribe based on effects. Section 403 of the Restatement (Third) of Foreign Relations Law attempted to deal with situations of concurrent jurisdiction by articulating a rule of customary international law that would have required a weighing of contacts and interests in each case in order to determine whether the exercise of prescriptive jurisdiction was reasonable. But state practice and *opinio juris* do not support a requirement of case-by-case balancing to establish reasonableness as a matter of customary international law. See Restatement (Fourth) of Foreign Relations Law § 407 Reporters' Note 3 (2018). The Restatement (Fourth) states: "International law recognizes no hierarchy of bases of prescriptive jurisdiction and contains no rules for assigning priority to competing jurisdictional claims." Id. § 407 cmt d.

This is not to say that nations fail to act reasonably in regulating persons and conduct outside their territories. It is rather to say that nations generally limit their exercises of prescriptive jurisdiction because of international comity rather than international law. The Restatement (Fourth) explains the distinction:

> As a matter of international comity, states often limit the exercise of jurisdiction to a greater extent than international law requires. International comity reflects deference to foreign states that international law does not mandate. . . . State choices to restrain the exercise of jurisdiction are not evidence of the limits set by customary international law if they do not result from a sense of international legal obligation.

Id. § 401 cmt a. Sometimes, the U.S. Congress expressly limits the geographic scope of federal statutes or creates exceptions to avoid conflicts with foreign laws, as in the case of antidiscrimination law discussed below. See infra pp. 107–114. When it does not, U.S. courts turn to various principles of statutory interpretation.

QUESTIONS

(1) Like other rules of customary international law, the rules governing jurisdiction must be based on a general practice that is accepted as law. See supra pp. 68–70. Why do you suppose that states have acted differently with respect to prescriptive, adjudicative, and enforcement jurisdiction, leading to different rules of customary international law?

(2) With respect jurisdiction to prescribe, what kinds of evidence would you look to in order to find state practice and *opinio juris*?

Additional reading: Restatement (Fourth) of Foreign Relations Law §§ 401, 407–413, 432 (2018); Dodge, Jurisdiction in the Fourth Restatement of Foreign Relations Law, 18 Y.B. Priv. Int'l L. 143 (2017); Ryngaert, Jurisdiction in International Law (2d ed. 2015); Int'l Law Comm'n, Report to the General Assembly, Annex V, [2006] 2(2) Y.B. Int'l L. Comm'n 231 (2006).

2.   PRINCIPLES OF INTERPRETATION

When Congress does not expressly address the geographic scope of a federal statutory provision, courts in the United States rely on three principles of interpretation to determine its reach: (1) the presumption against extraterritoriality; (2) the principle of reasonableness; and (3) the *Charming Betsy* canon of interpreting statutes not to violate international law.

The presumption against extraterritoriality dates to the early nineteenth century. See, e.g., The Apollon, 22 U.S. (9 Wheat.) 362, 370, 6 L. Ed. 111 (1824). During the first half of the twentieth century, the U.S. Supreme Court applied the presumption to determine the geographic scope of some statutes, see, e.g., American Banana Co. v. United Fruit Co., 213 U.S. 347, 29 S.Ct. 511, 53 L.Ed. 826 (1909) (Sherman Act); Foley Bros., Inc. v. Filardo, 336 U.S. 281, 69 S.Ct. 575, 93 L.Ed. 680 (1949) (Eight Hour Law), but not others, see, e.g., United States v. Bowman, 260 U.S. 94, 43 S.Ct. 39, 67 L.Ed. 149 (1922) (statute prohibiting false claims against the United States); Steele v. Bulova Watch Co., 344 U.S. 280, 73 S.Ct. 252, 97 L.Ed. 319 (1952) (Lanham Act). By the 1980s, the presumption seemed to have fallen into desuetude, and the Restatement (Third) of Foreign Relations Law did not include it.

Since 1989, however, the Supreme Court has applied the presumption against extraterritoriality in multiple cases. See Argentine Republic v. Amerada Hess Shipping Corp., 488 U.S. 428, 440–441, 109 S.Ct. 683, 691–692, 102 L.Ed.2d 818 (1989) (Foreign Sovereign Immunities Act); EEOC v. Arabian American Oil Co. (Aramco), 499 U.S. 244, 248, 111 S.Ct. 1227, 1230, 113 L.Ed.2d 274 (1991) (Title VII of 1964 Civil Rights Act); Smith v. United States, 507 U.S. 197, 203–204, 113 S.Ct. 1178, 1183, 122 L.Ed.2d 548 (1993) (Federal Tort Claims Act); Sale v. Haitian Centers Council, Inc., 509 U.S. 155, 173–174, 113 S.Ct. 2549,

2560, 125 L.Ed.2d 128 (1993) (Immigration and Nationality Act); Microsoft Corp. v. AT&T Corp., 550 U.S. 437, 454–456, 127 S.Ct. 1746, 1758–1759, 167 L.Ed.2d 737 (2007) (Patent Act); Morrison v. Nat'l Australia Bank Ltd., 561 U.S. 247, 255, 130 S.Ct. 2869, 2877–2878, 177 L.Ed.2d 535 (2010) (Securities Exchange Act); Kiobel v. Royal Dutch Petroleum Co., 569 U.S. 108, 115–117, 133 S.Ct. 1659, 1664–1665, 185 L.Ed.2d 671 (2013) (federal common law cause of action under the Alien Tort Statute); RJR Nabisco, Inc. v. European Community, 136 S.Ct. 2090, 2101, 195 L.Ed.2d 476 (2016) (Racketeer Influenced and Corrupt Organizations Act (RICO)). Today, the presumption is the principle of interpretation that The Supreme Court uses most frequently to determine the geographic scope of federal statutes.

The Supreme Court's 2010 decision in Morrison changed the presumption in significant ways. The question in Morrison was the geographic scope of Securities Exchange Act § 10(b), which prohibits fraud in connection with the purchase or sale of securities. More specifically, did § 10(b) apply when fraud occurred in the United States but the securities were purchased on a foreign stock exchange? Morrison divided the analysis into two steps. At step one, it asked whether the presumption had been rebutted by a "clear indication of extraterritoriality." Morrison, 561 U.S. at 265, 130 S.Ct. at 2883. The Court indicated that the presumption is not a "clear statement rule" and that "context can be consulted as well." Id. But the Court found no clear indication that Congress intended § 10(b) to apply extraterritorially. At step two, the Court asked whether the case involved a "domestic application" of the statute by examining the statute's "focus." Id. at 266, 130 S.Ct. at 2883. Before Morrison, the presumption was generally understood to turn on where the conduct occurred, and in Morrison the alleged fraud occurred in Florida. But the Court reasoned that a statutory provision might focus on something other than conduct and found that "the focus of the Exchange Act is not upon the place where the deception originated, but upon purchases and sales of securities in the United States." Id. Because § 10(b) focused on the transaction rather than the fraud, and because the transaction in Morrison occurred outside the United States, the Court concluded that applying U.S. law in that case would be impermissibly extraterritorial.

Morrison is the leading decision on the geographic scope of U.S. securities laws, and the case is excerpted in Problem 5. See infra pp. 350–358. In the case that follows, the Supreme Court formalized Morrison's two-step framework and applied it to another important statute.

RJR Nabisco, Inc. v. European Community

Supreme Court of the United States, 2016
136 S.Ct. 2090, 195 L.Ed.2d 476

[The Racketeer Influenced and Corrupt Organizations Act (RICO) makes it illegal to use a pattern of racketeering activity in particular ways relating to enterprises. Racketeering activity consists of certain state and federal offenses generally known as predicates—money laundering, for example. RICO also creates a civil cause of action for treble damages for "[a]ny person injured in his business or property" by a RICO violation. The European Community and 26 of its member states filed a civil suit under RICO, alleging that RJR Nabisco participated in a global money-laundering scheme in association with various organized crime groups. Under the alleged scheme, drug traffickers smuggled narcotics into Europe and sold them for euros that—through transactions involving black-market money brokers, cigarette importers, and wholesalers—were used to pay for large shipments of RJR cigarettes into Europe. The District Court dismissed the suit on the ground that RICO does not apply to racketeering activity occurring outside U.S. territory or to foreign enterprises, but the Second Circuit reversed concluding that RICO applies extraterritorially to the same extent as the predicate acts of racketeering. Justice Alito delivered the opinion of the Supreme Court.]

II

The question of RICO's extraterritorial application really involves two questions. First, do RICO's substantive prohibitions, contained in § 1962, apply to conduct that occurs in foreign countries? Second, does RICO's private right of action, contained in § 1964(c), apply to injuries that are suffered in foreign countries? We consider each of these questions in turn. To guide our inquiry, we begin by reviewing the law of extraterritoriality.

It is a basic premise of our legal system that, in general, "United States law governs domestically but does not rule the world." *Microsoft Corp. v. AT & T Corp.*, 550 U.S. 437, 454, 127 S.Ct. 1746, 167 L.Ed.2d 737 (2007). This principle finds expression in a canon of statutory construction known as the presumption against extraterritoriality: Absent clearly expressed congressional intent to the contrary, federal laws will be construed to have only domestic application. *Morrison v. National Australia Bank Ltd.*, 561 U.S. 247, 255, 130 S.Ct. 2869, 177 L.Ed.2d 535 (2010). The question is not whether we think "Congress would have wanted" a statute to apply to foreign conduct "if it had thought of the situation before the court," but whether Congress has affirmatively and unmistakably instructed that the statute will do so. *Id.* at 261. "When a statute gives no clear indication of an extraterritorial application, it has none." *Id.* at 255.

There are several reasons for this presumption. Most notably, it serves to avoid the international discord that can result when U.S. law is applied to conduct in foreign countries. See, *e.g.*, *Kiobel v. Royal Dutch Petroleum Co.*, 133 S.Ct. 1659, 1663–1664, 185 L.Ed.2d 671 (2013); *EEOC v. Arabian American Oil Co.*, 499 U.S. 244, 248, 111 S.Ct. 1227, 113 L.Ed.2d 274 (1991) (*Aramco*); *Benz v. Compania Naviera Hidalgo, S.A.*, 353 U.S. 138, 147, 77 S.Ct. 699, 1 L.Ed.2d 709 (1957). But it also reflects the more prosaic "commonsense notion that Congress generally legislates with domestic concerns in mind." *Smith v. United States*, 507 U.S. 197, 204, n. 5, 113 S.Ct. 1178, 122 L.Ed.2d 548 (1993). We therefore apply the presumption across the board, "regardless of whether there is a risk of conflict between the American statute and a foreign law." *Morrison*, 561 U.S. at 255.

Twice in the past six years we have considered whether a federal statute applies extraterritorially. In *Morrison*, we addressed the question whether § 10(b) of the Securities Exchange Act of 1934 applies to misrepresentations made in connection with the purchase or sale of securities traded only on foreign exchanges. We first examined whether § 10(b) gives any clear indication of extraterritorial effect, and found that it does not. 561 U.S. at 262–265. We then engaged in a separate inquiry to determine whether the complaint before us involved a permissible *domestic* application of § 10(b) because it alleged that some of the relevant misrepresentations were made in the United States. At this second step, we considered the " 'focus' of congressional concern," asking whether § 10(b)'s focus is "the place where the deception originated" or rather "purchases and sale of securities in the United States." *Id.* at 266. We concluded that the statute's focus is on domestic securities transactions, and we therefore held that the statute does not apply to frauds in connection with foreign securities transactions, even if those frauds involve domestic misrepresentations.

In *Kiobel*, we considered whether the Alien Tort Statute (ATS) confers federal-court jurisdiction over causes of action alleging international-law violations committed overseas. We acknowledged that the presumption against extraterritoriality is "typically" applied to statutes "regulating conduct," but we concluded that the principles supporting the presumption should "similarly constrain courts considering causes of action that may be brought under the ATS." 133 S.Ct. at 1664. We applied the presumption and held that the ATS lacks any clear indication that it extended to the foreign violations alleged in that case. *Id.* at 1665–1669. Because "all the relevant conduct" regarding those violations "took place outside the United States," *id.* at 1670, we did not need to determine, as we did in Morrison, the statute's "focus."

Morrison and Kiobel reflect a two-step framework for analyzing extraterritoriality issues. At the first step, we ask whether the presumption against extraterritoriality has been rebutted—that is, whether the statute gives a clear, affirmative indication that it applies extraterritorially. We must ask this question regardless of whether the statute in question regulates conduct, affords relief, or merely confers jurisdiction. If the statute is not extraterritorial, then at the second step we determine whether the case involves a domestic application of the statute, and we do this by looking to the statute's "focus." If the conduct relevant to the statute's focus occurred in the United States, then the case involves a permissible domestic application even if other conduct occurred abroad; but if the conduct relevant to the focus occurred in a foreign country, then the case involves an impermissible extraterritorial application regardless of any other conduct that occurred in U.S. territory.

What if we find at step one that a statute clearly *does* have extraterritorial effect? Neither *Morrison* nor *Kiobel* involved such a finding. But we addressed this issue in *Morrison*, explaining that it was necessary to consider § 10(b)'s "focus" only because we found that the statute does not apply extraterritorially: "If § 10(b) did apply abroad, we would not need to determine which transnational frauds it applied to; it would apply to all of them (barring some other limitation)." 561 U.S. at 267, n. 9. The scope of an extraterritorial statute thus turns on the limits Congress has (or has not) imposed on the statute's foreign application, and not on the statute's "focus."

III

With these guiding principles in mind, we first consider whether RICO's substantive prohibitions in § 1962 may apply to foreign conduct. Unlike in *Morrison* and *Kiobel*, we find that the presumption against extraterritoriality has been rebutted—but only with respect to certain applications of the statute.

A

The most obvious textual clue is that RICO defines racketeering activity to include a number of predicates that plainly apply to at least some foreign conduct. These predicates include the prohibition against engaging in monetary transactions in criminally derived property, which expressly applies, when "the defendant is a United States person," to offenses that "tak[e] place outside the United States." 18 U.S.C. § 1957(d)(2). Other examples include the prohibitions against the assassination of Government officials, § 351(i) ("There is extraterritorial jurisdiction over the conduct prohibited by this section"); § 1751(k) (same), and the prohibition against hostage taking, which applies to conduct that "occurred outside the United States" if either the hostage or the offender is a U.S. national, if the offender is found in the United States, or if the hostage taking is done to compel action by the U.S. Government, § 1203(b). At least one predicate—the prohibition against "kill[ing] a national of the United States, while such national is outside the United States"—applies only to conduct occurring outside the United States. § 2332(a).

We agree with the Second Circuit that Congress's incorporation of these (and other) extraterritorial predicates into RICO gives a clear, affirmative indication that § 1962 applies to foreign racketeering activity—but only to the extent that the predicates alleged in a particular case themselves apply extraterritorially. Put another way, a pattern of racketeering activity may include or consist of offenses committed abroad in violation of a predicate statute for which the presumption against extraterritoriality has been overcome. To give a simple (albeit grim) example, a violation of § 1962 could be premised on a pattern of killings of Americans abroad in violation of § 2332(a)—a predicate that all agree applies extraterritorially—whether or not any domestic predicates are also alleged.

We emphasize the important limitation that foreign conduct must violate "a predicate statute that manifests an unmistakable congressional intent to apply extraterritorially." 764 F.3d at 136. Although a number of RICO predicates have extraterritorial effect, many do not. The inclusion of *some* extraterritorial predicates does not mean that *all* RICO predicates extend to foreign conduct. This is apparent for two reasons. First, "when a statute provides for some extraterritorial application, the presumption against extraterritoriality operates to limit that provision to its terms." *Morrison*, 561 U.S. at 265. Second, RICO defines as racketeering activity only acts that are "indictable" (or, what amounts to the same thing, "chargeable" or "punishable") under one of the statutes identified in § 1961(1). If a particular statute does not apply extraterritorially, then conduct committed abroad is not "indictable" under that statute and so cannot qualify as a predicate under RICO's plain terms.

RJR resists the conclusion that RICO's incorporation of extraterritorial predicates gives RICO commensurate extraterritorial effect. It points out that "RICO itself" does not refer to extraterritorial application; only the underlying predicate statutes do. Brief for Petitioners 42. RJR thus argues that Congress could have intended to capture only *domestic* applications of extraterritorial predicates, and that any predicates that apply only abroad could have been "incorporated . . . solely for when such offenses are part of a broader pattern whose overall locus is domestic." *Id.* at 43.

The presumption against extraterritoriality does not require us to adopt such a constricted interpretation. While the presumption can be overcome only by a clear indication of extraterritorial effect, an express statement of extraterritoriality is not essential. "Assuredly context can be consulted as well." *Morrison*, 561 U.S. at 265, 130. Context is dispositive here. Congress has not expressly said that § 1962(c) applies to patterns of racketeering activity in foreign countries, but it has defined "racketeering activity"—and by extension a "pattern of racketeering activity"—to encompass violations of predicate statutes that *do* expressly apply extraterritorially. Short of an explicit declaration, it is hard to imagine how Congress could have more clearly indicated that it intended RICO to have (some) extraterritorial effect. This unique structure makes RICO the rare statute that clearly evidences extraterritorial effect despite lacking an express statement of extraterritoriality.

* * *

B

RJR contends that, even if RICO may apply to foreign patterns of racketeering, the statute does not apply to foreign *enterprises*. Invoking *Morrison*'s discussion of the Exchange Act's "focus," RJR says that the "focus" of RICO is the enterprise being corrupted—not the pattern of racketeering—and that RICO's enterprise element gives no clear indication of extraterritorial effect. Accordingly, RJR reasons, RICO requires a domestic enterprise.

This argument misunderstands *Morrison*. As explained above, only at the second step of the inquiry do we consider a statute's "focus." Here, however, there is a clear indication at step one that RICO applies extraterritorially. We therefore do not proceed to the "focus" step. The *Morrison* Court's discussion of the statutory "focus" made this clear, stating that "[i]f § 10(b) did apply abroad, we would not need to determine which transnational frauds it applied to; it would apply to all of them (barring some other limitation)." 561 U.S. at 267, n. 9. The same is true here. RICO—or at least §§ 1962(b) and (c)—applies abroad, and so we do not need to determine which transnational (or wholly foreign) patterns of racketeering it applies to; it applies to all of them, regardless of whether they are connected to a "foreign" or "domestic" enterprise. This rule is, of course, subject to the important limitation that RICO covers foreign predicate offenses only to the extent that the underlying predicate statutes are extraterritorial. But within those bounds, the location of the affected enterprise does not impose an independent constraint.

* * *

C

Applying these principles, we agree with the Second Circuit that the complaint does not allege impermissibly extraterritorial violations of §§ 1962(b) and (c).

The alleged pattern of racketeering activity consists of five basic predicates: (1) money laundering, (2) material support of foreign terrorist organizations, (3) mail fraud, (4) wire fraud, and (5) violations of the Travel Act. The Second Circuit observed that the relevant provisions of the money laundering and material support of terrorism statutes expressly provide for extraterritorial application in certain circumstances, and it concluded that those circumstances are alleged to be present here. 764 F.3d at 139–140. The court found that the fraud statutes and the Travel Act do not contain the clear indication needed to overcome the presumption against extraterritoriality. But it held that the complaint alleges *domestic* violations of those statutes because it "allege[s] conduct in the United States that satisfies every essential element of the mail fraud, wire fraud, and Travel Act claims." *Id.* at 142.

RJR does not dispute these characterizations of the alleged predicates. We therefore assume without deciding that the alleged pattern of racketeering activity consists entirely of predicate offenses that were either committed in the United States or committed in a foreign country in violation of a predicate statute that applies extraterritorially. The alleged enterprise also has a sufficient tie to U.S. commerce, as its members include U.S. companies, and its activities depend on sales of RJR's cigarettes conducted through "the U.S. mails and wires," among other things. App. to Pet. for Cert. 186a, Complaint ¶ 96. On these premises, respondents' allegations that RJR violated §§ 1962(b) and (c) do not involve an impermissibly extraterritorial application of RICO.

IV

We now turn to RICO's private right of action, on which respondents' lawsuit rests. Section 1964(c) allows "[a]ny person injured in his business or property by reason of a violation of section 1962" to sue for treble damages, costs, and attorney's fees. Irrespective of any extraterritorial application of § 1962, we conclude that § 1964(c) does not overcome the presumption against extraterritoriality. A private RICO plaintiff therefore must allege and prove a *domestic* injury to its business or property.

A

The Second Circuit thought that the presumption against extraterritoriality did not apply to § 1964(c) independently of its application to § 1962, reasoning that the presumption "is primarily concerned with the question of what *conduct* falls within a statute's purview." 764 F.3d at 151. We rejected that view in *Kiobel*, holding that the presumption "constrain[s] courts considering causes of action" under the ATS, a " 'strictly jurisdictional' " statute that "does not directly regulate conduct or afford relief." 133 S.Ct. at 1664. We reached this conclusion even though the underlying substantive law consisted of well-established norms of international law, which by definition apply beyond this country's borders. See id. at 1664–1666.

The same logic requires that we separately apply the presumption against extraterritoriality to RICO's cause of action despite our conclusion that the presumption has been overcome with respect to RICO's substantive prohibitions. "The creation of a private right of action raises issues beyond the mere consideration whether underlying primary conduct should be allowed or not, entailing, for example, a decision to permit enforcement without the check imposed by prosecutorial discretion." *Sosa v. Alvarez-Machain*, 542 U.S. 692, 727, 124 S.Ct. 2739,

159 L.Ed.2d 718 (2004). Thus, as we have observed in other contexts, providing a private civil remedy for foreign conduct creates a potential for international friction beyond that presented by merely applying U.S. substantive law to that foreign conduct. See, *e.g.*, *Kiobel*, 133 S.Ct. at 1665 ("Each of th[e] decisions" involved in defining a cause of action based on "conduct within the territory of another sovereign" "carries with it significant foreign policy implications").

Consider antitrust. In that context, we have observed that "[t]he application . . . of American private treble-damages remedies to anticompetitive conduct taking place abroad has generated considerable controversy" in other nations, even when those nations agree with U.S. substantive law on such things as banning price fixing. *F. Hoffmann-La Roche Ltd. v. Empagran S.A.*, 542 U.S. 155, 167, 124 S.Ct. 2359, 159 L.Ed.2d 226 (2004). Numerous foreign countries—including some respondents in this case—advised us in *Empagran* that "to apply [U.S.] remedies would unjustifiably permit their citizens to bypass their own less generous remedial schemes, thereby upsetting a balance of competing considerations that their own domestic antitrust laws embody." *Ibid*.

We received similar warnings in *Morrison*, where France, a respondent here, informed us that "most foreign countries proscribe securities fraud" but "have made very different choices with respect to the best way to implement that proscription," such as "prefer[ring] 'state actions, not private ones' for the enforcement of law." Brief for Republic of France as *Amicus Curiae*, O.T. 2009, No. 08–1191, p. 20; see *id.* at 23 ("Even when foreign countries permit private rights of action for securities fraud, they often have different schemes" for litigating them and "may approve of different measures of damages"). Allowing foreign investors to pursue private suits in the United States, we were told, "would upset that delicate balance and offend the sovereign interests of foreign nations." *Id.* at 26.

Allowing recovery for foreign injuries in a civil RICO action, including treble damages, presents the same danger of international friction. See Brief for United States as *Amicus Curiae* 31–34. This is not to say that friction would necessarily result in every case, or that Congress would violate international law by permitting such suits. It is to say only that there is a potential for international controversy that militates against recognizing foreign-injury claims without clear direction from Congress. Although "a risk of conflict between the American statute and a foreign law" is not a prerequisite for applying the presumption against extraterritoriality, *Morrison*, 561 U.S. at 255, where such a risk is evident, the need to enforce the presumption is at its apex.

Respondents urge that concerns about international friction are inapplicable in this case because here the plaintiffs are not foreign citizens seeking to bypass their home countries' less generous remedies but rather the foreign countries themselves. Brief for Respondents 52–53. Respondents assure us that they "are satisfied that the[ir] complaint . . . comports with limitations on prescriptive jurisdiction under international law and respects the dignity of foreign sovereigns." *Ibid.* Even assuming that this is true, however, our interpretation of § 1964(c)'s injury requirement will necessarily govern suits by nongovernmental plaintiffs that are not so sensitive to foreign sovereigns' dignity. We reject the notion that we should forgo the presumption against extraterritoriality and instead permit extraterritorial suits based on a case-by-case inquiry that turns on or looks to the consent of the affected sovereign. See *Morrison*, 561 U.S. at 261 ("Rather than guess anew in each case, we apply the presumption in all cases"); cf. *Empagran*, 542 U.S., at 168. Respondents suggest that we should be reluctant to permit a foreign corporation to be sued in the courts of this country for events occurring abroad if the nation of incorporation objects, but that we should discard those reservations when a foreign state sues a U.S. entity in this country under U.S. law—instead of in its own courts and under its own laws—for conduct committed on its own soil. We refuse to adopt this double standard. "After all, in the law, what is sauce for the goose is normally sauce for the gander." *Heffernan v. City of Paterson*, 136 S.Ct. 1412, 1418, 194 L.Ed.2d 508 (2016).

B

Nothing in § 1964(c) provides a clear indication that Congress intended to create a private right of action for injuries suffered outside of the United States. The statute provides a cause of action to "[a]ny person injured in his business or property" by a violation of § 1962. § 1964(c). The word "any" ordinarily connotes breadth, but it is insufficient to displace the presumption against extraterritoriality. See *Kiobel*, 133 S.Ct. at 1665–1666. The statute's reference to injury to "business or property" also does not indicate extraterritorial application. If anything, by cabining RICO's private cause of action to particular kinds of injury—excluding, for example, personal injuries—Congress signaled that the civil remedy is not coextensive with § 1962's substantive prohibitions. The rest of § 1964(c) places a limit on RICO plaintiffs' ability to rely on securities fraud to make out a claim. This too suggests that § 1964(c) is narrower in its application than § 1962, and in any event does not support extraterritoriality.

The Second Circuit did not identify anything in § 1964(c) that shows that the statute reaches foreign injuries. Instead, the court reasoned that § 1964(c)'s extraterritorial effect flows directly from that of § 1962. Citing our holding in *Sedima, S.P.R.L. v. Imrex Co.*, 473 U.S. 479, 105 S.Ct. 3275, 87 L.Ed.2d 346 (1985), that the "compensable injury" addressed by § 1964(c) "necessarily is the harm caused by predicate acts sufficiently related to constitute a pattern," *id.* at 497, the Court of Appeals held that a RICO plaintiff may sue for foreign injury that was caused by the violation of a predicate statute that applies extraterritorially, just as a substantive RICO violation may be based on extraterritorial predicates. 764 F.3d at 151. Justice GINSBURG advances the same theory. See *post*, at 2113–2114 (opinion concurring in part and dissenting in part). This reasoning has surface appeal, but it fails to appreciate that the presumption against extraterritoriality must be applied separately to both RICO's substantive prohibitions and its private right of action. It is not enough to say that a private right of action must reach abroad because the underlying law governs conduct in foreign countries. Something more is needed, and here it is absent.

* * *

C

Section 1964(c) requires a civil RICO plaintiff to allege and prove a domestic injury to business or property and does not allow recovery for foreign injuries. The application of this rule in any given case will not always be self-evident, as disputes may arise as to whether a particular alleged injury is "foreign" or "domestic." But we need not concern ourselves with that question in this case. As this case was being briefed before this Court, respondents filed a stipulation in the District Court waiving their damages claims for domestic injuries. The District Court accepted this waiver and dismissed those claims with prejudice. Respondents' remaining RICO damages claims therefore rest entirely on injury suffered abroad and must be dismissed.

* * *

[Justice Sotomayor took no part in the consideration or decision of this case. Justice Ginsburg filed a separate opinion (joined by Justices Breyer and Kagan) concurring in the Court's holding that RICO's criminal provisions apply extraterritorially to the same extent as its predicate acts but dissenting from Part IV's holding with respect to RICO's civil cause of action. She argued that § 1964(c)'s text incorporated § 1962 in the same way that § 1962 incorporated RICO's predicate acts. She also noted that § 1964(c) was modeled on the private right of action in U.S. antitrust law, which the Court had held to apply to foreign injuries at the time RICO was enacted. Justice Ginsburg then continued as follows.]

The Court nevertheless deems a domestic-injury requirement for private RICO plaintiffs necessary to avoid international friction. See *ante*, at 2106–2108. When the United States considers whether to initiate a prosecution or civil suit, the Court observes, it will take foreign-policy considerations into account, but private parties will not. It is far from clear, however, that the Court's blanket rule would ordinarily work to ward off international discord. Invoking the presumption against extraterritoriality as a bar to any private suit for injuries to business or property abroad, this case suggests, might spark, rather than quell, international strife. Making such litigation available to domestic but not foreign plaintiffs is hardly solicitous of international comity or respectful of foreign interests. Cf. *Pfizer*, 434 U.S. at 318–319 ("[A] foreign nation is generally entitled to prosecute any civil claim in the courts of the United States upon the same basis as a domestic corporation or individual might do. To deny him this privilege would manifest a want of comity and friendly feeling." (internal quotation marks omitted)).

* * *

To the extent extraterritorial application of RICO could give rise to comity concerns not present in this case, those concerns can be met through doctrines that serve to block litigation in U.S. courts of cases more appropriately brought elsewhere. Where an alternative, more appropriate forum is available, the doctrine of *forum non conveniens* enables U.S. courts to refuse jurisdiction. See *Piper Aircraft Co. v. Reyno*, 454 U.S. 235, 102 S.Ct. 252, 70 L.Ed.2d 419 (1981) (dismissing wrongful-death action arising out of air crash in Scotland involving only Scottish victims); Restatement (Second) of Conflict of Laws § 84 (1969). Due process constraints on the exercise of general personal jurisdiction shelter foreign corporations from suit in the United States based on conduct abroad unless the corporation's "affiliations with the [forum] in which suit is brought are so constant and pervasive 'as to render it essentially at home [there].' " *Daimler AG v. Bauman*, 134 S.Ct. 746, 751, 187 L.Ed.2d 624 (2014) (quoting *Goodyear Dunlop Tires Operations, S.A. v. Brown*, 564 U.S. 915, 919, 131 S.Ct. 2846, 180 L.Ed.2d 796 (2011) (alterations omitted). These controls provide a check against civil RICO litigation with little or no connection to the United States.

A second principle of interpretation is what the Restatement (Fourth) of Foreign Relations Law refers to as a principle of "reasonableness in interpretation." Restatement (Fourth) of Foreign Relations Law § 405 (2018). This principle draws heavily on the Supreme Court's 2004 decision in F. Hoffmann-La Roche Ltd. v. Empagran S.A., 542 U.S. 155, 124 S.Ct. 2359, 159 L.Ed.2d 226 (2004), interpreting the geographic scope of U.S. antitrust laws. In Empagran, the Court articulated a rule of statutory construction under which "ambiguous statutes" should be interpreted "to avoid unreasonable interference with the sovereign authority of other nations." Id. at 164. The Court made clear that not all interference with the sovereign authority of other nations is unreasonable: "No one denies that America's antitrust laws, when applied to foreign conduct, can interfere with a foreign nation's ability independently to regulate its own commercial affairs. But our courts have long held that application of our antitrust laws to foreign anticompetitive conduct is nonetheless reasonable, and hence consistent with principles of prescriptive comity, insofar as they reflect a legislative effort to redress *domestic* antitrust injury that foreign anticompetitive conduct has caused." Id. at 165. But in Empagran, the Court concluded that applying U.S. antitrust laws to foreign anticompetitive conduct in order to redress *foreign* antitrust injury would be unreasonable. The Restatement (Fourth) summarizes: "Interference with the sovereign authority of foreign states may be reasonable if application of federal law would serve the legitimate interests of the United States." Restatement (Fourth) of Foreign Relations Law § 405 cmt. b (2018).

What the principle of reasonableness means in practice is that the presumption against extraterritoriality does not preclude the possibility of other limitations on geographic scope based on prescriptive comity. For example, some U.S. courts have found the presumption against extraterritoriality to be rebutted by the Bankruptcy Code's definition of the estate to include all property "wherever located." 11 U.S.C. § 541(a). But they have nevertheless performed a choice of law analysis to determine whether to apply the Bankruptcy Code's provisions on avoiding transfers. See, e.g., In re French, 440 F.3d 145, 153 (4th Cir. 2006). The principle of reasonableness may also supplement a test developed by applying the presumption against extraterritoriality. In Parkcentral Glob. Hub Ltd. v. Porsche Auto. Holdings SE, 763 F.3d 198 (2d Cir. 2014) (per curiam), the Second Circuit declined to apply Securities Exchange Act § 10(b) despite the fact that the transactions at issue occurred in the United States, meeting the test the Supreme Court developed in Morrison. The Court held that § 10(b) should not be applied when the defendants were not themselves parties to the transactions and the claims were predominantly foreign. Id. at 216.

What form the additional comity limitations may take under this principle of interpretation will depend "on the text, history, and purpose of the particular provision." Restatement (Fourth) of Foreign Relations Law § 405 cmt. d (2018). In Empagran, the Supreme Court rejected a case-by-case approach, preferring a test that turned on the location of the antitrust injury. See Empagran, 542 U.S. at 168–169. In French, the Fourth Circuit adopted a multifactor choice-of-law analysis to determine whether the Bankruptcy Code's avoidance provisions should be applied. See In re French, 440 F.3d at 153. And in Parkcentral, the Second Circuit held that satisfying Morrison's transactional test was a necessary but not sufficient condition for applying § 10(b). See Parkcentral, 763 F.3d at 216. The principle of reasonableness allows U.S. courts to tailor the geographic scope of federal statutes more carefully than the presumption against extraterritoriality, but it does not require the same approach to every statute.

The third principle of interpretation is the *Charming Betsy* canon of interpreting federal statutes to avoid violations of international law. As the Restatement (Fourth) puts it: "Where fairly possible, courts in the United States construe federal statutes to avoid conflict with international law governing jurisdiction to prescribe." Restatement (Fourth) of Foreign Relations Law § 406 (2018). As we have seen, international law governing jurisdiction to prescribe permits extraterritorial jurisdiction in a wide variety of cases. See supra p. 92. So the *Charming Betsy* canon is unlikely to limit the geographic scope of federal statutes to a greater extent than the presumption against extraterritoriality and the principle of reasonableness. In modern times, it has been applied most frequently to determine the applicability of federal statutes to foreign-flagged ships. See, e.g., Spector v. Norwegian Cruise Line Ltd., 545 U.S. 119, 136 (2005) (interpreting Title III of American with Disabilities Act in light of international law regarding jurisdiction over foreign-flag ships); McCulloch v. Sociedad Nacional de Marineros de Honduras, 372 U.S. 10, 21 (1963) (interpreting the National Labor Relations Act to avoid conflict with "the well-established rule of international law that the law of the flag state ordinarily governs the internal affairs of a ship").

QUESTIONS

(1) The presumption against extraterritoriality articulated in Morrison and RJR is arguably more flexible than previous versions in at least two respects: (1) it is not a clear statement rule; and (2) it recognizes that the focus of a statutory provision may be on something other than conduct (for example, on the transaction, in the case of § 10(b), and on the injury to business or property, in the case of RICO's private right of action). Are these changes in the presumption positive or negative?

(2) What should a court do when a principle of interpretation changes? Should it apply the current presumption against extraterritoriality to all statutes? Or should it apply whatever version of the presumption, if any, prevailed at the time the statute was passed?

(3) Is it necessary to have a principle of reasonableness in interpretation in addition to the presumption against extraterritoriality? Does having multiple principles of interpretation increase the risk that courts will limit the geographic scope of statutes too much? Or does having multiple principles of interpretation provide helpful flexibility?

Additional reading: Buxbaum, The Scope and Limitations of the Presumption Against Extraterritoriality, 110 AJIL Unbound 62 (2016); Dodge, The Presumption Against Extraterritoriality in Two Steps, 110 AJIL Unbound 45 (2016); Dodge, Chevron Deference and Extraterritorial Regulation, 95 N.C. L. Rev. 911 (2017); Gardner, RJR Nabisco and the Runaway Canon, 102 Va. L. Rev. Online 134 (2016).

3. ANTIDISCRIMINATION LAW

Title VII of the 1964 Civil Rights Act provides: "It shall be an unlawful employment practice for an employer . . . to fail or refuse to hire or to discharge any individual, or otherwise to discriminate against any individual with respect to his compensation, terms, conditions, or privileges of employment, because of such individual's race, color, religion, sex, or national origin." 42 U.S.C. § 2000e–2(a)(1). In Equal Employment Opportunity Commission v. Arabian American Oil Co., 499

U.S. 244, 111 S.Ct. 1227, 113 L.Ed.2d 274 (1991), the Supreme Court applied the presumption against extraterritoriality to Title VII, holding that the provision did not apply to employment outside of the United States.

Congress, which was already in the process of considering significant amendments to Title VII, acted to reverse the decision in Aramco almost immediately. The relevant provisions of Title VII, as amended, follow—with the language added by the 1991 Civil Rights Act in italics:

42 U.S.C. § 2000e. Definitions

(f)   The term "employee" means an individual employed by an employer. . . . *With respect to employment in a foreign country, such term includes an individual who is a citizen of the United States.*

42 U.S.C. § 2000e–1. Exemption

(a) Inapplicability of subchapter to certain aliens and employees of religious entities

This subchapter shall not apply to an employer with respect to the employment of aliens outside any State. . . .

(b) Compliance with statute as violative of foreign law

It shall not be unlawful under section 2000e–2 or 2000e–3 of this title for an employer (or a corporation controlled by an employer), labor organization, employment agency, or joint labor-management committee controlling apprenticeship or other training or retraining (including on-the-job training programs) to take any action otherwise prohibited by such section, with respect to an employee in a workplace in a foreign country if compliance with such section would cause such employer (or such corporation), such organization, such agency, or such committee to violate the law of the foreign country in which such workplace is located.

(c) Control of corporation incorporated in foreign country

(1)   If an employer controls a corporation whose place of incorporation is a foreign country, any practice prohibited by section 2000e–2 or 2000e–3 of this title engaged in by such corporation shall be presumed to be engaged in by such employer.

(2)   Sections 2000e–2 and 2000e–3 of this title shall not apply with respect to the foreign operations of an employer that is a foreign person not controlled by an American employer.

(3)   For purposes of this subsection, the determination of whether an employer controls a corporation shall be based on—

> *(A)   the interrelation of operations;*

> *(B)   the common management;*

> *(C)   the centralized control of labor relations; and*

> *(D) the common ownership or financial control,*
> *of the employer and the corporation.*

The EEOC takes the position that one should initially look to a company's place of incorporation to determine its nationality. Companies incorporated in the United States are generally deemed to be American employers. But a company incorporated under foreign law may also be considered an American employer if other factors such as its principal place of business, the nationality of its dominant shareholders, and the nationality and location of its management suggest a significant connection to the United States. See Enforcement Guidance on Application of Title VII and the Americans with Disabilities Act to American Firms Overseas and to Foreign Firms in the United States, EEOC Notice 915.002 (Oct. 20, 1993).

The EEOC Enforcement Guidance also addresses the application of the control factors listed in § 2000e–1(c)(3), offering the following illustrative example involving the ADA, which the 1991 Civil Rights Act amended in the same way as Title VII:

> **Example:** Charging Party (CP), an American citizen who is hearing impaired, alleges that he was discriminatorily terminated from his job in the country of Tangeria by Tangoods, a 200-person firm incorporated in Tangeria with offices only in that country. Tangoods was created by a 2000-employee American company, Amerigoods, to supervise international marketing of Amerigoods' products. Amerigoods owns 25% of the stock of Tangoods. Some of the members of Tangoods' board of directors are officers and/or board members of Amerigoods, but the two companies have distinct corporate forms, have entirely separate staffs, and perform all management and operational functions, e.g., payroll, hiring, and firing, independently. Amerigoods sets corporate policies, applicable to Tangoods, on such matters as acceptable employee behavior, employee sales quotas, amounts of annual and sick leave, salary scales, severance pay, and pension accrual and payout. Amerigoods representatives inspect the Tangoods facilities on numerous regularly scheduled visits each year, and dictate changes in marketing and sales strategy as necessary for continued sales of Amerigoods' products.

> Because it is incorporated and does business exclusively outside the United States, Tangoods is not itself an American employer. It may, however, be controlled by an American employer. Amerigoods is a partial owner of Tangoods. In addition, there is substantial interrelationship of operations between the two companies; Tangoods exists and performs services principally for the benefit of Amerigoods, and Amerigoods representatives

monitor and modify Tangoods' operations to maintain sales. Although personnel operations are handled separately and there does not appear to be much overlap in managerial personnel, Amerigoods does set uniform corporate policies on some matters related to labor relations. There is also some overlap in board membership between the two companies. Under such circumstances, the Commission would consider Tangoods to be "controlled" by Amerigoods, and would assert jurisdiction over CP's charge challenging his termination.

One must also bear in mind the foreign compulsion defense found in § 2000e–1(b), which excuses compliance with Title VII if the discrimination is required by the law of the foreign country in which the workplace is located. To apply this defense, one must of course have an understanding of what is meant by "law." The case that follows dealt with that question under a similar exception contained in the Age Discrimination in Employment Act.

Mahoney v. RFE/RL, Inc.

United States Court of Appeals, District of Columbia Circuit, 1995
47 F.3d 447

*Dodge thinks
this is wrong
but binding.*

■ RANDOLPH, CIRCUIT JUDGE:

If an American corporation operating in a foreign country would have to "violate the laws" of that country in order to comply with the Age Discrimination in Employment Act, 29 U.S.C. § 623(f)(1), the company need not comply with the Act. The question here is whether this "foreign laws" exception in § 623(f)(1) applies when the overseas company, in order to comply with the Act, would have to breach a collective bargaining agreement with foreign unions.

RFE/RL, Inc. is a Delaware non-profit corporation. It is funded but not controlled by the federal government, *Ralis v. RFE/RL, Inc.*, 770 F.2d 1121, 1125 (D.C.Cir.1985), and is best known for its broadcast services, Radio Free Europe and Radio Liberty. RFE/RL's principal place of business is Munich, Germany. In 1982, the company entered into a collective bargaining agreement with unions representing its employees in Munich. One of the provisions of the labor contract, modeled after a nation-wide agreement in the German broadcast industry, required employees to retire at age sixty-five. In 1982, the Age Discrimination in Employment Act had no extraterritorial reach and, from all that appears, this portion of the RFE/RL collective bargaining agreement was entirely lawful. See *Ralis v. RFE/RL, Inc.*, 770 F.2d at 1124.

Congress amended the Act in 1984 to cover American citizens working for American corporations overseas. Pub.L. No. 98–459, 98 Stat. 1767, 1792–93 (codified as amended at 29 U.S.C. §§ 623(h), 630(f)). RFE/RL initially thought its American employees in Munich would therefore no longer have to retire at the age of sixty-five, as the collective bargaining agreement provided, and could continue to work until they were seventy if they so chose. In order to implement this understanding, the company applied to the "Works Council" for limited exemptions from its contractual obligation. Works Councils (*Betriebsräte*) exist in all German firms with twenty or more workers. *See* Christopher S. Allen, *Principles of the Economic System, in* GERMANY AND ITS BASIC LAW: PAST, PRESENT AND FUTURE; A GERMAN-AMERICAN SYMPOSIUM 339, 348 (Paul Kirchhof & Donald P. Kommers eds., 1993). They are bodies elected by both unionized and nonunionized employees. Their duties include insuring that management adheres to all provisions of union contracts. Departures from contractual requirements are illegal without the Works Council's approval. Rejecting RFE/RL's requests, the Works Council here determined that allowing only those employees who were American citizens to work past the age of sixty-five would violate not only the mandatory retirement provision, but also the collective bargaining agreement's provision forbidding discrimination on the basis of nationality.

RFE/RL appealed the Works Council's decisions with respect to several employees, including plaintiff De Lon, to the Munich Labor Court and lost. The Labor Court agreed with the Works Council that RFE/RL must uniformly enforce the mandatory retirement provisions because exemptions would unfairly discriminate against German workers. The Labor Court also held that the company's retaining employees over the age of sixty-five despite the collective bargaining agreement would be illegal. RFE/RL negotiated with the unions to delete the mandatory retirement provision from the collective bargaining agreement, but to no avail.

The company terminated plaintiff De Lon in 1987, and plaintiff Mahoney in 1988. Both plaintiffs were working for the company in Munich, both are United States citizens, and both were discharged pursuant to the labor contract because they had reached the age of sixty-five. The parties agree that RFE/RL thereby violated the Age Discrimination in Employment Act unless the "foreign laws" exception applied. The Act prohibits employers from discriminating against employees on the basis of age. 29 U.S.C. § 623. "Employee" includes "any individual who is a citizen of the United States employed by an employer in a workplace in a foreign country" (29 U.S.C. § 630(f)); and it is common ground that the Act covers RFE/RL.

* * *

The "foreign laws" exception to the Act states:

It shall not be unlawful for an employer, employment agency, or labor organization—

(1) to take any action otherwise prohibited under subsections (a), (b), (c), or (e) of this section where . . . such practices involve an employee in a workplace in a foreign

country, and compliance with such subsections would cause such employer, or a corporation controlled by such employer, to violate the laws of the country in which such workplace is located;

29 U.S.C. § 623(f)(1).

The district court held § 623(f)(1) inapplicable because the mandatory retirement provision "is part of a contract between an employer and unions—both private entities—and has not in any way been mandated by the German government. Second, the provision does not have general application, as laws normally do, but binds only the parties to the contract." *Mahoney*, 818 F.Supp. at 3. Although "the mandatory retirement provision in the union contract had 'legal' force in Germany in the sense that it was legally binding," the court found this to be "precisely the sense in which such contracts in this country may be said to have 'legal' force; yet they are not ordinarily thought of as 'laws.' " *Id.*

The decision of the Supreme Court in *Norfolk & Western Railway v. American Train Dispatchers' Ass'n*, 499 U.S. 117, 111 S.Ct. 1156, 113 L.Ed.2d 95 (1991), stands firmly against the district court's interpretation. But the parties unaccountably failed to mention the case to the district court, and failed again even to cite the decision on appeal. If *Norfolk & Western* had been brought to the district court's attention, we have no doubt that it would have ruled the other way.

Norfolk & Western held that a rail carrier's exemption under 49 U.S.C. § 11341(a) "from all other law" included a "carrier's legal obligations under a collective-bargaining agreement." 499 U.S. at 127, 111 S.Ct. at 1162. . . .

The point of *Norfolk & Western* is that when a company fails to comply with a labor contract it violates "law," which is why the statutory exemption from "law" relieved carriers of their contractual obligations. Section 623(f)(1) of the Age Discrimination in Employment Act is indistinguishable. *See West Virginia Univ. Hosps., Inc. v. Casey*, 499 U.S. 83, 98–99, 111 S.Ct. 1138, 1146–47, 113 L.Ed.2d 68 (1991). If RFE/RL had not complied with the collective bargaining agreement in this case, if it had retained plaintiffs despite the mandatory retirement provision, the company would have violated the German laws standing behind such contracts, as well as the decisions of the Munich Labor Court. In the words of § 623(f)(1), RFE/RL's "compliance with [the Act] would cause such employer . . . to violate the laws of the country in which such workplace is located." Domestic employers of course would never face a comparable situation; the Supremacy Clause of the Constitution would force any applicable state laws to give way, U.S. CONST. art. VI, cl. 2; and provisions in collective bargaining agreements contrary to the Act would be superseded. Congressional legislation cannot, however, set aside the laws of foreign countries. When an overseas employer's obligations under foreign law collide with its obligations under the Age Discrimination in

Employment Act, § 623(f)(1) quite sensibly solves the dilemma by relieving the employer of liability under the Act.

* * *

Plaintiffs complain that RFE/RL could have bargained harder for a change in the labor contract. But application of § 623(f)(1) does not depend on such considerations. The collective bargaining agreement here was valid and enforceable at the time of plaintiffs' terminations, and RFE/RL had a legal duty to comply with it. There is not, nor could there be, any suggestion that RFE/RL agreed to the mandatory retirement provision in order to evade the Age Discrimination in Employment Act. Such provisions are, the evidence showed, common throughout the Federal Republic of Germany, and RFE/RL entered into this particular agreement before Congress extended the Act beyond our borders.

* * *

QUESTIONS

(1) Is Title VII, as amended, consistent with customary international law's limits on prescriptive jurisdiction?

(2) In light of the 1991 amendments to Title VII, the EEOC's Enforcement Guidance, and the D.C. Circuit's decision in Mahoney, how should the following hypothetical situation be resolved:

> U.S. Oil, Inc. is a Delaware corporation with its principal place of business in Houston, Texas, which is primarily engaged in the business of exploring and drilling for oil. Tanoil, Inc. is a Tangerian corporation with its principal place of business at Omrah, Tangeria, which is owned by the Tangerian royal family. In order to explore for oil, U.S. Oil and Tanoil have formed an equity joint venture, the U.S.-Tangeria Oil Company (or USTO). USTO is incorporated under the laws of Tangeria and is 45% owned by U.S. Oil and 55% owned by Tanoil. Pursuant to the joint venture agreement, representatives of U.S. Oil occupy all of the senior management positions and four of the nine seats on USTO's board of directors.
>
> USTO has signed a concession agreement with the Tangerian Government, granting it the right to explore for oil in the new field and to drill for oil if any is found. USTO is not required to sell the oil it produces to U.S. Oil. The concession agreement provides that a U.S. Oil representative shall be in charge of hiring personnel for USTO, but that USTO shall, so far as is consistent with the efficient management of the company, give preference to citizens of Tangeria. The concession agreement also provides that USTO shall not employ any person of the Jewish faith, regardless of nationality. USTO ends up

hiring a large number of American citizens, many of them transferred from U.S. Oil.

Robert Shapiro is an American citizen of the Jewish faith and a geologist employed by U.S. Oil. Sensing an exciting opportunity for a person in his profession, Shapiro applies to transfer to USTO. When his request is denied on the ground that it would violate the concession agreement between USTO and the Tangerian government, Shapiro sues both U.S. Oil and USTO alleging discrimination on the basis of his religion in violation of Title VII.

CHAPTER IV

CORPORATE SOCIAL RESPONSIBILITY

Corporations dominate international economic life just as they do domestic economic life. Virtually all transnational operations such as those we study in the second half of this book take place through corporations. Those operations are primarily designed to generate profit for the benefit of shareholders. Yet they create a broad range of impacts beyond the realm of the financial: on the communities in which those operations are located; on the environment; and on individual stakeholders, including employees. Within the United States, the question of how to define the corporation's role and responsibilities as a social actor has generated decades of debate. Some commentators have argued that a corporation's sole responsibility is to maximize profits on behalf of its shareholders. As Milton Friedman famously stated, "there is one and only one social responsibility of business—to use its resources and engage in activities designed to increase its profits so long as it stays within the rules of the game."[1] Others promote a broader, stakeholder-oriented view of corporate governance, insisting that corporate decisionmaking and action must take into account the interests of various constituencies other than shareholders.[2]

Transposed to the transnational arena, the issue is even more complex. National laws on labor and employment, environmental protection, and other relevant subjects vary significantly, raising the question whether corporations fulfill their social and ethical obligations by complying with applicable norms at the place of their operations, or whether their home-state norms continue to play some role. Moreover, countries differ widely in their attitudes toward corporate responsibility itself. The corporate law under which a foreign subsidiary operates may require inputs into management decisionmaking that are not required in the United States. In Germany, for instance, employees enjoy statutory rights of participation in corporate governance. Even apart from the question of legal obligations, the actions that a company takes overseas can affect its reputation with important local constituencies, including shareholders and consumers. Finally, the increasing complexity of multinational enterprises (MNEs) and the facility with which they operate across national borders pose significant challenges to regulators.

This Chapter introduces some of the ethical issues that corporations confront in the course of transnational business activity, and various

---

[1] Friedman, Capitalism and Freedom 133 (1962).

[2] See Williams, Corporate Social Responsibility in an Era of Economic Globalization, 35 U.C. Davis L. Rev. 705, 716 (2002) (describing this view).

methods of holding them accountable for the consequences of that activity. Section A begins with anti-corruption efforts, a topic of importance to all business actors, large and small, engaged in all forms of cross-border activity. It focuses on the U.S. Foreign Corrupt Practices Act. Section B turns to the organization of MNEs and the particular regulatory challenges their activities present. Section C addresses voluntary codes of conduct, one common form of regulation. Section D turns to an alternative mechanism for holding MNEs accountable for their transnational operations: human rights litigation in domestic courts.

A. ANTI-CORRUPTION LAW

The Foreign Corrupt Practices Act of 1977 (FCPA) emerged from the explosive revelation in the mid-1970s of large payments made by U.S. firms, most conspicuously Lockheed Aircraft and Boeing, to such prominent foreign persons as Prime Minister Tanaka of Japan and Prince Bernhard of the Netherlands. While efforts to draw up an international agreement on the topic, sponsored by the United States, did not get very far, Congress did act. It produced the FCPA, which is tucked away chiefly in the Securities Exchange Act of 1934.

Primarily, the FCPA makes certain types of payments a crime, but it also requires U.S. issuers to maintain reasonable accounting procedures and internal fiscal controls to prevent such payments from going undetected by auditors. Such reasonable procedures and controls are those that "would satisfy prudent officials in the conduct of their own affairs." 15 U.S.C. § 78m(b)(7). Parallel amendments to the Internal Revenue Code attached tax disadvantages to the making of such payments.

The student's reaction may be to question why one should study this statute, since bribery is obviously a "bad thing." Lawyers at the advisory stage do have significant questions to wrestle with in at least two respects: (1) in advising as to the legality of payments made to sales agents or other intermediaries when there is some reason to believe that the money or some part thereof may pass to a state official; and (2) in evaluating the applicability of a statutory permission to pay what in the trade are known as "grease payments." The classic "grease payment" situation occurs when a firm finds that its equipment is sitting rotting on a dock in Ferengia because the customs officials will not apply their stamp to an invoice for it. They are duty bound to do so and, if one proceeded to the high court of Ferengia, one could presumably get the equivalent of a writ of mandamus ordering them to stamp the invoice. But that would be three years hence, given local judicial backlogs. The equipment would be useless, and the company would be in default on its contract. But $500 under the table will do the trick.

The FCPA's anti-bribery rules are set forth in three parallel provisions of Title 15. Section 78dd–1 applies to issuers, both foreign and domestic, who have registered securities with or are required to file reports to the Securities Exchange Commission. Section 78dd–2 applies to "domestic concerns," i.e., U.S. citizens, nationals, and residents, as well as corporations, partnerships, associations and other entities that have their principal places of business in the United States or are organized under U.S. law. Section 78dd–3 applies to other persons who act in furtherance of unlawful payments while within the territory of the United States. Each of these sections applies not only to the persons indicated but also to officers, directors, employees, agents, and stockholders acting on their behalf. The U.S. government has taken the position that individuals and companies may be liable for conspiring to violate the FCPA or for aiding and abetting even if they could not independently be charged with an FCPA violation (e.g., because a company is a foreign company and not an issuer). See A Resource Guide to the U.S. Foreign Corrupt Practices Act 34 (2012). In United States v. Hoskins, 902 F.3d 69 (2d Cir.2018), however, the Second Circuit rejected that position. Based on an extensive review of the Act's legislative history, the court concluded that "the FCPA defined precisely the categories of persons who may be charged for violating its provisions," id. at 71, and therefore that "the government may not override that policy using the conspiracy and complicity rules," id. at 95.

§ 78dd–1. Prohibited foreign trade practices by issuers

(a) Prohibition

It shall be unlawful for any issuer which has a class of securities registered pursuant to section 78*l* of this title or which is required to file reports under section 78*o*(d) of this title, or for any officer, director, employee, or agent of such issuer or any stockholder thereof acting on behalf of such issuer, to make use of the mails or any means or instrumentality of interstate commerce corruptly in furtherance of an offer, payment, promise to pay, or authorization of the payment of any money, or offer, gift, promise to give, or authorization of the giving of anything of value to—

(1) any foreign official for purposes of—

(A) (i) influencing any act or decision of such foreign official in his official capacity, (ii) inducing such foreign official to do or omit to do any act in violation of the lawful duty of such official, or (iii) securing any improper advantage; or

(B) inducing such foreign official to use his influence with a foreign government or instrumentality thereof to affect or influence any act or decision of such government or instrumentality, in order to assist such issuer in obtaining or retaining business for or with, or directing business to, any person;

(2) any foreign political party or official thereof or any candidate for foreign political office for purposes of—

(A) (i) influencing any act or decision of such party, official, or candidate in its or his official capacity, (ii) inducing such party, official, or candidate to do or omit to do an act in violation of the lawful duty of such party, official, or candidate, or (iii) securing any improper advantage; or

(B) inducing such party, official, or candidate to use its or his influence with a foreign government or instrumentality thereof to affect or influence any act or decision of such government or instrumentality, in order to assist such issuer in obtaining or retaining business for or with, or directing business to, any person; or

(3) any person, while knowing that all or a portion of such money or thing of value will be offered, given, or promised, directly or indirectly, to any foreign official, to any foreign political party or official thereof, or to any candidate for foreign political office, for purposes of—

(A) (i) influencing any act or decision of such foreign official, political party, party official, or candidate in his or its official capacity, (ii) inducing such foreign official, political party, party official, or candidate to do or omit to do any act in violation of the lawful duty of such foreign official, political party, party official, or candidate, or (iii) securing any improper advantage; or

(B) inducing such foreign official, political party, party official, or candidate to use his or its influence with a foreign government or instrumentality thereof to affect or influence any act or decision of such government or instrumentality, in order to assist such issuer in obtaining or retaining business for or with, or directing business to, any person.

(b) Exception for routine governmental action

Subsections (a) and (g) of this section shall not apply to any facilitating or expediting payment to a foreign official, political party, or party official the purpose of which is to expedite or to secure the performance of a routine governmental action by a foreign official, political party, or party official.

(c) Affirmative defenses

It shall be an affirmative defense to actions under subsection (a) or (g) of this section that—

(1) the payment, gift, offer, or promise of anything of value that was made, was lawful under the written laws and regulations of the foreign official's, political party's, party official's, or candidate's country; or

(2) the payment, gift, offer, or promise of anything of value that was made, was a reasonable and bona fide expenditure, such as travel and lodging expenses, incurred by or on behalf of a foreign official, party, party official, or candidate and was directly related to—

(A) the promotion, demonstration, or explanation of products or services; or

(B) the execution or performance of a contract with a foreign government or agency thereof.

* * *

(f) Definitions

For purposes of this section:

(1) (A) The term "foreign official" means any officer or employee of a foreign government or any department, agency, or instrumentality thereof, or of a public international organization, or any person acting in an official capacity for or on behalf of any such government or department, agency, or instrumentality, or for or on behalf of any such public international organization.

(B) For purposes of subparagraph (A), the term "public international organization" means—

(i) an organization that is designated by Executive Order pursuant to section 1 of the International Organizations Immunities Act (22 U.S.C. § 288); or

(ii) any other international organization that is designated by the President by Executive order for the purposes of this section, effective as of the date of publication of such order in the Federal Register.

(2) (A) A person's state of mind is "knowing" with respect to conduct, a circumstance, or a result if—

(i) such person is aware that such person is engaging in such conduct, that such circumstance exists, or that such result is substantially certain to occur; or

(ii) such person has a firm belief that such circumstance exists or that such result is substantially certain to occur.

(B) When knowledge of the existence of a particular circumstance is required for an offense, such knowledge is established if a person is aware of a high probability of the existence of such circumstance, unless the person actually believes that such circumstance does not exist.

(3) **(A)** The term "routine governmental action" means only an action which is ordinarily and commonly performed by a foreign official in—

> **(i)** obtaining permits, licenses, or other official documents to qualify a person to do business in a foreign country;

> **(ii)** processing governmental papers, such as visas and work orders;

> **(iii)** providing police protection, mail pick-up and delivery, or scheduling inspections associated with contract performance or inspections related to transit of goods across country;

> **(iv)** providing phone service, power and water supply, loading and unloading cargo, or protecting perishable products or commodities from deterioration; or

> **(v)** actions of a similar nature.

(B) The term "routine governmental action" does not include any decision by a foreign official whether, or on what terms, to award new business to or to continue business with a particular party, or any action taken by a foreign official involved in the decision-making process to encourage a decision to award new business to or continue business with a particular party.

The FCPA was amended in 1988 and 1998. The 1988 amendments narrowed the Act somewhat. They deleted the words "or having reason to know" after the word "knowing" in subsection (a)(3) and they added the exception for routine governmental action in subsection (b) to replace an exclusion of payments to foreign officials "whose duties are essentially ministerial or clerical." The 1998 amendments brought the FCPA into conformity with the 1997 OECD Convention on Combating Bribery of Foreign Public Officials in International Business Transactions, which is discussed below. There were five principal changes, the overall effect of which was to broaden the Act: (1) language prohibiting payments for the purpose of "securing any improper advantage" was added; (2) the definition of "foreign officials" was broadened to include officers and employees of public international organizations such as U.N. agencies; (3) new provisions were added to reach issuers and domestic concerns without regard to whether they used the mails or instrumentalities of interstate commerce; (4) § 78dd–3 was added to reach persons other than issuers and domestic concerns who act in furtherance of unlawful payments while within the territory of the United States; and (5) the

FCPA's penalty provisions were broadened to subject foreign nationals who are agents or employees of U.S. companies not just to civil penalties but to the same criminal penalties as agents and employees who are U.S. nationals. Relying on the legislative history of the Act and its amendments, the Fifth Circuit has held that the "obtaining or retaining business" language of the FCPA is broad enough to encompass payments to obtain more favorable tax treatment. See United States v. Kay, 359 F.3d 738 (5th Cir. 2004).

The FCPA provides for both civil and criminal penalties in suits brought by the U.S. Department of Justice and the Securities Exchange Commission. In 2012, these agencies published A Resource Guide to the U.S. Foreign Corrupt Practices Act to help businesses and individuals better understand the FCPA.[3] Courts have held that private parties have no implied cause of action under the Act. See Lamb v. Phillip Morris, Inc., 915 F.2d 1024 (6th Cir.1990), cert. denied 498 U.S. 1086, 111 S.Ct. 961, 112 L.Ed.2d 1048 (1991). But private parties have successfully brought civil suits under the Racketeer Influenced and Corrupt Organization Act (RICO) in cases involving the bribery of foreign officials, even though violations of the FCPA are not predicate acts under RICO. See Environmental Tectonics v. W.S. Kirkpatrick, Inc., 847 F.2d 1052 (3d Cir.1988), affirmed on other grounds, 493 U.S. 400, 110 S.Ct. 701, 107 L.Ed.2d 816 (1990).

The FCPA also establishes an opinion procedure by which parties contemplating particular payments can obtain guidance from the Department of Justice as to whether it would seek to enforce the Act against such payments. The desired result is a "no-action" letter of the following kind:

No. 11–01

Date: June 30, 2011

Foreign Corrupt Practices Act Review

Opinion Procedure Release

The Department has reviewed the FCPA Opinion Procedure request of a U.S. adoption service provider (the "Requestor") that was submitted on May 25, 2011. The company is a "domestic concern" under 15 U.S.C. § 78dd–2(h)(1)(B) of the FCPA and therefore is eligible to submit an opinion procedure request.

The Requestor proposes to pay certain expenses for a trip to the United States by one official from each of two foreign government agencies to learn more about the services provided by the Requestor. The two officials will be selected by their agencies, without the involvement of the Requestor, to travel to the United States.

---

[3]   https://www.justice.gov/sites/default/files/criminal-fraud/legacy/2015/01/16/guide.pdf.

The Requestor has no non-routine business pending before the foreign government agencies that employ these officials. The sponsored program will last for approximately two days (not including travel time). The Requestor intends to pay for economy class air fare, domestic lodging, local transport, and meals. The Requestor has asked for a determination of the Department's present enforcement intention under the FCPA.

The Requestor has represented, among other things, that:

- The Requestor has no non-routine business (e.g., licensing or accreditation) under consideration by the relevant foreign government agencies.

- The Requestor's routine business before the relevant foreign government agencies consists primarily of seeking approval of pending adoptions. Such routine business is guided by international treaty and administrative rules with identified standards.

- The Requestor will not select the particular officials who will travel. That decision will be made solely by the foreign government agencies.

- The Requestor will host only the designated officials, and not their spouses or family members.

- The Requestor intends to pay all costs directly to the providers. No cash will be provided directly to the officials.

- Any souvenirs that the Requestor gives the visiting officials would reflect Requestor's business and/or logo and would be of nominal value.

- Apart from the expenses identified above, the Requestor will not compensate the foreign government agencies or the officials for their visit, nor will it fund, organize, or host any other entertainment, side trips, or leisure activities for the officials, or provide the officials with any stipend or spending money.

- The visit will be for a two-day period (exclusive of travel time), and costs and expenses will be only those necessary and reasonable to educate the visiting officials about the operations and services of U.S. adoption service providers.

- The Requestor has invited another adoption service provider to participate in the visit.

In the following instances, with appropriate protections, the Department has recently issued favorable Opinion Releases with respect to sponsoring travel and related expenses for foreign officials:

- In FCPA Opinion Release 07–02, the Department issued an opinion in response to a private insurance company in the United States, declining to take enforcement action if the company proceeded with sponsoring domestic expenses for a trip by six officials from an Asian government for an educational program at the company's U.S. headquarters. The company represented that the purpose of the visit would be to familiarize the officials with the operation of a U.S. insurance company; that it would not select the officials who would participate; that it would pay costs directly to providers; and that it has no non-routine business pending before the agency that employs the officials.

- In FCPA Opinion Release 07–01, the Department issued an opinion in response to a private company in the United States, declining to take enforcement action if the company proceeded with sponsoring domestic expenses for a trip by a six-person delegation from an Asian government. The company represented that the purpose of the visit would be to familiarize the delegates with the nature and extent of the company's business operations; that it would not select the delegates; it would pay all costs directly to providers; and it did not currently conduct operations in the foreign country at issue.

Based upon all of the facts and circumstances, as represented by the Requestor, and consistent with these prior opinions, the expenses contemplated are reasonable under the circumstances and directly relate to "the promotion, demonstration, or explanation of [the Requestor's] products or services." 15 U.S.C. § 78dd–2(c)(2)(A). Therefore, the Department does not presently intend to take any enforcement action with respect to the planned program and proposed payments described in this request. The FCPA Opinion Release has no binding application to any party which did not join in the request, and can be relied upon by the Requestor only to the extent that the disclosure of facts and circumstances in its request is accurate and complete and continues to accurately and completely reflect such facts and circumstances. Additionally, this Opinion Release does not purport to endorse the adequacy of the Requestor's anti-corruption policies and procedures.

The 2012 Resource Guide published by the Department of Justice and Securities Exchange Commission provides further guidance with respect to gifts, travel, and entertainment:

Two years ago, Company A won a long-term contract to supply goods and services to the state-owned Electricity Commission in Foreign Country. The Electricity Commission is 100% owned, controlled, and operated by the government of Foreign Country, and employees of the Electricity Commission are subject to Foreign Country's domestic bribery laws. Some Company A executives are in Foreign Country for meetings with officials of the Electricity Commission. The General Manager of the Electricity Commission was recently married, and during the trip Company A executives present a moderately priced crystal vase to the General Manager as a wedding gift and token of esteem. Is Company A in violation of the FCPA?

No. It is appropriate to provide reasonable gifts to foreign officials as tokens of esteem or gratitude. It is important that such gifts be made openly and transparently, properly recorded in a company's books and records, and given only where appropriate under local law, customary where given, and reasonable for the occasion.

During the course of the contract described above, Company A periodically provides training to Electricity Commission employees at its facilities in Michigan. The training is paid for by the Electricity Commission as part of the contract. Senior officials of the Electricity Commission inform Company A that they want to inspect the facility and ensure that the training is working well. Company A pays for the airfare, hotel, and transportation for the Electricity Commission senior officials to travel to Michigan to inspect Company A's facilities. Because it is a lengthy international flight, Company A agrees to pay for business class airfare, to which its own employees are entitled for lengthy flights. The foreign officials visit Michigan for several days, during which the senior officials perform an appropriate inspection. Company A executives take the officials to a moderately priced dinner, a baseball game, and a play. Do any of these actions violate the FCPA?

No. Neither the costs associated with training the employees nor the trip for the senior officials to the Company's facilities in order to inspect them violates the FCPA. Reasonable and bona fide promotional expenditures do not violate the FCPA. Here, Company A is providing training to the Electricity Commission's employees and is hosting the Electricity Commission senior officials. Their review of the execution and performance of the contract is a legitimate business purpose.

Even the provision of business class airfare is reasonable under the circumstances, as are the meals and entertainment, which are only a small component of the business trip.

Would this analysis be different if Company A instead paid for the senior officials to travel first-class with their spouses for an all-expenses-paid, week-long trip to Las Vegas, where Company A has no facilities?

Yes. This conduct almost certainly violates the FCPA because it evinces a corrupt intent. Here, the trip does not appear to be designed for any legitimate business purpose, is extravagant, includes expenses for the officials' spouses, and therefore appears to be designed to corruptly curry favor with the foreign government officials. Moreover, if the trip were booked as a legitimate business expense—such as the provision of training at its facilities—Company A would also be in violation of the FCPA's accounting provisions. Furthermore, this conduct suggests deficiencies in Company A's internal controls.

It is important to keep in mind that other countries also have laws prohibiting the bribery of their own officials. However, other countries were initially slower than the United States to prohibit the bribery of *foreign* officials. One reason the American business community initially opposed the FCPA was that their foreign competitors were not subject to similar restrictions. The United States tried unsuccessfully in the 1970s, before the passage of the Act, to achieve a multilateral agreement on bribery. When Congress amended the FCPA in 1988, it expressed its sense that the President should again pursue such an agreement among the members of the OECD. These efforts bore fruit in late 1997 with the Convention on Combating Bribery of Foreign Public Officials in International Business Transactions, 37 I.L.M. 1 (1998). The United States has also joined the 1996 Inter-American Convention Against Corruption, 35 I.L.M. 724 (1996), the Council of Europe's 1999 Criminal Law Convention on Corruption, 38 I.L.M. 505 (1999), and the 2003 United Nations Convention Against Corruption, 43 I.L.M. 37 (2004).

The OECD Convention requires its signatories to criminalize the bribery of foreign officials and to prohibit accounting practices that would enable companies to hide such bribery. The Convention further commits its parties to render mutual legal assistance in criminal investigations of bribery and makes the bribery of foreign officials an extraditable offense. There are 43 parties to the Convention, including all 35 OECD countries plus Argentina, Brazil, Bulgaria, Costa Rica, Colombia, Oman, Russia, and South Africa. Enforcement is most active in Denmark, Germany, the Netherlands, Switzerland, the United Kingdom, and the United States.

Although U.S. efforts to have the Convention prohibit the tax deductibility of bribes failed, the OECD passed recommendations on the subject in 1996 and 2009. The United Nations Convention Against Corruption also requires states-parties to "disallow the tax deductibility of expenses that constitute bribes." As of 2013, almost all parties to the OECD Convention either prohibit the tax deductibility of bribes expressly or have an administrative practice deny such deductions.

QUESTIONS

(1) Suppose a U.S. computer company is approached by an official at the Civil Aviation Administration of China (CAAC) seeking to purchase computers to upgrade China's air-traffic control system. The official suggests that the company arrange and pay for an "inspection trip" to New York so that he and several of his colleagues can learn more about the company's products. Would the company violate the Foreign Corrupt Practices Act if it agreed to the trip? If it agreed to pay each of the officials coming on the trip a *per diem* of $500? If you decide that either payment is within an exemption to the Foreign Corrupt Practices Act, can you give the client an opinion that it is legal?

(2) Suppose a contract is concluded and the computers shipped to Shanghai, but the local Commodity Inspection Bureau insists that each computer must be disassembled for inspection unless the company pays a $10,000 fee to waive the inspection?

Additional reading: Zarin, Doing Business Under the Foreign Corrupt Practices Act (1995–); Deming, The Foreign Corrupt Practices Act and the New International Norms (2d ed. 2010); Department of Justice and Securities Exchange Commission, A Resource Guide to the U.S. Foreign Corrupt Practices Act (2012).

B. THE MULTINATIONAL ENTERPRISE

It has proven difficult to settle upon an agreed definition for multinational enterprises (MNEs). According to the OECD Guidelines for Multinational Enterprises, see infra pp. 132–139, they "usually comprise companies or other entities established in more than one country and so linked that they may co-ordinate their operations in various ways." First, it is important to recognize that an MNE is not a single entity, but rather a structure made up of many entities, each organized under the laws of some nation and tied together by links of stock ownership or other contractual arrangements.

Second, the entities that compose an MNE are creatures of national and not international law. Even the Societas Europaea (SE) is less an international corporation than a corporation chartered under the authority of the European Community acting as a nation. See infra pp. 303–304. National laws prescribe the corporate forms such entities may take, and may also limit the extent to which they may be owned by foreign corporations. It is because of the national character of such entities' constituent parts that the United Nations prefers the term transnational corporation (TNC) to multinational enterprise.

Third, the entities that compose an MNE tend to coordinate their operations in response to a common management strategy, which will generally be designed to maximize profits. This point should not be overstated. There is conflict in the specialized literature as to whether managements whose interests diverge from those of their stockholders in fact seek to maximize profits or some other value such as total sales, market shares, or asset size. The interests of the managements of the various entities that compose an MNE may also diverge in various respects, and decisions within an MNE are often the product of negotiation and compromise among different constituencies. Finally, one should recognize that an MNE cannot in any event approach each of the myriad decisions it must make in terms of direct profit-maximization, but must employ rules of thumb that are intended in the average to produce such results.[4]

Fourth, in comparison with "uninational" enterprises, MNEs enjoy a greater flexibility in organization. They may organize their managerial structure by product, by market, or by some combination of the two to achieve the proper balance of global efficiency and local sensitivity.[5] They may locate production facilities in different countries to take advantage of differences in costs of inputs such as labor and materials. And they may organize their operations to minimize tax and regulatory burdens.

According to common estimates, there are approximately 100,000 MNEs operating in the world today, and they play an increasingly important role in the global economy. Many MNEs coordinate vast and complex global value chains, using contractual partners as well as intra-enterprise affiliates in different countries to secure the intermediate goods and services that are ultimately incorporated into their end products. The United Nations Conference on Trade and Development (UNCTAD) has estimated that more than three-quarters of global trade occurs within these international production networks, most of it in the form of intra-group trade.[6] Some MNEs are enormous, and in the public mind, size is surely an outstanding feature of the MNE. Consider, for example, General Electric. As of 2017, it had assets of over $375 billion, annual sales of over $120 billion, and employed 313,000 people.[7] Critics sometimes argue that MNEs are bigger than many countries by comparing their sales to national GDPs. The comparison can be misleading because GDP is a measure of value added while sales are not. When UNCTAD did a proper comparison in 2002, it found that

---

[4]   See Vagts, The Multinational Enterprise: A New Challenge for Transnational Law, 83 Harv. L. Rev. 739, 755–756 (1970).

[5]   Muchlinski, Multinational Enterprises and the Law 8 (2d ed. 2007).

[6]   UNCTAD, World Investment Report 2013, at 135–136.

[7]   Marketwatch.

ExxonMobil was slightly larger than the economy of Pakistan and that General Motors was slightly larger than the economy of Peru.[8]

Most large MNEs are headquartered in developed countries, but MNEs based in developing and transition economies are gaining in the share of global production. In 2017, UNCTAD's top 100 MNEs included CK Hutchison Holdings (Hong Kong, China), Hon Hai Precision Industries (Taiwan), and four additional Chinese enterprises: China COSCO Shipping Corporation, China National Offshore Oil Corporation, Tencent Holdings, and HNA Group. While the expansion of the Chinese economy has recently outpaced growth in other parts of the world, in previous years MNEs from a number of other developing and transition economies have appeared on the top-100 list, including Vale SA (Brazil), Petronas (Malaysia), VimpelCom Ltd (Russian Federation), and Cemex S.A.B. de C.V. (Mexico).

1. THE ORGANIZATION OF THE MNE

As noted above, one characteristic of the MNE is its organizational flexibility. MNEs are organized in a variety of ways. Many MNEs from the United States and United Kingdom are organized in a pyramid structure. At the apex is a parent company, which controls several wholly or majority owned subsidiaries, which may in turn control wholly or majority owned subsidiaries of their own. Some MNEs have two parents. The Anglo-Dutch MNE Unilever is a prominent example. MNE structure may also be influenced by particular aspects of applicable local law. For instance, because Japan's Antimonopoly Law of 1947 prohibits holding companies, Japanese MNEs have taken the form of corporate groups called *keiretsu*, characterized by intra-group cross-shareholdings and strong coordinated management through inter-company conferences.[9]

Another characteristic of the world's largest MNEs is organizational complexity. Vertical ownership chains connecting a parent company with multiple levels of subsidiaries can be quite long, and involve many cross-border links. Horizontal complexity is created when multiple companies within the enterprise share ownership of other affiliates, including in the form of cross-shareholdings. And affiliates within large MNEs may take the form of joint ventures or other types of entities that are not fully controlled by the parent.[10] In addition to these forms of complexity within the MNE's corporate structure, one must consider the complexity of its operations. Many MNEs operate not only through their own affiliated companies, but also through value chains including independent actors, such as local suppliers of product components, that they seek to control through contractual rather than equity relationships.

---

[8] UNCTAD, World Investment Report 2002, at 90.

[9] On the various legal structures of MNEs, see Muchlinski, Multinational Enterprises and the Law 51–77 (2d ed. 2007).

[10] UNCTAD World Investment Report 2016, pp. 129–131.

These forms of complexity have significant implications for regulatory policy. Corporate accountability requires transparency regarding the ownership and control of entities engaged in various activities, which is often lacking in such an environment. Moreover, the organizational structures described above facilitate fluid movement of assets and capital across national borders in ways that challenge the effectiveness of national regulatory systems. As an example of these implications, consider the recent attention to the mechanisms used by U.S. technology companies to minimize their tax burdens. Simply by shifting assets to subsidiaries in low-tax jurisdictions, multinational enterprises can reduce significantly the tax payable on income produced by those assets. This problem is especially pronounced in the technology sector, where corporate assets take the form primarily of intellectual property rights that can easily be transferred between jurisdictions. In 2013, a Senate investigation concluded that the Apple group had shielded over $70 billion from taxation by utilizing offshore entities that were exempt not only from taxes but also from associated record-keeping and filing requirements.[11] This kind of activity led to a major initiative in the OECD and the G20 to combat "base erosion and profit shifting" (BEPS), whose objectives include increasing transparency as well as eliminating certain forms of preferential tax treatment.[12] We will return to the specific challenges of taxing MNEs in Problem 4. See infra pp. 333–342.

2. THE MULTINATIONAL ENTERPRISE AS HERO AND VILLAIN

It is not surprising that the MNE has become the center of keen political controversy, for it stands as a visible symbol of power. But the MNE is not itself the root of such controversy. The roots are deeper, in longer-run historical forces and in broader political or economic controversies within which the MNE figures. Indeed, analyzing an issue in terms of MNEs rather than within a more abstract framework such as international trade or global efficiency maximization tends both to reflect and to affect one's approach to and politics about the international system. MNEs are more specific and vulnerable targets for criticism than abstract laws of economics or remote theories of capitalism.

Proponents of the MNE as a medium for international trade and investment often stress the same considerations that underlie the policy and theoretical justifications for relatively free world trade and investment—namely maximizing the value of the world's production through profit-oriented investment and production decisions by private parties. MNEs may maximize the value of production by locating manufacturing industries wherever marginal returns upon investment

---

[11] See "Apple's Web of Tax Shelters Saved it Billions, Panel Finds," The New York Times, May 20, 2013.

[12] See OECD/G20 Inclusive Framework on BEPS, Progress Report July 2017–June 2018, available at www.oecd.org/tax/beps.

(in view of varying labor costs, markets, transportation factors and so on) are highest. Opponents of the MNE often draw upon longstanding critiques of Western capitalism and industrialization, with the MNE standing as a symbol of exploitation, domination, and imperialism. The freedom to shift production from one country to another, which proponents see as promoting efficiency, opponents fear will create a "race to the bottom" in which countries lower their labor and environmental standards in order to attract investment. The MNE thus becomes a threat to national sovereignty and democratic decision-making. And while some opponents see brands like Nike, Shell, and McDonald's as threats to local culture,[13] some proponents see MNEs as agents for overcoming the provincial and even dangerous organization of the world into nation states. It was only partly in jest that Thomas Friedman noted in 1996 that no two countries that both have a McDonald's had ever gone to war against each other.[14]

The actual effects of foreign direct investment are often two-edged, providing ammunition for both opponents and proponents of the MNE. The following passage from Muchlinski, Multinational Enterprises and the Law 87–88 (2d ed. 2007) is illustrative:

> Regarding employment effects, it is argued that MNEs can enhance employment levels in a host state by importing new jobs. However, this must be weighed against the possible job losses in less competitive domestic firms. Equally, the stability of the imported job must be taken into account. Is the job likely to be long term, or is it merely a short-term job given the extent of the foreign firm's commitment to the local economy? Furthermore, from the home state perspective, it is arguable that local jobs may be lost as domestic MNEs relocate employment to more advantageous foreign locations. On the other hand, the creation of overseas jobs may stimulate job creation in the home state as the MNE's international linkages develop.
>
> Turning to balance of payments considerations, a host state's balance may be improved by the inflow of new capital represented by a direct investment. However, this initial effect must be weighed against the longer term outflow of capital through repayments of loans and through dividend remittances. Should these exceed the initial investment, then a net loss to the balance of payments will result. A similar result may occur if the local affiliate is highly integrated into the international production network of the MNE and is obliged to purchase inputs from affiliates in other states to an amount that exceeds

---

[13] See, e.g., Klein, No Logo: Taking Aim at the Brand Bullies (2002).

[14] Friedman, A McTheory About War-Making, International Herald Tribune (Dec. 9, 1996). NATO's bombardment of Serbia in 1999 appears to have been the first exception to this rule.

the initial inflow of capital. However, such effects may be offset by a positive export performance from the MNE affiliate. . . .

On the question of technology and skills transfer, it is argued that MNEs, as the principal holders of advanced productive technology and managerial skills, can enhance a host economy through the transfer and dissemination of such competitive benefits. This argument depends on the willingness of the MNE to share its competitive advantages from local firms and workers. If the technology and know-how involved are unique, it is unlikely that the MNE will readily give up its lead by disseminating its knowledge. It would be most likely to set up a wholly owned subsidiary in the host state, so as to control the use of its technology and skills. Alternatively, it might enter into licensing agreements that impose restrictive terms on the licensee as to the use and dissemination of the technology. In either case employees using the technology may be subjected to restrictive covenants as to subsequent employment with competitors. . . .

Finally, on the question of the competitive effects of foreign direct investment on the host economy, it is often asserted that MNEs will spur domestic firms into greater efficiency by exposing them to new competition. However, . . . in the absence of significant spill-over effects that make new techniques available to local firms, and in the absence of adequate investment capital for local firms to develop, the net result may be that the foreign firm will drive the local competition out. Given the highly concentrated nature of many of the markets in which MNEs operate, significant anticompetitive effects may result.

Additional reading: Muchlinski, Multinational Enterprises and the Law (2d ed. 2007); Litvin, Empires of Profit: Commerce, Conquest and Corporate Responsibility (2003); Wallace, The Multinational Enterprise and Legal Control: Host State Sovereignty in an Era of Economic Globalization (2d ed. 2002); Backer, Multinational Corporations as Objects and Sources of Transnational Regulation, 14 ILSA J. Int'l & Comp. L. 499 (2008); Vagts, The Multinational Enterprise: A New Challenge for Transnational Law, 83 Harv. L. Rev. 739 (1970).

C. CODES OF CONDUCT

One of the fronts on which efforts to constrain the behavior of MNEs have advanced is voluntary codes of conduct. The OECD Guidelines for Multinational Enterprises, the ILO Tripartite Declaration of Principles Concerning Multinational Enterprises and Social Policy, the UN Global Compact, and the UN Norms on the Responsibilities of Transnational

Corporations and Other Business Enterprises with Regard to Human Rights each articulate principles generally applicable to all MNEs. Other initiatives have focused upon specific industries. The Voluntary Principles on Security and Human Rights and the Extractive Industries Transparency Initiative concentrate on energy and mining. The Fair Labor Association's Workplace Code of Conduct focuses primarily on manufacturing. The Equator Principles set forth benchmarks for project finance lending. The Kimberley Process aims to stem the flow of conflict diamonds. Besides participating in one or more of these initiatives, some MNEs have adopted their own corporate codes of conduct, beginning with Levi Strauss & Co. in 1991. Many of these retain independent auditors to monitor their compliance.

As an example, consider the following excerpts from the OECD Guidelines, first promulgated in 1976 and most recently revised in 2011.

Guidelines for Multinational Enterprises
Organization for Economic Cooperation and Development, 2011

* * *

I.   Concepts and Principles

1.   The *Guidelines* are recommendations jointly addressed by governments to multinational enterprises. They provide principles and standards of good practice consistent with applicable laws and internationally recognised standards. Observance of the *Guidelines* by enterprises is voluntary and not legally enforceable. Nevertheless, some matters covered by the *Guidelines* may also be regulated by national law or international commitments.

2.   Obeying domestic laws is the first obligation of enterprises. The *Guidelines* are not a substitute for nor should they be considered to override domestic law and regulation. While the *Guidelines* extend beyond the law in many cases, they should not and are not intended to place an enterprise in situations where it faces conflicting requirements. However, in countries where domestic laws and regulations conflict with the principles and standards of the *Guidelines*, enterprises should seek ways to honour such principles and standards to the fullest extent which does not place them in violation of domestic law.

3.   Since the operations of multinational enterprises extend throughout the world, international co-operation in this field should extend to all countries. Governments adhering to the *Guidelines* encourage the enterprises operating on their territories to observe the *Guidelines* wherever they operate, while taking into account the particular circumstances of each host country.

4.   A precise definition of multinational enterprises is not required for the purposes of the *Guidelines*. These enterprises operate in all

sectors of the economy. They usually comprise companies or other entities established in more than one country and so linked that they may co-ordinate their operations in various ways. While one or more of these entities may be able to exercise a significant influence over the activities of others, their degree of autonomy within the enterprise may vary widely from one multinational enterprise to another. Ownership may be private, State or mixed. The *Guidelines* are addressed to all the entities within the multinational enterprise (parent companies and/or local entities). According to the actual distribution of responsibilities among them, the different entities are expected to co-operate and to assist one another to facilitate observance of the *Guidelines*.

* * *

II. General Policies

Enterprises should take fully into account established policies in the countries in which they operate, and consider the views of other stakeholders. In this regard:

A. Enterprises should:

1. Contribute to economic, environmental and social progress with a view to achieving sustainable development.

2. Respect the internationally recognised human rights of those affected by their activities.

3. Encourage local capacity building through close co-operation with the local community, including business interests, as well as developing the enterprise's activities in domestic and foreign markets, consistent with the need for sound commercial practice.

4. Encourage human capital formation, in particular by creating employment opportunities and facilitating training opportunities for employees.

5. Refrain from seeking or accepting exemptions not contemplated in the statutory or regulatory framework related to human rights, environmental, health, safety, labour, taxation, financial incentives, or other issues.

6. Support and uphold good corporate governance principles and develop and apply good corporate governance practices, including throughout enterprise groups.

7. Develop and apply effective self-regulatory practices and management systems that foster a relationship of confidence and mutual trust between enterprises and the societies in which they operate.

8. Promote awareness of and compliance by workers employed by multinational enterprises with respect to company policies

through appropriate dissemination of these policies, including through training programmes.

9. Refrain from discriminatory or disciplinary action against workers who make *bona fide* reports to management or, as appropriate, to the competent public authorities, on practices that contravene the law, the *Guidelines* or the enterprise's policies.

10. Carry out risk-based due diligence, for example by incorporating it into their enterprise risk management systems, to identify, prevent and mitigate actual and potential adverse impacts as described in paragraphs 11 and 12, and account for how these impacts are addressed. The nature and extent of due diligence depend on the circumstances of a particular situation.

11. Avoid causing or contributing to adverse impacts on matters covered by the *Guidelines*, through their own activities, and address such impacts when they occur.

12. Seek to prevent or mitigate an adverse impact where they have not contributed to that impact, when the impact is nevertheless directly linked to their operations, products or services by a business relationship. This is not intended to shift responsibility from the entity causing an adverse impact to the enterprise with which it has a business relationship.

13. In addition to addressing adverse impacts in relation to matters covered by the *Guidelines*, encourage, where practicable, business partners, including suppliers and sub-contractors, to apply principles of responsible business conduct compatible with the *Guidelines*.

14. Engage with relevant stakeholders in order to provide meaningful opportunities for their views to be taken into account in relation to planning and decision making for projects or other activities that may significantly impact local communities.

15. Abstain from any improper involvement in local political activities.

B. Enterprises are encouraged to:

1. Support, as appropriate to their circumstances, cooperative efforts in the appropriate fora to promote Internet Freedom through respect of freedom of expression, assembly and association online.

2. Engage in or support, where appropriate, private or multi-stakeholder initiatives and social dialogue on responsible supply chain management while ensuring that these initiatives take due account of their social and economic effects on developing countries and of existing internationally recognised standards.

* * *

III. Disclosure

1. Enterprises should ensure that timely and accurate information is disclosed on all material matters regarding their activities, structure, financial situation, performance, ownership and governance. This information should be disclosed for the enterprise as a whole and, where appropriate, along business lines or geographic areas. Disclosure policies of enterprises should be tailored to the nature, size and location of the enterprise, with due regard taken of costs, business confidentiality and other competitive concerns.

* * *

IV. Human Rights

States have the duty to protect human rights. Enterprises should, within the framework of internationally recognised human rights, the international human rights obligations of the countries in which they operate as well as relevant domestic laws and regulations:

1. Respect human rights, which means they should avoid infringing on the human rights of others and should address adverse human rights impacts with which they are involved.

2. Within the context of their own activities, avoid causing or contributing to adverse human rights impacts and address such impacts when they occur.

3. Seek ways to prevent or mitigate adverse human rights impacts that are directly linked to their business operations, products or services by a business relationship, even if they do not contribute to those impacts.

4. Have a policy commitment to respect human rights.

5. Carry out human rights due diligence as appropriate to their size, the nature and context of operations and the severity of the risks of adverse human rights impacts.

6. Provide for or co-operate through legitimate processes in the remediation of adverse human rights impacts where they identify that they have caused or contributed to these impacts.

* * *

V. Employment and Industrial Relations

Enterprises should, within the framework of applicable law, regulations and prevailing labour relations and employment practices and applicable international labour standards:

1. a) Respect the right of workers employed by the multinational enterprise to establish or join trade unions and representative organisations of their own choosing.

b)   Respect the right of workers employed by the multinational enterprise to have trade unions and representative organisations of their own choosing recognised for the purpose of collective bargaining, and engage in constructive negotiations, either individually or through employers' associations, with such representatives with a view to reaching agreements on terms and conditions of employment.

c)   Contribute to the effective abolition of child labour, and take immediate and effective measures to secure the prohibition and elimination of the worst forms of child labour as a matter of urgency.

d)   Contribute to the elimination of all forms of forced or compulsory labour and take adequate steps to ensure that forced or compulsory labour does not exist in their operations.

e)   Be guided throughout their operations by the principle of equality of opportunity and treatment in employment and not discriminate against their workers with respect to employment or occupation on such grounds as race, colour, sex, religion, political opinion, national extraction or social origin, or other status, unless selectivity concerning worker characteristics furthers established governmental policies which specifically promote greater equality of employment opportunity or relates to the inherent requirements of a job.

* * *

5.   In their operations, to the greatest extent practicable, employ local workers and provide training with a view to improving skill levels, in co-operation with worker representatives and, where appropriate, relevant governmental authorities.

* * *

8.   Enable authorised representatives of the workers in their employment to negotiate on collective bargaining or labour-management relations issues and allow the parties to consult on matters of mutual concern with representatives of management who are authorised to take decisions on these matters.

VI. Environment

Enterprises should, within the framework of laws, regulations and administrative practices in the countries in which they operate, and in consideration of relevant international agreements, principles, objectives, and standards, take due account of the need to protect the environment, public health and safety, and generally to conduct their activities in a manner contributing to the wider goal of sustainable development. In particular, enterprises should:

1. Establish and maintain a system of environmental management appropriate to the enterprise, including:

    a) collection and evaluation of adequate and timely information regarding the environmental, health, and safety impacts of their activities;

    b) establishment of measurable objectives and, where appropriate, targets for improved environmental performance and resource utilisation, including periodically reviewing the continuing relevance of these objectives; where appropriate, targets should be consistent with relevant national policies and international environmental commitments; and

    c) regular monitoring and verification of progress toward environmental, health, and safety objectives or targets.

* * *

3. Assess, and address in decision-making, the foreseeable environmental, health, and safety-related impacts associated with the processes, goods and services of the enterprise over their full life cycle with a view to avoiding or, when unavoidable, mitigating them. Where these proposed activities may have significant environmental, health, or safety impacts, and where they are subject to a decision of a competent authority, prepare an appropriate environmental impact assessment.

4. Consistent with the scientific and technical understanding of the risks, where there are threats of serious damage to the environment, taking also into account human health and safety, not use the lack of full scientific certainty as a reason for postponing cost-effective measures to prevent or minimise such damage.

5. Maintain contingency plans for preventing, mitigating, and controlling serious environmental and health damage from their operations, including accidents and emergencies; and mechanisms for immediate reporting to the competent authorities.

* * *

VII. Combating Bribery, Bribe Solicitation and Extortion

1. Enterprises should not, directly or indirectly, offer, promise, give, or demand a bribe or other undue advantage to obtain or retain business or other improper advantage. Enterprises should also resist the solicitation of bribes and extortion. In particular, enterprises should:

2. Not offer, promise or give undue pecuniary or other advantage to public officials or the employees of business partners. Likewise, enterprises should not request, agree to or accept

undue pecuniary or other advantage from public officials or the
employees of business partners. Enterprises should not use
third parties such as agents and other intermediaries,
consultants, representatives, distributors, consortia,
contractors and suppliers and joint venture partners for
channeling undue pecuniary or other advantages to public
officials, or to employees of their business partners or to their
relatives or business associates.

3.   Develop and adopt adequate internal controls, ethics and
compliance programmes or measures for preventing and
detecting bribery, developed on the basis of a risk assessment
addressing the individual circumstances of an enterprise, in
particular the bribery risks facing the enterprise (such as its
geographical and industrial sector of operation) . . . .

4.   Prohibit or discourage, in internal company controls, ethics and
compliance programmes or measures, the use of small
facilitation payments, which are generally illegal in the
countries where they are made, and when such payments are
made, accurately record these in books and financial records.

* * *

VIII.   Consumer Interests

When dealing with consumers, enterprises should act in accordance with
fair business, marketing and advertising practices and should take all
reasonable steps to ensure the quality and reliability of the goods and
services that they provide. . . .

* * *

IX. Science and Technology

Enterprises should:

* * *

2.   Adopt, where practicable in the course of their business
activities, practices that permit the transfer and rapid diffusion
of technologies and know-how, with due regard to the protection
of intellectual property rights.

3.   When appropriate, perform science and technology development
work in host countries to address local market needs, as well as
employ host country personnel in an S & T capacity and
encourage their training, taking into account commercial needs.

4.   When granting licenses for the use of intellectual property
rights or when otherwise transferring technology, do so on
reasonable terms and conditions and in a manner that
contributes to the long term sustainable development prospects
of the host country.

* * *

X. Competition

Enterprises should:

1. Carry out their activities in a manner consistent with all applicable competition laws and regulations, taking into account the competition laws of all jurisdictions in which the activities may have anti-competitive effects.

2. Refrain from entering into or carrying out anti-competitive agreements among competitors, including agreements to:

    a) fix prices;

    b) make rigged bids (collusive tenders);

    c) establish output restrictions or quotas; or

    d) share or divide markets by allocating customers, suppliers, territories or lines of commerce.

* * *

XI. Taxation

1. It is important that enterprises contribute to the public finances of host countries by making timely payment of their tax liabilities. In particular, enterprises should comply with both the letter and the spirit of the tax laws and regulations of the countries in which they operate. . . . Tax compliance includes such measures as providing to the relevant authorities timely information that is relevant or required by law for purposes of the correct determination of taxes to be assessed in connection with their operations and conforming transfer pricing practices to the arm's length principle.

If, as paragraph I(1) states, the Guidelines are "voluntary and not legally enforceable," what might motivate a company to comply with them, or to adopt and implement its own voluntary code of conduct? Consider the following analysis:

> The logic follows a pattern that one might call the spotlight phenomenon. When U.S. corporations go abroad, they take more than their capital and technology with them. They also take their brand names, their reputations, and their international images. They bring in their wake the scrutiny of U.S.-based activist groups and the international media. When U.S. corporations are caught engaging in unfair or abusive practices, these groups spring into action, casting a shadow of scorn. . . . Once these campaigns reach the public arena, the perpetually hungry media brings attention to even small stories—especially those pitting giant U.S. corporations against hapless foreign workers.

Although this new form of muckraking creates its own potential hazards, it also affects the basic calculus of an investing firm. Suddenly, the advantages of lower-cost labor or lower-cost inputs from more abusive suppliers must be weighed against the crush of negative publicity, the cost of public relations, and the possibility of consumer protests. For consumer products firms, the impact is particularly intense since highly visible brand names provide an ideal target for smear campaigns and other public attacks.

* * *

As public concern coalesces around issues of human rights, the promulgation of codes and standards completes the spotlight phenomenon. Once firms have adhered to publicly acknowledged standards, they magnify the effect of their own violations. So long as firms could argue that subcontractors were beyond their reach, they could limit the public fallout from findings of abuse. With codes in place, however, firms can no longer hide behind an arm's length relationship of indifference. Once they have agreed to comply, they will be forced to—not by the sanction of law but by the sanction of the market. Firms will cut off abusive suppliers or make them clean up because it is now *in their financial interest* to do so. The spotlight does not change the morality of U.S. multinational managers. It changes their bottom-line interests.[15]

While compliance with codes of conduct remains voluntary for the most part, lawmakers in a number of countries have started to mandate disclosure in a few areas. For example, an EU Directive requires member states to mandate the disclosure by large companies of information "to the extent necessary for an understanding of the undertaking's development, performance, position and impact of its activity, relating to, as a minimum, environmental, social and employee matters, respect for human rights, anti-corruption and bribery matters."[16] In South Africa, the King Codes include sustainability reporting as part of the corporate governance framework. And Canada has enacted legislation requiring companies to disclose royalty payments made to foreign governments in connection with resource extraction, in an effort to deter corruption in the extractive industries.[17] The United States took a few steps in this direction as well, in the 2010 Dodd-Frank Act. Section 1502 of that act directed the Securities and Exchange Commission to promulgate regulations requiring companies that register with the SEC to disclose

---

[15] Spar, The Spotlight and the Bottom Line: How Multinationals Export Human Rights, 77 For. Aff. 7, 8–9 (Mar. Apr. 1998).

[16] Directive 2014/95/EU of the European Parliament and of the Council amending Directive 2013/34/EU as Regards Disclosure of Non-financial and Diversity Information by Certain Large Undertakings and Groups, 22 October 2014, L 330/1.

[17] Extractive Sector Transparency Measures Act, S.C. 2014, c. 39, s. 376.

annually if they manufacture products with certain "conflict minerals"—gold, tantalum, tin, and tungsten—originating in the Democratic Republic of the Congo or adjoining countries. Such companies would be required to provide audited reports on whether the conflict minerals they use funded armed groups. However, a number of groups challenged the SEC's rulemaking, in part on the basis that the required disclosure would violate corporations' First Amendment protections against compelled speech, and implementation has been in abeyance. See, e.g., National Assoc. of Manufacturers v. SEC, 748 F.3d 359 (D.C. Cir. 2014).

Although at a slower pace, some developments are underway to transpose not only disclosure obligations but also certain substantive obligations into hard law. A 2017 EU Regulation sets out a series of requirements regarding the maintenance of supply chains by EU entities engaged in the import of certain conflict minerals.[18] Obligations include various forms of supply chain due diligence, the implementation of risk management processes, and third-party audits.

QUESTION

(1) Consider the mechanisms through which voluntary guidelines and codes of conduct operate to affect behavior. Are all MNEs equally susceptible to pressure to adopt and follow such guidelines and codes?

Additional reading: Weissbrodt & Kruger, Norms on the Responsibilities of Transnational Corporations and Other Business Entities with Regard to Human Rights, 97 Am. J. Int'l L. 901 (2003); Ratner, Corporations and Human Rights: A Theory of Legal Responsibility, 111 Yale L.J. 443 (2001); Ruggie, Just Business: Multinational Corporations and Human Rights (2013).

D. HUMAN RIGHTS LITIGATION AGAINST CORPORATIONS

Another method of holding corporations accountable for the social and environmental impacts of their activity is ordinary civil litigation in domestic courts. Such litigation can take many forms. The plaintiffs may be the individuals or communities affected by corporate activity, or governmental entities suing to protect the interests of their citizens. They may seek monetary damages or injunctive relief. The claims may allege violation of domestic tort or statutory law, or of international law. Defendants may include individual corporate officers as well as corporations themselves—and may be charged with direct violations of applicable law, with failure adequately to supervise the activities of their foreign affiliates, or with aiding and abetting violations by others.

---

[18] Regulation (EU) 2017/821 of the European Parliament and of the Council Laying Down Supply Chain Due Diligence Obligations for Union Importers of Tin, Tantalum and Tungsten, Their Ores, and Gold Originating from Conflict-Affected and High-Risk Areas, 17 May 2017, L 130/1. The Regulation will apply as of January 1, 2021.

Because of concerns about the lack of an independent judiciary or other factors limiting the likelihood of an effective remedy, this type of litigation is rarely initiated in the countries where the relevant activity takes place. Rather, it is generally brought in a forum in the defendant's home country or, if available, some other country with a well-developed justice system. As you might expect, there are many barriers to such claims, including limitations on personal jurisdiction over non-resident defendants; the possibility in some systems of dismissal on the basis of *forum non conveniens*; substantive limitations on the responsibility of corporations for the acts of affiliated entities; questions regarding the extraterritorial application of domestic law; and so on. Nevertheless, transnational civil litigation plays a significant role in the business and human rights arena.

For the past twenty years, one of the most prominent vehicles for human rights litigation against multinational corporations has been a provision of the Judiciary Act of 1789 known as the Alien Tort Statute (ATS) or Alien Tort Claims Act (ATCA), 28 U.S.C.A. § 1350. The ATS gives the district courts jurisdiction over "any civil action by an alien for a tort only, committed in violation of the law of nations or a treaty of the United States." In Sosa v. Alvarez-Machain, 542 U.S. 692, 124 S.Ct. 2739, 159 L.Ed.2d 718 (2004), the Supreme Court endorsed the line of cases beginning with Filartiga v. Pena-Irala, 630 F.2d 876 (2d Cir. 1980), that allowed victims of serious human rights abuses abroad to sue in federal court. The Court cautioned, however, "that federal courts should not recognize private claims under federal common law for violations of any international law norm with less definite content and acceptance among civilized nations than the historical paradigms familiar when § 1350 was enacted." 542 U.S. at 732.

Whether corporations may be held liable under the ATS thus depends in part on what violations of international law are alleged. Even before Sosa, plaintiffs had failed to persuade the courts that environmental claims were well enough established to be actionable. See Flores v. Southern Peru Copper Corp., 343 F.3d 140, 161–172 (2d Cir. 2003); Beanal v. Freeport-McMoran, Inc., 197 F.3d 161, 166–167 (5th Cir. 1999). On the other hand, courts have held that the prohibition against nonconsensual medical experimentation is sufficiently established to meet the Sosa standard. See Abdullahi v. Pfizer, Inc., 562 F.3d 163, 174–188 (2d Cir. 2009).

A number of the corporate ATS cases have raised the question whether corporations may be held liable for aiding and abetting violations of international law by others. In one well-known case, Unocal was alleged to have been complicit in forced labor and other human rights violations by government of Myanmar (Burma) while building a 250-mile pipeline. See Doe I v. Unocal Corp., 395 F.3d 932 (9th Cir. 2002). The parties in Unocal settled after Sosa was decided, and the court of appeals decision was vacated, but the question of corporate liability for aiding and abetting after Sosa has arisen in other cases. Some courts have held that aiding and abetting liability requires that the corporation have acted with the purpose of facilitating the human rights violation. See Presbyterian Church of Sudan v. Talisman Energy, Inc., 582 F.3d 244, 257–259 (2d. Cir. 2009); Aziz v. Alcolac, Inc., 658 F.3d 388, 401 (4th Cir. 2011). Others have held that aiding and abetting liability requires only a *mens rea* of knowledge. See Doe v. Drummond Co. 782 F.3d 576, 609 (11th 2015) Doe v. Exxon Mobil Corp., 654 F.3d 11, 39 (D.C. Cir. 2011); see also Sarei v. Rio Tinto, PLC, 671 F.3d 736, 765 (9th Cir. 2011) (en banc) (noting but not resolving the *mens rea* question).

In a few cases, corporate defendants have argued that customary international law does not recognize corporate liability at all. Most courts have rejected this argument. See Doe v. Exxon Mobil Corp., 654 F.3d 11, 40–57 (D.C. Cir. 2011); Flomo v. Firestone Nat. Rubber Co., LLC, 643 F.3d 1013, 1017–1021 (7th Cir. 2011); Sarei v. Rio Tinto, PLC, 671 F.3d 736, 747–748 (9th Cir. 2011); Romero v. Drummond Co., Inc., 552 F.3d 1303, 1315 (11th Cir. 2008). But in Kiobel v. Royal Dutch Petroleum Co., the Second Circuit held that "[b]ecause corporate liability is not recognized as a 'specific, universal, and obligatory' norm, . . . it is not a rule of customary international law that we may apply under the ATS." 621 F.3d 111, 145 (2d Cir. 2010). The Kiobel case was brought by a group of Nigerian nationals living in the United States against Shell's British and Dutch parent companies and their Nigerian subsidiary, alleging that the defendants aided and abetted the Nigerian government in committing human rights violations in the oil-producing Ogoni region of Nigeria. Writing for the majority, Judge Cabranes noted:

> A legal culture long accustomed to imposing liability on corporations may, at first blush, assume that corporations must be subject to tort liability under the ATS, just as corporations are generally liable in tort under our domestic law (what international law calls "municipal law").[19] But the substantive law that determines our jurisdiction under the ATS is neither the domestic law of the United States nor the domestic law of any other country. By conferring subject matter jurisdiction over a limited number of offenses defined by *customary international law,* the ATS requires federal courts to look beyond rules of domestic law—however well-established they may be—to examine the specific and universally accepted rules

---

[19] The idea that corporations are "persons" with duties, liabilities, and rights has a long history in American domestic law. *See, e.g., N.Y. Cent. & Hudson River R.R. Co. v. United States,* 212 U.S. 481, 492, 29 S.Ct. 304, 53 L.Ed. 613 (1909) (rejecting the argument that, "owing to the nature and character of its organization and the extent of its power and authority, a corporation cannot commit a crime"). *See generally* Leonard Orland, *Corporate Criminal Liability* § 2.03–2.04 (2006) (discussing the policy behind, and history of, corporate criminal liability). It is an idea that continues to evolve in complex and unexpected ways. *See, e.g., Citizens United v. Fed. Election Comm'n,* 558 U.S. 50, 130 S.Ct. 876, 175 L.Ed.2d 753 (2010). The history of corporate rights and obligations under *domestic law* is, however, entirely irrelevant to the issue before us—namely, the treatment of corporations as a matter of *customary international law.*

that the nations of the world treat as binding *in their dealings with one another....*

Id. at 117–118. Judge Cabranes reviewed the decisions of international criminal tribunals, international treaties, and the works of scholars. Id. at 131–144. He concluded:

> No corporation has ever been subject to *any* form of liability (whether civil, criminal, or otherwise) under the customary international law of human rights. Rather, sources of customary international law have, on several occasions, explicitly rejected the idea of corporate liability. Thus, corporate liability has not attained a discernable, much less universal, acceptance among nations of the world in their relations *inter se,* and it cannot not, as a result, form the basis of a suit under the ATS.

> Acknowledging the absence of corporate liability under customary international law is not a matter of conferring "immunity" on corporations. It is, instead, a recognition that the States of the world, in their relations with one another, have determined that moral and legal responsibility for heinous crimes should rest on the individual whose conduct makes him or her " '*hostis humani generis,* an enemy of all mankind.' " *Sosa* 542 U.S. at 732, 124 S.Ct. 2739 (quoting *Filartiga v. Pena-Irala,* 630 F.2d 876, 890 (2d Cir.1980)). Nothing in this opinion limits or forecloses suits under the ATS against a corporation's employees, managers, officers, directors, or any other person who commits, or purposefully aids and abets, violations of international law. Moreover, nothing in this opinion limits or forecloses corporate liability under any body of law *other than the ATS*—including the domestic statutes of other States—and nothing in this opinion limits or forecloses Congress from amending the ATS to bring corporate defendants within our jurisdiction. Corporate liability, however, is simply not "accepted by the civilized world and defined with a specificity comparable to the features of the 18th-century paradigms" recognized as providing a basis for suit under the law prescribed by the ATS—that is, customary international law. *Sosa,* 542 U.S. at 725, 124 S.Ct. 2739.

Id. at 148–149.

Judge Leval issued a lengthy, and sharp, concurring opinion in the case. It began as follows:

> The majority opinion deals a substantial blow to international law and its undertaking to protect fundamental human rights. According to the rule my colleagues have created, one who earns profits by commercial exploitation of abuse of fundamental human rights can successfully shield those profits from victims' claims for compensation simply by taking the

precaution of conducting the heinous operation in the corporate form. Without any support in either the precedents or the scholarship of international law, the majority take the position that corporations, and other juridical entities, are not subject to international law, and for that reason such violators of fundamental human rights are free to retain any profits so earned without liability to their victims.

Adoption of the corporate form has always offered important benefits and protections to business—foremost among them the limitation of liability to the assets of the business, without recourse to the assets of its shareholders. The new rule offers to unscrupulous businesses advantages of incorporation never before dreamed of. So long as they incorporate (or act in the form of a trust), businesses will now be free to trade in or exploit slaves, employ mercenary armies to do dirty work for despots, perform genocides or operate torture prisons for a despot's political opponents, or engage in piracy— all without civil liability to victims. By adopting the corporate form, such an enterprise could have hired itself out to operate Nazi extermination camps or the torture chambers of Argentina's dirty war, immune from civil liability to its victims. By protecting profits earned through abuse of fundamental human rights protected by international law, the rule my colleagues have created operates in opposition to the objective of international law to protect those rights.

Id. at 149–150 (Leval, J., concurring).

In 2011, the Supreme Court granted certiorari to consider the question of corporate liability under customary international law. In an amicus brief, the United States government argued that the Second Circuit should not have examined the question of corporate liability in the abstract, but rather should have considered whether the particular international law norms at issue excluded corporations from their scope:

At the present time, the United States is not aware of any international-law norm, accepted by civilized nations and defined with the degree of specificity required by *Sosa*, that requires, or necessarily contemplates, a distinction between natural and juridical actors. See, *e.g.*, Torture Convention art. 1 (defining "torture" to include "*any act* by which severe pain or suffering * * * is intentionally inflicted on a person" for certain reasons, "by or at the instigation of or with the consent or acquiescence of a public official or other person acting in an official capacity") (emphasis added); Genocide Convention art. 2 (defining genocide to include "any of the following acts" committed with intent to destroy a group, without regard to the identity of the perpetrator); Common Article 3 (prohibiting "the following acts," without regard to the identity of the perpetrator). Both natural persons and corporations can violate international-law norms that require state action. And both natural persons and corporations can violate international-law norms that do not require state action. The court of appeals examined the question of corporate liability in the abstract, and therefore did not address whether any of the particular international-law norms identified by petitioners (or recognized by the district court as satisfying *Sosa*'s "demanding" standard, 542 U.S. at 738 n.30) exclude corporations from their scope. Because corporations (or agents acting on their behalf) can violate the types of international-law norms identified in *Sosa* to the same extent as natural persons, the question becomes whether or how corporations should be held accountable as a matter of federal common law for violations that are otherwise actionable in private tort suits for damages under the ATS.

Brief for the United States as Amicus Curiae Supporting Petitioners at 20–21, Kiobel v. Royal Dutch Petroleum Co., 569 U.S. 108, 133 S.Ct. 1659, 185 L.Ed.2d 671 (2013).

In the end, however, the Supreme Court did not reach the question of corporate liability.[20] After oral argument, it directed the parties to file supplemental briefs on a different question: "[w]hether and under what circumstances the [ATS] allows courts to recognize a cause of action for violations of the law of nations occurring within the territory of a sovereign other than the United States." 565 U.S. 1244, 132 S.Ct. 1738, 182 L.Ed.2d 270 (2012). The Supreme Court held that the presumption against extraterritoriality applies to causes of action under the ATS and dismissed the case. The Court concluded its opinion with the following paragraph:

> On these facts, all the relevant conduct took place outside the United States. And even where the claims touch and concern the territory of the United States, they must do so with sufficient force to displace the presumption against extraterritorial application. See *Morrison*, 561 U.S. 247, 130 S. Ct., at 2883–2888. Corporations are often present in many countries, and it would reach too far to say that mere corporate presence suffices. If Congress were to determine otherwise, a statute more specific than the ATS would be required.

Kiobel v. Royal Dutch Petroleum Co., 569 U.S. 108, 124–125, 133 S.Ct. 1659, 185 L.Ed.2d 671 (2013). The Kiobel majority did not go as far as Justices Alito and Thomas, who would have found the presumption overcome only where conduct *in the United States* "is sufficient to violate an international law norm that satisfies *Sosa*'s requirements of

---

[20] The previous term, in Mohamad v. Palestinian Authority, 566 U.S. 449, 132 S.Ct. 1702, 182 L.Ed.2d 720 (2012), the Supreme Court held that the Torture Victim Protection Act's statutory cause of action for torture and extrajudicial killing applied only to natural persons.

definiteness and acceptance among civilized nations." Id. at 127 (Alito, J., concurring).

In 2017, the Supreme Court granted certiorari once again to consider the question of corporate liability in Jesner v. Arab Bank, PLC, 138 S.Ct. 1386 (2018). The plaintiffs in Jesner alleged that Arab Bank, a foreign corporation, had financed terrorist attacks in Israel by funneling money through its New York branch. Writing for only three justices, Justice Kennedy suggested that international law might distinguish between corporations and natural persons, but found it unnecessary to resolve that question. Id. at 1402 (plurality opinion). Instead, the Court held that the ATS cause of action should not be extended to *foreign* corporations. Id. at 1403, 1407 (opinion of the Court). Thus, Jesner preserves the possibility of ATS claims against U.S. corporations, at least outside the Second Circuit, as a number of subsequent cases have recognized. See, e.g., Doe v. Nestle, S.A., 906 F.3d 1120, 1124 (9th Cir. 2018) (distinguishing between foreign and U.S. corporate defendants in a case involving allegations of child slave labor in the Ivory Coast); Al Shimari v. CACI Premier Tech., Inc., 320 F. Supp. 3d 781 (E.D. Va. 2018) (noting that the Supreme Court had explicitly confined its holding to foreign corporations and allowing a case to proceed against a U.S. corporation on the basis of its involvement in the alleged mistreatment of prisoners at Abu Ghraib).

In addition to the requirement that the claims "touch and concern" the United States with sufficient force to satisfy Kiobel, plaintiffs using the ATS face a number of other obstacles to bringing human rights claims against corporations. It can be difficult to establish personal jurisdiction over the foreign subsidiary that may have been most directly involved in the abuses, see, e.g., Kiobel v. Royal Dutch Petroleum Co., 2008 WL 591869 (S.D.N.Y) (dismissing claims against Shell's Nigerian subsidiary for lack of personal jurisdiction), while general jurisdiction over the parent company will exist only if the "corporation's affiliations with the State are so continuous and systematic as to render it essentially at home in the forum State." Daimler AG v. Bauman, 571 U.S. 117, 139, 134 S.Ct. 746, 187 L.Ed.2d 624 (2014) (international quotation marks omitted). Plaintiffs who are able to establish personal jurisdiction and overcome the presumption against extraterritoriality must still show that their claims meet Sosa's standard for acceptance and specificity and, in the case of aiding and abetting claims, that the defendant acted with the necessary *mens rea*.

In the wake of Kiobel, it is possible that more claims will be brought in state courts, which are subject to the same rules of personal jurisdiction but free from the limits that Sosa and Kiobel have placed on the ATS cause of action. It is also possible that more cases will be filed in foreign courts. In 2013, a Dutch decision found jurisdiction over Shell and its Nigerian subsidiary with respect to claims of environmental harm in Nigeria. Applying Nigerian law, the court held that the parent company was not liable in tort but that the subsidiary had committed negligence by insufficiently securing oil well-heads against sabotage, and was liable for damages. See Akpan v. Royal Dutch Shell Plc, No. 337050 (Hague Dist. Ct. 2013) (Neth.). In 2017, an appeals court in British Columbia rejected the argument of a Canadian mining company that corporations could never be liable for violations of customary international law. See Araya v. Nevsun Resources Ltd, 2017 BCCA 401 (2017). Another 2017 opinion, this one in the United Kingdom, permitted a group of villagers from Zambia to sue a U.K. company for alleged human rights violations of its Zambian subsidiary. See Lungowe v. Vedanta Resources Plc, [2017] EWCA Civ 1528 (2017).

QUESTIONS

(1) Assume that a U.S. oil company and its Nigerian subsidiary are alleged to have assisted the Nigerian military in torturing and killing opponents of oil drilling in the Niger Delta. How would you weigh the advantages and disadvantages of bringing suit in U.S. federal district court under the ATS, in U.S. state court, and in Nigerian court?

(2) The Second Circuit's Kiobel decision discusses the possibility of lawsuits under the ATS against individual actors within corporations, including their employees, managers, officers and directors. Is such litigation likely? Could it be an effective tool in securing compliance with human rights law?

Additional reading: Stephens et al., International Human Rights Litigation in U.S. Courts (2d ed. 2008); Dodge, Business and Human Rights Litigation in U.S. Courts Before and After Kiobel, in Business and Human Rights: From Principles to Practice 244 (Baumann-Pauly & Nolan eds., 2016); Payne & Pereira, Corporate Complicity in International Human Rights Violations, 12 Ann. Rev. L. & Soc. Sci. 63 (2016); Davis & Whytock, State Remedies for Human Rights, 98 B.U. L. Rev. 397 (2018).

PART TWO

PROBLEM EXERCISES IN TRANSNATIONAL BUSINESS

In Part Two, we turn from analysis of the background against which transnational business operations are carried out to a closer look at some particular transactions. We focus, in most of the problems, on a draft document as a means of organizing our analysis and unearthing the questions that lie in wait for one attempting such an arrangement. The draft documents are not always the ideal form for the project in question and are certainly not to be taken as models for other types of transactions involving different parties in different countries.

Most of the problem cases will involve the laws of the United States and of some other country, occasionally mediated by international law. In a rough way, they are designed to move in the direction of greater complexity, although it is difficult to scale them precisely along that dimension. In some cases, aspects of the problem are movable; that is, issues could be switched from one problem to another. For example, questions about currency risk or export controls could be raised in a number of places. Their potential applicability should not be forgotten just because they have been dealt with once before.

Many of the questions raised by the problem cases have no precise answers. Solutions will vary according to the risk preferences of the parties involved, their negotiating postures, and the experience of their counsel. To some extent, we look at the business aspects of those decisions, not drawing a sharp line between the business side and the legal side of the proposed deal. National policies in the fields we study here are often subject to rather sudden changes of direction. The student should be aware of the fact that foreign systems, too, are subject to statutory and judicial changes and that it is a difficult task to run down the very latest local information in the absence of modern computerized research systems and updating devices. That is, of course, one of the tasks to be assigned to foreign counsel. While some of the problems involve fairly extensive forays into foreign law, it is important to bear in mind that one will not, through this course, arrive at any advanced stage of expertise in matters of foreign law, but only at a higher level of sophistication about the pitfalls of dealing with foreign systems through foreign counsel.

PROBLEM 1

TRANSNATIONAL SALES

A. INTRODUCTION

The logical place to start looking at transborder business arrangements would be with the simplest variety. It would presumably look something like this: An American firm advertises its products on its website. A foreign company views the website and, after an exchange of emails, decides to buy one of the products. The transaction appears to be so straightforward that it is highly unlikely that a lawyer would be drawn into the deal; the parties would simply think it not worth the trouble and expense. They would rather turn the item over to a freight forwarder or somebody else in the business of shipping goods abroad. Such an intermediary will have in place routines for making out invoices, arranging transportation with an air freight carrier or an ocean transporter, filling out any forms required by the purchaser's country, providing for the payment of any customs duties or value added taxes imposed at the border, and similar matters. At some point, however, the head of the American firm starts to think about regularizing its export operations and consults you as to what would be called for by way of drafting of forms, creation of files and procedures, and so forth.

In 2016, more than 287,000 companies in the United States exported goods to other countries. More than 280,000 of these companies were small and medium sized enterprises (SMEs), firms with fewer than 500 workers. The goods they sold accounted for one third of the goods exported from the United States in 2016, worth nearly $430 billion.[1] SMEs sell items like machinery, computer parts, chemicals, plastics, and food.

An interest on the part of a small company's top management can compensate for the lack of a specialized export department like those of large firms. However, sometimes export activities become unexpectedly complicated. The United States imposes export controls on many items, and it may be necessary to obtain an export license. There may be problems with the payment for the item. Not only do payments systems differ from country to country, but a seller may also be reluctant to send an item abroad without some guarantee of payment. More generally, dispute resolution can become complex when more than one legal system is involved.

To serve as a focus for analysis, there follows a form of invoice used by an American computer manufacturer for domestic purposes. It is frequently the case that the only "contract" between a buyer and seller in the domestic setting is that constituted by the seller's invoice and the

---

[1] International Trade Administration, U.S. Exporting & Importing Companies: 2016.

buyer's acceptance of the goods. Assume that the American company uses the invoice in a sale of computers to a Chinese buyer. What issues would such a contract leave inappropriately treated or unresolved in the international context?

A checklist of problems that might arise in such a sale would include:

(1) The standard commercial law problems treated in the Uniform Commercial Code with respect to domestic transactions, complicated by uncertainty as to what law governs the transaction.

(2) Problems with export control regulations.

(3) Compliance with the tariff, quota, and other rules affecting the product in the country of destination, including health, safety, and other regulatory requirements not intended as limitations on imports.

(4) Problems of payment.

INVOICE

American Computer Company
755 Coenties Slip
New York, New York 10017
Conditions of Sale

Sold To:	Ship To:		FOB: New York Incoterms 2010
Invoice No.:	Customer No.:	Date of Order	When Ship
Order shipped	Product No.	Product Description	Total Price
		Subtotal: _____	
		Sales Tax: _____	
		Total: _____	

Terms are based on cash, net if paid within 30 days. Seller assumes no responsibility for damage to equipment if not used according to enclosed instructions.

Orders are accepted subject to our ability to obtain prompt shipment from suppliers. Seller will not be liable for damage resulting from failure to supply equipment.

Seller will not be liable for any claim in excess of the purchase price.

B. CHOICE OF LAW AND CHOICE OF FORUM

As discussed in Chapter II, the parties to an international transaction will often include clauses in their agreement selecting the law to govern their agreement and the forum (a national court or an international arbitral tribunal) to resolve their disputes. Sometimes, however, the parties to an export sales transaction may neglect to choose the governing law. Or sometimes, the parties may exchange standard forms with conflicting provisions on choice of law and choice of forum. In these situations, how will a court determine what law governs the contract? Are there any limits on the parties' ability to choose the governing law?

1. CISG

As a general matter, contract law is domestic law. But there is a widely adopted treaty that potentially applies to many international transactions for the sale of goods: the United Nations Convention on Contracts for the International Sale of Goods (CISG). Article 1(1) of the CISG states its basic scope of application:

> (1) This Convention applies to contracts of sale of goods between parties whose places of business are in different States:

> *(a)* When the States are Contracting States; or

> *(b)* When the rules of private international law lead to the application of the law of a Contracting State.

The United States has declared a reservation to Article 1(1)(b), which means that an American lawyer is unlikely to encounter that subsection in practice. That leaves Article 1(1)(a), under which the CISG will apply if the parties to the contract have their places of business in different countries, each of which has joined the CISG. The Convention entered into force with respect to the United States on January 1, 1988. As of January 2019, 89 countries are Contracting States,[2] including China, Canada, Mexico, Japan, Germany, South Korea, France, Italy, Brazil, the Netherlands, and Switzerland, whose combined trade in goods with the United States exceeded $2.6 trillion in 2017. Of the top U.S. trading partners, only the United Kingdom, India, Taiwan, and Ireland have not joined the CISG.

The CISG sets forth substantive law rules governing the formation of contracts for the sale of goods between parties whose places of business are in different states, as well as the rights and obligations of those

---

[2] As of January 1, 2019, the following are parties to the CISG: Albania, Argentina, Armenia, Australia, Austria, Azerbaijan, Bahrain, Belarus, Belgium, Benin, Bosnia and Herzegovina, Brazil, Bulgaria, Burundi, Canada, Chile, China, Colombia, Congo, Costa Rica, Croatia, Cuba, Cyprus, Czechia, Denmark, Dominican Republic, Ecuador, Egypt, El Salvador, Estonia, Fiji, Finland, France, Gabon, Georgia, Germany, Greece, Guinea, Honduras, Hungary, Iceland, Iraq, Israel, Italy, Japan, Kyrgyzstan, Latvia, Lebanon, Lesotho, Liberia, Lithuania, Luxembourg, Macedonia, Madagascar, Mauritania, Mexico, Moldova, Mongolia, Montenegro, the Netherlands, New Zealand, Norway, Palestine, Paraguay, Peru, Poland, Romania, Russia, St. Vincent and the Grenadines, San Marino, Serbia, Singapore, Slovakia, Slovenia, South Korea, Spain, Sweden, Switzerland, Syria, Turkey, Uganda, Ukraine, United States, Uruguay, Uzbekistan, Viet Nam, and Zambia. See www.uncitral.org/uncitral/en/uncitral_texts/sale_goods/1980CISG_status.html.

parties. It does not deal with such issues as incapacity, fraud, duress, mistake, and unconscionability, which continue to be governed by domestic law. See CISG Art. 4. Consumer contracts are expressly excluded from the CISG. See CISG Art. 2(a).

The CISG resulted from years of negotiation and attempts to strike a balance between the different national solutions for questions of contract law. Many provisions are quite different from those of the Uniform Commercial Code. For example, compare the following provision dealing with the "battle of the forms" with UCC § 2–207, set forth at infra pp. 160–161:

Article 19

(1) A reply to an offer which purports to be an acceptance but contains additions, limitations or other modifications is a rejection of the offer and constitutes a counter-offer.

(2) However, a reply to an offer which purports to be an acceptance but contains additional or different terms which do not materially alter the terms of the offer constitutes an acceptance, unless the offeror, without undue delay, objects orally to the discrepancy or dispatches a notice to that effect. If he does not so object, the terms of the contract are the terms of the offer with the modifications contained in the acceptance.

(3) Additional or different terms relating, among other things, to the price, payment, quality and quantity of the goods, place and time of delivery, extent of one party's liability to the other or the settlement of disputes are considered to alter the terms of the offer materially.

There are other important differences between the CISG and the UCC. The CISG does not contain a Statute of Frauds. Article 11 provides that "[a] contract of sale need not be concluded in or evidenced by writing and is not subject to any other requirements as to form. It may be proved by any means including witnesses." Nor does the CISG have a parol evidence rule. Article 8(3) says: "In determining the intent of a party or the understanding a reasonable person would have had, due consideration is to be given to all relevant circumstances of the case including the negotiations, any practices which the parties have established between themselves, usages and any subsequent conduct of the parties." See also MCC-Marble Ceramic Center, Inc. v. Ceramica Nuova d'Agostino, S.p.A., 144 F.3d 1384 (11th Cir.1998).

In contrast to the UCC, the CISG lacks a "perfect tender rule." The non-breaching party may declare a contract avoided only if the other party's failure to perform constitutes a "fundamental breach." The CISG contains a *Nachfrist* procedure borrowed from German law, however, which allows the non-breaching party to fix an additional, reasonable time for performance and to declare the contract avoided if the breaching party does not perform within that period. Like the UCC, the CISG allows a non-breaching buyer to seek either "market" or "cover" damages, as well as consequential damages. The CISG, however, allows the non-breaching party to seek specific performance unless it has resorted to a remedy that is inconsistent with this requirement, although a buyer may require the delivery of substitute goods under Article 46(2) only if non-conformity constitutes a fundamental breach of contract. Finally, Article 50 of the CISG (like China's Contract Law, infra p. 159) allows the buyer to reduce the price it pays for the goods in proportion to any non-conformity.

It is important to note that under Article 6 of the CISG, "[t]he parties may exclude the application of this Convention or . . . derogate from or vary the effect of its provisions." Thus, the Convention, like many systems of contract law, is optional rather than mandatory. In practice, it appears that parties often attempt to exclude application of the CISG.[3] The most likely reason is lack of familiarity, though views about the efficiency of the CISG's rules and the desire to gain an advantage by selecting one's own law may also play a role. But a choice-of-law clause has to be carefully drafted to make exclusion of the CISG effective. In Asante Technologies, Inc. v. PMC-Sierra, Inc., 164 F.Supp.2d 1142 (N.D.Cal. 2001), each party had included a choice of law clause in its standard form, one selecting the laws of California and the other the laws of British Columbia. The court said:

> Although selection of a particular choice of law, such as "the California Commercial Code" or the "Uniform Commercial Code" *could* amount to implied exclusion of the CISG, the choice of law clauses at issue here do not evince a clear intent to opt out of the CISG. For example, Defendant's choice of applicable law adopts the law of British Columbia, and it is undisputed that the CISG *is* the law of British Columbia. (International Sale of Goods Act ch. 236, 1996 S.B.C. 1 *et seq.* (B.C.).) Furthermore, even Plaintiff's choice of applicable law generally adopts the "laws of" the State of California, and California is bound by the Supremacy Clause to the treaties of the United States. U.S. Const. art. VI, cl. 2 ("This Constitution, and the laws of the United States which shall be made in pursuance thereof; and all treaties made, or which shall be made, under the authority of the United States, shall be the supreme law of the land.") Thus, under general California law, the CISG is applicable to contracts where the contracting parties are from different countries that have adopted the CISG. In the absence of clear language indicating that both contracting parties intended to opt out of the CISG, and in view of Defendant's Terms and Conditions which would apply the CISG, the Court

---

[3]   See John F. Coyle, The Role of the CISG in U.S. Contract Practice: An Empirical Study, 38 U. Pa. J. Int'l L. 195 (2016).

> rejects Plaintiff's contention that the choice of law provisions preclude the applicability of the CISG.

Id. at 1150. Even if both parties have included sufficiently explicit choice-of-law clauses excluding the CISG in their standard forms, unless those forms agree on the domestic law that should govern, a court may still have no alternative but to apply the CISG's rules to decide whether a contract was formed and which party's choice-of-law clause and other terms are part of the contract. See, e.g., Nucap Indus. Inc. v. Robert Bosch LLC, 273 F.Supp.3d 986, 1006 (E.D. Ill. 2017); Hanwha Corp. v. Cedar Pharmaceuticals, Inc., 760 F.Supp.2d 426, 431 (S.D.N.Y. 2011).

2. DOMESTIC LAW

With the important exception of the CISG discussed above, the modern law of sales is domestic law. In the United States, it is state rather than federal law. Nearly every state in the United States has adopted Article 2 of the Uniform Commercial Code (UCC), which applies to transactions in goods. Other transactions are subject to the common law of contracts, which varies from state to state. In China, contracts are governed by a unified national law, the 1999 Contract Law of the People's Republic of China.

The domestic law of contracts will govern if the CISG is not applicable, for example if parties' places of business are not both in CISG countries (e.g., a sale of goods contract between a Taiwanese buyer and a U.S. seller) or if the contract's choice-of-law clause has effectively excluded the CISG. Even when the CISG applies, the domestic law of contracts may also govern questions not covered by the Convention, such as the validity of the contract. See CISG Art. 7(2) ("Questions concerning matters governed by this Convention which are not expressly settled in it are to be settled in conformity with the general principles on which it is based or, in the absence of such principles, in conformity with the law applicable by virtue of the rules of private international law.").

Because the domestic law of contracts differs from jurisdiction to jurisdiction, *which* domestic law governs may significantly affect the rights and duties of the parties and how particular disputes between them will be resolved. If the contract contains a choice-of-law clause, the answer is generally straightforward. Most legal systems will enforce such clauses, subject to only limited exceptions. See, e.g., Restatement (Second) of Conflicts § 187(1) (1971) ("The law of the state chosen by the parties to govern their contractual rights and duties will be applied if the particular issue is one which the parties could have resolved by an explicit provision in their agreement directed to that issue."); UCC § 1–301(a) ("Except as otherwise provided in this section, when a transaction bears a reasonable relation to this state and also to another state or nation the parties may agree that the law either of this state or of such other state or nation shall govern their rights and duties."); Contract Law of the People's Republic of China Art. 126 ("The parties to a contract with a foreign element may choose the law to apply to the disposition of contractual disputes, except as otherwise provided for by law.").

When the contract does not have a choice-of-law clause and the CISG does not apply, a court will use the conflict-of-laws rules of its own jurisdiction to determine the applicable law. In the United States, those would be the conflicts rules of the state in which the court is located, even if the court is a federal court sitting in diversity. Klaxon Co. v. Stentor Electric Mfg. Co., 313 U.S. 487, 61 S.Ct. 1020, 85 L.Ed. 1477 (1941); Day & Zimmermann, Inc. v. Challoner, 423 U.S. 3, 96 S.Ct. 167, 46 L.Ed.2d 3 (1975) (per curiam). Common-law conflicts rules vary from state to state, but more states have adopted the approach of the Restatement (Second) of Conflicts than any other:

§ 188. Law Governing in Absence of Effective Choice by the Parties

(1) The rights and duties of the parties with respect to an issue in contract are determined by the local law of the state which, with respect to that issue, has the most significant relationship to the transaction and the parties under the principles stated in § 6.

(2) In the absence of an effective choice of law by the parties (see § 187), the contacts to be taken into account in applying the principles of § 6 to determine the law applicable to an issue include:

    (a) the place of contracting,

    (b) the place of negotiation of the contract,

    (c) the place of performance,

    (d) the location of the subject matter of the contract, and

    (e) the domicil, residence, nationality, place of incorporation and place of business of the parties.

These contacts are to be evaluated according to their relative importance with respect to the particular issue.

(3) If the place of negotiating the contract and the place of performance are in the same state, the local law of this state will usually be applied, except as otherwise provided in §§ 189–199 and 203.

§ 6. Choice-of-Law Principles

(1) A court, subject to constitutional restrictions, will follow a statutory directive of its own state on choice of law.

(2) When there is no such directive, the factors relevant to the choice of the applicable rule of law include

    (a) the needs of the interstate and international systems,

    (b) the relevant policies of the forum,

(c)   the relevant policies of other interested states and the relative interests of those states in the determination of the particular issue,

(d)   the protection of justified expectations,

(e)   the basic policies underlying the particular field of law,

(f)   certainty, predictability and uniformity of result, and

(g)   ease in the determination and application of the law to be applied.

In sale-of-goods cases, the common law of conflicts has been superseded by UCC § 1–301(b), which directs courts to apply the UCC "to transactions bearing an appropriate relation to this state." Note that a transaction may bear an "appropriate relation" to a state even if that state does not have the "most significant relationship" to the transaction. The UCC adopted this expansive conflicts rule to increase the number of cases to which the UCC would apply during its early days.

The 1999 Contract Law of the People's Republic of China also contains an article on applicable law, which provides a test for determining the applicable law in the absence of a choice by the parties:

Article 126. The parties to a contract with a foreign element may choose the law to apply to the disposition of contractual disputes, except as otherwise provided for by law. Where the parties to a contract with a foreign element make no such choice, the law of the state with the closest connection to the contract shall apply.

In regard to Chinese-foreign equity joint venture contracts, Chinese-foreign contractual joint venture contracts and contracts for Chinese-foreign co-operative exploration and exploitation of natural resources that are performed in the territory of the People's Republic of China, the law of the People's Republic of China shall apply.

Does it make a difference which domestic law of contracts is applied? There are some similarities in the commercial laws of different countries, due in part to cross-system borrowing. For example, some German influences infiltrated the UCC through one of its drafters, Karl Llewellyn, and China's first modern civil code was heavily influenced by German law. The drafters of China's 1999 Contract Law deliberately looked to the "beneficial experience of foreign countries," and many of that law's provisions closely follow the UNIDROIT Principles of International Commercial Contracts and the CISG. Still, domestic laws often diverge, because they arise from different legal cultures and respond to different commercial environments. Thus a given controversy between a buyer and seller could come out differently under different systems. We examine three constellations of problems not unknown in domestic sales law but likely to be particularly acute in transborder dealings.

For one example, suppose that the buyer asserts, after the goods have arrived, that they are not up to standard. One question is: what is the standard? Both § 2–313 of the UCC and Article 153 of China's Contract Law provide that a description of the quality of goods creates an express warranty. Article 62(1) of China's Contract Law further provides that the performance of a contract is to be judged "in accordance with the state standard or industry standard, . . . the usual standard or such a particular standard that conforms with the purpose of the contract." The latter two standards are equivalent to the implied warranties of merchantability and fitness found in § 2–314 and § 2–315 of the UCC.

Under the UCC's "perfect tender rule," a buyer has the right to reject a shipment of goods if they fail in any way to conform to the contract. The buyer must seasonably notify the seller of the rejection and must follow any reasonable instructions from the seller with respect to the goods. The buyer may seek as damages the difference between the contract price of the goods and either the market price or the "cover" price, as well as incidental and consequential damages, but generally may not seek specific performance of the contract unless the goods are unique. Under China's Contract Law, a buyer must notify the seller of any non-conformity within a reasonable time not exceeding two years. In contrast to the UCC, the buyer may not terminate a contract for defective performance unless the defect constitutes a fundamental breach. The buyer may seek damages for any non-conformity, but also has the option of two additional remedies not generally available under the UCC. First, under Article 110 of the Contract Law, the buyer may ask for specific performance unless such performance is impossible, impracticable, or not demanded within a reasonable time. Second, under Article 111, the buyer may claim a "reduction of the price," which essentially allows the buyer to modify the terms of the contract unilaterally and obtain the monetary benefit of a suit for damages without going to court.

Standard terms that limit remedies are also treated differently. Under UCC § 2–719 the seller may limit the buyer's remedies to repayment of the price and may exclude consequential damages unless the limitation is unconscionable, for example an exclusion for personal injuries in the case of consumer goods. Under Article 39 of China's Contract Law, a party using standard terms that exclude or limit its liability must bring them to the other party's attention "in a reasonable manner." A 2009 interpretation by the Supreme People's Court clarifies that the party using such standard terms bears the burden of proving that proper notice was given through special characters, symbols, fonts, or other signs, and the interpretation states that a party who did not receive proper notice may rescind the standard terms that exclude or limit liability. Article 53 of China's Contract Law further voids standard terms that exclude liability for property loss resulting from an intentional act or from gross negligence, as well as liability for personal injuries.

A second set of issues characteristic of international transactions is the problem of unexpected changes in conditions. For example, in 1956 hostilities in the Middle East closed the Suez Canal for a protracted period. All sorts of contractual arrangements were upset by this. The Uniform Commercial Code's provision on impracticability is set forth in § 2–615, which provides in part: "Delay in delivery or non-delivery in whole or in part by a seller . . . is not a breach of his duty under a contract for sale if performance as agreed has been made impracticable by the occurrence of a contingency the non-occurrence of which was a basic assumption on which the contract was made or by compliance in good faith with any applicable foreign or domestic government regulation or order whether or not it later proves to be invalid." Article 117 of China's Contract Law provides a defense of *force majeure* but requires "an objective circumstance that is unforeseeable, unavoidable and insurmountable." In its 2009 interpretation of China's Contract Law, the Supreme People's Court added a "change of circumstances" defense, allowing courts to modify or rescind a contract based on a major change that was unforeseeable and was not a "commercial risk."

Third, we have what is called "the battle of the forms." A buyer orders goods using its standard purchase order form, and the seller responds with its standard acknowledgment form or invoice, which contains additional or different terms. Is there a contract? What are its terms? The UCC departed from the common law's "mirror image rule" by providing that a reply that varied the terms of the offer could be an acceptance:

§ 2–207. Additional Terms in Acceptance or Confirmation

(1) A definite and seasonable expression of acceptance or a written confirmation which is sent within a reasonable time operates as an acceptance even though it states terms additional to or different from those offered or agreed upon, unless acceptance is expressly made conditional on assent to the additional or different terms.

(2) The additional terms are to be construed as proposals for addition to the contract. Between merchants such terms become part of the contract unless:

(a) the offer expressly limits acceptance to the terms of the offer;

(b) they materially alter it; or

(c) notification of objection to them has already been given or is given within a reasonable time after notice of them is received.

(3) Conduct by both parties which recognizes the existence of a contract is sufficient to establish a contract for sale although the writings of the parties do not otherwise establish a contract. In such case the terms of the particular contract consist of those terms on which the writings of the parties agree, together with any supplementary terms incorporated under any other provisions of this Act.

The relevant provisions of China's Contract Law, although allowing an acceptance to make some non-material modifications to an offer, are much closer in effect to the "mirror image rule" of the common law and to Article 19 of the CISG:

Article 30. The content of the acceptance shall accord with that of the offer. If the offeree makes material modification of the content of the offer, it is a new offer. Modification of the subject matter of the contract, quantity, quality, price or remuneration, time of performance, place or manner or performance, liability for breach of contract, means of dispute resolution and so forth is material modification of the content of the offer.

Article 31. If an acceptance makes non-material modification to the content of the offer, the acceptance is effective and the terms of the contract shall accord with those of the acceptance, unless the offeror expresses his objection in a timely manner or the offer indicates that the acceptance may not make any modification of the content of the offer.

3. FORMS AND INCOTERMS

From the foregoing it becomes apparent that if the parties sit down and apply themselves to drafting and negotiating a contract that deals specifically with the issues that have been raised, they have a lot of leeway within which to operate. Lawyers from different legal traditions will have different approaches to drafting contracts. It has long been noted that European and Asian lawyers are horrified at the length of documents produced by American lawyers. Observers have seen, however, that the length of contracts produced by such lawyers for transnational arrangements has been increasing. In an international arrangement where the parties do not share a common commercial culture and where they cannot be sure how a third party adjudicator will read their agreement, it is inevitable that thoughtful lawyers will feel a need to spell things out. Observers also point to drastic differences in negotiating styles between lawyers and business leaders in different countries. Americans are typically criticized as too eager to get to a written arrangement without going through the exploratory maneuvers other societies would regard as necessary to establishing that personal trust and confidence exist between the parties.

When the time comes to draft a contract, the international practitioner is inevitably going to be tempted to use forms. Indeed, one of the teaching devices used recurrently in this book is the standard form, although the reader should note that we have intentionally introduced problems into many of these forms for pedagogical purposes. In general, one should be cautious about casually accepting other drafters' handiwork. What they produced may not have been very good in the first place, or it may have been drafted with quite a different problem in mind.

One source of forms is the practitioner's own law firm. Particularly if there is recurrent need for a type of document, it is likely that one can retrieve a form from an electronic system and modify it on the screen. In advanced systems, you may encounter programs that help you do the job of adapting the form to your case, ones that ask you questions about the facts in your case and branch out in accordance with your responses. Another place to look is in books and articles that reproduce forms. You may be able to obtain copies of forms from other lawyers, from trade associations, from court records or from other files. And in recent years, companies such as Legal Zoom and Rocket Lawyer have emerged that provide on-line document services. There are, however, some special problems in employing forms designed for domestic use in international transactions, because such forms are likely to leave out clauses that are needed only in international contracts.

Related to forms are collections of clauses that can be incorporated by reference. The International Chamber of Commerce (ICC), for example, has published "Incoterms 2010,"[4] which defines 11 separate trade terms like "FOB," "FAS," and "CIF" that parties may incorporate by reference in their contracts. Such terms delineate the parties' respective obligations with respect to such matters as delivery, customs, cost of shipment, and risk of loss, and obviate the need for the parties to spell out such items in their contract. Some possibility for confusion exists because the commercial laws of individual legal systems may also define many of these terms, sometimes in ways that are inconsistent with the Incoterms. This is the case with UCC Article 2. To avoid confusion, the parties should specify that their contract is governed by the Incoterms (and by which version of the Incoterms). The Incoterms 2010 definition of "FOB" follows:

FOB
Free on Board
FOB (insert named port of shipment) Incoterms ® 2010
GUIDANCE NOTE
This rule is to be used only for sea or inland waterway transport.

---

[4] Earlier versions of the Incoterms were published by the ICC in 1936, 1953, 1967, 1976, 1980, 1990, and 2000.

"Free on Board" means that the seller delivers the goods on board the vessel nominated by the buyer at the named port of shipment or procures the goods already so delivered. The risk of loss of or damage to the goods passes when the goods are on board the vessel, and the buyer bears all costs from that moment onwards.

The seller is required either to deliver the goods on board the vessel or to procure goods already so delivered for shipment. The reference to "procure" here caters for multiple sales down a chain ("string sales"), particularly common in the commodity trades.

FOB may not be appropriate where goods are handed over to the carrier before they are on board the vessel, for example goods in containers, which are typically delivered at a terminal. In such situations, the FCA rule should be used.

FOB requires the seller to clear the goods for export, where applicable. However, the seller has no obligation to clear the goods for import, pay any import duty or carry out any import customs formalities.

A	The Seller's Obligations	B	The Buyer's Obligations
A1	**General obligations of the seller**	B1	**General obligations of the buyer**
	The seller must provide the goods and the commercial invoice in conformity with the contract of sale and any other evidence of conformity that may be required by the contract.		The buyer must pay the price as provided in the contract of sale.
	Any document referred to in A1–A10 may be an equivalent electronic record or procedure if agreed between the parties or customary.		Any document referred to in B1–B10 may be an equivalent electronic record or procedure if agreed between the parties or customary.
A2	**Licenses, authorizations, security clearances and other formalities**	B2	**Licenses, authorizations, security clearances and other formalities**
	Where applicable, the seller must obtain, at its own risk and expense, any export license or other official authorization and carry out all customs formalities necessary for the export of the goods.		Where applicable, it is up to the buyer to obtain, at its own risk and expense, any import license or other official authorization and carry out all customs formalities for the import of the goods and for their transport through any country.

A3 Contracts of carriage and insurance

a) Contract of carriage

The seller has no obligation to the buyer to make a contract of carriage. However, if requested by the buyer or if it is commercial practice and the buyer does not give an instruction to the contrary in due time, the seller may contract for carriage on usual terms at the buyer's risk and expense. In either case, the seller may decline to make the contract of carriage and, if it does, shall promptly notify the buyer.

b) Contract of insurance

The seller has no obligation to the buyer to make a contract of insurance. However, the seller must provide the buyer, at the buyer's request, risk, and expense (if any), with information that the buyer needs for obtaining insurance.

A4 Delivery

The seller must deliver the goods either by placing them on board the vessel nominated by the buyer at the loading point, if any, indicated by the buyer at the named port of shipment or by procuring the goods so delivered. In either case, the seller must deliver the goods on the agreed date or within the agreed period

B3 Contracts of carriage and insurance

a) Contract of carriage

The buyer must contract, at its own expense for the carriage of the goods from the named port of shipment, except where the contract of carriage is made by the seller as provided for in A3 a).

b) Contract of insurance

The buyer has no obligation to the seller to make a contract of insurance.

B4 Taking delivery

The buyer must take delivery of the goods when they have been delivered as envisaged in A4.

and in the manner customary at the port.

If no specific loading point has been indicated by the buyer, the seller may select the point within the named port of shipment that best suits its purpose.

| A5 | **Transfer of risks** | B5 | **Transfer of risks** |

The seller bears all risks of loss of or damage to the goods until they have been delivered in accordance with A4 with the exception of loss or damage in the circumstances described in B5.

The buyer bears all risks of loss of or damage to the goods from the time they have been delivered as envisaged in A4. If

a) the buyer fails to notify the nomination of a vessel in accordance with B7; or

b) the vessel nominated by the buyer fails to arrive on time to enable the seller to comply with A4, is unable to take the goods, or closes for cargo earlier than the time notified in accordance with B7;

then, the buyer bears all risks of loss of or damage to the goods:

(i) from the agreed date, or in the absence of an agreed date,

(ii) from the date notified by the seller under A7 within the agreed period, or, if no such date has been notified,

(iii) from the expiry date of any agreed period for delivery, provided that the goods have been clearly identified as the contract goods.

A6 Allocation of costs

The seller must pay

a) all costs relating to the goods until they have been delivered in accordance with A4, other than those payable by the buyer as envisaged in B6; and

b) where applicable, the costs of customs formalities necessary for export, as well as all duties, taxes and other charges payable upon export.

B6 Allocation of costs

The buyer must pay

a) all costs relating to the goods from the time they have been delivered as envisaged in A4, except, where applicable, the costs of customs formalities necessary for export, as well as all duties, taxes and other charges payable upon export as referred to in A6 b);

b) any additional costs incurred, either because:
   (i) the buyer has failed to give appropriate notice in accordance with B7, or
   (ii) the vessel nominated by the buyer fails to arrive on time, is unable to take the goods, or closes for cargo earlier than the time notified in accordance with B7, provided that the goods have been clearly identified as the contract goods; and

c) where applicable, all duties, taxes and other charges, as well as the costs of carrying out customs formalities payable upon import of the goods and the costs for their transport through any country.

A7   Notices to the Buyer

The seller must, at the buyer's risk and expense, give the buyer sufficient notice either that the goods have been delivered in accordance with A4 or that the vessel has failed to take the goods within the time agreed.

A8   Delivery document

The seller must provide the buyer, at the seller's expense, with the usual proof that the goods have been delivered in accordance with A4.

Unless such proof is a transport document, the seller must provide assistance to the buyer, at the buyer's request, risk and expense, in obtaining a transport document.

A9   Checking-packaging-marking

The seller must pay the costs of those checking operations (such as checking quality, measuring, weighing, counting) that are necessary for the purpose of delivering the goods in accordance with A4, as well as the costs of any pre-shipment inspection mandated by the authority of the country of export.

The seller must, at its own expense, package the goods, unless it is usual for the particular trade to transport the type of goods sold unpackaged. The seller may package the goods in the manner appropriate for their transport, unless the buyer

B7   Notices to the Seller

The buyer must give the seller sufficient notice of the vessel name, loading point and, where necessary, the selected delivery time within the agreed period.

B8   Proof of delivery

The buyer must accept the proof of delivery provided as envisaged in A8.

B9   Inspection of goods

The buyer must pay the costs of any mandatory pre-shipment inspection, except when such inspection is mandated by the authorities of the country of export.

has notified the seller of specific packaging requirements before the contract of sale is concluded. Packaging is to be marked appropriately.

A10 Assistance with information and related costs

The seller must, where applicable, in a timely manner, provide to or render assistance in obtaining for the buyer, at the buyer's request, risk and expense, any documents and information, including security-related information, that the buyer needs for the import of the goods and/or for their transport to the final destination.

The seller must reimburse the buyer for all costs and charges incurred by the buyer in providing or rendering assistance in obtaining documents and information as envisaged in B10.

B10 Assistance with information and related costs

The buyer must, in a timely manner, advise the seller of any security information requirements so that the seller may comply with A10.

The buyer must reimburse the seller for all costs and charges incurred by the seller in providing or rendering assistance in obtaining documents and information as envisaged in A10.

The buyer must, where applicable, in a timely manner, provide to or render assistance in obtaining for the seller, at the seller's request, risk and expense, any documents and information, including security-related information, that the seller needs for the transport and export of the goods and for their transport through any country.

The ICC has also produced the Uniform Customs and Practice for Documentary Credits (UCP), discussed in the next section, to spell out the agreements represented by bank letters of credit. The UCP and Incoterms may be said to constitute part of a modern version of *lex mercatoria*—the customary rules that governed international transactions before the rise of legal positivism. They are codifications of international commercial practice and may be applied by courts or arbitrators, either because the parties have expressly incorporated them into their agreement or as evidence of custom or trade usage, which is allowed to supplement the parties' written agreement under the UCC, CISG, and many other bodies of contract law.

A little bit further down the line are rules of law that say that "x will be the rule unless provided otherwise." You have presumably encountered this when studying the UCC sections dealing with implied warranties on the sale of goods. The CISG also sets forth a set of implied terms for international sale of goods contracts. As a general matter, both the UCC and CISG allow the parties to exclude or vary their default terms by agreement.

You will recall from Chapter II.B that a brief reference to the rules of some organization managing international arbitrations can bring into play a large body of requirements. When the parties' contract is formed with an exchange of forms or letters, however, such a reference can raise difficult issues, as the following case illustrates.

Filanto, S.p.A. v. Chilewich International Corp.

U.S. District Court for the Southern District of New York, 1992
789 F.Supp. 1229

[The defendant Chilewich was an export-import firm incorporated in the state of New York and having its principal place of business there. On February 28, 1989, Chilewich's agent in the United Kingdom signed a contract to supply footwear to Raznoexport, a Soviet entity. Section 10 of this "Russian Contract" provided: "All disputes or differences which may arise out of or in connection with the present Contract are to be settled, jurisdiction of ordinary courts being excluded, by the Arbitration at the USSR Chamber of Commerce and Industry, Moscow, in accordance with the Regulations of the said Arbitration."

To fulfill this contract Chilewich entered a series of agreements with the plaintiff Filanto, an Italian footwear manufacturer. Chilewich's previous orders had attempted to incorporate by reference the terms of the Russian Contract, including the arbitration clause, into its agreements with Filanto, but Filanto had attempted to exclude all the terms of the Russian Contract except those related to packing, shipment, and delivery. On March 13, 1990, Chilewich sent Filanto a Memorandum Agreement ordering 250,000 pairs of boots to be shipped in two installments. The Memorandum Agreement again attempted to incorporate by reference the terms of the Russian Contract, including the arbitration clause. On May 7, 1990, Chilewich opened a letter of credit in favor of Filanto. On August 7, 1990, Filanto returned a signed copy of the Memorandum Agreement, but with a cover letter purporting to exclude all terms of the Russian Contract except those related to packing, shipment, and delivery. Chilewich took delivery of the first shipment of 100,000 pairs of boots on September 15, 1990, but accepted only 60,000 of the remaining 150,000 pairs in January 1991. Filanto brought suit for breach of contract in U.S. district court, and Chilewich moved to dismiss based on the arbitration clause. Excerpts from the opinion of Chief Judge Charles Brieant follow.]

. . . The United States, Italy and the USSR are all signatories to [the Convention on the Recognition and Enforcement of Foreign Arbitral Awards (commonly known as the New York Convention)] and its implementing legislation makes clear that the Arbitration Convention governs disputes regarding arbitration agreements between parties to international commercial transactions. . . . The Arbitration Convention specifically requires courts to recognize any "agreement in writing under which the parties undertake to submit to arbitration. . . ." The term "agreement in writing" is defined as "an arbitral clause in a contract or an arbitration agreement, signed by the parties or contained in an exchange of letters or telegrams". . . .

As enforced

* * *

Courts interpreting this "agreement in writing" requirement have generally started their analysis with the plain language of the Convention, which requires "an arbitral clause in a contract or an arbitration agreement, signed by the parties or contained in an exchange of letters or telegrams," Article I(1), and have then applied that language in light of federal law, which consists of generally accepted principles of contract law, including the Uniform Commercial Code. . . .

However, as plaintiff correctly notes, the "general principles of contract law" relevant to this action, do *not* include the Uniform Commercial Code; rather, the "federal law of contracts" to be applied in this case is found in the United Nations Convention on Contracts for the International Sale of Goods (the "Sale of Goods Convention"), *codified at* 15 U.S.C. Appendix (West Supp. 1991).[5] This Convention, ratified by the Senate in 1986, is a self-executing agreement which entered into force between the United States and other signatories, including Italy, on January 1, 1988. . . . Although there is as yet virtually no U.S. case law interpreting the Sale of Goods Convention . . . , it may safely be predicted that this will change: absent a choice-of-law provision, and with certain exclusions not here relevant, the Convention governs *all* contracts between parties with places of business in different nations, so long as both nations are signatories to the Convention. Sale of Goods Convention Article 1(1)(a). Since the contract alleged in this case most certainly was formed, if at all, after January 1, 1988, and since both the United States and Italy are signatories to the Convention, the Court will interpret the "agreement in writing" requirement of the Arbitration Convention in light of, and with reference to, the substantive international law of contracts embodied in the Sale of Goods Convention.

---

[5] Of course, as with the Arbitration Convention, the Sale of Goods Convention is also "state law." U.S. Const. art. VI cl. 2; *Hauenstein v. Lynham*, 100 U.S. 483, 490, 25 L.Ed. 628, 631 (1880) ("[T]he Constitution, laws, and treaties of the United States are as much a part of the law of every state as its own local laws and Constitution").

Not surprisingly, the parties offer varying interpretations of the numerous letters and documents exchanged between them. The Court will briefly summarize their respective contentions.

Defendant Chilewich contends that the Memorandum Agreement dated March 13 which it signed and sent to Filanto was an offer. It then argues that Filanto's retention of the letter, along with its subsequent acceptance of Chilewich's performance under the Agreement—the furnishing of the May 11 letter of credit—estops it from denying its acceptance of the contract. Although phrased as an estoppel argument, this contention is better viewed as an acceptance by conduct argument, e.g., that in light of the parties' course of dealing, Filanto had a duty timely to inform Chilewich that it objected to the incorporation by reference of all the terms of the Russian contract. Under this view, the return of the Memorandum Agreement, signed by Filanto, on August 7, 1990, along with the covering letter purporting to exclude parts of the Russian Contract, was ineffective as a matter of law as a rejection of the March 13 offer, because this occurred some five months after Filanto received the Memorandum Agreement and two months after Chilewich furnished the Letter of Credit. Instead, in Chilewich's view, this action was a proposal for modification of the March 13 Agreement. Chilewich rejected this proposal, by its letter of August 7 to Byerly Johnson, and the August 29 fax by Johnson to Italian Trading SRL, which communication Filanto acknowledges receiving. Accordingly, Filanto under this interpretation is bound by the written terms of the March 13 Memorandum Agreement; since that agreement incorporates by reference the Russian Contract containing the arbitration provision, Filanto is bound to arbitrate.

Plaintiff Filanto's interpretation of the evidence is rather different. While Filanto apparently agrees that the March 13 Memorandum Agreement was indeed an offer, it characterizes its August 7 return of the signed Memorandum Agreement with the covering letter as a counteroffer. While defendant contends that under Uniform Commercial Code § 2–207 this action would be viewed as an acceptance with a proposal for a material modification, the Uniform Commercial Code, as previously noted does not apply to this case, because the State Department undertook to fix something that was not broken by helping to create the Sale of Goods Convention which varies from the Uniform Commercial Code in many significant ways. Instead, under this analysis, Article 19(1) of the Sale of Goods Convention would apply. That section, as the Commentary to the Sale of Goods Convention notes, reverses the rule of Uniform Commercial Code § 2–207, and reverts to the common law rule that "A reply to an offer which purports to be an acceptance but contains additions, limitations or other modifications is a rejection of the offer and constitutes a counter-offer". Sale of Goods Convention Article 19(1). Although the Convention, like the Uniform Commercial Code, does state that non-material terms do become part of the contract unless objected to, Sale of Goods Convention Article 19(2), the Convention treats inclusion (or deletion) of an arbitration provision as "material," Sale of Goods Convention Article 19(3). The August 7 letter, therefore, was a counteroffer which, according to Filanto, Chilewich accepted by its letter dated September 27, 1990. Though that letter refers to and acknowledges the "contractual obligations" between the parties, it is doubtful whether it can be characterized as an acceptance.

More generally, both parties seem to have lost sight of the narrow scope of the inquiry required by the Arbitration Convention. . . . All that this Court need do is to determine if a sufficient "agreement in writing" to arbitrate disputes exists between these parties. . . . Although that inquiry is informed by the provisions of the Sale of Goods Convention, the Court lacks the authority on this motion to resolve all outstanding issues between the parties. . . .

* * *

The Court is satisfied on this record that there *was* indeed an agreement to arbitrate between these parties.

There is simply no satisfactory explanation as to why Filanto failed to object to the incorporation by reference of the Russian Contract in a timely fashion. As noted above, Chilewich had in the meantime commenced its performance under the Agreement, and the Letter of Credit it furnished Filanto on May 11 *itself* mentioned the Russian Contract. An offeree who, knowing that the offeror has commenced performance, fails to notify the offeror of its objection to the terms of the contract within a reasonable time will, under certain circumstances, be deemed to have assented to those terms. Restatement (Second) of Contracts § 69 (1981). . . . The Sale of Goods Convention itself recognizes this rule: Article 18(1), provides that "A statement made by or other conduct of the offeree indicating assent to an offer is an acceptance". Although mere "silence or inactivity" does not constitute acceptance, Sale of Goods Convention Article 18(1), the Court may consider previous relations between the parties in assessing whether a party's conduct constituted acceptance, Sale of Goods Convention Article 8(3). In this case, in light of the extensive course of prior dealing between these parties, Filanto was certainly under a duty to alert Chilewich in timely fashion to its objections to the terms of the March 13 Memorandum Agreement—particularly since Chilewich had repeatedly referred it to the Russian Contract and Filanto had had a copy of that document for some time.

There [is another] convincing manifestation[ ] of Filanto's true understanding of the terms of this agreement. . . .

* * *

. . . Filanto, in a letter to Byerly Johnson dated June 21, 1991, explicitly stated that "[t]he April Shipment and the September shipment are governed by the Master Purchase Contract of February 28, 1989 [the

Russian Contract]"... . Furthermore, the letter, which responds to claims by Johnson that some of the boots that *were* supplied were defective, expressly relies on section 9 of the Russian Contract—another section which Filanto had in its earlier correspondence purported to exclude. The Sale of Goods Convention specifically directs that "[i]n determining the intent of a party . . . due consideration is to be given to . . . any subsequent conduct of the parties," Sale of Goods Convention Article 8(3). In this case, as the letter post-dates the partial performance of the contract, it is particularly strong evidence that Filanto recognized itself to be bound by *all* the terms of the Russian Contract.

In light of these factors, and heeding the presumption in favor of arbitration, *Moses H. Cone* [*Memorial Hospital v. Mercury Construction Corp.*, 460 U.S. 1, 24–26, 103 S.Ct. 927, 941–42, 74 L.Ed. 2d 765, 785–86 (1983)], which is even stronger in the context of international commercial transactions, *Mitsubishi Motors Corp. v. Soler Chrysler-Plymouth, Inc.*, 473 U.S. 614, 631, 105 S.Ct. 3346, 3356, 87 L.Ed.2d 444, 458 (1985), the Court holds that Filanto is bound by the terms of the March 13 Memorandum Agreement, and so must arbitrate its dispute in Moscow.[6]

* * *

QUESTIONS

(1) Which law governs the contract created by the buyer's receipt in China of the goods covered by the invoice, supra p. 152? Would U.S. and Chinese courts come to the same conclusion on this point? Would you advise the seller to include an American choice-of-law clause in its standard invoice form?

(2) If the seller wanted to opt out of the CISG, how should the choice-of-law clause be written?

(3) Are the clauses in the invoice limiting the seller's liability enforceable under New York law? Under Chinese law?

(4) Under this contract, who must pay the cost of shipping the goods from New York to China? If the goods are damaged during shipment, who bears the risk of loss?

(5) Suppose that the buyer, in a letter confirming its order, states that it will pay in 90 days, net. Does this permit a court to decide that a contract exists? If so, on what terms?

Additional reading: Ling, Contract Law in China (2002); Schlechtriem & Schwenzer, Commentary on the UN Convention on the International Sale of Goods (4th ed. 2016); Honnold & Flechtner, Uniform Law for International Sales Under the 1980 United Nations Convention (4th ed. 2009); Gillette & Walt, Sales Law: Domestic and International (3d ed. 2016).

---

[6] [Eds.] The court rejected an argument that Moscow, then involved in civil unrest, was not a suitable venue for arbitration.

C. TRANSPORTATION AND FINANCING IN INTERNATIONAL TRADE

Although the sales agreement will likely contain provisions dealing with transportation and payment, those questions may implicate bodies of law other than those that govern the contract itself. They may also bring third parties into the transaction, such as shipping companies and banks.

1. TRANSPORTATION

Which party is responsible for arranging transportation depends on the parties' agreement. Use of an Incoterm beginning with "E" or "F" makes the buyer responsible. Under a "C" or "D" Incoterm, the seller must arrange for transportation. Historically, most international trade in goods has traveled by sea, and much of the law of international transportation is derived from practices that developed for the carriage of goods by sea. It is important to note, however, that certain delivery terms such as FOB, CFR, and CIF are not appropriate to air, land, or multimodal transportation, and parties who plan to use such transportation should employ their non-maritime equivalents—FCA, CPT, and CIP.

The party responsible for arranging transportation will frequently rely on the services of a freight forwarder, who books space for the cargo and may also handle customs, arrange for insurance, and pay port and terminal charges. Assuming that the goods are traveling by sea, the carrier will issue a marine bill of lading. This bill of lading serves several functions. First, it is a receipt showing that the goods have been delivered for shipment and describing their quantity and condition. A "clean" bill of lading indicates that the goods show no apparent damage. An "on board" bill of lading further indicates that the goods have been loaded on the ship. Second, the bill of lading carries the right to receive physical delivery of the goods. If it is made out "to order," then the bill of lading is negotiable and may be transferred to another party, thereby transferring the right to receive the goods. Banks typically require negotiable bills of lading as security in the letter-of-credit transactions described below.

Finally, the bill of lading is the contract with the carrier and either contains its terms or incorporates them by reference to another document. These contracts are heavily regulated by national law and international conventions. There are three separate, and sometimes conflicting, international regimes governing carriage and bills of lading: the 1924 Hague Rules, which have been adopted by approximately 80 countries; the 1968 Hague-Visby Rules, an amendment of the Hague Rules adopted by more than 30 countries; and the 1978 Hamburg Rules, which have been adopted by relatively few important trading countries. The United States has enacted the Hague Rules into domestic law through the Carriage of Goods by Sea Act (COGSA), 46 U.S.C. §§ 1300–

1315. COGSA governs the contents of bills of lading and the liabilities of shippers, providing among other things for a $500 per package limitation on the carrier's liability for loss or damage, a limitation many commentators think is out of date. Although COGSA applies to all bills for the carriage of goods by sea to or from a U.S. port, it does not apply when damage to the goods occurs on land, in which case the carrier's liability is governed by the earlier Harter Act, 46 U.S.C. §§ 190–196. This legislative scheme has created a lack of uniformity for bills of lading even as a matter of U.S. domestic law.

Greater uniformity could be achieved through wide adoption of the Rotterdam Rules set forth in the 2008 United Nations Convention on Contracts for the International Carriage of Goods Wholly or Partly by Sea. Among other changes, the Rotterdam Rules extend the carrier's responsibility from the time the goods are received to the time they are delivered ("door-to-door" rather than "tackle-to-tackle" coverage) and would eliminate COGSA's $500 per package limitation. The United States has signed but not ratified the Convention, and the Rotterdam Rules will not go in effect for any country until 20 nations have ratified the Convention.

2. FINANCING

The financing of transnational sales involves risks that do not exist, or do not exist to the same degree, in domestic sales transactions. Over the years, mechanisms have been developed to help the parties to a transnational sale manage these risks.

The parties to a transnational sale often operate in different countries with different currencies. The contract of sale will usually provide for the price to be paid in one of these currencies, and the party whose currency is not chosen will then be exposed to what is known as currency or exchange-rate risk. This is simply the risk that the exchange rate between two currencies will shift to a party's disadvantage. Assume for example that American Computer Company agrees to buy computer equipment from China Computer Company at a price denominated in Chinese yuan. If the yuan subsequently strengthens against the dollar, American Computer Company will find that the equipment has become more expensive for it to buy. There are several ways for a buyer to "hedge" its currency risk. One is for the buyer to purchase enough of the seller's currency at the time the contract is made to cover the price when payment is due. Another option available for some currencies is to buy a forward exchange contract, typically with a bank, to purchase currency at a specified exchange rate at a date in the future. It locks in a particular exchange rate and ensures that the buyer will have the currency it needs when payment is due. A closely related alternative is the non-deliverable forward contract under which there is no physical delivery of the foreign currency and the bank instead pays or receives an amount reflecting the difference between the agreed exchange rate and the actual exchange rate on the forward date. A seller who agrees to take payment in the buyer's currency may hedge its currency risk in the same ways.

For the seller, there is also the risk that the buyer will default. The buyer's government might impose currency controls that prevent or delay payment, or the buyer might run into financial difficulties independent of its government. A seller may protect against the risk of non-payment for political or commercial reasons by purchasing export credit insurance from the U.S. Export-Import Bank.

More generally, for each party there is the risk that the other will not perform its contractual obligations. Of course, this risk exists in domestic transactions as well, but it is exacerbated in an international setting because each party may have less knowledge of the other's creditworthiness and because remedies for non-performance might have to be sought in the other party's legal system. Much of this risk, at least on a short-term basis, has been assumed by banks, particularly by banks that do business in the buyer's home community. They should be familiar with the buyer's credit standing and are in a better position to bring suit against the buyer and to absorb any eventual losses out of reserves against the whole of their portfolio of risks. A standard vehicle has been the letter of credit or documentary credit, a device that is not common in domestic transactions. A letter of credit provides that the seller will be paid by a bank upon the presentation of certain documents, including a bill of lading showing that the goods have been shipped. The letter of credit gives the buyer assurance that payment will not be made until the seller has delivered the goods to the carrier, and gives the seller assurance that it may look to a bank for payment as soon as shipment has been made.

If the parties intend to use a letter of credit, the sales contract should specify the kind to be used. Commercial letters of credit come in several variations. In theory, they can be "revocable" or "irrevocable," although in practice irrevocable letters of credit are almost always used. Credits that are silent on this point are deemed to be irrevocable. Letters of credit can be "advised" or "confirmed." As explained below, a confirmed letter of credit provides the seller with a promise to pay both from the issuing bank and from a confirming bank in the seller's own country; an advised letter of credit provides the seller with a promise to pay only from the issuing bank. Letters of credit can be "sight" credits, which entitle the seller to payment immediately upon the bank's determination that the documents conform to the terms of the letter of credit, or they can be "time" credits, which entitle the seller to payment at some specified time in the future. The parties might alternatively choose to use a standby letter of credit under which the bank is obligated to pay the seller only if the buyer does not.

If the sales contract calls for payment by letter of credit, the buyer, who in this context is often called the "applicant," will apply for such a credit at its bank. If the bank is satisfied with the buyer's creditworthiness, it will (for a fee) issue a letter of credit in favor of the seller, who is often called the "beneficiary." The letter of credit is a promise by the issuing bank to pay the seller a particular amount upon presentation of documents specified in the letter of credit. These documents usually include: the seller's draft or bill of exchange, which is simply the seller's demand for payment; the bill of lading; a commercial invoice; a packing list; and a certificate of origin. Depending upon the terms of the sales contract, the documents may also include an insurance certificate and an inspection certificate.

The issuing bank typically will then request that another bank in the seller's country either "advise" or "confirm" the letter of credit. An advising bank simply notifies the seller that a letter of credit has been opened in its favor. It acts as a conduit for the issuing bank, but does not itself make any promise to pay the seller. A confirming bank, on the other hand, adds its own promise to pay the seller upon the presentation of the conforming documents. A seller will generally prefer a confirmed letter of credit because it allows the seller to seek payment from a bank that is in its own country and is clearly subject to its own legal system, but of course banks charge an additional fee to confirm letters of credit.

The issuing bank will most often transmit the letter of credit to the advising or confirming bank using SWIFT (the acronym for the Society for Worldwide Interbank Financial Telecommunictions). The example below is presented in SWIFT MT 700, the format for documentary credits. Numbers to the left refer to "fields" in the SWIFT format. Note that, in contrast to the invoice at the start of this problem, in this example the U.S. company is the buyer and the Chinese company is the seller.[7]

SENDER:	NEW YORK BANK
	100 WALL STREET
	NEW YORK, NY 10005
RECEIVER:	BAODUI BANK
	100 JINRONG JIE
	BEIJING, CHINA 100140

SWIFT AUTHENTICATED MESSAGE
ISSUE OF DOCUMENTARY CREDIT (TYPE: 700)

:27:	SEQUENCE OF TOTAL:	
	1/1	
:40:	FORM OF DOCUMENTARY CREDIT:	
	IRREVOCABLE	
:20:	DOCUMENTARY CREDIT NUMBER:	
	12345	
:31C:	DATE OF ISSUE:	
	190109	
:40E:	APPLICABLE RULES:	

---

[7]   Adapted from Bank of America, Solutions for Exporters: An Exporter's Guide to Trade Services (2012).

UCP LATEST VERSION

:31D: DATE AND PLACE OF EXPIRY:
          190224 NEW YORK, NY

:50:   APPLICANT:
          AMERICAN COMPUTER CO.
          755 COENTIES SLIP
          NEW YORK, NY 10017

:59:   BENEFICIARY:
          ZHONGGUO DIANNAO GONGSI
          500 ZHONGGUANCUN DAJIE
          BEIJING, CHINA 100080

:32B: CURRENCY CODE, AMOUNT:
          USD 100,000

:41A: AVAILABLE WITH ... BY ... :
          NEW YORK BANK
          100 WALL STREET
          NEW YORK, NY 10005
          BY ACCEPTANCE

:42C: DRAFTS AT ... :
          90 DAYS SIGHT
          FOR 100 PCT INVOICE VALUE

:42A: DRAWEE:
          BAODUI BANK
          BEIJING, CHINA

:44E: PORT OF LOADING:
          TIANJIN, CHINA

:44F: PORT OF DISCHARGE:
          NEW YORK, NEW YORK

:44C: LATEST DATE OF SHIPMENT:
          190214

:45A: DESCRIPTION OF GOODS AND/OR SERVICES:
          COMPUTER EQUIPMENT ACCORDING TO
          P.O. NO. 54321
          FOB TIANJIN, CHINA

:46A: DOCUMENTS REQUIRED:
          SIGNED COMMERCIAL INVOICE IN
          ORIGINAL AND TWO COPIES
          PACKING LIST IN ORIGINAL AND TWO
          COPIES
          FULL SET OF CLEAN ON BOARD BILL OF
          LADING CONSIGNED TO ORDER OF SHIPPER
          CERTIFICATE OF ORIGIN

:71B: CHARGES:
          BANKING CHARGES ARE FOR ACCOUNT OF
          APPLICANT, EXCEPT FOR DOCUMENTARY
          DISCREPANCY CHARGES, IF ANY, WHICH
          ARE FOR ACCOUNT OF BENEFICIARY

:49:   CONFIRMATION INSTRUCTIONS:
          CONFIRM
          REGARDS

After the seller has delivered the goods to the carrier for shipment and obtained a bill of lading, it presents the bill of lading and other documents called for in the letter of credit to the confirming bank, the issuing bank, or a nominated bank acting on their behalf. The bank will check the documents to determine whether they appear on their face to be in compliance with the terms of the letter of credit and will pay the seller if they do. If they do not, the bank will notify the seller of the discrepancies, which the seller may attempt to correct. If the discrepancies cannot be corrected, the bank or the seller may seek a waiver from the buyer, which the buyer will often give if the discrepancies are minor and there are strong commercial reasons for going ahead with the deal. If the credit is a confirmed letter of credit, the confirming bank will forward the documents to the issuing bank, which will make its own examination of the documents. Once the issuing bank finds the documents to be conforming, it will release the documents to the buyer and debit its account. The buyer will then use the bill of lading to obtain the goods from the carrier.

Because the letter of credit requires payment based upon the presentation of conforming documents, the bank's examination of those documents is a critical step in the transaction. Banks have insisted on strict compliance, rejecting documents for trivial discrepancies, and courts have supported them. In the well-known words of an English court, "[t]here is no room for documents which are almost the same, or which will do just as well."[8] The current standards under which banks examine documents for compliance with letters of credit are set forth in the 2007 version of the Uniform Customs and Practices for Documentary Credits, commonly known as UCP 600.[9] UCP 600 is a set of rules produced by the ICC that virtually all banks incorporate by reference to govern their letters of credit:

Article 14

Standard for Examination of Documents

a.   A nominated bank acting on its nomination, a confirming bank, if any, and the issuing bank must examine a presentation to determine, on the basis of the documents alone, whether or not the documents appear on their face to constitute a complying presentation.

---

[8]   Equitable Trust Co. v. Dawson Partners, Ltd., 27 Lloyd's List L. Rep. 49, 52 (H.L.) (1926).

[9]   Earlier versions of the UCP were published in 1933, 1951, 1962, 1974, 1983, and 1993. There is also a supplement to the UCP for the presentation of electronic documents, known as the eUCP. Standby letters of credit are generally issued subject to ISP 98, a different set of rules produced by the ICC.

b. A nominated bank acting on its nomination, a confirming bank, if any, and the issuing bank shall each have a maximum of five banking days following the day of presentation to determine if a presentation is complying. This period is not curtailed or otherwise affected by the occurrence on or after the date of presentation of any expiry date or last day for presentation.

c. A presentation including one or more original transport documents subject to articles 19, 20, 21, 22, 23, 24 or 25 must be made by or on behalf of the beneficiary not later than 21 calendar days after the date of shipment as described in these rules, but in any event not later than the expiry date of the credit.

d. Data in a document, when read in context with the credit, the document itself and international standard banking practice, need not be identical to, but must not conflict with, data in that document, any other stipulated document or the credit.

e. In documents other than the commercial invoice, the description of the goods, services or performance, if stated, may be in general terms not conflicting with their description in the credit.

f. If a credit requires presentation of a document other than a transport document, insurance document or commercial invoice, without stipulating by whom the document is to be issued or its data content, banks will accept the document as presented if its content appears to fulfil the function of the required document and otherwise complies with sub-article 14(d).

g. A document presented but not required by the credit will be disregarded and may be returned to the presenter.

h. If a credit contains a condition without stipulating the document to indicate compliance with the condition, banks will deem such condition as not stated and will disregard it.

i. A document may be dated prior to the issuance date of the credit, but must not be dated later than its date of presentation.

j. When the addresses of the beneficiary and the applicant appear in any stipulated document, they need not be the same as those stated in the credit or in any other stipulated document, but must be within the same country as the respective addresses mentioned in the credit. Contact details (telefax, telephone, email and the like) stated as part of the beneficiary's and the applicant's address will be disregarded. However, when the address and contact details of the applicant appear as part of the consignee or notify party details on a transport document subject to articles 19, 20, 21, 22, 23, 24 or 25, they must be stated in the credit.

k.   The shipper or consignor of the goods indicated on any document need not be the beneficiary of the credit.

l.   A transport document may be issued by any party other than a carrier, owner, master or charterer provided that the transport document meets the requirements of articles 19, 20, 21, 22, 23 or 24 of these rules.

Article 15

Complying Presentation

a.   When an issuing bank determines that a presentation is complying, it must honour.

b.   When a confirming bank determines that a presentation is complying, it must honour or negotiate and forward the documents to the issuing bank.

c.   When a nominated bank determines that a presentation is complying and honours or negotiates, it must forward the documents to the confirming bank or issuing bank.

Article 16

Discrepant Documents, Waiver and Notice

a.   When a nominated bank acting on its nomination, a confirming bank, if any, or the issuing bank determines that a presentation does not comply, it may refuse to honour or negotiate.

b.   When an issuing bank determines that a presentation does not comply, it may in its sole judgement approach the applicant for a waiver of the discrepancies. This does not, however, extend the period mentioned in sub-article 14(b).

c.   When a nominated bank acting on its nomination, a confirming bank, if any, or the issuing bank decides to refuse to honour or negotiate, it must give a single notice to that effect to the presenter.

The notice must state:

i.   that the bank is refusing to honour or negotiate; and

ii.   each discrepancy in respect of which the bank refuses to honour or negotiate; and

iii. a)   that the bank is acting in accordance with instructions previously received from the presenter.

b)   that the issuing bank is holding the documents until it receives a waiver from the applicant and agrees to accept it, or receives further instructions from the presenter prior to agreeing to accept a waiver; or

c)   that the bank is returning the documents; or

d)   that the bank is acting in accordance with instructions previously received from the presenter.

d.   The notice required in sub-article 16(c) must be given by telecommunication or, if that is not possible, by other expeditious means no later than the close of the fifth banking day following the day of presentation.

e.   A nominated bank acting on its nomination, a confirming bank, if any, or the issuing bank may, after providing notice required by sub-article 16(c)(iii)(a) or (b), return the documents to the presenter at any time.

f.   If an issuing bank or a confirming bank fails to act in accordance with the provisions of this article, it shall be precluded from claiming that the documents do not constitute a complying presentation.

g.   When an issuing bank refuses to honour or a confirming bank refuses to honour or negotiate and has given notice to that effect in accordance with this article, it shall then be entitled to claim a refund, with interest, of any reimbursement made.

It is also important to understand that the letter of credit is independent of the underlying sales contract, so that neither the banks nor the buyer may resist a demand for payment accompanied by conforming documents on the ground that the seller has breached the sales contract. See UCP 600 Art. 4. As UCP Article 5 puts it, "[b]anks deal with documents and not with goods, services or performance to which the documents may relate." Courts, however, have created an exception for cases of fraud that is generally traced to the following case.

Sztejn v. J. Henry Schroder Banking Corporation

Supreme Court, Special Term, New York County, 1941
31 N.Y.S.2d 631, 177 Misc. 719

■ SHIENTAG, JUSTICE

This is a motion by the defendant, the Chartered Bank of India, Australia and China, (hereafter referred to as the Chartered Bank), made pursuant to Rule 106(5) of the Rules of Civil Practice to dismiss the supplemental complaint on the ground that it fails to state facts sufficient to constitute a cause of action against the moving defendant. The plaintiff brings this action to restrain the payment or presentment for payment of drafts under a letter of credit issued to secure the purchase price of certain merchandise, bought by the plaintiff and his coadventurer, one Schwarz, who is a party defendant in this action. The plaintiff also seeks a judgment declaring the letter of credit and drafts thereunder null and void. The complaint alleges that the documents accompanying the drafts are fraudulent in that they do not represent actual merchandise but instead cover boxes fraudulently filled with worthless material by the seller of the goods. The moving defendant urges that the complaint fails to state a cause of action against it because the Chartered Bank is only concerned with the documents and on their face these conform to the requirements of the letter of credit.

On January 7, 1941, the plaintiff and his coadventurer contracted to purchase a quantity of bristles from the defendant Transea Traders, Ltd. (hereafter referred to as Transea) a corporation having its place of business in Lucknow, India. In order to pay for the bristles, the plaintiff and Schwarz contracted with the defendant J. Henry Schroder Banking Corporation (hereafter referred to as Schroder), a domestic corporation, for the issuance of an irrevocable letter of credit to Transea which provided that drafts by the latter for a specified portion of the purchase price of the bristles would be paid by Schroder upon shipment of the described merchandise and presentation of an invoice and a bill of lading covering the shipment, made out to the order of Schroder.

The letter of credit was delivered to Transea by Schroder's correspondent bank in India, Transea placed fifty cases of material on board a steamship, procured a bill of lading from the steamship company and obtained the customary invoices. These documents describe the bristles called for by the letter of credit. However, the complaint alleges that in fact Transea filled the fifty crates with cowhair, other worthless material and rubbish with intent to simulate genuine merchandise and defraud the plaintiff and Schwarz. The complaint then alleges that Transea drew a draft under the letter of credit to the order of the Chartered Bank and delivered the draft and the fraudulent documents to the "Chartered Bank at Cawnpore, India, for collection for the account of said defendant Transea." The Chartered Bank has presented the draft along with the documents to Schroder for payment. The plaintiff prays for a judgment declaring the letter of credit and draft thereunder void and for injunctive relief to prevent the payment of the draft.

For the purposes of this motion, the allegations of the complaint must be deemed established and "every intendment and fair inference is in favor of the pleading". . . . Therefore, it must be assumed that Transea was engaged in a scheme to defraud the plaintiff and Schwarz, that the merchandise shipped by Transea is worthless rubbish and that the Chartered Bank is not an innocent holder of the draft for value but is merely attempting to procure payment of the draft for Transea's account.

It is well established that a letter of credit is independent of the primary contract of sale between the buyer and the seller. The issuing bank agrees to pay upon presentation of documents, not goods. This rule is necessary to preserve the efficiency of the letter of credit as an instrument for the financing of trade. One of the chief purposes of the letter of credit is to furnish the seller with a ready means of obtaining prompt payment for his merchandise. It would be a most unfortunate interference with business transactions if a bank before honoring drafts drawn upon it was obliged or even allowed to go behind the documents, at the request of the buyer and enter into controversies between the buyer and the seller regarding the quality of the merchandise shipped. If the buyer and the seller intended the bank to do this they could have so provided in the letter of credit itself, and in the absence of such a provision, the court will not demand or even permit the bank to delay paying drafts which are proper in form. . . . Of course, the application of this doctrine presupposes that the documents accompanying the draft are genuine and conform in terms to the requirements of the letter of credit. . . .

However, I believe that a different situation is presented in the instant action. This is not a controversy between the buyer and seller concerning a mere breach of warranty regarding the quality of the merchandise; on the present motion, it must be assumed that the seller has intentionally failed to ship any goods ordered by the buyer. In such a situation, where the seller's fraud has been called to the bank's attention before the drafts and documents have been presented for payment, the principle of the independence of the bank's obligation under the letter of credit should not be extended to protect the unscrupulous seller. It is true that even though the documents are forged or fraudulent, if the issuing bank has already paid the draft before receiving notice of the seller's fraud, it will be protected if it exercised reasonable diligence before making such payment. . . . However, in the instant action Schroder has received notice of Transea's active fraud before it accepted or paid the draft. The Chartered Bank, which under the allegations of the complaint stands in no better position than Transea, should not be heard to complain because Schroder is not forced to pay the draft accompanied by documents covering a transaction which it has reason to believe is fraudulent.

Although our courts have used broad language to the effect that a letter of credit is independent of the primary contract between the buyer and seller, that language was used in cases concerning alleged breaches of warranty; no case has been brought to my attention on this point involving an intentional fraud on the part of the seller which was brought to the bank's notice with the request that it withhold payment of the draft on this account. The distinction between a breach of warranty and active fraud on the part of the seller is supported by authority and reason. As one court has stated: "Obviously, when the issuer of a letter of credit knows that a document, although correct in form, is, in point of fact, false or illegal, he cannot be called upon to recognize such a document as complying with the terms of a letter of credit." . . .

No hardship will be caused by permitting the bank to refuse payment where fraud is claimed, where the merchandise is not merely inferior in quality but consists of worthless rubbish, where the draft and the accompanying documents are in the hands of one who stands in the same position as the fraudulent seller, where the bank has been given notice of the fraud before being presented with the drafts and documents for payment, and where the bank itself does not wish to pay pending an adjudication of the rights and obligations of the other parties. While the primary factor in the issuance of the letter of credit is the credit standing of the buyer, the security afforded by the merchandise is also taken into account. In fact, the letter of credit requires a bill of lading made out to the order of the bank and not the buyer. Although the bank is not interested in the exact detailed performance of the sales contract, it is vitally interested in assuring itself that there are some goods represented by the documents. . . .

On this motion only the complaint is before me and I am bound by its allegation that the Chartered Bank is not a holder in due course but is a mere agent for collection for the account of the seller charged with fraud. Therefore, the Chartered Bank's motion to dismiss the complaint must be denied. If it had appeared from the face of the complaint that the bank presenting the draft for payment was a holder in due course, its claim against the bank issuing the letter of credit would not be defeated even though the primary transaction was tainted with fraud. This I believe to the better rule despite some authority to the contrary. . . .

The plaintiff's further claim that the terms of the documents presented with the draft are at substantial variance with the requirements of the letter of credit does not seem to be supported by the documents themselves.

Accordingly, the defendant's motion to dismiss the supplemental complaint is denied.

The fraud exception or *Sztejn* exception was incorporated in UCC § 5–114. When Article 5 was revised in 1995, the exception was redrafted to remove ambiguities and moved to § 5–109:

§ 5–109. Fraud and Forgery

(a) If a presentation is made that appears on its face strictly to comply with the terms and conditions of the letter of credit, but a required document is forged or materially fraudulent, or honor of the presentation would facilitate a material fraud by the beneficiary on the issuer or applicant:

> (1) the issuer shall honor the presentation, if honor is demanded by (i) a nominated person who has given value in good faith and without notice of forgery or material fraud, (ii) a confirmer who has honored its confirmation in good faith, (iii) a holder in due course of a draft drawn under the letter of credit which was taken after acceptance by the issuer or nominated person, or (iv) an assignee of the issuer's or nominated person's deferred obligation that was taken for value and without notice of forgery or material fraud after the obligation was incurred by the issuer or nominated person; and

> (2) the issuer, acting in good faith, may honor or dishonor the presentation in any other case.

(b) If an applicant claims that a required document is forged or materially fraudulent or that honor of the presentation would facilitate a material fraud by the beneficiary on the issuer or applicant, a court of competent jurisdiction may temporarily or permanently enjoin the issuer from honoring a presentation or grant similar relief against the issuer or other persons only if the court finds that:

(1) the relief is not prohibited under the law applicable to an accepted draft or deferred obligation incurred by the issuer;

(2) a beneficiary, issuer, or nominated person who may be adversely affected is adequately protected against loss that it may suffer because the relief is granted;

(3) all of the conditions to entitle a person to the relief under the law of this State have been met; and

(4) on the basis of the information submitted to the court, the applicant is more likely than not to succeed under its claim of forgery or material fraud and the person demanding honor does not qualify for protection under subsection (a)(1).

QUESTIONS

(1) From the seller's point of view, what are the advantages of being paid through a letter of credit? Does American Computer Company's invoice call for payment by a letter of credit? Should it?

(2) Review the sample letter of credit on pp. 177–179 supra. Is it revocable or irrevocable, advised or confirmed, sight or time? What documents must the seller present to obtain payment? Who is responsible for paying the banks' fees?

(3) In a surprisingly large percentage of cases—50% or more—the documents presented by sellers under letters of credit contain discrepancies, yet it appears that banks routinely obtain waivers of such discrepancies from buyers. Since a seller who presents non-conforming documents is not entitled to payment unless the buyer waives the discrepancies, does this suggest that the bank's guarantee of payment is not the principal reason why letters of credit are used in transnational sales? What other function might they serve?

(4) Suppose your client Emptor's, a California department store chain, has entered a contract to buy 50,000 pairs of women's red pumps from Imelda Shoe Manufacturing, Inc., a Philippines company, with payment to be made through an irrevocable, confirmed, sight letter of credit upon the presentation of a bill of lading and other documents. Emptor's learns after confirmation of the letter of credit that other department stores that have ordered red pumps from Imelda have received women's black flats instead, although the bills of lading reflected the shipment of red pumps. If Emptor's is concerned it too may be shipped

black flats, what steps may it take to prevent payment on the letter of credit?

(5) UCP 600 contains no explicit exception that would allow payment to be stopped in cases of fraud. If a letter of credit provides that it is governed by UCP 600, may a buyer who can show that a required document is materially fraudulent still seek to enjoin payment under UCC § 5–109?

Additional reading: Jiménez, ICC Guide to Export/Import (4th ed. 2012); Sturley, Uniformity in the Law Governing the Carriage of Goods by Sea, 26 J. Mar. L. & Com. 553 (1995); Sturley, Modernizing and Reforming U.S. Maritime Law: The Impact of the Rotterdam Rules in the United States, 44 Tex. Int'l L.J. 427 (2009); Mann, The Role of Letters of Credit in Payment Transactions, 98 Mich. L. Rev. 2494 (2000), and comments thereon by Gillette, Corré, and Katz.

D. U.S. REGULATION OF EXPORT TRADE

In this section we focus on two types of regulation affecting exports from the United States: export controls and anti-boycott legislation. It is important to note that each of these regulations may apply to transactions other than export sales. U.S. export control regulations govern not just the sale of goods but also the transfer of technology, and may therefore be implicated in licensing transactions. U.S. anti-boycott legislation prohibits not just a refusal to do business for boycott reasons but also discrimination in employment for such reasons.

1. U.S. EXPORT CONTROLS

U.S. Export Administration Regulations (EAR) require a license from the Bureau of Industry and Security (BIS) within the Department of Commerce for the export of certain products and technologies.[10] "Export" is defined to include not only the shipment of a product or the transmission of technology out of the United States, but also releasing technology or source code to a foreign person in the United States. 15 C.F.R. § 734.13.

The starting point for determining whether a license is required is to find out whether the item in question is on the Commerce Control List (CCL), 15 C.F.R. Part 774, Supplement No. 1. The ten categories of the CCL are: (0) nuclear materials, facilities and equipment, and miscellaneous; (1) materials, chemicals, "microorganisms," and toxins; (2) materials processing; (3) electronics; (4) computers; (5) telecommunications and information security; (6) lasers and sensors; (7)

---

[10] Since the expiration of the Export Administration Act of 1979 in 2001, the Export Administration Regulations had been continued under the International Emergency Economic Powers Act (IEEPA), 50 U.S.C.A. §§ 1701–1706. In 2018, Congress repealed the Export Administration Act, replacing it with the Export Controls Act of 2018. 50 U.S.C.A. §§ 4811–4826. The Export Controls Act provides new legislative authorization for the existing regulations, which continue in effect until modified.

navigation and avionics; (8) marine; and (9) aerospace and propulsion. An illustrative listing follows:

4A001 Electronic computers and related equipment, having any of the following (*see* List of Items Controlled), and "electronic assemblies" and "specially designed" "components" therefor.

LICENSE REQUIREMENTS

Reasons for Control: NS, MT, AT, NP

Control(s)	Country Chart
NS applies to entire entry	NS Column 2.
MT applies to items in 4A001.a when the parameters in 4A101 are met or exceeded.	MT Column 1.
AT applies to entire entry	AT Column 1.

NP applies, unless a License Exemption is available. See § 742.3(b) of the EAR for information on applicable licensing review policies.

* * *

LICENSE EXCEPTIONS

LVS [shipments of limited value]: $5000 for 4A001.a; N/A for MT

GBS [shipments to Country Group B countries[11]]: N/A

CIV [civil end-users]: N/A

STA [strategic trade authorization]: License Exception STA may not be used to ship any commodity in 4A001.a.2 to any of the destinations listed in Country Group A:6 (See Suppement No. 1 to part 740 of the EAR [Albania, Hong Kong, India, Israel, Malta, Singapore, South Africa, and Taiwan].

LIST OF ITEMS CONTROLLED

* * *

Items:

a. "Specially designed" to have any of the following:

a.1. Rated for operations at an ambient temperature below 228 K (−45 °C) or above 358 K (85 °C);

Note: 4A001.a.1. does not apply to computers "specially designed" for civil automobile, railway train applications, or "civil aircraft" applications.

a.2. Radiation hardened to exceed any of the following specifications:

---

[11] [Eds.] This list, published at 15 C.F.R. Part 740, Supp. 1, includes approximately 170 countries, but not Russia or China.

a.2.a. A total dose of 5×10^3 Gy (Si);

a.2.b. A dose rate upset of 5×10^6 Gy (Si)/s; *or*

a.2.c. Single Event Upset of 1×10^{-8} Error/bit/day;

Note: 4A001.a.2. does not apply to computers "specially designed" for "civil aircraft" applications.

Note that the entry for each Export Control Classification Number or ECCN starts with a mention of the reason(s) for limiting exports of that item. These reasons, listed in § 738.2 and outlined in Part 742, are concerns about anti-terrorism (AT), chemical and biological weapons (CB), crime control (CC), chemical weapons convention (CW), encryption items (EI), firearms convention (FC), missile technology (MT), national security (NS), nuclear nonproliferation (NP), regional stability (RS), short supply (SS), United Nations embargo (UN), significant items (SI), and surreptitious listening (SL). Having concluded that one's intended export is on the CCL, one's next resort is to the Country Chart (Part 738, Supp. 1), which looks like this:

Pt. 738, Supp. No. 1   15 CFR Ch. VII (1–1–18 Edition)

SUPPLEMENT No. 1 TO PART 738—COMMERCE COUNTRY CHART

[Reason for control]

Countries	Chemical and biological weapons			Nuclear non-proliferation		National security		Missile tech	Regional stability		Firearms convention	Crime control			Anti-terrorism	
	CB 1	CB 2	CB 3	NP 1	NP 2	NS 1	NS 2	MT 1	RS 1	RS 2	FC 1	CC 1	CC 2	CC 3	AT 1	AT 2
Afghanistan	×	×		×		×	×	×	×	×		×		×		
Albania [2][3]	×	×		×		×	×	×	×	×		×		×		
Algeria	×	×		×		×	×	×	×	×		×		×		
Andorra	×	×		×		×	×	×	×	×		×		×		
Angola	×	×		×		×	×	×	×	×		×		×		
Antigua and Barbuda	×		×			×		×	×		×	×		×		
Argentina	×	×		×		×	×	×	×	×	×	×		×		
Armenia	×	×		×		×	×	×	×	×		×	×	×		
Aruba	×		×			×		×	×			×		×		
Australia [3][4]	×	×		×		×	×	×	×	×		×		×		
Austria [3][4]	×	×		×		×	×	×	×	×		×		×		
Azerbaijan	×	×		×		×	×	×	×	×		×	×	×		
Bahamas, The	×	×		×		×	×	×	×	×	×	×		×		
Bahrain	×	×		×		×	×	×	×	×		×		×		
Bangladesh	×	×		×		×	×	×	×	×		×		×		
Barbados	×		×			×		×	×		×	×		×		
Belarus	×	×		×		×	×	×	×	×		×	×	×		
Belgium [3]	×	×		×		×	×	×	×	×		×		×		
Belize	×	×		×		×	×	×	×	×	×	×		×		
Benin	×	×		×		×	×	×	×	×		×		×		
Bhutan	×	×		×		×	×	×	×	×		×		×		
Bolivia	×	×		×		×	×	×	×	×	×	×		×		
Bosnia and Herzegovina	×	×		×		×	×	×	×	×		×		×		
Botswana	×	×		×		×	×	×	×	×		×		×		
Brazil	×	×		×		×	×	×	×	×	×	×		×		
Brunei	×	×		×		×	×	×	×	×		×		×		
Bulgaria [3]	×	×		×		×	×	×	×	×		×		×		
Burkina Faso	×	×		×		×	×	×	×	×		×		×		
Burma	×		×	×		×	×	×	×	×		×	×	×		
Burundi	×		×	×		×	×	×	×	×		×		×		
Cameroon	×		×	×		×	×	×	×	×		×		×		
Canada																
Cape Verde	×	×		×		×	×	×	×	×		×		×		
Central African Republic	×	×		×		×	×	×	×	×		×		×		
Chad	×	×		×		×	×	×	×	×		×		×		
Chile	×	×		×		×	×	×	×	×	×	×		×		
China	×	×		×		×	×	×	×	×		×		×		
Colombia	×	×		×		×	×	×	×	×	×	×		×		
Comoros	×	×		×		×	×	×	×	×		×		×		

§ 738.4. Determining whether a license is required.

(a) *Using the CCL and the Country Chart*—(1) *Overview.* Once you have determined that your item is classified under a specific

ECCN, you must use information contained in the "License Requirements" section of that ECCN in combination with the Country Chart to decide whether a license is required. Note that not all license requirements set forth under the "License Requirements" section of an ECCN refer you to the Commerce Country Chart, but in some cases this section will contain references to a specific section in the EAR for license requirements. In such cases, this section would not apply.

(2) *License decision making process.* The following decision making process must be followed in order to determine whether a license is required to export or reexport a particular item to a specific destination:

(i) *Examine the appropriate ECCN in the CCL.* Is the item you intended to export or reexport controlled for a single Reason for Control?

(A) If yes, identify the single Reason for Control and the relevant Country Chart column identifier (e.g., CB Column 1).

(B) If no, identify the Country Chart column identifier for each applicable Reason for Control (e.g., NS Column 1, NP Column 1, etc.).

(ii) *Review the Country Chart.* With each of the applicable Country Chart Column identifiers noted, turn to the Country Chart (supplement no. 1 to part 738). Locate the correct Country Chart column identifier on the diagonal headings, and determine whether an "X" is marked in the cell next to the country in question for each Country Chart column identified in the applicable ECCN. If your item is subject to more than one reason for control, repeat this step using each unique Country Chart column identifier.

(A) If yes, a license application must be submitted based on the particular reason for control and destination, unless a License Exception applies. If "Yes" is noted next to any of the listed License Exceptions, you should consult part 740 of the EAR to determine whether you can use any of the available ECCN-driven License Exceptions to effect your shipment, rather than applying for a license. Each affirmative license requirement must be overcome by a License Exception. If you are unable to qualify for a License Exception based on each license requirement noted on the Country Chart, you must apply for a license. Note that other License Exceptions, not related to the CCL, may also apply to your transaction (See part 740 of the EAR).

(B) If no, a license is not required based on the particular reason for control and destination, [p]rovided that General Prohibitions Four through Ten do not apply to your proposed transaction and the License Requirement section does not refer you to any other part of the EAR to determine license requirements. For example, any applicable encryption registration and classification requirements described in § 740.17(b) of the EAR must be met for certain mass market encryption items to effect your shipment using the symbol "NLR." Proceed to parts 758 and 762 of the EAR for information on export clearance procedures and recordkeeping requirements. Note that although you may stop after determining a license is required based on the first Reason for Control, it is best to work through each applicable Reason for Control. A full analysis of every possible licensing requirement based on each applicable Reason for Control is required to determine the most advantageous License Exception available for your particular transaction and, if a license is required, ascertain the scope of review conducted by BIS on your license application.

———————

In 2007, the BIS adopted a special policy for high-technology exports to China, designed to facilitate exports to civilian end-users while preventing exports that would enhance China's military capability. The policy creates a Validated End-User (VEU) program, permitting exports without a license of certain items (not including items controlled for missile technology (MT) or crime control (CC) reasons) to customers in China who receive VEU authorization. See 15 C.F.R. § 748.15. At the same time, the BIS imposed new controls on about 20 product categories if they are destined for military end-uses in China. The Export Control Act of 2018 does not change any existing regulations but adopts three requirements that could result in further limits on exports to China: (1) it creates an ongoing interagency process to identify "emerging and foundational technologies" and to control their export; (2) it mandates a review of licensing requirements for countries subject to U.S. arms embargoes, including China; and (3) it orders the Commerce Department to consider impacts on the U.S. "defense industrial base" in making export licensing decisions.

One critical point to remember is that certain exports are prohibited outside of the ECCN system. The Department of State administers a separate set of controls on items with defense applications under the International Traffic in Arms Regulations (ITAR), 22 C.F.R. Subchapter M. These regulations contain a Munitions List, 22 C.F.R. Part 121, analogous to the CCL.[12] Certain countries are further subject to sanctions affecting exports, imports, or both. Presently this list includes Belarus, Burundi, Central African Republic, Cuba, Democratic Republic of the Congo, Iran, Libya, North Korea, Somalia, Sudan, Syria, and Zimbabwe. Such restrictions are generally codified as part of the Foreign Asset Control Regulations, 31 C.F.R. Chapter V, and are administered by the Department of the Treasury.[13]

———————

[12] See http://www.pmddtc.state.gov/regulations_laws.

[13] See https://www.treasury.gov/resource-center/sanctions/Programs/Pages/Programs.aspx.

In order to be effective, any system of export controls must contain prohibitions on reexports. The EAR currently prohibit the reexport of controlled items to listed countries; the reexport or export from abroad of foreign-made items incorporating more than a *de minimis* amount of controlled U.S. content; and the reexport or export from abroad of foreign-made items that are the direct product of controlled U.S. technology or software. 15 C.F.R. § 734.3. The application of export controls abroad can raise questions of prescriptive jurisdiction under international law. In 1982, the United States responded to the imposition of martial law in Poland by imposing export controls on goods and technology to be used in constructing a natural gas pipeline from the U.S.S.R. to Western Europe. The export controls applied not only to companies incorporated under U.S. law, but also to foreign companies owned or controlled by U.S. companies, prompting a formal protest by the European Community. See 21 I.L.M. 891. The following case reflects a Dutch court's attempt to grapple with such issues of prescriptive jurisdiction in response to a subsidiary's claim that the U.S. regulations excused it from performance of a contract.

Compagnie Européenne des Pétroles S.A. v. Sensor Nederland B.V.

District Court at The Hague, 1982
22 I.L.M. 66 (1983)

[In May 1982, Compagnie Européenne des Pétroles S.A. (C.E.P.), a company organized under French law and domiciled in Paris, ordered 2,400 strings of geophones for delivery to the U.S.S.R. from Sensor Nederland B.V. (Sensor), a Dutch company domiciled at The Hague. Sensor was a wholly-owned subsidiary of Geosource International (Nederland) B.V., which was in turn a wholly-owned subsidiary of Geosource, Inc., an American corporation domiciled in Houston, Texas. On July 27, 1982, Sensor informed C.E.P. that it would not be able to deliver the goods because of the U.S. export embargo imposed on June 22, 1982. C.E.P. sought specific performance.]

* * *

4. *Applicable law*

The international contract of sale was concluded by telex; the parties made no choice of law. In the event of failure by the parties to make such a choice, an international contract is governed by the law of the country with which it is most closely connected.

This is presumed to be the country where the party who is to effect the performance which is characteristic of the contract has its principal place of business at the time of conclusion of the contract.

This principle is embodied in Article 4 of the Convention on the Law applicable to Contractual Obligations, which convention was signed by the Netherlands on June 19, 1980. Although this Convention has not (yet) been ratified by the Netherlands, its Article 4 should already be applied as valid Netherlands private international law.

Applicability of Netherlands law implies in the present case that the Uniform Act governing the International Sale of Goods (Neth. O.J. 1971 No. 780) is also applicable to the contract.

5.   *The defence*

Sensor has submitted that it is subject to the Export Administration Regulations and that by virtue of § 385.2(c) of those Regulations it cannot fulfil its obligations towards C.E.P.

According to Sensor, the sanctions with which Sensor and Geosource are threatened in the event of infringement of the Export Administration Regulations constitute force majeure and justify a reliance on the "exonerating circumstances" of section 74 of the Uniform Act governing the International Sale of Goods.

6.   *§ 385.2(c) of the Export Administration Regulations*

6.1 The text of § 385.2(c) of the Export Administration Regulations reads as follows:

> "(1) As authorized by Section 6 of the Export Administration Act of 1979, prior written authorization by the Office of Export Administration is required for foreign policy reasons for the export or reexport to the U.S.S.R. of oil and gas exploration, production, transmission or refinement goods of U.S. origin as defined in CCL entries 6098F, 6191F, 6388F, 6389F, 6390F, 6391F, 6431F, 6491F, 6598F, 6685F, 6779F, and 6780F. Also included in the scope of this control are technical data of U.S. origin (other than that authorized under General License GTDA) related to oil and gas exploration, production, transmission and refinement and other goods that require a validated export license for shipment to the Soviet Union and that are intended for use in oil or gas exploration, production, transmission or refinement. The foreign product of such data is also controlled (§ 379.8). The term 'refinement' includes refinery operations directed to energy usage, but excludes petrochemical feedstock processes. In addition, prior written authorization is required for the export to the U.S.S.R. of non-U.S. origin goods and technical data by any person subject to the jurisdiction of the United States.
>
> "(2) For the purposes of this § 385.2(c) only, the term 'person subject to the jurisdiction of the United States' includes:
>
> > "(i)   Any person, wherever located, who is a citizen or resident of the United States;
> >
> > "(ii) Any person actually within the United States;

"(iii) Any corporation organized under the laws of the United States or of any state, territory, possession, or district of the United States; or

"(iv) Any partnership, association, corporation, or other organization, wherever organized or doing business, that is owned or controlled by persons specified in paragraphs (i), (ii), or (iii) of this section."

6.2 Under Section 11 of the Export Administration Act, any infringement of the regulation reproduced above is punishable by a fine of up to $10,000, by a term of imprisonment of up to ten years and by withdrawal of export licenses.

7.   Assessment of the extra-territorial jurisdiction rule of § 385.2(c)(2)(iv)

7.1 In what follows, it will be assumed that an export transaction such as that agreed upon between C.E.P. and Sensor falls within the scope of section (1) of § 385.2(c) and that the U.S. authorities have not granted an export license for that transaction.

It will also be assumed that Sensor is a "corporation" within the meaning of paragraph (iv) of section (2) of the American regulation.

7.2 Under point 4 above it has been found that the contract between C.E.P. and Sensor is governed by Netherlands law. To what extent, therefore, is it necessary to take into account a measure under U.S. law that operates in restraint of trade?

In answering that question, the first consideration must be that that measure extends to the transaction between C.E.P. and Sensor simply and solely via the jurisdiction rule of section (2)(iv). The object of that rule is manifestly to endow the measure with effects vis-a-vis corporations located outside the United States which conclude contracts outside the United States with non-American corporations.

That is the situation that arises in the present case. What particularly merits attention is the fact that, under international law as commonly interpreted, Sensor Nederland B.V. has Netherlands nationality, having been organized in the Netherlands under Netherlands law and both its registered office and its real centre of administration being located within the Netherlands. In accordance with this interpretation, the Treaty of Friendship, Commerce and Navigation between the Kingdom of the Netherlands and the United States of America of March 27, 1956, provides in Article XXIII, third paragraph:

"Companies constituted under the applicable laws and regulations within the territories of either Party shall be deemed companies thereof and shall have their juridical status recognized within the territories of the other Party."

7.3   The circumstance that the trade embargo imposed by the American authorities has been endowed with extra-territorial effects as hereinbefore described raises the question as to whether the jurisdiction rule that brings about such effects is compatible with international law.

7.3.1 The starting-point for answering such questions is the universally accepted rule of international law that in general it is not permissible for a State to exercise jurisdiction over acts performed outside its borders. Exceptions to this rule are, however, possible, for instance under the so-called "nationality principle" or the "protection principle" (the "universality principle" can be disregarded here).

7.3.2 The American jurisdiction rule would not appear to be justified by the nationality principle in so far as that rule brings within its scope companies of other than U.S. nationality.

The position would be different if, in the first place, the criterion "owned or controlled by persons specified in paragraphs (i), (ii), or (iii) of this section" were intended to be a yardstick for the (U.S.) nationality of the corporation—which is possible—and, moreover, if that criterion were accepted in international law side by side with the criterion hereinbefore referred to under 7.2; but in general, according to the views held outside the United States, this has to be regarded as in itself dubious, and in the relations between the United States and the Netherlands it is out of the question, having regard to the treaty provision hereinbefore cited under 7.2. The consequence of this is that the nationality principle offers insufficient basis for the jurisdiction rule here at issue.

7.3.3 Under the protection principle, it is permissible for a State to exercise jurisdiction over acts—wheresoever and by whomsoever performed—that jeopardize the security or creditworthiness of that State or other State interests. Such other State interests do not include the foreign policy interest that the U.S. measure seeks to protect. The protection principle cannot therefore be invoked in support of the validity of the jurisdiction rule here at issue.

7.3.4 It is also of importance to examine whether the acts of exportation covered by the American embargo, in so far as they are performed outside the United States, have direct and illicit effects within the territory of the United States. If that is the case, then those acts can be regarded as having been performed within the United States and on that ground brought within the jurisdiction of the United States under generally accepted rules of international law.

It cannot, however, be seen how the export to Russia of goods not originating in the United States by a non-American exporter could have any direct and illicit effects within the United States. Via this route too, therefore, the jurisdiction rule cannot be brought into compatibility with international law.

7.3.5 The foregoing does not entail that, measured by international law standards, the jurisdiction rule has to be denied all effects.

It is not unacceptable, for instance, that its effects should extend to American citizens who, wishing to evade the American embargo, to that end set up a non-American corporation outside the United States.

There is, however, no evidence to suggest that this has occurred in the present case.

If the jurisdiction rule nevertheless has the object of bringing a case such as that here at issue within the scope of the American measure, that rule must to that extent be deemed to be incompatible.

7.4   Under these circumstances the jurisdiction rule cannot have the consequence that the Netherlands courts will take the American embargo into account.

7.5   The foregoing does not in any way impair the jurisdiction rule of paragraphs (i), (ii) and (iii) of section (2).

Under the rules of Netherlands private international law, even where Netherlands law has to be applied to an international contract, as in the present case, the Netherlands courts are nevertheless, under certain circumstances, bound to accord priority over Netherlands law to the application of mandatory provisions of foreign law.

Among the circumstances under which the Netherlands courts are required to accord such priority is the situation in which the contract meets the condition of showing a sufficient nexus with the foreign country concerned.

That condition is not fulfilled in the present case.

8.   Conclusion

It follows from the foregoing that Sensor's reliance on the American embargo fails and that the claim, against which no defence other than that hereinbefore discussed has been adduced, must be allowed, Sensor being ordered to pay costs.

There are grounds for moderating the size of the per diem penalty.

9.   Decisions

The President:

Orders Sensor Nederland B.V. to deliver to Compagnie Européenne des Pétroles S.A. by October 18, 1982, at the latest, in the agreed manner, the 2,400 strings of geophones ordered by the latter, on pain of a penalty of Nfls 10,000.00, payable forthwith to Compagnie Européenne des Pétroles, for each day after October 18, 1982, that Sensor Nederland B.V. fails to deliver the said 2,400 strings of geophones. . . .

The United States never agreed with the European position and later terminated its boycott measures, claiming that it did so because it had achieved its objectives.

2. ANTI-BOYCOTT LEGISLATION

Another set of rules that may affect U.S. exports are those prohibiting Americans from cooperating with foreign boycotts, in particular that instituted by the Arab states and aimed at Israel. The boycott dates back to one of the earliest resolutions of the Arab League in 1945, which called for a boycott of "Zionist goods." Over time, this primary boycott of Israel was supplemented with a secondary boycott of companies that do business with Israel and even a tertiary boycott of companies that do business with companies that do business with Israel. American concerns about the boycott became more acute with the flexing of Arab economic power during the 1973 oil crisis. Congress passed the original anti-boycott law in 1977. Its provisions have been recodified in the Anti-Boycott Act of 2018, 50 U.S.C. §§ 4841–4843:

§ 4842. Foreign boycotts

(a) Prohibitions and exceptions

(1) . . . the President shall issue regulations prohibiting any United States person, with respect to his activities in the interstate or foreign commerce of the United States, from taking or knowingly agreeing to take any of the following actions with intent to comply with, further, or support any boycott fostered or imposed by a foreign country against a country which is friendly to the United States and which is not itself the object of any form of boycott pursuant to United States law or regulation:

(A) Refusing, or requiring any other person to refuse, to do business with or in the boycotted country, with any business concern organized under the laws of the boycotted country, with any national or resident of the boycotted country, or with any other person, pursuant to an agreement with, a requirement of, or a request from or on behalf of the boycotting country. The mere absence of a business relationship with or in the boycotted country with any business concern organized under the laws of the boycotted country, with any national or resident of the boycotted country, or with any other person, does not indicate the existence of the intent required to establish a violation of regulations issued to carry out this subparagraph.

(B) Refusing, or requiring any other person to refuse, to employ or otherwise discriminating against any United States person on the basis of race, religion, sex, or national origin of that person or of any owner, officer, director, or employee of such person.

(C) Furnishing information with respect to the race, religion, sex, or national origin of any United States person or of any owner, officer, director, or employee of such person.

(D) Furnishing information about whether any person has, has had, or proposes to have any business relationship (including a relationship by way of sale, purchase, legal or commercial representation, shipping or other transport, insurance, investment, or supply) with or in the boycotted country, with any business concern organized under the laws of the boycotted country, with any national or resident of the boycotted country, or with any other person which is known or believed to be restricted from having any business relationship with or in the boycotting country. Nothing in this paragraph shall prohibit the furnishing of normal business information in a commercial context as defined by the Secretary.

(E) Furnishing information about whether any person is a member of, has made contributions to, or is otherwise associated with or involved in the activities of any charitable or fraternal organization which supports the boycotted country.

(F) Paying, honoring, confirming, or otherwise implementing a letter of credit which contains any condition or requirement compliance with which is prohibited by regulations issued pursuant to this paragraph, and no United States person shall, as a result of the application of this paragraph, be obligated to pay or otherwise honor or implement such letter of credit.

* * *

Because the anti-boycott legislation applies to "any United States person," it becomes important to understand just who such persons are. The applicable regulations define this term to mean "any person who is a United States resident or national, including individuals, domestic concerns, and 'controlled in fact' foreign subsidiaries, affiliates, or other permanent foreign establishments of domestic concerns." 15 C.F.R. § 760.1(b)(1). Domestic concerns include partnerships, corporations, companies, associations and other entities organized under the laws of the United States or one of its states, territories, or possessions.

The reader will have noticed that under these regulations, the anti-boycott law also applies to foreign companies "controlled in fact" by domestic concerns. "*Control in fact* consists of the authority or ability of a domestic concern to establish the general policies or to control day-to-day operations of its foreign subsidiary, partnership, affiliate, branch, office, or other permanent foreign establishment." 15 C.F.R. § 760.1(c)(1). The regulations contain a rebuttable presumption of "control in fact" when:

(i) The domestic concern beneficially owns or controls (whether directly or indirectly) more than 50 percent of the outstanding voting securities of the foreign subsidiary or affiliate;

(ii) The domestic concern beneficially owns or controls (whether directly or indirectly) 25 percent or more of the voting securities of the foreign subsidiary or affiliate, if no other person owns or controls (whether directly or indirectly) an equal or larger percentage;

(iii) The foreign subsidiary or affiliate is operated by the domestic concern pursuant to the provisions of an exclusive management contract;

(iv) A majority of the members of the board of directors of the foreign subsidiary or affiliate are also members of the comparable governing body of the domestic concern;

(v) The domestic concern has authority to appoint the majority of the members of the board of directors of the foreign subsidiary or affiliate; or

(vi) The domestic concern has authority to appoint the chief operating officer of the foreign subsidiary or affiliate.

Besides defining the scope of the anti-boycott law, the regulations offer further guidance as to what is prohibited. The provisions on refusals to do business in 15 C.F.R. § 760.2 read in part as follows:

(3) Refusals to do business which are prohibited by this section include not only specific refusals, but also refusals implied by a course or pattern of conduct. There need not be a specific offer and refusal to constitute a refusal to do business; a refusal may occur when a United States person has a financial or commercial opportunity and declines for boycott reasons to consider or accept it.

* * *

(9) Agreements under this section may be either express or implied by a course or pattern of conduct. There need not be a direct request from a boycotting country for action by a United States person to have been taken pursuant to an agreement with or requirement of a boycotting country.

(10) This prohibition, like all others, applies only with respect to a United States person's activities in the interstate or foreign commerce of the United States and only when such activities are undertaken with intent to comply with, further, or support an unsanctioned foreign boycott. The mere absence of a business relationship with or in the boycotted country, with any business concern organized under the laws of the boycotted country, with national(s) or resident(s) of the boycotted country, or with any other person does not indicate the existence of the required intent.

* * *

On the question of intent, the regulations further state: "A United States person has the intent to comply with, further, or support an unsanctioned foreign boycott when such boycott is at least one of the reasons for that person's decision whether to take a particular prohibited action. . . ." 15 C.F.R. § 760.1(e)(2).

Finally, the regulations contain a limited exception for compliance with local laws. See 15 C.F.R. § 760.3(g). The exception allows United States persons resident in the boycotting country to observe local import laws and local laws governing its activities exclusively within the boycotting countries. The local laws may take the form of statutes, regulations, decrees or "other official sources having the effect of law in the host country," but do not include "presumed policies or understandings of policies." However, this exception does not apply to all kinds of activity. In particular, the regulations state that "[t]he exception for compliance with local law does not apply to boycott-based refusals to employ U.S. persons on the basis of race, religion, sex, or national origin even if the activity is exclusively within the boycotting country."

Enforcement of the boycott of Israel varies from country to country.[14] Recently, administrative actions by the BIS against companies violating U.S. anti-boycott laws have fluctuated between three and eight a year. In 2018, the Treasury Department listed nine countries as potentially requiring participation in, or cooperation with, the boycott—Iraq, Kuwait, Lebanon, Libya, Qatar, Saudi Arabia, Syria, United Arab Emirates, and Yemen.

QUESTIONS

(1) Assume that the computers American Computer Company wants to export to China are controlled by ECCN 4A001 for electronic computers. What are the reasons for control? Do any of those reasons for control apply to China? Do any license exemptions apply?

(2) Consider once again the hypothetical situation posed in Question (2) on pp. 113–114 of Chapter III. How should that situation be resolved under U.S. anti-boycott laws? In what ways do the foreign-laws exceptions of the anti-boycott regulations differ from those of Title VII? What might account for the differences?

Additional reading: Teslik, Congress, The Executive Branch, and Special Interests: The American Response to the Arab Boycott of Israel (1982).

E. INTERNATIONAL TRADE LAW

In contrast to the regulation of exports, which is generally left to domestic law, the regulation of imports is subject to an important system of international agreements under the auspices of the World Trade

---

[14] See 2018 National Trade Estimate Report on Foreign Trade Barriers 15–19.

Organization (WTO). The WTO agreements establish when WTO members may impose tariffs and other restrictions on imports. The United States has adapted its international trade law to conform to these agreements.

1. THE WTO SYSTEM

The WTO was created in 1994, but at the heart of the WTO system lies an older treaty—the General Agreement on Tariffs and Trade (GATT), first adopted in 1947. GATT was the product of a postwar revulsion against the excesses of protectionism. In 1947–48 representatives of 53 nations drafted the so-called Havana Charter, which in addition to reducing tariff rates would have set up an International Trade Organization (ITO) to administer and enforce its substantive provisions. Although the United States had been a prime initiator of the Havana Charter, it became apparent that the U.S. Senate would not give its consent. GATT was initially adopted as a temporary agreement to put into effect many of the Charter's terms.

GATT operated without a formal administering organization for forty-seven years. During that period, the GATT parties conducted a series of negotiating rounds that reduced tariff rates substantially and developed understandings on various subjects from government procurement to antidumping duties. There was also a system of dispute resolution to determine whether a country had violated GATT.

The WTO was established in 1994 by the Uruguay Round Final Act. The Uruguay Round readopted GATT (known as GATT 1994 to distinguish it from its predecessor GATT 1947). It also adopted several multilateral agreements dealing with trade in goods including agreements on Agriculture, Textiles, Antidumping, Subsidies and Countervailling Measures, Safeguards, Technical Barriers to Trade, and Sanitary and Phytosanitary Measures. Significantly, the Uruguay Round expanded the scope of the WTO system beyond the trade in goods by adopting a General Agreement on Trade in Services (GATS), an Agreement on Trade-Related Investment Measures (TRIMS), and an Agreement on Trade-Related Aspects of Intellectual Property Rights (TRIPS), the last of which we will return to in Problem 3. See infra pp. 266–268. And the Uruguay Round adopted an Understanding on Rules and Procedures Governing the Settlement of Disuptes (Dispute Settlement Understanding or DSU) that made important changes in the GATT's dispute resolution procedures. See infra pp. 205–207. All 164 WTO members must join all of these multilateral agreements. The text that follows provides a brief overview of the WTO system.

Tariffs

Article II of GATT imposes the obligation upon each party to "accord to the commerce of the other contracting parties treatment no less favourable than that provided for in the appropriate Part of the appropriate Schedule annexed to this Agreement." The schedules, which amount to 20,000 pages or so, set the tariff rates that each WTO member has agreed to extend to every other WTO member. These have been negotiated down to historically low levels over multiple rounds of GATT negotiations.

WTO members are free, of course, to reduce their tariff rates even further. But if they do so, they must generally extend the same lower tariff to all other WTO members. Article I's most-favored-nation (MFN) clause provides that "any advantage, favour, privilege or immunity granted by any contracting party to any product originating in or destined for any other country shall be accorded immediately and unconditionally to the like product originating in or destined for the territories of all other contracting parties."

One exception to this MFN obligation is found in Article XXIV, which permits the establishment of customs unions (like the European Union) and for free-trade areas (like NAFTA), which eliminate substantially all duties and other restrictions on trade among their members. The advantages and disadvantages of such regional trading agreements (RTAs) have been hotly debated.[15] On the one hand, because RTAs involve fewer countries, they tend to be quicker and easier to negotiate. A small number of like-minded countries may be able to achieve greater trade liberalization than the WTO can achieve. RTAs can also provide a testing ground for issues like competition, environment, investment, and labor on which no broad consensus exists. Finally, lack of progress in recent WTO negotiations seems to have left countries seeking further trade liberalization with no alternative. On the other hand, critics charge that the primary effect of RTAs is not to create trade but to distort it by shifting imports from more efficient producers outside the RTA to less efficient producers within it. They argue that RTAs undercut the bargaining position of developing countries, which are more powerful negotiating as a block within the WTO than in one-on-one negotiations with large developed countries like the United States. And they argue that RTAs undermine the WTO system—both in principle, by deviating from the MFN rule, and in practice, by diverting time and energy from WTO negotiations.

GATT expressly permits WTO members to impose additional duties under limited circumstances. Article VI authorizes antidumping duties to offset dumping—that is, the sale of products at less than their "normal value," typically defined as "the comparable price, in the ordinary course of trade, for the like product when destined for consumption in the exporting country." Article VI's provisions on antidumping duties are supplemented by an Antidumping Agreement that was adopted as part of the Uruguay Round.

---

[15] For a flavor of the debate, see Bhagwati & Panagariya, Bilateral Trade Treaties Are a Sham, Financial Times (July 13, 2003); Griswold, Bilateral Deals Are No Threat to Global Trade, Financial Times (July 27, 2003).

Article VI also authorizes countervailing duties to offset "any bounty or subsidy bestowed, directly, or indirectly, upon the manufacture, production or export of any merchandise." Article VI's provisions on countervailing duties are supplemented by the Agreement on Subsidies and Countervailing Measures (SCM Agreement), adopted as part of the Uruguay Round, which divides subsidies into three categories: (1) "prohibited subsidies" that are contingent on export performance or on the use of domestic rather than imported goods (also known as "red light" subsidies); (2) "actionable subsidies" that are permitted unless they cause injury to another WTO member (also known as "yellow light" subsidies); and (3) "non-actionable subsidies" that may not be countervailed (also known as "green light" subsidies). The third category expired in 2000 under the terms of the SCM Agreement.

Article XIX authorizes what the WTO calls "safeguard" measures, which are generally called "excape clause" measures in the United States. Specifically, Article XIX permits the temporary suspension of tariff concessions if "as a result of *unforeseen developments* . . . any product is being imported into the territory of that contracting party in such *increased quantities* and under such conditions as to cause or threaten *serious injury* to domestic producers in that territory of like or directly competitive products" (emphases added). Except in emergency circumstances, consultation with the countries adversely affected by the withdrawal must first take place. If the talks do not gain acquiescence by such countries in the action taken under Article XIX, they are authorized to withdraw "substantially equivalent concessions." The United States has invoked Article XIX several times, and retaliatory measures have in a few instances followed its action.

Restrictions Other than Tariffs

Other provisions of GATT limit the use of trade restrictions other than tariffs in an attempt to make tariffs as much as possible the sole authorized protective device. Articles III to XI bar a variety of national measures that serve, directly or indirectly, to curb importation.

Article III proscribes the use of internal taxes or other regulatory measures to protect domestic production. It generally requires "national treatment" for imports—that is, "treatment no less favorable than that accorded to like products of national origin in respect of all laws, regulations and requirements affecting their internal sale, offering for sale, purchase, transportation, distribution or use." Here a national-treatment standard serves the same general purpose as the most-favored-nation clause in Article I: eliminating discrimination.

The single most important prohibition in GATT appears in Article XI(1). That provision bars import restrictions other than duties, whether in the form of quotas limiting imports of a product or of licensing schemes that permit those administering them to use their discretion to restrict particular imports. The prohibition is softened by several exceptions in Article XI itself.

Exceptions

In addition to the exceptions already noted, GATT contains a number of general exceptions applicable to all GATT obligations. Article XX, entitled "General Exceptions," provides in part as follows:

> Subject to the requirement that such measures are not applied in a manner which would constitute a means of arbitrary or unjustifiable discrimination between countries where the same conditions prevail, or a disguised restriction on international trade, nothing in this Agreement shall be construed to prevent the adoption or enforcement by any contracting party of measures:
>
> (*a*)   necessary to protect public morals;
>
> (*b*)   necessary to protect human, animal or plant life or health;
>
> (*c*)   relating to the importations or exportations of gold or silver;
>
> (*d*) necessary to secure compliance with laws or regulations which are not inconsistent with the provisions of this Agreement, including those relating to customs enforcement, the enforcement of monopolies operated under paragraph 4 of Article II and Article XVII, the protection of patents, trade marks and copyrights, and the prevention of deceptive practices;
>
> (*e*)   relating to the products of prison labour;
>
> (*f*)   imposed for the protection of national treasures of artistic, historic or archaeological value;
>
> (*g*)   relating to the conservation of exhaustible natural resources if such measures are made effective in conjunction with restrictions on domestic production or consumption. . . .

* * *

There is also Article XXI, which (with some limitations) permits each contracting party to take "any action which it considers necessary for the protection of its essential security interests." There is some dispute whether Article XXI is completely "self-judging" or whether it permits review of a contracting party's good faith in invoking the exception. Finally, Article XXV(5) allows the contracting parties by a two-thirds vote to waive an obligation of GATT.

Dispute Settlement

In addition to establishing general rules about the conduct of national trade policies and serving as a forum for multilateral tariff negotiations, the GATT has served a third, critical function of resolving disputes. As part of the Uruguay Round agreements, the contracting states adopted an Understanding on Rules and Procedures Governing the Settlement of Disputes (Dispute Settlement Understanding or DSU), which considerably stiffened and "legalized" GATT's dispute resolution procedures.

The starting point is a newly established agency called the Dispute Settlement Body (DSB). If consultations and conciliation or mediation fail to resolve a problem between Members, a complaining party can ask the DSB to establish a panel composed of qualified experts who are not citizens of the states parties to the dispute. Under the DSU, this panel of experts hears arguments regarding one member's claims that another has enacted a measure violating a WTO agreement. The panel issues a report of its findings and, if it finds a violation, recommends that the member "withdraw[ ] the offending measure."

On one track, a panel report is brought before the DSB and is regarded as adopted sixty days after the report is circulated to the members unless "the DSB decides by consensus not to adopt the report." This provision inverts the pre-1994 practice under which an affirmative consensus was needed to make the report effective. Under that practice, the losing state could in effect "veto" a report by preventing a consensus from forming. The "reverse consensus" rule makes the report binding unless a consensus against the report develops among the WTO membership. Assuming that no winning party will be willing to join a consensus against a ruling in its favor, the reverse-consensus requirement virtually assures the automatic adoption of final reports.

The other track is chosen if a disputing state opts to resort to the standing Appellate Body established by the DSB. Appeals are heard by a three-member group selected from the seven-member Appellate Body within the WTO, whose expert members, appointed by the WTO and "broadly representative" of the organization's makeup, serve four-year terms subject to one-time reappointment. The Appellate Body's authority is "limited to issues of law" covered in the panel report and legal interpretations developed by the panel. A report by the Appellate Body shall be adopted by the DSB and "unconditionally accepted by the parties to the dispute" unless the DSB decides otherwise by consensus.

Because WTO rulings lack direct effect as domestic law, they do not "bind" domestic courts in the way, for example, that United States Supreme Court rulings bind state courts in the American national system. If a WTO member fails to change its law to comply with a final report, however, it must consult with the injured party and attempt to reach agreement on appropriate compensation. Failing such an agreement, the injured party may retaliate by suspending its own trade obligations to the offending party.

Over 500 cases were brought to WTO dispute-settlement in the first twenty years compared to some 300 disputes dealt with during the entire forty-seven year life of GATT 1947. The United States and China have both been active users of the WTO system. The United States has brought a total of 117 complaints, including 22 against China. China has brought a total of 17 complaints, including 12 against the United States.

2. U.S. TRADE LAW

The United States' laws on tariffs and other trade barriers constitute a large mass of rules, the domain of a specialized bar and a special customs court system. The infamous Smoot-Hawley Tariff Act of 1930 still sets the tariff rates in Column 2 of the Harmonized Tariff Schedule for non-WTO members. But it has been altered and amended by the Trade Act of 1974, the Trade Agreements Act of 1979, the Omnibus Trade and Competitiveness Act of 1988, and the Uruguay Round Implementation Act of 1994, among other statutes.

U.S. trade laws generally follow the template established by the WTO agreements. The United States implements its obligations under Article II of GATT by applying the rate of duty in Column 1 of the Harmonized Tariff Schedule to WTO members and others entitled to MFN treatment. The even lower rates listed in Column 1 Special are applied to countries given special status under the U.S. Generalized System of Preferences for developing countries and under U.S. Free Trade Agreements. The much higher rates in Column 2 apply to all other countries, though at the moment this includes only Cuba and North Korea.

Harmonized Tariff Schedule of the United States (2018) Revision 14
Annotated for Statistical Reporting Purposes

IV
22-6

Heading/ Subheading	Stat. Suf- fix	Article Description	Unit of Quantity	Rates of Duty		
				1		2
				General	Special	
2204		Wine of fresh grapes, including fortified wines; grape must other than that of heading 2009:				
2204.10.00		Sparkling wine..	....	19.8¢/liter 1/ 2/	Free (A*, AU, BH, CA, CL, CO, D, E, IL, KR, MA, MX, OM, P, PA, PE, SG) 8.8¢/liter (JO) 1/	$1.59/liter 1/
	30	Valued not over $1.59/liter...........................	liters			
		Valued over $1.59/liter:				
	65	Certified organic..................................	liters			
	75	Other.....................................	liters			
		Other wine; grape must with fermentation prevented or arrested by the addition of alcohol:				
2204.21		In containers holding 2 liters or less:				
2204.21.20	00	Effervescent wine..............................	liters............	19.8¢/liter 1/ 2/	Free (A+, AU, BH, CA, CL, CO, D, E, IL, KR, MA, MX, OM, P, PA, PE, SG) 8.8¢/liter (JO) 1/	$1.59/liter 1/

1/ Imports under this subheading may be subject to Federal Excise Tax (26 U.S.C. 5041).
2/ See 9903.88.03.

Harmonized Tariff Schedule of the United States (2018) Revision 14
Annotated for Statistical Reporting Purposes

IV
22-7

Heading/ Subheading	Stat. Suf- fix	Article Description	Unit of Quantity	Rates of Duty		2
				General	Special	
2204 (con.)		Wine of fresh grapes, including fortified wines; grape must other than that of heading 2009: (con.)				
		Other wine; grape must with fermentation prevented or arrested by the addition of alcohol: (con.)				
2204.21 (con.)		In containers holding 2 liters or less: (con.)				
		Other:				
		Of an alcoholic strength by volume not over 14 percent vol.:				
2204.21.30	00	If entitled under regulations of the United States Internal Revenue Service to a type designation which includes the name "Tokay" and if so designated on the approved label...............	liters........	6.3¢/liter 1/ 2/	Free (A, AU, BH, CA, CL, CO, D, E, IL, KR, MA, MX, OM, P, PA, PE, SG) 2.8¢/liter (JO) 1/	33¢/liter 1/
2204.21.50		Other................	....	6.3¢/liter 1/ 2/	Free (A+, AU, BH, CA, CL, CO, D, E, IL, KR, MA, MX, OM, P, PA, PE, SG) 2.8¢/liter (JO) 1/	33¢/liter 1/
		Valued not over $1.05/liter:				
	05	Red..................	liters			
	15	White..............	liters			
	25	Other..............	liters			
		Valued over $1.05/liter:				
	28	Icewine.............	liters			
		Other:				
		Red:				
	35	Certified Organic............	liters			
	40	Other..............	liters			
		White:				
	50	Certified Organic............	liters			
	55	Other.............	liters			
	60	Other..............	liters			
		Of an alcoholic strength by volume over 14 percent vol.:				
2204.21.60	00	If entitled under regulations of the United States Internal Revenue Service to a type designation which includes the name "Marsala" and if so designated on the approved label...............	liters........	5.3¢/liter 1/ 2/	Free (A, AU, BH, CA, CL, CO, D, E, IL, KR, MA, MX, OM, P, PA, PE, SG) 2.3¢/liter (JO) 1/	33¢/liter 1/
2204.21.80		Other................	....	16.9¢/liter 1/ 2/	Free (A+, AU, BH, CA, CL, CO, D, E, IL, KR, MA, MX, OM, P, PA, PE, SG) 7.5¢/liter (JO) 1/	33¢/liter 1/
	30	Sherry.............	liters			
	60	Other.............	liters			

1/ Imports under this subheading may be subject to Federal Excise Tax (26 U.S.C. 5041).
2/ See 9903.88.03.

Consistent with the WTO agreements, U.S. law authorizes upward departures from the rates set forth in the tariff schedules in the form of antidumping, countervailing, and "escape clause" duties. Cases may be initiated by affected domestic industries or by the U.S. Department of Commerce. Determinations in antidumping and countervailing duty cases are made by the International Trade Administration (ITA), which is part of the Department of Commerce, and the International Trade

Commission (ITC), which is an independent agency. Determinations in escape clause cases are made by the ITC alone. Determinations may be challenged in the Court of International Trade, whose decisions are appealable to the Court of Appeals for the Federal Circuit and ultimately to the U.S. Supreme Court.

Under the Tariff Act of 1930 (as amended), antidumping duties may be imposed if (1) goods are being sold at "less than fair value" and (2) such sales have caused or threaten to cause "material injury" to a domestic industry. The ITA makes the first determination by comparing the "export price" at which the goods are first sold outside the United States for exportation to the United States to their "normal value," the price charged in the exporter's domestic market. The ITC makes the "material injury" determination. Antidumping duties must equal the margin of dumping—that is, the difference between the normal value and the export price of the goods.

The Tariff Act of 1930 (as amended) also permits the imposition of countervailing duties if a foreign country "is providing, directly or indirectly, a countervailable subsidy." For WTO members and other countries that have assumed obligations substantially equivalent to the WTO's SCM Agreement, countervailing duties may only be imposed if the subsidy causes "material injury" to a domestic industry; for the limited number of other countries, no material injury determination is required. U.S. countervailing duty law applies to "export subsidies" that are contingent on export performance (corresponding to the WTO's "prohibited subsidies") as well as to "domestic subsidies" that are specific to an enterprise or industry (corresponding to the WTO's "actionable subsidies"). The ITA makes the subsidy determination, and the ITC makes the material injury determination. Countervailing duties must equal the amount of the countervailable subsidy.

The U.S. escape clause is found in Section 201 of the Trade Act of 1974 (as amended). It differs from the GATT's provision on safeguards chiefly in that the U.S. provision, while speaking of "serious injury" arising from imports in "increased quantities," does not require that these be "unforeseen developments." The ITC makes the required determinations and recommends relief to the President who makes the final decision. In 2002, President Bush imposed escape clause duties on steel. These duties were successfully challenged at the WTO, and the President rescinded them in 2003. In 2009, President Obama imposed duties on vehicle tires from China under a special safeguard provision (Section 421), with a lower standard of causation, applicable only to China. That provision expired in 2013.

A few provisions of U.S. law have proved particularly controversial. Section 301 of the Trade Act of 1974 gives the President power to impose unilateral sanctions on "unfair" foreign trade practices, discriminatory policies burdening U.S. exports, or unjustifiable restrictions on access to resources and supplies. The EU challenged Section 301 as contrary to the

Disputes Settlement Understanding of the Uruguay Round agreements, but in 1999 a WTO panel found no violation because the United States had committed to base any determination that a WTO member had violated its rights on a final decision by a WTO panel or the Appellate Body. See United States—Sections 301–10 of the Trade Act of 1974, WT/DS152/R. In 2018, based on a Section 301 determination by the U.S. Trade Representative that Chinese policies relating to technology transfer are unreasonable, President Trump initiated a dispute at the WTO and imposed additional duties on Chinese imports under Section 301.

Section 232 of the Trade Expansion Act of 1962 gives the President authority to impose duties or restrict imports to protect national security. In 2018, President Trump relied on this provision to increase tariffs on imports of steel and aluminum, including imports from some of the United States' closest allies. The European Union, Canada, Mexico, and India have each initiated disputes at the WTO challenging the tariffs as inconsistent with GATT. Although Article XXI of GATT contains an exception for national security, the extent to which this exception is "self-judging" remains unsettled.

QUESTIONS

(1) GATT adopts a general policy, reflected particularly in Article XI, that all restrictions on trade should take the form of tariffs rather than quotas or other non-tariff trade barriers. What considerations might support such a policy?

(2) Compare the language of GATT's general exceptions in Article XX to the language of GATT's security exceptions in Article XXI. See supra p. 205. Do the differences in language suggest greater discretion on the part of WTO members to impose trade restrictions based on national security? Why should restrictions based on national security be treated differently from restrictions to protect the environment, for example? Should there be any limits on imposing trade restrictions based on national security?

Additional reading: Trebilcock, Howse & Eliason, The Regulation of International Trade (4th ed. 2013); Jackson, Davey & Sykes, Legal Problems of International Economic Relations (6th ed. 2013); Pauwelyn, Guzman & Hillman, International Trade Law (3d ed. 2016).

PROBLEM 2

AGENCY AND DISTRIBUTORSHIP AGREEMENTS

A. INTRODUCTION

A U.S. manufacturer wishing to increase its sales abroad will frequently employ a foreign representative of some sort. Such representatives will generally have a better knowledge of the local market than the U.S. exporter. They may also have an independent reputation for trustworthiness with local buyers and may be better positioned than the U.S. firm to provide service to customers following a sale. In comparison with some other forms of doing business covered in this book, using a foreign representative requires a relatively small investment of resources by the U.S. firm—typically no more than the managerial time necessary to identify and come to an agreement with the appropriate local representative.

There are two basic sorts of foreign representatives—agents and distributors—and it is important at the outset to understand some distinctions between them. The most fundamental difference is that an agent arranges sales for the manufacturer, but never takes title to the goods; title passes directly from the manufacturer to the customer. A distributor, on the other hand, buys goods from the manufacturer and then resells them to the customer. This difference in the structure of the transaction makes a difference in how each sort of representative is paid. Agents typically receive a commission on sales they arrange for the manufacturer, while distributors make their money as profits when they resell the goods to the customer at a price higher than what the manufacturer charged them. The difference in structure also makes a difference in who bears the risk of the customer's nonpayment. Because the manufacturer using an agent sells directly to the customer, it is the manufacturer that bears the risk of nonpayment. (Sometimes an agent will agree to guarantee the customer's payment to the manufacturer, in which case the agent is known as a *del credere* agent.) Under a distributorship agreement, by contrast, the manufacturer is paid by the distributor before the goods are sold to the customer, and as a result the risk of the customer's nonpayment rests with the distributor.

Because distributors sell for their own account rather than on behalf of the manufacturer, they need not have authority to bind the manufacturer legally. Agents, who sell for the manufacturer's account, are sometimes given that authority, and enter into contracts with customers that bind the manufacturer. Sometimes, however, they too are denied such authority, typically with language in the agency agreement stating that all orders will be subject to the manufacturer's approval. The distinction between an agent with authority to bind the manufacturer and one without this authority may have tax consequences, which are discussed at infra pp. 254–255.

If agents may sometimes bind manufacturers, it is also true that manufacturers typically exercise greater control over agents than they do over distributors. The fact that distributors have title to the goods they sell gives them a degree of practical independence that agents lack. Additionally, there are legal limitations on the ability of manufacturers to control distributors that generally do not apply to agents. Under an agency agreement, for example, the manufacturer may determine the price to the customer, because the manufacturer sells directly to the customer. An agreement between the manufacturer and the distributor concerning the price to the customer, on the other hand, would likely violate U.S. or foreign antitrust law.

There are significant legal consequences that flow from using one sort of representative or the other. Many countries have protective legislation governing agency agreements and particularly their termination. Fewer countries extend the same sorts of protections to distributors. The European Union's Council Directive on Commercial Agents is discussed below in Section B. Distributorship agreements, on the other hand, will tend to raise antitrust concerns that agency agreements do not, and we consider such issues below in Section C. Finally, as we have already suggested, the choice of representative may have tax implications, which are discussed below in Section D.

As a focus for analysis, we consider the negotiation of a distributorship agreement by an American firm of modest size that manufactures a line of specialized electrical testing equipment. The firm's management is confident that the unique character of its apparatus will assure it of a market in Germany. After several trips by one of its executives to Europe, the firm located a potential distributor who seems to meet the requirements for a successful outlet in Germany. As American counsel for the firm, you are asked to pass on the legality and adequacy of the distributorship agreement before it is signed. You recognize that the question of the legality of the agreement implicates issues of German law and, because Germany is part of the European Union, of EU law. You may need to consult foreign counsel before advising the client.

Although the form of agreement that follows has been adapted from published sources, certain of its provisions are problematic, as you will no doubt discover during the course of your study. Even with a form of agreement that is not designed primarily for teaching purposes, you should be aware of the risk in using "standard form" contracts without an adequate grasp of what their authors had in mind or the significance of each clause, or without the exercise of independent judgment about its suitability for the enterprise at hand. The use of forms serves the goal of efficiency only if held within these basic constraints.

DISTRIBUTION AGREEMENT[1]

THIS AGREEMENT, made this ___ day of _____ by and between TECHNO MANUFACTURERS, INC., a corporation duly organized under the laws of the state of Colorado, U.S.A. (hereinafter "Manufacturer"), and IMPO AG, a corporation duly organized under the laws of the Federal Republic of Germany (hereinafter "Distributor"):

WHEREAS Manufacturer has developed and manufactures certain industrial products catalogued in Manufacturer's literature, together with certain service equipment (hereinafter "Techno Products"); and

WHEREAS, Distributor wishes to act as distributor of the entire line of Techno Products with respect to the Federal Republic of Germany (hereinafter "the Territory");

NOW, THEREFORE, in consideration of the mutual promises and covenants set forth in this Agreement, Manufacturer and Distributor agree as follows:

1. *Appointment.* Manufacturer hereby appoints Distributor, and Distributor hereby accepts appointment, as Manufacturer's exclusive distributor during the term of this Agreement with the right to sell or otherwise distribute Techno Products in the Territory, under Manufacturer's name and trademarks, subject to all the terms and conditions of this Agreement.

2. *Distribution Outside Territory.* Distributor shall limit its sales activities with respect to Techno Products to customers located in the Territory, and shall refrain from marketing or selling Techno Products outside the Territory.

3. *Noncompetition.* Distributor shall not manufacture or distribute any products that are directly or indirectly competitive with Techno Products.

4. *Relationship.* This Agreement does not make either party the employee, agent, or legal representative of the other for any purpose whatsoever. Neither party is granted any right or authority to assume or to create any obligation or responsibility, express or implied, on behalf of or in the name of the other party. In fulfilling its obligations pursuant to this Agreement each party shall be acting as an independent contractor.

5. *Marketing.* Distributor shall use its best efforts to promote the sale and use of Techno Products by all existing and potential customers in the Territory. Distributor shall furnish Manufacturer with an annual

[1] Adapted from examples in Clasen, International Agency and Distribution Agreements: Analysis and Forms (looseleaf 1990–), Nelson, Negotiating and Drafting Agency, Distribution, and Franchise Agreements, in Negotiating and Structuring International Commercial Transactions: Legal Analysis with Sample Agreements (Battram & Goldsweig eds., 1991), and Moore, Agreements for the Transmission of Technology Abroad: The Distributor Relationship, 45 Denver L.J. 43, 60–63 (1968).

[handwritten margin notes: "2 yearly reports", "hmmm", "vague?"]

business plan with respect to the marketing and sale of Techno Products, together with <u>semiannual</u> reports describing specific promotional activities undertaken during the reporting period. Distributor shall also provide Manufacturer with quarterly sales forecasts and reports setting forth recent sales figures, current inventory levels, competitive products and such other information concerning the marketing and sale of Techno Products as Manufacturer may reasonably request.

6. *Quota.* Distributor agrees to purchase and take delivery, during the term of this Agreement, of the quota (hereinafter "the Quota") of Techno Products established for such period as specified in Annex 1 of this Agreement. Distributor understands and agrees that the establishment and achievement of the Quota is the essence of this Agreement and that failure by Distributor to satisfy its obligations under this Article 6 shall constitute a breach of the Agreement on the basis of which Manufacturer shall be entitled to terminate this Agreement pursuant to Article 12.

7. *Purchase and Delivery.* Distributor shall purchase Techno Products from Manufacturer F.O.B. its plant at Junction City, Colorado, at such United States dollar prices as are scheduled in Manufacturer's export price list, payable in United States currency and upon terms of payment net 30 days from date of invoice with a ___% distributorship discount from list price.

8. *Import and Export.* Distributor shall be responsible for obtaining all licenses and permits and for satisfying all formalities that may be required to import Techno Products into the Territory in accordance with then prevailing law or regulations. Distributor shall supply Manufacturer on a timely basis with all necessary information and documentation requested by Manufacturer in order to permit Manufacturer to export Techno Products with respect to any sale or order solicited hereunder. Distributor shall not dispose of any U.S. origin Techno Products or know-how furnished to it pursuant to this Agreement to any party or in any manner that would constitute a violation of the export control regulations of the United States now or hereafter in effect if the disposition were made by a U.S. corporation, or a non-U.S. corporation subject to those regulations.

9. *Confidentiality.* Distributor acknowledges that during the course of this Agreement it may receive access to information concerning Manufacturer's marketing and business plans, sales strategies, advertising programs, pricing, costs, customers, technology and manufacturing methods and other information that Manufacturer designates or treats as confidential (hereafter "Confidential Information"). Distributor shall hold the Confidential Information in strict confidence and shall not use or disclose such Confidential Information except as required to perform its obligations under this Agreement.

10. *Trademarks.* All Techno Products sold by the Distributor shall bear Manufacturer's trademarks, and Distributor agrees not to remove or

efface such trademarks. Distributor shall not use any of Manufacturer's trademarks or trade names or any mark or name confusingly similar thereto, in any manner, except: (i) on letterhead, business cards, and signs in order to identify itself as an authorized distributor of Manufacturer, or (ii) in sales and promotional materials provided such materials have been previously approved by Manufacturer. Distributor shall not register any of Manufacturer's trademarks or any mark or name closely resembling them. Distributor shall advise Manufacturer of, and comply fully with, any legal requirements in the Territory to become a registered user of Manufacturer's trademarks.

11. *Term.* This Agreement shall continue in force for an initial period of three years after the date hereof and thereafter may be renewed by Manufacturer for additional periods of one year each by written notice to Distributor at least ninety calendar days prior to the expiration of the initial or any renewal period.

12. *Termination.* Notwithstanding the provisions of Article 11, this Agreement may be terminated by written notice to the other party as follows:

(a) by either party, effective immediately, if the other party should file a petition for bankruptcy, be declared bankrupt, become insolvent, make an assignment for the benefit of creditors, go into liquidation or receivership, or otherwise lose control of its business, or should the other party or a substantial part of its business come under the control of a third party;

(b) by either party in the event that the other party is in material breach of this Agreement and shall have failed to cure such breach within thirty days of receipt of written notice thereof from the first party;

(c) by either party, without any cause therefore, upon at least sixty days written notice thereof to the other party.

13. *Rights and Obligations Upon Termination.* In the event of the termination or nonrenewal of this Agreement for any reason, the parties shall have the following rights and obligations:

(a) Distributor shall cease all sales and marketing of Techno Products and shall return to Manufacturer and immediately cease all use of Confidential Information in the Distributor's possession.

(b) Distributor's obligations under Article 9 shall survive termination or nonrenewal of this Agreement for any reason.

(c) Distributor shall remove from its property and immediately discontinue all use of trademarks owned or controlled, now or hereafter, by Manufacturer and of any trademark that, in the opinion of Manufacturer, is confusingly similar thereto.

(d) Distributor shall turn over to Manufacturer Distributor's current customer mailing list for Techno Products.

(e) Distributor's obligations under Article 3 shall continue for a period of three years following the termination or nonrenewal of this Agreement for any reason.

(f) All indebtedness of Distributor to Manufacturer shall become immediately due and payable without further notice or demand.

(g) Manufacturer shall have the right, at its option to repurchase any part of Distributor's inventory of Techno Products at Manufacturer's invoiced price to Distributor for such products, less depreciation calculated on a thirty-six month, straight-line basis. If Manufacturer elects not to repurchase any such inventory, Distributor shall be entitled to sell the same but only during the six-month period following termination or nonrenewal.

14. *No Compensation.* In the event that either party terminates or decides not to renew this Agreement for any reason in accordance with the terms hereof, the parties hereby agree that, without prejudice to any other remedies which either party may have in respect of any breach of this Agreement, neither party shall be entitled to any indemnity, compensation, or like payment from the other as a result of such termination.

15. *Nonassignment.* Neither party shall have the right to assign or otherwise transfer its rights and obligations under this Agreement except with the prior written consent of the other party; provided, however, that a successor in interest by merger, by operation of law, assignment, purchase or otherwise of the entire business of either party shall acquire all rights and obligations of such party hereunder.

16. *Notices.* All notices under this Agreement shall be in English and shall be in writing and given by registered airmail to the parties at the addresses immediately below their signatures hereto, or to such other address of which either party may advise the other in writing. Notices will be deemed given when sent.

17. *Waiver.* No failure by either party to take any action or assert any right hereunder shall be deemed to be a waiver of such right in the event of the continuation or repetition of the circumstances giving rise to such right.

18. *Force Majeure.* Neither party shall be in breach of this Agreement by reason of any failure or delay in the performance of any obligation under this Agreement where such failure or delay arises out of any cause beyond the reasonable control and without the fault or negligence of such party.

19. *Severability.* The illegality or unenforceablity of any provision of this Agreement shall not affect the validity and enforceability of any other provisions of this Agreement.

20. *Disputes.* Any controversy or claim arising out of or relating to this Agreement shall be finally settled by arbitration in Denver, Colorado,

U.S.A. in accordance with the International Arbitration Rules of the American Arbitration Association in effect on the date of this Agreement, and judgment upon the award rendered by the arbitrator(s) may be entered in any court having jurisdiction thereof. The arbitration shall be conducted in the English language.

21. *Governing Law.* This Agreement shall be governed by, and interpreted and construed in accordance with, the laws of the State of Colorado, U.S.A.

22. *Entire Agreement.* This Agreement, including the Appendix hereto, represents the entire agreement between the parties and supersedes all prior discussions, agreements and understandings of every kind and nature between them. This Agreement may not be modified except in a writing signed by both parties.

TECHNO MANUFACTURERS, INC.

By _____

President

IMPO AG

By _____

Title: _____

QUESTIONS

We pose some questions that call for the application to this problem of matters considered elsewhere in this book.

(1) Review the materials on choice of forum clauses and arbitration at supra pp. 22–32, 40–62. Then consider Article 20 of the Distributorship Agreement. Why does it opt for an arbitration clause? If you were representing Impo, would you resist the attempt to provide for arbitration in the United States by an American organization? On what grounds? On what grounds might Techno resist?

(2) Consider the choice of law clause in Article 21. Is it sufficient to exclude application of the CISG? If not, do you think it would be desirable to do so?

(3) Under Article 7, who is responsible for the costs of transporting Techno Products from Colorado to Germany? Does the Agreement make proper use of the Incoterms?

Additional reading: ICC Model Contract on Commercial Agency (2015 edition); ICC Model Contract on Distributorship (2016 edition); Clasen, International Agency and Distribution Agreements: Analysis and Forms (looseleaf 1990–); Herold & Knoll, Negotiating and Drafting International Distribution, Agency, and Representative Agreements: The United States Exporter's Perspective, 21 Int'l Law. 939 (1987).

B. TERMINATION

1. A PRIMER ON THE EUROPEAN UNION

Although it was preceded by earlier steps towards European integration, the beginnings of the European Union (EU) are typically traced to the 1957 Treaty of Rome, which established the European Economic Community (EEC). The original members of the EEC were Belgium, France, Germany, Italy, Luxembourg, and the Netherlands. Denmark, Ireland, and the United Kingdom joined in 1973, Greece in 1981, Portugal and Spain in 1986, and Austria, Finland, and Sweden in 1995. On May 1, 2004, the EU expanded dramatically, admitting ten new members, mostly from Eastern Europe: Cyprus, Czechia, Estonia, Hungary, Latvia, Lithuania, Malta, Poland, Slovakia, and Slovenia. The eastward expansion continued with Bulgaria and Romania in 2007 and Croatia in 2013, bringing the total membership to 28 countries.

The European Union came into being in 1993 as a result of the Treaty of Maastricht, which among other things amended and renamed the Treaty of Rome. The Maastricht Treaty has in turn been amended by the Treaty of Amsterdam, the Treaty of Nice, and the Treaty of Lisbon, the last of which went into effect on December 1, 2009. In the process, the constituent treaties of the European Union have been renamed and renumbered several times, which can result in some confusion. For example, Articles 85 and 86 of the Treaty of Rome, which dealt with competition law, became Articles 81 and 82 of the EC Treaty in 1997, and became Articles 101 and 102 of the Treaty on the Functioning of the European Union in 2009. See infra pp. 238–240.

With the coming into force of the Lisbon Treaty in 2009, the European Union has a consolidated legal personality, replacing the previous "three pillars" of the EU, of which the European Community had been one. The EU now has two constituting treaties: the Treaty on European Union and the Treaty on the Functioning of the European Union. The EU's institutional framework consists of four principal bodies: the Council, the Commission, the Parliament, and the Court of Justice.

The Council is the political arm of the EU, consisting of the ministers of the member states. The Lisbon Treaty created a new position of President of the European Council, elected by the member states for a two-and-a-half-year term, to replace the presidency that had previously rotated among the member states every six months. The Council is also a legislative body, producing legislation with the participation of the Commission and the Parliament. The Council, however, does not initiate legislation. Instead it acts on proposals from the Commission, with the Parliament participating through a codecision, consultation, or assent procedure.

The (Commission) performs many of the functions commonly associated with an executive branch or a European government. In particular, it proposes new legislation, enforces existing EU law, and represents the EU in various international bodies. Under the principle of "subsidiarity," the Commission makes proposals only in areas in which action at the Community level would be more effective than action at a national level. The Commission consists of 28 members, including a president. Although the Commission members are selected by the member states, the Commission as a whole must be approved by the Parliament, which also has the power to dismiss the Commission by adopting a motion of censure. The Commission is supported by a large bureaucracy divided into many Directorates General (DGs) (e.g., the Directorate-General for the Environment, the Directorate-General for Competition).

The Parliament is a representative body elected directly by the peoples of the member states. It shares legislative and budgetary power with the Council and provides a check over the Commission by virtue of its power to approve and dismiss the Commission. However, it has a weaker and less direct role than the parliaments of the member states and the resulting "democratic deficit" has troubled many Europeans.

The Court of Justice of the European Union (CJEU) and the General Court (EGC) embody the judicial branch of the EU. The CJEU's largest source of jurisdiction is that over questions of EU law referred to it by the national courts of the member states. It also has jurisdiction to review actions of the Commission and controversies between the Council and the member states and between members. Each member state appoints one judge to serve for a renewable six-year term after consultation with the other member states. The CJEU rarely convenes as a full court, more commonly sitting as a Grand Chamber of 13 judges or in chambers of three or five. The judges are assisted by eight advocates general who make public submissions to the Court of Justice on cases brought before it. The EGC has original jurisdiction over certain categories of cases, particularly competition cases and cases brought by private individuals, with issues of law being appealable to the CJEU. Prior to 2009, the EGC was known as the Court of First Instance, and the CJEU was known as the European Court of Justice.

EC legislation may take various forms, but there is an important distinction between "regulations," which are binding and directly applicable in all member states, and "directives," which are binding as to the result to be achieved but leave to national authorities the choice of form and methods in implementing the relevant norms. The Commission may also issue "decisions" that are binding upon those to whom the decision is addressed. According to the case law of the CJEU, EC legislation has supremacy over the laws of the member states. It may also have "direct effect," creating not just obligations for member states but also rights for private parties, particularly if it takes the form of a regulation, but even to a limited extent if it is put in the form of a directive addressed to the member states. We shall encounter examples of directives and regulations in this Problem and an example of a Commission decision in Problem 5.

Additional reading: The literature on the European Union is immense. In order of increasing length and comprehensiveness are Folsom, European Union Law including BREXIT in a Nutshell (9th ed. 2017); Craig & de Búrca, EU Law: Text, Cases, and Materials (6th ed. 2015); Kuijper et al. eds., The Law of the European Union (5th ed. 2018); Smit & Herzog, The Law of the European Union (looseleaf, 2006–).

2. COMMERCIAL AGENT LEGISLATION

With the exceptions of the Automobile Dealers Act of 1956, 15 U.S.C.A. §§ 1221–1225, and some state statutes, American law does not provide special protection for agents and distributors. The situation abroad is quite different. Many European, Latin American, and Middle Eastern countries have enacted legislation to protect agents or distributors, particularly with respect to termination. These statutes seem to be motivated by a felt need to protect an "underdog" class of commercial actors, and perhaps by the sense of respect for vested rights that characterizes some societies. They are not aimed particularly at foreign interests, although their effect on the American style of handling such arrangements may be severe.

To advise a client properly about such a statute, an attorney will need to answer several questions.

(1) What kinds of representatives are covered by the law? It is more common to find legislation protecting agents than legislation protecting distributors. A German court decision of 16 February 1961, 34 B.G.H.Z. 282, explains why:

> It is typical of the commercial agent that he, in contrast to the manufacturer or independent dealer, practices his activity as a rule without putting in his own capital. He generally needs for his activity no substantial funds or equipment. The chief value of his business lies in the relations—created by him—with clients, his clientele. At the end of the contract he necessarily loses the clientele to the principal. Since his business is typically conducted without equipment or capital it vanishes at the contract's end since the clientele remains with the principal and is lost to the agent although it is the chief value of his business. The commercial agent is thus materially more strongly financially affected as a rule by the ending of a contract than an independent dealer who loses a relation to his supplier since the independent dealer keeps the capital and material assets inhering in his business.

There are exceptions, however. Belgian law has long protected distributors where the agreement is exclusive, nearly exclusive, or imposes significant obligations on the distributor such as meeting a quota or refraining from carrying competing products. See Law of 27 July 1961 on the Unilateral Termination of Exclusive Distributorship Agreements of Indefinite Duration, as amended by Law of 13 April 1971. Agents did not enjoy similar protection under Belgian law until the enactment of the Law of 13 April 1995 on Commercial Agency Contracts, which was passed to comply with European Council Directive 86/653 on Commercial Agents, discussed below. In 2014, both of these laws were consolidated into and replaced by Book X of the Belgian Economic Code.

(2) What sorts of obligations does the law impose? The U.S. Automobile Dealers Act of 1956 simply requires automobile manufacturers "to act in good faith in performing or complying with any of the terms or provisions of the franchise, or in terminating, canceling, or not renewing the franchise with said dealer." 15 U.S.C.A. § 1222. "Good faith" is defined as "the duty of each party to any franchise, and all officers, employees, or agents thereof to act in a fair and equitable manner toward each other so as to guarantee the one party freedom from coercion, intimidation, or threats of coercion or intimidation from the other party." 15 U.S.C.A. § 1221(e). Other countries' laws are often much more specific, covering such matters as the conclusion of the contract, compensation, termination of the contract, and restraints on competition, sometimes in great detail. For example, Article 10 of European Council Directive 86/653 on Commercial Agents (Agency Directive), which is concerned with when commissions are paid, provides:

1. The commission shall become due as soon as and to the extent that one of the following circumstances obtains:

   (a) the principal has executed the transaction; or

   (b) the principal should, according to his agreement with the third party, have executed the transaction; or

   (c) the third party has executed the transaction.

2. The commission shall become due at the latest when the third party has executed his part of the transaction or should have done so if the principal had executed his part of the transaction as he should have.

3. The commission shall be paid not later than on the last day of the month following the quarter in which it became due.

4. Agreements to derogate from paragraphs 2 and 3 to the detriment of the commercial agent shall not be permitted.

(3) To what extent can the parties vary these obligations by agreement? The reader will have noticed that paragraphs 2 and 3 of Article 10, just quoted, may not be varied by agreement to the detriment of the agent. By contrast, Article 6 of the same directive, which deals with the level of remuneration, applies only in the absence of an agreement on remuneration by the parties.

A perennial question is whether the parties may avoid such legislation through a choice-of-law clause, a choice-of-forum clause, or some combination of the two. In Volkswagen Interamericana, S.A. v. Rohlsen, 360 F.2d 437 (1st Cir. 1966), the court refused to give effect to a choice-of-forum clause selecting Mexican courts in a suit under the Automobile Dealers Act:

> The very purpose of the act is to give the dealer certain rights against a manufacturer independent of the terms of the agreement itself. . . . This protection would be of little value if a manufacturer could contractually limit jurisdiction to a forum practically inaccessible to the dealer. The act cannot be so easily thwarted.

It is not clear whether a federal court today would reach the same result in light of M/S Bremen v. Zapata Off-Shore Company, 407 U.S. 1, 92 S.Ct. 1907, 32 L.Ed.2d 513 (1972), Mitsubishi Motors Corp. v. Soler Chrysler-Plymouth, Inc., 473 U.S. 614, 105 S.Ct. 3346, 87 L.Ed.2d 444 (1985), Carnival Cruise Lines, Inc. v. Shute, 499 U.S. 585, 111 S.Ct. 1522, 113 L.Ed.2d 622 (1991), and AT&T Mobility LLC v. Concepcion, 563 U.S. 333, 131 S.Ct. 1740, 179 L.Ed.2d 742 (2011). See supra Chapter II. Whether the parties may avoid the EU's Agency Directive by providing that their contract is to be governed by the law of country that is not a member of the European Union is the subject of the European Court of Justice's decision in Ingmar GB Ltd. v. Eaton Leonard Technologies Inc., [2000] ECR I-9305, which is excerpted below. See infra pp. 228–229.

Although many European countries had enacted laws protecting agents, these laws varied substantially in their details. To harmonize such laws, the European Council in 1986 adopted Directive 86/653 on Commercial Agents, 1986 O.J. (L 382) 17 (to which we have already referred). The Council explained in the Directive's second recital that "differences in national laws concerning commercial representation substantially affect the conditions of competition and the carrying-on of that activity within the Community and are detrimental both to the protection available to commercial agents vis-à-vis their principals and to the security of commercial transactions" and that "those differences are such as to inhibit substantially the conclusion and operation of commercial representation contracts where principal and commercial agents are established in different Member States." The provisions of Council Directive 86/653 were primarily based on provisions in German and French law.

It is important to note that this piece of EU legislation is in the form of a directive addressed to the member states. It requires member states to change their domestic laws to implement the directive, but leaves them some discretion as to the precise form such laws will take. Thus, a representative seeking to enforce the rights provided for in the Agency

Directive would bring suit under domestic law in the domestic court of a member state.

Among the Agency Directive's most important provisions are those regarding the termination of an agreement:

Council Directive (86/653/EEC) of 18 December 1986 on the Coordination of the Laws of the Member States Relating to Self-Employed Commercial Agents

1986 O.J. (L 382) 17

* * *

CHAPTER I

Scope

Article 1

1. The harmonization measures prescribed by this Directive shall apply to the laws, regulations and administrative provisions of the Member States governing the relations between commercial agents and their principals.

2. For the purposes of this Directive, "commercial agent" shall mean a self-employed intermediary who has continuing authority to negotiate the sale or the purchase of goods on behalf of another person, hereinafter called the "principal", or to negotiate and conclude such transactions on behalf of and in the name of that principal.

3. A commercial agent shall be understood within the meaning of this Directive as not including in particular:

— a person who, in his capacity as an officer, is empowered to enter into commitments binding on a company or association,

— a partner who is lawfully authorized to enter into commitments binding on his partners,

— a receiver, a receiver and manager, a liquidator or a trustee in bankruptcy.

[handwritten margin note: commercial not agent]

* * *

CHAPTER IV

Conclusion and termination of the agency contract

* * *

Article 14

An agency contract for a fixed period which continues to be performed by both parties after that period has expired shall be deemed to be converted into an agency contract for an indefinite period.

Article 15

1.   Where an agency contract is concluded for an indefinite period either party may terminate it by notice.

2.   The period of notice shall be one month for the first year of the contract, two months for the second year commenced, and three months for the third year commenced and subsequent years. The parties may not agree on shorter periods of notice.

3.   Member States may fix the period of notice at four months for the fourth year of the contract, five months for the fifth year and six months for the sixth and subsequent years. They may decide that the parties may not agree to shorter periods.

4.   If the parties agree on longer periods than those laid down in paragraphs 2 and 3, the period of notice to be observed by the principal must not be shorter than that to be observed by the commercial agent.

5.   Unless otherwise agreed by the parties, the end of the period of notice must coincide with the end of a calendar month.

6.   The provision of this Article shall apply to an agency contract for a fixed period where it is converted under Article 14 into an agency contract for an indefinite period, subject to the proviso that the earlier fixed period must be taken into account in the calculation of the period of notice.

Article 16

Nothing in this Directive shall affect the application of the law of the Member States where the latter provides for the immediate termination of the agency contract:

(a)   because of the failure of one party to carry out all or part of his obligations;

(b)   where exceptional circumstances arise.

Article 17

1.   Member States shall take the measures necessary to ensure that the commercial agent is, after termination of the agency contract, indemnified in accordance with paragraph 2 or compensated for damage in accordance with paragraph 3.

2.   (a)   The commercial agent shall be entitled to an indemnity if and to the extent that:

— he has brought the principal new customers or has significantly increased the volume of business with existing customers and the principal continues to derive substantial benefits from the business with such customers, and

— the payment of this indemnity is equitable having regard to all the circumstances and, in particular, the commission lost by the commercial agent on the business transacted with such customers. Member States may provide for such circumstances also to include the application or otherwise of a restraint of trade clause, within the meaning of Article 20;

(b)   The amount of the indemnity may not exceed a figure equivalent to an indemnity for one year calculated from the commercial agent's average annual remuneration over the preceding five years and if the contract goes back less than five years the indemnity shall be calculated on the average for the period in question;

(c)   The grant of such an indemnity shall not prevent the commercial agent from seeking damages.

3.   The commercial agent shall be entitled to compensation for the damage he suffers as a result of the termination of his relations with the principal.

Such damage shall be deemed to occur particularly when the termination takes place in circumstances:

—   depriving the commercial agent of the commission which proper performance of the agency contract would have procured him whilst providing the principal with substantial benefits linked to the commercial agent's activities,

—   and/or which have not enabled the commercial agent to amortize the costs and expenses that he had incurred for the performance of the agency contract on the principal's advice.

4.   Entitlement to the indemnity as provided for in paragraph 2 or to compensation for damage as provided for under paragraph 3, shall also arise where the agency contract is terminated as a result of the commercial agent's death.

5.   The commercial agent shall lose his entitlement to the indemnity in the instances provided for in paragraph 2 or to compensation for damage in the instances provided for in paragraph 3, if within one year following termination of the contract he has not notified the principal that he intends pursuing his entitlement.

* * *

Article 18

The indemnity or compensation referred to in Article 17 shall not be payable:

(a)   where the principal has terminated the agency contract because of default attributable to the commercial agent which would justify immediate termination of the agency contract under national law;

(b)   where the commercial agent has terminated the agency contract, unless such termination is justified by circumstances attributable to the principal or on grounds of age, infirmity or illness of the commercial agent in consequence of which he cannot reasonably be required to continue his activities;

(c) where, with the agreement of the principal, the commercial agent assigns his rights and duties under the agency contract to another person.

Article 19

The parties may not derogate from Articles 17 and 18 to the detriment of the commercial agent before the agency contract expires.

———————

The Agency Directive was implemented in the United Kingdom by the Commercial Agents (Council Directive) Regulations 1993, which entered into force on January 1, 1994 and gave rise to the following case.

Ingmar GB Ltd. v. Eaton Leonard Technologies Inc.

European Court of Justice (5th Chamber), 2000
[2000] ECR I-9305

[By an agreement dated January 1, 1989, Eaton, a California manufacturer of sophisticated tube and pipe bending machines for the automotive and aircraft industries, appointed Ingmar, a company established in the United Kingdom, as its exclusive agent for the United Kingdom. A clause in the agreement provided that California law would govern. After the agreement was terminated in 1996, Ingmar brought suit before the High Court of Justice of England and Wales, Queen's Bench Division, seeking compensation under the provision of the United Kingdom's regulations that implements Article 17 of the Agency Directive. The High Court held that the U.K. regulations did not apply because the agreement was governed by California law. On appeal, the Court of Appeal of England and Wales (Civil Division) asked the European Court of Justice for a preliminary ruling on the following question:

> Under English law, effect will be given to the applicable law as chosen by the parties, unless there is a public policy reason, such as an overriding provision, for not so doing. In such circumstances, are the provisions of Council Directive 86/653/EEC, as implemented in the laws of the Member States, and in particular those provisions relating to the payment of compensation to agents on termination of their agreements with their principals, applicable when:
>
> (a) a principal appoints an exclusive agent in the United Kingdom and the Republic of Ireland for the sale of its products therein; and
>
> (b) in so far as sales of the products in the United Kingdom are concerned, the agent carries out its activities in the United Kingdom; and

(c) the principal is a company incorporated in a non-EU State, and in particular in the State of California, USA, and situated there; and

(d) the express applicable law of the contract between the parties is that of the State of California, USA?]

* * *

21 The purpose of Articles 17 to 19 of the Directive, in particular, is to protect the commercial agent after termination of the contract. The regime established by the Directive for that purpose is mandatory in nature. Article 17 requires Member States to put in place a mechanism for providing reparation to the commercial agent after termination of the contract. Admittedly, that article allows the Member States to choose between indemnification and compensation for damage. However, Articles 17 and 18 prescribe a precise framework within which the Member States may exercise their discretion as to the choice of methods for calculating the indemnity or compensation to be granted.

22 The mandatory nature of those articles is confirmed by the fact that, under Article 19 of the Directive, the parties may not derogate from them to the detriment of the commercial agent before the contract expires. It is also borne out by the fact that, with regard to the United Kingdom, Article 22 of the Directive provides for the immediate application of the national provisions implementing the Directive to contracts in operation.

23 Second, it should be borne in mind that, as is apparent from the second recital in the preamble to the Directive, the harmonising measures laid down by the Directive are intended, *inter alia*, to eliminate restrictions on the carrying-on of the activities of commercial agents, to make the conditions of competition within the Community uniform and to increase the security of commercial transactions.

24 The purpose of the regime established in Articles 17 to 19 of the Directive is thus to protect, for all commercial agents, freedom of establishment and the operation of undistorted competition in the internal market. Those provisions must therefore be observed throughout the Community if those Treaty objectives are to be attained.

25 It must therefore be held that it is essential for the Community legal order that a principal established in a non-member country, whose commercial agent carries on his activity within the Community, cannot evade those provisions by the simple expedient of a choice-of-law clause. The purpose served by the provisions in question requires that they be applied where the situation is closely connected with the Community, in particular where the commercial agent carries on his activity in the territory of a Member State, irrespective of the law by which the parties intended the contract to be governed.

Upon remand from the Court of Appeal, the High Court of Justice awarded Ingmar £183,600 in compensation under the Commercial Agents (Council Directive) Regulations 1993.

In 1980, the member states of the European Community concluded a Convention on the Law Applicable to Contractual Obligations, 1998 O.J. (C 27) 2 (consolidated version), commonly known as the Rome Convention. Its provisions on choice of law and mandatory rules were not applied in *Ingmar* because the Convention had not entered into force when the parties' agreement was signed. On December 17, 2009, the Rome Convention was superseded by Regulation (EC) No. 593/2008 on the Law Applicable to Contractual Obligations (Rome I Regulation), 2008 O.J. (L 177) 6, except with respect to Denmark. Consider how the following provisions of the Rome I Regulation might affect the question in *Ingmar*:

Article 3

Freedom of choice

1.   A contract shall be governed by the law chosen by the parties. The choice shall be made expressly or clearly demonstrated by the terms of the contract or the circumstances of the case. By their choice the parties can select the law applicable to the whole or to part only of the contract.

* * *

3.   Where all other elements relevant to the situation at the time of the choice are located in a country other than the country whose law has been chosen, the choice of the parties shall not prejudice the application of provisions of the law of that other country which cannot be derogated from by agreement.

* * *

Article 9

Overriding mandatory provisions

1.   Overriding mandatory provisions are provisions the respect for which is regarded as crucial by a country for safeguarding its public interests, such as its political, social or economic organisation, to such an extent that they are applicable to any situation falling within their scope, irrespective of the law otherwise applicable to the contract under this Regulation.

2.   Nothing in this Regulation shall restrict the application of the overriding mandatory provisions of the law of the forum.

3.   Effect may be given to the overriding mandatory provisions of the law of the country where the obligations arising out of the contract have to be or have been performed, in so far as those overriding mandatory provisions render the performance of the contract unlawful. In considering whether to give effect to those

provisions, regard shall be had to their nature and purpose and to the consequences of their application or non-application.

*   *   *

Article 23

Relationship with other provisions of Community law

With the exception of Article 7, this Regulation shall not prejudice the application of provisions of Community law which, in relation to particular matters, lay down conflict-of-law rules relating to contractual obligations.

*   *   *

QUESTIONS

(1) Compare the provisions of the Agency Directive with the Automobile Dealers Act. Which has the advantage in terms of clarity, fairness and enforceability?

(2) Is the Distribution Agreement at supra pp. 215–219 subject to the Agency Directive?

(3) Suppose that the parties were moved by advantages they perceived from an antitrust perspective (infra pp. 232–248) to shift from an independent distributor relationship to an agency agreement. How would that affect the posture of the parties under German legislation implementing the Agency Directive?

(4) Assuming that the parties' agreement is subject to German legislation implementing the Agency Directive, what changes would have to be made to the agreement's provisions concerning notice of and indemnity upon termination?

(5) Note that Articles 11 and 12 of the agreement provide for an initial term of three years, renewable by the manufacturer, but permit either party to terminate without cause. Assuming again that the agreement is subject to German legislation implementing the Agency Directive, would it be preferable to provide for a shorter term with an option to renew or to provide for termination without cause?

(6) In contrast to Eaton in the Ingmar case, Techno has included an arbitration clause as well as a choice-of-law clause in its proposed agreement. Will this enable Techno to succeed in resisting a claim for indemnity upon termination where Eaton failed?

Additional reading: Corporate Counsel's Guide to Distribution Counseling ch. 50 (looseleaf, 2006–); Jacobs, International Distribution and Franchising, 7 Int. Q. 302 (1995).

C. EXCLUSIVITY

1. THE USE OF EXCLUSIVE CONTRACTS

The materials that follow treat problems posed by exclusive distributorship arrangements under the antitrust laws of the United States and of the European Union. This section describes some characteristics of these contracts.

Contracts of exclusive distributorship between the manufacturer and the wholesaler (distributor) or retailer (dealer) of a product restrict the selling rights of either or both parties, usually territorially. Because those restrictions arise from agreements between companies that operate at different levels in the chain of production and distribution, they constitute vertical restraints. The comments below treat three typical restraints.

Territorial Exclusivity

In their simplest form, exclusive distributorship contracts confer exclusive rights upon the distributor to sell the product within a defined territory. In the European Union, the exclusive territory is generally a member nation. For example, Berlinco, a German manufacturer of widgets, may agree to sell to Parisco, a French distributor, and also agree not to sell widgets to any other person in France. Berlinco might enter into comparable contracts with distributors in other European countries.

Note the effect of such "sole-outlet" arrangements. Unless French dealers or consumers make the effort to purchase Berlinco widgets from suppliers in foreign countries, or unless foreign suppliers are willing to advertise or open branches in France, Parisco may have a monopoly of the French market for Berlinco widgets. There may be no "intrabrand" competition. How much freedom this gives Parisco with respect to pricing and other policies will depend upon the extent to which it faces meaningful competition from distributors of other brands of widgets—upon the extent of "interbrand" as opposed to "intrabrand" competition. For example, if Berlinco widgets are readily interchangeable with other brands (if, for example, we are talking about different toothpaste brands), competition for consumers in the widget market would remain keen.

Manufacturers and distributors offer varied justifications for the possible anticompetitive effects of these agreements. The protection given Parisco may encourage it to make the investment of funds and energy to introduce a new product or promote more intensively one already on the market. That protection may be an essential condition to various commitments by Parisco. For example, if widgets were complex products such as electronic equipment requiring servicing, the firms might contend that the agreement gave Parisco the minimum assurance against competition that would lead it to develop an expert sales staff, post-sales service operations, and so on. It further assures Parisco that other distributors will not be able to take advantage of its efforts and benefit from the developing market for Berlinco widgets without comparable investments of their own. The arrangement thus is said to spur rather than limit competition among brands. Of course, the force of this argument will depend upon the degree to which there is effective interbrand competition.

Territorial Restrictions

A second restraint might perfect this arrangement by adding territorial restrictions upon sales by distributors. Parisco agrees not to sell widgets to any dealer or consumer outside its exclusive French territory, or indeed to any dealer or consumer in France whom Parisco knows to be a resident of a foreign country. Contracts between Berlinco and exclusive distributors in other countries may contain comparable clauses. Thus a network of truly exclusive territories has been created. The consumer loses the option available to him under the sole-outlet agreement to shop in other national markets. Intrabrand competition among Berlinco widget distributors disappears. Again, the anticompetitive effects of this arrangement will depend upon a variety of factors, including the extent to which there is meaningful interbrand competition. Justifications offered for this restriction are similar to those noted above. Either or both firms may claim that it is indispensable to the business arrangement, in the sense that Parisco would not have undertaken its selling efforts without assurance of absolute territorial protection.

Noncompete Obligations

A third restraint might prevent Parisco from handling any products competitive with the widgets purchased from Berlinco. The anticompetitive effects of this "noncompete" arrangement may be severe, if Berlinco's competitors were thereby foreclosed from finding satisfactory distributor outlets to reach the French market.

This simplified description of exclusive distributorship arrangements bypasses arguments of a more subtle character that may be relevant or critical to a determination of their legality. Extensive economic data may prove essential to an evaluation of the effect of a given arrangement and the sufficiency of the justifications offered for it. For example, the extent of interbrand competition may determine Parisco's freedom to set prices or other sales policies; price differentials, if any, between Berlinco widgets in France and other countries may evidence whether Parisco has a virtual monopoly of the French widget market; the size and reputation of Parisco *vis-à-vis* other distributors in the field may determine the extent to which a "noncompete" provision limits opportunities for Berlinco's competitors.

2. CONSEQUENCES UNDER U.S. ANTITRUST LAW

The fundamental texts of U.S. antitrust law are Sections 1 and 2 of the Sherman Act, 15 U.S.C.A. §§ 1–2, which read as follows:

§ 1. Trusts, etc., in restraint of trade illegal; penalty

Every contract, combination in the form of trust or otherwise, or conspiracy, in restraint of trade or commerce among the several States, or with foreign nations, is declared to be illegal. Every person who shall make any contract or engage in any combination or conspiracy hereby declared to be illegal shall be deemed guilty of a felony, and, on conviction thereof, shall be punished by fine not exceeding $100,000,000 if a corporation, or, if any other person, $1,000,000, or by imprisonment not exceeding ten years, or by both said punishments, in the discretion of the court.

§ 2. Monopolizing trade a felony; penalty

Every person who shall monopolize, or attempt to monopolize, or combine or conspire with any other person or persons, to monopolize any part of the trade or commerce among the several States, or with foreign nations, shall be deemed guilty of a felony, and, on conviction thereof, shall be punished by fine not exceeding $100,000,000 if a corporation, or, if any other person, $1,000,000, or by imprisonment not exceeding ten years, or by both said punishments, in the discretion of the court.

The U.S. Department of Justice may prosecute violations of the Sherman Act as civil or criminal offenses. Private plaintiffs may also obtain injunctive relief or treble damages for violations of the Act. The Sherman Act is supplemented by a number of other laws, including the Clayton Act and the Hart-Scott-Rodino Antitrust Improvements Act, which deal with mergers and will be discussed further in Problem 5.

As the U.S. Supreme Court has noted, the Sherman Act's language "has a generality and adaptability comparable to that found to be desirable in constitutional provisions," Sugar Institute v. United States, 297 U.S. 553, 600, 56 S.Ct. 629, 80 L.Ed. 859 (1936), and like the U.S. Constitution it cannot be understood without reference to the extensive case law interpreting it. Of prime importance is the distinction the Supreme Court has drawn between restraints that are analyzed under a "rule of reason" and restraints considered *per se* violations of the Act. The Court summarized the distinction in State Oil Co. v. Khan, 522 U.S. 3, 10, 118 S.Ct. 275, 279, 139 L.Ed.2d 199 (1997):

> Although the Sherman Act, by its terms, prohibits every agreement "in restraint of trade," this Court has long recognized that Congress intended to outlaw only unreasonable restraints. See, *e.g., Arizona v. Maricopa County Medical Soc.,* 457 U.S. 332, 342–343, 102 S.Ct. 2466, 2472–2473, 73 L.Ed.2d 48 (1982) (citing *United States v. Joint Traffic Assn.,* 171 U.S. 505, 19 S.Ct. 25, 43 L.Ed. 259 (1898)). As a consequence, most antitrust claims are analyzed under a "rule of reason," according to which the finder of fact must decide whether the questioned practice imposes an unreasonable restraint on competition, taking into

account a variety of factors, including specific information about the relevant business, its condition before and after the restraint was imposed, and the restraint's history, nature, and effect. 457 U.S., at 343, and n. 13, 102 S.Ct., at 2472, and n. 13 (citing *Board of Trade of Chicago v. United States*, 246 U.S. 231, 238, 38 S.Ct. 242, 243–244, 62 L.Ed. 683 (1918)).

Some types of restraints, however, have such predictable and pernicious anticompetitive effect, and such limited potential for procompetitive benefit, that they are deemed unlawful *per se*. *Northern Pacific R. Co. v. United States,* 356 U.S. 1, 5, 78 S.Ct. 514, 518, 2 L.Ed.2d 545 (1958). *Per se* treatment is appropriate "[o]nce experience with a particular kind of restraint enables the Court to predict with confidence that the rule of reason will condemn it." *Maricopa County, supra,* at 344, 102 S.Ct., at 2473. . . .

Among the few restraints still considered *per se* violations are tying, where the seller has market power, see Eastman Kodak Co. v. Image Technical Services, Inc., 504 U.S. 451, 112 S.Ct. 2072, 119 L.Ed.2d 265 (1992), and agreements between competitors to fix prices, see Catalano, Inc. v. Target Sales, Inc., 446 U.S. 643, 647, 100 S.Ct. 1925, 1927, 64 L.Ed.2d 580 (1980), or to divide markets, see Palmer v. BRG of Georgia, Inc., 498 U.S. 46, 49, 111 S.Ct. 401, 402, 112 L.Ed.2d 349 (1990). It is worth noting that in several respects the "rule of reason" read into the Sherman Act bears an analogy to paragraph (3) of Article 101 of the Treaty on the Functioning of the European Union. See infra p. 239.

The Sherman Act's application to commerce with foreign nations is the subject of both judicial decisions and statutory law. With respect to import commerce, the Supreme Court held in Hartford Fire Insurance Co. v. California, 509 U.S. 764, 796, 113 S.Ct. 2891, 125 L.Ed.2d 612 (1993), that "the Sherman Act applies to foreign conduct that was meant to produce and did in fact produce some substantial effect in the United States." With respect to export commerce or commerce outside the United States, the Foreign Trade Antitrust Improvements Act of 1982, 15 U.S.C.A. § 6a, adopts a similar effects test.

Early antitrust litigation in the United States concerned primarily horizontal agreements—for example, price fixing or division of territories among competitors. Although certain kinds of vertical agreements had long been significant in antitrust enforcement—resale price maintenance agreements, for example—the exclusive distributorship contract had not. Thus the American experience has been unlike that of the European Union, where exclusive distributorship contracts became an early focus of litigation and regulation.

In a series of cases during the 1960s and 70s, the U.S. Supreme Court wrestled with the question whether territorial exclusivity and territorial restrictions violate Section 1 of the Sherman Act. See White Motor Co. v. United States, 372 U.S. 253, 83 S.Ct. 696, 9 L.Ed.2d 738

(1963); United States v. Arnold, Schwinn & Co., 388 U.S. 365, 87 S.Ct. 1856, 18 L.Ed.2d 1249 (1967); Continental T.V., Inc. v. GTE Sylvania, Inc., 433 U.S. 36, 97 S.Ct. 2549, 53 L.Ed.2d 568 (1977). Ultimately, the Court reversed the position it had taken in Schwinn and held in Sylvania that nonprice vertical restrictions should be analyzed under the "rule of reason":

> Vertical restrictions reduce intrabrand competition by limiting the number of sellers of a particular product competing for the business of a given group of buyers. . . .

> Vertical restrictions promote interbrand competition by allowing the manufacturer to achieve certain efficiencies in the distribution of his products. These "redeeming virtues" are implicit in every decision sustaining vertical restrictions under the rule of reason. Economists have identified a number of ways in which manufacturers can use such restrictions to compete more effectively against other manufacturers. . . . For example, new manufacturers and manufacturers entering new markets can use the restrictions in order to induce competent and aggressive retailers to make the kind of investment of capital and labor that is often required in the distribution of products unknown to the consumer. Established manufacturers can use them to induce retailers to engage in promotional activities or to provide service and repair facilities necessary to the efficient marketing of their products. Service and repair are vital for many products, such as automobiles and major household appliances. The availability and quality of such services affect a manufacturer's goodwill and the competitiveness of his product. Because of market imperfections such as the so-called "free rider" effect, these services might not be provided by retailers in a purely competitive situation, despite the fact that each retailer's benefit would be greater if all provided the services than if none did. . . .

> * * *

> . . . [Vertical] restrictions, in varying forms, are widely used in our free market economy. As indicated above, there is substantial scholarly and judicial authority supporting their economic utility. There is relatively little authority to the contrary. Certainly, there has been no showing in this case, either generally or with respect to Sylvania's agreements, that vertical restrictions have or are likely to have a "pernicious effect on competition" or that they "lack any . . . any redeeming virtue." Ibid. Accordingly, we conclude that the *per se* rule stated in *Schwinn* must be overruled. . . .

> In sum, we conclude that the appropriate decision is to return to the rule of reason that governed vertical restrictions

prior to *Schwinn.* When anticompetitive effects are shown to result from particular vertical restrictions they can be adequately policed under the rule of reason, the standard traditionally applied for the majority of anticompetitive practices challenged under § 1 of the Act.

GTE Sylvania, 433 U.S. at 54–59, 97 S.Ct. at 2560–2562.

More recently, the Supreme Court has extended the rule of reason to cover price restrictions in vertical agreements. In State Oil Co. v. Khan, 522 U.S. 3, 118 S.Ct. 275, 139 L.Ed.2d 199 (1997), the Supreme Court held that maximum price-fixing should no longer be considered a *per se* violation in vertical agreements, and in Leegin Creative Leather Products, Inc. v. PSKS, Inc., 551 U.S. 877, 127 S.Ct. 2705, 168 L.Ed.2d 623 (2007), the Court did the same with respect to minimum price-fixing.

The justifications for vertical price restraints are similar to those for other vertical restraints. See *GTE Sylvania*, 433 U.S., at 54–57. Minimum resale price maintenance can stimulate interbrand competition—the competition among manufacturers selling different brands of the same type of product—by reducing intrabrand competition—the competition among retailers selling the same brand. See *id.*, at 51–52. The promotion of interbrand competition is important because "the primary purpose of the antitrust laws is to protect [this type of] competition." *Khan*, 522 U.S., at 15. A single manufacturer's use of vertical price restraints tends to eliminate intrabrand price competition; this in turn encourages retailers to invest in tangible or intangible services or promotional efforts that aid the manufacturer's position as against rival manufacturers. Resale price maintenance also has the potential to give consumers more options so that they can choose among low-price, low-service brands; high-price, high-service brands; and brands that fall in between.

Absent vertical price restraints, the retail services that enhance interbrand competition might be underprovided. This is because discounting retailers can free ride on retailers who furnish services and then capture some of the increased demand those services generate. *GTE Sylvania, supra*, at 55. Consumers might learn, for example, about the benefits of a manufacturer's product from a retailer that invests in fine showrooms, offers product demonstrations, or hires and trains knowledgeable employees. R. Posner, Antitrust Law 172–173 (2d ed. 2001). . . .

Leegin, 551 U.S. at 890–891, 127 S.Ct. at 2715.

It is important to note that the limitations U.S. antitrust law imposes upon distributorship agreements generally do not apply to agency agreements. This result is justified on the ground that because an agent is not "independent" of its principal there can be no contract or conspiracy in restraint of trade. See Simpson v. Union Oil Co., 377 U.S. 13, 84 S.Ct. 1051, 12 L.Ed.2d 98 (1964). Accordingly, U.S. courts have allowed provisions in agency agreements, such as provisions fixing prices, that would have been considered *per se* violations in an agreement with a distributor. See United States v. General Electric Co., 272 U.S. 476, 47 S.Ct. 192, 71 L.Ed. 362 (1926).

It is also important to remember that the Sherman Act applies to foreign commerce only when the agreement in question has a substantial effect in the United States. See supra p. 235. Restraints on competition in an agreement between a U.S. manufacturer and a foreign distributor are unlikely to cause such an effect unless those restraints effectively prevent other U.S. manufacturers from accessing the foreign market. Nor would Section 3 of the Clayton Act, 15 U.S.C.A. § 14, which prohibits noncompete agreements the effect of which "may be to substantially lessen competition or tend to create a monopoly," apply to agreements with foreign distributors, since it governs only sales for "use, consumption, or resale within the United States."

However, the relatively lax treatment under U.S. law of vertical agreements, and particularly of vertical agreements for the export of U.S. products, may not be used to insulate what are really horizontal agreements among competitors to divide markets. Thus, an agreement in which a U.S. manufacturer appoints a foreign competitor as its exclusive distributor or agent in the foreign country and the foreign competitor appoints the U.S. manufacturer as its exclusive distributor or agent in the United States may be found to violate the Sherman Act. See, e.g., Timken Roller Bearing Co. v. United States, 341 U.S. 593, 71 S.Ct. 971, 95 L.Ed. 1199 (1951); United States v. Masonite Corp., 316 U.S. 265, 62 S.Ct. 1070, 86 L.Ed. 1461 (1942).

3. CONSEQUENCES UNDER EUROPEAN UNION COMPETITION LAW

The following materials are designed to give the reader a basic familiarity with the antitrust laws of the European Union. For a fuller exposition of the legal structure of the Community and of its law-making institutions, the Court of Justice, the Commission, the Council and the Parliament, see supra pp. 220–222.

The analysis starts with Articles 101 and 102 of the Treaty on the Functioning of the European Union, 2010 O.J. (C 83) 47 (consolidated version). Between 1997 and 2009, these were known as Articles 81 and 82 of the EC Treaty, and before 1997 as Articles 85 and 86 of the Treaty of Rome.

Article 101

1. The following shall be prohibited as incompatible with the common market: all agreements between undertakings, decision by associations of undertakings and concerted practices

which may affect trade between Member States and which have as their object or effect the prevention, restriction or distortion of competition within the common market, and in particular those which:

    (a)   directly or indirectly fix purchase or selling prices or any other trading conditions;

    (b)   limit or control production, markets, technical development, or investment;

    (c)   share markets or sources of supply;

    (d)   apply dissimilar conditions to equivalent transactions with other trading parties, thereby placing them at a competitive disadvantage;

    (e)   make the conclusion of contracts subject to acceptance by the other parties of supplementary obligations which, by their nature or according to commercial usage, have no connection with the subject of such contracts.

2.   Any agreements or decisions prohibited pursuant to this Article shall be automatically void.

3.   The provisions of paragraph 1 may, however, be declared inapplicable in the case of:

    —   any agreement or category of agreements between undertakings;

    —   any decision or category of decisions by associations of undertakings;

    —   any concerted practice or category of concerted practices;

which contributes to improving the production or distribution of goods or to promoting technical or economic progress, while allowing consumers a fair share of the resulting benefit, and which does not:

    (a)   impose on the undertakings concerned restrictions which are not indispensable to the attainment of these objectives;

    (b)   afford such undertakings the possibility of eliminating competition in respect of a substantial part of the products in question.

Article 102

Any abuse by one or more undertakings of a dominant position within the common market or in a substantial part of it shall be prohibited as incompatible with the common market in so far as it may affect trade between Member States.

Such abuse may, in particular, consist in:

(a) directly or indirectly imposing unfair purchase or selling prices or other unfair trading conditions;

(b) limiting production, markets or technical development to the prejudice of consumers;

(c) applying dissimilar conditions to equivalent transactions with other trading parties, thereby placing them at a competitive disadvantage;

(d) making the conclusion of contracts subject to acceptance by the other parties of supplementary obligations which, by their nature or according to commercial usage, have no connection with the subject of such contracts.

These two articles will remind the reader, respectively, of Sections 1 and 2 of the Sherman Act. See supra p. 233. And they raise the same question regarding their geographic scope—that is, whether they apply to international arrangements such as the one here being examined. Note that Article 101 covers agreements "which may affect trade between the Member States" and that Article 102 applies to abuse "of a dominant position within the common market or a substantial part of it." In the Wood Pulp case, Åhlström Osakeyhtiö v. Commission, [1988] ECR 5193, the European Court of Justice upheld the authority of the Commission to impose fines under Article 101 (then Article 85 of the Treaty of Rome) on foreign wood pulp producers who had agreed on prices to be charged to buyers in the European Community. The Court stated that such conduct involved two elements: the formation of the agreement, and its implementation (that is, the application of the agreed-upon prices in transactions with buyers). It concluded that the decisive factor in determining whether the Community had jurisdiction to regulate the transactions was the place of implementation. Because the pricing agreement was implemented within the common market, the Community had jurisdiction to apply its rules to the conduct. Id. at ¶¶ 16–17. Although the Court avoided characterizing the result as such, it thus approved the application of EU competition law to foreign commerce on the basis of its domestic effects, much as the Supreme Court has done in interpreting U.S. antitrust law. See supra at p. 235.

Effective May 1, 2004—the date on which the EU grew from 15 to 25 member states—the European Commission put into place a series of reforms, commonly known as the "Modernization Package," the general thrust of which was to decentralize the enforcement of EU competition law and to depend more heavily on national courts and competition authorities. The Modernization Package is embodied in Council Regulation No. 1/2003, 2003 O.J. (L 1) 1, which replaced Council Regulation No. 17, and is elaborated in a number of notices and guidelines issued by the Commission.

Under Article 101(3), an agreement with anticompetitive effects may nevertheless be permitted if it provides sufficient countervailing benefits for consumers. One way in which this provision has been implemented is through a series of "block exemptions," regulations under which the Commission exempts entire categories of agreements or practices. An example is the Block Exemption Regulation discussed below. The Modernization Package continues this system of block exemptions.

Prior to May 1, 2004, the parties to an agreement that did not fit within a block exemption had the alternative of seeking a "negative clearance" from the Commission. Council Regulation No. 1/2003 abolished this notification system and gave national competition authorities and courts the authority to apply Article 101(3), which means that they, rather than the Commission, now determine in individual cases whether a restrictive agreement is permitted because of its countervailing benefits.

Of course, decentralization carries the risk that enforcement of EU Competition law will not be uniform. To limit this risk, the Commission issued as part of the Modernization Package a set of Guidelines on the application of Article 101(3), which complements other Commission guidelines dealing with particular types of agreements. The Commission also issued a Notice on cooperation between the Commission and the courts of the EU Member States that allows judges to ask the Commission for information and opinions on cases before them and a Notice on cooperation within the Network of Competition Authorities that provides guidance on work-sharing and the exchange of information. For genuinely novel questions of law, the Commission may issue a "guidance letter" at the request of a business, but these letters are not binding on the Commission, national competition authorities, or national courts.

In Consten and Grundig v. Commission, [1966] E.C.R. 299, the European Court of Justice held that vertical distribution agreements came within the scope of Article 101 (then Article 85). In 1967 the Commission issued its first block exemption, Regulation 67/67, 1967 O.J. 10, which spelled out conditions under which Article 101 would not be regarded as applicable to distribution agreements. The current block exemption, known as the Block Exemption Regulation 330/2010, 2010 O.J. (L 102) 1, entered into force on June 1, 2010.

The Regulation's recitals recognize the procompetitive aspects of distribution agreements:

(6) Certain types of vertical agreements can improve economic efficiency within a chain of production or distribution by facilitating better coordination between the participating undertakings. In particular, they can lead to a reduction in the transaction and distribution costs of the parties and to an optimisation of their sales and investment levels.

(7) The likelihood that such efficiency-enhancing effects will outweigh any anti-competitive effects due to restrictions contained in vertical agreements depends on the degree of market power of the parties to the agreement and, therefore, on the extent to which those undertakings face competition from other suppliers of goods or services regarded by their customers as interchangeable or substitutable for one another, by reason of the products' characteristics, their prices and their intended use.

(8) It can be presumed that, where the market share held by each of the undertakings party to the agreement on the relevant market does not exceed 30%, vertical agreements which do not contain certain types of severe restrictions of competition generally lead to an improvement in production or distribution and allow consumers a fair share of the resulting benefits.

The block exemption declares that Article 101(1) is not applicable to vertical agreements—that is, agreements between entities that operate at different levels in the chain of production or distribution—so long as each party's market share does not exceed 30%. Article 4 contains a list of "hardcore restrictions"—contractual terms that will cause the agreement to lose the protection of the block exemption. Article 5 contains a further list of "excluded restrictions"—terms that will not take the entire agreement outside the scope of the block exemption but that are not themselves exempt from Article 101(1) and that therefore may be unenforceable under Article 101(2). If an agreement or term falls outside the scope of the block exemption, it must be analyzed under Article 101 on an individual basis. On the one hand, there is no presumption that a vertical agreement falling outside the block exemption because the market share thresholds are exceeded will violate Article 101. On the other hand, there is a presumption that agreements containing hardcore restrictions violate Article 101.

Commission Regulation (EU) No. 330/2010 of 20 April 2010 on the Application of Article 101(3) of the Treaty on the Functioning of the European Union to Categories of Vertical Agreements and Concerted Practices

2010 O.J. (L 102) 1

* * *

Article 1

Definitions

1.   For the purposes of this Regulation, the following definitions shall apply:

(a) "vertical agreement" means an agreement or concerted practice entered into between two or more undertakings each of which operates, for the purposes of the agreement or the concerted practice, at a different level of the production or distribution chain, and relating to the conditions under which the parties may purchase, sell or resell certain goods or services;

(b) "vertical restraint" means a restriction of competition in a vertical agreement falling within the scope of Article 101(1) of the Treaty;

(c) "competing undertaking" means an actual or potential competitor; "actual competitor" means an undertaking that is active on the same relevant market; "potential competitor" means an undertaking that, in the absence of the vertical agreement, would, on realistic grounds and not just as a mere theoretical possibility, in case of a small but permanent increase in relative prices be likely to undertake, within a short period of time, the necessary additional investments or other necessary switching costs to enter the relevant market;

(d) "non-compete obligation" means any direct or indirect obligation causing the buyer not to manufacture, purchase, sell or resell goods or services which compete with the contract goods or services, or any direct or indirect obligation on the buyer to purchase from the supplier or from another undertaking designated by the supplier more than 80% of the buyer's total purchases of the contract goods or services and their substitutes on the relevant market, calculated on the basis of the value or, where such is standard industry practice, the volume of its purchases in the preceding calendar year;

* * *

(h) "buyer" includes an undertaking which, under an agreement falling within Article 101(1) of the Treaty, sells goods or services on behalf of another undertaking;

(i) "customer of the buyer" means an undertaking not party to the agreement which purchases the contract goods or services from a buyer which is party to the agreement.

* * *

Article 2

Exemption

1.   Pursuant to Article 101(3) of the Treaty and subject to the provisions of this Regulation, it is hereby declared that Article 101(1) of the Treaty shall not apply to vertical agreements.

This exemption shall apply to the extent that such agreements contain vertical restraints.

2.   The exemption provided for in paragraph 1 shall apply to vertical agreements entered into between an association of undertakings and its members, or between such an association and its suppliers, only if all its members are retailers of goods and if no individual member of the association, together with its connected undertakings, has a total annual turnover exceeding EUR 50 million. Vertical agreements entered into by such associations shall be covered by this Regulation without prejudice to the application of Article 101 of the Treaty to horizontal agreements concluded between the members of the association or decisions adopted by the association.

3.   The exemption provided for in paragraph 1 shall apply to vertical agreements containing provisions which relate to the assignment to the buyer or use by the buyer of intellectual property rights, provided that those provisions do not constitute the primary object of such agreements and are directly related to the use, sale or resale of goods or services by the buyer or its customers. The exemption applies on condition that, in relation to the contract goods or services, those provisions do not contain restrictions of competition having the same object as vertical restraints which are not exempted under this Regulation.

4.   The exemption provided for in paragraph 1 shall not apply to vertical agreements entered into between competing undertakings. However, it shall apply where competing undertakings enter into a non-reciprocal vertical agreement and:

(a)   the supplier is a manufacturer and a distributor of goods, while the buyer is a distributor and not a competing undertaking at the manufacturing level; or

(b)   the supplier is a provider of services at several levels of trade, while the buyer provides its goods or services at the retail level and is not a competing undertaking at the level of trade where it purchases the contract services.

5.   This Regulation shall not apply to vertical agreements the subject matter of which falls within the scope of any other block exemption regulation, unless otherwise provided for in such a regulation.

Article 3

Market share threshold

1.   The exemption provided for in Article 2 shall apply on condition that the market share held by the supplier does not exceed 30% of the relevant market on which it sells the contract goods or services and the market share held by the buyer does not exceed 30% of the relevant market on which it purchases the contract goods or services.

2.   For the purposes of paragraph 1, where in a multi party agreement an undertaking buys the contract goods or services from one undertaking party to the agreement and sells the contract goods or services to another undertaking party to the agreement, the market share of the first

undertaking must respect the market share threshold provided for in that paragraph both as a buyer and a supplier in order for the exemption provided for in Article 2 to apply.

Article 4

Restrictions that remove the benefit of the block exemption—hardcore restrictions

[handwritten: Hardcore! — assumed pot. anticomp.]

The exemption provided for in Article 2 shall not apply to vertical agreements which, directly or indirectly, in isolation or in combination with other factors under the control of the parties, have as their object:

(a) the restriction of the buyer's ability to determine its sale price, without prejudice to the possibility of the supplier to impose a maximum sale price or recommend a sale price, provided that they do not amount to a fixed or minimum sale price as a result of pressure from, or incentives offered by, any of the parties;

[handwritten: (can set a ceiling) (can't say you can only sell above this price) — no price term.]

(b) the restriction of the territory into which, or of the customers to whom, a buyer party to the agreement, without prejudice to a restriction on its place of establishment, may sell the contract goods or services, except:

(i) the restriction of active sales into the exclusive territory or to an exclusive customer group reserved to the supplier or allocated by the supplier to another buyer, where such a restriction does not limit sales by the customers of the buyer,

(ii) the restriction of sales to end users by a buyer operating at the wholesale level of trade, . . .

* * *

Article 5

Excluded restrictions

[handwritten: excluding: — just the restr. may be invalid!]

1. The exemption provided for in Article 2 shall not apply to the following obligations contained in vertical agreements:

(a) any direct or indirect non-compete obligation, the duration of which is indefinite or exceeds five years;

(b) any direct or indirect obligation causing the buyer, after termination of the agreement, not to manufacture, purchase, sell or resell goods or services; . . .

* * *

For the purposes of point (a) of the first subparagraph, a non compete obligation which is tacitly renewable beyond a period of five years shall be deemed to have been concluded for an indefinite duration.

2. By way of derogation from paragraph 1(a), the time limitation of five years shall not apply where the contract goods or services are sold by the buyer from premises and land owned by the supplier or leased by the

supplier from third parties not connected with the buyer, provided that the duration of the non-compete obligation does not exceed the period of occupancy of the premises and land by the buyer.

3.   By way of derogation from paragraph 1(b), the exemption provided for in Article 2 shall apply to any direct or indirect obligation causing the buyer, after termination of the agreement, not to manufacture, purchase, sell or resell goods or services where the following conditions are fulfilled:

   (a)   the obligation relates to goods or services which compete with the contract goods or services;

   (b)   the obligation is limited to the premises and land from which the buyer has operated during the contract period; . . .

   (d)   the duration of the obligation is limited to a period of one year after termination of the agreement.

Paragraph 1(b) is without prejudice to the possibility of imposing a restriction which is unlimited in time on the use and disclosure of know-how which has not entered the public domain.

In 1962, the Commission issued an official notice stating that generally agreements with commercial agents would not fall within Article 101(1) (then Article 85(1)). 1962 O.J. 2921. In connection with the adoption of the Block Exemption Regulation, the Commission in 2010 issued new Guidelines on Vertical Restraints, 2010 O.J. (C 130) 1, paragraphs 12–21 of which discuss the applicability of Article 101(1) to agents. An intermediary will be considered an agent for the purposes of Article 101(1) if it "does not bear any, or bears only insignificant, risks in relation to the contracts concluded and/or negotiated on behalf of the principal." Title to the goods must not vest in the agent, and the agent must not contribute to the cost of purchasing or transporting the goods, maintain stocks of the goods at its own cost or risk, undertake responsibility towards third parties for damage caused by the goods, take responsibility for the customer's non-performance of the contract, be obliged to invest in sales promotion, or make market-specific investments in equipment, premises, or the training of personnel.

If an agency agreement meets these conditions, "all obligations imposed on the agent in relation to the contracts concluded and/or negotiated on behalf of the principal fall outside Article 101(1)." In particular, an agency agreement may include territorial restrictions and prices and conditions at which the agent must sell the goods. Provisions relating to the relationship between the agent and the principal, on the other hand, may infringe Article 101(1). "Exclusive agency provisions will in general not lead to anti-competitive effects. However, single branding provisions and post-term non-compete provisions, which concern inter-brand competition, may infringe Article 101(1) if they lead to or contribute to a (cumulative) foreclosure effect on the relevant market."

Non-compete obligations in agency agreements may benefit from the Block Exemption Regulation if they meet the requirements of Article 5. Apart from Article 101(1), the Agency Directive, see supra pp. 225–228, also limits non-compete obligations following termination of an agreement:

Article 20

1.   For the purposes of this Directive an agreement restricting the business activities of a commercial agent following termination of the agency contract is hereinafter referred to as a restraint of trade clause.

2.   A restraint of trade clause shall be valid only if and to the extent that:

    (a) it is concluded in writing and

    (b) it relates to the geographical area or the group of customers and the geographical area entrusted to the commercial agent and to the kind of goods covered by his agency under the contract.

3.   A restraint of trade clause shall be valid for not more than two years after termination of the agency contract.

4.   This Article shall not affect provisions of national law which impose other restrictions on the validity or enforceability of restraint of trade clauses or which enable the courts to reduce the obligations on the parties resulting from such an agreement.

QUESTIONS

(1) If an American firm elects as its European distributor a German merchant and decides to have its lawyers draft an agreement to cover the relationship, by what law will that agreement be governed? Must it comply with both antitrust laws? Which country has the greatest interest in seeing that the agreement is not more restrictive than necessary?

(2) In what respects is the European law more restrictive or more permissive than its American counterpart? Would any provisions of the draft at supra pp. 215–219 need to be changed in order to pass muster?

(3) By way of background, what differences do you see in the way in which the European and the American rules developed? In what ways does the European system allocate its functions differently as between legislative, executive and judicial branches? What general historical factors seem to have played a role in causing that type of allocation?

Additional reading: Elhauge & Geradin, Global Antitrust Law and Economics ch. 4 (3d ed. 2018). On the application of U.S. antitrust law to vertical restraints, see Areeda & Hovencamp, Antitrust Law: An Analysis of Antitrust Principles and Their Application vol. VIII (4th ed. 2013); Mastromanolis, Insights from U.S. Antitrust Law on Exclusive and Restricted Territorial Distribution, 15 U. Pa. J. Int. Bus. 559 (1995).

On vertical restraints under EU law, see Van Bael & Bellis, Competition Law of the European Community ch. 3 (5th ed. 2009); Goyder, EU Distribution Law (5th ed. 2011).

D. TAXATION

1. U.S. INCOME TAX TREATMENT

The tax consequences of U.S. export activity depend not on whether the exporter uses a distributor or an agent to sell its goods, but on such questions as whether the gains from those sales are considered U.S. source or foreign source income. Many other tax systems also distinguish between domestic and foreign source income, making the definition of "source" a critical matter. Not surprisingly, it is difficult to develop an internationally acceptable set of definitions that might serve to curb exorbitant national claims. The problem is comparable to that of determining whether a country is entitled to regulate transnational conduct because it has its origin or effect within it. See supra pp. 91–114. Which countries are sufficiently involved to levy taxes on the income of an enterprise that buys goods in Country A, processes them in B, and sells them in C? Moreover, factual determinations regarding the source of income have become difficult with the advent of electronic commerce. Are sales made where the server is located? Where the seller's warehouse is located? At the destination of the goods?[2]

We start our study of the application of source concepts with the American rules on export sales, which are stated in Sections 861(a)(6), 862(a)(6), 863(b), and 865 of the Internal Revenue Code. The following case suggests some of the problems posed by a relatively "simple" sales transaction involving the sale of purchased inventory (i.e., the sale of goods that the seller did not produce). It involves the operations of a now-defunct form of entity known as a "Western Hemisphere Trade Corporation." The legislation creating this form was Congress's first effort to relieve American exporters of U.S. tax burdens. The rules applicable to Western Hemisphere Trade Corporations taxed their export sales income at a rate that was effectively 14 percentage points lower than the rate applicable to income earned within the United States.

A.P. Green Export Co. v. United States
Court of Claims, 1960
284 F.2d 383

[This was a suit for refund of income taxes. Plaintiff was formed to operate as a Western Hemisphere Trade Corporation. It bought brick from its parent company, which it sold to customers in Canada and Central and South America. Plaintiff maintained no sales force or

---

[2]   See Azam, Global Taxation of Cross-Border E-Commerce Income, 31 Va. Tax. Rev. 639 (2012).

business establishment abroad. It received orders at and sent offers from its headquarters in Missouri, to which acceptances were sent by customers. Goods were priced CIF at the port of entry, or occasionally FOB factory. Transportation costs were included in the quoted prices and were usually prepaid by plaintiff. Insurance policies were purchased by plaintiff for its benefit but were negotiable and covered the goods for some days after arrival abroad. Documents were surrendered on acceptance by the buyer. Payments were by 30-day sight drafts, frequently discounted by plaintiff's bank before acceptance.

The government took the position that plaintiff did not qualify as a Western Hemisphere Trade Corporation because (1) it was only exporting abroad and had no investment there, and (2) it did not meet the requirements of the then Code provisions as to the foreign source of its gross income. To this second point, the source rules of the 1939 Code, particularly those in Section 119, were relevant. Section 862 still defines the source of sales income in similar terms.

The court rejected both positions. The part of its opinion, by Chief Judge Jones, relating to the second point is set forth below.]

II.   Place of Sale

The place of sale is a conclusion which follows the application of the proper test to a series of commercial transactions. The choice of the proper test becomes very difficult when the effects of the determination sought go beyond the traditional area of the law of sales.

The title-passage test as determinative of where a sale has occurred, and, by reference to section 119, where plaintiff's income was derived, is open to serious criticism, for it causes the incidence of the United States tax to depend upon the vagaries of the law of sales. The time and place of passage of title to ascertained goods is subject to the consensual arrangements of the parties. Williston on Sales, sec. 259, 2d ed.; cf. Uniform Sales Act, sec. 18. This all-important consent is most frequently expressed by the parties, but if not it is determined at the time of controversy by a number of presumptions set up by the law of sales. These fairly complex rules regarding passage of title are extremely important in determining such questions as the risk of loss of goods in transit, or the rights of successive creditors, but have little or no bearing on the question of where income is earned and how it should be apportioned among the various countries in which business is conducted. . . . The title-passage test has been further criticized as imposing inequitable tax burdens on taxpayers engaged in substantially similar transactions, such as upon exporters, some of whose customers require that property in the goods passes in the United States. . . .

Whatever its weaknesses, however, the title-passage test as determinative of place of sale and source of income has been overwhelmingly adopted by the courts in recent decisions. . . . We believe no other suitable test providing an adequate degree of certainty for the taxpayer has been proposed. The use of vague "contacts" or "substance of the transaction" criteria would make it more difficult for corporations engaged in Western Hemisphere trade to plan their operations so as to receive the deductions granted them only if they derive their income from sources outside the United States. Tests based upon the destination of the property sold or on the locus of the selling activity are equally vulnerable to the charge of unfair discrimination. See United States v. Balanovski, 236 F.2d 298, at page 305.

If then the passage of title does control the place of sale and the source of income, logic demands that we specify the place where title to the goods passed. It is a black letter rule of the law of sales that title to specific goods passes from the seller to the buyer in any manner and on any condition explicitly agreed on by the parties. Amtorg Trading Corp. v. Higgins, 2 Cir., 150 F.2d 536; United States v. Balanovski, supra; Williston on Sales, sec. 259, rev. ed. (1948); cf. Uniform Commercial Code, sec. 2–401. Examination of the sales contracts before us shows that the parties expressed their intentions as follows:

> "Title to these goods and the responsibility for their shipment and safe carriage shall be in the A.P. Green Export Company until their delivery to the customer at destination."

Such a clear statement, undoubtedly binding upon the parties in an ordinary sales or contract dispute, would seem to end our inquiry into the intention of the parties. But the Government urges that the terms of shipment raise presumptions that the parties intended to pass title in the United States contrary to their stated intentions, and that we must acknowledge the effect of these presumptions. We find no merit in this contention. It is true that in some instances the shipping terms, particularly the c.i.f. (cost, insurance, and freight) transactions, indicate presumptively that title passed at the place of shipment. . . . But the authorities are agreed that these presumptions are useful in ascertaining intention only if no *express* intention of the parties appears. See Williston on Sales, supra, sec. 261, et seq., and cases cited. The Government does not suggest the expressions in the contract were fraudulent. It does maintain that we must disregard the *stated* intentions of the parties in determining where title passed because the ultimate motive for these statements was the plaintiff's desire to avoid a tax.

We believe the Government has erred in failing to distinguish two separate legal consequences flowing from the same act of expression by the parties, the consequences being the passage of title and the avoidance of a tax. Title passes in a sales transaction as a result of the mutual arrangement of the buyer and the seller, whatever the reason or motivation for the consent. It would be an unjustified distortion of this law for us to disregard the parties' stated intention to pass title outside the United States because they were principally motivated by a desire to avoid a tax. This is *not* to say that under the tax law, in an atmosphere of tax avoidance, we may not find that the passage of title no longer governs the place of sale and the source of income. The next section of our opinion covers this problem. It is perfectly clear, however, that the parties intended to pass title to the goods outside the United States; this being determinative, we find that title to the goods did pass outside the United States.

III. Tax Avoidance

We now come to the problem of tax avoidance to which we have just referred. The Government urges that we examine the transactions here in the penetrating light of Gregory v. Helvering, 293 U.S. 465, 55 S.Ct. 266, 79 L.Ed. 596, for it claims that plaintiff's principal purpose in organizing and operating the export corporation was tax avoidance.

Organizing a Western Hemisphere trade corporation does not constitute tax avoidance and the Commissioner of Internal Revenue has so ruled. . . . Neither the motives, occasion for, nor the time of the *organization* of the plaintiff corporation affects its eligibility for tax relief. The Code provisions themselves have created this new business norm, a norm motivated entirely by a tax result.

The questions concerning the methods of operating the export corporation are not so easily answered. The facts show that the plaintiff delayed the passage of title with at least one eye on the Revenue Code. See finding 25. May we, therefore, depart from the title-passage test in determining the place of sale and source of plaintiff's income? The defendant says we must and submits in support a ruling by the Commissioner which states:

> "Where the sales transaction is arranged for the primary purpose of tax avoidance, the foregoing rules [passage of title test] will not be applied. In such case, all factors of the transaction such as negotiations, execution of the agreement, location of the property and place of payment will be considered, and the sale will be treated as having been consummated at the place where the substance of the sale occurred." [G.C.M. 25131, 1947–2 Cum.Bull. 85.]

The defendant also relies on United States v. Balanovski, 131 F. Supp. 898, reversed in part, 2 Cir., 236 F.2d 298, 306, certiorari denied, 352 U.S. 968, 77 S.Ct. 357, 1 L.Ed.2d 322. At first glance the Balanovski case seems to give little support to the defendant's position. There, the facts showed that goods were purchased in the United States and sold to the Argentine Government. In determining the source of income of the Argentine broker, Balanovski, the district court applied a "substance of the transaction" test and determined that Balanovski had not earned income in the United States. The Court of Appeals for the Second Circuit reversed the district court on the exact point of where the sales had taken place. It rejected the "substance of the transaction" test and rested its decision on the traditional ground of looking to the point of passage of title.

But the final passage of Judge Clark's opinion in Balanovski, supra, is notable:

> "Of course this test [title-passage] may present problems, as where passage of title is formally delayed to avoid taxes. Hence it is not necessary, nor is it desirable, to require rigid adherence to this test under all circumstances."

The Government concludes from this that in instances where passage of title is formally delayed to avoid taxes the court would feel free to look beyond the question of where title passed. Furthermore, it is suggested that the court tacitly accepted a "substance of the transaction" criterion as only by examining the indicia of substance would it be possible to decide whether passage of title was delayed merely to avoid taxes.

Along with this we must consider the statement of Judge Learned Hand in the Gregory case that "a transaction, otherwise within an exception of the tax law, does not lose its immunity, because it is actuated by a desire to avoid, or, if one choose, to evade, taxation. Any one may so arrange his affairs that his taxes shall be as low as possible; he is not bound to choose that pattern which will best pay the Treasury; there is not even a patriotic duty to increase one's taxes." 69 F.2d 809, at page 810. . . . It is undeniable that this is a doctrine essential to industry and commerce in a society like our own in which as far as possible business is always shaped to the form best suited to keep down taxes. . . . The question always is whether the transaction under scrutiny is in fact what it appears to be in form. A corporate reorganization may be illusory; a contract of sale may be intended only to deceive others. In such cases the transaction as a whole is different from its appearance. It is the intent that controls, but the intent which counts is one which contradicts the apparent transaction, not the intent to escape taxation. Chisholm v. Commissioner, 2 Cir. 79 F.2d 14.

Why the parties in the present case wished to make the sales as they did is one thing, but that is irrelevant under the Gregory case so long as the consummated agreements were no different than they purported to be, and provided the retention of title was not a sham but had a commercial purpose apart from the expected tax consequences. . . . Plaintiff's operations meet these tests. The facts show that the parties did intend title to pass outside the United States. There was no sham. Retaining title until delivery served a legitimate business purpose apart from the expected tax consequences. A moment's contemplation of the current headline disputes among countries all over the world underscores the prudence of exporters who retain title to goods until delivery. A sudden trade embargo, a seizure or a nationalization of an industry, a paralyzing nationwide strike—under these circumstances the exporter who retains title diverts his shipments with little difficulty to friendlier ports and markets. Of additional significance is the fact that retaining title permits the shipper to insure his goods in the United States. If loss occurs he can recover directly and in dollars with the obvious benefits of avoiding circuitous litigation and the fluctuations of foreign currency. . . .

Our conclusion from all of the above is that the sales were made outside the United States. However, our conclusion would be no different if we followed the defendant's suggestion and went beyond the passage of title to the other elements "of substance" in the transactions. Orders were solicited outside the United States. In every case, the contract of sale was made outside the United States; the destinations of the goods and the competitive markets for the goods were outside the United States. In most cases, the place of payment was outside the United States.

Accordingly, the plaintiff is entitled to recover its back taxes for the years 1952 and 1953, together with interest as provided by law. Judgment will be entered to that effect.

In 1976 Congress abolished the Western Hemisphere Trade Corporation, effective in 1980. But other devices designed to promote American exports persisted. In 1972 Congress invented the Domestic International Sales Corporation (DISC). Its export sales earnings were, to the extent of roughly fifty percent, subject to deferral as long as the earnings were plowed back into property used to generate further exports. Note that these earnings were, by normal standards, clearly U.S. source income of a U.S. corporation. The DISC was challenged, particularly by European countries, as an illegal subsidy under GATT. A GATT panel found that the DISC did in fact constitute a forbidden subsidy, although it also found fault with the taxation of foreign sales income by other states.[3]

In response, Congress in 1984 substituted the Foreign Sales Corporation (FSC). The FSC, unlike the DISC, had to be a foreign corporation and have activities outside of the United States. It was exempted from tax with respect to its "exempt foreign trade income"— income from the sale or lease of goods or performance of services abroad. European countries again challenged this device and prevailed before WTO panel and the Appellate Body. In 2000 the United States passed a new statute—the Extraterritorial Income Exclusion Act or ETI—that replaced the FSC with an exclusion of extraterritorial income, applicable to all foreign sales regardless of where the property was manufactured and whether it was exported, but grandfathered FSC benefits for certain existing transactions. This law was also adjudged to violate GATT. Congress tried again in 2004 with the American Jobs Creation Act, which replaced the ETI with a tax break for domestic production irrespective of the product's final destination. The Jobs Act again grandfathered benefits for certain existing transactions under the FSC and ETI, which

[3] See Jackson, The Jurisprudence of International Trade: The DISC Case in GATT, 72 Am. J. Int'l L. 747 (1979).

was again found to violate GATT. Faced with the threat of EU trade sanctions authorized by the WTO, Congress finally repealed the grandfathered tax breaks in 2006.

The 2017 Tax Cuts and Jobs Act (TCJA) amended some of the rules regarding the source of income generated by sales of goods. Gain from the sale of purchased inventory, as in the example above, is still sourced at the place of sale. However, gain from the sale of goods produced by the seller is treated differently. Under Section 863(b) of the Internal Revenue Code as amended, such gain is sourced to the location of production. If the goods in question are produced entirely in the United States, then income earned by selling those goods is characterized as U.S. source income, even if they are sold overseas. Conversely, income earned by selling foreign-produced goods in the United States is characterized as foreign source income. In the case of goods produced partly within and partly outside the United States, the income must be allocated and apportioned between the countries involved on the basis of production activities.

QUESTIONS

(1) Does the rule in the Green case seem too rigid and mechanical from the point of view of the American interest in capturing a fair share of the revenue? Do you agree with the court's conclusion that the retention of title "served a legitimate business purpose"?

(2) Under generally accepted accounting principles, income is not realized until goods are sold and title passes. Is that principle helpful in finding an appropriate solution to this problem?

(3) Is the TCJA's rule that looks to the place of production preferable to one that looks to the place of sale? If so, should that rule be extended to purchased inventory, or is there some reason to distinguish between goods produced by the seller and goods purchased by the seller?

2. FOREIGN TAX TREATMENT

The exporter's tax status under the law of Germany, where the goods are distributed, depends very largely on the question whether a permanent establishment is created. Article 7(1) of the income tax treaty entered into between Germany and the United States provides:

> The business profits of an enterprise of a Contracting State shall be taxable only in that State unless the enterprise carries on business in the other Contracting State through a permanent establishment situated therein. If the enterprise carries on business as aforesaid, the business profits of the enterprise may be taxed in the other State but only so much of them as is attributable to that permanent establishment.

Other things being equal, a U.S. exporter will prefer to avoid creating a permanent establishment overseas and subjecting itself to foreign tax.

Filing tax returns in a foreign jurisdiction may be burdensome, particularly for a relatively small exporter. Although the exporter may credit taxes paid to a foreign jurisdiction against its U.S. taxes, limitations on the foreign tax credit may prevent full utilization of the credit. See infra pp. 339–340.

Article 5 of the treaty defines "permanent establishment" in some detail. See infra pp. 551–552. With respect to agents and distributors, Article 5(5) provides that "where a person (other than an agent of an independent status to whom paragraph 6 applies) is acting on behalf of an enterprise and has, and habitually exercises, in a Contracting State an authority to conclude contracts in the name of the enterprise, that enterprise shall be deemed to have a permanent establishment in that State. . . ." Because distributors act on their own behalf and lack authority to bind the exporter, use of a foreign distributor will generally not create a permanent establishment. The exporter may use an agent and avoid creating a permanent establishment either by denying the agent authority to conclude contracts in its name—typically with language in the agency agreement stating that all orders will be subject to the exporter's approval—or by using "a broker, general commission agent, or any other agent of an independent status." Article 5(6). In Taisei Fire & Marine Insurance Co. v. Commissioner, 104 T.C. 535 (1995), the U.S. Tax Court held that an agent could be considered to have "independent status" if it were legally and economically independent of its principal, although that decision would not, of course, bind German taxing authorities in their application of the treaty.

In countries other than the United States, one must pay close attention to the sales tax, or, as in the case of Europe, the value-added tax.[4] Bear in mind two differences from the characteristic sales tax one encounters in the United States. First, the VAT is not payable simply on the final sale to a consumer, but at each sale along the way. Second, VAT rates may exceed 20% (the German standard rate is currently 19%), as compared with the typical U.S. sales-tax rate of 4 to 7%. The critical portions of the German law, which is captioned *"Umsatzsteuergesetz (Mehrwertsteuer),"* i.e., "Turnover Tax (Valued Added Tax)," follow:

Section 1:

(1)   The following turnovers shall be subject to the turnover tax:

1.   Deliveries and other performances which an enterprise makes in [Germany] in exchange for consideration within the scope of the enterprise. . . .

4.   Importation of items into the customs territory. . . .

---

[4]   VATs in Europe have been progressively harmonized by a series of EU directives. A directive enacted in 2018 established a permanent minimum standard rate of 15% for VATs throughout the EU. Council Directive 2018/912/EU, 2018 O.J. (L 162) 1.

Section 10:

(1) In the case of deliveries and other performances ... the turnover shall be measured by the consideration. Consideration shall be everything which the recipient ... must expend ... in order to obtain the delivery or other performance, but less the turnover tax.

Section 11:

(1) In the case of imports ... the value added shall be computed on the value of the imported goods according to the customs law provisions in effect concerning customs value. ...

(3) ... The value ... shall be increased by the amount of customs duty. ...

Section 12:

(1) The tax on each taxable transaction shall amount to nineteen per cent of the taxable base amount. ...

Section 15:

(1) The enterprise may deduct the following input tax amounts:

     1. The tax ... for deliveries or other performances effected for that enterprise by other enterprises ...

     2. The importation tax paid on items imported into the customs area for the enterprise ...

     3. The tax for acquiring items for the enterprise within the Community.

QUESTIONS

(1) Does the Distribution Agreement, supra pp. 215–219, subject Techno to the payment of German income taxes on revenues derived from sales through Impo? What portions of the U.S. German Tax Convention bear on this question?

(2) Does the choice between the distributor mode and the agency mode affect the local income tax consequences? Does it affect the turnover tax computation? (Track the computation of the VAT through both ways of selling.)

Additional reading: Herzfeld & Doernberg, International Taxation in a Nutshell (11th ed. 2018).

PROBLEM 3

A LICENSING AGREEMENT

A. INTRODUCTION

In Problems 1 and 2, we examined the legal issues arising from a U.S. company's export business. For some companies, producing an item in the United States and exporting it would be financially non-competitive—perhaps due to tariffs, transport, or manufacturing costs. For an American manufacturer owning significant intellectual property rights—patents, trademarks, copyrights, and unpatented trade secrets or "know-how"—licensing may provide an alternative path to enter a foreign market. If a suitable local licensee can be found, a holder of patent and other rights can realize a return on its investment without running such risks.

Under a typical licensing arrangement, the licensor allows a licensee to use its patented technology, along with its brand name and associated trademarks, in producing and selling the licensor's products within a particular geographic area. The licensee pays for those rights in the form of royalties on resulting sales. (How royalty payments are structured is, in the first instance, up to the parties, and will depend upon their respective financial and accounting goals. Paragraph 4 of the licensing agreement that follows illustrates three common kinds of royalties: an initial royalty; a royalty based on production, sales, or revenue; and a minimum royalty. Some jurisdictions frown upon particular types of royalty payments.) With such an arrangement, a holder of patent and other rights can realize a return on its investment in a foreign market without taking on the downsides of engaging in foreign production itself, such as expropriation risk, foreign exchange difficulties, or diversion of executive talents.

Of course, the licensor has no great measure of control over how the licensee's operation is conducted. Will the foreign management be effective in producing or selling the item? Also, a licensee may be in a position to block the American firm from entering its market during the term of the license and, at its end, may have developed its own competitive position to such a degree as to make it impractical for the American firm to compete there.

Various policies of the potential licensee's government bear on the desirability of this alternative. Thus, while a licensing arrangement is on its face an arrangement between two private parties, it must conform to the government policies of the parties' home states. Those policies may be reflected not only in the patent and trademark laws of the two jurisdictions but also in other bodies of law such as taxation, antitrust, and export controls.

Consider now the following licensing agreement. You are counsel for an American company, Data Devices, Inc., which has developed a compact and cheap computer capable of use by small businesses. Data Devices benefits from its distinctive processes for making small electronic components. It has a handful of patents on improvements it has made in computers and in processes for making them. Previously it restricted its activities to the United States, and thus has no experience abroad. Recently an industrialist from a Latin American country visited Data Devices' plant and was impressed by its product. In turn, the company's management was convinced that the Latin American firm was capable of turning out a high-quality product and had excellent sales connections in its region.

In reviewing the agreement that follows, you should bear in mind that licensing agreements have become quite specialized depending on the industry involved and the relationship between the parties. They can also run to great length. The sample agreement presented here is briefer and more general than many you would encounter in practice. It also contains provisions that may prove to be problematic under the laws of one or more jurisdictions.

LICENSE AGREEMENT[1]

An *Agreement* made this _____ day of _____ 20__ between Data Devices, Inc., a Delaware corporation having a place of business at Chicago, Illinois, hereinafter called the *Licensor,* and Compañía Mercada S.A., a Guatador corporation, having a place of business at Estancia, Guatador, hereinafter called the *Licensee.*

WITNESSETH:

Whereas Licensor has invented and developed a method (hereinafter called "the process") for the manufacture of a computer (hereinafter called "the product") and possesses valuable secret knowledge, formulae, information, data, and related skills useful in performing the process;

Whereas Licensor has applied for and obtained patents for both the process and the product in the United States and in Guatador, as set forth in Annex A (hereinafter called "the patents");

Whereas Licensor has obtained trademarks for the product amongst others in the United States and in Guatador, as set forth in Annex B (hereinafter called "the trademarks");

Whereas Licensee is an established manufacturer and trader in the electronics industry in Guatador and desires to obtain *Licensor's* know-how and the right to work *Licensor's* patents in Guatador, including the

---

[1]   This license agreement is adapted from Goldschmid, International License Contracts, A Practical Guide (1968) and Oestricher & Zych, Drafting International Technology License Agreements, in Negotiating and Structuring International Commercial Transactions: Legal Analysis with Sample Agreements (Battram & Goldsweig eds. 1991).

right to manufacture the product and sell it under *Licensor's* trademark in Guatador;

Now therefore in consideration of the mutual promises, obligations and covenants set forth herein, the parties agree as follows:

1. *License Grant*

Licensor hereby grants *Licensee* an exclusive license to manufacture, use, and sell the product in Guatador under the trademark, to practice the patent and know-how, and to use any information and technical assistance respecting the process and product which *Licensor* may give *Licensee* in future. *Licensee* shall not manufacture, use, or sell the product, use the trademark, practice the patent or know-how, or use any information or technical assistance respecting the process and product outside Guatador.

2. *Disclosure of Improvements*

During the term of this Agreement, *Licensor* shall make available to *Licensee* any improvement, information, and know-how related to the process or product, which *Licensor* has acquired as a result of its research and development or in any other lawful way and which *Licensor* has the right to pass on to *Licensee,* for which no additional royalty shall be payable.

3. *Grant-Back*

Licensee shall promptly disclose to *Licensor* any improvement or invention pertaining to the process or product. At *Licensor's* request, *Licensee* shall assign to *Licensor* without charge the entire right, title, and interest to and in any such improvement or invention, as well as the right to file any patent applications therefor.

4. *Royalties*

As full consideration for the rights granted in this Agreement, *Licensee* shall pay to *Licensor* the following:

(a) *Initial Royalty. Licensee* shall pay to *Licensor* U.S.$10,000 upon the execution of this Agreement.

(b) *Royalty on Sales.* Not later than sixty (60) days after the end of each calendar quarter, *Licensee* shall pay to *Licensor* a sum equal to five percent (5%) on *Licensee's* net sales of the product in Guatador during such calendar quarter. The term "net sales" shall mean the gross amount invoiced by *Licensee* on sales of the product, less returns, rebates, trade discounts, cash discounts, sales taxes, and transportation charges allowed to purchaser on the purchase price. Such sum shall be paid in U.S. currency at the rate of conversion on the date of remittance.

(c) *Minimum Royalty.* Irrespective of the sales achieved in any given year, *Licensee* shall pay to *Licensor* U.S.$10,000 upon each anniversary of the date of this Agreement.

5. Records

Licensee shall maintain complete and accurate records of all sales on which royalty is due hereunder in accordance with generally accepted accounting standards. *Licensee* shall permit access by *Licensor* to all such records during normal business hours. In the event that *Licensor* discovers that such records have not been maintained or are not accurate or that *Licensee* has failed to make payment of any royalties required by the Agreement, *Licensee* shall reimburse *Licensor* for the cost of reviewing such records, including reimbursement of all reasonable accountants' and attorneys' fees.

6. Sub-License

Licensee shall not grant any sub-license of any of the rights granted by this Agreement without the prior written consent of *Licensor*.

7. Assignment

Licensee shall not assign this Agreement or any right granted herein without the prior written consent of *Licensor*.

8. Confidentiality

Licensee shall treat as secret and confidential all know-how and information received under this Agreement, except to the extent that they have come into the public domain. *Licensee* shall not disclose such know-how and information to any persons other than those employees requiring the know-how and information in the performance of their duties. This obligation of confidentiality shall not cease with the expiry or termination of this Agreement.

9. Technical Assistance

Licensor shall provide, at *Licensee's* sole expense, sufficient technical assistance to enable *Licensee* to manufacture the product.

10. Trademark

Licensee shall affix the trademark to all products manufactured or sold pursuant to this Agreement. *Licensor* undertakes to maintain the trademark in Guatador by renewing its registration well in time. *Licensee* agrees to use and display *Licensor's* trademark at all times in such a manner as to exclude any doubt of *Licensor's* ownership, and so as to safeguard *Licensor's* interests, particularly to prevent the trademark from becoming generic.

11. Quality

All products manufactured or sold pursuant to this Agreement shall meet the quality specifications set forth in Annex C. *Licensee* shall permit *Licensor* access to its manufacturing facilities during normal working hours for the purpose of ensuring that *Licensee's* manufacturing practices conform to the requirements of this Paragraph 11.

12. *Non-Competition*

Licensee shall not, during the term of this Agreement, engage in the manufacture, use, or sale of any good that competes with or has a similar use or application as the product.

13. *Warranties*

Licensor hereby warrants and represents that it is the sole owner of the patents; that the patents are validly issued and in effect; that to its knowledge no claim has been made contesting the validity of any of the patents and that practicing the art disclosed in the patents will not constitute an infringement of the rights of any third party. *Licensor* shall indemnify and hold harmless *Licensee* against any loss, damage, or claim arising from or relating to any breach of the warranties contained in this Paragraph 13. *Licensor* shall have the right to control the defense of any such suit or claim, including, without limitation, the right to choose counsel and to settle and dispose of any such suit or claim as it deems appropriate in its sole discretion.

14. *Non-Contestation of Rights*

Licensee shall not contest the validity of *Licensor's* patents or trademarks, or *Licensor's* property rights to know-how, information, and improvements that *Licensor* has made available to *Licensee* under this Agreement.

15. *Infringement*

Licensee shall notify *Licensor* promptly of any infringement of *Licensor's* patents or trademarks in Guatador and shall provide *Licensor* with any available evidence thereof. *Licensor* may, at its sole discretion, take legal steps to enforce its patent or trademark rights, but is under no obligation to do so. *Licensee* shall assist *Licensor* in the prosecution of any claim or action arising from or related to any such infringement.

16. *Term*

This Agreement is deemed to have come into force on the date first mentioned above and shall continue up to the date of expiry of *Licensor's* latest patent in Guatador relating to the product or the process, unless terminated earlier as provided in Paragraph 17. Upon the expiry or termination of this Agreement, *Licensee* shall immediately cease the manufacture, use, and sale of the product, the use of the trademark, and the use of the patent, know-how, information, and improvements made available under this Agreement.

17. *Termination*

(a) *Licensor* may terminate this Agreement by giving three calendar months' notice by registered letter:

(i) should *Licensee* have failed to start manufacture of the product within six months after the date of this Agreement;

(ii) should *Licensee* have failed to start sales of the product within four months from the start of production;

(iii) should *Licensee* have breached any term of this Agreement; or

(iv) in the event of a change in the controlling interest in *Licensee's* firm at the date of this Agreement.

Provided, however, that any notice served under sub-paragraphs (i), (ii), or (iii) hereunder shall be considered null and void if *Licensee* cures the default before expiry of the notice period.

(b) Either party may terminate the Agreement with immediate effect by giving notice by registered letter:

(i) in case of a suit filed or threatened in Guatador against *Licensee* for patent infringement due to *Licensee's* working *Licensor's* patent under the license granted hereunder if *Licensor* refuses to take up the defense, or if *Licensor* loses a suit in which he has taken up the defense, or if a court injunction is issued against *Licensee*; or

(ii) in case of dissolution or bankruptcy of the other party.

18. Entire Agreement

This Agreement constitutes the entire agreement between *Licensor* and *Licensee* with regard to its subject matter, and no prior, simultaneous or collateral promises or representations not expressly contained herein shall be of any force or effect.

19. Language

This Agreement has been executed both in the English and Spanish languages. In case of doubt, the English version shall prevail.

20. Applicable Law

This Agreement shall be governed by and construed under the laws of the State of Illinois, one of the United States of America.

21. Arbitration

All disputes arising out of or in connection with this Agreement shall be finally settled under the Rules of Arbitration of the International Chamber of Commerce by one or more arbitrators appointed in accordance with the said Rules.

For and on behalf of: For and on behalf of:
Data Devices, Inc.   Compañía Mercada, S.A.

_____   _____

QUESTIONS

(1) Consider Articles 3 and 16 of the agreement. When you combine their effect, how long might the agreement last?

(2) Consider the choice-of-law and arbitration clauses (Articles 20 and 21). Do they seem to provide the best mode of dispute resolution for the licensor? Is either of them missing anything important? Suppose that the licensee's country does not recognize such clauses. Will their absence materially undercut the licensor's position?

(3) Under the agreement, what happens if U.S. rules on the export of technology change so that it becomes impossible for the licensor to transfer the technology—although it was legal at the time of the transfer? What happens if the licensee is found by the U.S. authorities to have re-transferred technology (or products of technology) in violation of U.S. rules?

Additional reading: A massive, multivolume looseleaf treatise with forms is Epstein, Eckstrom's Licensing in Foreign and Domestic Operations (looseleaf, 1972–). See also Campbell, International Licensing (looseleaf, 1997–); Liberman, Chrocziel & Levine, International Licensing and Technology Transfer: Practice and the Law (looseleaf, 2008–).

B. Introduction to Intellectual Property Law

1. Types of Intellectual Property

To understand a licensing transaction, one needs at least an elementary knowledge of what is being licensed—that is, intellectual property. Basically, intellectual property comes in four categories: patents, copyrights, trademarks, and trade secrets. The common quality of each is that the owner of the property is given the right to exclude others from using something the owner has created by application of inventive talents and/or investment of funds. There is inevitable tension between the element of monopoly given to the owner of the property and the general idea of free competition enshrined in the antitrust laws. Intellectual property legislation is based on the idea that overall there will be more competition and more efficiency if enterprises are motivated to innovate by the knowledge that their competitors will not be able to "free ride" on their accomplishments—that is to set up competing production without having incurred the research and development costs, and the concurrent risks of failure and loss, involved in bringing a new product or service to market.

Let us take each of these items separately and describe first how the United States system protects each of them. A patent is designed to give protection to the inventor of "any new and useful process, machine, manufacture or composition of matter. . . ." 35 U.S.C.A. § 101. In order to obtain a patent the inventor must file an application describing the claimed invention; the application must make it clear to the reader how the invention is to be practiced so that when the patent expires, others can be fully competitive in that technology. The application is then reviewed by the Patent and Trademark Office staff, who measure it against the state of the art to see if it is, in fact, novel, useful, and non-obvious. There are procedures through which a rival inventor can contest the issuance of a patent to the applicant. When the patent issues, it gives the owner an exclusive right to make, use, offer to sell, and sell the invention within the United States. Prior to the 1994 Agreement on Trade-Related Aspects of Intellectual Property Rights (TRIPS Agreement), the term of a U.S. patent was 17 years, starting from the date of issue. To comply with the TRIPS Agreement, the term was changed so that it is now 20 years, beginning from the date of the application. Once obtained, a patent may be enforced by suing infringers. Infringers may defend by contesting the validity of the patent, as well as denying that their actions constituted infringement. If successful, the patent holder may obtain money damages (not less than a reasonable royalty) or an injunction or both. A patent may also be sold to another party—an assignment. Licenses can be issued allowing limited uses of the invention by other parties. They can be exclusive or non-exclusive and may be limited by territory, etc.

A copyright is designed to protect expressions rather than ideas. Copyright protection subsists in "original works of authorship fixed in any tangible medium of expression." 17 U.S.C.A. § 102. One would think of a book, a song, or a painting as being appropriate for copyright protection—but computer software and databases are as well. The borderline between the subject matter of patents and of copyrights is becoming increasingly difficult to maintain, particularly in the area of computer programs. Obtaining a copyright involves the deposit of copies of the work in question (as well as affixing the claim to copies of the work). The Copyright Office reviews applications for compliance with formal requirements, but conducts no examination comparable to the patent reviews conducted by the Patent and Trademark Office. A copyright is protected only against copying, as indicated by "substantial similarity;" thus, a person who produced a work similar to that under copyright would be permitted to show that it was the product of independent work. There are complicated questions about the "fair use" of another's expressions—for quotations in scientific literature, for reviews, for parodies, etc. In 1998 Congress extended the term of a copyright, which is now the life of the author plus 70 years. For corporate authors, the term of a copyright is now the shorter of 95 years from the date of publication or 120 years from the date of creation.

A trademark permits a seller of a product or service to market those items in a distinctive manner that will distinguish them from the products of others. Thus, the trademark "Coca Cola" distinguishes that product from other soft drinks. It also tells the customer that the source is a given company of that name. A trademark protects the goodwill of the producer—that is, the substantial investment that it may have made in advertising, customer service, and other things that build and maintain customer acceptance of the item. Under the Lanham Act of 1946, 15 U.S.C.A. §§ 1051–1127, one may register a mark with the Patent and Trademark Office. (However, in the United States, trademark rights begin upon use of the mark, not upon registration.) There is no specified term to a trademark, although rights thereunder can be lost by failure to maintain control over the uniformity and quality of the product, by non-use, and by other lapses. The holder of a mark can bring actions against persons who use the mark or something deceptively similar to sell their products.

A trade secret is information that is not generally known, and whose confidentiality creates economic value for the owner. (The classic example of a trade secret is the formula for Coca-Cola.) The advantages of the trade secret over the patent are, first, that it can be used to cover items that are not sufficiently novel to obtain patent protection and, second, that it does not expire at the end of any specified time. The downside of trade secret protection is that the secret is lost if it is discovered by legitimate means. For example, a competitor could buy a novel device, have technicians "reverse engineer" it by taking it apart and noting how its components work, and then imitate it. Traditionally, trade secrets were protected by including confidentiality clauses in contracts, but state and federal law have now added additional levels of protection. The Uniform Law Commission has promulgated a Uniform Trade Secrets Act, authorizing suits for injunctive relief and for damages, that has been adopted in every state but Massachusetts, New York, and North Carolina. In 1996, Congress passed the Economic Espionage Act of 1996, 18 U.S.C.A. §§ 1831–1839, which made the theft or misappropriation of trade secrets a federal crime. And in 2016, Congress passed the Defend Trade Secrets Act of 2016, which amends the Economic Espionage Act to create a private right of action for injunctive relief and damages. 18 U.S.C.A. § 1836(b). The Act also authorizes ex parte seizure orders, but only in extraordinary circumstances to prevent the dissemination of a trade secret.

The patent, copyright and trademark systems of other countries differ substantially from the U.S. pattern. Although such differences will be less significant in the case of other countries with a strong industrial and technological base, there may still be differences in the rigor of the search for prior art, the standards applied in judging "novelty," and the degree of protection afforded the patent when issued. Some countries have given the author of works of art "moral rights" against debasement of the conception even by those who purchased the works. Trademark systems vary in their requirements as to the use of the mark.

Traditionally, each of these varied intellectual property systems has been regarded as independent and territorially limited. Thus, a U.S. patent gives an exclusive right to make, use, offer to sell, and sell the product within the United States. Products made abroad that are covered by U.S. patents can be excluded at the border, as can unpatented products made with patented processes. However, a person manufacturing in Sweden a product that is covered by a U.S. patent, but not a Swedish one, is committing no violation of law. See Microsoft Corp. v. AT & T Corp., 550 U.S. 437, 127 S.Ct. 1746, 167 L.Ed.2d 737 (2007). The same limitation applies in the cases of the other three types of intellectual property, though there have been cases in which U.S. courts have enjoined trademark infringements that took place at least in part outside the United States. See Steele v. Bulova Watch Co., 344 U.S. 280, 73 S.Ct. 252, 97 L.Ed. 319 (1952). It follows that the owner of intellectual property rights must, early on, make a decision as to where it is worthwhile making the applications and filings needed to secure protection. The fees themselves are quite substantial, to say nothing of the costs of having lawyers and patent agents do the work.

2. INTERNATIONAL AGREEMENTS CONCERNING INTELLECTUAL PROPERTY

The separateness of national systems began to be the subject of concern in the late nineteenth century. In the 1883 Paris Convention on the Protection of Industrial Property, the major industrialized countries agreed to conform their industrial property laws to certain standards. For one thing, they guaranteed foreign inventors national treatment in granting legal protection. In 1886, these countries concluded the Berne Convention for the Protection of Literary and Artistic Works, which protects authors, composers, and artists.[2] In 1970, the World Intellectual Property Organization (WIPO) was created, which today administers the Paris and Berne Conventions along with 22 others.

The harmonization of intellectual property protection took a major leap forward with the conclusion of the TRIPS Agreement as part of the Uruguay Round package of GATT agreements (see supra p. 202). The United States and other industrialized countries used the leverage afforded them by their positions as markets for the goods of developing countries to insist that these countries improve their protection of intellectual property. Under the TRIPS Agreement, WTO members must amend their domestic laws to provide a minimum level of intellectual property protection. The TRIPS Agreement built on the existing international framework by requiring WTO members to comply with most provisions of the Paris and Berne Conventions. See TRIPS Arts. 2 & 9. Articles 3 and 4 of TRIPS imposed obligations of national and most-favored-nation treatment, as is common in GATT agreements.

Part II of the TRIPS Agreement sets forth minimum requirements concerning the availability, scope, and term of seven kinds of intellectual property protection: copyrights, trademarks, geographical indications, industrial designs, patents, layout-designs of integrated circuits, and

---

[2] While the United States joined the Paris Convention in 1887, it did not become a party to the Berne Convention until 1989.

trade secrets. Several of its provisions are worth noting. Article 10, for example, provides that computer programs and compilations of data are entitled to copyright protection. Article 27 provides that "patents shall be available for any inventions, whether products or processes, in all fields of technology, provided that they are new, involve an inventive step and are capable of industrial application." There is an exclusion for "diagnostic, therapeutic and surgical methods for the treatment of humans or animals" and for "plants and animals other than micro-organisms," although countries that exclude plant varieties from patentability must provide a *sui generis* system for their protection. Significantly, however, there is no exclusion for pharmaceuticals, for which many less developed countries had previously refused to grant patent protection. Article 33 provides that the term of a patent shall be at least 20 years from the filing date, which necessitated the change in United States law mentioned above.

Perhaps the most sweeping provisions are those in Part III of TRIPS, which require WTO members to ensure that enforcement measures will "permit effective action against any act of infringement of intellectual property rights." See TRIPS Art. 41. Remedies must include the right to injunctive relief and damages. In the case of trademark counterfeiting and copyright piracy, they must also include seizure of the offending goods by customs authorities and criminal penalties for willful violations. Some of these provisions seem very ambitious for countries with understaffed legal systems. Article 41 further provides that "[p]rocedures concerning the enforcement of intellectual property rights shall be fair and equitable. They shall not be unnecessarily complicated or costly, or entail unreasonable time-limits or unwarranted delays." Query whether U.S. procedures for intellectual property protection might be considered "unnecessarily complicated or costly."

Scattered among the provisions just discussed are several others that bear upon the materials that follow. Article 40 authorizes WTO members to apply their laws to prevent adverse effects on competition:

Article 40

1.　Members agree that some licensing practices or conditions pertaining to intellectual property rights which restrain competition may have adverse effects on trade and may impede the transfer and dissemination of technology.

2.　Nothing in this Agreement shall prevent Members from specifying in their legislation licensing practices or conditions that may in particular cases constitute an abuse of intellectual property rights having an adverse effect on competition in the relevant market. As provided above, a Member may adopt, consistently with the other provisions of this Agreement, appropriate measures to prevent or control such practices, which may include for example exclusive grantback conditions, conditions preventing challenges to validity and coercive package licensing, in the light of the relevant laws and regulations of that Member.

* * *

As we shall see below, the Andean Community, the United States, and the European Union all attempt to prevent such adverse effects, though in quite different ways.

Article 31 of the TRIPS Agreement allows for the compulsory licensing of patents. When a third party who wishes to use a patented technology has been unable to obtain authorization from the patent holder on reasonable commercial terms or in cases of national emergency or extreme urgency, a government may authorize the third party to use the technology or may use the technology itself, provided that the patent holder is paid "adequate remuneration in the circumstances of each case." The question of compulsory licensing has become an issue of concern with respect to pharmaceuticals, particularly those useful in treating HIV, and the full text of Article 31 is set forth in the discussion of that question below. See infra pp. 271–273.

Finally, Article 6 of the TRIPS leaves WTO members free to adopt their own rules concerning the "exhaustion" of intellectual property rights—that is, the extent to which such rights survive the first sale of an item and allow the intellectual property owner to control its resale. Article 6 provides that "[f]or the purposes of dispute settlement under this Agreement, . . . nothing in this Agreement shall be used to address the issue of the exhaustion of intellectual property rights." The rules concerning exhaustion determine the extent to which an intellectual property owner may prevent parallel importation and thus the extent to which it may charge different prices in different markets. See infra pp. 283–295.

Additional reading: Sinnott et al., Baxter World Patent Law and Practice (looseleaf, 1974–); Geller, Nimmer & Bently, International Copyright Law and Practice (looseleaf, 1988–).

C. INTELLECTUAL PROPERTY AND DEVELOPING COUNTRIES

For less developed countries a basic question arises: why have an intellectual property system at all? The benefits of a patent system will inure almost entirely to enterprises from industrialized countries that derive royalties from licenses granted to persons in the developing world or profits from export sales protected by patents. And protecting those enterprises' exclusive rights to produce certain goods might increase the price of those goods to local consumers—including necessary items such as medicine. Such concerns over the perceived imbalance in the risks and advantages of implementing intellectual property regimes became largely moot with the inclusion of TRIPS in the agenda of the Uruguay Round. In order to achieve trade advantages, less developed countries have in general accepted the position of the United States and other developed countries on these issues. Nevertheless, licensing arrangements in developing countries continue to generate some particular issues.

1. REGULATING LICENSING AGREEMENTS: THE ROLE OF TECHNOLOGY TRANSFER LAWS

Some less developed countries have responded to the imbalance between foreign intellectual property owners and local licensees and consumers by enacting technology transfer laws that regulate licensing agreements. An early and prominent example was Andean Commission Decision 24 on the Common Regime of Treatment of Foreign Capital and Trademarks, Patents, Licenses, and Royalties issued in 1970. 10 I.L.M. 152 (1971), as amended, 16 I.L.M. 138 (1977). Decision 24 represented a common position on foreign investment and technology transfer by the members of the Andean Pact, a subregional organization founded in 1969 by Bolivia, Chile, Colombia, Ecuador, and Peru. Chile pulled out of the Andean Pact in 1976 because of disagreement with its restrictive attitude toward foreign investment. Venezuela joined in 1973 but withdrew in 2006. Among its provisions, Decision 24 required government approval of licensing agreements. Article 20 forbade the member governments from approving agreements that contained a number of clauses listed therein.

The Andean Pact's attitude towards foreign investment and licensing began to change in the 1980s. In 1987 Decision 24 was repealed and replaced by Decision 220. 27 I.L.M. 974 (1988). In 1991 Decision 220 was itself replaced by Decision 291, 30 I.L.M. 1283 (1991), which remains in effect today. Decision 291 is complemented by three other decisions that establish the legal framework for protecting various kinds of intellectual property consistent with the TRIPS Agreement: Decision 345 on the Protection of the Rights of Breeders of New Plant Varieties; Decision 351 on Copyright and Neighboring Rights; and Decision 486 on the Common Industrial Property Regime, supplemented by Decision 689, adopted in 2008, which covers other kinds of intellectual property including patents, trademarks, and industrial secrets.[3]

In spite of the decided shift in attitudes toward intellectual property licensing represented by the more recent decisions of the Andean Community (so called since 1996), one can detect certain similarities between the current regime for regulating licensing and the regime established by Decision 24. Licensing agreements must still be registered with the competent national agency in order to be valid. Article 57 of Decision 486, for example, provides: "Any license that is granted for the

---

[3] Decision 486 replaced Decision 344, Oct. 21, 1993, 34 I.L.M. 1635 (1995), effective December 1, 2000. Decisions 345, 351, and 486 are available in Spanish and English on the Andean Community's website, www.comunidadandina.org and in WIPO Lex, the global database maintained by the World Intellectual Property Organization, www.wipo.int/wipolex.

exploitation of a patent shall be registered with the competent national office. Failure to register shall render the license invalid with respect to third parties." Article 58 further provides that "[t]he competent national authority shall not register any license agreements for patent exploitation that do not conform to the provisions of the Common Regime for the Treatment of Foreign Capital and for Trademarks, Patents, Licenses, and Royalties [Decision 291], or that do not conform to Andean Community or domestic antitrust provisions." Moreover, Article 14 of Decision 291 contains a list of clauses identical to Article 20 of Decision 24, the difference being that these clauses (with the exception for territorial restrictions on exports to other Andean Community nations) are now disfavored rather than forbidden:

Article 14. For the purposes of registering contracts on the transfer of foreign technology, trademarks or patents, the Member Countries may take into consideration that said contracts do not contain the following:

a)   Clauses that tie the supply of technology or the use of a trademark to the obligation of the recipient country or the recipient company to acquire from a particular source capital equipment, intermediate products, raw materials or other technologies, or to permanently utilize personnel indicated by the company providing the technology;

b)   Clauses by which the company selling the technology or granting the utilization of a trademark reserves the right to set the sale or resale prices of the products manufactured using that technology;

c)   Clauses that contain restrictions with respect to the volume and structure of production;

d)   Clauses that prohibit the utilization of competing technologies;

e)   Clauses that establish a total or partial purchase option in favor of the supplier of the technology;

f)   Clauses that require the purchaser of the technology to transfer to the supplier the inventions or improvements deriving from the utilization of said technology;

g)   Clauses that require the payment of royalties to the owners of patents or trademarks for patents or trademarks that are not used or have expired; and

h)   Other clauses of like effect.

Save in exceptional cases duly authorized by the competent national agency of the recipient country, clauses that prohibit or limit in any manner the exportation of products manufactured using the respective technology shall not be permitted.

In no case shall clauses of this nature be permitted in relation to subregional trade or the export of similar products to third countries.

QUESTION

(1) Would any of the provisions in the licensing agreement between Data Devices and Mercada, supra pp. 258–262, be problematic if Guatador were a member of the Andean Community?

2. THE TRIPS AGREEMENT AND PUBLIC HEALTH

As noted above, one concern regarding the establishment of intellectual property regimes in developing countries was that granting patent protection for pharmaceuticals would limit local governments' ability to respond to public health crises. For example, take a drug such as an antibiotic. The drug will be marketed for several dollars in the United States and Europe, that price being justified by the high costs of developing the drug and taking it through the protracted and expensive testing processes needed to obtain approval from the FDA and comparable government agencies abroad. However, it will cost only a few pennies to produce that same drug for local use in, say, Tanzania. Why not make the drug available to the impoverished population of Tanzania without patent protection through local manufacture? After all, there is very little likelihood that grant of patent protection will encourage anybody to develop new products in Tanzania. And, in any case, maintenance of a decent patent system in the country will be very expensive and use up a high percentage of the country's Ph.D.s trained in the natural sciences.

As we have seen, the TRIPS agreement included in the Uruguay Round requires all countries to implement and enforce intellectual property laws in order to accede to the WTO. See supra pp. 266–268. It does not exclude medicines from the scope of patent protection. It does, however, include a mechanism that attempts to preserve the ability of WTO members to respond to public health crises. Recall that under Article 6, WTO members are allowed to set their own rules with respect to "the issue of the exhaustion of intellectual property rights." See supra p. 268. Article 31 permits WTO members to create "compulsory licensing" regimes pursuant to that authority—essentially, procedures whereby a government can allow the manufacture of a patented product without the consent of the patent owner. The circumstances in which compulsory licensing is available are narrow.

Article 31

Other Use Without Authorization of the Right Holder

Where the law of a Member allows for other use of the subject matter of a patent without the authorization of the right holder, including use by the government or third parties authorized by the government, the following provisions shall be respected:

(a) authorization of such use shall be considered on its individual merits;

(b) such use may only be permitted if, prior to such use, the proposed user has made efforts to obtain authorization from the right holder on reasonable commercial terms and conditions and that such efforts have not been successful within a reasonable period of time. This requirement may be waived by a Member in the case of a national emergency or other circumstances of extreme urgency or in cases of public non-commercial use. In situations of national emergency or other circumstances of extreme urgency, the right holder shall, nevertheless, be notified as soon as reasonably practicable. In the case of public non-commercial use, where the government or contractor, without making a patent search, knows or has demonstrable grounds to know that a valid patent is or will be used by or for the government, the right holder shall be informed promptly;

(c) the scope and duration of such use shall be limited to the purpose for which it was authorized, and in the case of semi-conductor technology shall only be for public non-commercial use or to remedy a practice determined after judicial or administrative process to be anti-competitive;

(d) such use shall be non-exclusive;

(e) such use shall be non-assignable, except with that part of the enterprise or goodwill which enjoys such use;

(f) any such use shall be authorized predominantly for the supply of the domestic market of the Member authorizing such use;

(g) authorization for such use shall be liable, subject to adequate protection of the legitimate interests of the persons so authorized, to be terminated if and when the circumstances which led to it cease to exist and are unlikely to recur. The competent authority shall have the authority to review, upon motivated request, the continued existence of these circumstances;

(h) the right holder shall be paid adequate remuneration in the circumstances of each case, taking into account the economic value of the authorization;

(i) the legal validity of any decision relating to the authorization of such use shall be subject to judicial review or other independent review by a distinct higher authority in that Member;

(j)   any decision relating to the remuneration provided in respect of such use shall be subject to judicial review or other independent review by a distinct higher authority in that Member;

* * *

This framework did not prevent ongoing tension between governments in developing countries and pharmaceuticals manufacturers. In 1997 the South African Parliament passed the Medicines and Related Substances Control Amendment Act, which among other things authorized the importation of drugs that could be made more cheaply abroad. This provision was designed in particular to allow South Africa to import generic antiretroviral drugs from India to treat HIV, the virus that causes AIDS. In 1998 the South African Pharmaceutical Manufacturers Association brought suit in South Africa alleging that the Act violated the TRIPS Agreement and the South African Constitution. The suit was dropped in April 2001 following a damaging public relations campaign waged by NGOs against the pharmaceutical companies.

And since the mid-1990s, Brazil has maintained a highly successful HIV treatment program using locally produced generic antiretroviral drugs. In early 2001, the United States Trade Representative requested the establishment of a WTO panel, alleging that Brazil's industrial property law of 1996 violated the TRIPS Agreement. Specifically, the United States argued that the provision allowing for compulsory licensing of patents unless the patented product was manufactured in Brazil violated TRIPS Article 27.1, which provides that "patents shall be available and patent rights enjoyable without discrimination as to the place of invention, the field of technology and whether products are imported or locally produced." The United States withdrew its complaint in June 2001, after its position had been condemned by the U.N. Commission on Human Rights among others.

The Article 31 framework had one significant limitation: it was of no assistance to member states with limited or no pharmaceutical manufacturing capabilities, which could not make effective use of compulsory licensing to meet public health needs. Public health was a major topic of discussion at the WTO's 2001 ministerial conference at Doha, Qatar, which resulted in a Declaration on the TRIPS Agreement and Public Health. 41 I.L.M. 755 (2002). The so-called Doha Declaration emphasized each member state's freedom to grant compulsory licenses and to determine what constitutes a national emergency or other circumstance of extreme urgency under Article 31, as well as each member's right to establish "without challenge" its own rules of exhaustion of intellectual property rights under Article 6.

Paragraph 6 of the Doha Declaration also recognized the limitation mentioned above. To address this problem, the WTO General Council approved a waiver of TRIPS Article 31(f) in 2003, which it subsequently proposed to make permanent by adding Article 31bis to amend the TRIPS Agreement. This article extends compulsory licensing to cover the manufacture of pharmaceuticals in one country for export to another, to meet the latter's public health needs:

Article 31bis

1.   The obligations of an exporting Member under Article 31(f) shall not apply with respect to the grant by it of a compulsory licence to the extent necessary for the purposes of production of a pharmaceutical product(s) and its export to an eligible importing Member(s) in accordance with the terms set out in paragraph 2 of the Annex to this Agreement.

2.   Where a compulsory licence is granted by an exporting Member under the system set out in this Article and the Annex to this Agreement, adequate remuneration pursuant to Article 31(h) shall be paid in that Member taking into account the economic value to the importing Member of the use that has been authorized in the exporting Member. Where a compulsory licence is granted for the same products in the eligible importing Member, the obligation of that Member under Article 31(h) shall not apply in respect of those products for which remuneration in accordance with the first sentence of this paragraph is paid in the exporting Member.

Eligible importing members include all least developed countries and other member states that lack sufficient pharmaceutical manufacturing capabilities. Paragraph 2 of the Annex, referred to in Article 31bis(1) establishes the following requirements:

(a)   the eligible importing Member(s) has made a notification to the Council for TRIPS, that:

(i)   specifies the names and expected quantities of the product(s) needed;

(ii)   confirms that the eligible importing Member in question, other than a least developed country Member, has established that it has insufficient or no manufacturing capacities in the pharmaceutical sector for the product(s) in question in one of the ways set out in the Appendix to this Annex; and

(iii)   confirms that, where a pharmaceutical product is patented in its territory, it has granted or intends to grant a compulsory licence in accordance with Articles 31 and 31bis of this Agreement and the provisions of this Annex;

(b)   the compulsory licence issued by the exporting Member under the system shall contain the following conditions:

(i)   only the amount necessary to meet the needs of the eligible importing Member(s) may be manufactured under the licence and the entirety of this production shall be exported to the Member(s) which has notified its needs to the Council for TRIPS;

(ii) products produced under the licence shall be clearly identified as being produced under the system through specific labelling or marking. Suppliers should distinguish such products through special packaging and/or special colouring/shaping of the products themselves, provided that such distinction is feasible and does not have a significant impact on price; and

(iii) before shipment begins, the licensee shall post on a website the following information:

— the quantities being supplied to each destination as referred to in indent (i) above; and

— the distinguishing features of the product(s) referred to in indent (ii) above;

(c) the exporting Member shall notify the Council for TRIPS of the grant of the licence, including the conditions attached to it. The information provided shall include the name and address of the licensee, the product(s) for which the licence has been granted, the quantity(ies) for which it has been granted, the country(ies) to which the product(s) is (are) to be supplied and the duration of the licence. The notification shall also indicate the address of the website referred to in subparagraph (b)(iii) above.

The Annex further commits eligible importing members to "take reasonable measures within their means, proportionate to their administrative capacities and to the risk of trade diversion to prevent re-exportation of the products" and requires all members to "ensure the availability of effective legal means to prevent the importation into, and sale in, their territories of products produced under the system and diverted to their markets inconsistently with its provisions." Article 31bis went into effect in 2017 following acceptance by two thirds of the WTO's members.

A number of jurisdictions have changed their laws to permit compulsory licensing for export to eligible countries. See, e.g., Regulation (EC) No. 816/2006 on Compulsory Licensing of Patents Relating to the Manufacture of Pharmaceutical Products for Export to Countries with Public Health Problems, 2006 O.J. (L 157) 1. As of December 2017, only one notification had been filed taking advantage of the system, relating to the export to Rwanda of a drug under Canadian patent.[4] Yet at the

---

[4]   See www.wto.org/english/tratop_e/trips_e/public_health_e.htm.

same time, the prices for many HIV drugs in less developed countries have dropped significantly. Pharmaceutical companies are providing some HIV drugs at or near cost through programs like the Accelerating Access Initiative. And where compulsory licensing is a possibility, the "right holder"—that is, the corporation holding a patent on a particular product, such as a drug—confronts a question of strategy. It may prefer to negotiate a licensing agreement with a local company on less than favorable terms rather than face compulsory licensing of the sort described above. Brazil, India, and Thailand (countries with substantial pharmaceutical manufacturing capabilities) have granted compulsory licenses for HIV and other drugs, and countries like Brazil have used the threat of compulsory licenses to negotiate for lower prices. On the other hand, the ability of some countries to respond to public health crises has also been affected by the inclusion of so-called "TRIPs-plus" provisions, setting more restrictive standards for the enforcement of intellectual property rights than TRIPs requires, in bilateral and regional investment treaties.

QUESTIONS

(1) Does the TRIPS Agreement appear to place any limits on a WTO member's decision to allow parallel imports of pharmaceuticals that are lawfully produced abroad?

(2) What limitations does the text of the TRIPS Agreement place on a WTO member's decision to grant a compulsory license for pharmaceuticals to combat public health crises? How does Article 31bis alter those limitations?

(3) In what ways might compulsory licensing and parallel imports be combined? Would it be permissible under TRIPS to export antiretroviral drugs produced under a compulsory license from Brazil to South Africa?

(4) If compulsory licensing and parallel imports of HIV drugs were to become widespread, what effect might this have on the incentives of drug makers to produce new generations of HIV drugs? To maintain such incentives, should compulsory licensing and parallel imports be limited to less developed countries?

Additional reading: Helfer, Alter & Guerzovich, Islands of Effective International Adjudication, Constructing an Intellectual Property Rule of Law in the Andean Community, 103 Am. J. Int'l L. 1 (2009); Atik & Lidgard, Embracing Price Discrimination: TRIPS and the Suppression of Parallel Trade in Pharmaceuticals, 27 U. Pa. J. Int'l Econ. L. 1043 (2006); Kapczynski, Harmonization and Its Discontents: A Case Study of TRIPS Implementation in India's Pharmaceutical Sector, 97 Cal. L. Rev 1571 (2009); Symposium, Global Health and the Law, 41 J.L. Med. & Ethics 9 (2013) (Flood & Lemmens, eds.); Report of the United

Nations Secretary-General's High-Level Panel on Access to Medicines (September 2016).

D. ANTITRUST ASPECTS OF INTELLECTUAL PROPERTY

It should be evident that there is an inherent tension between intellectual property law and antitrust law. Intellectual property rights by definition exclude others from utilizing the protected innovation. Legal systems supposedly have balanced those factors out and achieved a reasonable compromise between the two, although it would be hard to demonstrate empirically that the right solution has been achieved. The hard problems come up when owners of such property seek to achieve what others regard as inappropriate extensions of the rights conferred by the patent or other rights. Some obvious examples: Can the owner of a patent on a given piece of machinery insist as a condition to a license that the licensee use the patentee's unpatented components? Can one specify the price at which the products of a patented process are resold? Another source of contention has been "grantback" clauses obligating the licensee to let the licensor use any improvements which the licensee develops— often for free. Is it an antitrust violation to acquire patents that one does not intend to use, knowing that others might have used them to compete with the holder? Is it monopolization to acquire so many patents that the field is blanketed and newcomers are frightened away from even attempting to operate in it?

Difficult as these problems are when they arise domestically—that is, when it is a matter of conflict between the patent law of A and the antitrust law of A—they are magnified when the conflict is between the patent law of A and the antitrust law of B. For example, suppose that the plaintiff in a U.S. antitrust case claims that the defendant committed fraud upon the patent office in Spain and has been exploiting those fraudulent patents to protect its monopoly. Or suppose that an American court, as part of a remedy for antitrust violations it has found, orders a U.S. party to terminate a license agreement with a foreign manufacturer.

1. LICENSING UNDER U.S. ANTITRUST LAW

The U.S. Department of Justice and Federal Trade Commission have issued Antitrust Guidelines for the Licensing of Intellectual Property, most recently updated in 2017, that touch upon many of these problems. The Guidelines apply equally to domestic and international arrangements, although it is important to recall that anticompetitive agreements must affect U.S. commerce to come within the reach of U.S. antitrust laws. See supra p. 235.

The Licensing Guidelines generally adopt a favorable attitude towards licensing agreements and the restrictions they contain. The Guidelines "recognize that intellectual property licensing allows firms to combine complementary factors of production and is generally procompetitive." Licensing Guidelines § 2.0. The Guidelines do not presume that intellectual property creates market power, because there will often be a sufficient substitute for the product or process in question that prevents the exercise of such power. *Id.* § 2.2. And the Guidelines expressly state that an intellectual property owner is not ordinarily required "to create competition in its own technology." *Id.* § 3.1. More stringent rules are applied to cross licenses where two patent holders give rights to each other and create risks of market division.

Licensing agreements are treated as vertical agreements unless the licensor and licensee "would have been actual or potential competitors in a relevant market in the absence of the license." *Id.* § 3.3. Indeed, licensing may be treated even more permissively than other vertical agreements for, as the Guidelines explain, "the fact that intellectual property may in some cases be misappropriated more easily than other forms of property may justify the use of some restrictions that might be anticompetitive in other contexts." *Id.* § 4.1.2. Most restraints in licensing agreements are evaluated under the rule of reason. *Id.* § 3.4. Among the few restraints that may be considered *per se* antitrust violations are price-fixing, output restraints, and market division among horizontal competitors. *Id.* Under the rule of reason, even if a restraint has an anticompetitive effect, it may be permitted if the restraint is necessary to achieve procompetitive efficiencies and the procompetitive efficiencies outweigh the anticompetitive effects. *Id.* § 4.2.[5] Consider the Licensing Guidelines' discussion in the following example of a vertical agreement containing exclusivity and a non-compete obligation:

Example 7

Situation: NewCo, the inventor and manufacturer of a new flat panel display technology, lacking the capability to bring a flat panel display product to market, grants BigCo an exclusive license to sell a product embodying NewCo's technology. BigCo does not currently sell, and is not developing (or likely to develop), a product that would compete with the product embodying the new technology and does not control rights to another display technology. Several firms offer competing displays, BigCo accounts for only a small proportion of the outlets for distribution of display products, and entry into the manufacture and distribution of display products is relatively easy. Demand for the new technology is uncertain and successful market penetration will require considerable promotional effort. The license contains an exclusive dealing restriction preventing BigCo from selling products that compete with the product embodying the licensed technology.

---

[5]   For a discussion of *per se* violations and the rule of reason in U.S. antitrust law, see *supra* pp. 233–237.

Discussion: This example illustrates both types of exclusivity in a licensing arrangement. The license is exclusive in that it limits the ability of the licensor to grant other licenses. In addition, the license has an exclusive dealing component in that it restricts the licensee from selling competing products.

> The inventor of the display technology and its licensee are in a vertical relationship and are not actual or potential competitors in the manufacture or sale of display products or in the sale or development of technology. Hence, the grant of an exclusive license does not affect competition between the licensor and the licensee. The exclusive license may promote competition in the manufacturing and sale of display products by encouraging BigCo to develop and promote the new product in the face of uncertain demand by rewarding BigCo for its efforts if they lead to large sales. Although the license bars the licensee from selling competing products, this exclusive dealing aspect is unlikely in this example to harm competition by anticompetitively foreclosing access, raising competitors' costs of inputs, or facilitating anticompetitive pricing because the relevant product market is unconcentrated, the exclusive dealing restraint affects only a small proportion of the outlets for distribution of display products, and entry is easy. On these facts, the evaluating Agency would be unlikely to challenge the arrangement.

Section 5 of the Licensing Guidelines discusses a number of specific provisions commonly found in licensing agreements. One such provision is a "grantback" clause, which the Guidelines define as "an arrangement under which a licensee agrees to extend to the licensor of intellectual property the right to use the licensee's improvements to the licensed technology." *Id.* § 5.6. The Guidelines continue:

> The Agencies will evaluate a grantback provision under the rule of reason, considering its likely effects in light of the overall structure of the licensing arrangement and conditions in the relevant markets. An important factor in the Agencies' analysis of a grantback will be whether the licensor has market power in a relevant technology or research and development market. If the Agencies determine that a particular grantback provision is likely to reduce significantly licensees' incentives to invest in improving the licensed technology, the Agencies will consider the extent to which the grantback provision has offsetting procompetitive effects, such as (1) promoting dissemination of licensees' improvements to the licensed technology, (2) increasing the licensors' incentives to disseminate the licensed technology, or (3) otherwise increasing competition and output in a relevant technology or research and development market. In addition, the Agencies will consider the extent to which

grantback provisions in the relevant markets generally increase licensors' incentives to innovate in the first place.

Finally, to encourage licensing in the absence of market power, the Licensing Guidelines establish a "safety zone." Absent extraordinary circumstances, the Department of Justice and Federal Trade Commission will not challenge a restraint in a licensing agreement if (1) the restraint is not facially anticompetitive, i.e., a *per se* antitrust violation, and (2) the licensor and its licensees collectively do not account for more than 20% of any market significantly affected by the restraint. *Id.* § 4.3.

2.   LICENSING UNDER EU COMPETITION LAW

In Problem 2, we examined the basic structure of EU competition law. See supra pp. 238–241. As we saw, Article 101 of the Treaty on the Functioning of the European Union broadly prohibits agreements between companies that create anticompetitive effects within the common market. However, under Article 101(3), certain categories of agreements may be exempted from this prohibition through the use of block exemptions. In 2004, the European Commission adopted a Technology Transfer Block Exemption Regulation (TTBER), which was subsequently revised in 2014. Commission Regulation (EU) No. 316/2014, 2014 O.J. (L 93) 17. The current TTBER applies to licensing agreements entered into on or after May 1, 2014. Agreements concluded before that date became subject to the new TTBER on May 1, 2015.

The TTBER applies only to agreements between two parties for the licensing of patents, know-how, software copyrights, and a few other defined categories of intellectual property (see Article 1(b)). It is important to note that the TTBER treats agreements between competing parties more strictly than agreements between non-competing parties. Under Article 3, the exemption applies to agreements between competing parties where their combined market share does not exceed 20% and to agreements between non-competing parties where their individual market shares do not exceed 30%. If these thresholds are exceeded after the agreement is entered, the agreement may lose the benefit of the block exemption after a two-year grace period.

Article 4 contains lists of hardcore restrictions, one applicable to agreements between competing parties and one applicable to agreements between non-competing parties, that may not be included in a licensing agreement without losing the benefit of the TTBER. These include the types of restrictions that have the most significant anti-competitive effect, such as restrictions on resale price and the territorial division of markets. The following examples are drawn from the list of restrictions applicable to agreements between non-competing parties:

Article 4
Hardcore restrictions

* * *

2.   Where the undertakings party to the agreement are not competing undertakings, the exemption provided for in Article 2 shall not apply to agreements which, directly or indirectly, in isolation or in combination with other factors under the control of the parties, have as their object any of the following:

(a)   the restriction of a party's ability to determine its prices when selling products to third parties, without prejudice to the possibility of imposing a maximum sale price or recommending a sale price, provided that it does not amount to a fixed or minimum sale price as a result of pressure from, or incentives offered by, any of the parties;

(b)   the restriction of the territory into which, or of the customers to whom, the licensee may passively sell the contract products, except:

(i)   the restriction of passive sales into an exclusive territory or to an exclusive customer group reserved for the licensor,

* * *

Article 5 contains a list of excluded restrictions that are not themselves protected by the block exemption but the inclusion of which will not cause the entire agreement to lose the benefit of the TTBER. These are the same for both competing and non-competing parties. Consider the following provisions:

Article 5
Excluded restrictions

1.   The exemption provided for in Article 2 shall not apply to any of the following obligations contained in technology transfer agreements:

(a)   any direct or indirect obligation on the licensee to grant an exclusive licence or to assign rights, in whole or in part, to the licensor or to a third party designated by the licensor in respect of its own improvements to, or its own new applications of, the licensed technology;

(b)   any direct or indirect obligation on a party not to challenge the validity of intellectual property rights which the other party holds in the Union, without prejudice to the possibility, in the case of an exclusive license, of providing for termination of the technology transfer agreement in the event that the licensee challenges the validity of any of the licensed technology rights.

* * *

Article 6 allows the Commission or the competition authority of a member state to withdraw the benefit of the block exemption even though an agreement complies with its provisions, although such a withdrawal is extremely unlikely.

When it adopted the current TTBER, the European Commission also issued Technology Transfer Guidelines, 2014 O.J. (C 89) 3. These Guidelines elaborate on the application of the TTBER, the analysis of restrictions excluded from the TTBER under Article 5, and the analysis of agreements that fall outside the TTBER. The Guidelines emphasize that "the vast majority of [license] agreements are . . . pro-competitive," Technology Transfer Guidelines ¶ 17, and state that "there is no presumption of illegality of agreements that fall outside the scope of the block exemption provided that they do not contain hardcore restrictions of competition." Id. ¶ 156. Where an individual assessment of an excluded restriction or an entire agreement is necessary, the Guidelines call for a weighing of the negative and positive effects of a restrictive licensing agreement within the context of Article 101(3), which requires *inter alia* that the efficiency gains fully offset the likely negative impacts and a showing that less restrictive alternatives would be significantly less efficient. The Guidelines also provide current guidance on emerging issues, including those related to "patent pools" (multilateral patent licensing agreements).

QUESTIONS

(1) Consider the provisions in the licensing agreement between Data Devices and Mercada on territorial exclusivity and territorial restrictions (paragraph 1), grant-back (paragraph 3), non-competition (paragraph 12), and non-contestation of rights (paragraph 14). Under the 2017 Licensing Guidelines, would U.S. authorities be likely to challenge any of these provisions on antitrust grounds?

(2) If Mercada were a Spanish company, would any of those provisions be problematic under the EU's Technology Transfer Block Exemption Regulation? Can you suggest any ways of redrafting them to fit within the TTBER?

(3) Would you consider the TTBER's approach to licensing agreements more similar to that of the United States or to that of the Andean Community? Of the three approaches, which seems most desirable in terms of efficiency and predictability?

Additional reading: Waller, Antitrust and American Business Abroad ch. 11 (3d ed., looseleaf 1997–); Van Bael & Bellis, Competition Law of the European Community ch. 6 (5th ed. 2009).

E. INFRINGING AND GRAY MARKET GOODS

The manufacture and sale of goods in violation of intellectual property rights is common. Sometimes, that activity involves the manufacture of counterfeits—that is, products that are designed to look like genuine goods sold under well-known labels, but that often fall woefully short of the associated quality standards. In some circumstances, counterfeit goods may not only deceive consumers but also create significant public health risks. For example, there was one well-publicized incident in China involving counterfeit baby formula sold bearing the trademarks of leading manufacturers. The formula contained melanine, leading to the death of at least six infants and illness of thousands more. In addition, of course, the availability of counterfeit goods adversely affects the manufacturer of the genuine article. That company may lose sales, to the extent that potential buyers choose counterfeit versions instead. (Consider for instance the loss associated with the widespread piracy of copyrighted works including CDs, DVDs, and software.) Moreover, particularly in the case of consumer goods such as golf clubs, electronics, or apparel, the company may lose customer goodwill over the long term if buyers of the counterfeit versions associate their poor quality with the brand in question.

As a general matter, if an owner of U.S. intellectual property rights finds that goods infringing those rights are being imported into the United States, it may seek damages and an injunction in federal court. The importation of a patented invention constitutes patent infringement. 35 U.S.C.A. § 271(a). Section 32 of the Lanham Act makes it trademark infringement to use in commerce "any reproduction, counterfeit, copy, or colorable imitation" of a registered trademark, 15 U.S.C.A. § 1114(1), while Section 42 further prohibits the importation of merchandise bearing trademarks that "copy or simulate" a U.S. registered trademark. 15 U.S.C.A. § 1124. Section 106 of the Copyright Act grants a copyright owner the exclusive right to reproduce and to distribute copies of a copyrighted work, with the consequence that the importation of unauthorized copies of the owner's work constitutes copyright infringement. 17 U.S.C.A. § 106. And the Defend Trade Secrets Act of 2016 authorizes injunctive relief and damages when a misappropriated trade secret is related to a product or service used in interstate or foreign commerce. 18 U.S.C.A. § 1836(b).

Alternatively, an owner of U.S. intellectual property rights may take action against infringing goods under Section 337 of the Tariff Act of 1930. 19 U.S.C.A. § 1337. Section 337 makes it an unfair trade practice to import articles that infringe valid and enforceable U.S. patents, copyrights, and trademarks or that use misappropriated trade secrets. The Federal Circuit has held that Section 337 applies even if the trade secret was misappropriated abroad. See TianRui Group Co. Ltd. v. International Trade Commission, 661 F.3d 1322 (Fed.Cir.2011). Section 337 authorizes the U.S. International Trade Commission (ITC) to issue exclusion orders directing the Customs Service not to admit such articles to the United States and cease and desist orders to violators, backed by substantial civil penalties. Such orders are subject to policy review by the President, and in 2013 President Obama disapproved an exclusion order barring importation of certain Apple iPhones and iPads for infringing a patent owned by Samsung, the first time a president had reversed such an order since 1987. Although an intellectual property owner may not seek damages under Section 337, it is a popular remedy because it provides significantly faster relief than bringing suit in federal court, and may increase the intellectual property owner's leverage in settlement negotiations. In 1988, a GATT panel ruled that Section 337 violated the obligation of "national treatment" under GATT Article 3 by subjecting imported products to a remedy not available for domestic ones. See United States—Section 337 of the Tariff Act of 1930, GATT Panel Report, Nov. 7, 1989, GATT B.I.S.D. (36th Supp.) 345 (1990). Amendments to Section 337 enacted in 1994 were designed to cure these defects, although it is not clear that the amendments succeeded in doing so.[6]

Whether an owner of intellectual property rights may prevent the parallel importation of "gray market" goods is a more complicated question. An item is considered a gray market good if the intellectual property owner has authorized the creation of the good or copy, or the affixing of the trademark, but has not authorized the item's importation to the market in question. For example, an owner of U.S. and foreign intellectual property rights may have licensed those rights to a foreign licensee, intending its product to be produced and sold in a particular foreign market. It may then find that a third party is purchasing the product in that market and importing it to the United States. Such parallel imports undercut an intellectual property owner's ability to control the mode and channels of distribution for its products. For example, the manufacturer might wish to have its products sold at higher price in some markets than in others, in order to defray higher marketing or servicing costs or to maintain the reputation of a product as a luxury item. Contractual restrictions in a licensing agreement may prevent the licensee from selling outside the designated territory, but will not bind third parties who purchase the product from the licensee. As noted above, Article 6 of the TRIPS Agreement left it to the domestic law of each WTO member to determine when intellectual property rights have been exhausted. See supra p. 268.

Under U.S. law, two statutory provisions afford trademark owners some protection against gray market goods. The first is Section 42 of the Lanham Act, mentioned above, which prohibits the importation of merchandise bearing trademarks that "copy or simulate" a U.S. registered mark. The second is Section 526 of the Tariff Act of 1930, 19 U.S.C.A. § 1526, which provides for seizure by Customs officials of

---

[6]   See, e.g., Rogers & Whitlock, Is Section 337 Consistent with the GATT and the TRIPs Agreement?, 17 Am. U. Int'l L. Rev. 459 (2002).

"merchandise of foreign manufacture if such merchandise . . . bears a trademark owned by a citizen of, or by a corporation or association created or organized within, the United States," as well as for damages and injunctive relief against the violator. Interpreting Section 526 in K Mart Corporation v. Cartier, Inc., 486 U.S. 281, 108 S.Ct. 1811, 100 L.Ed.2d 313 (1988), the U.S. Supreme Court upheld a Customs Service regulation providing that goods manufactured by a parent, subsidiary, or affiliate of the trademark owner were not goods "of foreign manufacture" and were therefore not excludable. However, it struck down a regulation similarly treating goods manufactured by independent foreign licensees, holding that they were goods of foreign manufacture and therefore excludable. A few years later, interpreting Section 42 of the Lanham Act in Lever Brothers Co. v. United States, 981 F.2d 1330 (D.C.Cir.1993), the Court of Appeals for the D.C. Circuit held that even goods manufactured by a foreign affiliate of the trademark owner were excludable if the foreign made goods were physically different from those sold in the United States. In 1999, the Customs Service responded with a regulation permitting the importation of physically different goods if those goods were labeled to alert consumers. The current regulation reads in relevant part as follows:[7]

§ 133.23 Restrictions on importation of gray market articles.

(a) *Restricted gray market articles defined.* "Restricted gray market articles" are foreign-made articles bearing a genuine trademark or trade name identical with or substantially indistinguishable from one owned and recorded by a citizen of the United States or a corporation or association created or organized within the United States and imported without the authorization of the U.S. owner. "Restricted gray market goods" include goods bearing a genuine trademark or trade name which is:

(1) *Independent licensee.* Applied by a licensee (including a manufacturer) independent of the U.S. owner, or

(2) *Foreign owner.* Applied under the authority of a foreign trademark or trade name owner other than the U.S. owner, a parent or subsidiary of the U.S. owner, or a party otherwise subject to common ownership or control with the U.S. owner (see §§ 133.2(d) and 133.12(d) of this part), from whom the U.S. owner acquired the domestic title, or to whom the U.S. owner sold the foreign title(s); or

(3) *"Lever-rule".* Applied by the U.S. owner, a parent or subsidiary of the U.S. owner, or a party otherwise subject to common ownership or control with the U.S. owner (see §§ 133.2(d) and 133.12(d) of this part), to goods that the Customs Service has determined to be physically and materially different

---

[7]   19 C.F.R. § 133.23.

from the articles authorized by the U.S. trademark owner for importation or sale in the U.S. (as defined in § 133.2 of this part).

(b) *Labeling of physically and materially different goods.* Goods determined by the Customs Service to be physically and materially different under the procedures of this part, bearing a genuine mark applied under the authority of the U.S. owner, a parent or subsidiary of the U.S. owner, or a party otherwise subject to common ownership or control with the U.S. owner (see §§ 133.2(d) and 133.12(d) of this part), shall not be detained under the provisions of paragraph (c) of this section where the merchandise or its packaging bears a conspicuous and legible label designed to remain on the product until the first point of sale to a retail consumer in the United States stating that: "This product is not a product authorized by the United States trademark owner for importation and is physically and materially different from the authorized product." The label must be in close proximity to the trademark as it appears in its most prominent location on the article itself or the retail package or container. Other information designed to dispel consumer confusion may also be added.

(c) *Denial of entry.* All restricted gray market goods imported into the United States shall be denied entry and subject to detention as provided in § 133.25, except as provided in paragraph (b) of this section.

* * *

Copyright owners have sometimes attempted to use Section 602 of the U.S. Copyright Act to prevent the parallel importation of goods bearing a copyrighted label. Section 602(a) provides that "[i]mportation into the United States, without the authority of the owner of copyright under this title, of copies or phonorecords of a work that have been acquired outside the United States is an infringement of the exclusive right to distribute copies or phonorecords under section 106." The Supreme Court rejected those attempts in a pair of cases. Quality King Distributors, Inc. v. L'anza Research International, Inc., 523 U.S. 135, 118 S.Ct. 1125, 140 L.Ed.2d 254 (1998), involved a "round trip" situation: the products bearing the copyrighted label were manufactured in the United States, shipped abroad and sold, and eventually reimported into the country without the authorization of the copyright owner. The U.S. Supreme Court held that L'anza could not prevent the parallel importation of its product under Section 602(a) because Section 602(a) makes unauthorized importation a violation of Section 106, and Section 106 is limited by the "first sale" doctrine of Section 109, under which the first sale of a copyrighted work exhausts the owner's right to control its subsequent sale. Kirtsaeng v. John Wiley & Sons, Inc., 568 U.S. 519, 133 S.Ct.1351, 185 L.Ed.2d 392 (2013), involved the parallel importation of copies made abroad. Wiley & Sons, a textbook publisher, had assigned to its foreign subsidiary the rights to publish, manufacture and sell foreign editions of its English-language textbooks. These books contained language to the effect that they were authorized for sale only in the relevant foreign regions, and that exportation to other regions without the publisher's consent was illegal. Kirtsaeng, a Thai mathematics student living in the United States, arranged for his friends and family to purchase foreign edition textbooks at Thai bookstores and ship them to him in the United States, where he then resold them at a profit. The Supreme Court extended the L'anza rule to this situation, holding that if the copy had been "lawfully made" (i.e., with the permission of the copyright owner), then, regardless of the location of initial manufacture, the first sale doctrine permitted its buyer to resell it without the copyright owner's permission.

Finally, patent holders have invoked U.S. patent law to try to prevent parallel imports. As the following case explains, such efforts collide with the "first sale" doctrine, as in the copyright context.

Impression Products, Inc. v. Lexmark International, Inc.

Supreme Court of the United States, 2017
137 S.Ct. 1523, 198 L.Ed.2d 1

■ ROBERTS, CHIEF JUSTICE

A United States patent entitles the patent holder (the "patentee"), for a period of 20 years, to "exclude others from making, using, offering for sale, or selling [its] invention throughout the United States or importing the invention into the United States." 35 U.S.C. § 154(a). Whoever engages in one of these acts "without authority" from the patentee may face liability for patent infringement. § 271(a).

When a patentee sells one of its products, however, the patentee can no longer control that item through the patent laws—its patent rights are said to "exhaust." The purchaser and all subsequent owners are free to use or resell the product just like any other item of personal property, without fear of an infringement lawsuit.

This case presents two questions about the scope of the patent exhaustion doctrine: First, whether a patentee that sells an item under an express restriction on the purchaser's right to reuse or resell the product may enforce that restriction through an infringement lawsuit. And second, whether a patentee exhausts its patent rights by selling its product outside the United States, where American patent laws do not apply. We conclude that a patentee's decision to sell a product exhausts all of its patent rights in that item, regardless of any restrictions the patentee purports to impose or the location of the sale.

I

The underlying dispute in this case is about laser printers—or, more specifically, the cartridges that contain the powdery substance, known as toner, that laser printers use to make an image appear on paper. Respondent Lexmark International, Inc. designs, manufactures, and sells toner cartridges to consumers in the United States and around the globe. It owns a number of patents that cover components of those cartridges and the manner in which they are used.

When toner cartridges run out of toner they can be refilled and used again. This creates an opportunity for other companies—known as remanufacturers—to acquire empty Lexmark cartridges from purchasers in the United States and abroad, refill them with toner, and then resell them at a lower price than the new ones Lexmark puts on the shelves.

Not blind to this business problem, Lexmark structures its sales in a way that encourages customers to return spent cartridges. It gives purchasers two options: One is to buy a toner cartridge at full price, with no strings attached. The other is to buy a cartridge at roughly 20-percent off through Lexmark's "Return Program." A customer who buys through the Return Program still owns the cartridge but, in exchange for the lower price, signs a contract agreeing to use it only once and to refrain from transferring the empty cartridge to anyone but Lexmark. To enforce this single-use/no-resale restriction, Lexmark installs a microchip on each Return Program cartridge that prevents reuse once the toner in the cartridge runs out.

Lexmark's strategy just spurred remanufacturers to get more creative. Many kept acquiring empty Return Program cartridges and developed methods to counteract the effect of the microchips. With that technological obstacle out of the way, there was little to prevent the remanufacturers from using the Return Program cartridges in their resale business. After all, Lexmark's contractual single-use/no-resale agreements were with the initial customers, not with downstream purchasers like the remanufacturers.

Lexmark, however, was not so ready to concede that its plan had been foiled. In 2010, it sued a number of remanufacturers, including petitioner Impression Products, Inc., for patent infringement with respect to two groups of cartridges. One group consists of Return Program cartridges that Lexmark sold within the United States. Lexmark argued that, because it expressly prohibited reuse and resale of these cartridges, the remanufacturers infringed the Lexmark patents when they refurbished and resold them. The other group consists of all toner cartridges that Lexmark sold abroad and that remanufacturers imported into the country. Lexmark claimed that it never gave anyone authority to import these cartridges, so the remanufacturers ran afoul of its patent rights by doing just that.

* * *

II

A

First up are the Return Program cartridges that Lexmark sold in the United States. We conclude that Lexmark exhausted its patent rights in these cartridges the moment it sold them. The single-use/no-resale restrictions in Lexmark's contracts with customers may have been clear and enforceable under contract law, but they do not entitle Lexmark to retain patent rights in an item that it has elected to sell.

The Patent Act grants patentees the "right to exclude others from making, using, offering for sale, or selling [their] invention[s]." 35 U.S.C. § 154(a). For over 160 years, the doctrine of patent exhaustion has imposed a limit on that right to exclude. See *Bloomer v. McQuewan*, 14 How. 539, 14 L.Ed. 532 (1853). The limit functions automatically: When a patentee chooses to sell an item, that product "is no longer within the limits of the monopoly" and instead becomes the "private, individual property" of the purchaser, with the rights and benefits that come along with ownership. *Id.*, at 549–550. A patentee is free to set the price and negotiate contracts with purchasers, but may not, "*by virtue of his patent,* control the use or disposition" of the product after ownership passes to the purchaser. *United States v. Univis Lens Co.*, 316 U.S. 241, 250, 62 S.Ct. 1088, 86 L.Ed. 1408 (1942) (emphasis added). The sale "terminates all patent rights to that item." *Quanta Computer, Inc. v. LG Electronics, Inc.*, 553 U.S. 617, 625, 128 S.Ct. 2109, 170 L.Ed.2d 996 (2008).

This well-established exhaustion rule marks the point where patent rights yield to the common law principle against restraints on alienation. The Patent Act "promote[s] the progress of science and the useful arts by granting to [inventors] a limited monopoly" that allows them to "secure the financial rewards" for their inventions. *Univis*, 316 U.S., at 250, 62 S.Ct. 1088. But once a patentee sells an item, it has "enjoyed all the rights secured" by that limited monopoly. *Keeler v. Standard Folding Bed Co.*, 157 U.S. 659, 661, 15 S.Ct. 738, 39 L.Ed. 848 (1895). Because "the purpose of the patent law is fulfilled . . . when the patentee has received his reward for the use of his invention," that law furnishes "no basis for restraining the use and enjoyment of the thing sold." *Univis*, 316 U.S., at 251, 62 S.Ct. 1088.

* * *

Turning to the case at hand, we conclude that this well-settled line of precedent allows for only one answer: Lexmark cannot bring a patent infringement suit against Impression Products to enforce the single-use/no-resale provision accompanying its Return Program cartridges. Once sold, the Return Program cartridges passed outside of the patent monopoly, and whatever rights Lexmark retained are a matter of the contracts with its purchasers, not the patent law.

* * *

III

Our conclusion that Lexmark exhausted its patent rights when it sold the domestic Return Program cartridges goes only halfway to resolving this case. Lexmark also sold toner cartridges abroad and sued Impression Products for patent infringement for "importing [Lexmark's] invention into the United States." 35 U.S.C. § 154(a). Lexmark contends that it may sue for infringement with respect to all of the imported cartridges—not just those in the Return Program—because a foreign sale does not trigger patent exhaustion unless the patentee "expressly or implicitly transfer[s] or license[s]" its rights. Brief for Respondent 36–37. . . .

This question about international exhaustion of intellectual property rights has also arisen in the context of copyright law. Under the "first sale doctrine," which is codified at 17 U.S.C. § 109(a), when a copyright owner sells a lawfully made copy of its work, it loses the power to restrict the purchaser's freedom "to sell or otherwise dispose of . . . that copy." In *Kirtsaeng v. John Wiley & Sons, Inc.,* we held that this " 'first sale' [rule] applies to copies of a copyrighted work lawfully made [and sold] abroad." 568 U.S., at 525, 133 S.Ct. 1351. We began with the text of § 109(a), but it was not decisive: The language neither "restrict [s] the scope of [the] 'first sale' doctrine geographically," nor clearly embraces international exhaustion. *Id.,* at 528–533, 133 S.Ct. 1351. What helped tip the scales for global exhaustion was the fact that the first sale doctrine originated in "the common law's refusal to permit restraints on the alienation of chattels." *Id.,* at 538, 133 S.Ct. 1351. That "common-law doctrine makes no geographical distinctions." *Id.,* at 539, 133 S.Ct. 1351. The lack of any textual basis for distinguishing between domestic and international sales meant that "a straightforward application" of the first sale doctrine required the conclusion that it applies overseas. *Id.,* at 540, 133 S.Ct. 1351 (internal quotation marks omitted).

Applying patent exhaustion to foreign sales is just as straightforward. Patent exhaustion, too, has its roots in the antipathy toward restraints on alienation, see *supra,* at 1528–1533, and nothing in the text or history of the Patent Act shows that Congress intended to confine that borderless common law principle to domestic sales. . . . And differentiating the patent exhaustion and copyright first sale doctrines would make little theoretical or practical sense: The two share a "strong similarity . . . and identity of purpose," *Bauer & Cie v. O'Donnell,* 229 U.S. 1, 13, 33 S.Ct. 616, 57 L.Ed. 1041 (1913), and many everyday products—"automobiles, microwaves, calculators, mobile phones, tablets, and personal computers"—are subject to both patent and copyright protections, see *Kirtsaeng,* 568 U.S., at 545, 133 S.Ct. 1351; Brief for Costco Wholesale Corp. et al. as *Amici Curiae* 14–15. There is a "historic kinship between patent law and copyright law," *Sony Corp. of America v. Universal City Studios, Inc.,* 464 U.S. 417, 439, 104 S.Ct. 774, 78 L.Ed.2d

574 (1984), and the bond between the two leaves no room for a rift on the question of international exhaustion.

Lexmark sees the matter differently. The Patent Act, it points out, limits the patentee's "right to exclude others" from making, using, selling, or importing its products to acts that occur in the United States. 35 U.S.C. § 154(a). A domestic sale, it argues, triggers exhaustion because the sale compensates the patentee for "surrendering [those] *U.S. rights.*" Brief for Respondent 38. A foreign sale is different: The Patent Act does not give patentees exclusionary powers abroad. Without those powers, a patentee selling in a foreign market may not be able to sell its product for the same price that it could in the United States, and therefore is not sure to receive "the reward guaranteed by U.S. patent law." *Id.,* at 39 (internal quotation marks omitted). Absent that reward, says Lexmark, there should be no exhaustion. In short, there is no patent exhaustion from sales abroad because there are no patent rights abroad to exhaust.

The territorial limit on patent rights is, however, no basis for distinguishing copyright protections; those protections "do not have any extraterritorial operation" either. 5 M. Nimmer & D. Nimmer, Copyright § 17.02, p. 17–26 (2017). Nor does the territorial limit support the premise of Lexmark's argument. Exhaustion is a separate limit on the patent grant, and does not depend on the patentee receiving some undefined premium for selling the right to access the American market. A purchaser buys an item, not patent rights. And exhaustion is triggered by the patentee's decision to give that item up and receive whatever fee it decides is appropriate "for the article and the invention which it embodies." *Univis,* 316 U.S., at 251, 62 S.Ct. 1088. The patentee may not be able to command the same amount for its products abroad as it does in the United States. But the Patent Act does not guarantee a particular price, much less the price from selling to American consumers. Instead, the right to exclude just ensures that the patentee receives one reward— of whatever amount the patentee deems to be "satisfactory compensation," *Keeler,* 157 U.S., at 661, 15 S.Ct. 738—for every item that passes outside the scope of the patent monopoly.

* * *

. . . Exhaustion does not arise because of the parties' expectations about how sales transfer patent rights. More is at stake when it comes to patents than simply the dealings between the parties, which can be addressed through contract law. Instead, exhaustion occurs because, in a sale, the patentee elects to give up title to an item in exchange for payment. Allowing patent rights to stick remora-like to that item as it flows through the market would violate the principle against restraints on alienation. Exhaustion does not depend on whether the patentee receives a premium for selling in the United States, or the type of rights that buyers expect to receive. As a result, restrictions and location are irrelevant; what matters is the patentee's decision to make a sale.

Impression Products addressed the exhaustion of product patent rights under 35 U.S.C.A. § 271(a). Congress addressed parallel imports and process patents in 35 U.S.C.A. § 271(g), which provides that "[w]hoever without authority imports into the United States . . . a product which is made by a process patented in the United States shall be liable as an infringer. . . ." Although U.S. courts have not yet addressed the question, it seems likely that they will extend Impression Products to process patents, so that an authorized sale abroad would exhaust the patent rights.

Of course, gray market goods are not a concern solely of the United States. Within the European Union, the ability of manufacturers to restrict the importation of gray market goods is governed by the 2015 Trade Mark Directive, which recast an earlier version. Directive (EU) 2015/2436 of the European Parliament and of the Council to Approximate the Laws of the Member States Relating to Trade Marks, 2015 O.J. (L 336) 1.[8] Article 10 of this Directive provides: "The registration of a trade mark shall confer on the proprietor exclusive rights therein. . . . [T]he proprietor of that registered trade mark shall be entitled to prevent all third parties not having his consent from using [the trade mark] in the course of trade. . ." This right, however, is limited by the following provision on exhaustion of trademark rights:

Article 15

Exhaustion of the rights conferred by a trade mark

1.   A trade mark shall not entitle the proprietor to prohibit its use in relation to goods which have been put on the market in the Union under that trade mark by the proprietor or with the proprietor's consent.

2.   Paragraph 1 shall not apply where there exist legitimate reasons for the proprietor to oppose further commercialization of the goods, especially where the condition of the goods is changed or impaired after they have been put on the market.

The previous version of the Directive applied throughout the European Economic Area (EEA) (the EU countries plus Iceland, Liechtenstein, and Norway). As of this writing the incorporation of the recast Directive into the EEA Agreement is anticipated but not yet complete.

In Zino Davidoff SA v. A & G Imports Ltd. and Levi Strauss & Co. v. Tesco Stores Ltd., [2001] E.C.R. I-8691, two trademark owners brought suit under UK law to prevent discount stores from purchasing their products—toiletries and jeans, respectively—outside the EEA, importing

---

[8]   The EU has adopted a dual system in the area of trademark protection. In addition to recognizing trademarks granted under the laws of individual member states, it also protects "European trademarks," which are issued at the Union level. Regulation (EU) 2017/1001 of the European Parliament and of the Council on the European Union Trade Mark, 2017 O.J. (L 154) 1.

them to the United Kingdom, and reselling them there. The discount stores argued that the trademark owners should be deemed to have consented to such uses of their trademarks by placing their goods on the market in non-EEA countries. The European Court of Justice answered, in relevant part, as follows:

> 32   It must . . . be borne in mind that in Articles [10 and 15] of the Directive the Community legislature laid down the rule of Community exhaustion, that is to say, the rule that the rights conferred by a trade mark do not entitle the proprietor to prohibit use of the mark in relation to goods bearing that mark which have been placed on the market in the EEA by him or with his consent. In adopting those provisions, the Community legislature did not leave it open to the Member States to provide in their domestic law for exhaustion of the rights conferred by a trade mark in respect of products placed on the market in non-member countries (Case C-355/96 Silhouette International Schmied [1998] ECR I-4799, paragraph 26).

> 33   The effect of the Directive is therefore to limit exhaustion of the rights conferred on the proprietor of a trade mark to cases where goods have been put on the market in the EEA and to allow the proprietor to market his products outside that area without exhausting his rights within the EEA. By making it clear that the placing of goods on the market outside the EEA does not exhaust the proprietor's right to oppose the importation of those goods without his consent, the Community legislature has allowed the proprietor of the trade mark to control the initial marketing in the EEA of goods bearing the mark (Case C-173/98 Sebago and Maison Dubois [1999] ECR I-4103, paragraph 21).

> 34   By its questions, the national court is seeking chiefly to determine the circumstances in which the proprietor of a trade mark may be regarded as having consented, directly or indirectly, to the importation and marketing within the EEA by third parties who currently own them, of products bearing that trade mark, which have been placed on the market outside the EEA by the proprietor of the mark or with his consent.

* * *

> 45   In view of its serious effect in extinguishing the exclusive rights of the proprietors of the trade marks in issue in the main proceedings (rights which enable them to control the initial marketing in the EEA), consent must be so expressed that an intention to renounce those rights is unequivocally demonstrated.

> 46   Such intention will normally be gathered from an express statement of consent. Nevertheless, it is conceivable that

consent may, in some cases, be inferred from facts and circumstances prior to, simultaneous with or subsequent to the placing of the goods on the market outside the EEA which, in the view of the national court, unequivocally demonstrate that the proprietor has renounced his rights.

* * *

53   It follows from the answer to the first question referred in the three cases C-414/99 to C-416/99 that consent must be expressed positively and that the factors taken into consideration in finding implied consent must unequivocally demonstrate that the trade mark proprietor has renounced any intention to enforce his exclusive rights.

54   It follows that it is for the trader alleging consent to prove it and not for the trade mark proprietor to demonstrate its absence.

55   Consequently, implied consent to the marketing within the EEA of goods put on the market outside that area cannot be inferred from the mere silence of the trade mark proprietor.

56   Likewise, implied consent cannot be inferred from the fact that a trade mark proprietor has not communicated his opposition to marketing within the EEA or from the fact that the goods do not carry any warning that it is prohibited to place them on the market within the EEA.

57   Finally, such consent cannot be inferred from the fact that the trade mark proprietor transferred ownership of the goods bearing the mark without imposing contractual reservations or from the fact that, according to the law governing the contract, the property right transferred includes, in the absence of such reservations, an unlimited right of resale or, at the very least, a right to market the goods subsequently within the EEA.

58   A rule of national law which proceeded upon the mere silence of the trade mark proprietor would not recognise implied consent but rather deemed consent. This would not meet the need for consent positively expressed required by Community law.

59   In so far as it falls to the Community legislature to determine the rights of a trade mark proprietor within the Member States of the Community it would be unacceptable on the basis of the law governing the contract for marketing outside the EEA to apply rules of law that have the effect of limiting the protection afforded to the proprietor of a trade mark by Articles [10(1) and 15(1)] of the Directive.

Subsequent cases have explored the concept of "consent" under Article 15(1) in connection with initial sales *within* the EEA. Several of these involve the distribution of luxury goods under licensing agreements that explicitly prohibit licensees from selling the goods to discount retailers (an act that can diminish the prestige of the brand). The European Court of Justice has held that if a licensee sells goods within the EEA in breach of such a clause, it does so without the consent of the trademark owner, whose rights are therefore not exhausted. Case C-59/08, Copad SA v. Christian Dior Couture SA, 2009 E.C.R. I-03421.

QUESTIONS

(1) Assuming that Data Devices has properly registered its trademarks, would it be able to prevent a third party from buying computers manufactured by Mercada in Guatador and reselling them in the United States?

(2) Could Data Devices use either its product or process patents to prevent a third party from buying computers manufactured by Mercada in Guatador and reselling them in the United States?

(3) If L'anza cannot rely on Section 602(a) of the Copyright Act to prevent the reimportation of goods it sells abroad, would it have any better luck under U.S. trademark or patent law?

(4) Assuming that Data Devices has properly registered its trademarks, would it be able to prevent a third party from buying computers manufactured by Mercada in Guatador and reselling them in the EEA?

(5) Recall that less developed countries have considered it important to allow parallel imports of products they do not produce domestically, including pharmaceuticals. See supra pp. 271–276. The European Union and United States, by contrast, have been more willing to allow intellectual property owners to prevent parallel imports of gray market goods. Can you think of reasons why this might be so? Might developed country limitations on parallel imports actually benefit less developed countries by making intellectual property owners willing to sell their products for less in less developed countries?

Additional reading: Davis, St. Quintin & Tritton, Tritton on Intellectual Property in Europe (5th ed. 2018); Abbott, First Report (Final) to the Committee on International Trade Law of the International Law Association on the Subject of Parallel Importation, 1 J. Int'l Econ. L. 607 (1998); Sugden, Gray Markets: Prevention, Detection and Litigation (2009).

PROBLEM 4

ESTABLISHMENT OF AN OPERATION ABROAD

A. INTRODUCTION

Foreign direct investment (FDI) is investment by an enterprise from one country in an enterprise from another, involving a long-term relationship and a significant degree of control by the foreign investor. In this Problem we are concerned with the establishment of a new operation owned and controlled by a foreign investor—what is sometime called "greenfield investment." Other kinds of foreign direct investment include the acquisition of an existing foreign company and the establishment of a joint venture with a foreign partner; these are the subjects of Problems 5 and 6 respectively. For statistical purposes direct investment is often defined as one involving more than ten percent of the capital stock of a foreign enterprise. Smaller investments in equity as well as holdings of bonds and other forms of indebtedness, some of which are discussed in Problem 8, are regarded as portfolio investment.

Many of the same factors that make licensing attractive might also lead a company to consider establishing an operation of its own abroad. Production in a foreign country may allow a company to avoid transportation costs or tariffs in serving that country's market. Because of lower labor costs or better access to raw materials, it may be cheaper to produce a product abroad and export it to serve other markets, including that of the company's home country. In comparison with licensing, however, foreign direct investment allows a company a greater measure of control—over its intellectual property and the quality of the product, for example. A company may also be able to earn a greater return by establishing its own operation abroad, in part because it need not share its earnings with a foreign licensee, distributor, or agent.

But foreign direct investment also faces hazards that the transactions we have studied thus far do not. First, a company must acquire the knowledge of local markets and conditions necessary to make its foreign operation successful—something that was less vital when a foreign partner was responsible for selling, or for producing and selling, the product abroad. History is replete with examples of foreign companies that encountered difficulties understanding and responding to local conditions.[1] Second, investing abroad exposes a company to a variety of regulatory risks. The host country might impose exchange controls, preventing a foreign investor from repatriating the profits from

---

[1] See Litvin, Empires of Profit: Commerce, Conquest and Corporate Responsibility (2003) (discussing examples from the English East India Company to Nike).

its operations or the proceeds from selling its investment. The host country might impose regulations that make the investment less profitable than the investor had anticipated. The host country might even nationalize or expropriate the foreign investor's assets.

Despite such risks, foreign direct investment has boomed. In 2016, while representing a two percent decline from the previous year, worldwide FDI inflows were $1.75 trillion. In recent years, FDI inflows to developing countries have frequently exceeded those to developed countries, although in 2016 they suffered a decline of 14% from the previous year and accounted for significantly less than half of the total. Mexico attracted approximately $26.7 billion in foreign direct investment during 2016, bringing its total stock of FDI to $474 billion.[2]

As a focus for discussion, consider the following:

Pestco, a Delaware corporation headquartered in Omaha, Nebraska, produces pesticides for agricultural use at two facilities in the Omaha area. Pestco's environmental record is relatively good, although a spill of toxic chemicals at one of its Omaha plants in 2010 sent three workers to the hospital, led to substantial remediation costs, and damaged its reputation in the local community.

Since the advent of the North American Free Trade Agreement (NAFTA) in 1994, Pestco has seen its sales to Mexico increase substantially, due in part to the lowering of Mexican tariffs on its products and in part to a greater demand for Mexican agricultural products caused by the lowering of U.S. tariffs. Pestco expects that demand in Mexico for the kinds of pesticides it produces will continue to grow over the next decade and it is considering establishing a new manufacturing facility specifically to serve that market.

Two locations for the new facility are under consideration. The first is in El Paso, Texas. El Paso's location just across the border from Mexico promises some savings in transportation costs to Mexico compared with Pestco's Omaha plants. Unemployment is relatively high in El Paso, and the local Chamber of Commerce is eager to attract Pestco in order to generate jobs and tax revenue. A new facility in El Paso would be subject to the same federal environmental regulations as Pestco's Omaha plants, but Pestco is, of course, quite familiar with these regulations.

The second location is in Juarez, Mexico, just across the border from El Paso. Labor is substantially cheaper in Juarez— Pestco could expect to pay its least skilled workers about one quarter of what it would spend in the United States on wages and benefits. But productivity is also lower in Mexico—about

---

[2]   UNCTAD, World Investment Report 2017, at 2, 224, 228.

one third what it is in the United States, according to the OECD. Pestco is not presently familiar with Mexican environmental regulations governing the production of pesticides, but it suspects that these may be less stringent than their U.S. counterparts. The possibility that Pestco might establish a facility in Juarez was the subject of a recent article in the business pages of the Omaha World-Herald, which has generated protests from both labor and environmental groups in the United States, the former concerned about the export of jobs and the latter about potentially lax Mexican environmental regulation.

In addition to the considerations noted above, there are a number of legal issues that may bear upon the decisions of a company like Pestco about whether, where, and in what form to establish a foreign operation. As we shall see, businesses may operate abroad through a variety of forms—most frequently, some type of corporation. Section A reviews how corporations are assigned a "nationality," and outlines some of the implications of that assignment. An alternative is to operate in a foreign jurisdiction through a branch, without creating a separate juridical entity. Section B is concerned with the choice between a subsidiary and a branch, and discusses in particular limitations of liability and tax considerations—two of the factors that most commonly influence that choice. Section C deals with the restrictions that host countries may place on foreign investment, using Mexico's Foreign Investment Act of 1993 and a provision of the U.S. Telecommunications Act as examples. Section D addresses some of the additional tax issues that arise in connection with the ongoing operation of enterprises with significant foreign operations.

B. CORPORATE NATIONALITY AND THE RIGHTS OF FOREIGN COMPANIES

1. ESTABLISHING A CORPORATION'S NATIONALITY

There is something a bit strange about saying that a corporation is a "national" or "citizen" of a country. But from early on it has been necessary to fit corporations into rules designed for flesh-and-blood individuals. For example, American courts long ago had to resolve the question whether corporations could be citizens of a state or foreign country for purposes of diversity jurisdiction under Article III of the Constitution. It was held that they were citizens for that purpose but were not entitled to claim "privileges and immunities" under Article IV. Note that in the United States, with each of its 50 states creating corporations, it is common to speak of a corporation's residence or domicile rather than its citizenship.

In the transnational business environment, the nationality of a corporation may be important for a number of purposes. First, under the so-called "internal affairs" rule, the rights and duties of a corporation's directors, managers, and shareholders are determined by the law of its domicile. In the United States and the United Kingdom, this is the law of the jurisdiction of incorporation. Thus, a corporation with its headquarters in New York may be incorporated under the laws of Delaware—as a majority of the largest American firms are—and have its internal affairs governed by Delaware law. In a number of Continental European countries, by contrast, the internal affairs of a corporation are governed by the law of its "real seat"—its *siège* or *sitz*—which is to say the law of the place from which its day-to-day affairs are directed. Indeed, some "real seat" jurisdictions like Germany refused, until recently, to recognize the corporate status of a company managed from Germany unless it was also incorporated under German law.

Second, the rights of a corporation under international law may depend upon its nationality. In the Barcelona Traction Case, 1970 I.C.J. 3 (Feb. 5) (Belg. v. Spain), for example, the International Court of Justice held that only Canada had standing to bring a claim of expropriation on behalf of a company incorporated in Canada and having its registered office there, despite the fact that 88% of the corporation's shareholders were Belgian nationals. The nationality of a corporation may also determine whether it is entitled to claim rights under a treaty. As we saw in Chapter II, the U.S. Supreme Court held in Sumitomo Shoji America, Inc. v. Avagliano, 457 U.S. 176, 102 S.Ct. 2374, 72 L.Ed.2d 765 (1982), that Sumitomo's wholly-owned subsidiary was not covered by the U.S.-Japan Friendship, Commerce, and Navigation Treaty because it was incorporated under New York law and was therefore not a company of Japan for purposes of the treaty. See supra pp. 85–89. Tax treaties typically contain elaborate provisions designed to limit their benefits to nationals of one country operating in the other. See infra pp. 575–580.

Third, a corporation may incur obligations under national law by reason of its nationality. Corporations organized under U.S. law, for example, are subject to U.S. taxation on their worldwide income, while foreign corporations are subject to U.S. taxation only on their U.S. source income. See infra p. 314. As we have seen, the obligation not to discriminate against U.S. citizens abroad applies to U.S. corporations and to foreign corporations controlled by U.S. corporations, but not to foreign corporations not controlled by U.S. corporations. See supra pp. 107–114.

Fourth, restrictions on a corporation's activities may be imposed by reason of its foreign nationality. Section 310 of the Communications Act of 1934, 47 U.S.C.A. § 310, for example, restricts the holding of broadcast licenses by foreign corporations and by U.S. corporations owned or controlled above certain percentages by foreign corporations. See infra p. 330. The Exon-Florio Amendment, 50 U.S.C.A. § 4565, subjects to special national security review corporate takeovers "by or with any foreign person which could result in foreign control of any person engaged in interstate commerce in the United States." See infra pp. 385–390. Other countries also limit the participation of foreign corporations in certain sectors of their economy. See infra pp. 316–329.

In determining a corporation's nationality for purposes of deciding what law will govern its internal affairs, countries have looked almost exclusively to the state of incorporation or to the place of management, as described above. While these tests have also been important in determining a corporation's nationality for other purposes, the following factors have sometimes also been considered pertinent or conclusive:

(a) nationality of shareholders;

(b) nationality of directors;

(c) nationality of officers;

(d) nationality of employees;

(e) nationality of the holders of debt obligations;

(f) nationality of the owners of patents or trademarks which the corporation is licensed to use;

(g) the nation in which the industrial or commercial activities of the corporation are centered; and

(h) the nation with which, under some all-embracing standard, the corporation is most significantly identified.

In choosing among these factors, or a combination of them, a number of considerations must be borne in mind. First, the resulting standard should be administrable. That is, the authorities enforcing it should be able to ascertain the necessary facts without too much delay or doubt. Second, the outcome of any official determination should be predictable. Otherwise foreign investors might be intimidated from participating in forms or in areas of business activity that were not meant to be proscribed, or domestic investors might be discouraged from joint enterprises with some element of foreign capital or entrepreneurship. Finally, the test should be reasonably evasion-proof and should not lend itself to accommodating superficial disguises.

Within the European Union, the ability of corporations to choose their nationalities—and thereby to avoid certain requirements contained in domestic legislation—is protected by the "right of establishment" conferred by the following provisions of the Treaty on the Functioning of the European Union:

Article 49

(ex Article 43 TEC)

Within the framework of the provisions set out below, restrictions on the freedom of establishment of nationals of a Member State in the territory of another Member State shall be prohibited. Such prohibition shall also apply to restrictions on the setting-up of agencies, branches or subsidiaries by nationals of any Member State established in the territory of any Member State.

* * *

Article 52

(ex Article 46 TEC)

1. The provisions of this chapter and measures taken in pursuance thereof shall not prejudice the applicability of provisions laid down by law, regulation or administrative action providing for special treatment for foreign nationals on grounds of public policy, public security or public health.

* * *

Article 54

(ex Article 48 TEC)

Companies or firms formed in accordance with the law of a Member State and having their registered office, central administration or principal place of business within the Community shall, for the purposes of this Chapter, be treated in the same way as natural persons who are nationals of Member States.

These provisions have generated a series of important opinions by the Court of Justice of the European Union (CJEU). In 1999, the CJEU considered a case involving two Danish nationals, residing in Denmark, who sought to avoid Danish law's minimum capitalization requirement of DKK 200,000 for a corporation. They incorporated Centros Ltd. under U.K. law, which imposed no such minimum capitalization requirement, and then attempted to register a branch of the company to do business in Denmark. The Danish Trade and Companies Board refused the registration on the ground that Centros, which did no business in the United Kingdom, was seeking to establish not a branch but a principal establishment in violation of Danish minimum capital rules. In Centros Ltd. v. Erhvervs-og Selskabsstyrelsen, 1999 E.C.R. I-1459, the CJEU held that the Board's decision violated the right of establishment:

> [T]he fact that a national of a Member State who wishes to set up a company chooses to form it in the Member State whose rules of company law seem to him the least restrictive and to set up branches in other Member States cannot, in itself, constitute an abuse of the right of establishment. The right to form a company in accordance with the law of a Member State and to set up branches in other Member States is inherent in the exercise, in a single market, of the freedom of establishment guaranteed by the Treaty.

Of course, a company may exercise its right to choose its nationality not only in the decision where to incorporate originally, but in a subsequent decision to reincorporate elsewhere. In an important line of cases, the CJEU has addressed whether various national restrictions on reincorporation—some imposed by the state of original incorporation, and some imposed by the state in which reincorporation was sought— were compatible with the right of establishment under the Treaty. In Daily Mail, Case C-81/87, The Queen v. H.M. Treasury and Comm'rs of Inland Revenue, ex parte Daily Mail and Gen. Trust PLC, 1988 E.C.R. 5483, the CJEU recognized the right of the country of incorporation to veto a change in nationality. In that case, a U.K. company sought to transfer its central management, and thus its residence for tax purposes, to the Netherlands in order to avoid U.K. taxes on an asset sale and share repurchase plan. The CJEU held that the company had no right under the treaty to move its residence without the U.K.'s consent, emphasizing that companies "exist only by virtue of the varying national legislation which determines their incorporation and functioning."

Subsequent cases have chipped away at this authority, however. For example, in Cartesio, Case C-210/06, Cartesio Oktató és Szolgáltató bt., 2008 E.C.R. I-9641, the CJEU opined in dicta that a member state could not require a local company seeking to reincorporate elsewhere to wind up its business before doing so. The Court reinforced that position in Polbud, Case C-106/16, Polbud Wykonawstwo sp. z o.o, 2017 E.C.R. I-804, a case involving a local company that sought to relocate its registered office in another country. Addressing the reverse question—a restriction on inbound reincorporations—the Court held in 2012 that Hungary could not treat the conversion of a foreign company into a Hungarian one differently than it would treat the conversion of a domestic company. Case C-378/10, VALE Építési kft, 2012 E.C.R. I-440. Whether these decisions might ultimately increase the competition for corporate charters and lead to the emergence of a "Delaware of Europe" is difficult to say.

As the cases above reflect, the laws of various European states may continue to limit the flexibility of corporations in making cross-border moves. Another alternative for corporations in the European Union became available in 2004 with the entry into force of the European Council Regulation on the Statute for a European Company. Council Regulation (EC) No. 2157/2001, 2001 O.J. (L 294) 1. The purpose of the regulation is to provide a form of organization—known as a Societas Europaea or SE—that is adapted to doing business on an EU-wide basis. A company incorporated under the law of a member state may transform into an SE if it has had a subsidiary incorporated under the law of another member state for at least two years. SEs may also be created as subsidiaries, holding companies, or through mergers. They must have a subscribed capital of at least 120,000 euros and must have their registered offices in an EU member state. The SE regulation was more than 30 years in the making. The final version is less comprehensive than earlier drafts and leaves issues not covered by the regulation to be resolved under the laws of the member state in which the SE has its registered office.

The SE form offers several advantages. It tends to make mergers with other European companies easier. It also allows companies to change their domiciles more freely, which may allow them to avoid higher-tax jurisdictions. The SE allows companies from countries like Germany that mandate codetermination—that is, employee representation in management—to lessen its impact. When Allianz, Europe's largest insurer, went from being an AG to an SE in 2006, it was able to reduce its supervisory board from 20 members to 12. Although half these members must still be employee representatives, one is now British, one French, and only four German, in comparison to the ten German employee representatives who had served on Allianz AG's supervisory board.[3] As of 2018, more than 3,000 SEs had been registered, among them leading European companies including Airbus, Allianz, BASF, and SAP.

QUESTIONS

(1) Does it make sense to use different tests to determine a corporation's nationality with respect to its internal and its external affairs?

(2) Does Centros allow the EU member states, or the EU Council, sufficient scope to protect shareholders, creditors, and the public?

(3) In the wake of Centros and its progeny, would you expect a small country like the Netherlands or Denmark to reform its corporate law in an effort to attract reincorporations and emerge as a "Delaware of Europe"? What obstacles would you foresee?

Additional reading: On corporate nationality, see Mabry, Multinational Corporations and U.S. Technology Policy: Rethinking the Concept of Corporate Nationality, 87 Geo. L.J. 563 (1999); Vagts, The Corporate Alien: Definitional Questions in Federal Restraints on Foreign Enterprise, 74 Harv. L. Rev. 1489 (1961). On Centros and its progeny, see Bratton, McCahery & Vermeulen, How Does Corporate Mobility Affect Lawmaking? A Comparative Analysis, 57 Am. J. Comp. L. 347 (2009); Dammann, Freedom of Choice in European Corporate Law, 29 Yale J. Int'l L. 477 (2004); Mucciarelli, The Function of Corporate Law and the Effects of Reincorporations in the U.S. and the EU, 20 Tul. J. Int'l & Comp. L. 421 (2012). On the Societas Europaea, see Kübler, A Shifting Paradigm of European Company Law?, 11 Colum. J. Eur. L. 219 (2005).

---

[3]   Simensen & Wiesmann, Unions Weakened on Supervisory Board, Financial Times (Apr. 12, 2007).

2. THE RIGHTS OF FOREIGN CORPORATIONS

A corporation deemed under some test to be "foreign" faces the question whether it is authorized to engage in particular activities in another jurisdiction. For instance, can it bring suit in order to protect its rights? Can it negotiate and enter into a contract? Can it purchase and own personal or real property? These activities, viewed as isolated acts or investments of the foreign corporation, raise the issue of recognizing "legal" existence outside the home country for a particular purpose. But at some stage the activities abroad will cease to be sporadic. They will shade into the regular doing of business, the taking of an active part in some other nation's commercial or industrial life. Different questions of policy arise with respect to such conduct of a foreign corporation, in contrast with its appearance in court or the negotiation of an occasional contract.

Within the U.S. federal system, the states have resolved the question of foreign corporations' general capacity to do business in a fairly uniform way. Whatever may be their constitutional power today to exclude such corporations entirely from the transaction of local business, states have chosen to admit them upon compliance with certain requirements. In most situations, these requirements are not of an onerous nature: providing certain information, submitting to the jurisdiction of local courts, and assuming certain fiscal obligations. Such requirements are felt to serve an essential protective purpose, but stop short of the comprehensive set of rules in the corporation laws applicable to domestic corporations. For certain kinds of corporations, particularly those operating in highly regulated industries such as insurance or banking, the requirements may become substantial and indeed approximate the full range of local regulation brought to bear upon domestic corporations transacting comparable business. The following provisions of the New York Business Corporation Law typify "qualification" laws of general applicability.

§ 1301. AUTHORIZATION OF FOREIGN CORPORATIONS.

(a) A foreign corporation shall not do business in this state until it has been authorized to do so as provided in this article. A foreign corporation may be authorized to do in this state any business which may be done lawfully in this state by a domestic corporation, to the extent that it is authorized to do such business in the jurisdiction of its incorporation, but no other business.

(b) Without excluding other activities which may not constitute doing business in this state, a foreign corporation shall not be considered to be doing business in this state, for the purposes of this chapter, by reason of carrying on in this state any one or more of the following activities:

(1) Maintaining or defending any action or proceeding, whether judicial, administrative, arbitrative or otherwise, or

effecting settlement thereof or the settlement of claims or disputes.

(2) Holding meetings of its directors or its stockholders.

(3) Maintaining bank accounts.

(4) Maintaining offices or agencies only for the transfer, exchange and registration of its securities, or appointing and maintaining trustees or depositaries with relation to its securities.

(c) The specification in paragraph (b) does not establish a standard for activities which may subject a foreign corporation to service of process under this chapter or any other statute of this state.

* * *

§ 1304. APPLICATION FOR AUTHORITY; CONTENTS.

(a) A foreign corporation may apply for authority to do business in this state. An application . . . shall set forth:

(1) The name of the foreign corporation.

(2) The fictitious name the corporation agrees to use in this state pursuant to section 1301 of this chapter, if applicable.

(3) The jurisdiction and date of its incorporation.

(4) The purpose or purposes for which it is formed, it being sufficient to state, either alone or with other purposes, that the purpose of the corporation is to engage in any lawful act or activity for which corporations may be organized under this chapter, provided that it also state that it is not formed to engage in any act or activity requiring the consent or approval of any state official, department, board, agency or other body without such consent or approval first being obtained. By such statement all lawful acts and activities shall be within the purposes of the corporation, except for express limitations therein or in this chapter, if any.

(5) The county within this state in which its office is to be located.

(6) A designation of the secretary of state as its agent upon whom process against it may be served and the post office address within or without this state to which the secretary of state shall mail a copy of any process against it served upon him.

* * *

§ 1306. POWERS OF AUTHORIZED FOREIGN CORPORATIONS.

An authorized foreign corporation shall have such powers as are permitted by the laws of the jurisdiction of its incorporation but no greater powers than those of a domestic corporation formed for the business set forth in the application for authority.

§ 1307. TENURE OF REAL PROPERTY.

A foreign corporation may acquire and hold real property in this state in furtherance of its corporate purposes and may convey the same by deed or otherwise in the same manner as a domestic corporation.

* * *

§ 1312. ACTIONS OR SPECIAL PROCEEDINGS BY UNAUTHORIZED FOREIGN CORPORATIONS.

(a) A foreign corporation doing business in this state without authority shall not maintain any action or special proceeding in this state unless and until such corporation has been authorized to do business in this state and it has paid to the state all fees and taxes imposed under the tax law or any related statute, as defined in section eighteen hundred of such law, as well as penalties and interest charges related thereto, accrued against the corporation. This prohibition shall apply to any successor in interest of such foreign corporation.

(b) The failure of a foreign corporation to obtain authority to do business in this state shall not impair the validity of any contract or act of the foreign corporation or the right of any other party to the contract to maintain any action or special proceeding thereon, and shall not prevent the foreign corporation from defending any action or special proceeding in this state.

Section 102(7) of the law excerpted above defines the term "foreign corporation" to mean one "formed under laws other than the statutes of this state."

In other countries the rules confronted by a foreign corporation vary widely, determined as they are by a complex of political attitudes, particularly in countries still in the throes of development. A country such as Germany may simply impose requirements of registration, similar to New York's, upon a foreign corporation that transacts business in it through a local branch. Another country may insist upon local incorporation of a subsidiary, may impose special requirements such as the duty to obtain governmental authorization for each corporate venture, or may prohibit operations in certain or all fields that are conducted directly or indirectly by aliens. To a considerable degree these questions of the right of aliens to conduct local business through a local branch or subsidiary, questions referred to generally as pertaining to the "right of establishment," are regulated on the international scene by bilateral treaties of friendship, commerce, and navigation or by multilateral treaties. As we have seen, the provisions of the Treaty on the Functioning of the European Union concerning the right of establishment have been given an expansive interpretation by the Court of Justice of the European Union as between EU member states. See supra pp. 301–303.

C. CHOICE OF CORPORATE FORM

If a company wishes to establish a more permanent presence abroad, one of the decisions it must make is whether to incorporate a separate entity under local law or to operate simply through its own undifferentiated branch. Moreover, in many legal systems, there is more than one form of corporation from which to choose: in Germany, for example, forms include the large public corporation (*Aktiengesellschaft* or AG), the small or close corporation (*Gesellschaft mit beschränkter Haftung* or GmbH), and, for small start-ups, the entrepreneurial company with limited liability (*Unternehmergesellschaft haftungsbeschränkt* or UG). Some legal systems permit unusual forms that may offer particular advantages: for instance, the Swiss association (*Verein*) has attracted significant use by multinational service firms, including accounting and legal enterprises, because it achieves a decentralized structure in which the liability of each independent office is separate from that of the others. One should consult local counsel to determine the options available and their advantages and limitations.

The decision whether to operate as a branch or to incorporate a local subsidiary will turn on various factors. To begin with, it may depend in part on local administrative practices and preferences. In Mexico, a foreign company is technically permitted to establish a branch (*Sucursal de Sociedad Extranjera*). But the Mexican government has historically preferred that foreign investors establish wholly or partially owned Mexican entities and has discouraged the establishment of branches by delaying the necessary approvals.

Foreign investors in Mexico have therefore tended to establish subsidiaries, choosing one of the three types of entities with limited liability available under Mexican law: the public corporation (*Sociedad Anónima* or S.A.), the corporation with variable capital (*Sociedad Anónima de Capital Variable* or S.A. de C.V.), or the limited liability company (*Sociedad de Responsibilidad Limitada* or S. de R.L.).[4] The *Sociedad Anónima* is similar to a U.S. corporation. It may transact business and bring suit in its own name. The liability of its shareholders is limited to the amounts of their capital contributions. There is no limit on the duration of an S.A. and its shares may be transferred freely. However, the capital of an S.A. must be fixed in its charter and may not be increased or reduced without amending the charter and obtaining approvals from the Mexican government.

---

[4]   See generally Zamora et al., Mexican Law ch. 19 (2004); Vargas, Mexican Law for the American Lawyer ch. 7 (2009).

The *Sociedad Anónima de Capital Variable* is similar to the *Sociedad Anónima* but without the same rigidity of capital structure. An S.A. de C.V. has a minimum fixed capital, but its charter may provide for an unlimited amount of variable capital for which shares may be issued when additional capital is needed without prior government approval. Most major corporations in Mexico take this form.

The *Sociedad de Responsibilidad Limitada* lies somewhere between a corporation and a partnership. It may transact business and bring suit in its own name, and the liability of its members is limited to their capital contributions. However, ownership interests in an S. de R.L. may not be represented by shares of stock, may not be sold to the public, and may not be transferred without the consent of members holding a majority of its capital stock. The S. de R.L. is frequently the choice for establishing an equity joint venture between a foreign investor and a Mexican party. The S. de R.L. may be treated as either a branch or a partnership for U.S. tax purposes.

The decision whether to operate through a branch or a subsidiary may also affect the applicability of various treaties designed to protect foreign investors. As noted above, the U.S. Supreme Court held in the Sumitomo case that a New York subsidiary of a Japanese company was not entitled to claim the benefits of the U.S.-Japan Friendship, Commerce, and Navigation Treaty because under the terms of the treaty the subsidiary was a company of the United States rather than a company of Japan. See supra pp. 85–89. Chapter Eleven of NAFTA, by contrast, applies to the investments of investors from one NAFTA country in the territory of another NAFTA country regardless of whether the investment takes the form of a branch or a subsidiary. Under NAFTA Article 1139, "investment" includes "an enterprise," and "enterprise" includes both enterprises organized under the laws of a NAFTA country and the branches of such enterprises. The same tends to be true of other U.S. international investment agreements (IIAs). See U.S. Model Bilateral Investment Treaty art. 1 (2012) (defining "investment" and "enterprise" in similar terms). Problem 7 discusses the protection of foreign investment under IIAs in greater detail. See infra pp. 470–482.

The following sections address two other factors that are particularly important in choosing the form of a foreign investment: limited liability and tax considerations.

1. LIMITED LIABILITY

One advantage of using a corporate form to do business abroad is the "limited liability" of subsidiaries. Because a foreign branch is not an entity distinct from the parent company, the parent is liable for the branch's debts and other liabilities. A foreign subsidiary, on the other hand, is a juridical entity distinct from its parent. As a general matter, shareholders are not responsible for the debts of a corporation. The parent company's liability for its foreign subsidiary's operations is thus "limited" to the amount of capital the parent has invested in the subsidiary. Salomon v. Salomon & Co., [1897] A.C. 22 (H.L.) upheld this principle even where one shareholder held 20,001 of a company's 20,007 shares of stock and the other six were held by his family members. "Either the limited company was a legal entity or it was not. If it was, the business belonged to it and not to Mr. Salomon. . . . [I]t is impossible to say at the same time that there is a company and there is not." Id. at 31.

However, the limited liability of shareholders is not absolute. "The law permits the incorporation of a business for the very purpose of enabling its proprietors to escape personal liability . . . but, manifestly, the privilege is not without its limits. Broadly speaking, the courts will disregard the corporate form, or, to use accepted terminology, 'pierce the corporate veil,' whenever necessary 'to prevent fraud or to achieve equity.' " Walkovszky v. Carlton, 18 N.Y.2d 414, 417, 223 N.E.2d 6, 7, 276 N.Y.S.2d 585, 587 (1966). As the foregoing quotation indicates, the tests applied to pierce the corporate veil are often vague and indeterminate. Justice Traynor indicated some of the circumstances that might lead a court to disregard the corporate form in Minton v. Cavaney, 56 Cal.2d 576, 579, 364 P.2d 473, 475, 15 Cal.Rptr. 641, 643 (1961): "The equitable owners of a corporation, for example, are personally liable when they treat the assets of the corporation as their own and add or withdraw capital from the corporation at will . . . ; when they hold themselves out as being personally liable for the debts of the corporation . . . ; or when they provide inadequate capitalization and actively participate in the conduct of corporate affairs."

U.S. multinationals must, of course, be concerned not just with American law on piercing the corporate veil but also with the laws of those foreign jurisdictions in which their subsidiaries operate, as Union Carbide Corporation discovered in the wake of the gas leak disaster in Bhopal, India. On the night of December 2, 1984, poisonous methyl isocyanate gas escaped from a pesticide factory in Bhopal, a city in the state of Madhya Pradesh. More than 2,000 people died and more than 200,000 suffered some degree of injury, in some cases so severe as to be disabling. The plant belonged to Union Carbide India, Ltd. (UCI), a company organized under the laws of India. UCI was owned 50.9% by Union Carbide Corporation, a multinational enterprise headquartered in Danbury, Connecticut with assets of over $10 billion and annual sales of $9 billion. The government of India owned 22% of UCI, and the remaining 27.1% of its shares were publicly held by Indian citizens. At the time Indian law generally required that no more than 40% of the stock of such firms be owned by foreigners, but an exception had been made in this case. UCI's directors were Indian nationals, as were the bulk of the employees at Bhopal. UCI had twelve other plants in India, although none of them produced the insecticide made there. UCI's net worth at the end of 1983 was estimated to be approximately $27 million.

There has never been an authoritative determination of the cause(s) of the disaster. There is at least some indication that each of the following may have played a role: (1) sabotage by parties unknown, (2) negligence by Indian employees of UCI in operating the equipment and in failing to react promptly to use safety equipment and warn the population when it appeared that poisonous methyl isocyanate was escaping, (3) failure by Indian governmental authorities to exercise effective regulatory control over the operations at Bhopal, (4) deficiencies in the basic design of the plant as it was drawn up in the United States using as a model a similar plant in West Virginia, (5) modifications made to the original design by engineers in India, motivated in part by a need to comply with Indian legal requirements calling for the use of components made in India, and (6) failure of the Indian authorities to react promptly to the disaster and to use the most advanced medical techniques available.

American lawyers soon descended upon Bhopal and sought to enlist plaintiffs in suits against Union Carbide. The first suit was filed in the United States just four days after the disaster. On February 6, 1985, this suit and 144 others were consolidated in the U.S. District Court for the Southern District of New York under the provisions of Title 28 dealing with multidistrict litigation. On March 29, 1985, India adopted the Bhopal Gas Leak Disaster (Processing of Claims) Act (the Bhopal Act), which gave the Indian government exclusive authority to represent victims of the Bhopal disaster in courts around the world. Shortly thereafter, the government of India filed a complaint on behalf of all victims of the disaster in the U.S. District Court for the Southern District of New York. On May 12, 1986, Judge Keenan dismissed the consolidated claims on grounds of *forum non conveniens*, contingent upon Union Carbide's submission to the jurisdiction of the courts of India. In re Union Carbide Corp. Gas Plant Disaster at Bhopal, India in December, 1984, 634 F.Supp. 842 (S.D.N.Y. 1986), aff'd 809 F.2d 195 (2d Cir.), cert. denied, 484 U.S. 871, 108 S.Ct. 199, 98 L.Ed.2d 150 (1987).

In September 1986, the government of India filed suit against Union Carbide Corporation in Bhopal seeking $3 billion in damages under a theory of "multinational enterprise liability," claiming that Union Carbide had "an absolute and non-delegable duty to ensure that the . . . hazardous plant did not cause any danger or damage to the people and the State by the operation of the ultrahazardous and dangerous activity at the . . . plant."[5] In December 1987, the Bhopal District Court ordered Union Carbide to pay $270 million in interim relief. Union Carbide appealed to the Madhya Pradesh High Court, which upheld the grant of

---

[5] Complaint, Union of India v. Union Carbide Corp., No. 1113 (D. Bhopal, India 1986), quoted in Covell, The Bhopal Disaster Litigation: It's Not Over Yet, 16 N.C. J. Int'l J. L. & Comm. Reg. 279, 284 (1991).

interim relief while reducing it to $190 million.[6] On the question of lifting the corporate veil, Judge Seth had this to say:

> In the opinion of this Court, much water has flown down the Ganges since it was first held in *Saloman v. Saloman & Company* (1897 A.C. 22) as an absolute principle that a corporation or company has a legal and separate entity of its own. As far back as in 1965, it was declared by the Supreme Court in *Tata Engineering and Locomotive Co. Ltd. v. State of Bihar* (A.I.R. 1965 SC 40) that in course of time the doctrine that a corporation or company has a legal and separate entity of its own has been subject to certain exceptions by the application of the fiction that the veil of the corporation can be lifted and its face examined in substance. . . .
>
> Similarly, in a recent decision of the Supreme Court in *Life Insurance Corporation of India v. Escorts Ltd.* (A.I.R. 1986 SC 1370), it has been observed thus by Chinappa Reddy, J.:
>
>> "Generally and broadly speaking, we may say that the corporate veil may be lifted where a statute itself contemplates lifting the veil, or fraud or improper conduct is intended to be prevented or a taxing statute or a beneficent statute is sought to be evaded or where associated companies are inextricably connected as to be in reality part of one concern. It is neither necessary nor desirable to enumerate the class of cases where lifting the veil is permissible, since, that must necessarily depend on the relevant statutory or other provision, the objects sought to be achieved, the impugned conduct, the involvement of the element of public interest, the effect on parties who may be affected etc."

* * *

> Accordingly, there is no reason why when the corporate veil can be lifted in the cases of tax evasions, . . . it cannot be lifted on purely equitable considerations in a case of tort which has resulted in a mass disaster and in which on the face of it the assets of the alleged subsidiary company are utterly insufficient to meet the just claims of [a] multitude of disaster victims. The concept in question regarding "lifting the veil" has been an expanding concept and the Court shall fail in its duty if it does not apply the said concept in a case of the nature of the Bhopal suit.

As to whether Union Carbide could be considered to have control over UCI, Judge Seth continued:

---

[6]   Union Carbide Corp. v. Union of India (Madhya Pradesh H.C.) No. 26/88 (1988), reprinted in Rosencranz, Divan & Noble, Environmental Law and Policy in India 359–381 (1991).

As per the very facts pleaded by the defendant-UCC it is clear that it held the majority of equity share capital of the Indian company at all material times. It is also clear from the Articles of Association of the Indian company that the defendant-UCC controlled more than half of the total voting power of the Indian company at all material times. Thus, the defendant-UCC not only controlled the composition of the Board of Directors of the Indian company but also had full control over the management of the Indian company. If, as alleged by the defendant-UCC, it chose to follow the policy of keeping itself at arms length from the Indian company in certain respects, it was entirely its choice and such policy could not absolve it from its liability.

Both sides appealed to the Indian Supreme Court. In February 1989, the Court fashioned a settlement under which Union Carbide agreed to pay $470 million to the government of India to settle all civil claims and criminal charges. The Court credited against this amount $5 million that Union Carbide had previously given to the Red Cross, and UCI contributed $45 million. See Union Carbide Corp. v. Union of India, 1990 A.I.R. (S.C.) 273. The Indian Supreme Court subsequently rejected challenges to the validity of the Bhopal Act, see Sahu v. Union of India, 1990 A.I.R. (S.C.) 1480, and to the settlement, although the Court overruled that part of its order quashing the criminal proceedings against Union Carbide, its former chief executive officer Warren Anderson, and others. See Union Carbide Corp. v. Union of India, 1992 A.I.R. (S.C.) 248. Neither Anderson nor Union Carbide appeared for arraignment, and in 1992 the Bhopal District Court declared them "absconders" and ordered the attachment of Union Carbide's remaining assets in India.

Attempts by private Indian parties to relitigate the matter in U.S. court have been unsuccessful. In Bi v. Union Carbide Chemicals & Plastics Co., 984 F.2d 582 (2d Cir.), cert. denied, 510 U.S. 862, 114 S.Ct. 179, 126 L.Ed.2d 138 (1993), the court held that the Bhopal Act deprived the plaintiffs of standing to sue. And in Bano v. Union Carbide Corp., 273 F.3d 120 (2d Cir. 2001), the court held that claims against Union Carbide and Anderson under the Alien Tort Statute were barred by the settlement orders of the Indian Supreme Court. In related litigation, a federal court held in 2012 that neither Union Carbide nor Anderson was liable for injuries to local residents allegedly caused by exposure to polluted soil and water at the site of the Bhopal plant. Sahu v. Union Carbide Corp., 2012 WL 2422757 (S.D.N.Y. 2012).

QUESTIONS

(1) Given the structure of Union Carbide Corporation's investment in India, to what extent would it have expected to be liable in the event of an industrial accident at its Bhopal plant?

(2) How much control does it appear that Union Carbide Corporation had over the day-to-day operations of Union Carbide India Limited? Should the amount of control a parent has over a subsidiary affect the parent's liability for the actions of the subsidiary?

(3) Reflecting upon the disaster at Bhopal, should multinationals structure operations differently? Should they insist upon 100% ownership? Shift to licensing local producers?

2. TAX CONSIDERATIONS

There are two basic principles upon which nations assert the power to tax: the status of the taxpayer and the source of the income. Almost all tax systems contain elements of both the status and source principles, although the way in which they are applied to arrive at a determination of taxable income varies from country to country. Most countries have adopted systems that are primarily territorial in nature—that is, they tax only income derived from sources within their borders, such as wages earned through local employment or revenues earned through the operation of a local business. The United States, in contrast, has historically followed a global taxation model. While non-resident aliens and foreign corporations are subject to taxation only on their U.S. source income, United States citizens, resident aliens, and domestic corporations are subject to taxation on their global income. A corporation is considered "domestic" if it is "created or organized in the United States or under the law of the United States or of any State." 26 U.S.C. § 7701(a)(4). The Code achieves this result through a series of provisions that curtail an initially sweeping assertion of the tax power. See, e.g., 26 U.S.C. § 61(a) ("gross income means all income from whatever source derived"). This model was never completely absolute, however; as we shall see, it was qualified in a number of ways in order to mitigate the overall burden on taxpayers with significant foreign source income.

Tax treatment has exerted a considerable influence upon the legal forms used by American businesses to conduct their foreign operations. For many years, the use of subsidiaries was particularly advantageous. The U.S. corporate tax rate stood at 35%, which was significantly higher than the corporate tax rate in most other countries. While the earnings of a U.S. company's foreign branch would be immediately taxable as income to the company, the relevant Code provisions permitted what commentators described as "tax deferral" of income that was earned by foreign subsidiaries. In brief, income earned overseas by the foreign subsidiary of a U.S. company was subject to taxation only in the relevant foreign country. (That is, such income was non-U.S. source, earned by a non-U.S. taxpayer, and therefore generated no U.S. income tax liability.) Only at the point when the subsidiary issued a dividend to its U.S. parent would it generate U.S. tax consequences, since the dividend payment would be taxable income of the parent. As a result of this structure, U.S. corporations routinely reinvested the foreign earnings of their subsidiaries abroad rather than "repatriating" those earnings to the United States in the form of dividends, thus deferring eventual payment of U.S. taxes. Congress frequently expressed concern about the level of foreign earnings retained overseas, occasionally enacting provisions such as one-time tax breaks intended to encourage their repatriation (and their reinvestment domestically for purposes such as worker hiring and training, infrastructure, research and development, capital investments, or the financial stabilization of the parent company).

The sweeping tax reform legislation enacted in 2017, commonly referred to as the Tax Cuts and Jobs Act (TCJA), sought to disincentivize the tax deferral of foreign-earned income. First, it reduced the corporate tax rate from 35% to 21%. Second, it introduced a new provision that allows a U.S. corporation owning at least 10% of a foreign company to deduct 100% of the foreign-source portion of any dividends received from that company. 26 U.S.C. § 245A. The effect of this provision is to shift the U.S. tax system to a more territorial approach that taxes U.S.-source income but not foreign-source income. With respect to foreign earnings and profits accumulated before 2017, the TCJA also imposes a "transition tax." It provides that U.S. shareholders owning at least 10% of a foreign subsidiary must include as taxable income their pro rata share of earnings accumulated since 1986, to the extent such earnings have not previously been subject to U.S. tax. The rate applicable to accumulated earnings is 15.5% (8% for non-cash earnings), and the law permits the taxpayer to spread the resulting tax liability over a period of up to eight years. We will return to these provisions in Section D. See infra at pp. 333–337.

The TCJA also introduced two new taxes that act as a backstop to ensure that U.S. companies do not shift too much of their income generating activities abroad. First, it introduced a new tax on "global intangible low-taxed income" (GILTI). In effect, U.S. companies will now be required to pay U.S. income tax (although at the low rate of 10.5%) on earnings of their foreign subsidiaries in excess of a fixed return of 10% on foreign assets. 26 U.S.C. § 951A; see infra p. 334. Second, it introduced a new Base Erosion Anti-Abuse Tax (BEAT), which subjects U.S. companies with income of $500 million or more to a minimum tax of 10% calculated not just on their ordinary income but also on payments to foreign affiliates for such things as services, interest, rents, and royalties. Companies subject to the tax must pay the higher of their taxes calculated the usual way or the BEAT. 26 U.S.C. § 59A; see infra p. 337.

The 2017 tax reform introduced a number of other changes to the taxation regime that will affect a U.S. company's choice of form for foreign operations. One such change directly affects the treatment of foreign branch income. Recall that a branch is simply part of the relevant corporation. As a result, its income is consolidated with other income earned by that corporation. The same is true of its losses—and historically the primary advantage to operating overseas as a branch rather than as an incorporated subsidiary was that any losses incurred by the branch could be used to offset earnings elsewhere, thus reducing the overall taxable income of the company. While the new legislation continues that treatment of losses, it limits the availability of tax credits for foreign tax paid on the income earned by branches. See infra at pp. 339–340.

QUESTIONS

(1) Under what circumstances would it be advantageous for a U.S. firm to conduct its manufacturing operations in Mexico through a branch rather than a foreign subsidiary?

(2) If Pestco were to decide to establish an operation in Juarez, Mexico, what would be the advantages and disadvantages of each of the four options available to it under Mexican law?

D. RESTRICTIONS ON FOREIGN INVESTMENT

As noted in the introduction to this Chapter, there has been tremendous growth in foreign direct investment over the past decades, and many countries have engaged in significant legal reform in order to attract such investment. Nevertheless, barriers to foreign investment persist. They may include, among others, formal restrictions such as limitations on foreign ownership (either across the board or in particular sectors and industries); onerous approval procedures and other administrative practices; and operating restraints such as local employment requirements. The number and type of such restrictions vary across countries.[7]

1. FOREIGN INVESTMENT IN MEXICO

Mexico has had a long and sometimes difficult relationship with foreign investment. During the administration of Porfirio Diaz from 1876 to 1911, foreign investors in general and U.S. investors in particular came to dominate the Mexican economy, holding huge amounts of land and controlling the mining, banking, railroad, electricity, and oil industries. In 1910 a decade of revolution began, which produced among other things the 1917 Constitution that is still in force today. Articles 27 and 28 of the Constitution represented a reaction against foreign investment. Article 27 vested original ownership of all lands, waters, and natural resources in the Mexican state, which was given the express right to regulate them to achieve a more equitable distribution of wealth. Foreigners could be granted the right to own land and to operate concessions for the exploitation of natural resources only if they agreed to a "Calvo Clause" under which they would be considered Mexican nationals and could not invoke the protection of their home governments

---

[7] See generally OECD FDI Regulatory Restrictiveness Index, available at www.oecd.org.

upon penalty of forfeiting their property. Article 27 also prohibited foreigners from owning land in a restricted zone of one hundred kilometers along Mexico's borders and fifty kilometers along its shores. Article 28 reserved certain activities to the state, including the issuance of money, postal services, and telegraph services.

Mexico soon began to expropriate and redistribute large land-holdings, many of them owned by foreigners. Then, in 1938, President Cárdenas expropriated the oil concessions. This led to a famous exchange of letters between U.S. Secretary of State Cordell Hull and the Mexican Minister of Foreign Affairs concerning the expropriation of agrarian properties, but with Mexico's expropriation of U.S. oil interests looming in the background.[8] The United States took the position that "no government is entitled to expropriate private property, for whatever purpose, without provision for prompt, adequate, and effective payment therefor," while Mexico maintained that only national treatment was required "for expropriations of a general and impersonal character like those which Mexico has carried out for the purpose of redistribution of the land." It continued:

> The political, social, and economic stability and the peace of Mexico depend on the land being placed anew in the hands of the country people who work it; a transformation of the country, that is to say, the future of the nation, could not be halted by the impossibility of paying immediately the value of the properties belonging to a small number of foreigners who seek only a lucrative end.

Ultimately Mexico and the United States agreed to methods for determining the value of both the agrarian claims and the oil claims, and Mexico paid approximately $40 million to settle the former and $24 million to settle the latter.

From 1940 to 1958, Mexico pursued a more open policy towards foreign investment, halting expropriations and even permitting foreign companies once again to explore and drill for oil. Mexico shifted course in 1958 with the administration of President Lopez Mateos, which nationalized the telephone company and foreign-owned power companies. Article 27 of the Constitution was amended to prohibit the granting and continuation of oil and gas concessions and the exploitation of these resources was expressly reserved to the state. Foreign investment in other sectors of the economy was restricted by a series of statutes culminating in the rather restrictive 1973 Act to Promote Mexican Investment and Regulate Foreign Investment.[9]

Mexico's debt crisis, which began in 1982, and its resulting need to attract greater foreign investment led, once again, to a change of policy. In 1989, Mexico issued Foreign Investment Regulations far more liberal

---

[8]   Reproduced in 3 Hackworth, Digest of International Law 655–661 (1942).

[9]   Translated in 12 I.L.M. 463 (1973).

than the 1973 Act they were supposedly designed to implement. This tension was resolved in 1993 when Mexico adopted a new Foreign Investment Act that closely followed the 1989 Regulations. At the same time, Mexico joined the North American Free Trade Agreement (NAFTA), which entered into force on January 1, 1994. Chapter Eleven of NAFTA provides substantial protections for Canadian and U.S. investors in Mexico (and vice versa), as well as a system of arbitration for resolving investment disputes.

Since it was first passed in 1993, Mexico's Foreign Investment Act has been amended a number of times, most recently in August 2014. These amendments have generally liberalized the law by modifying or eliminating restrictions on foreign investment in basic petrochemicals, satellite communications, railroads, retail gasoline sales, broadcasting, financial services, and basic and cellular phone services. The following excerpts are taken from the English translation of the law on the Ministry of Economy's website.[10]

FOREIGN INVESTMENT LAW
TITLE ONE
GENERAL PROVISIONS
CHAPTER I
On the purpose of the Law

ARTICLE 1. This law is of public policy and for general adherence throughout the Republic. Its purpose is to establish rules to attract foreign investment to the country and promote its contribution to national development.

ARTICLE 2. For the purposes hereof, the following terms shall have the following meanings:

I. Commission: the National Foreign Investment Commission;

II. Foreign investment:

    a) Participation by foreign investors, in any percentage, in the capital stock of Mexican companies;

    b) Investments by Mexican companies in which foreign capital has majority interest; and

    c) Participation by foreign investors in activities and acts contemplated herein.

III. Foreign investor: an individual or entity of any nationality other than Mexican, and foreign entities with no legal standing;

IV. Registry: the National Foreign Investment Registry;

V. Ministry: the Ministry of Economy;

---

[10] See   http://www.economia.gob.mx/files/comunidad_negocios/ied/foreign_investment_ law.pdf.

VI. Restricted Zone: a strip of the national territory one hundred kilometers wide along the borders and fifty kilometers wide along the coast, as referred to in Section I of Article 27 of the Political Constitution of the United Mexican States; and

VII. Foreigners Exclusion Clause: an express agreement or covenant forming an integral part of the corporate by-laws and setting forth that such corporations shall not admit, directly or indirectly, foreign investors or corporations with foreigners admission clause, as partners or stockholders.

ARTICLE 3. For the purposes hereof, investments made in this country by foreigners with the stay status of permanent residents shall be considered Mexican investment, except those made in activities contemplated in Titles One and Two hereof.

ARTICLE 4. Foreign investment may participate in any proportion in the capital of Mexican companies, acquire fixed assets, enter new fields of economic activity or manufacture new product lines, open and operate establishments, and expand or relocate existing establishments, except as otherwise provided herein.

The rules for the participation of foreign investment in the activities of the financial sector provided for in this Law shall be applied without prejudice to those established by the specific laws for those activities.

For the purpose of determining the foreign investment percentage in economic activities subject to certain maximum limits of foreign participation, foreign investment indirectly conducted in such activities through the stock of Mexican companies with a majority Mexican investment shall not be taken into account as long as such Mexican companies are not controlled by the foreign investment.

CHAPTER II

On reserved activities

ARTICLE 5. The activities determined by the relevant laws in the following strategic areas are reserved exclusively for the State:

I. Exploration and extraction of oil and other hydrocarbons, as provided by Articles 27, seventh paragraph, and 28, fourth paragraph, of the Political Constitution of the United Mexican States and the respective secondary Law;

II. Repealed by an Order published in the Official Gazette of the Federation on August 11, 2014;

III. Planning and control of the national electric system, as well as the public services of transmission and distribution of electricity, as provided by Articles 27, paragraph sixth, and 28, paragraph fourth, of the Political Constitution of the United Mexican States and the respective secondary Law;

IV. Generation of nuclear energy;

V.   Radioactive minerals;

VI.   Repealed by an Order published in the Official Gazette of the Federation on June 7, 1995.

VII.   Telegraph;

VIII.   Radiotelegraphy;

IX.   Postal service;

X.   Repealed by an Order published in the Official Gazette of the Federation on May 12, 1995.

XI.   Bank note issuing;

XII.   Minting of coins;

XIII.   Control, supervision and surveillance of ports, airports and heliports; and

XIV.   Others as expressly provided by applicable legal provisions.

ARTICLE 6. The economic activities and companies mentioned hereunder are reserved exclusively to Mexicans or to Mexican companies with foreigners exclusion clause:

I.   Domestic land transportation for passengers, tourism and freight, not including messenger or courier services;

II.   Repealed by an Order published in the Official Gazette of the Federation on August 11, 2014;

III.   Repealed by an Order published in the Official Gazette of the Federation on July 14, 2014;

IV.   Repealed by an Order published in the Official Gazette of the Federation on August 20, 2008.

V.   Development banking institutions, under the terms of the law governing the matter; and

VI.   Rendering of professional and technical services set forth expressly by applicable legal provisions.

Except as set forth in Title Five hereof, foreign investment may not participate directly in the activities and companies mentioned in this article nor through trusts, contracts, partnerships or by-law agreements, pyramiding schemes, or other mechanisms granting any control or participation.

CHAPTER III

On activities and acquisitions
under specific regulations

ARTICLE 7. In the economic activities and corporations mentioned hereafter, foreign investment may participate in the following percentages:

I. Up to 10% in:

Cooperative companies for production;

II. Up to 25% in:

a) Domestic air transportation;

b) Air taxi transportation; and

c) Specialized air transportation;

III. Up to 49% in:

[a) through o), repealed];

p) Manufacture and commercialization of explosives, firearms, cartridges, ammunitions and fireworks, not including acquisition and use of explosives for industrial and extraction activities nor the preparation of explosive compounds for use in said activities;

q) Printing and publication of newspapers for circulation solely throughout Mexico;

r) Series "T" shares in companies owning agricultural, ranching, and forestry lands;

s) Fresh water, coastal, and exclusive economic zone fishing not including fisheries;

t) Integral port administration;

u) Port pilot services for inland navigation under the terms of the law governing the matter;

v) Shipping companies engaged in commercial exploitation of ships for inland and coastal navigation, excluding tourism cruises and exploitation of marine dredges and devices for port construction, conservation and operation;

w) Supply of fuel and lubricants for ships, airplanes, and railway equipment; and

x) Broadcasting. This maximum foreign investment will be subject to the reciprocity that exists in the country of constitution of the investor or economic agent who exercise control, in the last instance, directly or indirectly.

IV. Repealed by an Order published in the Official Gazette of the Federation on December 24, 1996.

Except as set forth in Title Five hereof, foreign investment participation limits in the activities and companies mentioned in this article may not be surpassed directly nor through trusts, contracts, partnerships or by-law agreements, pyramiding schemes or other mechanisms granting any control or a higher participation than the one established.

ARTICLE 8. A favorable resolution by the Commission is required for foreign investment to participate in a percentage higher than 49% in the economic activities and companies referred to hereafter:

I.   Port services in order to allow ships to conduct inland navigation operation, such as towing, mooring and barging.

II.   Shipping companies engaged in the exploitation of ships solely for high-seas traffic;

III. Concessionaire or permissionaire companies of air fields for public service;

IV.   Private education services of pre-school, elementary, middle school, high school, college or any combination;

V.   Legal services;

VI.   Repealed by an Order published in the Official Gazette of the Federation on January 10, 2014;

VII. Repealed by an Order published in the Official Gazette of the Federation on January 10, 2014;

VIII. Repealed by an Order published in the Official Gazette of the Federation on January 10, 2014;

IX.   Repealed by an Order published in the Official Gazette of the Federation on July 14, 2014;

X.   Repealed by an Order published in the Official Gazette of the Federation on August 11, 2014;

XI.   Repealed by an Order published in the Official Gazette of the Federation on August 11, 2014;

XII. Construction, operation and exploitation of general railways, and public services of railway transportation.

ARTICLE 9. A favorable resolution from the Commission is required for foreign investment to participate, directly or indirectly, in a percentage higher than 49% of the capital stock of Mexican companies when the aggregate value of the assets of such companies at the date of acquisition exceeds the amount determined annually by such Commission.[11]

* * *

TITLE THREE

COMPANIES

Incorporation of and modification to companies

ARTICLE 15. The Ministry of Economy shall authorize the corporate or business names intended to be used on the incorporation of companies. The foreigners exclusion clause or the agreement provided for in Section

---

[11] [Eds.] Article 9 applies to acquisitions of existing Mexican companies. With respect to Canadian and U.S. investors, NAFTA required Mexico to raise this threshold to $150 million (adjusted for inflation since January 1, 1995). See 32 I.L.M. 605, 719 (1994).

I of Article 27 of the Constitution shall be inserted in the by-laws of the companies incorporated.

ARTICLE 16. The procedure referred to in the preceding article is required for companies that change their corporate or business name.

The companies that replace their foreigners exclusion clause with the foreigners admission clause shall notify such event to the Ministry of Foreign Affairs within thirty business days following the above mentioned change.

If these companies own real estate located in the restricted zone intended for non-residential purposes, they shall give the notice provided by Section I of Article 10 within the period set forth in the preceding paragraph.

ARTICLE 16A. Any application of the permits provided in Articles 15 and 16 shall be resolved upon by the Ministry of Economy within two business days following the date of the application.

TITLE FOUR
INVESTMENTS BY FOREIGN LEGAL ENTITIES

ARTICLE 17. Notwithstanding the provisions in any international treaty and convention to which Mexico is party, the following individuals shall obtain authorization from the Ministry:

I. Foreign legal persons intending to engage in business acts on a regular basis in the Mexican Republic, and

II. Foreign legal persons to which Article 2736 of the Civil Code for the Federal District regarding local jurisdiction and, for the Mexican Republic regarding federal jurisdiction refers, who intend to establish themselves in the Republic, if they are not regulated by different laws.

ARTICLE 17A. The authorizations to which the preceding article refers shall be granted when the following requirements are met:

a) That said persons prove that they are duly organized in accordance with the laws of their own country;

b) That the corporate charter and other organizational documents are not contrary to Mexican public policy established in law; and

c) In the case of the persons to which the preceding article, Section I refers, they shall establish themselves in the Republic or maintain an office or branch therein, or in the case of the persons to which the preceding article, Section II refers, they shall maintain a representative in the place in Mexico in which they will operate, in charge of their obligations.

Any application which meets the requirements set forth above shall be granted within fifteen business days following the date of the application. Concluded the aforesaid period without any resolution forthcoming, the application shall be deemed to have been granted.

The Ministry shall remit to the Ministry of Foreign Affairs a copy of the applications and the authorizations granted hereunder.

TITLE FIVE

NEUTRAL INVESTMENT

CHAPTER I

The concept of neutral investment

ARTICLE 18. Neutral investment is the investment made in Mexican companies or in trusts authorized under this Title and shall not be taken into account for determining the percentage of foreign investment in the capital stock of Mexican companies.

CHAPTER II

Neutral investment represented by instruments issued by trustee institutions

ARTICLE 19. The Ministry may authorize trustee institutions to issue neutral investment instruments which shall solely grant pecuniary rights to their holders and, if applicable, limited corporate rights, but without granting their holders voting rights in Regular Shareholders' Meetings.

The Ministry will have a maximum period of thirty-five business days from the day immediately following application to grant or deny the authorization. Upon the lapsing of the aforesaid period without any resolution forthcoming, the application shall be deemed to have been granted.

CHAPTER III

Neutral investment represented by special series of stocks

ARTICLE 20. The investment in stocks without voting rights or with limited corporate rights shall be considered neutral, provided that the authorization from the Ministry is granted, and when applicable, from the National Banking and Securities Commission.

The Ministry will have a maximum period of thirty-five business days from the day immediately following application to grant or deny the authorization. Upon the lapsing of the aforesaid period without any resolution forthcoming, the application shall be deemed to have been granted.

* * *

TITLE SIX
NATIONAL FOREIGN INVESTMENT COMMISSION
CHAPTER I
Structure of the Commission

ARTICLE 23. The Commission shall be composed of the Ministers of the Interior; Foreign Affairs; Finance and Public Credit; Social Development; Environment, Natural Resources and Fishery; Energy; Commerce and Industrial Development; Communications and Transportation; Labor and Social Welfare; and Tourism, who may appoint an Under-Secretary as alternative. Likewise, those authorities and private and social representatives who may have relation to the issues to be addressed, may be invited to participate in the Commission sessions. These may participate with the right to speak but not to vote.

The Commission shall meet at least twice a year and will decide upon the issues within its purview by a majority vote. In case of a draw the chairman of such Commission will have a casting vote.

ARTICLE 24. The Commission shall be chaired by the Minister of Commerce and Industrial Development and shall have an Executive Secretary and a Committee of Representatives for its operation.

ARTICLE 25. The Committee of Representatives shall be composed of the civil servants appointed by each of the Ministers who sit on the Commission, shall meet at least once every four months and shall have the authority delegated to it by such Commission.

CHAPTER II
Duties of the Commission

ARTICLE 26. The Commission shall have the following authority and powers:

I.   To issue political guidelines on foreign investment matters and to design mechanisms to promote foreign investment in Mexico;

II.   To resolve, through the Ministry, on the viability and, as the case may be, on the terms and conditions for the participation of foreign investment in activities or acquisitions with specific regulation, pursuant to Articles 8 and 9 hereof;

III. To be the mandatory consulting entity on foreign investment matters for governmental agencies and entities of the Federal Public Administration;

IV. To establish the criteria for the application of legal and regulatory provisions on foreign investment, through the issuance of general resolutions; and

V.   All others entrusted to it pursuant to this Law.

* * *

CHAPTER III

Operation of the Commission

ARTICLE 28. The Commission must resolve upon the requests submitted to its consideration within a period which shall not exceed forty five business days from the date of the respective request, as set forth in the regulations hereof. If the Commission fails to resolve within the period indicated hereinabove, the request shall be considered approved as submitted. Upon express request from the interested party, the Ministry shall issue the corresponding authorization.

ARTICLE 29. In order to evaluate the requests submitted to its approval, the Commission shall observe the following criteria:

I.   Impact upon employment and training of workers;

II.   Technological contribution;

III.   Compliance with environmental provisions included in the ecological regulations governing the matter; and

IV.   In general, its contribution to increase the competitiveness of the country's productive system.

On resolving upon the legal feasibility of a request, the Commission may only impose requirements which do not distort international trade.

ARTICLE 30. For reasons of national security, the Commission may prevent acquisitions by foreign investment.

TITLE SEVEN

NATIONAL FOREIGN INVESTMENT REGISTRY

ARTICLE 31. The Registry shall not be public and shall be divided into the sections set forth by its regulations, which will also determine its organization, and the information which must be provided to such Registry.

ARTICLE 32. The following must register with the Registry:

I.   Mexican companies in which there is participation, including through trusts, of:

    a)   Foreign investment;

    b)   Mexicans who have or acquire another nationality and who have their domicile outside Mexican territory; or

    c)   Neutral investment.

II.   Those who regularly engage in business acts in Mexico, in case they are:

    a)   Foreign individuals or companies;

    b)   Mexicans who have or acquire another nationality and who have their domicile outside Mexican territory; and

III.   Trusts on shares or corporate equity interest, on real estate, and on neutral investment whereby rights in favor of the foreign investment or of Mexicans who have or acquire another nationality and who have their domicile outside Mexican territory shall be derived.

The obligation to register shall be incumbent upon the individuals and companies to which Sections I and II refer, and in the case of Section III, by the trustee institution. The registration must be done within 40 business days from the date of the creation of the company or the equity participation by foreign investment; of formalization or official recording by Public Notary of the documents relating to the foreign company; or of the creation of the relevant trust or granting of beneficial rights in favor of the foreign investment.

ARTICLE 33. The Registry shall issue registration certificates when the request contains the following data:

I. In the case of Sections I and II:

    a) Name, trade or corporate name, domicile, date of incorporation, if applicable, and main economic activity to be performed;

    b) Name and domicile of legal representative;

    c) Name and domicile of persons authorized to hear and receive notices;

    d) Name, trade or corporate name, nationality and stay status, if applicable, domicile of the foreign investors abroad or in the country and the percentage of their interest;

    e) Amount of the capital stock subscribed and paid-in or subscribed and payable; and

    f) Estimated date for startup of operations and estimated amount of total investment with a forecast schedule;

II. In the case of Section III:

    a) Name of the trustee bank;

    b) Name, trade or corporate name, domicile and nationality of the foreign investment or of the trust settler or foreign investors;

    c) Name, trade or corporate name, domicile and nationality of foreign investment or of foreign investors appointed trust beneficiaries;

    d) Date of incorporation, purposes and duration of the trust; and

    e) Description, value, purposes and, if applicable, location of the property in trust.

Once the Registry has issued the registration and renewals thereof, the Registry shall have the authority to request declarations with respect to the information submitted. Notice should be given to the Registry on any modification to the information submitted as set forth in this article, pursuant to what is provided for in its Regulations.

* * *

ARTICLE 35. The subjects required to register in the Registry shall annually renew their registration record, for which purpose the filing of an economic-financial questionnaire as set forth by the respective regulations shall be sufficient.

* * *

TITLE EIGHT
PENALTIES

ARTICLE 37. The Ministry will be able to revoke the authorizations granted in the case of acts performed in violation of the provisions of this Law.

The acts, covenants or partnerships and bylaw agreements declared null and void by the Ministry due to their noncompliance hereunder, shall have no legal effect between the parties and shall not be enforced before third parties.

ARTICLE 38. Infringements to the provisions under this Law and its regulatory provisions shall be subject to the following penalties:

I.   If the foreign investment engages in activities, acquisitions or any other acts which require a favorable resolution from the Commission, without having obtained such resolution previously, a fine ranging from one thousand to five thousand wages shall be imposed;

II.   If foreign companies regularly engage in business acts in the Mexican Republic, without having obtained prior authorization from the Ministry, a fine ranging from five hundred to one thousand wages shall be imposed;

III.   If acts in violation to what is set forth in this Law or its regulatory provisions on the matter of neutral investment are performed, a fine ranging from one hundred to three hundred wages shall be imposed;

IV.   In case of non-performance, untimely performance, submittance of incomplete or incorrect information with respect to the registration, reporting or notice obligations with the Registry on the part of the obligated individuals, a fine ranging from thirty to one hundred wages shall be imposed;

V.   If fraud is incurred in order to allow the enjoyment or disposal of real estate in the restricted zone by foreign individuals or entities or to Mexican companies which do not have foreigners exclusion clause, in violation to what is set forth by Titles Two and Three hereof, the violator shall be sanctioned with a fine of up to the amount of the transaction; and

VI.   Any other violations to this Law or to its regulatory provisions shall bear a fine ranging from one hundred to one thousand wages.

For the purposes of this article, "wage" shall be understood as the daily general minimum wage in force in the Federal District at the time in which the violation is determined.

For the determination and imposition of any penalty, the interested party shall be previously heard and, in case of pecuniary penalties, the nature and seriousness of the violation, the earning power of the violator, the time elapsed from the date the obligations should have been performed and their compliance or regularization, and the total value of the operation shall be taken into consideration.

The Ministry shall have the authority to impose penalties, except for the violation referred to in Section V of this article and others related to Titles Two and Three, which shall be applied by the Ministry of Foreign Affairs.

The imposition of penalties referred to in this Title shall be without prejudice to the appropriate civil or criminal liabilities.

QUESTIONS

(1) Consider the limitations on foreign investment contained in Articles 5–8 of Mexico's Foreign Investment Act of 1993. What sectors of the economy does Mexico appear to be particularly concerned to protect from foreign investment? Do these limitations make sense in light of Mexico's history with foreign investment?

(2) Article 29 of Mexico's Foreign Investment Act of 1993 sets forth criteria for the National Commission of Foreign Investments to consider in approving applications for foreign investment. What goals do these criteria appear to reflect? Would Pestco's establishment of a pesticide manufacturing facility in Juarez appear to be consistent with these goals?

Additional reading: Torres Landa, The Changing Times: Foreign Investment in Mexico, 23 N.Y.U. J. Int'l L. & Pol. 801 (1991); Chua, The Privatization-Nationalization Cycle: The Link Between Markets and Ethnicity in Developing Countries, 95 Colum. L. Rev. 223, 228–238 (1995); Vargas, Mexico's Foreign Investment Act of 1993, in 1 Mexican Law: A Treatise for Legal Practitioners and International Investors (Vargas ed., 1998); Vargas, Mexico's Foreign Investment Regulations of 1998, 23 Hous. J. Int'l L. 1 (2000).

2. FOREIGN INVESTMENT IN THE UNITED STATES

The general practice of the United States has been to welcome foreign investment. Nevertheless, U.S. law places certain limits on the activities of corporations that are considered "foreign" under various criteria. For example, the Nuclear Regulatory Commission may not issue licenses for facilities that produce or use nuclear materials to any entity that is owned or controlled by an alien, foreign corporation, or foreign government. U.S. domestic airlines must have at least 75% of their voting shares owned or controlled by U.S. citizens and at least two thirds of their directors and managing officers must be U.S. citizens. Similar rules prevail as to U.S.-flag merchant shipping. The Exon-Florio Amendment, first enacted in 1988 and made permanent in 1992, gives the President broad authority to block foreign acquisitions of U.S. companies on a case-by-case basis to protect national security. We shall consider Exon-Florio further in Problem 5. See infra pp. 385–390.

Since 1912, Congress has also imposed restrictions on foreign investment in U.S. broadcasters. The current restrictions are found in § 310 of the Communications Act of 1934, 47 U.S.C.A. § 310, as amended most recently by the Telecommunications Act of 1996:

§ 310.   License ownership restrictions

(a) Grant to or holding by foreign government or representative

The station license required under this chapter shall not be granted to or held by any foreign government or the representative thereof.

(b) Grant to or holding by alien or representative, foreign corporation, etc.

No broadcast or common carrier or aeronautical en route or aeronautical fixed radio station license shall be granted to or held by—

(1) any alien or the representative of any alien;

(2) any corporation organized under the laws of any foreign government;

(3) any corporation of which more than one-fifth of the capital stock is owned of record or voted by aliens or their representatives or by a foreign government or representative thereof or by any corporation organized under the laws of a foreign country;

(4) any corporation directly or indirectly controlled by any other corporation of which more than one-fourth of the capital stock is owned of record or voted by aliens, their representatives, or by a foreign government or representative thereof, or by any corporation organized under the laws of a foreign country, if the Commission finds that the public interest will be served by the refusal or revocation of such license.

––––––––––

The original purpose of these restrictions on foreign ownership was to protect broadcast transmissions from undue foreign influence, which might raise national security concerns. The restrictions contained in Section 310(a) and in Sections 310(b)(1)–(3) are strict limitations that the Federal Communications Commission (FCC) has no authority to waive. For many years, the 25% threshold set forth in Section 310(b)(4) was also viewed by industry participants and other observers as a strict limitation. With the increasing globalization of the telecommunications industry, however, complaints arose that the inability to access foreign capital was creating barriers to entry for certain participants, including small business entities. Commenters highlighted changes in the media landscape since the adoption of Section 310, including the growth in competition that broadcasters face from platforms such as Google and Twitter that are not subject to the same foreign ownership restrictions. They also suggested that national security risks today are created not by broadcast transmissions but by the possibility of cyber-attacks launched by foreign interests over communications networks.

The Commission undertook a review of its practices under Section 310(b)(4), and in 2013 issued a declaratory ruling stating that it would consider applications for foreign ownership exceeding the statutory threshold on a case-by-case basis "based on the specific facts and unique circumstances presented by each application before it."[12] That ruling signaled a liberalization of the Commission's approach to foreign ownership in the broadcast industry, and indeed the Commission subsequently issued several orders approving foreign ownership in excess of 25%. See Univision Holdings, Inc., Declaratory Ruling, DA 17-4 (Jan 3., 2017) (permitting aggregate foreign ownership up to 49%); Hemisphere Media Group, Inc., Declaratory Ruling, DA 17-79 (Jan. 18, 2017) (permitting aggregate foreign ownership of 49.99%). In one of these orders, the Commission for the first time approved 100% foreign ownership of broadcast licenses. The relevant petition was filed by Frontier Media, LLC, an Alaska company wholly owned by two Australian citizens, which sought to obtain indirect ownership of a group of broadcast licenses in Alaska and Texas. The section of the order relating to the requisite public interest analysis is brief, and concludes simply that no national security concerns had been identified. Rather, the analysis highlights the investment concerns that motivated the 2013 ruling:

> [W]e find that grant of the Petition would: (1) increase the likelihood of continued service to small communities by authorizing investment by individuals who are ready, willing, and able to operate the stations based on their extensive experience operating them to date; (2) facilitate foreign investment in the U.S. broadcast radio market; and (3) potentially encourage reciprocal investment opportunities for U.S. companies in foreign markets. For these reasons, we find that grant of the Petition will serve the public interest.

Frontier Media, LLC, Declaratory Ruling, DA 17-190 (Feb. 23, 2017).

---

[12] In the Matter of Commission Policies and Procedures Under Section 310(b)(4) of the Communications Act, Foreign Investment in Broadcast Licensees, MB Docket No. 13–50, ¶ 11 (November 14, 2013).

In one case involving Pandora Media, the parent company of the radio streaming service, the Commission considered the particular challenges faced by publicly traded companies seeking to establish compliance with the foreign ownership restrictions. Pandora Radio LLC, Declaratory Ruling, FCC 15-52 (May 4, 2015). The ownership of Pandora Media was widely dispersed, with no single individual or entity holding an interest of 5% or more in the company. Moreover, at least half of the company's shares were held by intermediaries, making a determination of the specific identity of the shares' beneficial owners highly impractical. As a result, Pandora concluded, it was unable to establish compliance with the statutory thresholds—even though it had no reason to believe that its foreign ownership exceeded them. The Commission recognized these difficulties and approved Pandora's petition on the condition that Pandora monitor its foreign ownership in a variety of ways. Building on that decision, the Commission subsequently adopted a new compliance methodology in a 2016 ruling.[13] The new approach permits publicly traded companies to rely on various public sources of information regarding their ownership, including the filings that must be made with the Securities and Exchange Commission by any shareholder acquiring more than 5% of the shares of such a company. Only shareholdings that are known, or that should be known, to be in foreign hands count toward the ownership limit.

The 2016 ruling, which went into effect in April 2017, also streamlines the process for approving petitions regarding foreign ownership. For example, once an applicant has received approval for a specific foreign owner whose stake exceeds 25%, it may increase that owner's stake to 49.99% without further action. Likewise, an applicant that has received approval for a specific foreign owner whose stake exceeds 50% may increase that owner's stake to 100% without further action. In addition, a declaratory ruling pertaining to a particular licensee will cover any additional subsidiaries or affiliates later formed or acquired, as long as the overall foreign ownership structure remains within the bounds of the ruling.

QUESTIONS

(1) Does restricting broadcasting activity to Americans make sense in national security terms? What sort of anti-American activities by foreigners does the statute envisage?

(2) Suppose that U.S. legislation treated newspaper ownership in the same way that it treats broadcasters. In what ways are the two media different? Would that raise constitutional issues?

---

[13] Review of Foreign Ownership Policies for Broadcast, Common Carrier and Aeronautical Radio Licensees under Section 310(b)(4) of the Communications Act of 1934, as Amended, Report and Order, 31 FCC Rcd 11272 (2016).

(3) In Citizens United v. Fed. Election Comm'n, 558 U.S. 310 (2010), the Supreme Court held that the Constitution did not permit the federal government to limit independent expenditures by corporations— for-profit as well as non-profit—on political speech. In his separate opinion, Justice Stevens noted that the majority decision "would appear to afford the same [First Amendment] protection to multinational corporations controlled by foreigners as to individual Americans." Id. at 424. Election laws prohibit foreign nationals, including companies incorporated under the laws of a foreign country, from making campaign contributions or donations in the United States. Are there arguments for similarly restricting domestic corporations if they are under foreign control? Would such restrictions be constitutional?

Additional reading: Addis, Who's Afraid of Foreigners? The Restrictions on Alien Ownership of Electronic Media, 32 Colum. Hum. Rts. L. Rev. 133 (2000); Hastings, Foreign Ownership of Broadcasting: The Telecommunications Act of 1996 and Beyond, 29 Vand. J. Transnat'l L. 817 (1996); Massaro, Foreign Nationals, Electoral Spending, and the First Amendment, 34 Harv. J. L. & Pub. Pol'y 663 (2011).

E. TAX ISSUES AFFECTING FOREIGN OPERATIONS

In this section, we attempt to provide a general overview of some of the international tax issues that arise in connection with ongoing foreign operations. We begin with a word of caution. On the one hand, it is quite unrealistic to work in the area of foreign investment without taking tax into account. Tax considerations have a major effect on the way in which foreign operations are structured, and most practitioners in the international field have at least a basic knowledge of international tax, enough so that they can understand the client's motivations and know when to ask for specialized help. On the other hand, including tax matters incurs the risk of misleading superficiality. International tax is a specialty of its own with all of the attributes that go with such a characterization. There are courses and casebooks in the field; there are international tax services, roundtables, and colloquia. Moreover, 2017 brought major changes in the form of the Tax Cuts and Jobs Act (TCJA). That legislation changed the tax treatment of international business activity in a number of significant ways; however, at the time of this writing, rulemaking under the new law is not yet complete. For these reasons, the discussion that follows remains at a fairly general level. In the world of practice, a lawyer structuring foreign business operations would be sure to keep in close touch with the firm's international tax lawyer down the hall.

1. TAX-MINIMIZING TECHNIQUES AND LEGISLATIVE REACTIONS TO THEM

The materials above suggest two techniques by which American businesses with foreign operations could lighten their domestic tax burdens. First, a domestic corporation could establish a foreign subsidiary to conduct its manufacturing and selling operations, thereby eliminating all U.S. taxation of the foreign earnings until dividend payments or liquidation. Second, a domestic corporation that was involved with its foreign subsidiaries in an integrated international venture could adjust the prices charged to those foreign subsidiaries in order to shift as much of the income derived from that venture as possible to low-tax jurisdictions.

Over time, several of these techniques came to be viewed as abuses of the Code's provisions. One target of concern related to the practice of U.S. corporations in accumulating the earnings of their foreign subsidiaries overseas, thus insulating that income from U.S. taxation until it was repatriated in the form of dividends. See supra pp. 314–316. This concern was previously addressed in Subpart F of the Code. That Subpart treats all or part of the undistributed income of certain corporations as if it had in fact been distributed to the shareholders, and imposes a tax, payable by the *shareholders,* on this attributable income. However, the rules affected primarily a limited form of business structure that had become significant—the so-called "tax haven" or "base company" structure. In other words, they targeted U.S. companies that deliberately shifted mobile income to low-tax jurisdictions in an effort to shield their foreign earnings from an "appropriate" level of taxation.

Subpart F, however, created new opportunities for tax avoidance. For instance, royalty income paid between entities that are disregarded for U.S. tax purposes does not trigger taxation under Subpart F, an opportunity that was widely exploited by technology companies. Reportedly, such a strategy enabled Microsoft to lower its U.S. tax bill for 2011 by $2.43 billion. See Senators Levin and Coburn, Memorandum on Offshore Profit Shifting and the U.S. Tax Code 23 (Sept. 20, 2012). The 2017 tax reform bill returned to the issue. As noted above, it introduced new provisions intended to encourage the repatriation of foreign earnings by U.S. parent companies by effectively eliminating the tax payable on dividends from foreign-source income. See supra p. 315. It also introduced a new tax on "global intangible low tax income" (GILTI), which includes but is not limited to earnings from patents and other intellectual property rights held in low-tax jurisdictions. Income on foreign assets that exceeds a 10% rate of return is subject to this tax. In a provision that operates similarly to Subpart F, new Section 951A of the tax code deems this income to be repatriated in the year it is earned, thus subjecting it to immediate taxation (although at the low rate of 10.5%) by the United States. The intent is to discourage MNEs from holding valuable assets, and earning the income derived from those assets, outside the United States.

Another corporate practice that drew the attention of regulators was "transfer pricing"—the process by which MNEs fix the prices for goods and services that pass from one of their affiliates to another. Intra-firm trade of this type accounts for a significant portion of exports worldwide. Because these dealings do not take place at arm's length, however, questions arise as to how to price the transfers—and opportunities arise for MNEs to manipulate the pricing in order to lessen their overall tax burdens. Sometimes the pricing disadvantages the U.S. tax position; sometimes it favors the United States at the expense of another country's fiscal authorities. Pricing also has implications for *ad valorem* tariff structures as well as exchange control systems; Section 1059A says that the cost of an item imported into the United States cannot be higher than its customs value. And pricing has internal consequences within the MNE, which uses the profits achieved by an activity for internal decision-making purposes, such as evaluating the performance of its managers and deciding where to allocate its new capital investments.

According to studies, the IRS loses tens of billions of dollars each year as a result of transfer pricing.[14] Such large amounts have drawn the attention of enforcement authorities and have resulted in a number of lengthy and expensive disputes. In 2006 GlaxoSmithKline settled a sixteen-year dispute with the IRS by agreeing to pay more than $3 billion.[15] The price paid for the inability to find a simple working solution for these problems has been substantial. Part of it falls upon the taxpayer, which must bear the expense of preparing and defending its tax returns. But the burdens on the IRS and the Tax Court are also substantial.

Before we look at the legal solutions, we need to understand the problem in more concrete terms. Consider a fairly typical example:

> Amco manufactures widgets, at a cost of $50 each, which retail at a price of $100 both in the United States and in Guatador. Amco sells widgets to non-affiliated American wholesalers at $75, realizing profits of $25 on each sale taxable in the United States at a rate of 35%. With respect to distribution in Guatador, Amco sells widgets to its Guatadoran subsidiary Subco at a price of $55, which Subco resells at a price of $100. Amco earns $5 on each sale, taxable at the U.S. rate of 21%, and Subco earns $45 on each sale, taxable at the Guatadoran rate of 10%. It may seem obvious that something is wrong about the $55–$75 discrepancy, but closer examination may justify at least part of it. The lower price for foreign sales

---

[14] See, e.g., Clausing, Multinational Firm Tax Avoidance and Tax Policy, 62 Nat'l Tax J. 703 (Dec. 2009) (estimating the losses at $30 billion annually).

[15] Moving Pieces: Global Companies Have Plenty of Latitude to Minimize Their Tax Bills, The Economist (Feb. 24, 2007).

may reflect the greater costs of Subco's selling effort in entering a new market or the lower manufacturing costs and higher wholesale mark-up of foreign competitors. Even if some $75 sales are made abroad to other wholesalers, Amco might argue that its credit experience with Subco is better than with non-affiliated wholesalers, or that it can rely on Subco to concentrate on selling only its goods whereas independent wholesalers disperse their efforts and achieve poorer results.

Congress has largely left the resolution of this type of problem to the IRS, attempting in Section 482 to do no more than provide the agency with authority to adjust prices on transactions between corporations subject to common control. The Treasury Department has issued several series of regulations under the section. The current regulation dates to 1994 and was last amended in 2011. As to transfers of tangibles, it lists six possible methods: (1) The comparable uncontrolled price or "CUP." The regulation sets forth as an example a situation in which the taxpayer sells the same item to a controlled and to an uncontrolled party, there being only minor and readily calculable differences in such things as shipping costs. The price of the sale to the outside party (CUP) can be used to fix the "inside" sale price. (2) The resale price method can be used for sales in which the taxpayer resells goods it has purchased without substantially adding value to those goods. In such situations, the gross profit margin realized in some reasonable category of uncontrolled sales can be used as a standard. (3) The cost plus method contrasts with the resale price method in that it is applicable to situations in which the goods are manufactured or substantially altered by a member of the corporate group. In that case, one takes the costs to be assigned to the production of the goods and adds thereto a markup comparable to that used on CUPs. (4) The comparable profits method compares the transaction in question with uncontrolled transactions and assigns to the questioned sale a level of profit similar to that on the uncontrolled sales. (5) The profit split measures the contributions to the value added of the buyer and the seller and assigns a price on that basis. (6) A taxpayer may also use "unspecified methods" if it can satisfy the IRS as to their equivalence to an arm's length price. See 26 C.F.R. § 1.482–3.

Similar problems arise with respect to other transactions. The regulations provide that interest on loans and advances is to be judged according to its relation to the "applicable Federal rate." 26 C.F.R. § 1.482–2(a). If the entity making the loan itself borrowed the money, the rate it paid in its capacity as debtor will also govern the rate it is regarded as having received as re-lender. Transfers of intangibles—that is, intellectual property—are also to be dealt with on an arm's length basis. Preference is again for comparison with uncontrolled transactions, if such there be. A table indicates that an appropriate approach is to take the royalty rates charged in 15 like transactions and utilize the mean to fix the rate. 26 C.F.R. § 1.482–4.

To ease the agonies of taxpayers, the IRS has established procedures for "advance pricing agreements." Companies can present their proposed allocation system for prior IRS approval and can rely on its being respected for a period of three to five years if applied consistently. The number of APAs has increased dramatically since they were first introduced in 1991, and more than 1,000 have now been concluded.

A further layer of complexity is added by the fact that tax authorities outside the United States are also apt to question transfer prices (and in the opposite direction). A large number of countries have adopted the OECD's Transfer Pricing Guidelines—last substantially revised in 2017—but differences among national systems remain.[16]

In 2017, the TCJA also added a provision known as the Base Erosion Anti-Abuse Tax (BEAT), which more generally addresses the concern that multinational enterprises may structure intercompany transactions in order to avoid otherwise applicable U.S. tax. BEAT applies only to large companies—those with income of $500 million or more. Such companies are subject to a minimum tax of 10% calculated not just on their ordinary income but also on "base erosion" payments made to foreign affiliates, including payments for services, interest, rents, and royalties. The provision operates to offset certain tax deductions that U.S. companies obtain through transactions with their foreign affiliates. In effect, it imposes a minimum tax—the "base erosion minimum tax amount"—on outbound payments to related parties. 26 U.S.C. § 59A. Companies subject to the tax must pay whichever is higher—the tax due on their corporate income calculated using the normal allowable deductions or the BEAT.

2. ACCOMMODATION AMONG NATIONAL TAX SYSTEMS: UNILATERAL AND BILATERAL TECHNIQUES

It should be evident that applying the tax laws of more than one nation to transactions that cross national boundaries often leads to problems of overlapping or "double" taxation. Indeed, the interplay among different tax systems occasionally results in the escape of certain income from all the tax systems involved, a phenomenon exploited by some MNEs. See supra p. 334. These problems of "overlap" or "underlap" may arise because nations use explicitly different principles as bases for income taxation: one may refer principally to the geographical source of income, a second to the state of incorporation of the taxpayer, a third to the seat of the corporate taxpayer. Or they may arise because two countries, although using what appears to be the same approach to income taxation, may read different meanings into the same label. For example, two countries following a source principle limiting the national tax power to domestic source income may follow different rules in

---

[16] See Ault & Arnold, Comparative Income Taxation: A Structural Analysis 529–535 (3d ed. 2010).

determining the source of income from an international sales transaction. Even if all these legal differences can be adjusted through uniform national rules, inconsistent accounting concepts can allocate items of income or expense to different periods or to different parts of an international corporate family, thus producing inconsistent tax results. This part of the Problem covers various techniques used to address the problem of "double taxation."

Consider the possible meanings that phrase can bear. (1) Is there double taxation simply because two countries impose taxes relating to income from the same transaction, perhaps an international sale or dividend payment? In other words, does the "double" mean only that two tax authorities are involved without consideration of the aggregate tax burden? (2) If one stressed the actual tax burden, is there double taxation when nation X imposes a 15% withholding tax on dividends paid by a corporation in X to a corporation in nation Y, and Y imposes a tax at a rate of 15% on foreign dividend income, if the same dividend income paid entirely within either country would have been subject to a tax on the recipient at a rate of 40%? (3) Before one can protest against double taxation, should the total tax burden under X and Y law involve a tax liability greater than that which would have been incurred under X *or* Y law, if all relevant events and persons had been located in either X or Y?

Apart from these questions, there remains the problem of how broadly one defines the single transaction that allegedly gives rise to double taxation. An international dividend payment, an international sales transaction, and the business operations of a foreign branch are fairly clear examples of situations where two tax systems may assert claims against a unified transaction or business operation. Suppose, however, that a foreign subsidiary is subject to an income tax in its country of incorporation, and that its dividend payments out of retained earnings to the parent are then subject to tax on the parent in its country. Is there one transaction or two? If there are two, can one still talk meaningfully of double taxation?

Whatever the difficulty in giving a satisfactory definition to this phrase, the cumulative tax burden frequently appears to be oppressive under any test. For this reason, nations have taken steps to mitigate the burden. Some of these steps, perhaps the most important, have been unilateral. A number of countries that tax the global income earned by their residents and nationals—most prominently the United States—have mainly adopted a credit approach. They permit the taxpayer either to credit against the taxes owed on its global income taxes paid to a foreign country or to deduct such foreign taxes from its taxable income. Other countries—including many in Continental Europe—rely primarily on an exemption approach that exempts from domestic taxation entirely some or all classes of foreign-source income. In practice, almost all countries employ some combination of these two approaches.[17]

In addition to these unilateral solutions, the tax treaty represents an increasingly important technique for limiting the national taxing power through bilateral arrangements.[18] These treaties attack the problems of double or overlapping taxation by providing for the surrender, generally by the source country, of the right to tax certain income or by creating or confirming through the treaty the right to a foreign tax credit against taxes imposed by the taxpayer's country of origin. As of the end of 2017, there were over 3,000 such treaties.[19]

3.   THE FOREIGN TAX CREDIT

Since 1918, U.S. tax laws have allowed taxpayers to credit against their federal income tax certain amounts that they have paid to foreign taxing authorities. To consider the operation of a foreign tax credit in its simplest form, imagine a U.S. person who earns $10,000 in State X. Assume that the taxpayer owes $2,000 in U.S. income tax on those earnings, but must also pay $1,800 in income tax to State X (because it is income sourced there). The foreign tax credit would permit the taxpayer to apply a credit of $1,800 to its U.S. tax liability, thus mitigating the problem of double taxation. It bears emphasis that the foreign tax credit is limited to "income" and closely allied taxes. A foreign levy is a tax only if it requires a compulsory payment to the government. Penalties, fines, interest, and customs duties are not considered taxes. To be eligible for the credit, a foreign tax must have the predominant characteristic of income tax in the U.S. system—that is, it must be designed to reach net gain. See 26 C.F.R. § 1.901–2(a). The consequence has been that a number of foreign taxes, which may amount to a substantial or principal part of the American corporation's (or its foreign subsidiary's) tax burden, may not qualify for the credit. Given the diverse approaches to taxation in different countries, and the lesser weight given to income taxes in many countries, one can question the theory behind the U.S. restriction.

The foreign tax credit has been subject to limitations that have changed in form, but have maintained a single general purpose: to ensure that the amount credited is no greater than the U.S. taxes that would have been imposed on the foreign income involved. The limit can be expressed as a formula:

---

[17]   See Ault & Arnold, Comparative Income Taxation: A Structural Analysis 446–474 (3d ed. 2010).

[18]   Unilateral measures to reduce double taxation may, of course, reduce the executive's bargaining power to negotiate treaties with other countries. In Section 896 Congress sought to undo this effect by giving the executive power to reverse such concessions with respect to a country refusing to reciprocate. Note the other retaliatory provisions found in Sections 883, 891, and 901(c).

[19]   UNCTAD, World Investment Report 2017, at 141.

Tax credit = U.S. tax before credit × foreign income/total income.

In effect, this limit ensures that the United States does not subsidize the decision of other countries to impose income tax at higher rates. The American taxpayer is subject to a total income tax burden at the higher of the United States or the foreign rate.

The tax rules require taxpayers to segregate income by type into separate "baskets" for purposes of determining available credit. The limit described above is applied to each particular type of income. This has the effect of limiting the ability of the taxpayer to offset income that is highly taxed abroad by including it with income that bears little taxation. Immediately prior to the enactment of the TCJA, there were only two baskets: one for passive income, and one for all other types of income. The TCJA added two more: one for GILTI and one for foreign branch income. See 26 U.S.C. § 904(d)(1)(A) and (B). Note the effect of the latter on foreign operations that are conducted through branches. Under the new rule, a U.S. company's credit for foreign taxes paid on foreign branch income will apply only against any U.S. tax payable on such income; the credit cannot be used to reduce U.S. tax payable on other types of earnings. This change will affect groups that incur losses in some foreign branches and gains in others. For instance, consider a U.S. group that earns income of $10,000 in foreign branch A but incurs a loss of $15,000 in foreign branch B. The group would pay foreign income tax in state A on its income there. Because its overall position in its foreign branch basket is a loss of $5,000, however, it would incur no U.S. tax on foreign branch income, and would therefore not be able to apply as a credit the amount of foreign tax paid in state A.

4. TAX TREATIES

As of 2016, the United States is party to 58 income tax treaties covering 66 countries.[20] These treaties reach the vast majority of foreign trade and investment involving U.S. companies. They cover nearly every country in Europe, even states once behind the Iron Curtain such as Russia and the Ukraine. They also include major countries in Asia such as India, Indonesia, Japan, South Korea, and the People's Republic of China. They do not include any countries in sub-Saharan Africa except South Africa or any countries in Latin America save Mexico and Venezuela. It has been doubted that a treaty of the type negotiated between developed countries is suited to the needs of less developed countries. Because the net flow of income (as distinguished from investment) is dominantly from developing to developed countries, the surrenders of revenue found in Articles 7(4), 10(2)–(3), 11(1), and 12(1) of

---

[20] The United States has also entered into a number of treaties regulating estate taxes. Tax information exchange agreements (TIEAs) have been concluded with a number of countries—including many important offshore financial centers—that do not have full-blown tax treaties with the United States.

the U.S.-German Tax Convention may fall disproportionately on the developing state. See Annex, infra pp. 547–582.

The current system of tax treaties dates from the 1920s. A number of scholars have called for a fundamental rethinking of that system in light of changes such as the growth of portfolio investment, the rise of multinational enterprises, and changes in other countries' corporate tax policies. Others have warned against throwing the baby out with the bathwater.[21]

A tax treaty does not form a logical, self-contained structure. It attempts to regulate a number of disparate problems that have arisen under the tax laws of two countries, and is tailored to the relationship between two specific countries. However, patterns can be discerned. Many of the United States' trading partners take as their starting point the OECD Model Tax Convention on Income and on Capital, which was promulgated in 1963 and last updated in 2010. These OECD drafts reflect the consensus achieved and compromises reached by fiscal experts from a large number of developed countries. There is also the United Nations Model Double Taxation Convention Between Developed and Developing Countries, first published in 1980 and revised in 2011, which is designed to address the particular concerns of less developed countries.

The United States has long had its own series of model tax treaties, which it uses as a starting point in negotiations with other countries. The most recent model was issued in 2016, replacing the 2006 version. The changes include a number of provisions intended to address the challenges of base erosion and profit shifting. In addition to those challenges, the topics that generally seem to have attracted the most attention in recent tax treaties include: (1) endeavors to cope with the tendency of advanced tax systems to integrate corporate and individual income taxes so as to diminish the dual load borne by dividend income; (2) efforts to increase cooperation between the two states' revenue authorities, going so far even as to authorize them to institute arbitration proceedings; and (3) efforts to fend off the attempts of sophisticated taxpayers from third countries to avail themselves of tax benefits under treaties.

The U.S.-German Tax Convention included in the Annex provides a useful illustration of these treaties, and you should make a general survey of that instrument. Articles 4 and 5 include critical definitions: those of "residence" and "permanent establishment." To appreciate the importance of these definitions, consider Article 7, dealing with business profits. It clarifies that the creation of a "fixed place of business"—such as a branch or a management office—is what triggers the authority of the state in which that establishment is located to tax its profits. Note that

---

[21] Compare Roin, Rethinking Tax Treaties in a Strategic World with Disparate Tax Systems, 81 Va. L. Rev. 1753 (1995); and Avi-Yonah, The Structure of International Taxation: A Proposal for Simplification, 74 Tex. L. Rev. 1301 (1996); with Graetz & O'Hear, The Original Intent of U.S. International Taxation, 46 Duke L.J. 1021 (1997).

Article 23 enshrines in the treaty the provisions of both countries' laws regarding foreign tax credits. And throughout the treaty, you will see a basic mechanism at work by which the parties agree to allocate the power to tax certain forms of income to one—but not both—of the countries, in that way eliminating the possibility of double taxation. See, e.g., Article 11 (stating that interest income shall be taxable only in the state where the taxpayer is resident); Article 12 (royalties shall be taxable only in the state where the payee is resident). You will note that the effect of these provisions is generally to limit or eliminate tax imposed by the *source* country.

Additional reading: The simplest introduction to international tax is Herzfeld & Doernberg, International Taxation in a Nutshell (11th ed. 2018). More extensive works are McDaniel, Repetti & Ring, Introduction to United States International Taxation (6th ed. 2014) and Bittker & Lokken, Fundamentals of International Taxation (2018 ed.). Rhoades & Langer, U.S. International Taxation and Tax Treaties provides a thorough treatment. Tax Notes International, a weekly service, provides news about U.S., foreign, and international tax developments. For a systematic overview of foreign tax systems, see Ault & Arnold, Comparative Income Taxation: A Structural Analysis (3d ed. 2010). A terse review of international tax is Avi-Yonah, The Structure of International Taxation: A Proposal for Simplification, 74 Tex. L. Rev. 1301 (1996).

PROBLEM 5

MERGERS AND ACQUISITIONS

A. INTRODUCTION

An alternative to establishing a new branch or subsidiary abroad is to acquire an existing foreign company, and mergers and acquisitions have become an important form of foreign direct investment. Indeed, in the years immediately preceding the global financial crisis, the value of cross-border mergers and acquisitions had approached 80% of the figure for foreign investment inflows worldwide.[1] However, the crisis caused a collapse in merger and acquisition activity, and cross-border transactions fell from a high of over $1.5 trillion in 2007 to just $250 billion in 2009.[2] Activity was slow to rebound, due in part to the fiscal crisis within the Eurozone and to sluggish growth in developing countries. It picked up significantly after 2014, although as of 2018 it had not quite returned to pre-crisis levels.

From a foreign investor's perspective, one of the principal advantages of acquiring an existing company is speed. It is much faster for a company wishing to enter a foreign market to purchase an existing operation than to build a new one from scratch. An established company's most valuable assets may be its distribution network or its goodwill with local customers, things that would take a foreign investor years to establish on its own. Mergers and acquisitions may also allow the firms involved to become more efficient, either by achieving synergies or by eliminating redundancies, although promised gains in efficiency often fail to materialize. Finally, mergers and acquisitions may be driven by fear—fear that if a company does not grow larger by acquiring others it may itself become a target for acquisition. Historically, mergers and acquisitions have been a more important vehicle for investment in developed economies. In developing countries greenfield investment has dominated, in part because of the relative lack of companies that are potential candidates for takeovers.

The two waves of merger activity from 1999 to 2001 and from 2005 to 2007 were increasingly international.[3] This was due in large part to the greater involvement of European firms. Europe, at least outside of the United Kingdom, had long been considered unreceptive to mergers and acquisitions. Vodafone's hostile takeover of the German firm Mannesmann in 2000 did much to change perceptions about the possibilities for mergers and acquisitions on the Continent. The EU has

---

[1] That is, $716 billion in cross-border mergers and acquisitions as compared to $916 in FDI inflows. See UNCTAD, World Investment Report 2006, at xxvii.

[2] UNCTAD, World Investment Report 2008, at xv; World Investment Report 2013, at 8.

[3] UNCTAD, World Investment Report 2006, at 13–15; Black, The First International Merger Wave (and the Fifth and Last U.S. Wave), 54 U. Miami L. Rev. 799 (2000).

also adopted a number of measures, including its 2004 Directive on Takeover Bids discussed below, designed to promote a single market for corporate control.

A number of high-profile takeover bids in 2006–2007 involving European companies drew attention to the area: Dutch firm Mittal Steel's successful takeover of Luxembourg-based Arcelor; Italian electricity provider Enel's unsuccessful bid for the French company Suez; German energy firm E.ON's unsuccessful bid for Spanish electric giant Endesa; and Enel's successful acquisition of a substantial stake in Endesa. These deals and others produced a nationalist backlash, with politicians intervening in attempts to prevent foreign takeovers of leading companies.[4] Emblematic of this trend was French Decree 2005–1739, issued at the end of 2005, requiring government approval for takeovers in 11 sectors of the economy. In a 2012 report, the European Commission noted that the low level of takeovers from 2008 on made it difficult to assess the overall impact of the Directive on Takeover Bids.[5]

The most recent merger wave, from 2014 to 2017, also had a strong international character, with cross-border transactions accounting for over 30 percent of all activity during each of those years. It was driven in part by China's increased interest in outbound investment, which will likely continue as that country pursues its "One Belt, One Road" initiative to create a transport and logistics network linking Asia, Europe, the Middle East, and Africa.

B. SHARE PURCHASE AGREEMENT

To focus your analysis, assume that your client, a publicly held company named American Kitchens, is negotiating with a family in Germany to acquire Deutsche Küchen Werke GmbH (DKW), a German company that manufactures modern-style pottery at a single factory in Cologne, Germany. Although its style is very up-to-date, the firm was founded in 1817 and has been making pottery continuously since then. During its most recent fiscal year, DKW had sales of $30 million, including approximately $5 million in the United States. American Kitchens is a U.S. manufacturer and seller of kitchen equipment. During its most recent fiscal year, American Kitchens had sales of $180 million, including approximately $30 million in the European Union.

American Kitchens is prepared to pay about €90 million for the acquisition, which would include about $6 million worth of inventory and a lease on an office in New York, which the buyer expects to close down since it has its own network of sales agencies. Also among the target firm's assets is a long-term relationship with the firm that owns the finest deposit of clay suitable for the making of such china. There is a

---

[4]   See To the Barricades, The Economist (Mar. 14, 2006).

[5]   Report on the Application of Directive 2004/25/EC on Takeover Bids, 2012 O.J. (COM 347) 4.

workforce of about 250 persons: a good deal more of the operation involves expert hand labor than is the case with most of the buyer's operations.

The buyer's general counsel furnishes you with a draft agreement,[6] which has resulted from preliminary negotiations between the buyer and the sellers.

SHARE PURCHASE AGREEMENT

This Share Purchase Agreement ("Agreement") is made as of ___, 20__ by American Kitchens, Inc. ("Buyer"), a Delaware corporation with its place of business at Philadelphia, Pennsylvania, USA, and ___ ("Sellers"), owners of all the issued and outstanding shares ("Shares") in Deutsche Küchen Werke GmbH ("Company"), a German corporation with its place of business in Cologne, Germany.

1.   Sale and Transfer of the Shares

The Sellers hereby agree to sell and the Buyer agrees to purchase the Shares for €90 million ("Purchase Price") free and clear of all encumbrances. The Shares shall be transferred at Closing with the benefits of all rights attached to them as at the date of this Agreement, including all rights to dividends.

2.   The Closing

The purchase and sale of the Shares ("Closing") shall occur at the offices of _____, on _____, 20__ ("Closing Date"), provided the conditions set forth in Articles 6 and 7 have been satisfied.

3.   Sellers' Warranties

Sellers represent and warrant to Buyer:

(a)   The Company is validly existing and incorporated under the laws of Germany. The Company is not insolvent and is capable of paying its debts and no action has been brought or threatened so as to have the Company declared insolvent. Sellers have delivered to Buyer true and accurate copies of the constitutional documents of the Company.

(b)   Sellers have full power and capacity to enter into and to perform this Agreement. This Agreement constitutes the legal, valid, and binding obligation of Sellers, enforceable against them in accordance with its terms.

(c)   The Shares constitute the whole of the issued and outstanding capital of the Company and are fully paid.

(d)   Sellers have delivered to Buyer financial statements of the Company for each of its last five fiscal years ("Accounts"). The Accounts comply with and have at all times been prepared in accordance with the generally accepted accounting principles and practices of Germany. The

---

[6]   Adapted from ABA Model Stock Purchase Agreement with Commentary (1995) and ICC Model Mergers & Acquisitions Contract: Share Purchase Agreement (2004).

Accounts give a true and fair view of the assets and liabilities and of the profits and losses for the periods to which the Accounts relate.

(e) Annex A contains a complete and accurate list of all real property, leaseholds, or other interests therein owned by the Company. The Company owns all of the property and assets that it purports to own, including all the properties and assets reflected in the Accounts.

(f) Except as set forth in Annex B, the Company has no liabilities or obligations of any kind (known or unknown, accrued or contingent, or otherwise) except for liabilities reflected or reserved against in the Accounts and current liabilities incurred in the ordinary course of business since the date thereof.

(g) Except as set forth in Annex C, the Company is in full compliance with all legal requirements applicable to it or to the operation of its business or the ownership or use of any of its assets. All government permits relevant thereto are in good standing and no legal proceeding against the Company has been commenced or, to the knowledge of the Sellers, threatened.

4. Buyer's Warranties

Buyer represents and warrants to Sellers:

(a) Buyer is validly existing and incorporated under the laws of Delaware.

(b) Buyer has full power and capacity to enter into and to perform this Agreement. This Agreement constitutes the legal, valid, and binding obligation of Buyer, enforceable against it in accordance with its terms.

(c) Buyer is acquiring the Shares for its own account and not with a view to their distribution within the meaning of Section 2(11) of the Securities Act.

5. Sellers' Obligations Prior to the Closing

Prior to the Closing the Sellers will:

(a) Cause the Company to afford Buyer and its representatives free access to the Company's personnel, properties, books, records, and other data and to furnish Buyer copies of all contracts or other documents as Buyer may reasonably request.

(b) Cause the Company to conduct the business only in the ordinary course of business.

(c) Notify the Buyer in writing of any material adverse change in the business, operations, assets, prospects, or condition of the Company ("Material Adverse Change").

(d) Notify the Buyer in writing of any fact or condition that causes or constitutes a breach of any of Sellers' representations or warranties.

(e) Make all filings required to consummate the sale of the Shares.

6.   Conditions to Buyer's Obligation

Buyer's obligation to purchase the Shares is subject to the satisfaction at or prior to the Closing of each of the following conditions (any of which may be waived by the Buyer):

(a) All of Sellers' representations and warranties in this Agreement must have been accurate in all material respects as of the date of this Agreement and as of the Closing Date.

(b) All of the covenants and obligations that Sellers are required to perform or comply with pursuant to this Agreement at or prior to the Closing must have been duly performed or complied with in all material respects.

(c) Since the date of this Agreement, there must not have been any Material Adverse Change.

[handwritten margin note: Tell if you make material adverse change & let buyer terminate if there is one]

7.   Conditions to Sellers' Obligation

Sellers' obligation to sell the Shares is subject to the satisfaction at or prior to the Closing of each of the following conditions (any of which may be waived by the Sellers):

(a) All of Buyer's representations and warranties in this Agreement must have been accurate in all material respects as of the date of this Agreement and as of the Closing Date.

(b) All of the covenants and obligations that Buyer is required to perform or comply with pursuant to this Agreement at or prior to the Closing must have been duly performed or complied with in all material respects.

8.   Termination

This Agreement may, by notice given prior to or at the Closing, be terminated:

(a) By either Buyer or Sellers if a material breach of any provision of this Agreement has been committed by the other party and has not been waived.

(b) By Buyer if any of the conditions in Article 6 has not been satisfied as of the Closing Date and Buyer has not waived such condition or by Sellers if any of the conditions in Article 7 has not been satisfied as of the Closing Date and Sellers have not waived such condition.

(c) By mutual consent of Buyer and Sellers.

The right of termination does not prevent any party from claiming possible damages.

9.   Restrictive Covenants

(a) Sellers shall not, directly or indirectly, engage in, assist, or finance any activity that may be directly or indirectly in competition with the Company's business as of the Closing Date for a period of two years from the Closing Date with respect to the territory where the Company is engaged as of the Closing Date.

[handwritten margin note: noncompete 2yrs]

(b) Sellers shall not, directly or indirectly, solicit, recruit, assist others in recruiting or hiring, or discuss employment arrangements with any employee of the Company without the prior written consent of the Buyer.

(c) Sellers shall keep confidential all information relating to the business of the Company that has not become part of the public domain ("Confidential Information") and shall refrain from using such Confidential Information.

10. Confidentiality and Announcements

Each party shall keep confidential and shall not disclose in whole or in part to any third party this Agreement or any information contained within or related to this Agreement except as is:

(a) required by applicable law or by the rules of any relevant stock exchange;

(b) necessary to obtain government approvals connected with this Agreement;

(c) ordered by a court of competent jurisdiction;

(d) already in the public domain or becomes part of the public domain; or

(e) agreed to in writing by the other party.

The parties shall consult with each other as to the form of any announcement made under this Article 10. The obligations of this Article 10 shall survive any termination of this Agreement.

11. Costs

Except as expressly provided in this Agreement each party will bear its respective expenses incurred in connection with the preparation, execution, and performance of this Agreement.

12. Assignment

Neither party may assign any of its rights under the Agreement; nothing in this agreement will be construed to give any person other than the parties any legal or equitable right, remedy, or claim under this Agreement.

13. Resolution of Disputes

In case of dispute, the courts of Cologne, Germany shall have exclusive jurisdiction.

14. Applicable Law

This Agreement shall be governed by the law of Germany.

IN WITNESS WHEREOF, the parties have executed and delivered this Agreement as of the date first written above.

Buyer _____   Seller _____

                                Seller _____

QUESTIONS

(1) In an international transaction, should arbitration be substituted for the choice of forum clause?

(2) In executing this agreement, are there any particular formal requirements that need to be taken into account? (Hint: recall the discussion in Chapter I of the role of the notary in civil law jurisdictions. See supra p. 4.)

(3) As we shall see later, two antitrust authorities might take an interest in this sale—and might interfere. Should the agreement reflect that risk? How?

C. SECURITIES AND CORPORATIONS LAW

1. SECURITIES ASPECTS OF TRANSNATIONAL ACQUISITIONS

Mergers and acquisitions frequently involve the sale of stock, and thus implicate U.S. or foreign laws regulating the sale of securities. The American securities lawyer is accustomed to operating in the environment created by legislation developed beginning in the 1930s. One of the centerpieces of that legislation is Rule 10b-5,[7] adopted pursuant to Section 10(b) of the Securities Exchange Act of 1934, which reads as follows:

> It shall be unlawful for any person, directly or indirectly, by the use of any means or instrumentality of interstate commerce, or of the mails or of any facility of any national securities exchange,
>
> (a) To employ any device, scheme, or artifice to defraud,
>
> (b) To make any untrue statement of a material fact or to omit to state a material fact necessary in order to make the statements made, in the light of the circumstances under which they were made, not misleading, or
>
> (c) To engage in any act, practice, or course of business which operates or would operate as a fraud or deceit upon any person,
>
> in connection with the purchase or sale of any security.

Rule 10b-5 is famous among other things for the fact that it outlaws insider trading, the practice of persons privy to corporate information buying from or selling to outsiders who do not know that data. (Although at its origin this was strictly an American rule, regarded abroad as extremely naive and overambitious, it has now been widely imitated, notably as a result of EU directives that instructed the member states to

---

[7]   17 C.F.R. § 240.10b–5.

introduce rules on the topic.[8]) But it also prohibits the sort of ordinary fraud one might encounter in a sale of securities—for instance, material misrepresentations made by a seller regarding its results of operations in order to induce a buyer to pay a higher price.

The Share Purchase Agreement set forth above involves a transaction negotiated by the parties face-to-face. American litigants have tried—and failed—to persuade courts that the sale of all of the stock of a corporation does not really involve the "sale of a security" within the meaning of the Rule. A party defrauded in the course of such a transaction might therefore consider asserting a claim for damages under U.S. securities laws. In a cross-border case, doing so would raise certain questions. First, the application of Rule 10b-5 to a transnational purchase/sale raises jurisdictional questions relating to the extraterritorial application of the securities laws. Second, in an agreement like the Share Purchase Agreement above, the parties may have included a choice of law clause in favor of foreign law. This raises the question whether a court would enforce that clause, eliminating the possibility of a lawsuit under U.S. law. The following materials address these two questions in turn.

As we saw in Chapter III, in situations where a U.S. law is ambiguous as to its own geographic scope, courts apply a presumption against extraterritorial application. See supra pp. 94–105. In the following case, the Supreme Court applied that presumption to Section 10(b) and Rule 10b-5.

Morrison v. National Australia Bank Ltd.

Supreme Court of the United States, 2010
561 U.S. 247, 130 S.Ct. 2869, 177 L.Ed.2d 535

[In 1998, National Australia Bank (National) purchased HomeSide Lending, a company headquartered in Florida that was in the business of servicing mortgages. National's ordinary shares were traded on the Australian Stock Exchange and not on any exchange in the United States, although National's American Depository Receipts (ADRs), which represent the right to receive a specified number of ordinary shares, were listed on the New York Stock Exchange. In 2001, National had to write down the value of HomeSide's assets, causing National's share prices to fall. Petitioners, Australians who purchased National's ordinary shares before the write-downs, sued respondents—National, HomeSide, and officers of both companies—in Federal District Court for violation of §§ 10(b) and 20(a) of the Securities and Exchange Act of 1934 and SEC Rule 10b-5. They claimed that HomeSide and its officers had manipulated financial models to make the company's mortgage-servicing

---

[8] See Directive 2003/6/EC of 28 January 2003 on Insider Dealing and Market Manipulation, 2003 O.J. (L 96) 16. This directive was subsequently replaced by a regulation establishing a uniform regime throughout the EU. Regulation (EU) 596/2014 of the European Parliament and of the Council on Market Abuse, 2014 O.J. (L 173) 1.

rights appear more valuable than they really were. Respondents moved to dismiss for lack of subject matter jurisdiction under Federal Rule of Civil Procedure 12(b)(1) and for failure to state a claim under Rule 12(b)(6). The District Court granted the 12(b)(1) motion and the Second Circuit affirmed.

Writing for the Court, Justice Scalia first held that that if U.S. law did not reach the conduct in question, the District Court should have dismissed for failure to state a claim under Rule 12(b)(6) rather than for lack of subject matter jurisdiction under Rule 12(b)(1). The Court concluded that the District Court had subject matter jurisdiction under the Securities Exchange Act's jurisdictional provision, 15 U.S.C. § 78aa, to decide whether § 10(b) applied to National's conduct. Justice Scalia then continued as follows.]

III

A

It is a "longstanding principle of American law 'that legislation of Congress, unless a contrary intent appears, is meant to apply only within the territorial jurisdiction of the United States.' " *EEOC* v. *Arabian American Oil Co.*, 499 U.S. 244, 248, 111 S.Ct. 1227, 113 L.Ed.2d 274 (1991) (*Aramco*) (quoting *Foley Bros., Inc.* v. *Filardo*, 336 U.S. 281, 285, 69 S.Ct. 575, 93 L.Ed. 680 (1949)). This principle represents a canon of construction, or a presumption about a statute's meaning, rather than a limit upon Congress's power to legislate, see *Blackmer* v. *United States*, 284 U.S. 421, 437, 52 S.Ct. 252, 76 L.Ed. 375 (1932). It rests on the perception that Congress ordinarily legislates with respect to domestic, not foreign matters. *Smith* v. *United States*, 507 U.S. 197, 204, n. 5, 113 S.Ct. 1178, 122 L.Ed.2d 548 (1993). Thus, "unless there is the affirmative intention of the Congress clearly expressed" to give a statute extraterritorial effect, "we must presume it is primarily concerned with domestic conditions." *Aramco, supra*, at 248, 111 S.Ct. 1227 (internal quotation marks omitted). The canon or presumption applies regardless of whether there is a risk of conflict between the American statute and a foreign law, see *Sale* v. *Haitian Centers Council, Inc.*, 509 U.S. 155, 173–174, 113 S.Ct. 2549, 125 L.Ed. 128 (1993). When a statute gives no clear indication of an extraterritorial application, it has none.

Despite this principle of interpretation, long and often recited in our opinions, the Second Circuit believed that, because the Exchange Act is silent as to the extraterritorial application of § 10(b), it was left to the court to "discern" whether Congress would have wanted the statute to apply. . . .

* * *

The Second Circuit . . . established that application of § 10(b) could be premised upon either some effect on American securities markets or investors (*Schoenbaum*) or significant conduct in the United States (*Leasco*). It later formalized these two applications into (1) an "effects test," "whether the wrongful conduct had a substantial effect in the United States or upon United States citizens," and (2) a "conduct test," "whether the wrongful conduct occurred in the United States." *SEC* v. *Berger*, 322 F.3d 187, 192–193 (C.A.2 2003). These became the north star of the Second Circuit's § 10(b) jurisprudence, pointing the way to what Congress would have wished. . . .

[The Court recounts criticism of these tests, including that their application proved inconsistent and unpredictable.]

The criticisms seem to us justified. The results of judicial-speculation-made-law—divining what Congress would have wanted if it had thought of the situation before the court—demonstrate the wisdom of the presumption against extraterritoriality. Rather than guess anew in each case, we apply the presumption in all cases, preserving a stable background against which Congress can legislate with predictable effects.

B

Rule 10b-5, the regulation under which petitioners have brought suit, was promulgated under § 10(b), and "does not extend beyond conduct encompassed by § 10(b)'s prohibition." *United States* v. *O'Hagan*, 521 U.S. 642, 651, 117 S.Ct. 2199, 138 L.Ed.2d 724 (1997). Therefore, if § 10(b) is not extraterritorial, neither is Rule 10b-5.

On its face, § 10(b) contains nothing to suggest it applies abroad:

> "It shall be unlawful for any person, directly or indirectly, by the use of any means or instrumentality of interstate commerce or of the mails, or of any facility of any national securities exchange . . . [t]o use or employ, in connection with the purchase or sale of any security registered on a national securities exchange or any security not so registered, . . . any manipulative or deceptive device or contrivance in contravention of such rules and regulations as the [Securities and Exchange] Commission may prescribe. . . ." 15 U.S.C. 78j(b).

Petitioners and the Solicitor General contend, however, that three things indicate that § 10(b) or the Exchange Act in general has at least some extraterritorial application.

First, they point to the definition of "interstate commerce," a term used in § 10(b), which includes "trade, commerce, transportation, or communication . . . between any foreign country and any State." 15 U.S.C. § 78c(a)(17). But "we have repeatedly held that even statutes that contain broad language in their definitions of 'commerce' that expressly refer to '*foreign* commerce' do not apply abroad." *Aramco*, 499 U.S., at 251, 111 S.Ct. 1227; see id., at 251–252, 111 S.Ct. 1227 (discussing cases). The general reference to foreign commerce in the definition of "interstate commerce" does not defeat the presumption against extraterritoriality.

Petitioners and the Solicitor General next point out that Congress, in describing the purposes of the Exchange Act, observed that the "prices established and offered in such transactions are generally disseminated and quoted throughout the United States and foreign countries." 15 U.S.C. § 78b(2). The antecedent of "such transactions," however, is found in the first sentence of the section, which declares that "transactions in securities as commonly conducted upon securities exchanges and over-the-counter markets are affected with a national public interest." § 78b. Nothing suggests that this *national* public interest pertains to transactions conducted upon *foreign* exchanges and markets. The fleeting reference to the dissemination and quotation abroad of the prices of securities traded in domestic exchanges and markets cannot overcome the presumption against extraterritoriality.

Finally, there is § 30(b) of the Exchange Act, 15 U.S.C. § 78dd(b), which *does* mention the Act's extraterritorial application: "The provisions of [the Exchange Act] or of any rule or regulation thereunder shall not apply to any person insofar as he transacts a business in securities without the jurisdiction of the United States," unless he does so in violation of regulations promulgated by the Securities and Exchange Commission "to prevent . . . evasion of [the Act]." (The parties have pointed us to no regulation promulgated pursuant to § 30(b).) The Solicitor General argues that "[this] exemption would have no function if the Act did not apply in the first instance to securities transactions that occur abroad." Brief for United States as *Amicus Curiae* 14.

We are not convinced. In the first place, it would be odd for Congress to indicate the extraterritorial application of the whole Exchange Act by means of a provision imposing a condition precedent to its application abroad. And if the whole Act applied abroad, why would the Commission's enabling regulations be limited to those preventing "evasion" of the Act, rather than all those preventing "violation"? The provision seems to us directed at actions abroad that might conceal a domestic violation, or might cause what would otherwise be a domestic violation to escape on a technicality. At most, the Solicitor General's proposed inference is possible; but possible interpretations of statutory language do not override the presumption against extraterritoriality. See *Aramco, supra*, at 253, 111 S.Ct. 1227.

The Solicitor General also fails to account for § 30(a), which reads in relevant part as follows:

> "It shall be unlawful for any broker or dealer . . . to make use of the mails or of any means or instrumentality of interstate commerce for the purpose of effecting on an exchange not within or subject to the jurisdiction of the United States, any transaction in any security the issuer of which is a resident of, or is organized under the laws of, or has its principal place of business in, a place within or subject to the jurisdiction of the

United States, in contravention of such rules and regulations as the Commission may prescribe. . . ." 15 U.S.C. § 78dd(a).

Subsection 30(a) contains what § 10(b) lacks: a clear statement of extraterritorial effect. Its explicit provision for a specific extraterritorial application would be quite superfluous if the rest of the Exchange Act already applied to transactions on foreign exchanges—and its limitation of that application to securities of domestic issuers would be inoperative. Even if that were not true, when a statute provides for some extraterritorial application, the presumption against extraterritoriality operates to limit that provision to its terms. See *Microsoft Corp.* v. *AT & T Corp.*, 550 U.S. 437, 455–456, 127 S.Ct. 1746, 167 L.Ed.2d 737 (2007). No one claims that § 30(a) applies here.

The concurrence claims we have impermissibly narrowed the inquiry in evaluating whether a statute applies abroad, citing for that point the dissent in *Aramco*, see *post*, at 2891. But we do not say, as the concurrence seems to think, that the presumption against extraterritoriality is a "clear statement rule," *ibid.*, if by that is meant a requirement that a statute say "this law applies abroad." Assuredly context can be consulted as well. But whatever sources of statutory meaning one consults to give "the most faithful reading" of the text, *post*, at 2892, there is no clear indication of extraterritoriality here. The concurrence does not even try to refute that conclusion, but merely puts forward the same (at best) uncertain indications relied upon by petitioners and the Solicitor General. As the opinion *for the Court* in *Aramco* (which we prefer to the dissent) shows, those uncertain indications do not suffice.

In short, there is no affirmative indication in the Exchange Act that § 10(b) applies extraterritorially, and we therefore conclude that it does not.

IV

A

Petitioners argue that the conclusion that § 10(b) does not apply extraterritorially does not resolve this case. They contend that they seek no more than domestic application anyway, since Florida is where HomeSide and its senior executives engaged in the deceptive conduct of manipulating HomeSide's financial models; their complaint also alleged that Race and Hughes made misleading public statements there. This is less an answer to the presumption against extraterritorial application than it is an assertion—a quite valid assertion—that that presumption here (as often) is not self-evidently dispositive, but its application requires further analysis. For it is a rare case of prohibited extraterritorial application that lacks all contact with the territory of the United States. But the presumption against extraterritorial application would be a craven watchdog indeed if it retreated to its kennel whenever some domestic activity is involved in the case. The concurrence seems to imagine just such a timid sentinel, see *post*, at 2892, but our cases are to the contrary. In *Aramco*, for example, the Title VII plaintiff had been hired in Houston, and was an American citizen. See 499 U.S., at 247, 111 S.Ct. 1227. The Court concluded, however, that neither that territorial event nor that relationship was the "focus" of congressional concern, *id.*, at 255, 111 S.Ct. 1227, but rather domestic employment. See also *Foley Bros.*, 336 U.S., at 283, 285–286, 69 S.Ct. 575.

Applying the same mode of analysis here, we think that the focus of the Exchange Act is not upon the place where the deception originated, but upon purchases and sales of securities in the United States. Section 10(b) does not punish deceptive conduct, but only deceptive conduct "in connection with the purchase or sale of any security registered on a national securities exchange or any security not so registered." 15 U.S.C. § 78j(b). See *SEC* v. *Zandford*, 535 U.S. 813 (2002). Those purchase-and-sale transactions are the objects of the statute's solicitude. It is those transactions that the statute seeks to "regulate," see *Superintendent of Ins. of N.Y.* v. *Bankers Life & Casualty Co.*, 404 U.S. 6, 12 (1971); it is parties or prospective parties to those transactions that the statute seeks to "protec[t]," *id.*, at 10. See also *Ernst & Ernst* v. *Hochfelder*, 425 U.S. 185, 195 (1976). And it is in our view only transactions in securities listed on domestic exchanges, and domestic transactions in other securities, to which § 10(b) applies.

The primacy of the domestic exchange is suggested by the very prologue of the Exchange Act, which sets forth as its object "[t]o provide for the regulation of securities exchanges . . . operating in interstate and foreign commerce and through the mails, to prevent inequitable and unfair practices on such exchanges. . . ." 48 Stat. 881. We know of no one who thought that the Act was intended to "regulat[e]" foreign securities exchanges—or indeed who even believed that under established principles of international law Congress had the power to do so. The Act's registration requirements apply only to securities listed on national securities exchanges. 15 U.S.C. § 78–1–(a).

With regard to securities not registered on domestic exchanges, the exclusive focus on *domestic* purchases and sales is strongly confirmed by § 30(a) and (b), discussed earlier. The former extends the normal scope of the Exchange Act's prohibitions to acts effecting, in violation of rules prescribed by the Commission, a "transaction" in a United States security "on an exchange not within or subject to the jurisdiction of the United States." § 78dd(a). And the latter specifies that the Act does not apply to "any person insofar as he transacts a business in securities without the jurisdiction of the United States," unless he does so in violation of regulations promulgated by the Commission "to prevent evasion [of the Act]." § 78dd(b). Under both provisions it is the foreign location of the *transaction* that establishes (or reflects the presumption of) the Act's inapplicability, absent regulations by the Commission.

The same focus on domestic transactions is evident in the Securities Act of 1933, 48 Stat. 74, enacted by the same Congress as the Exchange Act, and forming part of the same comprehensive regulation of securities trading. See *Central Bank of Denver, N.A.* v. *First Interstate Bank of Denver, N.A.*, 511 U.S. 164, 170–171, 114 S.Ct. 1439, 128 L.Ed.2d 119 (1994). That legislation makes it unlawful to sell a security, through a prospectus or otherwise, making use of "any means or instruments of transportation or communication in interstate commerce or of the mails," unless a registration statement is in effect. 15 U.S.C. § 77e(a)(1). The Commission has interpreted that requirement "not to include . . . sales that occur outside the United States." 17 CFR § 230.901 (2009).

Finally, we reject the notion that the Exchange Act reaches conduct in this country affecting exchanges or transactions abroad for the same reason that *Aramco* rejected overseas application of Title VII to all domestically concluded employment contracts or all employment contracts with American employers: The probability of incompatibility with the applicable laws of other countries is so obvious that if Congress intended such foreign application "it would have addressed the subject of conflicts with foreign laws and procedures." 499 U.S., at 256, 111 S.Ct. 1227. Like the United States, foreign countries regulate their domestic securities exchanges and securities transactions occurring within their territorial jurisdiction. And the regulation of other countries often differs from ours as to what constitutes fraud, what disclosures must be made, what damages are recoverable, what discovery is available in litigation, what individual actions may be joined in a single suit, what attorney's fees are recoverable, and many other matters. See, *e.g.*, Brief for United Kingdom of Great Britain and Northern Ireland as *Amicus Curiae* 16–21. The Commonwealth of Australia, the United Kingdom of Great Britain and Northern Ireland, and the Republic of France have filed *amicus* briefs in this case. So have (separately or jointly) such international and foreign organizations as the International Chamber of Commerce, the Swiss Bankers Association, the Federation of German Industries, the French Business Confederation, the Institute of International Bankers, the European Banking Federation, the Australian Bankers' Association, and the Association Francaise des Entreprises Privées. They all complain of the interference with foreign securities regulation that application of § 10(b) abroad would produce, and urge the adoption of a clear test that will avoid that consequence. The transactional test we have adopted—whether the purchase or sale is made in the United States, or involves a security listed on a domestic exchange—meets that requirement.

B

The Solicitor General suggests a different test, which petitioners also endorse: "[A] transnational securities fraud violates [§] 10(b) when the fraud involves significant conduct in the United States that is material to the fraud's success." Brief for United States as *Amicus Curiae* 16; see

Brief for Petitioners 26. Neither the Solicitor General nor petitioners provide any textual support for this test. The Solicitor General sets forth a number of purposes such a test would serve: achieving a high standard of business ethics in the securities industry, ensuring honest securities markets and thereby promoting investor confidence, and preventing the United States from becoming a "Barbary Coast" for malefactors perpetrating frauds in foreign markets. Brief for United States as *Amicus Curiae* 16–17. But it provides no textual support for the last of these purposes, or for the first two as applied to the foreign securities industry and securities markets abroad. It is our function to give the statute the effect its language suggests, however modest that may be; not to extend it to admirable purposes it might be used to achieve.

If, moreover, one is to be attracted by the desirable consequences of the "significant and material conduct" test, one should also be repulsed by its adverse consequences. While there is no reason to believe that the United States has become the Barbary Coast for those perpetrating frauds on foreign securities markets, some fear that it has become the Shangri-La of class-action litigation for lawyers representing those allegedly cheated in foreign securities markets. See Brief for Infineon Technologies AG as *Amicus Curiae* 1–2, 22–25; Brief for European Aeronautic Defence & Space Co. N.V. et al. as *Amici Curiae* 2–4; Brief for Securities Industry and Financial Markets Association et al. as *Amici Curiae* 10–16; Coffee, Securities Policeman to the World? The Cost of Global Class Actions, N.Y.L.J. 5 (2008); S. Grant & D. Zilka, The Current Role of Foreign Investors in Federal Securities Class Actions, PLI Corporate Law and Practice Handbook Series, PLI Order No. 11072, pp. 15–16 (Sept.–Oct.2007); Buxbaum, Multinational Class Actions Under Federal Securities Law: Managing Jurisdictional Conflict, 46 Colum. J. Transnat'l L. 14, 38–41 (2007).

As case support for the "significant and material conduct" test, the Solicitor General relies primarily on *Pasquantino* v. *United States*, 544 U.S. 349, 125 S.Ct. 1766, 161 L.Ed.2d 619 (2005). In that case we concluded that the wire-fraud statute, 18 U.S.C. § 1343 (2009 ed., Supp. II), was violated by defendants who ordered liquor over the phone from a store in Maryland with the intent to smuggle it into Canada and deprive the Canadian Government of revenue. 544 U.S., at 353, 371, 125 S.Ct. 1766. Section 1343 prohibits "any scheme or artifice to defraud,"—fraud *simpliciter*, without any requirement that it be "in connection with" any particular transaction or event. The *Pasquantino* Court said that the petitioners' "offense was complete the moment they executed the scheme inside the United States," and that it was "[t]his domestic element of petitioners' conduct [that] the Government is punishing." 544 U.S., at 371, 125 S.Ct. 1766. Section 10(b), by contrast, punishes not all acts of deception, but only such acts "in connection with the purchase or sale of any security registered on a national securities exchange or any security not so registered." Not deception alone, but deception with respect to certain purchases or sales is necessary for a violation of the statute.

The Solicitor General points out that the "significant and material conduct" test is in accord with prevailing notions of international comity. If so, that proves that *if* the United States asserted prescriptive jurisdiction pursuant to the "significant and material conduct" test it would not violate customary international law; but it in no way tends to prove that that is what Congress has done.

Finally, the Solicitor General argues that the Commission has adopted an interpretation similar to the "significant and material conduct" test, and that we should defer to that. In the two adjudications the Solicitor General cites, however, the Commission did not purport to be providing its own interpretation of the statute, but relied on decisions of federal courts—mainly Court of Appeals decisions that in turn relied on the Schoenbaum and Leasco decisions of the Second Circuit that we discussed earlier. See *In re United Securities Clearing Corp.*, 52 S.E.C. 92, 95, n. 14, 96, n. 16 (1994); *In re Robert F. Lynch*, Exchange Act Release No. 11737, 8 S.E.C. Docket 75, 77, n. 15 (1975). We need "accept only those agency interpretations that are reasonable in light of the principles of construction courts normally employ." *Aramco*, 499 U.S., at 260, 111 S.Ct. 1227 (SCALIA, J., concurring in part and concurring in judgment). Since the Commission's interpretations relied on cases we disapprove, which ignored or discarded the presumption against extraterritoriality, we owe them no deference.

* * *

Section 10(b) reaches the use of a manipulative or deceptive device or contrivance only in connection with the purchase or sale of a security listed on an American stock exchange, and the purchase or sale of any other security in the United States. This case involves no securities listed on a domestic exchange, and all aspects of the purchases complained of by those petitioners who still have live claims occurred outside the United States. Petitioners have therefore failed to state a claim on which relief can be granted. We affirm the dismissal of petitioners' complaint on this ground.

In the wake of Morrison, lower courts have wrestled with how to determine the location of transactions in securities that are not listed on an exchange. Plaintiffs seeking to situate their investment transactions within the United States identified a broad range of potentially relevant factors, including the dissemination of offering materials in the United States; actions taken within the United States to solicit their investment; and the wiring of money to the United States. In Absolute Activist Value Master Fund Ltd. v. Ficeto, 677 F.3d 60 (2d Cir. 2012), the Second Circuit Court of Appeals adopted a test that seems to be emerging as the basis of judicial consensus regarding the meaning of Morrison's second prong:

[R]ather than looking to the identity of the parties, the type of security at issue, or whether each individual defendant engaged in conduct within the United States, we hold that a securities transaction is domestic when the parties incur irrevocable liability to carry out the transaction within the United States or when title is passed within the United States.

After Morrison, courts have struggled with a second question as well: If applying Section 10(b) to a U.S. transaction would likely cause conflict with foreign law, may a court still consider the reasonableness of doing so in the particular case? Courts are divided on this point. In Parkcentral Global Hub Ltd. v. Porsche Auto. Holdings SE, 763 F.3d 198 (2d Cir. 2014), the Second Circuit Court of Appeals held that it could. "While a domestic transaction or listing is *necessary* to state a claim under § 10(b), a finding that these transactions were domestic would not *suffice* to compel the conclusion that the plaintiffs' invocation of § 10(b) was appropriately domestic." Id. at 216. It went on to state that in cases where the "potential for regulatory and legal overlap and conflict" was obvious, courts should "make their way with careful attention to the facts of each case" in order to determine whether the transaction in question was "so predominantly foreign as to be impermissibly extraterritorial." Id. at 216–217. In Stoyas v. Toshiba Corp., 896 F.3d 933 (9th Cir. 2018), by contrast, the Ninth Circuit Court of Appeals rejected this approach. "[Parkcentral] carves-out 'predominantly foreign' securities fraud claims from Section 10(b)'s ambit, disregarding Section 10(b)'s text. . . Parkcentral's test for whether a claim is foreign is an open-ended, under-defined multi-factor test, akin to the vague and unpredictable tests that Morrison criticized and endeavored to replace with a 'clear,' administrable rule." Id. at 950.

After the decision in Morrison, Congress amended the jurisdictional provisions of the Securities Exchange Act in Section 929P(b) of the 2010 Dodd-Frank Act, restoring the ability of the SEC and the DOJ to bring enforcement actions under Section 10(b) in cases involving "conduct within the United States that constitutes significant steps in furtherance of the violation, even if the securities transaction occurs outside the United States and involves only foreign investors" or "conduct occurring outside the United States that has a foreseeable effect within the United States." Because the language of the amendment addresses only the jurisdictional provisions of the Exchange Act and not the geographic scope of § 10(b) itself, courts have disagreed about whether the amendment was effective. Compare SEC v. Chicago Convention Center, LLC, 961 F. Supp. 2d 905, 909–917 (N.D. Ill. 2013) (suggesting that Dodd-Frank may not have successfully amended Securities Exchange Act), with SEC v. Scoville, 913 F.3d 1204, 1214–1218 (10th Cir. 2019) (concluding that Congress unmistakeably indicated that the antifraud provisions apply extraterritorially in suits brought by the government). However, the U.S. government has other tools to pursue securities fraud that may not be available to private parties. While § 10(b) of the Exchange Act refers only to fraud in connection with the "purchase or sale" of securities, § 17(a) of the Securities Act criminalizes fraud in the "offer or sale" of securities. In SEC v. Goldman Sachs & Co., 790 F. Supp. 2d 147 (S.D.N.Y 2011), the district court dismissed several counts alleging that the defendant violated § 10(b) on the ground that there was no "purchase or sale" in the United States, but held that the SEC had sufficiently alleged that the defendant made "offers" in the United States. "These communications included phone calls Tourre participated in from New York City and/or emails he sent from New York City to IKB and ABN regarding ABACUS and constituted domestic 'offers' of securities or security-based swaps." Id. at 165. The potentially broader reach of § 17(a) does not help defrauded investors seeking damages, however, because most circuits have held that § 17(b) does not create a private right of action. See, e.g., Finkel v. Stratton Corp., 962 F.2d 169, 174–175 (2d Cir. 1992).

Assuming that a fraud claim arising out of a share purchase agreement does fall within the scope of U.S. law, what effect would a foreign forum-selection and choice of law clause in that agreement have on the applicability of U.S. securities law? In some respects, there would seem to be little at stake in the choice between U.S. and foreign law in such a case. Most foreign countries provide remedies for fraud and misrepresentation under their securities laws too, as well as remedies for breach of contract. And while it is true that there are aspects of U.S. law (not found in all legal systems) that provide advantages to securities fraud plaintiffs, some of these are relevant only in the context of class actions brought by large groups of investors—for instance, the "fraud on the market" theory, which relieves plaintiffs of the need to prove that they relied specifically on the alleged misrepresentations, and the "opt out" device used in U.S. class actions. Nevertheless, some perceived advantages of the U.S. system, such as broad U.S. discovery processes, are relevant in all cases. Moreover, American counsel might prefer an American trial simply because of their familiarity with American law, or the hope that an American judge (or jury) will be more sympathetic and generous than another tribunal. A plaintiff in the position of American Kitchens might therefore seek to contest the enforcement of foreign forum-selection and choice of law clauses.

In a series of cases decided in the 1990s, the U.S. Circuit Courts of Appeals upheld clauses choosing English law and English courts in contracts between Lloyd's of London and its members, despite the fact that this would preclude those members from bringing U.S. securities law claims.[9] In those cases, U.S. investors had argued that enforcement

---

[9]   See Lipcon v. Underwriters at Lloyd's, London, 148 F.3d 1285 (11th Cir.1998), cert. denied, 525 U.S. 1093, 119 S.Ct. 851, 142 L.Ed.2d 704 (1999); Richards v. Lloyd's of London, 135 F.3d 1289 (9th Cir.) (en banc), cert. denied, 525 U.S. 943, 119 S.Ct. 365, 142 L.Ed.2d 301 (1998); Haynsworth v. The Corporation, 121 F.3d 956 (5th Cir.1997), cert. denied, 523 U.S. 1072, 118 S.Ct. 1513, 140 L.Ed.2d 666 (1998); Allen v. Lloyd's of London, 94 F.3d 923 (4th Cir.1996); Bonny

of clauses choosing English courts and English law would violate the public policy of the United States as embodied in its securities laws. See, e.g., Bonny v. Society of Lloyd's, 3 F.3d 156 (7th Cir. 1993), cert. denied, 510 U.S. 1113, 114 S.Ct. 1057, 127 L.Ed.2d 378 (1994). The Courts of Appeals rejected this argument, concluding, in the words of the Seventh Circuit, "that English law affords plaintiffs a cause of action for fraud similar to that available for the claims they have brought under Rule 10b-5." Id. at 161.

QUESTIONS

(1) Assume that American Kitchens has inspected the operations of DKW in Germany and has entered a tentative agreement with its owners to purchase their shares. Although American Kitchens believes that it has received accurate financial and operational data from DKW, it wants to preserve its ability to initiate a lawsuit under Rule 10b-5 should the data prove to have been misleading. Could it structure the transaction in a way that might make this more likely—for instance, by providing in the Share Purchase Agreement that the closing will occur at its attorney's offices in Philadelphia? Does it matter? That is, would American Kitchens really be better off under 10b-5 than under the German law of fraud? If so, is that for procedural reasons, because U.S. courts would be more sensitive in "feel" about asserted securities fraud, or because of differences in substance?

(2) Even if American Kitchens could not bring an action for damages under Rule 10b-5, could the SEC prosecute the DKW manager who sent the misleading financial data under § 17(a) of the Exchange Act?

(3) If American Kitchens objects to the exclusive jurisdiction of German courts and DKW objects to the exclusive jurisdiction of U.S. courts, might arbitration prove an acceptable middle ground? In this connection, consider Scherk v. Alberto-Culver Co., 417 U.S. 506, 94 S.Ct. 2449, 41 L.Ed.2d 270 (1974) (holding that securities fraud claims are arbitrable), discussed in Mitsubishi Motors Corp. v. Soler Chrysler-Plymouth, Inc., 473 U.S. 614, 105 S.Ct. 3346, 87 L.Ed.2d 444 (1985). See supra pp. 44–52. Would the choice of German law preclude the arbitrators from considering claims under Rule 10b-5?

Additional reading: Steinberg, Gevurtz & Chaffee, Global Issues in Securities Law (2013). On the extraterritorial application of the Exchange Act's antifraud provisions, see Hazen, Treatise on the Law of Securities Regulation, 6 Law Sec. Reg. § 17.4 (2013); Buxbaum, Remedies

---

v. Society of Lloyd's, 3 F.3d 156 (7th Cir.1993), cert. denied, 510 U.S. 1113, 114 S.Ct. 1057, 127 L.Ed.2d 378 (1994); Roby v. Corporation of Lloyd's, 996 F.2d 1353 (2d Cir.), cert. denied, 510 U.S. 945, 114 S.Ct. 385, 126 L.Ed.2d 333 (1993); Riley v. Kingsley Underwriting Agencies, Ltd., 969 F.2d 953 (10th Cir.), cert. denied, 506 U.S. 1021, 113 S.Ct. 658, 121 L.Ed.2d 584 (1992).

for Foreign Investors Under U.S. Federal Securities Law, 75 L. & Contemp. Probs. 161 (2012).

2. TENDER OFFERS AND TAKEOVER DEFENSES

The securities aspects of a takeover are much more complex if the stock that is being sought is owned not by a small group of individuals, but by a wide spectrum of public shareholders. In the United States the Williams Act has, since 1968, regulated the making of public tender offers.[10] It requires that the party making the offer give the offerees elaborately specified information that would be useful to them in deciding whether or not to sell. Under the Williams Act, a tender offer must be held open for a minimum of 20 business days, and if the bidder changes its bid the offer must remain open for at least 10 more days. Offerees may withdraw their acceptances while the tender offer remains open. The Williams Act also requires that all offerees be treated equally during the course of the operation—for example, that offerees be treated on a pro rata basis if the offer is oversubscribed. It does not, however, contain any mandatory bid provision requiring a bidder who gains control to buy out the remaining shareholders at a comparable price. Finally, Regulation 14E under the Act contains an antifraud provision similar to Rule 10b-5. Because of concerns that compliance with the Williams Act was causing foreign issuers to exclude U.S. investors from tender offers, the SEC has issued rules exempting tender offers for foreign securities from the Act if U.S. investors hold ten percent or less of those securities and exempting tender offers for foreign securities from some (but not all) of the Act if U.S. investors hold more than ten but less than forty percent.[11]

Public tender offers also raise questions regarding the obligations of the target company's board of directors and in particular whether the target company may respond to a hostile tender offer with defensive measures designed to thwart the bid. In the United States, these are questions of state corporate law, which under the so-called "internal affairs" doctrine are governed by the laws of the state of incorporation. Delaware law gives directors fairly broad authority to resist a hostile bid if they perceive a threat to the corporation.[12] Common defenses have acquired a host of colorful names: (1) a "poison pill," which gives existing

---

[10] 82 Stat. 454 (1968), 15 U.S.C.A. §§ 78m(d)–(e), 78n(d)–(f).

[11] Cross-Border Tender and Exchange Offers, Business Combinations and Rights Offerings, Securities Act Release No. 7759, Exchange Act Release No. 42,054 (Oct. 22, 1999), as amended by Commission Guidance and Revisions to the Cross-Border Tender Offer, Exchange Offer, Rights Offerings, and Business Combination Rules and Beneficial Ownership Reporting Rules for Certain Foreign Institutions, Securities Act Release No. 8957, Exchange Act Release No. 58,597 (October 9, 2008). See Basnage, Curtin & Rubin, Cross-Border Tender Offers and Other Business Combination Transactions and the U.S. Federal Securities Laws: An Overview, 61 Bus. Law. 1071 (2006).

[12] See Unocal Corp. v. Mesa Petroleum Co., 493 A.2d 946 (Del. 1985). The board's discretion becomes more limited if it concludes that a takeover is inevitable or if the board puts the company up for sale. See Revlon, Inc. v. MacAndrews & Forbes Holdings, Inc., 506 A.2d 173 (Del. 1985).

shareholders the right to large amounts of stock, debt securities, or cash if the hostile bidder gains control; (2) "golden parachutes," granting large severance payments to existing managers in the event of a change in control; (3) selling the corporation's "crown jewels" (in other words, its most valuable assets) to another company; (4) a "lock-up," which involves granting preferential options on assets or stock to a company other than the hostile bidder; (5) seeking a "white knight," that is, a competing bid for the corporation from a company more friendly to the corporation's existing management; (6) paying "greenmail" to the hostile bidder by acquiring its stock in the corporation at a premium; and (7) the so-called "Pac Man" defense, in which the target launches its own hostile bid for control of the bidder. The prevalence of hostile takeovers in the United States declined after the 1980s, although the merger wave of the mid-2000s included quite a few. Even when the incidence of hostile bids is low, their possibility still exerts a disciplining effect on management, inclining them to be more receptive to friendly bids for fear that such bids might otherwise become hostile.

The problem of the public tender offer did not impinge on the awareness of regulators in other countries until much later. In most of Europe—and in countries in other parts of the world—it has been rare for the stock of even major companies to be held by as wide a range of individual public shareholders as in the United States. In a country such as Germany, many stockholders deposit their shares with banks, which in that country are allowed to perform the functions of stockbrokers. This is strongly indicated by the fact that shares are normally created in bearer form. This makes them particularly vulnerable to loss or theft, so having them locked in a bank's vault makes the owner feel much more secure. There is also a technical problem with making tender offers to holders of bearer shares because one does not have a company register of their names and addresses. One would, therefore, have to operate solely through the financial press—and, of course, the network of knowledgeable bankers and advisers. Until quite recently hostile takeovers were rare in Continental Europe, though this has changed since 2000 when Vodafone completed its acquisition of Mannesmann.

Efforts to harmonize takeover laws in the EU member states came to a conclusion in 2004, after 15 years of work, with the adoption of Directive 2004/25/EC on Takeover Bids, 2004 O.J. (L 142) 12. To protect minority shareholders, Article 5 of the Takeover Directive requires any bidder passing a threshold set by each member state to make a mandatory bid for all the remaining voting securities of the company at the highest price the bidder paid for the securities in the run-up to the takeover. Article 15 allows a bidder passing a threshold of 90–95% (as determined by the law of each member state) to "squeeze-out" minority shareholders at a fair price, while Article 16 allows minority shareholders a corresponding right of "sell-out" under the same circumstances.

The most important provisions of the Takeover Directive are Articles 9 and 11. Article 9 establishes a rule of board neutrality—that is, that from at least the time the bid is made public until it succeeds or fails, "the board of the offeree company shall obtain the prior authorization of the general meeting of shareholders given for this purpose before taking any action, other than seeking alternative bids, which may result in the frustration of the bid." Article 11 contains a breakthrough rule making pre-bid defenses like share-transfer and voting restrictions inapplicable during the bid period and after the bidder succeeds in obtaining at least 75% of the company's voting rights. But in a key compromise, Articles 9 and 11 were made optional, and many EU members have chosen not to adopt them.[13] In these countries, companies must still be allowed to opt into Articles 9 and 11 on an individual basis, but may suspend those rules if they become the targets of bidders who are not subject to the same rules. See Article 12(3). The end result of all this is that European takeover law continues to consist of a patchwork of differing national laws.

Since 1994, German corporate law has seen enormous reforms on many fronts.[14] Germany adopted a Takeover Law (*Wertpapiererwerbs- und Übernahmegesetz* or *WpÜG*) effective January 1, 2002, which was amended in 2006 to implement the EU's Takeover Directive. The Takeover Law applies to public tender offers for securities of companies domiciled in Germany and listed on an organized market in the European Economic Area (the EU plus Norway, Iceland, and Liechtenstein), and, with a somewhat different scope of application, to public tender offers for securities of companies domiciled elsewhere within the European Economic Area but listed in Germany. Like the Williams Act in the United States, the Takeover Law regulates the mechanics of tender offers, requiring the bidder to disclose a variety of information in its offering documents, first to the German Federal Securities Supervisory Office and then to the public. If information in the offering documents is incorrect or incomplete, a person who accepted the offer may seek damages from those responsible for the documents. Under the Takeover Law, a public tender offer must remain open for a minimum of four weeks and a maximum of ten following publication of the offering documents, although the time may be extended if the bidder revises its offer or if there is an alternative takeover bid. The Takeover Law requires the bidder to offer adequate consideration for the target's shares, which means the price must equal or exceed the higher of (1) the average price of the target's shares within the three months prior to publication of the decision to launch the tender offer (or, in the case of a mandatory offer, within the three months prior to the date on which control of 30% of the target's voting rights was acquired), and (2) the highest price paid by the

---

[13] See Report on the Implementation of the Directive on Takeover Bids, https://eur-lex.europa.eu/legal-content/EN/TXT/?uri=CELEX:52012DC0347.

[14] See Noack & Zetzsche, Corporate Governance Reform in Germany: The Second Decade, 16 Eur. Bus. L. Rev. 1033 (2005).

bidder to acquire the target's shares within the six months prior to publication of the offering documents. The Law further requires that if securities are offered for the target's shares, those securities must be listed on an organized market in the European Economic Area, a provision that may limit the ability of U.S. firms to offer shares to acquire German ones.[15]

In contrast to U.S. law, the German Takeover Law does not allow partial tender offers. Thus a bidder must offer to acquire all of the target's shares, although the bidder may be allowed to exclude shareholders residing outside the European Economic Area. (Recall the SEC's Cross-Border Tender and Exchange Offer Rule, supra p. 362, which was designed to address the tendency to exclude U.S. shareholders from foreign tender offers.) Also in contrast to U.S. law, the Takeover Law requires a bidder who obtains at least 30% of the target company's voting rights to make a mandatory bid for all outstanding voting securities of the company, as required by Article 5 of the Takeover Directive. Germany has set the threshold for the "squeeze-out" and "sell-out" rights required by Articles 15 and 16 of the Takeover Directive at 95%. So a bidder who passes that threshold may "squeeze out" the remaining minority shareholders but may also be required to accept their offer to "sell out" their holdings.

Finally, although the German Takeover Law opts out of Articles 9 and 11 of the Takeover Directive, other provisions of German law may achieve roughly the same effect. Article 33 of the Takeover Law contains a duty of board neutrality. This duty does not apply to decisions to seek a competing bid from a "white knight" or (in derogation of Article 9) to measures authorized by the target company's supervisory board (*Aufsichtsrat*).[16] Nevertheless, the favorite tactic of American boards— the "poison pill"—is not available under German corporate law. Although Germany has also opted out of Article 11's breakthrough rule, multiple voting rights and voting caps have been prohibited for listed companies since 2003 and restrictions on the transferability of shares are rarely used as takeover defenses.

QUESTIONS

(1) Assume that DKW is publicly listed on a German exchange. Over the past three months, American Kitchens has quietly been purchasing its shares on this exchange and, having now acquired 3% of

---

[15] Since 2005, this has required U.S. companies to convert their financial statements to standards issued by the International Accounting Standards Board.

[16] Under the German practice of co-determination, workers' representatives compose up to half of such supervisory boards, with shareholder representatives holding a tie-breaking vote if needed. See generally Baums & Ulmer, Employees' Co-Determination in the Member States of the European Union (2004); Vagts, Reforming the "Modern" Corporation: Perspectives from the German, 80 Harv. L. Rev. 23 (1966).

those shares, has decided to launch a public tender offer. What barriers would it face under the German Takeover Law?

(2) If DKW's management decided to resist the takeover bid, do you think it could do so effectively?

Additional reading: Gilson & Black, The Law and Finance of Corporate Acquisitions (2d ed. 1995); Noack & Zetzsche, Corporate Governance Reform in Germany: The Second Decade, 16 Eur. Bus. L. Rev. 1033 (2005); Kirchner & Painter, Takeover Defenses under Delaware Law, the Proposed Thirteenth EU Directive and the New German Takeover Law: Comparison and Recommendations for Reform, 50 Am. J. Comp. L. 451 (2002); Armour & McCahery, eds., After Enron: Improving Corporate Law and Modernising Securities Regulation in Europe and the US (2006).

D. ANTITRUST LAW

The acquisition of one significant competitor in one country by another in a second country may have implications for the antitrust policy of both states. Since 1976 the United States has required pre-merger notification for large acquisitions under the Hart-Scott-Rodino Antitrust Improvements Act. Since 1989 the European Union has done the same under its Merger Regulation. During the 1990s there was an explosion of merger notification systems around the world, so that by the year 2000 more than 60 jurisdictions had adopted a system of some sort.[17] A U.S. Department of Justice Advisory Committee observed that "the marked increase in the number of jurisdictions possessing merger review regimes renders it increasingly likely that international mergers and acquisitions will be reviewed by multiple jurisdictions" and that "it is not unheard of for merging parties to file notifications with a dozen or more jurisdictions."[18] As we shall see, different authorities sometimes take different views of the anticompetitive effects of the same transaction. See infra pp. 377–385.

1. U.S. ANTITRUST LAW WITH RESPECT TO MERGERS

In 1914, the U.S. Congress enacted the Clayton Act, Section 7 of which prohibits any person engaged in commerce from acquiring the stock or assets of any other person engaged in commerce where "the effect of such acquisition may be substantially to lessen competition, or to tend to create a monopoly." 15 U.S.C.A. § 18. In 1950, Congress strengthened the Clayton Act with the Celler-Kefauver Act. Then, in 1976, Congress enacted the Hart-Scott-Rodino Antitrust Improvements Act, 15 U.S.C.A. § 18a, providing for pre-merger notification of large acquisitions. Since 2004, the relevant monetary thresholds have been adjusted annually

---

[17] See International Competition Policy Advisory Committee to the Attorney General and Assistant Attorney General for Antitrust, Final Report, Annex 2-C (2000).

[18] Id. at 87, 92.

for inflation. In the discussion that follows, the threshholds effective as of 2018 are included in brackets.

In general, Hart-Scott-Rodino, as substantially amended in 2000, requires pre-merger notification to the Department of Justice or the Federal Trade Commission (FTC) if, as a result of the acquisition, the acquiring person would (1) hold more than $200 million [$337.60 million] of the acquired person's voting securities and/or assets or (2) hold more than $50 million [$84.4 million] of the acquired person's voting securities and/or assets, if the acquiring person has assets or annual sales of $100 million [$168.8 million] or more and the acquired person has assets or annual sales of $10 million [$16.9 million] or more, or the acquiring person has assets or annual sales of $10 million [$16.9 million] or more and the acquired person has assets or annual sales of $100 million [$168.8 million] or more. If pre-merger notification is required, the acquiring party must observe a waiting period of 30 days after filing the notification—15 days in the case of a cash tender offer. The Department of Justice or FTC may require additional information and may extend the waiting period for an additional 30 days after receipt of such information (10 days in the case of a cash tender offer). If after review the Department of Justice or FTC concludes that the acquisition would violate Section 7 of the Clayton Act, it may bring suit in federal court to enjoin the acquisition.[19]

Hart-Scott-Rodino applies equally to acquisitions involving foreign parties that affect U.S. commerce. But the FTC and the Department of Justice have authority to exempt transactions that are not likely to violate U.S. antitrust laws, and they have exercised that authority to exempt some transactions involving foreign parties including, for example, the following:[20]

§ 802.51 Acquisitions of voting securities of a foreign issuer.

(a) *By U.S. persons.* (1) The acquisition of voting securities of a foreign issuer by a U.S. person shall be exempt from the requirements of the act unless the issuer (including all entities controlled by the issuer) either: holds assets located in the United States (other than investment assets, voting or nonvoting securities of another person, and assets included pursuant to § 801.40(d)(2) of this chapter) having an aggregate total value of over $50 million (as adjusted) [$84.4 million]; or made aggregate sales in or into the United States of over $50 million (as adjusted) [$84.4 million] in its most recent fiscal year.

(2) If interests in multiple foreign issuers are being acquired from the same acquired person, the assets located in the United States and sales in or into the United States of all the issuers must

---

[19] The Department of Justice and FTC have published guidelines for their analysis of such mergers. See Horizontal Merger Guidelines (1992, revised 2010); Commentary on the Horizontal Merger Guidelines (2006).

[20] 16 C.F.R. § 802.51.

be aggregated to determine whether either $50 million (as adjusted) [$84.4 million] limitation is exceeded.

(b) *By foreign persons.* (1) The acquisition of voting securities of a foreign issuer by a foreign person shall be exempt from the requirements of the act unless the acquisition will confer control of the issuer and the issuer (including all entities controlled by the issuer) either: holds assets located in the United States (other than investment assets, voting or nonvoting securities of another person, and assets included pursuant to § 801.40(d)(2) of this chapter) having an aggregate total value of over $50 million (as adjusted); [$84.4 million] or made aggregate sales in or into the United States of over $50 million (as adjusted) [$84.4 million] in its most recent fiscal year.

(2) If controlling interests in multiple foreign issuers are being acquired from the same acquired person, the assets located in the United States and sales in or into the United States of all the issuers must be aggregated to determine whether either $50 million (as adjusted) [$84.4 million] limitation is exceeded.

(c) Where a foreign issuer whose securities are being acquired exceeds the threshold in paragraph (b)(1) of this section, the acquisition nevertheless shall be exempt where:

(1) Both acquiring and acquired persons are foreign;

(2) The aggregate sales of the acquiring and acquired persons in or into the United States are less than $110 million (as adjusted) [$185.7 million] in their respective most recent fiscal years;

(3) The aggregate total assets of the acquiring and acquired persons located in the United States (other than investment assets, voting or nonvoting securities of another person, and assets included pursuant to § 801.40(d)(2) of this chapter) are less than $110 million (as adjusted) [$185.7 million]; and

(4) The transaction does not meet the criteria of Section 7A(a)(2)(A).[21]

2. EU MERGER REGULATION

Provisions on mergers were not included in the 1957 Treaty of Rome. The merger wave of the 1960s raised concern about this omission, and in 1973 the European Court of Justice held in Europemballage Corp. & Continental Can Co. v. Commission, Case No. 6/72, [1973] E.C.R. 215, that mergers that strengthened a dominant position fell within Article 86 of the Treaty of Rome (now Article 102 of the Treaty on the Functioning of the European Union). It was not until 1989, however, that

---

[21] [Eds.] Section 7A(a)(2)(A) requires pre-merger notification if "as a result of such acquisition, the acquiring person would hold an aggregate total amount of the voting securities and assets of the acquired person . . . in excess of $200,000,000" as adjusted for inflation. 15 U.S.C.A. § 18a(a)(2)(A).

the European Council adopted a regulation requiring pre-merger notification to the Commission, 1989 O.J. (L 395) 1. In 2004, the European Council replaced this regulation with a new Merger Regulation, effective May 1, 2004, portions of which are set forth below.[22]

The new Merger Regulation made several important changes in EU's system of merger control. First, it changed the substantive standard of review. The original Merger Regulation prohibited any concentration that "creates or strengthens a dominant position as a result of which effective competition would be significantly impeded in the common market or in a substantial part of it." This "dominance" test was replaced in the 2004 Regulation by a prohibition of mergers that "significantly impede effective competition in particular as a result of the creation or strengthening of a dominant position." The new test brought the EU's substantive standard closer to the "substantially lessen competition" test used in the United States. It also made clear that mergers with anticompetitive effects in oligopolistic markets are prohibited even if the merged company is not "dominant." Second, the new Merger Regulation allows the parties to file a notification before entering a binding merger agreement so long as they can demonstrate a good faith intention to conclude such an agreement. Third, the new Merger Regulation changes the timetable for review. During the first phase, the Commission now has 25 working days to review a transaction, which may be extended by 10 working days to allow for negotiations with the parties. If the Commission decides to carry out an in-depth inquiry, it has a further 90 working days during the second phase, which may be extended by 15 working days if remedies are offered and by a further 20 working days at the request of the parties. Finally, the new Merger Regulation allows the parties to a transaction that is not covered by the regulation but is subject to notification in three or more member states to request review by the Commission instead, so long as none of these member states object. This "one-stop shop" provision was expected to be particularly important with the expansion of the EU in 2004 from 15 to 25 members, and now to 28 members.

---

[22] The European Commission has issued Merger Guidelines, 2004 O.J. (C 31) 5, that elaborate on its interpretation of the Merger Regulation's substantive standard and an implementing regulation, 2004 O.J. (L 133) 1 (as amended in 2008 and again in 2013), that deals in greater detail with questions of procedure.

Council Regulation (EC) No. 139/2004 of January 20 2004 on the Control of Concentrations Between Undertakings (the EC Merger Regulation)

2004 O.J. (L 24) 1

* * *

Article 1

Scope

1.   Without prejudice to Article 4(5) and Article 22, this Regulation shall apply to all concentrations with a Community dimension as defined in this Article.

2.   A concentration has a Community dimension where:

(a)   the combined aggregate worldwide turnover of all the undertakings concerned is more than EUR 5 000 million; and

(b)   the aggregate Community-wide turnover of each of at least two of the undertakings concerned is more than EUR 250 million,

unless each of the undertakings concerned achieves more than two-thirds of its aggregate Community-wide turnover within one and the same Member State.

3.   A concentration that does not meet the thresholds laid down in paragraph 2 has a Community dimension where:

(a)   the combined aggregate worldwide turnover of all the undertakings concerned is more than EUR 2 500 million;

(b)   in each of at least three Member States, the combined aggregate turnover of all the undertakings concerned is more than EUR 100 million;

(c)   in each of at least three Member States included for the purpose of point (b), the aggregate turnover of each of at least two of the undertakings concerned is more than EUR 25 million; and

(d)   the aggregate Community-wide turnover of each of at least two of the undertakings concerned is more than EUR 100 million,

unless each of the undertakings concerned achieves more than two-thirds of its aggregate Community-wide turnover within one and the same Member State.

* * *

Article 2

Appraisal of concentrations

1.   Concentrations within the scope of this Regulation shall be appraised in accordance with the objectives of this Regulation and the following provisions with a view to establishing whether or not they are compatible with the common market.

In making this appraisal, the Commission shall take into account:

(a) the need to maintain and develop effective competition within the common market in view of, among other things, the structure of all the markets concerned and the actual or potential competition from undertakings located either within or outwith the Community;

(b) the market position of the undertakings concerned and their economic and financial power, the alternatives available to suppliers and users, their access to supplies or markets, any legal or other barriers to entry, supply and demand trends for the relevant goods and services, the interests of the intermediate and ultimate consumers, and the development of technical and economic progress provided that it is to consumers' advantage and does not form an obstacle to competition.

2. A concentration which would not significantly impede effective competition in the common market or in a substantial part of it, in particular as a result of the creation or strengthening of a dominant position, shall be declared compatible with the common market.

3. A concentration which would significantly impede effective competition, in the common market or in a substantial part of it, in particular as a result of the creation or strengthening of a dominant position, shall be declared incompatible with the common market.

4. To the extent that the creation of a joint venture constituting a concentration pursuant to Article 3 has as its object or effect the coordination of the competitive behaviour of undertakings that remain independent, such coordination shall be appraised in accordance with the criteria of Article 81(1) and (3) of the Treaty, with a view to establishing whether or not the operation is compatible with the common market.

5. In making this appraisal, the Commission shall take into account in particular:

— whether two or more parent companies retain, to a significant extent, activities in the same market as the joint venture or in a market which is downstream or upstream from that of the joint venture or in a neighbouring market closely related to this market,

— whether the coordination which is the direct consequence of the creation of the joint venture affords the undertakings concerned the possibility of eliminating competition in respect of a substantial part of the products or services in question.

Article 3
Definition of concentration

1. A concentration shall be deemed to arise where a change of control on a lasting basis results from:

(a) the merger of two or more previously independent undertakings or parts of undertakings, or

(b)   the acquisition, by one or more persons already controlling at least one undertaking, or by one or more undertakings, whether by purchase of securities or assets, by contract or by any other means, of direct or indirect control of the whole or parts of one or more other undertakings.

2.   Control shall be constituted by rights, contracts or any other means which, either separately or in combination and having regard to the considerations of fact or law involved, confer the possibility of exercising decisive influence on an undertaking, in particular by:

(a)   ownership or the right to use all or part of the assets of an undertaking;

(b)   rights or contracts which confer decisive influence on the composition, voting or decisions of the organs of an undertaking.

3.   Control is acquired by persons or undertakings which:

(a)   are holders of the rights or entitled to rights under the contracts concerned; or

(b)   while not being holders of such rights or entitled to rights under such contracts, have the power to exercise the rights deriving therefrom.

4.   The creation of a joint venture performing on a lasting basis all the functions of an autonomous economic entity shall constitute a concentration within the meaning of paragraph 1(b).

* * *

Article 4

Prior notification of concentrations and pre-notification referral at the request of the notifying parties

1.   Concentrations with a Community dimension defined in this Regulation shall be notified to the Commission prior to their implementation and following the conclusion of the agreement, the announcement of the public bid, or the acquisition of a controlling interest.

Notification may also be made where the undertakings concerned demonstrate to the Commission a good faith intention to conclude an agreement or, in the case of a public bid, where they have publicly announced an intention to make such a bid, provided that the intended agreement or bid would result in a concentration with a Community dimension.

* * *

4.   Prior to the notification of a concentration within the meaning of paragraph 1, the persons or undertakings referred to in paragraph 2 may inform the Commission, by means of a reasoned submission, that the concentration may significantly affect competition in a market within a Member State which presents all the characteristics of a distinct market

and should therefore be examined, in whole or in part, by that Member State.

The Commission shall transmit this submission to all Member States without delay. The Member State referred to in the reasoned submission shall, within 15 working days of receiving the submission, express its agreement or disagreement as regards the request to refer the case. Where that Member State takes no such decision within this period, it shall be deemed to have agreed.

Unless that Member State disagrees, the Commission, where it considers that such a distinct market exists, and that competition in that market may be significantly affected by the concentration, may decide to refer the whole or part of the case to the competent authorities of that Member State with a view to the application of that State's national competition law.

The decision whether or not to refer the case in accordance with the third subparagraph shall be taken within 25 working days starting from the receipt of the reasoned submission by the Commission. The Commission shall inform the other Member States and the persons or undertakings concerned of its decision. If the Commission does not take a decision within this period, it shall be deemed to have adopted a decision to refer the case in accordance with the submission made by the persons or undertakings concerned.

If the Commission decides, or is deemed to have decided, pursuant to the third and fourth subparagraphs, to refer the whole of the case, no notification shall be made pursuant to paragraph 1 and national competition law shall apply. Article 9(6) to (9) shall apply *mutatis mutandis*.

5.   With regard to a concentration as defined in Article 3 which does not have a Community dimension within the meaning of Article 1 and which is capable of being reviewed under the national competition laws of at least three Member States, the persons or undertakings referred to in paragraph 2 may, before any notification to the competent authorities, inform the Commission by means of a reasoned submission that the concentration should be examined by the Commission.

The Commission shall transmit this submission to all Member States without delay.

Any Member State competent to examine the concentration under its national competition law may, within 15 working days of receiving the reasoned submission, express its disagreement as regards the request to refer the case.

Where at least one such Member State has expressed its disagreement in accordance with the third subparagraph within the period of 15 working days, the case shall not be referred. The Commission shall, without delay, inform all Member States and the persons or undertakings concerned of any such expression of disagreement.

Where no Member State has expressed its disagreement in accordance with the third subparagraph within the period of 15 working days, the concentration shall be deemed to have a Community dimension and shall be notified to the Commission in accordance with paragraphs 1 and 2. In such situations, no Member State shall apply its national competition law to the concentration.

* * *

Article 6

Examination of the notification and initiation of proceedings

1. The Commission shall examine the notification as soon as it is received.

(a) Where it concludes that the concentration notified does not fall within the scope of this Regulation, it shall record that finding by means of a decision.

(b) Where it finds that the concentration notified, although falling within the scope of this Regulation, does not raise serious doubts as to its compatibility with the common market, it shall decide not to oppose it and shall declare that it is compatible with the common market.

A decision declaring a concentration compatible shall be deemed to cover restrictions directly related and necessary to the implementation of the concentration.

(c) Without prejudice to paragraph 2, where the Commission finds that the concentration notified falls within the scope of this Regulation and raises serious doubts as to its compatibility with the common market, it shall decide to initiate proceedings. Without prejudice to Article 9, such proceedings shall be closed by means of a decision as provided for in Article 8(1) to (4), unless the undertakings concerned have demonstrated to the satisfaction of the Commission that they have abandoned the concentration.

2. Where the Commission finds that, following modification by the undertakings concerned, a notified concentration no longer raises serious doubts within the meaning of paragraph 1(c), it shall declare the concentration compatible with the common market pursuant to paragraph 1(b).

The Commission may attach to its decision under paragraph 1(b) conditions and obligations intended to ensure that the undertakings concerned comply with the commitments they have entered into vis-à-vis the Commission with a view to rendering the concentration compatible with the common market.

* * *

Article 7

Suspension of concentrations

1.   A concentration with a Community dimension as defined in Article 1, or which is to be examined by the Commission pursuant to Article 4(5), shall not be implemented either before its notification or until it has been declared compatible with the common market. . . .

* * *

Article 8

Powers of decision of the Commission

1.   Where the Commission finds that a notified concentration fulfils the criterion laid down in Article 2(2) and, in the cases referred to in Article 2(4), the criteria laid down in Article 81(3) of the Treaty, it shall issue a decision declaring the concentration compatible with the common market.

A decision declaring a concentration compatible shall be deemed to cover restrictions directly related and necessary to the implementation of the concentration.

2.   Where the Commission finds that, following modification by the undertakings concerned, a notified concentration fulfils the criterion laid down in Article 2(2) and, in the cases referred to in Article 2(4), the criteria laid down in Article 81(3) of the Treaty, it shall issue a decision declaring the concentration compatible with the common market.

The Commission may attach to its decision conditions and obligations intended to ensure that the undertakings concerned comply with the commitments they have entered into vis-á-vis the Commission with a view to rendering the concentration compatible with the common market.

A decision declaring a concentration compatible shall be deemed to cover restrictions directly related and necessary to the implementation of the concentration.

3.   Where the Commission finds that a concentration fulfils the criterion defined in Article 2(3) or, in the cases referred to in Article 2(4), does not fulfil the criteria laid down in Article 81(3) of the Treaty, it shall issue a decision declaring that the concentration is incompatible with the common market.

4.   Where the Commission finds that a concentration:

(a)   has already been implemented and that concentration has been declared incompatible with the common market, or

(b)   has been implemented in contravention of a condition attached to a decision taken under paragraph 2, which has found that, in the absence of the condition, the concentration would fulfil the criterion laid down in Article 2(3) or, in the cases referred to in Article 2(4), would not fulfil the criteria laid down in Article 81(3) of the Treaty, the Commission may:

— require the undertakings concerned to dissolve the concentration, in particular through the dissolution of the merger or the disposal of all the shares or assets acquired, so as to restore the situation prevailing prior to the implementation of the concentration; in circumstances where restoration of the situation prevailing before the implementation of the concentration is not possible through dissolution of the concentration, the Commission may take any other measure appropriate to achieve such restoration as far as possible,

— order any other appropriate measure to ensure that the undertakings concerned dissolve the concentration or take other restorative measures as required in its decision.

* * *

Article 10

Time limits for initiating proceedings and for decisions

1.   Without prejudice to Article 6(4), the decisions referred to in Article 6(1) shall be taken within 25 working days at most. That period shall begin on the working day following that of the receipt of a notification or, if the information to be supplied with the notification is incomplete, on the working day following that of the receipt of the complete information.

That period shall be increased to 35 working days where the Commission receives a request from a Member State in accordance with Article 9(2) or where, the undertakings concerned offer commitments pursuant to Article 6(2) with a view to rendering the concentration compatible with the common market.

2.   Decisions pursuant to Article 8(1) or (2) concerning notified concentrations shall be taken as soon as it appears that the serious doubts referred to in Article 6(1)(c) have been removed, particularly as a result of modifications made by the undertakings concerned, and at the latest by the time limit laid down in paragraph 3.

3.   Without prejudice to Article 8(7), decisions pursuant to Article 8(1) to (3) concerning notified concentrations shall be taken within not more than 90 working days of the date on which the proceedings are initiated. That period shall be increased to 105 working days where the undertakings concerned offer commitments pursuant to Article 8(2), second subparagraph, with a view to rendering the concentration compatible with the common market, unless these commitments have been offered less than 55 working days after the initiation of proceedings.

The periods set by the first subparagraph shall likewise be extended if the notifying parties make a request to that effect not later than 15 working days after the initiation of proceedings pursuant to Article 6(1)(c). The notifying parties may make only one such request. Likewise, at any time following the initiation of proceedings, the periods set by the first subparagraph may be extended by the Commission with the agreement of the notifying parties. The total duration of any extension or extensions effected pursuant to this subparagraph shall not exceed 20 working days.

4.   The periods set by paragraphs 1 and 3 shall exceptionally be suspended where, owing to circumstances for which one of the undertakings involved in the concentration is responsible, the Commission has had to request information by decision pursuant to Article 11 or to order an inspection by decision pursuant to Article 13.

* * *

3.   CONCURRENT JURISDICTION: THE BOEING/MCDONNELL DOUGLAS MERGER

Both the United States' Hart-Scott-Rodino Act and the EU's Merger Regulation may apply to transactions involving a foreign party, or indeed two foreign parties, so long as their respective thresholds are met. For some transactions, notifications to both jurisdictions are required, which raises the possibility of conflicting or inconsistent decisions. There are several reasons why U.S. and EU authorities might reach different conclusions regarding the same transaction. First, the transaction might have different effects within each jurisdiction, with only one of them feeling a sufficient effect to warrant action.

Second, there are differences in the substantive laws to be applied. In the United States, the Clayton Act prohibits acquisitions whose effect "may be substantially to lessen competition, or to tend to create a monopoly." The EU's original Merger Regulation focused on whether a transaction would create or strengthen a "dominant position," and although the 2004 Merger Regulation ("significantly impede effective competition in particular as a result of the creation or strengthening of a dominant position") moved the EU closer to the U.S. formulation, differences remain. Historically, the European Commission has been more likely to presume that anticompetitive effects will arise from transactions involving a party with a very high market share. The Commission has also tended to be more concerned than U.S. authorities about effects on competitors, including what are called "portfolio effects," that is, the tendency of customers to shift purchases to producers who carry a full line of products.

Third, there are procedural differences. The Merger Regulation permits third parties, including competitors, to submit comments to the Commission if they can show a sufficient interest in the outcome of the transaction. The European Commission also has authority to block a transaction by itself, subject to appeal to the General Court and the Court of Justice of the European Union. U.S. officials have no such authority. Although the parties to a transaction opposed by the Department of Justice or the FTC typically comply voluntarily, U.S. officials must seek an injunction in federal court to block a transaction if the parties do not.

Some observers feel that this has led U.S. enforcement authorities to be more careful and perhaps less political in determining whether to oppose a transaction. In recent years, the General Court (formerly the Court of First Instance) has become more active in reviewing the Commission's merger decisions. The Commission has also sought to address perceived shortcomings through the adoption of several best-practice guidelines, including the DG Competition Best Practices on the Conduct of EC Merger Control Proceedings (2004) and the DG Competition Best Practice Guidelines on Divestiture Commitments (2013).

As we shall see, full-blown conflict between U.S. and EU regulators in addressing cross-border mergers is rare. One of the best examples of the issues that can arise in international merger review remains an episode from 1997 involving the review of a proposed merger between two U.S. airplane manufacturers, Boeing and McDonnell Douglas. On July 7, 1997 the FTC approved the merger. The European Commission objected, however, and cleared the merger only after Boeing agreed to a number of important concessions. Note that the Commission's decision was made under the pre-2004 Merger Regulation.

Statement of Chairman Robert Pitofsky and Commissioners Janet D. Steiger, Roscoe B. Starek III and Christine A. Varney[23] in the Matter of The Boeing Company/McDonnell Douglas Corporation

File No. 971–0051
[July 1, 1997]

After an extensive and exhaustive investigation, the Federal Trade Commission has decided to close the investigation of The Boeing Company's proposed acquisition of McDonnell Douglas Corporation. For reasons discussed below, we have concluded that the acquisition would not substantially lessen competition or tend to create a monopoly in either defense or commercial aircraft markets.

There has been speculation in the press and elsewhere that the United States antitrust authorities might allow this transaction to go forward—particularly the portion of the transaction dealing with the manufacture of commercial aircraft—because aircraft manufacturing occurs in a global market, and the United States, in order to compete in that market, needs a single powerful firm to serve as its "national champion." A powerful United States firm is all the more important, the argument proceeds, because that firm's success contributes much to improving the United States' balance of trade and to providing jobs for U.S. workers.

The national champion argument does not explain today's decision. Our task as enforcers, conferred in clear terms by Congress in enacting the

---

[23] [Eds.] Commissioner Mary L. Azcuenaga filed a separate statement disagreeing with the FTC's decision not to pursue the matter further.

antitrust statutes, is to ensure the vitality of the free market by preventing private actions that may substantially lessen competition or tend to create a monopoly. In the Boeing-McDonnell Douglas matter, the Commission's task was to review a merger between two direct competitors.

We do not have the discretion to authorize anticompetitive but "good" mergers because they may be thought to advance the United States' trade interests. If that were thought to be a wise approach, only Congress could implement it. In any event, the "national champion" argument is almost certainly a delusion. In reality, the best way to boost the United States' exports, address concerns about the balance of trade, and create jobs is to require United States' firms to compete vigorously at home and abroad. . . .

On its face, the proposed merger appears to raise serious antitrust concerns. The transaction involves the acquisition by Boeing, a company that accounts for roughly 60% of the sales of large commercial aircraft, of a non-failing direct competitor in a market in which there is only one other significant rival, Airbus Industrie, and extremely high barriers to entry. The merger would also combine two firms in the U.S. defense industry that develop fighter aircraft and other defense products. Nevertheless, for reasons we will now discuss, we do not find that this merger will substantially lessen competition in any relevant market.

* * *

The evidence collected during the staff investigation, including the virtually unanimous testimony of forty airlines that staff interviewed, revealed that McDonnell Douglas's commercial aircraft division, Douglas Aircraft Company, can no longer exert a competitive influence in the worldwide market for commercial aircraft. Over the past several decades, McDonnell Douglas has not invested at nearly the rate of its competitors in new product lines, production facilities, company infrastructure, or research and development. As a result, Douglas Aircraft's product line is not only very limited, but lacks the state of the art technology and performance characteristics that Boeing and Airbus have developed. Moreover, Douglas Aircraft's line of aircraft do not have common features such as cockpit design or engine type, and thus cannot generate valuable efficiencies in interchangeable spare parts and pilot training that an airline may obtain from a family of aircraft, such as Boeing's 737 family or Airbus's A-320 family.

In short, the staff investigation revealed that the failure to improve the technology and efficiency of its commercial aircraft products has lead to a deterioration of Douglas Aircraft's product line to the point that the vast majority of airlines will no longer consider purchasing Douglas aircraft and that the company is no longer in a position to influence significantly the competitive dynamics of the commercial aircraft market.

Our decision not to challenge the proposed merger does not reflect a conclusion that McDonnell Douglas is a failing company or that Douglas Aircraft is a failing division. Nor does our decision not to challenge the proposed merger reflect a conclusion that Douglas Aircraft could maintain competitively significant sales, but has simply decided to redeploy or retire its assets. While McDonnell Douglas's prospects for future commercial aircraft sales are virtually non-existent, its commercial aircraft production assets are likely to remain in the market for the near future as a result of a modest backlog of aircraft orders. . . .

The merger also does not threaten competition in military programs. Though both Boeing and McDonnell Douglas develop fighter aircraft, there are no current or future procurements of fighter aircraft by the Department of Defense in which the two firms would likely compete. Finally, there are no other domestic military markets in which the products offered by the companies are substitutes for each other. The Department of Defense, in a letter to the Commission dated July 1, 1997, indicated that competition would remain in the defense industry post-merger.

While the merger seems to pose no threat to the competitive landscape in either the commercial aircraft or in various defense markets, we find the twenty year exclusive contracts Boeing recently entered with three major airlines potentially troubling. Boeing is the largest player in the global commercial aircraft market and though the contracts now foreclose only about 11% of that market, the airlines involved are prestigious. They represent a sizeable portion of airlines that can serve as "launch" customers for aircraft manufacturers, that is, airlines that can place orders large enough and have sufficient market prestige to serve as the first customer for a new airplane. We intend to monitor the potential anticompetitive effects of these, and any future, long term exclusive contracts.

Commission Decision of 30 July 1997 Declaring a Concentration Compatible with the Common Market and the Functioning of the EEA Agreement

(Case No IV/M.877—Boeing/McDonnell Douglas)

* * *

(97/816/EC)

* * *

IV. THE COMMUNITY DIMENSION

(7)   Boeing and MDC have a combined aggregate worldwide turnover in excess of ECU 5 billion (Boeing ECU 17 billion, MDC ECU 11 billion). Each of them has a Community-wide turnover in excess of ECU 250 million . . . , but they do not both achieve more than two thirds of their aggregate Community-wide turnover within one and

the same Member State. The notified operation therefore has a Community dimension.

* * *

VI. COOPERATION WITH THE US AUTHORITIES

(11) In compliance with the Agreement between the European Communities and the Government of the United States of America regarding the application of their competition laws ('the Agreement'), the European Commission and the Federal Trade Commission have carried out all necessary notifications. . . . On 1 July 1997, the Federal Trade Commission reached a majority decision not to oppose the merger.

(12) On 13 July 1997, pursuant to Articles VI and VII of the Agreement, the US Department of Defence and Department of Justice, on behalf of the US Government, informed the European Commission of concerns that: (i) a decision prohibiting the proposed merger could harm important US defence interests; (ii) despite any measures the Commission could impose on a third party purchaser, a divestiture of Douglas Aircraft Company (DAC) would be likely to be unsuccessful in preserving DAC as a stand-alone manufacturer of new aircraft, resulting in an inefficient disposition of whatever of DAC's new aircraft manufacturing operations that potentially could be salvaged by Boeing, and in the loss of employment in the United States; and (iii) any divestiture of DAC to a third party that would not operate DAC as a manufacturer of new aircraft would be anti-competitive in that it would create a firm with the incentive and means to raise price and diminish service in respect of the provision of spare parts and service to DAC's fleet-in-service, a large portion of which is owned by US airlines. The Commission took the above concerns into consideration to the extent consistent with Community law. In particular, as far as US defence interests are concerned, the Commission has in any event limited the scope of its action to the civil side of the operation since it has not established that a dominant position has been strengthened or created in the defence sector as a result of the proposed concentration.

* * *

VII. COMPETITIVE ASSESSMENT

(40) Boeing, as the company itself states in its 1995 annual report, has led the world production of commercial aeroplanes for more than three decades and has built more jet aircraft than all the other manufacturers combined. Given the typical long operating life of these products, Boeing has by far the broadest customer base which gives it a significant competitive advantage *vis-à-vis* its competitors.

(41) It is estimated that Boeing has a share of around 60% of the current worldwide fleet in service of western-built, large passenger aircraft.

The share of MDC is around 24% and that of Airbus only around 14% even more than 25 years after Airbus began operations. The remaining 2% are related to Lockheed aircraft still in operation. Lockheed has, however, no longer been active in the production of commercial aircraft since 1984. It is true that the existence of a large fleet in service is not a guarantee of the success of a supplier of commercial aircraft, particularly when a supplier offers only a limited range of aircraft types. However, where a large fleet in service is combined with a broad product range, the existing fleet in service can be a key factor which may often determine decisions of airlines on fleet planning or acquisitions. Cost savings arising from commonality benefits, such as engineering spares inventory and flight crew qualifications, are very influential in an airline's decision-making process for aircraft type selections and may frequently lead to the acquisition of a certain type of aircraft even if the price of competing products is lower. The importance of the existing fleet in service for the choice of new aircraft has been underlined by all airlines which replied to the Commission's questions on this point.

* * *

(43) Boeing has recently entered into exclusive arrangements for the supply of large commercial jet aircraft to American Airlines (American), Delta Airlines (Delta), and Continental Airlines (Continental). . . .

* * *

(45) The fact that three of the biggest airlines in the world have locked themselves into a 20-year supply agreement with a single supplier is already an indication that Boeing enjoys a dominant position in the large commercial aircraft market. . . .

* * *

(49) . . . Boeing itself effectively admits that there are massive barriers to entry to this market. Initial development and investment costs are huge (over US $10 billion to develop a new wide-body jet, according to Boeing). The production process itself is characterized by very significant learning curve effects and economies of scale and scope, which must be attained if a new entrant is to compete effectively over time. Very strict safety regulations need to be complied with at US, European and other national levels.

* * *

(53) The proposed concentration would lead to a strengthening of Boeing's dominant position in large commercial aircraft through:

— the addition of MDC's competitive potential in large commercial aircraft to Boeing's existing position in this market,

— the large increase in Boeing's overall resources and in Boeing's defence and space business which has a significant spill-over effect on Boeing's position in large commercial aircraft and makes this position even less assailable.

1. *Impact of MDC's commercial aircraft business*

(54) The immediate effect of the proposed concentration would be that:

 (a) Boeing would increase its market share in the overall market for large commercial aircraft from 64% to 70%;

 (b) by taking over the activities of MDC, Boeing would, in future, be faced with only one competitor in this market;

 (c) Boeing would increase its customer base from 60% to 84% of the current fleet in service;

 (d) Boeing would increase its capacity in commercial aircraft, particularly in terms of skilled work force;

 (e) Boeing would increase its ability to induce airlines to enter into exclusivity deals, thereby further foreclosing the market.

* * *

2. *Overall effects resulting from the defence and space business of MDC*

(72) The overall effects resulting from the take-over of MDC's defence and space business would lead to a strengthening of Boeing's dominant position through:

 (a) an increase in Boeing's overall financial resources;

 (b) an increase in Boeing's access to publicly funded R & D and intellectual property portfolio;

 (c) an increase in Boeing's bargaining power *vis-à-vis* suppliers;

 (d) opportunities for offset and 'bundling deals.'

* * *

VIII.   CONCLUSION

(113) For the reasons outlined above, the Commission has reached the conclusion that the proposed concentration would lead to the strengthening of a dominant position through which effective competition would be significantly impeded in the common market within the meaning of Article 2(3) of the Merger Regulation.

IX. REMEDIES

[In order to remove the Commission's competition concerns, Boeing undertook, among other things, to do the following: (1) to maintain DAC in a separate legal entity for 10 years; (2) not to use its privileged access to DAC's existing fleet in service to leverage its opportunities for persuading current DAC operators to purchase Boeing Aircraft; (3) not to enforce its exclusivity rights under its agreements with American, Delta, and Continental; (4) not to enter any additional exclusive agreements until 1 August 2007; (5) to grant to other commercial aircraft manufacturers non-exclusive, reasonable royalty licenses for government-funded patents that would be used in the manufacture or sale of aircraft; (6) to report annually to the Commission for 10 years on non-classified aeronautics R & D projects; and (7) not to exert undue influence on its suppliers to refuse to deal with other manufacturers or to grant preferential treatment to Boeing.]

———————————

In 2001, another merger divided U.S. and EU antitrust authorities, when General Electric's proposed acquisition of Honeywell was cleared by the U.S. Department of Justice and subsequently prohibited by the European Commission. GE was the world's largest producer of large and small jet aircraft engines. Honeywell was a leading producer of avionics products and also of engines for corporate jets. Both antitrust authorities assumed that the merged firm would engage in "bundling," offering consumers a package of complementary products at a lower price that could not be matched by competitors. But while the U.S. Department of Justice viewed this as a benefit to consumers, the European Commission concluded that it would enable GE to drive competitors from the marketplace and raise prices to consumers over the longer-term. In 2005, the Court of First Instance (today renamed the General Court) upheld the Commission's decision though it found serious flaws in the Commission's analysis.

Conflicts such as those presented in the Boeing/McDonnell Douglas and GE/Honeywell mergers—while rare—have caused U.S. and EU antitrust authorities to focus on deepening their cooperation. Since 1991, the two jurisdictions have had an Agreement Regarding the Application of Their Competition Laws,[24] to which the European Commission's Boeing decision refers. See supra p. 381. That Agreement requires U.S. and EU authorities to notify each other whenever the enforcement activities of one may affect the other, to coordinate their enforcement activities, to take into account each other's interests, and to consult with each other upon request. The Agreement was supplemented in 1998 by a further Agreement on the Application of Positive Comity Principles in the Enforcement of Their Competition Laws,[25] which permits one party to request that the other party take enforcement action against anticompetitive activities occurring in the other party's territory that adversely affect the first party. The United States and European Union also established a joint working group that issued a set of Best Practices on Cooperation in Merger Investigations, with provisions for

———————————

[24] 30 I.L.M. 1491 (1991). In 1994, the European Court of Justice ruled that this agreement had not been properly concluded, but the defect was cured the following year with a new agreement that was retroactive to the effective date of the original agreement. See European Communities—United States Competition Agreement, 34 I.L.M. 850 (1995).

[25] 37 I.L.M. 1070 (1998).

coordinating the timing of merger investigations and sharing information and analysis. In addition, they participate in multilateral fora promoting cooperation in antitrust enforcement, such as the OECD's Global Forum on Competition and the International Competition Network.

QUESTIONS

(1) Would American Kitchens and DKW be required to file notification of their deal with either U.S. or EU authorities?

(2) What seems to account for the different results reached by U.S. and EU authorities in the Boeing case? To what extent might procedural differences, differences in substantive law, and differences in where the anticompetitive effects were felt have played a role?

Additional reading: Elhauge & Geradin, Global Antitrust Law and Economics (3d ed. 2018); Joelson, An International Antitrust Primer (4th ed. 2017); Van Bael & Bellis, Competition Law of the European Community (5th ed. 2010); Gerber, Global Competition: Law, Markets and Globalization (2010). For country-by-country descriptions of takeover rules, see Rowley & Baker, International Mergers: The Antitrust Process (3d ed. looseleaf 2003–). On the issues raised by multijurisdictional merger review, see Kovacic, Transatlantic Turbulence: The Boeing-McDonnell Douglas Merger and International Competition Policy, 68 Antitrust L.J. 805 (2001); Symposium: Can We Regulate Competition Internationally? A Case Study of the Attempted GE/Honeywell Merger, 23 U. Pa. J. Int'l Econ. L. 457 (2002); Dodge, An Economic Defense of Concurrent Antitrust Jurisdiction, 38 Tex. Int'l L.J. 27 (2003); Leddy et al., Transatlantic Merger Control: The Courts and the Agencies, 43 Cornell Int'l L.J. 25 (2010).

E. EXON-FLORIO

Some foreign acquisitions of U.S. companies may have implications for national security—for instance, where the target company produces technology that is critical to the United States' defense capability. In such cases, the acquisition faces additional scrutiny. The foundation of the relevant regulatory framework is the Exon-Florio Amendment, 50 U.S.C. § 4565, to the Defense Production Act. Exon-Florio gives the President of the United States authority to suspend or prohibit any transaction that could result in foreign control of any person engaged in commerce in the United States if he finds that "there is credible evidence . . . that the foreign interest exercising control might take action that threatens to impair the national security." Id. § 4565(d). The implementing regulations, which were revised in 2008, define "control" as "the power, direct or indirect, whether or not exercised, through the ownership of a majority or a dominant minority of the total outstanding voting interest in an entity, board representation, proxy voting, a special share, contractual arrangements, formal or informal arrangements to act in concert, or other means, to determine, direct, or decide important matters affecting an entity. . . ." 31 C.F.R. § 800.204.

The President has delegated the authority to review acquisitions under Exon-Florio to an inter-agency committee called the Committee on Foreign Investment in the United States, or CFIUS, which is chaired by the Treasury Department and currently consists of nine members: the Secretaries of the Treasury, Energy, Commerce, Defense, Homeland Security, and State; the Attorney General; the U.S. Trade Representative; and the Director of the Office of Science and Technology. CFIUS receives notices of foreign acquisitions from the parties involved, after which it has 45 days to decide whether to initiate an investigation. If CFIUS decides an investigation is warranted, it has 45 days to complete the investigation and make a recommendation to the President, who then has 15 days to decide whether to block the transaction or allow it to proceed. Under the current rules, giving notice under Exon-Florio is voluntary. The parties to a transaction raising national security concerns nevertheless have an incentive to do so and gain approval, because the President can order divestiture of unapproved transactions.

When Exon-Florio was first adopted in 1988, Congress was particularly concerned about Japanese acquisitions of U.S. high-technology companies that might have made the United States dependent on foreign suppliers for such things as semiconductors. Fujitsu's proposed (though ultimately unsuccessful) takeover of Fairchild Semiconductor was cited as the sort of threat that the Amendment was designed to avoid. Exon-Florio was amended in 1992 and again in 2007 to elaborate upon the factors that the President may consider. The current list reads as follows:

(f) Factors to be considered

For purposes of this section, the President or the President's designee may, taking into account the requirements of national security, consider—

(1) domestic production needed for projected national defense requirements,

(2) the capability and capacity of domestic industries to meet national defense requirements, including the availability of human resources, products, technology, materials, and other supplies and services,

(3) the control of domestic industries and commercial activity by foreign citizens as it affects the capability and capacity of the United States to meet the requirements of national security,

(4) the potential effects of the proposed or pending transaction on sales of military goods, equipment, or technology to any country—

(A) identified by the Secretary of State—

  (i) under section 6(j) of the Export Administration Act of 1979, as a country that supports terrorism;

  (ii) under section 6(*l*) of the Export Administration Act of 1979, as a country of concern regarding missile proliferation; or

  (iii) under section 6(m) of the Export Administration Act of 1979, as a country of concern regarding the proliferation of chemical and biological weapons;

 (B) idcntificd by the Secretary of Defense as posing a potential regional military threat to the interests of the United States; or

 (C) listed under section 309(c) of the Nuclear Non-Proliferation Act of 1978 on the "Nuclear Non-Proliferation-Special Country List" (15 C.F.R. Part 778, Supplement No. 4) or any successor list;

(5) the potential effects of the proposed or pending transaction on United States international technological leadership in areas affecting United States national security;

(6) the potential national security-related effects on United States critical infrastructure, including major energy assets;

(7) the potential national security-related effects on United States critical technologies;

(8) whether the covered transaction is a foreign government-controlled transaction, as determined under subsection (b)(1)(B);

(9) as appropriate, and particularly with respect to transactions requiring an investigation under subsection (b)(1)(B), a review of the current assessment of—

 (A) the adherence of the subject country to nonproliferation control regimes, including treaties and multilateral supply guidelines, which shall draw on, but not be limited to, the annual report on "Adherence to and Compliance with Arms Control, Nonproliferation and Disarmament Agreements and Commitments" required by section 403 of the Arms Control and Disarmament Act;

 (B) the relationship of such country with the United States, specifically on its record on cooperating in counter-terrorism efforts, which shall draw on, but not be limited to, the report of the President to Congress under section 7120 of the Intelligence Reform and Terrorism Prevention Act of 2004; and

 (C) the potential for transshipment or diversion of technologies with military applications, including an analysis of national export control laws and regulations;

(10) the long-term projection of United States requirements for sources of energy and other critical resources and material; and

(11) such other factors as the President or the Committee may determine to be appropriate, generally or in connection with a specific review or investigation.

The President has used his authority to block a transaction only a handful of times. In 1990, President Bush ordered the Chinese National Aero-Technology Corporation, a company with close ties to the People's Liberation Army, to divest itself of control over MAMCO, a U.S. aircraft parts company that used technology subject to U.S. export controls. In 2012, President Obama ordered the Chinese-owned Ralls Corporation to divest itself of wind turbine companies it had acquired (without making notification to CFIUS) that planned to install Chinese-manufactured turbines within the vicinity of restricted air space at a naval training facility. He subsequently blocked the sale of AIXTRON, Inc., a U.S.-based but German-owned semiconductor manufacturer, to Grand Chip Investment GmbH, which was itself based in Germany but under Chinese ownership.

As of 2018, President Trump had likewise twice exercised his authority to block transactions. The first situation involved the proposed acquisition of Lattice Semiconductor Corp., based in Oregon, by Canyon Bridge Capital Partners, an equity fund with the backing of the Chinese government. A group of congressional representatives had expressed concern that the deal would permit China to acquire critical U.S. technology. The second involved a hostile takeover bid for Qualcomm Inc. by Broadcom Ltd., a Singapore concern. Again, the objection to the proposed transaction was one that involved China: that Broadcom might reduce research and development activities at Qualcomm, thereby diminishing U.S. capacity in the race against Chinese concerns to develop new wireless technology.[26]

More frequently, participants in transactions that implicate national security have entered into "mitigation agreements" that they negotiate with CFIUS in order to obtain approval of their transaction. Mitigation agreements have been used to restrict the access of foreign workers to sensitive technologies, for example, or in the case of communications companies to ensure compliance with U.S. law enforcement requests to conduct surveillance.

The political climate has changed considerably in recent years, and the current focus of congressional concern—as the episodes described above illustrate—is China's access to U.S. technology. In 2018, as part of the National Defense Authorization Act for Fiscal Year 2019, Congress

---

[26] See How Fear of Huawei Killed $117 Billion Broadcom Deal, Bloomberg News (Mar. 13, 2018).

enacted the Foreign Investment Risk Review Modernization Act (FIRRMA). Once this law has been fully put into effect through implementing regulations, FIRRMA will result in some significant changes to current practice. First, it significantly expands the review authority to encompass a broader range of transactions. As amended, Exon-Florio will cover not only mergers, acquisitions, and takeovers, but also real estate transactions and non-passive investment transactions that raise security concerns. It will therefore cover some transactions that do not involve a transfer of control at all—including investment transactions that would give the investor access to "material non-public technical information" of the company in question.

FIRRMA includes a provision outlining the factors that Congress wants CFIUS to consider in reviewing covered transactions:

> (1) whether a covered transaction involves a country of special concern that has a demonstrated or declared strategic goal of acquiring a type of critical technology or critical infrastructure that would affect United States leadership in areas related to national security;

> (2) the potential national security-related effects of the cumulative control of, or pattern of recent transactions involving, any one type of critical infrastructure, energy asset, critical material, or critical technology by a foreign government or foreign person;

> (3) whether any foreign person engaging in a covered transaction with a United States business has a history of complying with United States laws and regulations;

> (4) the control of United States industries and commercial activity by foreign persons as it affects the capability and capacity of the United States to meet the requirements of national security, including the availability of human resources, products, technology, materials, and other supplies and services, and in considering "the availability of human resources," should construe that term to include potential losses of such availability resulting from reductions in the employment of United States persons whose knowledge or skills are critical to national security, including the continued production in the United States of items that are likely to be acquired by the Department of Defense or other Federal departments or agencies for the advancement of the national security of the United States;

> (5) the extent to which a covered transaction is likely to expose, either directly or indirectly, personally identifiable information, genetic information, or other sensitive data of United States citizens to access by a foreign government or

foreign person that may exploit that information in a manner that threatens national security; and

(6) whether a covered transaction is likely to have the effect of exacerbating or creating new cybersecurity vulnerabilities in the United States or is likely to result in a foreign government gaining a significant new capability to engage in malicious cyber-enabled activities against the United States, including such activities designed to affect the outcome of any election for Federal office.

The Act also changes various aspects of review procedure. Most importantly, it subjects certain categories of transactions to mandatory notification. It directs CFIUS to develop regulations defining those categories, which must include acquisitions by foreign entities in which a foreign government has a "substantial interest." The Act also creates a new, expedited form of notice called a "declaration"—essentially, a short-form notification to which CFIUS must respond within 30 days, either informing the parties that they may proceed, requesting a full notice, or initiating unilateral review of the proposed transaction. Finally, it gives CFIUS the authority to levy significant fees on transaction participants, up to the lesser of $300,000 or one percent of the value of the proposed transaction.

QUESTIONS

(1) What factors would you look for in determining whether to provide notice to CFIUS of a foreign company's acquisition of stock in a U.S. corporation?

(2) Recall the restrictions on foreign ownership of U.S. broadcasters found in Section 310(b) of the Communications Act. See supra p. 330. How do they compare to Exon-Florio's approach in terms of predictability and effectiveness?

Additional reading: Graham & Marchick, US National Security and Foreign Direct Investment (2006); Moran, Three Threats: An Analytical Framework for the CFIUS Process (2009); Alvarez, Political Protectionism and United States International Investments Obligations in Conflict: The Hazards of Exon-Florio, 30 Va. J. Int'l L. 1 (1989).

F. PRIVATIZATION

Privatization is a special kind of acquisition that involves the takeover of a state-owned company. In many countries, important enterprises have been state-owned. This was, of course, true in Eastern Europe and the Soviet Union prior to the collapse of Communism. It remains true in China despite dramatic increases in foreign direct investment. In other parts of the world, waves of nationalization and privatization have often followed each other in a cycle. Mexico, for example, nationalized large sectors of the economy from 1915 to 1940, including the oil industry. This was followed by a period of partial reprivatization from 1940 to 1958, which was in turn followed by a period of renationalization from 1958 to 1983, during which the government purchased controlling interests in many companies, including power producers and the telephone company. Since 1983, Mexico has embarked on an ambitious program of privatization.[27]

The most recent wave of privatizations began in the United Kingdom in the early 1980s, after Margaret Thatcher became Prime Minister. By the mid-1990s, the British government had sold state-owned firms employing hundreds of thousands of people for more than $100 billion. Many Latin American governments initiated privatization programs in the late 1980s and early 1990s in response to the debt crisis, and many Eastern European governments did the same after the collapse of Communism. When German reunification took place in 1991, the property of the former German Democratic Republic was privatized or liquidated through an agency called the Treuhand. Other countries have also instituted privatization programs, sometimes with prodding from international institutions such as the World Bank and the IMF. In recent years China has been a leading source of privatizations—although generally in the form of transactions that reduce rather than eliminate the government's stake in its state-owned firms.

Governments may decide to privatize state-owned enterprises for many reasons, including ideology, budgetary concerns, and a desire to improve performance. Ideology was an important factor in Prime Minister Thatcher's decision to privatize state-owned companies in the United Kingdom and in Eastern Europe privatization programs, which were seen as part of those countries' rejection of Communism.

Budgetary concerns played an important role in Latin American countries attempting to recover from the debt crisis of the 1980s. Privatization may have a positive impact on a government's budget in three ways. First, the proceeds from privatization provide revenues that a government may use to cover shortfalls in its budgets or to reduce its debts. Second, if the state-owned enterprise has been losing money, as is frequently the case, privatization will end the need for subsidies and the consequent drain on public resources. Third, once the privatized company begins to show a profit, the government can expect still more revenue in the form of taxes.

Finally, there is the desire to improve the performance of the companies concerned, not just to earn tax revenue for the government, but to improve service for consumers. The privatization of telephone companies, for example, has often had among its principal goals the increase in the number of telephone lines and public telephones, reducing the wait for installation of telephone service, and reducing the time

---

[27] See Chua, The Privatization-Nationalization Cycle: The Link Between Markets and Ethnicity in Developing Countries, 95 Colum. L. Rev. 223, 228–238 (1995).

required to obtain a dial tone. In order to obtain such improvements in performance, it is often necessary to attract a foreign investor with experience in the particular industry and ready access to the capital necessary to purchase new equipment and to finance other improvements.

For the foreign investor, acquiring a state-owned company presents special difficulties. First, the transaction is liable to be more politically charged than the acquisition of a privately owned company, particularly if the company provides some basic service like telephones or electricity. The shift from public to private ownership may itself be controversial and the shift to *foreign* private ownership even more so. Second, privatizations are more likely to face opposition from employees and their representatives, who felt that their jobs at the state-owned enterprise were relatively secure and fear that privatization will mean layoffs. Third, there may be little or no existing regulatory framework to govern the privatized company, such a framework having been unnecessary when its managers were civil servants. Both the government and the foreign investor will want to be sure of how the company will be regulated after privatization—the government to ensure that the public's interests are protected; the foreign investor to ensure that it will be able to earn a sufficient return to make the investment profitable. As a consequence, the regulatory framework is often the subject of intense negotiations between the government and foreign investors during the privatization process. Fourth, a state-owned firm may have less information about its own assets and liabilities than a private firm would because there is less of an incentive to keep good accounts when earning a profit is not a priority and when the state will make up any losses that develop. Thus, there may be greater uncertainty about exactly what the foreign investor is buying, and the investor may have to accept less in the way of representations and warranties than it typically would in a private transaction. Fifth, if the state-owned enterprise had previously been nationalized, there may be issues related to the claims of its former owners and their heirs. This has been of particular concern in Eastern Europe, where some governments have allowed former owners to seek restitution of their properties while others have limited them to compensation.

To illustrate some of these difficulties, it may be useful to consider briefly the privatization of the Venezuelan telephone company, Compañía Anónima Nacional Teléfonos de Venezuela (CANTV). CANTV was privatized in two stages. In 1991, the government of Venezuela sold 40% of CANTV's capital stock to a consortium led by GTE for approximately $1.9 billion and transferred an additional 11% to a share purchase program for CANTV employees. In 1996, the government sold the remaining 49% of CANTV in an initial public offering for approximately $1 billion. Prior to the privatization, Venezuela had a low ratio of telephone lines to inhabitants, a large backlog of demand for telephone service, and a severely congested network of old and poorly maintained equipment. The first stage of the privatization was structured as a single-bid auction in which only prequalified consortia of investors were allowed to bid. In addition to the GTE consortium, a consortium led by Bell Atlantic and Bell Canada prequalified. The members of each consortium were required to sign confidentiality agreements so that they could not collude during the auction. Venezuela provided information about CANTV to the consortia in a confidential memorandum, but this information was less extensive than one would have expected in the acquisition of a private company because CANTV's internal systems were simply not capable of generating the same sort of information. Venezuela provided only limited representations and warranties regarding CANTV's debts and its pension liabilities.

The structure of the transaction was determined by both legal and political considerations. Reducing the government's ownership to less than 50% meant that CANTV would no longer be considered a public sector company and would thus be freed from certain restrictions on its operations under Venezuelan law. By remaining CANTV's biggest shareholder with 49% of its capital stock, however, the government was able to reduce political opposition to the privatization. The 11% transferred to the employees' share purchase program also helped to ensure union support for the privatization. The GTE consortium agreed to hold its 40% through a Venezuelan subsidiary VenWorld, and GTE agreed to retain at least 50% of VenWorld's voting rights and 40% of its capital stock for a period of time.

Although owning only 40% of CANTV's shares, the GTE consortium was assured of control through provisions in the Stock Purchase Agreement and CANTV's by-laws creating different classes of stock. The consortium's 40% constituted all of the Class A shares of CANTV, which were entitled to elect five of nine directors on the CANTV board. Venezuela's 49% constituted all of CANTV's Class B shares, which were entitled to elect two directors, and the employees' 11% constituted all of CANTV's Class C shares were also entitled to elect two directors. Upon transfer to third parties, each of these classes of shares automatically converted into Class D shares, thus ensuring that representation on the board of directors would not change until 2001. From 2001 forward, Venezuela was entitled to elect one director regardless of the number of shares that it owns—a provision common to privatizations that is known as a "golden share."

Both CANTV's modernization goals and the framework for its regulation were set forth in a 35-year Concession Agreement between CANTV and the Venezuelan government. Under the Agreement, CANTV was to be the exclusive provider of fixed telephone services in Venezuela until 2000. The Agreement also set forth a rate structure that allowed telephone rates to keep pace with inflation and to capture the profits earned as a result of lower operating costs. Finally, the Concession

Agreement required CANTV to install new digital lines, expand the number of public telephones, reduce the time needed to obtain a dial tone, and increase the percentage of calls completed on the first attempt.

The second stage of CANTV's privatization consisted of an initial public offering of Venezuela's remaining 49% stake in 1996, which raised approximately $1 billion. There were several reasons for the lower valuation of the company that this reflected compared with 1991. For a time, currency controls prevented CANTV from purchasing new equipment abroad, slowing its modernization program. CANTV also had substantial difficulty collecting on its bills to government agencies, which was particularly damaging in an inflationary economic environment.

In 2007, President Hugo Chavez renationalized CANTV. Verizon (successor to GTE) by then owned 28.5% of CANTV, for which Venezuela agreed to pay $572 million. While this was said to represent fair value for Verizon's stake, it was approximately 15% less than Verizon had earlier been offered by a Mexican bidder.[28] President Chavez also nationalized Venezuela's largest electricity company, Electricidad de Caracas, and pressed to renegotiate a number of oil projects with multinational companies. We shall consider these renegotiations further in Problem 7. See infra pp. 488–492.

QUESTIONS

(1) Why was an auction to prequalified investors more appropriate than an initial public offering for the first stage of CANTV's privatization?

(2) Consider the various classes of shares and their voting rights. Why was it more important for the GTE consortium to be able to elect a majority of CANTV's board of directors than to own a majority of its capital stock? Why do you suppose that Venezuela insisted on retaining a "golden share"?

Additional reading: Reality Check: The Distributional Impact of Privatization in Developing Countries (Nellis & Birdsall eds., 2005); Guislain, The Privatization Challenge: A Strategic, Legal, and Institutional Analysis of International Experience (1997); Estrin & Pelletier, Privatization in Developing Countries: What Are the Lessons of Recent Experience?, 33 World Bank Research Observer 65 (2018); Huyghebaert et al., Ownership Dynamics After Partial Privatization: Evidence From China, 54 J. L. & Econ. 389 (2011). On the privatization of Venezuela's telephone company, see Gizang & Sabater, A Case Study: The Privatization of the Venezuelan Telecommunications Industry, in Privatization: Current Issues (Brown & Ridley eds., 1994); Lavey, Making and Keeping Regulatory Promises, 55 Fed. Comm. L.J. 1 (2002). On problems with Russia's privatizations, see Black, Kraakman &

---

[28] Webb-Vidal, Verizon's Venezuela Deal Buoys Investors, Financial Times (February 13, 2007).

Tarassova, Russian Privatization and Corporate Governance: What Went Wrong?, 52 Stan. L. Rev. 1731 (2000).

PROBLEM 6

AN INTERNATIONAL JOINT VENTURE

A. INTRODUCTION

Joint ventures may be defined broadly as common projects between independent parties, usually companies, that share both the management responsibilities and the financial risks. Joint ventures fall into two basic legal categories: "equity joint ventures" in which the parties establish another corporation in which they both own interests; and "contractual joint ventures" in which the parties do not establish another corporation but simply specify their rights and obligations by contract, constituting in effect a partnership.

Sharing control can be difficult, and there seem to be two principal reasons why firms agree to do it. First, government regulation may require foreign investment to take the form of a joint venture either generally or in particular areas of the economy. Recall Mexico's Foreign Investment Act, considered in Problem 4, supra pp. 318–329, which limits foreign investment to specified percentages in such sectors as air transportation and domestic newspapers. A foreign investor who wishes to operate in one of these areas has no choice but to find a local partner.

Second, even when not required by law, two companies may choose to enter a joint venture because neither company alone has all of the ingredients necessary to make the venture succeed. Foreign investors frequently seek out local partners who are familiar with local conditions (including government regulations and the bureaucracy that administers them), local supply chains, local product markets, channels for distribution, labor conditions, and local customs. The local partner might also bring to the joint venture existing production and distribution facilities and an established reputation. The foreign partner, on the other hand, is generally expected to contribute to the joint venture its technology, management skills, financing, and perhaps access to markets for export.

In China, joint ventures were the original vehicles for encouraging foreign investment in the post-Mao era. China adopted a Law on Chinese-Foreign Equity Joint Ventures in 1979 and a Law on Chinese-Foreign Contractual Joint Ventures in 1988. Since 1990, China has also permitted Wholly Foreign-Owned Enterprises (WFOEs). With the lifting of many restrictions on foreign investment following China's 2001 accession to the WTO, WFOEs became the preferred vehicle for foreign investment in China. Still, in recent years China has approved more than 6,000 equity joint ventures annually. The dynamics of Chinese-foreign joint ventures have also shifted over time as China's economy and its enterprises have become larger and more sophisticated. Foreign enterprises are feeling greater pressure to establish footholds in China, while China has less need for foreign capital and management expertise than it once did. The general tendency of these trends has been to increase the leverage of the Chinese party in a joint venture.

A number of issues tend to be of particular importance in negotiating joint ventures. The first is control. Will the foreign and the local partner each own 50% of an equity joint venture, for example, or will there be a majority and a minority partner? If there is to be a minority partner, will its interests be protected by requiring a supermajority or unanimity for certain decisions? How will responsibilities be divided between the board of directors and the joint venture's managers, and how will the latter be selected? A second important issue is technology transfer. What technologies will the foreign partner license to the joint venture? How will their use be restricted to protect the foreign partner's intellectual property rights? Who will own new technologies or improvements developed by the joint venture? A third is valuation. Assuming that the parties bring assets other than cash to the joint venture—intellectual property rights or an existing distribution network, for example—how is each party's contribution to be valued? A fourth is dispute resolution. Differences may be expected to develop over the life of the joint venture, and if these differences cannot be resolved through negotiation, should they be submitted to arbitration or taken to court? And a fifth is exit, that is, how a party may leave the joint venture. May it sell its interest to a third party? If so, should the other partner be given a right of first refusal? May the joint venture continue to use technology from the foreign partner after it leaves the joint venture?

From a tax perspective, a joint venture may generally elect to be treated either as a corporation or as a partnership under the IRS's check-the-box regulations, so long as the joint venture does not take a form the IRS considers a *per se* corporation.[1] In Europe, the German *Aktiengesellschaft*, the French *Société Anonyme*, and the Spanish *Sociedad Anónima* are *per se* corporations; in China, the joint stock company or *Gufen Youxian Gongsi* is. In the past, to encourage foreign investment, China provided tax incentives to foreign-invested enterprises, including joint ventures and wholly foreign-owned enterprises. Since 2008, however, China has unified its tax treatment of foreign and domestic enterprises, both of which are now taxed at a basic rate of 25%. Tax breaks are still available for foreign investment in certain encouraged industries and in the central and western regions of China.

Section B sets forth a sample contract for an equity joint venture in the People's Republic of China. As you read it, consider how each of the

---

[1]   See 26 C.F.R. §§ 301.7701–1, –2, and –3.

issues mentioned above is treated. Section C discusses the legal framework for foreign investment in China, and for equity joint ventures in particular. Section D considers some of the tensions that may be expected to arise over the life of a joint venture and some methods for resolving disputes. And Section E discusses some of the problems that joint ventures raise under antitrust law in various jurisdictions.

B. A U.S.-CHINESE JOINT VENTURE CONTRACT

The establishment of a joint venture typically proceeds through several steps. The first, and probably the most important, is the identification of an appropriate joint venture partner. For the foreign party, this means finding a local partner that can bring to the joint venture those things that the foreign party lacks, such as good working relationships with the local bureaucracy, a local supply chain, experience in local markets, and perhaps established production facilities or distribution networks. After preliminary negotiations, the parties may then sign a non-binding letter of intent or memorandum of understanding.[2] The parties must reserve a name for the joint venture with the local Administration of Industry and Commerce (AIC).

In China, the next step in establishing an equity joint venture is to prepare a preliminary feasibility study, which is one of the documents the parties will submit when registering the joint venture with the AIC. For the foreign party, the feasibility study offers an opportunity to perform further due diligence on its Chinese partner.

The parties will then negotiate a "joint venture agreement," which sets forth the main points of their agreement, and a more detailed "joint venture contract," which sets forth their rights and obligations, although the parties may agree to dispense with the former and simply conclude a joint venture contract.

Prior to 2016, foreign-invested entities—including joint ventures—were required to obtain approval from China's Ministry of Commerce (MOFCOM) before registering with the AIC. Since October 1, 2016, however, foreign-invested entities need only register online with MOFCOM unless they operate in an industry on the so-called "negative list." Foreign-invested entities in industries on the negative list, found in MOFCOM's Catalogue of Industries for Guiding Foreign Investment, still require MOFCOM approval.

After registering with MOFCOM, the parties must then register with the local AIC in order to receive a business license and commence operations. As a focus for discussion, consider the following sample joint venture contract. Note that this is a very simple joint venture contract

---

[2] On negotiating in China, see Graham & Lam, The Chinese Negotiation, in Harvard Business Review on Doing Business in China (2004).

and that many such contracts will be significantly longer and more complex.

Joint Venture Contract

Adhering to the principles of equality and mutual benefit, the parties hereby agree as follows:

1. *Parties.*

The parties to this contract (hereinafter "the Parties") are: American Hair Products, Inc. (hereinafter "American"), a corporation organized under the laws of the State of Delaware, United States of America, with its legal address at 500 Spring Street, Los Angeles, California, United States of America, and People's Manufacturing Corporation (hereinafter "People's"), a corporation organized under the laws of the People's Republic of China, with its legal address at 75 Nanjing Road, Tianjin, People's Republic of China.

2. *Establishment of the Joint Venture.*

In accordance with the Law of the People's Republic of China on Sino-Foreign Equity Joint Ventures and other applicable Chinese laws and regulations, the Parties agree to establish a joint venture to be known as Double Happiness Hair Products Corporation (hereinafter "the Joint Venture"), with its legal address at 75 Nanjing Road, Tianjin, People's Republic of China.

3. *Form of the Joint Venture.*

The Joint Venture shall be organized as a limited liability company governed by the laws of the People's Republic of China. The liability of the Parties shall be limited to the amounts of their respective capital contributions. The profits and losses of the Joint Venture shall be shared by the Parties in proportion to their contributions to the registered capital of the Joint Venture.

4. *Purpose of the Joint Venture.*

The purpose of the Joint Venture is to combine the knowledge and experience of the Parties into a jointly managed organization to increase the variety of hair care products and to raise their quality.

5. *Scope of the Joint Venture*

The scope of the Joint Venture is to engage in the manufacture, sourcing, production, marketing, and sale of hair care products.

6. *Total Investment.*

The Parties' total investment in the Joint Venture shall be RMB 200 million (*i.e.* U.S.$30 million), which shall consist of the Parties' contributions to the registered capital of the Joint Venture and loans from the Parties to the Joint Venture.

7. *Registered Capital.*

The registered capital of the Joint Venture shall be RMB 100 million (*i.e.* U.S.$15 million), of which American shall contribute RMB 60 million (*i.e.* U.S.$9 million) and People's shall contribute RMB 40 million (*i.e.* U.S.$6 million). American's contribution to the registered capital shall be in U.S. Dollars, industrial property rights, and proprietary technology. People's contribution to the registered capital shall be in Chinese Renminbi.

8. *Responsibilities of the Parties.*

(1) American shall have the following responsibilities:

(a) procuring for the Joint Venture all necessary machinery, equipment, and raw materials from abroad;

(b) installing and testing the machinery and equipment for the Joint Venture;

(c) training the personnel of the Joint Venture; and

(d) such other responsibilities as the Joint Venture may entrust to it.

(2) People's shall have the following responsibilities:

(a) registering the Joint Venture and obtaining a business license from the relevant authorities in the People's Republic of China;

(b) contracting for the provision of electricity, water, telephone service, etc. for the Joint Venture;

(c) facilitating customs procedures for machinery, equipment, and raw materials imported from abroad;

(d) procuring machinery, equipment, and raw materials within the People's Republic of China;

(e) recruiting local personnel;

(f) assisting foreign personnel in applying for entry visas and in complying with other legal requirements of the People's Republic of China;

(g) marketing and distributing the products of the Joint Venture in the People's Republic of China; and

(h) such other responsibilities as the Joint Venture may entrust to it.

9. *Technology Transfer.*

American shall transfer to the Joint Venture advanced technology suited to the production of hair care products in the People's Republic of China, including industrial property rights and proprietary technology, as provided in the Technology Transfer Agreement between American and the Joint Venture attached as Annex A to this Contract.

American's transfer of technology to the Joint Venture shall be valued at RMB 15 million (*i.e.* U.S.$2.25 million) for the purposes of American's contribution to the registered capital of the Joint Venture.

The Joint Venture and its personnel shall safeguard the confidentiality of American's technology. American shall license to the Joint Venture any improvements it makes in the technology. The Joint Venture shall license to American any improvements it makes in the technology.

10. *Trademarks.*

Trademarks for the Joint Venture shall be registered in the People's Republic of China and in relevant markets abroad and shall be the property of the Joint Venture.

11. *Board of Directors.*

The Joint Venture's board of directors shall be composed of five directors, of which American shall elect three and People's shall elect two. Each director shall serve for a renewable term of three years. American shall appoint the chairman of the board, who shall act as the legal representative of the Joint Venture. People's shall appoint the vice-chairman of the board.

The board of directors shall decide all matters by majority vote, except for the following, which shall require unanimous approval:

(a) amendment of the Joint Venture's articles of association;

(b) termination or dissolution of the Joint Venture;

(c) increase or assignment of the registered capital of the Joint Venture;

(d) merger of the Joint Venture with another economic organization.

12. *Meetings.*

The board of directors shall meet at least once a year. Directors may participate in meetings of the board by conference call and any director may authorize any other director to act for him by proxy. Four directors shall constitute a quorum.

13. *Board of Supervisors*

The Joint Venture's board of supervisors shall be composed of three supervisors, one appointed by each of the Parties and one democratically elected by the employees. Each supervisor shall serve for a renewable term of three years. The board of supervisors shall have the powers: to examine the Joint Venture's financial affairs; to supervise the directors' and managers' execution of their duties; to institute proceedings against directors and managers in a people's court for violations of laws, administrative regulations, or the Joint Venture's articles of association; and other powers specified in the Company Law of the People's Republic of China.

14. *Management.*

The Joint Venture shall have a general manager recommended by American and a deputy general manager recommended by People's. The general manager and the deputy general manager shall be appointed by the board of directors, which shall also have the power to dismiss them without cause. The general manager shall carry out the various resolutions of the board of directors and shall organize and lead the daily operational and managerial work of the Joint Venture. The deputy general manager shall assist the general manager.

15. *Labor Management.*

Labor contracts covering employment, recruitment, dismissal and resignation of staff and workers of the Joint Venture, and their salaries, welfare benefits, labor insurance, labor protection, and labor discipline shall conform to the applicable labor laws and regulations of the People's Republic of China. The Joint Venture shall enter into labor contracts with every employee.

16. *Accounting.*

The fiscal year of the joint venture shall run from January 1 to December 31. The Joint Venture's accounts shall be kept in accordance with Chinese Accounting Standards and shall be written in both Chinese and English. The Joint Venture shall submit quarterly and annual financial reports to each of the Parties.

17. *Tax*

The Joint Venture shall pay all taxes applicable to it under the laws of the People's Republic of China.

The employees of the Joint Venture shall pay all taxes applicable to them under the Law of the People's Republic of China on Individual Income Tax and other applicable laws, and the Joint Venture shall withhold and pay such taxes.

18. *Breach of Contract.*

In the event that one Party materially breaches this Contract, and such breach is not remedied within seven days following the receipt of written notice from the other Party, the Party that is not in breach of this Contract may elect to continue to operate the Joint Venture or to dissolve it pursuant to Paragraph 22. A Party that breaches this Contract shall be liable for any losses to the Joint Venture caused by its breach.

19. *Force Majeure.*

A Party shall not be liable for any failure to perform its obligations under this Contract caused by *force majeure*, such as earthquake, flood, fire, war, civil disturbance, or governmental regulation, provided that the Party failing to perform notifies the other Party of the *force majeure* without delay. In the event that the *force majeure* causes heavy losses to the Joint Venture, the Parties shall decide, through consultations, whether to continue the Joint Venture or to dissolve it pursuant to Paragraph 22.

20. *Term.*

The term of the Joint Venture shall be 10 years from the date on which its business license is issued. The term of the Joint Venture may be extended if mutually agreed by both Parties.

21. *Transfer of Equity.*

Each Party may transfer all or part of its investment in the Joint Venture to a third party only with the consent of the other Party.

A Party (hereinafter "Transferor") that wishes to transfer all or part of its investment to a third party must give the other Party (hereinafter "Nontransferor") a right of first refusal. Notice to the Nontransferor shall be in writing and shall state the name of the third party, the purchasing price, and the other material terms. The Nontransferor shall have thirty (30) days to exercise the right of first refusal. If the Nontransferor does not exercise the right of first refusal within thirty (30) days, the Transferor shall be entitled to make the transfer to the third party.

22. *Dissolution and Liquidation.*

The Joint Venture may be dissolved in the following situations:

(a) expiration of the term of the Joint Venture, unless the Parties mutually agree to extend such term pursuant to Paragraph 20;

(b) inability to continue operations because of heavy losses;

(c) inability to continue operations because of breach of this Contract by one of the Parties;

(d) inability to continue operations because of *force majeure* as defined in Paragraph 19;

(e) inability to obtain the desired objectives of the Joint Venture.

In the event of an inability to continue operations because of a breach of this Contract by one of the Parties, the other Party shall make an application for dissolution to the relevant authorities of the People's Republic of China. In all other situations, the board of directors shall make such application.

The board of directors shall form the liquidation committee of the Joint Venture and shall use its best efforts to sell all of the assets and pay all of the liabilities of the Joint Venture. Any remaining property shall be distributed to the Parties in proportion to their investments in the Joint Venture.

23. *Applicable Law.*

The formation of this Contract, its validity, interpretation, execution, and the settlement of disputes arising under it shall be governed by the laws of the People's Republic of China.

24. *Settlement of Disputes.*

Any dispute arising from or in connection with this Contract shall, if possible, be settled through friendly consultation or mediation. Any dispute that cannot be settled through consultation or mediation shall be submitted to the Tianjin International Economic and Financial Arbitration Center of the China International Economic and Trade Arbitration Commission (CIETAC) for arbitration in Tianjin, People's Republic of China, which shall be conducted in accordance with the CIETAC arbitration rules in effect at the time of applying for arbitration. The arbitral award shall be final and binding upon both parties.

25. *Language.*

This Contract shall be written in both Chinese and English, with both versions being equally authentic. In the event of any discrepancy between the two versions, the Chinese version shall prevail.

26. *Execution.*

This Contract is signed at Tianjin, People's Republic of China by the authorized representatives of American and People's on the _____ day of _____ 20__.

_____

on behalf of American Hair Products, Inc.

_____

on behalf of People's Manufacturing Corporation

QUESTIONS

(1) Review the responsibilities of the parties set forth in Paragraph 8. Do they provide an indication of what each party expects the other to bring to the joint venture?

(2) In-kind contributions to registered capital must be valued by a Chinese appraisal organization and approved by the relevant government authorities. If these valuations differ from those of the parties, it may affect the parties' respective contributions to registered capital and thus their rights to share in the profits of the joint venture. Does the contract adequately provide for this possibility?

(3) If American Hair Products is concerned about its ability to control the day-to-day operations of the joint venture, which of the following should be most important to it: (a) the ability to elect a majority of the joint venture's directors; (b) the ability to appoint the chairperson of the board; or (c) the ability to appoint the joint venture's general manager?

(4) In what ways does the Joint Venture Contract protect the interests of the minority partner? Do those protections seem adequate? Do they seem excessive?

(5) Some issues related to the transfer of American's patents and know-how are dealt with in Paragraph 9. As counsel for American, would you be satisfied with the ways in which they are handled? What further provisions would you want to include in the Technology Transfer Agreement to protect American's interests? Should American consider licensing its technology to the joint venture rather than transferring it as a contribution to registered capital?

(6) If American becomes disenchanted with its partner's performance, what options would it have under the Joint Venture Contract?

Additional reading: Prescott & Swartz, Joint Ventures in the International Arena (2d ed. 2010); Wolf, The Complete Guide to International Joint Ventures with Sample Clauses and Contracts (3d ed. 2011).

C. CHINESE REGULATION OF FOREIGN INVESTMENT

Foreign investment projects in China are classified based upon the relevant industry into four categories: encouraged, permitted, restricted, and prohibited. The State Development and Reform Commission (SDRC) and MOFCOM publish a Catalogue for the Guidance of Foreign Investment Industries, which lists industries in the encouraged, restricted, and prohibited categories.[3] Industries not listed in one of these three categories (like the manufacture of hair care products) fall in the permitted category.

Chinese law permits foreign investment to take a variety of forms. A foreign company may engage in limited activities without creating a separate legal entity by establishing a representative office to facilitate contacts with businesses in China. As noted above, foreign companies are also allowed to establish wholly-owned subsidiaries known as wholly foreign-owned enterprises or WFOEs, which have become the preferred form of foreign investment in China since 2001.

However, a substantial amount of foreign investment in China still takes the form of joint ventures. In some industries, like exploration for oil and gas, Chinese law requires this. Even when it is not required, many foreign investors have thought it useful to have a Chinese partner with existing manufacturing facilities, access to local supply chains and distribution networks, and familiarity with the local bureaucracy. Chinese law permits both contractual joint ventures and equity joint

---

[3] An English translation of the Catalogue may be found at http://www.fdi.gov.cn/180000 0121_39_4851_0_7.html. In 2018 China further liberalized its investment restrictions, for example by planning to phase out equity restrictions in the area of automobile manufacturing. See Special Administrative Measures on Access to Foreign Investment 2018.

ventures. Although contractual joint ventures are more flexible (not requiring the joint venture partners, for example, to share profits in proportion to their capital contributions), equity joint ventures have been perceived as more predictable and outnumber contractual joint ventures by more than ten to one.

The text of China's Equity Joint Venture Law follows, along with excerpts from its implementing regulations. You will note that the sample joint venture contract has been tailored to conform with the law and regulations.

Law on Sino-Foreign Equity Joint Ventures[4]

Adopted July 1, 1979
Amended April 4, 1990 and March 15, 2001

Article 1. In order to expand international economic cooperation and technological exchange, the People's Republic of China shall permit foreign companies, enterprises and other economic entities or individuals (hereinafter referred to as foreign partners) to establish, within the territory of the People's Republic of China, equity joint ventures with Chinese companies, enterprises or other economic entities (hereinafter referred to as Chinese partners), in accordance with the principles of equality and mutual benefit that are subjected to the approval by the Chinese government.

Article 2. The Chinese government, pursuant to the provisions of agreements, contracts and articles of association which it has approved, shall protect foreign partners' investment in equity joint ventures, profits due to them and their other legal rights and interests in accordance with the law.

All activities of an equity joint venture shall be governed by the laws and regulations of the People's Republic of China.

The State shall not subject equity joint ventures to nationalization or expropriation. In special circumstances, however, in order to meet public interest requirements, the State may expropriate an equity joint venture in accordance with the legal procedures, but certain compensation must be paid.

Article 3. Equity joint venture agreements, contracts and articles of association to which the various parties to an equity joint venture are signatories shall be submitted to the state department in charge of foreign economics and trade (hereinafter referred to as an examining and approval authority) for examination and approval. An examining and approval authority shall decide whether or not to grant the approval within three months. Once approved, an equity joint venture shall

---

[4] http://english.mofcom.gov.cn/aarticle/lawsdata/chineselaw/200301/20030100062855.html.

register with a state administration for industry and commerce and commence its operations after obtaining a business license.

Article 4. An equity joint venture shall take the form of a limited liability company.

The proportion of investment contributed by a foreign partner as its share of the registered capital of an equity joint venture shall in general be no less than 25 per cent.

Equity joint venture partners shall share profits and bear risks and losses in proportion to their contribution to the registered capital of an equity joint venture.

The transfer of one party's share of the registered capital shall be effected only with the consent of the other parties to the equity joint venture.

Article 5. Each party to an equity joint venture may contribute cash, capital goods, industrial property rights, etc., as its investment in the enterprise.

Technology and equipment contributed as investment by a foreign partner must genuinely be an advanced technology and equipment appropriate to China's needs. If losses occur due to deception resulting from the intentional supply of outdated technology or equipment, compensation shall be paid.

The investment contribution of a Chinese partner may include providing site-use rights for an equity joint venture during its period of operations. If the site-use rights are not part of the Chinese partner's investment contribution, the equity joint venture shall be required to pay site-use fees to the Chinese government.

The various items of investment mentioned above shall be specified in the equity joint venture contract and articles of association. The value of each item (excluding the site) shall be determined by the equity joint venture partners through joint assessment.

Article 6. An equity joint venture shall establish a board of directors composed of a certain number of members determined through consultation by the equity joint venture partners and stipulated in the equity joint venture contract and articles of association. Each equity joint venture partner shall be responsible for the appointment and replacement of its own directors. The chairperson and deputy chairperson shall be selected by the equity joint venture partners through consultation or shall be elected by the board or directors. Where the chairperson is appointed from one party to an equity joint venture, the deputy chairperson shall be appointed from the other party. The board of directors, in accordance with the principles of equality and mutual benefit, shall decide all the important matters of an equity joint venture.

A board of directors is empowered to discuss and take action on, pursuant to the provisions of the articles of association of the equity joint venture, all the important issues concerning the enterprise, namely, enterprise development plans, production and operational projects, its income and expenditure budget, profit distribution, labor and wage plans, suspension of operations; as well as the appointment or hiring of general manager, deputy general manager, chief engineer, the chief accountant and auditor, and determining their functions and powers, remuneration, etc.

The general and deputy general managers (or general and deputy factory heads) shall be appointed separately by each of the joint venture partners.

Matters such as the recruitment, dismissal, remuneration, welfare benefits, labor protection and labor insurance of employees of an equity joint venture shall be stipulated in contracts concluded in accordance with the law.

Article 7. Employees of an equity joint venture may establish a trade union organization according to the law for the promotion of trade union activities and the protection of the legal rights and interests of employees.

An equity joint venture shall provide its enterprise trade union with the necessary facilities for its activities.

Article 8. After payment of equity joint venture income tax on an enterprise's gross profits, pursuant to the tax laws of the People's Republic of China, and after deductions therefrom as stipulated in its articles of association regarding reserve funds, employee bonus and welfare funds and enterprise development funds, the net profit of an equity joint venture shall be distributed between the equity joint venture partners in proportion to their investment contribution to the enterprise's registered capital.

An equity joint venture may enjoy preferential treatment in the form of tax reductions or exemptions in accordance with the provisions of the relevant state tax laws and administrative regulations.

A foreign partner that reinvests its share of an equity joint venture's net profit within the Chinese territory may apply for a rebate on that portion of income tax already paid.

Article 9. An equity joint venture shall present its business license to a bank or other financial institution authorized by a state exchange control organ to engage in foreign exchange dealings and shall open a foreign exchange account.

An equity joint venture shall conduct its foreign exchange transactions in accordance with the Regulations of the People's Republic of China for Foreign Exchange Control.

An equity joint venture may, in its business operations, obtain funds directly from foreign banks.

The various items of insurance required by an equity joint venture shall be furnished by insurance companies within the Chinese territory.

Article 10. An equity joint venture, within its approved scope of operations and in accordance with the principles of fairness and reasonableness, may purchase raw materials, fuels, and other such materials from both domestic and international markets.

An equity joint venture shall be encouraged to sell its products outside China. It may sell its export products on foreign markets through its own direct channels or its associated agencies or through China's foreign trade establishments. Its products may also be sold on the domestic Chinese market.

If deemed necessary, an equity joint venture may establish branch organizations outside China.

Article 11. Net profit received by a foreign partner after executing obligations prescribed by the relevant laws, agreements and contracts, funds received on the termination or suspension of an equity joint venture's operations and other relevant funds may be remitted abroad in accordance with the exchange control regulations and in the currency specified in the equity joint venture contract.

A foreign partner shall be encouraged to deposit in the Bank of China foreign exchange that it is entitled to remit abroad.

Article 12. Wage income and other legitimate income earned by equity joint venture employees of foreign nationality may be remitted abroad in accordance with the exchange control regulations after payment of individual income tax pursuant to tax laws of the People's Republic of China.

Article 13. The duration of an equity joint venture's term of operations may differ, depending on the line of business and other differing circumstances. The term of operations of some types of equity joint ventures shall be set, while the term of operations of other types of equity joint ventures may be set in some cases, but not set in others. In the case of an equity joint venture which has its term of operations set, the term may be extended subject to the agreement of all equity joint venture partners and the lodging of an application with the examining and approval authority six months before the expiry of the joint venture term. The examining and approval authority shall decide whether to approve or reject an application within one month of its receipt.

Article 14. In the event of an equity joint venture incurring heavy losses, one party failing to execute its obligations as prescribed in the equity joint venture contract or articles of association, or force majeure, etc., the contract may be terminated subject to the negotiation and agreement reached by all parties of an equity joint venture, the approval of the examining and approval authority and registration with a state administration for industry and commerce. If a loss is incurred due to a breach of contract, the party that violated the contract provision shall bear the financial liability for the loss.

Article 15. Any dispute arising between equity joint venture partners that the board of directors is unable to settle through consultation may be resolved through conciliation or arbitration by a Chinese arbitral body or through arbitration conducted by an arbitral body agreed on by all parties of an equity joint venture.

If the parties of an equity joint venture have not stipulated an arbitration clause in their contract or do not reach a written arbitration agreement after a dispute has arisen, they may file a lawsuit in a people's court.

Article 16. This Law shall take effect from the date of its promulgation.

As is true in most legal systems, a statute will often be elaborated by administrative regulations and interpretations. The Equity Joint Venture Regulations[5] deal in greater detail with a number of key issues. To protect the rights of the minority partner, for example, Article 33 requires unanimous board approval to amend the joint venture's articles of association, terminate the joint venture, increase or reduce its registered capital, or engage in a merger or division. Article 43 regulates the technology transfer agreement as follows:

Article 43. The technology transfer agreements signed by a joint venture shall be submitted for approval to the examination and approval authority.

Technology transfer agreements shall comply with the following stipulations:

(1) the fees for use of technology shall be fair and reasonable;

(2) unless otherwise agreed upon by both parties, the technology exporting party shall not put any restrictions upon the quantity, price or region of sale of the products that are to be exported by the technology importing party;

(3) the term for a technology transfer agreement is generally no longer than ten years;

(4) after the expiry of a technology transfer agreement, the technology importing party shall have the right to use the technology continuously;

---

[5]   english.mofcom.gov.cn/aarticle/lawsdata/chineselaw/200301/20030100064563.html.

    (5)   conditions for mutual exchange of information on the improvement of technology by both parties of the technology agreement shall be reciprocal;

    (6)   the technology importing party shall have the right to buy the equipment, parts and raw materials needed from sources they deem suitable;

    (7)   no unreasonably restrictive clauses prohibited by the Chinese law and regulations shall be included.

Note that some of these stipulations apply to the licensing of technology, others to the transfer of ownership of technology, and others to both.

    The Equity Joint Venture Law and Regulations are supplemented by other guidance, which can take a bewildering variety of forms, including circulars, notices, opinions, and interpretations. For example, the right of first refusal found in Paragraph 21 of the Joint Venture Contract, supra p. 404, was drafted to take advantage of guidance provided by the Supreme People's Court. Article 11 of the Provisions of the Supreme People's Court on Several Issues Concerning the Trial of Disputes Involving Foreign-Funded Enterprises, issued in 2010, states:

    Article 11. A shareholder of either party to a foreign-funded enterprise shall obtain the unanimous consent of all its shareholders when transferring all or some of its equity to a third party other than the existing shareholders, and if any shareholder pleads for revocation of the contract on equity transfer on the ground that it has not agreed to the transfer, it shall be upheld by the people's court unless:

    (1)   there is evidence to prove that the shareholder has agreed upon the transfer;

    (2)   the transferor has sent a written notice on the equity transfer issues, and the shareholder has failed to respond within 30 days upon receipt of the written notice; or

    (3)   the shareholder neither agrees to the transfer nor purchases the transferred equity.

QUESTIONS

    (1) Foreign investment laws often establish a limitation on the maximum amount of equity a foreign investor may own. See, e.g., Mexico's Foreign Investment Act of 1993, supra pp. 318–329. Article 4 of China's Equity Joint Venture Law, by contrast, establishes a minimum percentage contribution to the registered capital of a joint venture. What might have motivated such a requirement?

    (2) How do the Equity Joint Venture Regulations' provisions on technology transfer compare to those of the Andean Community and the

European Union studied in Problem 3? See supra pp. 269–271, 280–282. Do any of these provisions seem to be of particular concern?

Additional reading: Chow, The Legal System of the People's Republic of China in a Nutshell (3d ed. 2015); Zimmerman, China Law Deskbook (4th ed. 2014); Cao, Corporate Income Tax Law and Practice in the People's Republic of China (2011); China Law Blog, www.chinalaw blog.com.

D. RESOLVING DIFFERENCES

Differences will inevitably arise during the life of a joint venture. It may be possible to anticipate areas in which tensions are likely and to draft the joint venture contract to deal with some of them. At a minimum, the parties will need to give careful thought to the dispute resolution provisions of their agreement.

1. TENSIONS IN THE JOINT VENTURE RELATIONSHIP

Although the partners to a joint venture will obviously have some interests in common, they will just as obviously have some that are not. The Chinese saying "same bed, different dreams" (同床异梦) nicely captures the situation in which joint venture partners may find themselves. One can predict in a general way how differences and tensions are going to develop over the life of a joint venture:

Technology

Characteristically the local partner will want the most advanced technology for the joint venture. The foreign partner, on the other hand, may be content to use technology that might be regarded as outmoded back home but seems adequate for local circumstances. The foreign partner may wish to place restrictions on the use of its technology to safeguard its intellectual property rights. The local partner may resist these restrictions or simply ignore them, using the technology to improve its own products, which then compete with the joint venture's. The local partner may also come to resent the continuing payment of royalties to the foreign partner once the technology has been learned and has come to seem obvious. There is also the question of who owns improvements made by the joint venture; the local partner will tend to see these as the property of the joint venture, while the foreign partner will tend to see them as part of its own technology.

Procurement

Each joint venture partner may have preferences about the firms from which goods and services are purchased. In many less developed countries there is a tendency for companies to make purchases from related or "friendly" firms, which the foreign partner may view with suspicion. On the other hand, if the joint venture purchases materials from the foreign partner, the foreign partner may resist any attempt by the joint venture to redirect those purchases even if other sources of supply become cheaper.

Personnel

The foreign partner will be skeptical of the presence of family members and friends in the management of the joint venture, something that may seem quite natural to the local partner. (Whom can one trust if not one's cousin?) The foreign partner may also be troubled to find that the local personnel it has trained are often transferred to the local partner's own operation. The local partner, on the other hand, may resent the rotation of managers from the foreign partner, who bring with them a certain arrogance and seem to leave just when they have started to understand something about local conditions.

Expansion

The local partner—sometimes under local government pressure—may wish to export to foreign markets. This may trouble the foreign partner, which may be supplying those markets either through its own manufacturing or through licensees. The roles may be reversed as to local markets, with the foreign partner wishing to expand into other product lines and the local partner being constrained by ties of family, school, or guild from entering into competition with other local firms. Expansion may also require additional infusions of capital, which the local partner may have more difficulty providing.

Dividends and Investment Policy

In the typical case, the local partner will want a higher percentage of the joint venture's profits paid out as dividends while the foreign partner may prefer to reinvest the profits in the joint venture. The greater size of the foreign partner may give it a longer profit horizon, and it may see advantages in deferring the payment of its home country's taxes (although recent changes to U.S. tax law have largely removed these advantages, see supra p. 315). The local partner may feel pressure from its government to show a return more quickly. On the other hand, in a country with considerable political tensions the roles may reverse. The foreign partner will see opportunities at home or in third countries that promise as good a rate of return with less risk, while the local partner will be under pressure from the government not to let funds go abroad and will be inured to local risks.

Compliance with Law

The foreign partner may think that complying with all legal requirements in the host country will take too long or be too expensive. It may believe that the local partner's relationship with certain government officials will provide sufficient protection. The local partner may sometimes encourage the foreign partner in this belief. Government officials, however, may be promoted, transferred, or even prosecuted for corruption. Moreover, illegality in some aspect of a joint venture may be exploited by the local party or by the local government to gain further concessions from the foreign party.

Culture

Managers from different companies and from different countries often have different ways of doing things. Cultural differences may be magnified in a relationship in which one party is expected to provide the technology and management expertise. There is a tendency for foreign managers to view their local partners as lazy and resistant to change and for local managers to view their foreign counterparts as arrogant and condescending. Such attitudes can obviously create friction in day-to-day working relationships.

The unraveling of the Danone-Wahaha joint venture between 2007 and 2009 illustrates a number of problems that joint ventures may encounter in the People's Republic of China. Founded in 1996, this joint venture grew to be China's largest bottled water and beverage company, with 15% of the Chinese market. Once considered a joint-venture showcase, it now stands as a prime example of mistakes to be avoided.

The Chinese partner in the joint venture was Hangzhou Wahaha Group, originally a state-owned enterprise owned by the Hangzhou city government. Hangzhou Wahaha Group's founder Zong Qinghou built the Wahaha trademark into a valuable brand by selling nutritional drinks for children. (In Chinese, "Wahaha" sounds like a baby laughing.) The foreign joint venture partners were the French company Danone Group and a Hong Kong corporation, Bai Fu Qin. Danone and Bai Fu Qin did not invest in the joint venture directly but rather through a Singapore corporation, Jin Jia Investment. Hangzhou Wahaha Group's sole contribution to the joint venture was the Wahaha trademark, valued at US$13.2 million, while Jin Jia contributed US$66.1 million in cash.

Some of the joint venture's problems grew from issues regarding control. At the outset, Hangzhou Wahaha Group owned 49% of the joint venture's shares and Jin Jia owned 51%. Danone and Bai Fu Qin each owned 50% of Jin Jia and thus each owned 25.5% of the joint venture. Although the Chinese partner owned less than 50% of the joint venture's shares, it saw itself as the majority partner. But in 1998 Danone bought out Bai Fu Qin, becoming the 51% owner of the joint venture and causing resentment on the part of its Chinese partner.

Changing the ownership structure, however, did not change control of the joint venture on the ground. From the start, the joint venture was managed entirely by Hangzhou Wahaha Group and its chairman Zong. Danone's prior lack of success in the Chinese market may have led it to take a hands-off approach, but as a result the joint venture's management and employees developed loyalties to the Chinese joint venture partner and Zong. As events would show, Danone lacked even a basic ability to monitor the joint venture's activities.

Other problems arose from the failure to follow legal formalities. In 1996 China's Trademark Office rejected transfer of the Wahaha trademark from the Chinese partner to the joint venture on the ground that the trademark belonged to state, although Hangzhou Wahaha Group had become a private company after formation of the joint venture. Rather than appeal this decision, the parties decided to work around it by entering an exclusive license agreement for the trademark in 1999. The full license agreement was to run for 50 years, but to obtain government approval the parties registered only an abbreviated version, representing the agreement as a non-exclusive 10-year license. This put Danone in a weak position to enforce its rights if problems arose.

Both the trademark license agreement and the joint venture agreement prohibited Hangzhou Wahaha Group from using the Wahaha trademark and from competing with the joint venture. But beginning in 2000, Zong created a series of companies, owned partly by Hangzhou Wahaha Group and partly by members of his family, which sold the same products as the joint venture using the Wahaha trademark. Because of its hands-off approach, Danone did not learn of the parallel companies until 2005.

After negotiations to integrate the parallel companies into the joint venture failed, Danone in 2007 began arbitration at the Stockholm Chamber of Commerce, as provided in the joint venture agreement. Hangzhou Wahaha Group and Zong responded to claims about competing with the joint venture by initiating suits in Chinese courts against three Danone-appointed directors alleging that their service as directors or managers of other competing Chinese companies violated China's Company Law. Hangzhou Wahaha Group also successfully challenged the validity of the trademark license agreement before a tribunal of the Hangzhou Arbitration Commission, a decision upheld by the Hangzhou Intermediate People's Court.

In September 2009, the Stockholm Chamber of Commerce tribunal ruled for Danone. On the same day, the parties announced that they had reached a settlement under which Zong agreed to buy Danone's 51% interest in the joint venture for US$450 million.[6] Combined with a reported US$380 million in dividends over the life of the joint venture, Danone made a substantial profit on its initial investment. But it ultimately lost control to its Chinese partner of a very profitable investment—one that near the end accounted for more than 5% of Danone's profits worldwide.

---

[6]   Mitchell & Dyer, French Food Group's Chinese Venture Leaves a Bitter Taste, Financial Times (Nov. 10, 2009).

QUESTIONS

(1) Consider the Joint Venture Contract between American Hair Products and People's Manufacturing Corporation, supra pp. 400–405. Do tensions seem likely to arise in any of the areas noted above?

(2) What might Danone have done differently to avoid the problems in its joint venture with Wahaha?

2. DISPUTE RESOLUTION IN U.S.-CHINESE JOINT VENTURES

Although equity joint venture contracts must be governed by Chinese law,[7] the parties have numerous options for dispute resolution. Choosing U.S. courts is not a good option unless both parties have assets in the United States or in a third country that will enforce a U.S. judgment. Chinese courts almost never enforce U.S. judgments against assets in China. Under Article 282 of the Civil Procedure Law of the People's Republic of China, Chinese courts enforce foreign judgments only "in accordance with an international treaty concluded or acceded to by the People's Republic of China or under the principle of reciprocity." There is no judgments treaty between China and the United States, and Chinese courts have been reluctant to find that U.S. courts reciprocally enforce Chinese judgments. U.S. parties are sometimes reluctant to choose Chinese courts because of doubts concerning those courts' independence from powerful local interests.

Parties who wish to settle their disputes through arbitration have a choice of arbitrating in China or abroad. Under Article 128 of the Contract Law of the People's Republic of China, only "foreign-related" contracts may provide for arbitration outside of China. The Supreme People's Court has interpreted this requirement to be satisfied: (1) when either or both parties are foreign citizens or foreign legal persons; (2) when either or both parties have their habitual residences outside the territory of the People's Republic of China; (3) when the subject matter of the contract is outside the territory of the People's Republic of China; (4) when the legal fact that leads to establishment, change or termination of the civil relation happens outside the territory of the People's Republic of China; or (5) in "other circumstances." See Interpretation on Several Issues Concerning the Law on the Application of Laws to Foreign-Related Civil Relations art. 1, Fa Shi [2012] No. 24 (Dec. 28, 2012).

With respect to joint ventures, Article 15 of the Equity Joint Venture Law specifically permits the parties to provide for the resolution of disputes through arbitration "by a Chinese arbitral body or through an arbitral body agreed on by all parties of an equity joint venture." See supra p. 411. Disputes between a joint venture and another Chinese

---

[7] See Contract Law of the People's Republic of China, Art. 126 (1999), supra p. 158; Regulations for the Implementation of the Law of the People's Republic of China on Sino-foreign Equity Joint Ventures, Art. 12.

entity, by contrast, are considered "domestic," and the arbitration of such disputes must be seated in China. You will have noted that the sample joint venture contract above provides for arbitration before a Chinese arbitral body, the China International Economic and Trade Arbitration Commission (CIETAC).

CIETAC is one of the busiest arbitration centers in the world, handling more than two thousand cases annually. CIETAC consists of an arbitration commission in Beijing and sub-commissions in Chongqing, Fuzhou, Hangzhou, Shanghai, Shenzhen, Tianjin, and Wuhan. In 2012, CIETAC also established a branch office in Hong Kong, known as the CIETAC Hong Kong Arbitration Center. Under the CIETAC Rules, the parties may agree to have their arbitration administered by the commission in Beijing or by one of CIETAC's sub-commissions or centers. But where the parties do not agree or their agreement is ambiguous, the Beijing commission administers the arbitration. The introduction of this rule in 2012 led the Shanghai and Shenzhen sub-commissions to split from the Beijing commission. In 2015, the Supreme People's Court issued an interpretation on jurisdictional issues arising from the CIETAC split, deciding that arbitration agreements concluded before the split that refer to the Shanghai or Shenzhen sub-commissions may be heard by the breakaway sub-commissions and Chinese courts should enforce their awards.

CIETAC maintains a panel of more than 1,200 arbitrators, including more than 300 foreign arbitrators. Under the 2015 CIETAC Rules, arbitrators from outside this list may be appointed if the parties agree, subject to confirmation by the Chairman of CIETAC. CIETAC's mandatory fee schedule is low by international standards. While this makes CIETAC a lower-cost option for dispute resolution, it can also make it difficult to attract good foreign arbitrators.

The choice of CIETAC arbitration has several implications. First, CIETAC arbitration is obviously governed by the CIETAC arbitration rules, which may differ in certain respects from the arbitration rules of other institutions. Consider the following provisions from the 2015 CIETAC Rules:[8]

Article 7. Place of Arbitration

1.   Where the parties have agreed on the place of arbitration, the parties' agreement shall prevail.

2.   Where the parties have not agreed on the place of arbitration or their agreement is ambiguous, the place of arbitration shall be the domicile of CIETAC or its sub-commission/arbitration center administering the case. CIETAC may also determine the place of arbitration to be another location having regard to the circumstances of the case.

---

[8]   www.cietac.org/index.php?m=Page&a=index&id=106&l=en.

3.   The arbitral award shall be deemed as having been made at the place of arbitration.

* * *

Article 24. Duties of Arbitrator

An arbitrator shall not represent either party, and shall be and remain independent of the parties and treat them equally.

Article 25. Number of Arbitrators

1.   The arbitral tribunal shall be composed of one or three arbitrators.

2.   Unless otherwise agreed by the parties or provided by these Rules, the arbitral tribunal shall be composed of three arbitrators.

Article 26. Nomination or Appointment of Arbitrator

1.   CIETAC maintains a Panel of Arbitrators which uniformly applies to itself and all its sub-commissions/arbitration centers. The parties shall nominate arbitrators from the Panel of Arbitrators provided by CIETAC.

2.   Where the parties have agreed to nominate arbitrators from outside CIETAC's Panel of Arbitrators, an arbitrator so nominated by the parties or nominated according to the agreement of the parties may act as arbitrator subject to the confirmation by the Chairman of CIETAC.

Article 27. Three-Arbitrator Tribunal

1.   Within fifteen (15) days from the date of receipt of the Notice of Arbitration, the Claimant and the Respondent shall each nominate, or entrust the Chairman of CIETAC to appoint, an arbitrator, failing which the arbitrator shall be appointed by the Chairman of CIETAC.

2.   Within fifteen (15) days from the date of the Respondent's receipt of the Notice of Arbitration, the parties shall jointly nominate, or entrust the Chairman of CIETAC to appoint, the third arbitrator, who shall act as the presiding arbitrator.

3.   The parties may each recommend one to five arbitrators as candidates for presiding arbitrator and shall each submit a list of recommended candidates within the time period specified in the preceding Paragraph 2. Where there is only one common candidate on the lists, such candidate shall be the presiding arbitrator jointly nominated by the parties. Where there is more than one common candidate on the lists, the Chairman of CIETAC shall choose the presiding arbitrator from among the common candidates having regard to the circumstances of the case, and he/she shall act as the presiding arbitrator jointly nominated by the parties. Where there is no common candidate on the lists, the presiding arbitrator shall be appointed by the Chairman of CIETAC.

4.   Where the parties have failed to jointly nominate the presiding arbitrator according to the above provisions, the presiding arbitrator shall be appointed by the Chairman of the CIETAC.

* * *

Article 31. Disclosure

1.   An arbitrator nominated by the parties or appointed by the Chairman of the CIETAC shall sign a Declaration and disclose any facts or circumstances likely to give rise to justifiable doubts as to his/her impartiality or independence.

2.   If circumstances that need to be disclosed arise during the arbitral proceedings, the arbitrator shall promptly disclose such circumstances in writing.

3.   The Declaration and/or the disclosure of the arbitrator shall be submitted to the Arbitration Court to be forwarded to the parties.

Article 32. Challenge to the Arbitrator

1.   Upon receipt of the Declaration and/or the written disclosure of an arbitrator, a party wishing to challenge the arbitrator on the grounds of the disclosed facts or circumstances shall forward the challenge in writing within ten (10) days from the date of such receipt. If a party fails to file a challenge within the above time period, it may not subsequently challenge the arbitrator on the basis of the matters disclosed by the arbitrator.

2.   A party having justifiable doubts as to the impartiality or independence of an arbitrator may challenge that arbitrator in writing and shall state the facts and reasons on which the challenge is based with supporting evidence.

3.   A party may challenge an arbitrator in writing within fifteen (15) days from the date it receives the Notice of Formation of the Arbitral Tribunal. Where a party becomes aware of a reason for a challenge after such receipt, the party may challenge the arbitrator in writing within fifteen (15) days after such reason has become known to it, but no later than the conclusion of the last oral hearing.

4.   The challenge by one party shall be promptly communicated to the other party, the arbitrator being challenged and the other members of the arbitral tribunal.

5.   Where an arbitrator is challenged by one party and the other party agrees to the challenge, or the arbitrator being challenged voluntarily withdraws from his/her office, such arbitrator shall no longer be a member of the arbitral tribunal. However, in neither case shall it be implied that the reasons for the challenge are sustained.

6.   In circumstances other than those specified in the preceding Paragraph 5, the Chairman of CIETAC shall make a final decision on the challenge with or without stating the reasons.

7.   An arbitrator who has been challenged shall continue to serve on the arbitral tribunal until a decision on the challenge has been made by the Chairman of CIETAC.

* * *

Article 51. Scrutiny of Draft Award

The arbitral tribunal shall submit its draft award to CIETAC for scrutiny before signing the award. CIETAC may bring to the attention of the arbitral tribunal issues addressed in the award on the condition that the arbitral tribunal's independence in rendering the award is not affected.

* * *

Article 81. Language

1.   Where the parties have agreed on the language of arbitration, their agreement shall prevail. In the absence of such agreement, the language of arbitration to be used in the proceedings shall be Chinese. CIETAC may also designate another language as the language of arbitration having regard to the circumstances of the case.

2.   If a party or its representative(s) or witness(es) requires interpretation at an oral hearing, an interpreter may be provided either by the Arbitration Court or by the party.

3.   The arbitral tribunal or the Arbitration Court may, if it considers it necessary, require the parties to submit a corresponding translation of their documents and evidence into Chinese or other languages.

Second, CIETAC's Rules provide that the arbitral tribunal may conciliate a dispute submitted to it if both parties agree. Conciliation ends and the arbitration proceedings resume when one of the parties so requests or the tribunal concludes that further efforts at conciliation would be futile. There has long been a preference in China for resolving disputes through mediation,[9] and today perhaps a third of CIETAC disputes are conciliated. Article 47(9) of the CIETAC rules provides: "Where conciliation is not successful, neither party may invoke any opinion, view or statement, and any proposal or proposition expressing acceptance or opposition by either party or by the arbitral tribunal in the process of conciliation as grounds for any claim, defense or counterclaim in the subsequent arbitral proceedings, judicial proceedings, or any other

---

[9]   See Cohen, Chinese Mediation on the Eve of Modernization, 54 Cal. L. Rev. 1201 (1966).

proceedings." Nevertheless, arbitrators may form opinions during the process of conciliation that may be difficult to put aside. Once the arbitrators have indicated their views during the course of conciliation, the parties may also feel pressure to settle so as not to anger the tribunal. To address this concern, the 2012 Rules added Article 47(8), which provides for conciliation outside the arbitral tribunal.

Third, the enforcement by Chinese courts of CIETAC awards is not governed by the New York Convention if such awards are made in China.[10] (The enforcement of CIETAC awards outside China in countries that are party to the New York Convention is governed by the Convention.) Articles 70 and 71 of the 1994 Arbitration Law of the People's Republic of China[11] require that a party resisting enforcement of a foreign-related arbitral award made in China, or applying to have such an award set aside, must show one of the circumstances set forth in Article 274 of the Civil Procedure Law of the People's Republic of China, as amended in 2012:

> **Article 274.** If a defendant provides evidence to prove that the arbitration award made by a foreign-affair arbitration institution of the People's Republic of China involves any of the following circumstances, the people's court shall, after examination and verification by a collegial bench, rule to disallow the enforcement of the award:
>
> (1) The parties have not stipulated any clause regarding arbitration in their contract or have not subsequently reached a written agreement on arbitration;
>
> (2) The defendant is not duly notified of the appointment of the arbitrators or the arbitration proceeding, or the defendant fails to express his defense due to the reasons for which he is not held responsible;
>
> (3) The formation of the arbitration panel or the arbitration procedure is not in conformity with rules of arbitration; or
>
> (4) The matters decided by arbitration exceed the scope of the arbitration agreement or the authority of the arbitration institution.
>
> If a people's court determines that the enforcement of an award will violate the social and public interest, the court shall make a ruling to disallow the enforcement of the arbitration award.[12]

---

[10] China made both reciprocity and commercial reservations upon acceding to the New York Convention in 1987.

[11] english.mofcom.gov.cn/aarticle/lawsdata/chineselaw/200411/20041100311032.html.

[12] This provision was originally Article 260 of the 1991 Civil Procedure Law, but was renumbered 258 when the law was amended in 2007, and was renumbered 274 when the law was again amended in 2012. For domestic awards, Article 237 of the Civil Procedure Law provides additional grounds for non-enforcement, including falsified or concealed evidence, corruption, and "twisting the law."

As an alternative to CIETAC arbitration, the parties to a joint venture contract may choose a foreign arbitral body, such as the International Chamber of Commerce, the London Court of International Arbitration, the International Center for Dispute Resolution, the Stockholm Chamber of Commerce, or the Singapore International Arbitration Centre. Under Article 283 of the 2012 Civil Procedure Law, the enforcement in China of awards rendered by foreign arbitral bodies is governed by the New York Convention, and the grounds for refusing to enforce such awards are therefore limited to those stated in Article V of the Convention. See supra pp. 42–43. The Hong Kong International Arbitration Center is another alternative. Since Hong Kong reverted to Chinese sovereignty in 1997, the New York Convention has not applied to the enforcement of Hong Kong awards in China, but the 1999 Arrangement Concerning Mutual Enforcement of Arbitral Awards Between the Mainland and the Hong Kong Special Administrative Region reproduces the grounds for non-enforcement under the New York Convention almost word for word. China's Supreme People's Court has confirmed that this Arrangement also applies to awards by other arbitral institutions in Hong Kong and to ad hoc awards. The latter is particularly significant because, as a general matter, China does not permit or recognize ad hoc arbitrations.

Statistics on the enforcement of arbitral awards in China are difficult to come by. A 2016 survey of publicly reported cases by a law firm showed that foreign arbitral awards were enforced about 70% of the time, with enforcement rates improving in recent years.[13]

Although there is no appeal from a decision to enforce or refuse enforcement of an arbitral award, since 1995 the Supreme People's Court has attempted to increase enforcement by establishing a reporting system. Before refusing to enforce a foreign or foreign-related arbitral award, and before acting to set aside a foreign-related arbitral award, an Intermediate People's Court must submit a report to the High People's Court. If the High People's Court agrees that the award should not be enforced or should be set aside, it must submit a report to the Supreme People's Court. Only if the Supreme People's Court approves may the Intermediate People's Court refuse to enforce an award or set it aside. In 2018, a similar reporting system was extended to domestic arbitral awards. While this may provide additional protection in disputes between joint ventures and other Chinese companies (which are considered domestic), it may also increase the number of reported cases and slow down the reporting system.

---

[13] Enforcing Foreign Arbitral Awards in China—A Review of the Past Twenty Years, http://www.kwm.com/en/knowledge/insights/enforcing-foreign-arbitral-awards-in-china-20160 915.

Questions

(1) Should any of the provisions in CIETAC's arbitration rules cause concern for a foreign joint venture partner? Could any of these concerns be ameliorated by changes to the arbitration clause?

(2) Compare the grounds for refusing to enforce an award in Article 274 of China's Civil Procedure Law to those in Article V of the New York Convention, supra pp. 42–43. Is there any reason to prefer one to the other?

Additional reading: Bosshart, Luedi & Wang, Past Lessons for China's New Joint Ventures, McKinsey Quarterly (Dec. 2010); Walsh, Wang & Xin, Same Bed, Different Dreams: Working Relationships in Sino-American Joint Ventures, 34 J. World Bus. 69 (1999); Miller, Glen, Jasperson & Karmokolias, International Joint Ventures in Developing Countries: Happy Marriages?, International Finance Corporation Discussion Paper Number 29 (1996). On the Danone-Wahaha joint venture, see Lee & Tan, Joint Ventures in China—Lessons to Be Learned from Danone v. Wahaha, in International Joint Ventures 543 (Campbell & Netzer eds., 2009). On dispute resolution in China, see Managing Business Disputes in Today's China: Duelling with Dragons (Moser ed., 2007); von Wunschheim, Enforcement of Commercial Arbitral Awards in China (2013); Judicial Independence in China: Lessons for Global Rule of Law Promotion (Peerenboom ed., 2010).

E. Antitrust

Because joint ventures involve cooperation between potential competitors, they may raise concerns under antitrust or competition laws. Yet joint ventures do not always fit comfortably into the frameworks established for horizontal agreements, vertical agreements, and mergers. This Section considers the treatment of joint ventures under U.S. antitrust law, EU competition law, and China's Anti-Monopoly Law.

1. Joint Ventures Under U.S. Antitrust Law

In United States v. Penn-Olin Chemical Co., 378 U.S. 158, 84 S.Ct. 1710, 12 L.Ed.2d 775 (1964), the U.S. Supreme Court stated:

> The joint venture, like the "merger" and the "conglomeration," often creates anticompetitive dangers. It is the chosen competitive instrument of two or more corporations previously acting independently and usually competitively with one another. The result is "a triumvirate of associated corporations." If the parent companies are in competition, or might compete absent the joint venture, it may be assumed that neither will compete with the progeny in its line of commerce. Inevitably, the operations of the joint venture will be frozen to

those lines of commerce which will not bring it into competition with the parents, and the latter, by the same token will be foreclosed from the joint venture's market.

This is not to say that the joint venture is controlled by the same criteria as the merger or conglomeration. The merger eliminates one of the participating corporations from the market while a joint venture creates a new competitive force therein. . . .

Overall, the same considerations apply to joint ventures as to mergers, for in each instance we are but expounding a national policy enunciated by the Congress to preserve and promote a free competitive economy. . . .

The Penn-Olin case involved a domestic joint venture that was organized and owned by two major chemical concerns to produce sodium chlorate in the Southeastern United States. The Court found that, on the record before it, Section 1 of the Sherman Act had not been violated. However, it concluded that Section 7 of the Clayton Act applied to the joint formation and ownership of subsidiaries as well as to mergers with or acquisition of existing companies. The Court remanded the case for further proceedings and gave the following guidance:

We note generally the following criteria which the trial court might take into account in assessing the probability of a substantial lessening of competition: the number and power of the competitors in the relevant market; the background of their growth; the power of the joint venturers; the relationship of their lines of commerce; the competition existing between them and the power of each in dealing with the competitors of the other; the setting in which the joint venture was created; the reasons and necessities for its existence; the joint venture's line of commerce and the relationship thereof to that of its parents; the adaptability of its line of commerce to non-competitive practices; the potential power of the joint venture in the relevant market; an appraisal of what the competition in the relevant market would have been if one of the joint venturers had entered it alone instead of through Penn-Olin; the effect, in the event of this occurrence, of the other joint venturer's potential competition; and such other factors as might indicate potential risk to competition in the relevant market. In weighing these factors the court should remember that the mandate of the Congress is in terms of the probability of a lessening of substantial competition, not in terms of tangible present restraint.

On remand, the district court held that, on the record before it, there was no reasonable probability that either parent corporation would have entered the Southeastern sodium chlorate market if Penn-Olin had not been organized. 246 F.Supp. 917 (D.Del.1965). This decision was affirmed by an equally divided Supreme Court, 389 U.S. 308, 88 S.Ct. 502, 19 L.Ed.2d 545 (1967). See also Texaco Inc. v. Dagher, 547 U.S. 1, 126 S.Ct. 1276, 164 L.Ed.2d 1 (2006) (holding that *per se* rule against horizontal price fixing did not apply to joint venturers who did not compete with each other in the relevant market).

Although Penn-Olin involved a domestic joint venture, other leading cases have dealt with various sorts of international joint ventures. Several of these have condemned joint ventures that were designed to divide markets among the joint venture partners. In Timken Roller Bearing Co. v. United States, 341 U.S. 593, 71 S.Ct. 971, 95 L.Ed. 1199 (1951), the Supreme Court upheld the District Court's finding that Timken Roller Bearing, an Ohio corporation, had violated the Sherman Act by entering agreements with two foreign joint ventures, British Timken and French Timken, to allocate territories and fix prices. The Court rejected Timken's argument that these restraints on trade were ancillary to a legitimate joint venture: "Nor do we find any support in reason or authority for the proposition that agreements between legally separate persons and companies to suppress competition among themselves and others can be justified by labeling the project a 'joint venture.' Perhaps every agreement and combination to restrain trade could be so labeled." Id. at 598, 71 S.Ct. at 974–975. See also United States v. American Tobacco Co., 221 U.S. 106, 31 S.Ct. 632, 55 L.Ed. 663 (1911).

On the other hand, as a leading District Court opinion has noted, "[i]t is settled that joint manufacturing ventures, even in domestic markets, are not made unlawful per se by the Sherman Act, but become unlawful only if their purpose or their effect is to restrain trade or to monopolize." United States v. Imperial Chemical Industries, 100 F.Supp. 504, 557 (S.D.N.Y. 1951). Judge Ryan continued:

> But the proof here shows an American concern, already established in a foreign local market, and a British concern, which has a foothold in the same foreign local market, combining to form a jointly owned company to the end that the same foreign market may be developed for their mutual benefit and profits divided on an agreed basis. To this, and as an incident to the formation of the foreign company, we find added by agreement not only joint contribution of capital investment but a pooling of patents and processes owned by the parent companies. . . . [T]he very purpose with which the foreign companies here involved were conceived and the circumstances under which they were born place them under the bar.

Another leading District Court decision emphasized the effect of a foreign manufacturing joint venture on exports by domestic competitors. In United States v. Minnesota Mining & Mfg. Co., 92 F.Supp. 947 (D.Mass.1950), American producers of coated abrasives controlling four-fifths of exports from the United States formed the Durex Corporation, which, through its foreign subsidiaries, conducted manufacturing operations in several foreign countries. Judge Wyzanski found that these joint ventures had the prohibited effect of "precluding their American competitors from receiving business they might otherwise have received from the markets served by these jointly owned foreign factories." Id. at 961. The court also rejected several arguments that the arrangements, though anticompetitive, were beneficial to American interests overall:

> It is no excuse for the violations of the Sherman Act that supplying foreign customers from foreign factories is more profitable and in that sense is, as defendants argue, "in the interest of American enterprise". . . . Financial advantage is a legitimate consideration for an individual non-monopolistic enterprise. It is irrelevant where the action is taken by a combination and the effect, while it may redound to the advantage of American finance, restricts American commerce. For Congress in the Sherman Act has condemned whatever unreasonably restrains American commerce regardless of how it fattens profits of certain stockholders. Congress has preferred to protect American competitors, consumers and workmen.

> Nor is it any excuse that the use of foreign factories has increased the movement of raw materials from American to foreign shores. We may disregard the point that the books are not in balance when raw materials actually transported are set off against finished products potentially transported. It is more significant that Congress has not said you may choke commerce here if you nourish it there.

Id. at 962.

As Penn-Olin indicates, joint ventures are typically subject to the same provisions of U.S. antitrust law as other sorts of potentially anticompetitive conduct, including Section 1 of the Sherman Act and Section 7 of the Clayton Act. There are, however, a few kinds of joint ventures for which Congress has enacted specific legislation. In 1919, Congress passed the Webb-Pomerene Act, 40 Stat. 517 (1919), 15 U.S.C.A. §§ 61–66, which allows domestic firms to form export cartels known as Webb-Pomerene Associations so long as domestic competition is not affected:

> Nothing contained in the Sherman Act shall be construed as declaring to be illegal an association entered into for the sole purpose of engaging in export trade and actually engaged solely in such export trade, or an agreement made or act done in the course of export trade by such association, provided such association, agreement, or act is not in restraint of trade within the United States, and is not in restraint of export trade of any domestic competitor of such association: *Provided*, That such association does not, either in the United States or elsewhere, enter into any agreement, understanding, or conspiracy, or do

any act which artificially or intentionally enhances or depressed prices within the United States of commodities of the class exported by such association, or which substantially lessens competition within the United States, or otherwise restrains trade therein.

Id. § 62. In 1982, Congress enacted a similar statute, the Export Trading Company Act, 96 Stat. 124 (1982), 15 U.S.C.A. §§ 4001–4021, which allows firms contemplating export activities to apply to the Secretary of Commerce for a Certificate of Review which would immunize the applicant from civil or criminal antitrust liability for actions covered by the certificate that do not adversely affect trade within the United States or the export trade of competitors.

Congress has also acted to protect research and development joint ventures and production joint ventures through the National Cooperative Research Act, 98 Stat. 1815 (1984), and the National Cooperative Research and Production Act, 107 Stat. 117 (1993), which are codified together at 15 U.S.C.A. §§ 4301–4306. These Acts provide that such joint ventures disclosed to the Department of Justice and Federal Trade Commission are to be evaluated under a rule of reason and that private plaintiffs against them are limited to actual (rather than treble) damages. The protection for production joint ventures is available only if the joint venture's principal production facilities are located in the United States and the joint venture's partners are either U.S. persons or foreign persons from countries that treat U.S. persons at least as well as their own nationals with respect to production joint ventures.

Further guidance on the antitrust treatment of joint ventures is provided in the Joint Venture Guidelines issued by the Federal Trade Commission and the Department of Justice in 2000. See Antitrust Guidelines for Collaborations Among Competitors, 4 Trade Reg. Rep. (CCH) & 13,161 (2000). The Guidelines begin by noting: "Such collaborations often are not only benign but procompetitive. Indeed, in the last two decades, the federal antitrust agencies have brought relatively few civil cases against competitor collaborations." Some agreements among competitors are *per se* illegal, including agreements to fix prices or output, rig bids, or divide markets. "If, however, participants in an efficiency-enhancing integration of economic activity enter into an agreement that is reasonably related to the integration and reasonably necessary to achieve its procompetitive benefits, the Agencies analyze the agreement under the rule of reason, even if it is of a type that might otherwise be considered per se illegal." Id. § 3.2. The Joint Venture Guidelines summarize the analysis of agreements under the rule of reason as follows:

> The Agencies' analysis begins with an examination of the nature of the relevant agreement. As a part of this examination, the Agencies ask about the business purpose of the agreement and examine whether the agreement, if already in operation, has

caused anticompetitive harm. In some cases, the nature of the agreement and the absence of market power together may demonstrate the absence of anticompetitive harm. In such cases, the Agencies do not challenge the agreement. Alternatively, where the likelihood of anticompetitive harm is evident from the nature of the agreement, or anticompetitive harm has resulted from an agreement already in operation, then, absent overriding benefits that could offset the anticompetitive harm, the Agencies challenge such agreements without a detailed market analysis.

If the initial examination of the nature of the agreement indicates possible competitive concerns, but the agreement is not one that would be challenged without a detailed market analysis, the Agencies analyze the agreement in greater depth. The Agencies typically define relevant markets and calculate market shares and concentration as an initial step in assessing whether the agreement may create or increase market power or facilitate its exercise. The Agencies examine the extent to which the participants and the collaboration have the ability and incentive to compete independently. The Agencies also evaluate other market circumstances, e.g. entry, that may foster or prevent anticompetitive harms.

If the examination of these factors indicates no potential for anticompetitive harm, the Agencies end the investigation without considering procompetitive benefits. If investigation indicates anticompetitive harm, the Agencies examine whether the relevant agreement is reasonably necessary to achieve procompetitive benefits that likely would offset anticompetitive harms.

Id. § 1.2.

Echoing the analysis in Penn-Olin, the Joint Venture Guidelines note that the competitive effects of competitor collaborations may differ from those of mergers. First, most mergers completely end competition between the merging parties, while most competitor collaborations preserve some competition between the participants. Second, mergers are designed to be permanent, while competitor collaborations often are not. The Guidelines make clear, however, that the Agencies will analyze a joint venture as a merger if the participants are competitors, the joint venture eliminates all competition between them in the relevant market, and the joint venture does not terminate by its own terms within a sufficiently limited period of time (generally 10 years). Id. § 1.3

Finally, the Joint Venture Guidelines set forth two "safety zones," while emphasizing that "competitor collaborations are not anticompetitive merely because they fall outside the safety zones." Id. § 4.1. First, "[a]bsent extraordinary circumstances, the Agencies do not challenge a competitor collaboration when the market shares of the collaboration and its participants collectively account for not more than twenty percent of each relevant market in which competition may be affected." Id. § 4.2. Second, absent extraordinary circumstances, the Agencies do not challenge research and development collaborations "where three or more independently controlled research efforts in addition to those of the collaboration possess the required specialized assets or characteristics and the incentive to engage in R & D that is a close substitute for the R & D activity of the collaboration." Id. § 4.3.

In connection with foreign joint ventures, it is also important to recall that under the Foreign Trade Antitrust Improvements Act of 1982 (FTAIA), 15 U.S.C.A. § 6a & § 45a, discussed in Problem 2, supra p. 235, neither the Sherman Act nor the FTC Act applies to anticompetitive conduct involving export commerce or commerce within or among foreign nations unless such conduct has "a direct, substantial, and reasonably foreseeable effect" on domestic commerce, import commerce, or the export commerce of a person in the United States. In other words, joint ventures will be subject to U.S. antitrust law only to the extent that they cause anticompetitive effects in the United States. In United States v. LSL Biotechnologies, 379 F.3d 672 (9th Cir.2004), the Department of Justice challenged a provision in a joint venture agreement between a U.S. company and an Israeli company to produce tomato seeds that precluded the Israeli company from competing in North America. The Court of Appeals upheld the District Court's dismissal on the ground that restraints on competition with respect to tomato seeds in Mexico did not have the "direct" effect on the price of tomatoes in the United States required by the FTAIA.

2. JOINT VENTURES UNDER EU COMPETITION LAW

That a joint venture may not be subject to U.S. antitrust law by virtue of the FTAIA or because of the specific exemptions of the Webb-Pomerene and Export Trading Company Acts does not insulate it from scrutiny under foreign antitrust law. In the Wood Pulp Case, Åhlström Osakeyhtiö v. Commission, [1988] ECR 5193, see supra p. 240, the Court of Justice of the European Union (then the European Court of Justice) rejected the argument that U.S. wood pulp exporters were immunized from the application of Article 101 of the Treaty on the Functioning of the European Union (TFEU) (then Article 85 of the Treaty of Rome) because they had formed a Webb-Pomerene Association. The Court noted: "There is not, in this case, any contradiction between the conduct required by the United States and that required by the Community since the Webb-Pomerene Act merely exempts the conclusion of export cartels from the application of United States anti-trust laws but does not require such cartels to be concluded." Id. at 5244.

The treatment of joint ventures under European Union law has evolved over time. The European Commission has generally distinguished between "cooperative" joint ventures that fall within

Article 101 of the TFEU and "concentrative" joint ventures that fall within Article 102.[14] Under EU law, as under U.S. law, joint ventures are sometimes analyzed as mergers. Indeed, the parties will often prefer to have their joint venture reviewed by the European Commission under the Merger Regulation because it provides greater certainty that the joint venture does not violate EU competition law.

To come within the Merger Regulation discussed in Problem 5, supra pp. 368–377, joint ventures must meet the threshold turnover requirements of Article 1 and must be "full-function" joint ventures—that is, they must "perform[ ] on a lasting basis all the functions of an autonomous economic entity." Merger Regulation Art. 3(4). This latter requirement is elaborated in the Commission's 2007 Consolidated Jurisdictional Notice:[15]

> (94) Full function character essentially means that a joint venture must operate on a market, performing the functions normally carried out by undertakings operating in the same market. In order to do so the joint venture must have a management dedicated to its day-to-day operations and access to sufficient resources including finance, staff, and assets (tangible and intangible) in order to conduct on a lasting basis its business activities within the area provided for in the joint-venture agreement. . . .

> (95) A joint venture is not full-function if it only takes over one specific function within the parent companies' business activities without its own access to or presence on the market. This is the case, for example, for joint ventures limited to R & D or production. . . .

* * *

> (103) Furthermore, the joint venture must be intended to operate on a lasting basis. The fact that the parent companies commit to the joint venture the resources described above normally demonstrates that this is the case. In addition, agreements setting up a joint venture often provide for certain contingencies, for example, the failure of the joint venture or fundamental disagreement as between the parent companies. . . . This kind of provision does not prevent the joint venture from being considered as operating on a lasting basis. The same is normally true where the agreement specifies a period for the duration of the joint venture where this period is sufficiently long in order to bring about a lasting change in the structure of the undertakings concerned, or where

---

[14] The text of Articles 101 and 102 is set forth in Problem 2. See supra pp. 238–240.

[15] 2008 O.J. (C 95) 1.

the agreement provides for the possible continuation of the joint venture beyond this period.

(104) By contrast, the joint venture will not be considered to operate on a lasting basis where it is established for a short finite duration. This would be the case, for example, where a joint venture is established in order to construct a specific project such as a power plant, but it will not be involved in the operation of the plant once its construction has been completed.

In Case C-248/16, Austria Asphalt GmbH & Co. OG v. Bundeskartellanwalt (2017), the Court of Justice of the European Union held that only joint ventures that perform on a lasting basis all the functions of an autonomous economic entity fall within the Merger Regulation, because it is only these joint ventures that bring about a lasting change in the structure of the market. Id. at ¶ 22.

3. JOINT VENTURES UNDER CHINA'S ANTI-MONOPOLY LAW

China's Anti-Monopoly Law, which came into force on August 1, 2008, does not expressly mention joint ventures but does have a chapter dealing with mergers and other "concentrations of undertakings." Article 4 of the 2014 Guiding Opinion on the Notification of Concentration of Business Operators makes clear that any newly established joint venture under the joint control of at least two companies falls within this chapter. In contrast to the EU Merger Regulation, there is no requirement that the joint venture have a "full function character."

For the first decade MOFCOM administered the Anti-Monopoly Law's chapter on concentration of undertakings, but in 2018 responsibility for all competition regulation was centralized in a new State Administration for Market Regulation (SAMR). The parties to a joint venture are required to file a notification with SAMR if they meet the turnover thresholds set forth in Article 3 of the 2008 Provisions of the State Council on the Notification Thresholds of Concentrations of Business Operators. Specifically, notification is required if during the last financial year (1) the combined turnover of all parties to the concentration was more than RMB 10 billion (U.S.$1.5 billion) worldwide or more than RMB 2 billion (U.S.$300 million) in the People's Republic of China and (2) at least two of the parties each had turnover in the People's Republic of China of more than RMB 400 million (U.S.$60 million). China has repeatedly fined joint ventures that failed to make the required notifications.

Under Article 28 of the Anti-Monopoly Law, SAMR has authority to prohibit a joint venture or other concentration if it "leads, or may lead, to elimination or restriction of competition." Under Article 29, SAMR also has authority "to impose additional, restrictive conditions for lessening the negative impact exerted by such concentration on competition." In 2014, China prohibited the world's three largest container-shipping companies (Maersk, MSC, and CMA CGM) from establishing an association because of concerns about competition in shipping routes to China. Also in 2014, China imposed conditions on a joint venture with Toyota to make batteries for hybrid cars.

QUESTIONS

(1) Would you expect the proposed joint venture agreement, supra pp. 400–405, to raise U.S. antitrust concerns? If the parties explicitly agreed that People's Manufacturing and Double Happiness would limit their sales to China and that American Hair Products would not sell its products in China, would that raise U.S. antitrust concerns?

(2) Would you expect the proposed joint venture agreement to raise concerns under China's Anti-Monopoly Law? Would the parties be required to file notification with SAMR?

(3) From the parties' point of view, are there any advantages to a system that reviews proposed joint ventures for antitrust concerns before the joint ventures are established? Do the "safety zones" in the U.S. Joint Venture Guidelines provide the same advantages?

Additional reading: On U.S. antitrust law, see 2 Waller, Antitrust and American Business Abroad, ch. 12 (3d ed., looseleaf 1997–) and 2 Fugate, Foreign Commerce and the Antitrust Laws, ch. 11 (5th ed. 1996–). On EU competition law, see Morais, Joint Ventures and EU Competition Law (2013). On China's Anti-Monopoly Law, see Blewett & Bai, Merger Control in China: A Practical Guide, uk.practicallaw.com/W-004-7032 (2017).

PROBLEM 7

A CONCESSION AGREEMENT

A. INTRODUCTION

In the early twentieth century, grants of mineral rights were typically made through contracts known as concession agreements. The classic example was the 1901 D'Arcy concession in which the Shah of Persia granted a foreign investor exclusive oil rights to 500,000 square miles of territory for a period of 60 years in exchange for a $100,000 bonus, $100,000 of the investor's stock, and a 16 percent royalty on the oil produced. Classic concession agreements generally did not obligate investors to explore or drill for oil, did not allow host states to participate in the ventures, and provided compensation only through royalties.

Time has played a critical role in shifting the balance of power in concession agreements from foreign investors to host states. This has been true both with respect to the evolution of such agreements generally and with respect to the renegotiation of individual agreements. From the 1940s to the 1970s, the terms of concession agreements changed dramatically. In 1943, American oil companies negotiated an agreement with Venezuela that agreed in principle to share the proceeds of their operations 50–50. In 1950, Saudi Arabia renegotiated its deal with the Arabian American Oil Company (ARAMCO) to apply the 50–50 principle, structuring a large part of its take in the form of taxes from which ARAMCO had previously been exempt. Application of the foreign tax credit to this arrangement resulted in a large shift in revenues from the U.S. treasury to that of Saudi Arabia.

The formation of OPEC in 1960 dramatically altered the balance of power in favor of the oil-producing states. In 1972, oil companies agreed to a new way of compensating host states. Under new participation agreements, states were allowed to buy into companies holding the concessions for payment of their "updated book value." State participation was to start at 25% and rise to 51% by 1983. But this arrangement did not survive the further shift of power that occurred with the Arab Oil Embargo of 1973–74. In 1974, for example, Saudi Arabia took a 60% stake in ARAMCO; in 1976, it took back 100% of the mineral rights for the payment of book value. ARAMCO stayed on as operator of the oil fields, receiving a payment of 21 cents per barrel.

Over the same period, the process of decolonization brought new nations to the United Nations General Assembly, where they began to display their numerical power. Three successive resolutions of that body expressed the views of the new majority. The first came in 1962, Resolution No. 1803 (XVII) on Permanent Sovereignty over Natural Resources, which stated:

2.   The exploration, development and disposition of such resources, as well as the import of the foreign capital required for these purposes, should be in conformity with the rules and conditions which the peoples and nations freely consider to be necessary or desirable with regard to the authorization, restriction or prohibition of such activities.

In 1966, Resolution No. 2158 (XXI), also captioned Permanent Sovereignty over National Resources, said that the Assembly:

5.   *Recognizes* the right of all countries, and in particular of the developing countries, to secure and increase their share in the administration of enterprises which are fully or partly operated by foreign capital and to have a greater share in the advantages and profits derived therefrom on an equitable basis, with due regard to development needs and objectives of the peoples concerned and to mutually acceptable contractual practices, and calls upon the countries from which such capital originates to refrain from any action which would hinder exercise of that right.

And in 1974, Resolution No. 3281, the Charter of Economic Rights and Duties of States, reemphasized the right of each state to regulate and exercise authority of foreign investment.

Today, contractual arrangements in the oil and gas industry can take a variety of forms. Modern concession agreements, like the one reproduced in Section B, see infra pp. 438–458, give the foreign investor the right to explore for, produce, and sell oil and gas from a specific area for a specific period of time, with the investor bearing the costs and risks of exploration and the government collecting royalties, taxes, and sometimes other payments.

Under production-sharing agreements, the foreign company similarly bears the costs and risks of exploration, but the division of the financial rewards is structured differently. After payment to the government of a royalty based on the production of oil and gas, the company is entitled to a certain percentage of the production from which it may recover its costs (called "cost oil"). The remaining production (called "profit oil") is then divided between the company and the government according to the production-sharing provisions of the contract. The company may also be liable for corporate income tax on the profit it earns. Indonesia introduced the first production sharing agreement in 1966 as an arrangement that avoided giving oil companies ownership of the resource in the ground (though you will see that Brazil's concession contract also avoids doing this). Today, production-sharing agreements are widely used, particularly in developing countries.

With service contracts, the foreign company does not assume the costs and risks of exploration and is not entitled to any share of the production. The company is simply hired to perform specific services related to exploration or development. Service contracts are common in Iran, Iraq, and Kuwait.

Each of these alternatives—concession agreements, production-sharing agreements, and service contracts—may be used in conjunction with a joint venture between a foreign company and a national oil company. From the government's perspective, the participation of the national oil company offers an opportunity to train its personnel and an additional way to participate in the financial rewards. Sometimes the government's interest is "carried," which means that the company bears all the costs of the exploration with the government having the right to acquire a certain percentage of the venture after oil and gas is found by paying the same percentage of the exploration costs.

Changes in the balance of power have shaped not just changes in the general forms of these agreements, but also the renegotiation of specific agreements. Over the life of a particular agreement, relations between the parties are likely to follow a predictable trajectory. At the start, state officials are pleased that somebody wishes to explore for minerals within their realm. They are duly impressed by the risks that the exploration involves and by the technical skills of the foreign investor. Ten years later, after a successful start, perceptions have changed. The risks that once seemed so daunting are now in the past, and the operation appears smooth and easy. Local personnel have been trained to take over the technical and managerial aspects of the project, and the state's financial resources have expanded to the point where it may be able to run the project itself. Meanwhile, the foreign party still has a large investment at stake, which it cannot simply pull out and move somewhere else. Intelligent managers are conscious of their vulnerability and may be willing to renegotiate if reasonable terms can be had. See infra pp. 488–492.

Section B introduces some of the problems that must be attended to in drafting a concession agreement, including control, the distribution of revenue, the extent of the foreign investor's involvement in the larger economy, and changes over the life of the agreement. Sections C, D, E, and F then consider some specific legal issues raised by concession agreements, including choice of forum, choice of law, the level of protection afforded by international law, political risk insurance, and questions concerning renegotiation.

B. DRAFTING PROBLEMS IN CONCESSION AGREEMENTS

We set forth below a modern concession agreement used by Brazil.[1] The agreement grants the concessionaire the exclusive right to explore for oil and natural gas in a defined "concession area" and to produce oil and gas if it is found. Under the 1988 Brazilian Constitution, the federal

---

[1]   Other examples of petroleum and mineral agreements may be found at https://resource contracts.org.

government owns all mineral resources within Brazilian territory. The national oil company Petrobras had a monopoly on oil and gas until 1995, when the Constitution was amended to permit exploration and production by private companies. In 1997, Law No. 9,478/1997 (the Petroleum Law) established a regime for concession agreements with private companies. In 2010, Law No. 12,351/2010 (the Pre-Salt Law) established a regime for production-sharing agreements in the pre-salt layers of Brazil's continental shelf. Both regimes permit foreign companies to participate in the public bid process. If a foreign company wins the bid, it must set up a company under Brazilian law, with its headquarters and management in Brazil, to enter into the agreement with the government.

Brazil's concession agreement separates the concessionaire's obligations into phases. During the exploration phase, the concessionaire is required to conduct an exploration program meeting certain minimum requirements. If oil or gas is discovered, the concessionaire may conduct an assessment and make a declaration of "commercial feasibility"—that is, a declaration that it makes economic sense to produce the oil or gas. The production phase begins on the date that the declaration of commercial feasibility is submitted and lasts for a term of 27 years. The oil or gas is produced according to an overall production plan and yearly production programs, each approved by the National Agency of Petroleum (ANP). After production is complete, the fields must be decommissioned according to an approved decommissioning program. You will see that the government agency remains heavily involved throughout the life of the agreement.

The concession agreement below contains many provisions that are frequently found in such agreements. These include: minimum work obligations during the exploration phase; the relinquishment of parts of the concession area found not to contain oil or gas, or where the production of oil or gas has been completed; the approval of annual work programs and budgets during the production phase; local content requirements with respect to goods, services, and employment; financial payments to the government in the form of bonuses, royalties, taxes, and certain other payments; and (of course) provisions on dispute resolution.

CONCESSION AGREEMENT FOR EXPLORATION AND PRODUCTION OF OIL AND GAS

entered into by and between

The NATIONAL AGENCY OF PETROLEUM, NATURAL GAS AND BIOFUELS—ANP (hereinafter referred to as "ANP"), a special independent agency organized by Law No. 9,478 of August 6, 1997, . . .

and

_____, organized under the laws of Brazil, with its principal place of business at _____, enrolled in the National Register of

Legal Entities (CNPJ/MF) under No. _____ (hereinafter referred to as "Concessionaire") . . . .

WHEREAS

pursuant to items V and IX of article 20 and the main section of article 176 of the Constitution of the Federative Republic of Brazil and article 3 of Law No. 9,478/97, the Oil and Gas Deposits existing in the national territory, the continental shelf, and the exclusive economic zone belong to the Federal Government;

pursuant to item I of article 177 of the Constitution of the Federative Republic of Brazil and article 4 of Law No. 9,478/97, the Research and Exploration of the Oil and Gas Deposits existing in the national territory, the continental shelf, and the exclusive economic zone are the monopoly of the Federal Government;

pursuant to paragraph one of article 177 of the Federal Constitution and article 5 of Law No. 9,478/97, the Federal Government may allow state-owned or private companies incorporated under the Brazilian laws, with principal place of business and management in the Country, to develop activities of Exploration and Production of Oil and Gas, upon concession, as established in the prevailing laws and regulations;

* * *

pursuant to articles 36 to 42 of Law No. 9,478/97, the Concessionaire participated in the bidding process for award of this Concession Agreement, and the bidding process in which it was declared the winner was awarded and approved for the Block defined in Annex I;

* * *

ANP and the Concessionaire enter into this Concession Agreement for Exploration and Production of Oil and Gas for the Block identified in Annex I under the following terms and conditions.

CHAPTER I—BASIC PROVISIONS
SECTION ONE—DEFINITIONS

Legal Definitions

1.1.   The definitions contained in article 6 of Law No. 9,478/1997, in article 2 of Law No. 12,351/2010, and in article 3 of Decree No. 2,705/1998 are hereby incorporated into this Agreement and, consequently, are valid for all its purposes and effects whenever they are used herein, either in the singular or plural, in the masculine or feminine gender.

Contractual Definitions

1.2.   Also for the purposes and effects of this Agreement, the definitions contained in this paragraph shall also be valid whenever the following words and phrases are used herein, in the singular or plural, in the masculine or feminine gender:

* * *

1.2.18. Brazilian Supplier: any manufacturer or supplier of goods manufactured or services provided in Brazil through limited liability companies incorporated under the Brazilian laws or companies that use goods manufactured in the Country under special customs regimes and tax incentives applicable to the Oil and Gas industry.

* * *

1.2.21. Applicable Laws and Regulations: the set of all laws, decrees, regulations, resolutions, ordinances, normative instructions, or any other regulatory acts that are or may be applicable to the Parties or to the activities of Exploration, Assessment, Development, and Production of Oil and Gas, as well as to decommissioning of the facilities.

* * *

1.2.23. Best Practices of the Oil Industry: The best and safest procedures and technologies available in the oil and gas industry worldwide intended to: (a) ensure the operational safety of the facilities, preserving life, physical integrity, and human health; (b) preserve the environment and protect adjacent communities; (c) prevent or reduce as much as possible the risk of spill of oil, natural gas, by-products, and other chemicals that may be hazardous to the environment; (d) preserve oil and gas resources, which implies the use of adequate methods and processes to maximize the recovery of hydrocarbons in a technical, economic, and environmentally sustainable way, with the corresponding control of the reserve decline, and to mitigate surface losses; (e) minimize consumption of natural resources in the Operations. In order to perform the Best Practices of the Oil Industry, the Concessionaires shall rely on the standards issued by ANP and other Brazilian public bodies, incorporating technical standards and recommendations of internationally recognized bodies and associations of the oil industry, whenever such measures increase the chances to achieve the objectives listed above.

* * *

1.2.44. Social Responsibility: the Concessionaire is responsible for the impacts of its decisions and previous and current activities on society and the environment through an ethical and transparent behavior that (a) contributes to sustainable development, including the health and well-being of society; takes into account the stakeholders' expectations; (b) complies with the applicable laws and regulations and is consistent with the international rules of behavior; and (c) is integrated into the Concessionaire and shown in its relationships related to the Concessionaire's activities within its sphere of influence.

* * *

SECTION TWO—SUBJECT MATTER

Exploration and Production of Oil and Gas

2.1.   The subject matter of this Agreement is:

a)   to conduct Exploration Operations in the Concession Area undertaken in the Minimum Exploration Program or in addition thereto;

b)   in case of a Discovery, at the Concessionaire's discretion, to perform a Discovery Assessment under a Discovery Assessment Plan approved by ANP;

c)   if the commercial feasibility of the Discovery is verified by the Concessionaire, to Produce Oil and Gas in the Concession Area according to a Development Plan approved by ANP.

Costs, Losses, and Risks Associated with the Execution of Operations

2.2.   The Concessionaire shall always and exclusively bear all costs and risks related to the execution of the Operations and its consequences.

2.3.   The Concessionaire shall bear all losses it may incur, including the ones resulting from an act of God or force majeure event, as well as accidents or events of nature affecting the Exploration and Production of Oil and Gas in the Concession Area.

* * *

Ownership of Oil and/or Gas

2.7.   The Oil and Gas Deposits existing in the national territory, the continental shelf, and the exclusive economic zone belong to the Federal Government pursuant to items V and IX of article 20 of the Federal Constitution and article 3 of Law No. 9,478/97.

2.7.1.   The Concessionaire shall have the ownership only of the Oil and Gas that are effectively produced and granted thereto at the Production Measurement Point, through original acquisition and according to this Agreement.

2.7.2.   The Concessionaire shall be subject to charges related to the government taxes and shares, as well as those provided for in the Applicable Laws and Regulations.

Other Natural Resources

2.8.   The Concessionaire is prohibited to use, enjoy, or dispose, in any way and at any title, total or partially, of any other natural resources that may exist in the Concession Area other than Oil and Gas, except when duly authorized by the competent authorities, according to the Applicable Laws and Regulations.

    2.8.1.   Discovery of natural resources other than Oil and Gas by chance shall be notified to ANP within no more than seventy-two (72) hours.

* * *

SECTION THREE—CONCESSION AREA

Identification

3.1.   The Operations shall be conducted exclusively in the Concession Area described and delimited in Annex I.

Voluntary Relinquishment

3.2.   The Concessionaire may, at any time during the Exploration Phase, voluntarily relinquish areas forming part of the Concession Area.

* * *

CHAPTER II—EXPLORATION AND ASSESSMENT
SECTION FIVE—EXPLORATION PHASE

* * *

Minimum Exploration Program

5.3.   The Concessionaire shall perform the obligations related to the Minimum Exploration Program within the terms and under the conditions described in Annex II.

* * *

5.17.   Failure to execute, in full or in part, the Minimum Exploration Program at the End of the Exploration Phase entails the lawful termination of the Agreement, without prejudice to the execution of the financial guarantees for exploration activities and application of appropriate sanctions.

* * *

Concessionaire's Options after Completion of the Minimum Exploration Program

5.18.   After completion of the Minimum Exploration Program and up to the end of the term expected for the Exploration Phase, the Concessionaire may, upon prior formal written notice to ANP:

    a)   assess any Discovery regarding the remaining Concession Area;

b)   inform the Commercial Feasibility of the Discovery, initiating the Production Phase;

c)   retain the areas in which postponement of the Declaration of Commercial Feasibility is applicable, under paragraphs 8.4 and 8.5; or

d)   fully relinquish the Concession Area.

* * *

SECTION SIX—FINANCIAL GUARANTEES OF THE MINIMUM EXPLORATION PROGRAM

Provision of Financial Guarantee

6.1.   The Concessionaire shall provide to ANP one or more financial guarantees for the Minimum Exploration Program.

Types of Financial Guarantees

6.2.   The Concessionaire may provide to ANP the following instruments as financial guarantees:

a)   irrevocable letter of credit;

b)   performance bond;

c)   oil pledge agreement;

d)   posting of bond.

* * *

Return of the Financial Guarantees

6.9.   In the absence of outstanding issues, ANP shall issue the certificate of completion of the Minimum Exploration Program within thirty (30) days after its completion and, then, it shall return the respective financial guarantees.

* * *

SECTION SEVEN—DISCOVERY AND ASSESSMENT

Notification of Discovery

7.1.   Any Discovery of Oil and/or Gas in the Concession Area must be notified by the Concessionaire to ANP on an exclusive basis within no more than seventy-two (72) hours.

Assessment, Discovery Assessment Plan and Final Discovery Assessment Report

7.2.   The Concessionaire may, at its discretion, proceed with the Assessment of a Discovery of Oil and/or Gas at any time during the Exploration Phase.

7.3.   If the Concessionaire decides to proceed with the Discovery Assessment, it must submit a proposed Discovery Assessment Plan for ANP's approval.

7.4.   ANP shall have a term of up to sixty (60) days after receipt of the Discovery Assessment Plan to approve it or reasonably notify the Concessionaire for it to make modifications.

* * *

SECTION EIGHT—DECLARATION OF COMMERCIAL FEASIBILITY

Declaration of Commercial Feasibility

8.1.   Upon compliance with the Discovery Assessment Plan approved by ANP, the Concessionaire, through notice to ANP, may, at its sole discretion, submit the Declaration of Commercial Feasibility for the Discovery.

* * *

8.2.   Failure by the Concessionaire to submit the Declaration of Commercial Feasibility in a timely manner entails the lawful termination of the Agreement regarding the relevant area retained for the Discovery Assessment.

* * *

Postponement of the Declaration of Commercial Feasibility

8.4.   If the main accumulation of hydrocarbons discovered and assessed in a Concession Area is Natural Gas, the Concessionaire may request to ANP an authorization to postpone the Declaration of Commercial Feasibility in up to five (5) years, in the following cases:

   a)   lack of market for the Natural Gas to be produced, expected to be created in less than five (5) years;

   b)   lack or inadequacy of infrastructure for transportation of the Natural Gas to be produced by the Concessionaire, expected to be implemented in less than 5 (five) years.

8.5.   If the main accumulation of hydrocarbons discovered and assessed in a Concession Area is Oil, the Concessionaire may request to ANP an authorization to postpone the Declaration of Commercial Feasibility in up to five (5) years, in the following cases:

   a)   lack of technology for the Production, outflow, or refining, expected to be created in less than 5 (five) years.

   b)   the volume of the Discovery is such that its commercial feasibility depends on additional Discoveries to be made in the same Block or in adjacent Blocks, aiming at the joint Development of all Operations.

8.6.   The Concessionaire may request ANP that the period for postponement of the delivery of the Declaration of Commercial Feasibility is extended for five (5) additional years.

* * *

CHAPTER III—DEVELOPMENT AND PRODUCTION
SECTION NINE—PRODUCTION PHASE

Start and Duration

9.1.   The Production Phase of each Development Area shall begin on the date of submission of the Declaration of Commercial Feasibility and shall last for twenty-seven (27) years.

9.2.   References to the extension or termination of this Agreement in this Section are made to each Development Area or Field on an individual basis, which may correspond to different Production Phases.

* * *

Termination

9.6.   At any time during the Production Phase, the Concessionaire may terminate this Agreement, in whole or in part, upon notice to ANP at least one hundred and eighty (180) days before the date intended to terminate the Agreement.

* * *

Relinquishment of the Field

9.7.   Once the Production Phase is completed, pursuant to paragraph 9.1, the Field shall be relinquished to ANP.

* * *

9.9.   The Concessionaire must submit to ANP a Facility Decommissioning Program, detailing all actions required for the decommissioning of the facilities, within no less than three hundred and sixty-five (365) days before the end of Production.

    9.9.1.   The Facility Decommissioning Program shall strictly comply with the Applicable Laws and Regulations and the Best Practices of the Oil Industry, also pursuant to the provisions in Section Twenty-One and the other relevant provisions applicable to the reversal of properties provided for in paragraphs 18.6 and 18.7.

* * *

SECTION TEN—DEVELOPMENT PLAN

Content

10.1.   The Development Plan shall observe:

    a)   rationalization of the Production;

    b)   the control of the decline in reservoirs;

    c)   reduction in the burning of Natural Gas and greenhouse gas emissions to the atmosphere;

    d)   system for reuse or reinjection of the Associated Gas; provided that only the burning of Natural Gas in flares shall be allowed for reasons of safety, emergency, and commissioning, pursuant to the Applicable Laws and Regulations;

e) the proper treatment of contaminants and natural resources resulting from the Production activities, avoiding disposal into the environment; and

f) incorporation of criteria related to the decommissioning of the facilities in the definitions of the field development project.

Terms

10.2. The Concessionaire shall submit the Development Plan to ANP within one hundred and eighty (180) days from receipt by the operator of a communication of approval of the Final Discovery Assessment Report.

* * *

Approval and Implementation of the Development Plan

10.7. ANP shall have one hundred and eighty (180) days from the date of receipt of the Development Plan to approve it or request the Concessionaire to make the modifications it deems applicable.

* * *

10.9. The Concessionaire shall conduct all Operations according to the Development Plan approved by ANP.

* * *

Reviews and Amendments

10.12. The Development Plan shall be reviewed or amended in the following cases:

a) as required by ANP or at the request of the Concessionaire if, at any time, it fails to comply with the Applicable Laws and Regulations or the Best Practices of the Oil Industry;

b) at the request of the Concessionaire, in case of changes in the technical or economic conditions assumed in its preparation.

* * *

SECTION ELEVEN—PRODUCTION START DATE AND ANNUAL PRODUCTION PROGRAMS

Start of Production

11.1. The Start Date of the Field Production shall occur within no more than five (5) years, extendable at ANP's discretion, from the date of submission of the Declaration of Commercial Feasibility.

* * *

Annual Production Program

11.2. The Annual Production Program shall not provide for a variation equal to or higher than ten percent (10%) of the amount provided for in the Development Plan.

* * *

Approval of the Annual Production Program

11.6. ANP shall have thirty (30) days from receipt of the Annual Production Program to approve it or request the Concessionaire to make the modifications it deems applicable.

* * *

CHAPTER IV—EXECUTION OF OPERATIONS
SECTION FOURTEEN—EXECUTION BY THE CONCESSIONAIRE

Concessionaire's Exclusivity

14.1. The Concessionaire shall have the exclusive right to execute the Operations in the Concession Area pursuant to the terms, conditions, and effectiveness of the Agreement.

Appointment of the Operator by the Concessionaire

14.2. The Operator is designated by the Concessionaire to, on its behalf:

a) conduct and perform all Operations provided for in this Agreement;

b) submit all plans, programs, guarantees, proposals, and communications to ANP; and

c) receive all replies, requests, proposals, and other communications from ANP.

* * *

Diligence to Conduct Operations

14.12. The Concessionaire shall plan, prepare, implement, and control the Operations in a diligent, efficient and appropriate manner, pursuant to the Applicable Laws and Regulations and the Best Practices of the Oil Industry, always respecting the provisions in this Agreement and not performing any act that characterizes or may characterize a violation of the economic order.

14.12.1. The Concessionaire shall, in all Operations:

a) adopt the measures required for preservation of oil resources and other natural resources and for the protection of human life, heritage, and environment, pursuant to Section Twenty-One;

b) respect the applicable technical, scientific, and safety rules and procedures, including as to the recovery of fluids, aiming at the rationalization of production and the control of the decline in the reservoirs; and

c)   employ, whenever appropriate and economically justified, at ANP's discretion, technical experiences and more advanced technologies, including the ones that can increase the economic yield and the Production of the Deposits.

* * *

SECTION FIFTEEN—CONTROL OF OPERATIONS AND ASSISTANCE BY ANP

Monitoring and Inspection by ANP

15.1.   ANP shall permanently monitor and inspect the Operations directly or through arrangements with bodies of the Federal Government, States, or the Federal District.

* * *

Access and Control

15.2.   ANP shall have free access to the Concession Area and the ongoing Operations, equipment, and facilities of the Concessionaire, as well as all records, studies, and technical data available, for purposes of monitoring and inspection.

* * *

SECTION EIGHTEEN—PROPERTIES

Properties, Equipment, Facilities and Materials

18.1.   The Concessionaire is exclusively responsible for directly supplying, purchasing, renting, leasing, chartering, or otherwise obtaining, at its own account and risk, all properties, furniture, and real properties, including, without limitation, the facilities, buildings, systems, equipment, machines, materials, and supplies required to execute the Operations.

* * *

Licenses, Authorizations and Permits

18.2.   The Concessionaire shall be fully responsible, pursuant to paragraph 14.14, for obtaining all licenses, authorizations, and permits required for acquisition or use of the properties referred to in paragraph 18.

* * *

SECTION NINETEEN—PERSONNEL, SERVICES AND SUBCONTRACTS

Personnel

19.1.   The Concessionaire shall, directly or in any other way, recruit and hire all personnel required to execute the Operations at its own account and risk, being, for all purposes of this Agreement, the sole and exclusive employer.

* * *

Services

19.6.   The Concessionaire must directly perform, contract, or otherwise obtain, at its own account and risk, all services required for performance of this Agreement.

* * *

19.8.   The Concessionaire shall be strictly held liable for the activities of its subcontractors resulting, directly or indirectly, in damages or losses to ANP or the Federal Government.

* * *

SECTION TWENTY—LOCAL CONTENT

Concessionaire's Commitment with the Local Content

20.1.   The Concessionaire shall meet the following minimum mandatory percentages of Global Local Content:

20.1.1.   In the Onshore Exploration Phase: Global Local Content of 50%.

20.1.2.   In the Offshore Exploration Phase, with water depth over 100 meters: Global Local Content of 18%.

20.1.3.   In the Development Stage or for each Development module, in case of module development, of Onshore Fields: Global Local Content of 50%.

20.1.4.   In the Development Stage or for each Development module, in case of module development, of Offshore Fields with water depth over 100 meters, for the following Macro-Groups:

a)   Well Construction: 25%.

b)   Production Collection and Outflow System: 40%.

c)   Stationary Production Unit: 25%.

20.2.   The Concessionaire shall ensure preference to Brazilian Suppliers whenever their bids have more favorable conditions of price, deadline, and quality, or conditions equivalent to the ones submitted by foreign suppliers.

20.3.   The procedures for contracting goods and services directed to performance of this Agreement shall:

a)   include Brazilian Suppliers among the suppliers invited to submit bids;

b)   provide the main non-technical documents and specifications of the contract also in Portuguese to the Brazilian companies invited;

c) accept equivalent specifications of Brazilian Suppliers, as long as the Best Practices of the Oil Industry are complied with.

* * *

Penalty for Failure to Respect the Local Content

20.12. Failure to respect the Local Content shall subject the Concessionaire to a penalty, which shall be calculated on the monetary amount not observed, in the following percentage, as the case may be:

a) If the percentage of the Unused Local Content (NR) is below sixty-five percent (65%) of the Minimum Local Content, the penalty shall be forty percent (40%) of the amount of the Unused Local Content.

b) If the percentage of the Unused Local Content (NR) is equal to or higher than sixty-five percent (65%), the penalty shall begin at forty percent (40%), reaching seventy-five percent (75%) of the amount of the Minimum Local Content in case of 100% Unused Local Content (NR), according to the formula:

$$M (\%) = NR (\%) - 25\%.$$

Where NR (%) is the percentage of Unused Local Content.

* * *

SECTION TWENTY-ONE—OPERATIONAL SAFETY AND ENVIRONMENT

Environmental Control

21.1. The Concessionaire shall have a safety and environment management system that complies with the Best Practices of the Oil Industry and the Applicable Laws and Regulations.

21.2. The Concessionaire shall, in the performance of the Agreement:

a) ensure preservation of an ecologically balanced environment;

b) mitigate the occurrence of impacts and/or damages to the environment;

c) ensure safety of the Operations for purposes of protecting human life, the environment, and the Federal Government's heritage;

d) ensure protection of the Brazilian historical and cultural heritage;

e) repair the degraded environment pursuant to the technical solution required by the applicable environmental authority;

f) meet the Safety Recommendations issued by ANP pursuant to the Applicable Laws and Regulations.

* * *

Social Responsibility

21.7. The Concessionaire shall provide a Social Responsibility and sustainability management system that meets the Social Responsibility guidelines and the Applicable Laws and Regulations.

Liability for Damages and Losses

21.8. Without prejudice to the provisions in paragraph 21.1, the Concessionaire shall undertake full and strict liability for all environmental damages that may result from execution of the Operations, directly or indirectly.

   21.8.1. The Concessionaire shall indemnify the damages resulting from the Operations.

   21.8.2. The Concessionaire shall indemnify the Federal Government and ANP, pursuant to paragraphs 2.2 to 2.6, for any and all lawsuit, appeal, claim or legal oppositions, arbitration court, audit, inspection, investigation, or dispute of any kind, as well as for any damages, compensations, punishments, fines, or penalties of any kind, related to or resulting from such damages and losses.

SECTION TWENTY-TWO—INSURANCE

Insurance

22.1. The Concessionaire shall obtain and keep in force, during the effectiveness of the Agreement, without entailing limitation of its liability under this Agreement, insurance coverage for all cases required by the Applicable Laws and Regulations.

* * *

22.2. At ANP's sole discretion and provided that previously authorized by it, self-insurance may be accepted.

* * *

CHAPTER V—GOVERNMENT SHARES AND INVESTMENTS IN RESEARCH, DEVELOPMENT AND INNOVATION
SECTION TWENTY-THREE—SHARES

Government and Third-Party Shares

23.1. In addition to the signature bonus, paid before the date of execution of the Agreement, the Concessionaire shall pay to the Federal Government and third parties the following shares, pursuant to the Applicable Laws and Regulations:

a) Royalties;

b) special share;

c) payment for land occupancy or withholding; and

d) payment of a share to the landowner.

23.2. For the fields that may pay special share, regardless of the amounts indicated in Table 2 of the call for bids of the Fourteenth Bidding Round and in Annex V to this Agreement, the royalty rate shall be ten percent (10%).

23.3. ANP may, in the scope of the extensions of the effectiveness of this agreement and considering the expected production and other relevant factors pursuant to the Applicable Laws and Regulations, grant a royalty reduction to up to five percent (5%) over the incremental production generated by a potential new investment plan to be executed in field.

* * *

SECTION TWENTY-FOUR—RESOURCES FOR RESEARCH, DEVELOPMENT AND INNOVATION

24.1. If the Special Share is payable for a Field in any quarter of the calendar year, the Concessionaire shall be required to pay Expenses Identified as Research, Development, and Innovation in the fields of interest and topics relevant to the industry of Oil, Natural Gas, and Biofuels, in an amount equal to one percent (1%) of the Gross Revenue of the Production for such Field.

* * *

24.2. Thirty percent (30%) to forty percent (40%) of the resources provided for in paragraph 24.1 shall be invested in national universities or research and development institutes accredited by ANP.

24.3. Thirty percent (30%) to forty percent (40%) of the resources provided for in paragraph 24.1 shall be directed to technological programs for development and qualification of domestic suppliers.

24.4. The remaining balance of the Expenses Identified as Research, Development, and Innovation, upon compliance with paragraphs 24.2 and 24.3, may be invested in activities of research, development, and innovation developed at facilities of the very Concessionaire or its Affiliates located in Brazil or of national suppliers of the Industry of Oil, Natural Gas, and Biofuels, or at universities or research and development institutes accredited by ANP.

* * *

SECTION TWENTY-FIVE—TAXES

Tax Regime

25.1. The Concessionaire shall be subject to the tax regime in the federal, state and municipal scopes, undertaking to comply with it under the terms, deadlines, and conditions defined in the Applicable Laws and Regulations.

* * *

SECTION TWENTY-SIX—CURRENCY AND FOREIGN CURRENCY

Currency

26.1. The currency shall be Real, for all purposes and effects of this Agreement.

Foreign Currency

26.2. The entry and remittance of foreign currency shall observe the Brazilian laws, including the regulations issued by the monetary authorities of the Country.

SECTION TWENTY-SEVEN—ACCOUNTING AND AUDIT

Accounting

27.1. According to the Applicable Laws and Regulations, the Concessionaire shall:

a) keep all documents, books, papers, records, and other procedural documents;

b) keep all supporting documents required for determination of the Local Content and of the Government and Third-Party Shares supporting the accounting bookkeeping;

c) make the applicable entries;

d) submit the accounting and financial statements;

e) submit to ANP, on a quarterly basis, the Quarterly Expense Report under the Applicable Laws and Regulations; and

f) submit to ANP the Local Content Report under the Applicable Laws and Regulations.

Audit

27.2. ANP may perform audit, including for the declarations of calculation of the Government Shares, under the Applicable Laws and Regulations.

* * *

CHAPTER VI—GENERAL PROVISIONS
SECTION TWENTY-EIGHT—ASSIGNMENT OF THE AGREEMENT

Assignment

28.1. The Concessionaire's rights and obligations under this Agreement may be subject to Assignment, in whole or in part, subject to ANP's prior authorization.

* * *

28.4.   The Operator and the other members of the Consortium shall have, respectively, at least a thirty-percent (30%) and a five-percent (5%) share in the Agreement throughout its effectiveness.

28.5.   The Concessionaires shall notify ANP about changes in their corporate control within thirty (30) days from registration of the charter with the effective registration agency, under the Applicable Laws and Regulations.

* * *

SECTION THIRTY—TERMINATION OF THE AGREEMENT

Lawful Termination

30.1.   This Agreement shall be lawfully terminated:

   a)   upon lapse of the effective period provided for in Section Four;

   b)   upon completion of the Exploration Phase without performing the Minimum Exploration Program;

   c)   at the end of the Exploration Phase, in case there has been no Commercial Discovery;

   d)   in case the Contractor fully relinquishes the Concession Area;

   e)   upon failure to deliver the Development Plan within the term established by ANP;

   f)   upon ANP's disapproval of the Development Plan;

   g)   upon refusal of the Consortium Members to execute, in whole or in part, the production individualization agreement after ANP's decision; or

   h)   upon adjudication of bankruptcy or non-approval of any Concessionaire's request for judicial reorganization by the competent court;

Termination upon Mutual Agreement Between the Parties

30.2.   This Agreement may be terminated at any time upon mutual agreement between the Parties, without prejudice to performance of the obligations under this agreement.

Unilateral Termination

30.3.   At any time during the Production Phase, the Concessionaire may terminate this Agreement only upon notice to ANP at least one hundred and eighty (180) days before the date intended to terminate the Agreement.

* * *

Consequences of Termination

30.5.   In any of the cases of termination provided for in this Agreement or in the Applicable Laws and Regulations, the Concessionaire shall not be entitled to any reimbursement.

30.6.   Once this Agreement is terminated, the Concessionaire shall be liable for losses and damages arising from its default and termination, paying all applicable indemnifications and compensations, as provided by law and herein.

SECTION THIRTY-ONE—ACT OF GOD, FORCE MAJEURE AND SIMILAR CAUSES

Full or Partial Exemption

31.1.   The obligations undertaken in this Agreement shall only be released in the events of acts of God, force majeure, and similar causes that justify non-performance, such as administrative action or omission, factum principis, and unexpected disruptions.

* * *

31.2.   Notification of events that may be considered an act of God, force majeure, or similar cause shall be immediate and shall specify such circumstances, its causes and consequences.

* * *

Amendment and Termination of the Agreement

31.3.   After the act of God, force majeure, or similar causes are overcome, the Concessionaire shall perform the affected obligations, and the term for performance of these obligations shall be extended for the period corresponding to the duration of the event.

* * *

Environmental Permitting

31.4.   ANP may extend or suspend the lapse of the contract term in case of evidenced delay in the permitting procedure due to exclusive fault of the applicable environmental authorities.

* * *

Losses

31.7.   The Concessionaire shall individually and exclusively assume all losses arising from the situation of act of God or force majeure.

SECTION THIRTY-TWO—CONFIDENTIALITY

Obligation of the Concessionaire

32.1.   Any and all data and information acquired, processed, produced, developed, or, in any way, obtained as a result of the Operations and the Agreement are strictly confidential and, therefore, shall not be disclosed by the Concessionaire without the prior consent of ANP, except when:

   a)   data and information are already public or become public through a third party authorized to disclose them;

   b)   there is a requirement for disclosure arising from legal obligation or court order;

c)   the disclosure is made according to the rules and limits imposed by the stock exchange in which the Concessionaire's shares are traded;

* * *

ANP's Commitment

32.3.   ANP undertakes not to disclose any data and information obtained as a result of the Operations and related to the areas withheld by the Concessionaire, pursuant to article 5, paragraph 2, of Decree No. 7,724/2012.

* * *

SECTION THIRTY-FOUR—LEGAL REGIME

Governing Law

34.1.   This Agreement shall be executed, governed, and construed according to the Brazilian laws.

    34.1.1.   The parties shall observe the Applicable Laws and Regulations upon execution of this agreement.

* * *

Reconciliation

34.2.   The Parties undertake to use all efforts as to amicably resolve upon any and all dispute or controversy arising from this Agreement or related thereto.

    34.2.1.   Such efforts shall include at least the request for a specific reconciliation meeting by the unsatisfied party, followed by its request and factual and lawful reasons.

    34.2.2.   The request shall be met, and the meeting shall be scheduled by the other party within thirty (30) days from the request, in ANP's offices. The representatives of the parties shall have powers to compromise on the matter.

    34.2.3.   After the meeting, if no agreement is immediately reached, the parties shall have at least thirty (30) additional days to negotiate an amicable solution.

34.3.   The Parties may, upon agreement, resort to an independent expert in order to obtain a well-grounded opinion that may lead to the settlement of the dispute or controversy.

    34.3.1.   In case such agreement is signed, arbitration may only be filed after issuance of the expert's opinion.

* * *

Arbitration

34.5.   After the procedure set forth in paragraph 34.2, if one of the Parties considers there are conditions for an amicable solution to the dispute or controversy referred to in such paragraph, it may submit such issue to arbitration ad hoc, using the Arbitration Rules of the United Nations Commission on International Trade Law—UNCITRAL as a parameter, according to the following precepts:

a) the arbitrators shall be appointed as determined by the Arbitration Rules of UNCITRAL;

b) three arbitrators shall be appointed. Each Party shall choose an arbitrator. The two arbitrators so appointed shall designate the third arbitrator, who shall preside over the panel;

c) upon agreement of the Parties, a sole arbitrator may be appointed in the events the amounts involved are not high;

d) the city of Rio de Janeiro, Brazil, shall be the seat of the arbitration and the place where the arbitration award is rendered;

e) the language of the arbitration proceeding shall be the Portuguese. However, the Parties may support the proceeding with testimonies or documents in any other language, as decided by the arbitrators, with no need for a sworn translation;

f) any and all expenses required for installation and development of the arbitration, such as costs and advance payment of arbitrator's and expert's fees, shall be exclusively borne by the Concessionaire. ANP shall reimburse such amounts only upon a final conviction, as decided by the arbitrators;

g) on the merits, the arbitrators shall decide based on the Brazilian laws;

h) the arbitration award shall be final and its content shall bind the Parties. Any amounts possibly payable by ANP shall be paid off by a special judicial order, except in the event of administrative acknowledgement of the request; and

i) if preliminary injunctions or urgent protective measures are required before arbitration, the interested Party may request them directly from the Judiciary Branch, based on the Applicable Laws and Regulations, and they shall be cancelled if arbitration is not filed within thirty (30) days from the date of effectiveness of the decision.

34.6. The Parties may, by mutual agreement, choose to file the arbitration with the International Court of Arbitration of the International Chamber of Commerce or with another widely recognized, reputable arbitration panel, according to the rules of the chamber chosen, provided that the provisions of sub-items "b" to "i" of paragraph 34.5 are observed.

* * *

34.7. The Parties hereby represent to be aware that the arbitration addressed by this Section refers exclusively to disputes arising from the Agreement or related thereto and is intended to settle only litigations related to the equity rights available, under Law No. 9,307/1996.

Jurisdiction

34.8. For the provisions in item "i" of paragraph 34.5 and matters not related to the equity rights available, as provided by Law No. 9,307/96, the Parties elect the jurisdiction of the Federal Courts—Judiciary Section of Rio de Janeiro, Brazil, as the sole competent court, to the exclusion of any other court, however privileged it may be.

SECTION THIRTY-FIVE—FINAL PROVISIONS

* * *

35.3. Any amendments or addenda to this Agreement shall observe the Applicable Laws and Regulations and shall only be valid if formally made in writing and signed by the representatives of the Parties.

There are a number of fundamental things worth noting about the concession agreement set forth above. First, the concessionaire bears all the risk that no producible oil or gas will be discovered. The money it spends on exploration cannot be recovered from Brazil if oil and gas are not found. The concessionaire is also strictly liable for any damages caused during exploration and production.

Second, the concession agreement imposes minimum work obligations on the concessionaire only during the exploration phase. The parties simply cannot know before oil or gas is discovered what further obligations will make sense. For the later phases, the agreement establishes procedures under which the concessionaire will propose further plans that the government agency will review and approve. These include the Discovery Assessment Plan, the Development Plan, the Annual Production Plans, and the Facility Decommissioning Programs. The concession agreement also provides for the modification of plans and the extension of deadlines under certain circumstances. It requires regular reports to the government and notices of certain events. And it gives the government access to the concessionaire's facilities and records. In other words, the concession agreement establishes a framework for the future relationship between the concessionaire and the government—a relationship that may last more than three decades if oil or gas is discovered.

Third, the concession agreement establishes a detailed fiscal regime for sharing the money generated by the project. (1) Paragraph 23.1 refers to a signature bonus, which is a one-time payment on or before the concession agreement is signed. In Brazil, the government's invitation to bid will establish a minimum signature bonus that every bid must include, although bidders may offer higher signature bonuses in an effort to win the bid. (2) The concessionaire must pay a monthly royalty based on the total volume of oil and gas produced in a field during that month. In Brazil, the standard royalty is 10%, though the ANP may reduce this to 5% for blocks classified as inactive marginal fields. (3) The concessionaire must also pay what the agreement calls a "special share," also sometimes called a special participation payment. These are additional payments that allow the government to share in the good fortune when the volume of production is particularly high. The special share is calculated as a percentage of net production revenues (adjusted for royalties, exploration investments, operating costs, depreciation, and taxes), with the percentage ranging from 10% to 40% depending on the characteristics of the field, the years of production, and the volume of production. (4) Section 24 of the agreement provides that whenever a special share is payable, the concessionaire must also invest 1% of the gross revenues from that field in research and development at national universities and institutes, programs for the development of Brazilian suppliers, and the concessionaire's own research programs in Brazil. (5) The concessionaire must pay an annual fee to the government for areas occupied or retained for future exploration. This functions like a rental payment, and varies from BRL 10 to BRL 5,000 per square kilometer depending on the characteristics of the block. The fee for occupation creates an incentive for the concessionaire to explore the concession area and to relinquish to the government areas it does not intend to use. (6) If the block is owned by a private landowner, the concessionaire must make monthly payments to the landowner, typically 1% of the value of the oil and gas produced. (7) Section 25 provides that the concessionaire is subject to Brazilian taxes. In general Brazilian corporations are taxed at a rate of 34%, consisting of a basic rate of 15%, a surtax of 10% for profits exceeding BRL 240,000, and a social contribution tax of 9%. The corporate income tax is paid only on profit. Many expenditures, including the royalties paid to the government, are tax deductible.[2]

Fourth, the concession agreement provides benefits to the government apart from the payments just described. In particular, Section 20 sets forth minimum requirements for local content to promote growth and jobs in the Brazilian economy. To facilitate local content, the concessionaire must invite Brazilian suppliers to submit bids and must provide the bid specifications in Portuguese. The concessionaire must give preference to Brazilian suppliers when their bids are equivalent to those of foreign suppliers. Section 20 also sets forth penalties for failure to comply with local content requirements, though the effect of these

---

[2]   For more details, see Brazil, in Ernst & Young, Global Oil and Gas Tax Guide (2018).

provisions may be to set the price at which the concessionaire can buy its way out of the requirements if it wishes.

QUESTIONS

(1) In what ways does this concession agreement differ from the classic concession agreements described at the start of this Problem?

(2) Concession agreements may grant a foreign investor rights over a large part of a country's territory. In what ways does Brazil's concession agreement limit the rights that are granted and seek to minimize the impact of the investor's presence?

(3) Consider the various components of the government's "take": the signature bonus, the 10% royalty on production, the "special share" for particularly successful fields, the fee for occupancy, and the corporate income tax. How do they vary with respect to timing—that is, when and how regularly can the government count on receiving each of these payments? How do they vary with respect to profitability—that is, which of them give the government a greater share if the project becomes more successful?

(4) In what ways does the concession agreement reflect environmental concerns? Do the protections for the environment seem sufficient?

Additional reading: Yergin, The Prize: The Epic Quest for Oil, Money and Power (1991); Smith et al., Materials on International Petroleum Transactions ch. 6 (3d ed. 2010); Oil Contracts: How to Read Them and Understand Them (Open Oil 2013), http://openoil.net/wp-content/uploads/2013/11/oil-contracts-v1.2-dec-13.pdf.

C. SOME LEGAL ASPECTS OF CONCESSION AGREEMENTS

Under many systems of municipal law, distinctive principles apply to contracts between a government and a private party. They include different rules as to apparent authority, impossibility of performance, assignment of contracts, and remedies for breach of contract. And of course sovereign immunity may preclude suit by the aggrieved private party, a topic considered in Problem 8. See infra pp. 522–527.

Problems of a more fundamental nature, however, arise from the fact that the government is not only a contracting party but also a lawmaker. It may, for example, enact new environmental or safety laws that impose additional burdens on the foreign investor. It may change the tax rates applicable to corporations generally or to the foreign operation in particular. It may even change the rules of contract law that govern the agreement.

There is, of course, an undeniable need for the governmental party to preserve sufficient flexibility to enact laws that it considers to be in the general interest without incurring excessive liabilities. Such considerations have led to the growth of special doctrines in many legal systems—for example, the French law of the *contrat administratif* that allows the government party to make certain changes to a contract unilaterally.[3] On the other hand, the foreign investor may be unwilling to enter an agreement without some assurance that the rules governing its operation will not change in ways that fundamentally alter the bargain.

These problems are compounded by the length of time for which concession agreements run. In order to conduct initial exploration, build the necessary infrastructure, and commence production, the investor needs to have a long-term commitment in place. Consider for example what would have to be done before a mine in the central part of Papua New Guinea could actually begin shipping ore. It may be many years before such an operation generates enough income to repay the investment and yield a profit. But time does not stand still. Over ten or twenty years, the economic, social, and political situation in the host country may change radically. One endemic problem is that the relative positions of the parties to a concession agreement tend to shift. The host state, originally delighted to have won the interest of a foreign investor, becomes more and more confident in its own ability to manage the enterprise, which has now become a more routinized and steady operation. The foreign investor also becomes more susceptible to pressure as its "sunk costs" increase.

In the sections that follow, we consider some of the legal issues that arise from these considerations. We begin with the dispute resolution clauses. As we will see, international arbitration is frequently used to shield the foreign investor (at least partially) from the domestic courts of the host state. A concession agreement may also address the conflict between government as party and government as regulator through its choice of law clause or through a "stabilization clause" that attempts to freeze the law applicable to the foreign investment. We then consider the international law that applies to the breach or repudiation of concession agreements. This includes customary international law, but also the provisions of International Investment Agreements (IIAs) that increasingly govern this area. There is also the possibility of purchasing insurance to protect against some kinds of political risks. Finally, we look at the issue of renegotiation to account for changes over the life of the agreement, with varying amounts of pressure applied by the host government.

1.   CHOICE OF DISPUTE RESOLUTION MECHANISMS IN CONCESSION AGREEMENTS

The drafters of a concession agreement face a number of choices in selecting a mechanism for resolving the disputes that may arise during

---

[3]   See 1 Vedel & Delvolvé, Droit Administratif 363–443 (12th ed. 1992).

its operation. They may opt for domestic courts. It is extraordinarily rare for the courts of the foreign investor's home country to be chosen, for this would be taken as an insult by the host state. On the other hand, it is relatively common for concession agreements to select the courts of the host state, particularly for the resolution of contractual issues. For example, Article 16.4 of the 1995 Concession Contract for Water and Sewage Service between the province of Tucumán, Argentina and Compañia de Aguas del Aconquija S.A. (an affiliate of the French company Compagnie Générale des Eaux, which subsequently became Vivendi Universal) provided:

> For purposes of interpretation and application of this Contract the parties submit themselves to the exclusive jurisdiction of the Contentious Administrative Tribunals of Tucumán.

In the era of International Investment Agreements (IIAs), the choice of the host state's courts may seem less risky because of a relatively consistent line of authority holding that such clauses, even if exclusive, do not deprive international arbitral tribunals of authority to decide treaty claims. See McLachlan et al., International Investment Arbitration: Substantive Principles 117–119 & n. 107 (2d ed. 2017). IIAs are discussed further below. See pp. 470–482.

Another alternative, of course, is international arbitration. The neutrality that arbitration offers may be viewed by the foreign investor as an advantage over the domestic courts of the host state. Under Paragraph 34 of the Brazilian concession agreement above, if a dispute cannot be resolved amicably through reconciliation, it may be submitted to *ad hoc* arbitration under the Arbitration Rules of the United Nations Commission on International Trade Law (UNCITRAL). The arbitration clause covers only "disputes arising from the Agreement or related thereto and is intended to settle only litigations related to the equity rights available, under Law No. 9,307/1996," which is Brazil's arbitration law. Under that law, certain matters like taxes are not capable of settlement by arbitration. For such matters and for interim measures, Paragraph 34.8 designates the Federal Courts of Rio de Janeiro as the exclusive forum.

An *ad hoc* arbitration is one that is not administered by an arbitral institution, and the UNCITRAL Arbitration Rules are typically used in such arbitrations. Under the Rules, if the parties do not agree on an appointing authority, the Secretary-General of the Permanent Court of Arbitration in The Hague may designate the appointing authority. The UNCITRAL Arbitration Rules were last revised in 2010, with a provision on transparency in investor-state arbitration added in 2013. They are subject to modification by the parties, and you will see that Paragraph 34.5 of the concession agreement deals specifically with several important questions, including the number of arbitrators (three), the seat of arbitration (Rio de Janeiro), the language of the proceeding (Portuguese), and the allocation of costs (to the concessaire unless the government loses). Instead of *ad hoc* arbitration, the parties to a concession agreement may choose one of the institutions widely used for international commercial arbitrations such as the International Chamber of Commerce (ICC), the London Court of International Arbitration (LCIA), or the Stockholm Chamber of Commerce (SCC), each of which has its own rules.

There is also the International Centre for Settlement of Investment Disputes (ICSID), which was created in 1966 specifically to hear cases between states and private investors. To be eligible for arbitration under the ICSID Convention, both the host state and the foreign investor's home state must be parties to the Convention—and 159 states are parties to the ICSID Convention as of 2018. If either the foreign investor's home state or the host state, but not both, is a party to the Convention, the dispute may be decided instead under the ICSID Additional Facility rules. A critical difference between arbitration under the ICSID Convention and arbitration under any of the other institutions or rules mentioned above (including the ICSID Additional Facility rules) is that awards under the ICSID Convention are not subject to review by domestic courts under the framework established by the New York Convention. See supra pp. 41–44. Instead Article 52 of the ICSID Convention provides a separate procedure for the annulment of awards. The grounds for annulment of an ICSID award are limited like those under the New York Convention. However, relatively few investment awards have been set aside by domestic courts under the New York Convention, while there have been a number of annulments under the ICSID Convention, some quite controversial.[4]

2. CHOICE OF LAW IN CONCESSION AGREEMENTS

We dealt with choice of law clauses in Problem 1. See supra pp. 152–161. This issue presents special difficulties in contracts between a private party and a government because of the government's ability to change its own law, potentially to the detriment of the private party.

Despite this risk, modern concession agreements often expressly choose the law of the host state to govern the agreement. Paragraph 34.1 of the Brazilian concession agreement above, for example, provides: "This Agreement shall be executed, governed, and construed according to the Brazilian laws."

The law of the host state will also typically be applied if the parties fail to choose the governing law. For example, Article 42(1) of the ICSID Convention provides:

> The Tribunal shall decide a dispute in accordance with such rules of law as may be agreed by the parties. In the absence of such agreement, the Tribunal shall apply the law of the

---

[4] See ICSID, Updated Background Paper on Annulment for the Administrative Council of ICSID (2016).

Contracting State party to the dispute (including its rules on the conflict of laws) and such rules of international law as may be applicable.

It is worth noting that under Article 42(1) as it has been interpreted, international law may not only fill gaps in the law of the host state, but may also limit the application of the host state's law to those rules that are consistent with international law. Although a number of concession contracts have not specified the applicable law, it is generally advisable to do so.

Some older concession agreements sought to address the conflict between the government as party and the government as regulator by selecting principles of law common to more than one country. For example, Article 46 of the 1954 Iran Consortium Agreement provided:

> In view of the diverse nationalities of the parties to this Agreement, it shall be governed by and interpreted and applied in accordance with principles of law common to Iran and the several nations in which the other parties to this Agreement are incorporated, and in the absence of such common principles, then by and in accordance with principles of law recognized by civilized nations in general, including such of those principles as may have been applied by international tribunals.[5]

One practical drawback of this option, however, is that it may plunge the parties and the arbitrators into complex exercises in comparative law. Today, it is more common to address the risk of changes in the applicable law through a stabilization clause.

3. STABILIZATION CLAUSES

Another technique for addressing the conflict between government as party and government as regulator is the so-called "stabilization clause," the aim of which is to prevent, limit, or compensate for changes in the regulatory regime that may harm the foreign investor. In its classic form, the stabilization clause "freezes" the law applicable to the concession agreement. Thus, Article 41(B) of the 1954 Iran Consortium Agreement provided:

> No general or special legislative or administrative measures or any other act whatsoever of or emanating from Iran or any governmental authority in Iran (whether central or local) shall annul this Agreement, amend or modify its provisions or prevent or hinder the due and effective performance of its terms. Such annulment, amendment or modification shall not take place except by agreement of the parties to this Agreement.

---

[5] The Agreement appears in 2 Hurewitz, Diplomacy in the Near and Middle East 348 (1956).

Such "freezing" clauses are often characterized as outdated, but they appear in many modern concession agreements and are expressed in various ways.[6] Pakistan's 2009 Model Petroleum Concession Agreement simply states: "The Rules, Income Tax Ordinance 2001, Regulations of Mines and Oilfields and Mineral Development (Government Control) Act, 1948 and other laws that are in force on the Effective Date shall remain applicable for the purposes hereof, whether or not the same are subsequently amended or revised."[7] A 2006 concession agreement with Ghana, on the other hand, incorporates stabilization of the legal regime as a contractual undertaking by the government:

> As of the Effective Date of this Agreement and throughout its Term, the State guarantees Contractor the stability of the terms and conditions of this Agreement as well as the fiscal and contractual framework hereof specifically including those terms and conditions and that framework that are based upon or subject to the provisions of the laws and regulations of Ghana (and any interpretations thereof) including, without limitation, the Petroleum Income Tax Law, the Petroleum Law, the GNPC Law and those other laws, regulations and decrees that are applicable hereto.

The agreement further provides that "[a]ny legislative or administrative act of the State or any of its agencies or subdivisions which purports to vary any such right or obligation shall, to the extent sought to be applied to this Agreement, constitute a breach of this Agreement by the State."[8] Of course, a stabilization clause need not attempt to freeze all the laws applicable to a foreign investor. It may seek to stabilize only those laws that are most important to the financial success of the investment— typically its tax laws and laws governing the repatriation of capital.

Some modern concession agreements include "equilibrium" clauses that provide for a rebalancing of the parties' rights and obligations in the event of a legislative change in order to reestablish the initial equilibrium of the agreement. This may be done as an alternative to a traditional stabilization clause or in combination with it. With such a clause, it is important to state how the rebalancing will occur. Will it be subject to negotiation by the parties? Will it be left to the decision of an arbitrator? Consider the following provision from Morocco's 2014 Model Concession Contract:

> In the event that a change in Regulations has a significant adverse effect on the economic benefits that PETCO [Petroleum Company] would have received if such change had not been

---

[6]   For a survey of recent practice with respect to stabilization clauses, see International Finance Corporation, Stabilization Clauses and Human Rights (2008).

[7]   Pakistan Model Petroleum Concession Agreement for Onshore Area, Art. 30.5 (2009).

[8]   Petroleum Agreement Among Government of the Republic of Ghana et al. and Tullow Ghana Ltd. et al., Arts. 26.2–26.3 (2006).

made, the terms of this Agreement will be as soon as possible adjusted in order to compensate PETCO for such adverse effect.

ONHYM [Office National des Hydrocarbures et des Mines] shall use every effort with the STATE to preserve or re-establish in favor of PETCO the economic terms and conditions prevailing at the time of signature. If despite the efforts of ONHYM, this should not prove to be possible, PETCO shall notify in writing to ONHYM a proposal for the necessary changes to be made to the terms of this Agreement in order to compensate for such adverse effect, and the Parties shall endeavor to agree on such changes to the terms hereof.

If the Parties fail to agree on such changes within a term of sixty (60) days from the date on which PETCO delivers a notice on this regard to ONHYM, the matter may be referred to Arbitration under Article 22.[9]

To say that stabilization clauses are enforceable, as many tribunals and commentators have, is not to say that legislation breaching such a clause may be enjoined. As a general matter, arbitrators lack injunctive power and are limited to awarding damages. Thus, in the Aminoil Award the tribunal first concluded that the stabilization clause was valid and enforceable and then construed it not to prohibit nationalization so long as compensation was paid—a judgment perhaps worthy of Solomon, another noted Middle Eastern arbitrator. See Kuwait v. American Independent Oil Co. (AMINOIL), 21 I.L.M. 976, 1018–1024 (1982).

QUESTIONS

(1) Consider Paragraph 34 of the Brazilian Concession Agreement, which provides for *ad hoc* arbitration under the UNCITRAL Arbitration Rules and chooses Brazilian law without a stabilization clause. Do these provisions give adequate security to foreign investors?

(2) Do stabilization clauses benefit only the foreign investor? If so, then why have host countries been willing to agree to them?

Additional reading: Schreuer et al., The ICSID Convention: A Commentary 545–639 (2d ed. 2009); Parra, Applicable Law in Investor-State Arbitration, in Contemporary Issues in International Arbitration and Mediation (Rovine ed., 2008); Erkan, International Energy Investment Law: Stability Through Contractual Clauses (2011); Cameron, International Energy Investment Law: The Pursuit of Stability (2010); Maniruzzaman, Drafting Stabilisation Clauses in International Energy Contracts: Some Pitfalls for the Unwary, 2007 Int'l Energy L. & Tax. R. 23.

---

[9] Petroleum Agreement Regarding the Exploration for and Exploitation of Hydrocarbons Between Office National des Hydrocarbures et des Mines (ONHYM) Acting on Behalf of the State and PETCO, Art. 16.2 (2014).

D. INTERNATIONAL LAW ON THE BREACH OR REPUDIATION OF CONCESSION AGREEMENTS

Under what circumstances may the breach or repudiation of a concession agreement violate not just the system of laws chosen to govern the agreement but also international law? For many years, this was a question primarily of customary international law. But the advent of IIAs has expanded the protection that international law affords to contracts. We will consider these two sources of international law in turn.

1. CUSTOMARY INTERNATIONAL LAW

Customary international law protects foreign investors against expropriation of property and against repudiation or breach of contract under certain circumstances. The Restatement (Third) of Foreign Relations Law summarized these rules of customary international law as follows:

§ 712. State Responsibility for Economic Injury to Nationals of Other States

A state is responsible under international law for injury resulting from:

(1) a taking by the state of the property of a national of another state that

   (a) is not for a public purpose, or

   (b) is discriminatory, or

   (c) is not accompanied by provision for just compensation;

For compensation to be just under this Subsection, it must, in the absence of exceptional circumstances, be in an amount equivalent to the value of the property taken and be paid at the time of taking, or within a reasonable time thereafter with interest from the date of taking, and in a form economically usable by the foreign national;

(2) a repudiation or breach by the state of a contract with a national of another state

   (a) where the repudiation or breach is (i) discriminatory; or (ii) motivated by noncommercial considerations, and compensatory damages are not paid; or

   (b) where the foreign national is not given an adequate forum to determine his claim of repudiation or breach, or is not compensated for any repudiation or breach determined to have occurred; or

(3) other arbitrary or discriminatory acts or omissions by the state that impair property or other economic interests of a national of another state.

Note that the Restatement (Third) treats expropriations of property separately from repudiations or breaches of contracts.

It is clear that the customary international law rules on expropriation cover both formal transfers of ownership (direct expropriations) and actions that effectively deprive the investor of the benefits of ownership (indirect expropriations). They cover expropriations that result from a single act and those that result from a series of acts (creeping expropriations). As in domestic law, the central problem is how to determine when government regulation goes so far as to become a taking of property. Comment *g* to Section 712 provides the following guidance:

> Subsection (1) applies not only to avowed expropriations in which the government formally takes title to property, but also to other actions of the government that have the effect of "taking" the property, in whole or in large part, outright or in stages ("creeping expropriation"). A state is responsible as for an expropriation of property under Subsection (1) when it subjects alien property to taxation, regulation, or other action that is confiscatory, or that prevents, unreasonably interferes with, or unduly delays, effective enjoyment of an alien's property or its removal from the state's territory. Depriving an alien of control of his property, as by an order freezing his assets, might become a taking if it is long extended. A state is not responsible for loss of property or for other economic disadvantage resulting from bona fide general taxation, regulation, forfeiture for crime, or other action of the kind that is commonly accepted as within the police power of states, if it is not discriminatory, Comment *f*, and is not designed to cause the alien to abandon the property to the state or sell it at a distress price.

IIAs have added words to the definitions of expropriation. See infra pp. 471–472. But they have not been able to draw a clear line between regulation and expropriation or to remove the need for case-by-case determinations.

Another issue with respect to expropriation is the standard of compensation required by customary international law. In 1938, during a dispute with Mexico over the expropriation of agricultural lands, U.S. Secretary of State Cordell Hull wrote that "no government is entitled to expropriate private property, for whatever purpose, without provision for prompt, adequate, and effective payment therefor"—the so-called Hull Doctrine—while Mexico maintained that only national treatment was required "for expropriations of a general and impersonal character like those which Mexico has carried out for the purpose of redistribution of the land."[10] During the 1960s and 70s, a series of U.N. General Assembly

---

[10]   3 Hackworth, Digest of International Law 655–661 (1942).

resolutions called for "appropriate compensation" in cases of expropriation. Although there may be no consensus today on what customary international law requires, IIAs have tended to resolve the question by adopting a standard that reflects the U.S. position. See infra pp. 471–472.

It has long been recognized that the repudiation or breach of a contract by a state may also give rise to liability under customary international law. The Umpire in the Rudloff Case stated, "[t]he taking away or destruction of rights acquired, transmitted and defined by a contract is as much a wrong, entitling the sufferer to redress, as the taking away or destruction of tangible property." Rudloff Case (U.S. v. Ven.) (Jurisdiction), 9 U.N. Rep. Int'l Arb. Awards 244, 250 (1903–05) (American-Venezuelan Comm.). On the other hand, it is equally clear that a state's breach of an ordinary commercial agreement does not give rise to international responsibility. If the central problem with expropriations is how to distinguish government regulations from government takings, the central problem with repudiations and breaches of contract is how to distinguish actions taken as party to the contract (which give rise to liability only under the domestic law governing the contract) from actions taken as a governmental authority (which may violate customary international law).

An ambitious study of many years ago concluded: "If one examines these cases carefully, one finds that, so far as they can be said to contain any common ground at all, it is the feature of the use of governmental power to defeat the obligations of the contract."[11] When the state breaches or repudiates a contract for governmental rather than commercial reasons, its action may be analogized to an expropriation. Indeed, a number of international tribunals have permitted claims for the expropriation of contractual rights. See, e.g., Phillips Petroleum Co. Iran v. Islamic Republic of Iran, 21 Iran-U.S. Cl. Trib. Rep. 79, 106 (1989); Certain German Interests in Polish Upper Silesia (Germ. v. Pol.), 1926 P.C.I.J. (ser. A) No. 7, at 44 (May 25); Norwegian Shipowners' Claim (Nor. v. U.S.), 1 U.N. Rep. Int'l Arb. Awards 307, 334 (1922).

The Restatement (Third) offers the following guidance in Comment h:

> A state party to a contract with a foreign national is liable for a repudiation or breach of that contract under applicable national law, but not every repudiation or breach by a state of a contract with a foreign national constitutes a violation of international law. Under Subsection (2), a state is responsible for such a repudiation or breach only if it is discriminatory, Comment f, or if it is akin to an expropriation in that the contract is repudiated or breached for governmental rather than commercial reasons and the state is not prepared to pay

---

[11] Dunn, The Protection of Nationals 167 (1932).

damages. A state's repudiation or failure to perform is not a violation of international law under this section if it is based on a bona fide dispute about the obligation or its performance, if it is due to the state's inability to perform, or if nonperformance is motivated by commercial considerations and the state is prepared to pay damages or to submit to adjudication or arbitration and to abide by the judgment or award.

As this Comment suggests, there are a number of defenses a state may raise to avoid liability for breaching an agreement that might not be available in the case of an expropriation of property. The government may argue, for example, that the investor has violated its obligations under the contract, and that the government is therefore entitled to vary or terminate its own obligations. It may argue that its performance is excused by necessity or by *force majeure*. Or the government may claim that it was induced to enter the contract because of misrepresentations by the investor and is therefore entitled to rescind the contract.

2. INTERNATIONAL INVESTMENT AGREEMENTS

The protection of foreign investment under international law has been affected in recent years by the dramatic increase in the number of International Investment Agreements (IIAs). Many IIAs take the form of Bilateral Investment Treaties (BITs), but investment protections have also been incorporated into other kinds of treaties, including free-trade agreements like NAFTA. From 1995 to 2005, the number of BITs more than doubled, reaching a total of 2,495 such treaties. By early 2019, there were 2,971 BITs (2,367 of which were in force) and 384 other IIAs (312 of which were in force).[12] Over the same period, the number of investment disputes exploded—rising from six at the end of 1995 to 904 by early 2019.[13] Not all countries have joined the rush to conclude IIAs. Although Brazil signed 14 BITs between 1994 and 1999, it ratified none of them. Since 2015, Brazil has developed a new model called Cooperation and Facilitation Investment Agreements (CFIAs), which are discussed below. Some other countries are now terminating their IIAs or developing additional alternatives. See infra pp. 481–482. But IIAs remain an important source of protection for investors from countries that have them, including investors from the United States.[14]

---

[12] See http://investmentpolicyhub.unctad.org/IIA.

[13] See http://investmentpolicyhub.unctad.org/ISDS. Many of the awards in these cases are publicly available at sites such as www.italaw.com and icsid.worldbank.org.

[14] The United States currently has BITs with Albania, Argentina, Armenia, Azerbaijan, Bahrain, Bangladesh, Belarus (not in force), Bolivia (terminated in 2012 but still in force for existing investments until 2022), Bulgaria, Cameroon, Democratic Republic of the Congo, Republic of the Congo, Croatia, Czech Republic, Ecuador, Egypt, El Salvador (not in force), Estonia, Georgia, Grenada, Haiti (not in force), Honduras, Jamica, Jordan, Kazakhstan, Kyrgyzstan, Latvia, Lithuanian, Moldova, Mongolia, Morocco, Mozambique, Nicaragua (not in force), Panama, Poland, Romania, Russia (not in force), Rwanda, Sengal, Slovakia, Sri Lanka, Trinidad and Tobago, Tunisia, Turkey, Ukraine, Uruguay, and Uzbekistan (not in force). See https://www.state.gov/e/eb/ifd/bit/117402.htm. The United States currently has free-trade

Substantive Protections

IIAs protect investments by investors of one treaty partner in the territory of another treaty partner. Typically, they include various substantive protections, like protection against expropriation, national treatment, most-favored-nation treatment, fair and equitable treatment, and full protection and security. Typically, they also include dispute resolution provisions that allow a foreign investor to bring investment claims directly against the host state. By allowing direct claims, IIAs sought to replace the system of diplomatic protection (also called espousal) under which the investor's home state would take up the investor's claim as its own and attempt to negotiate compensation from the host state. Many states publish model BITs that serve as the basis for negotiating new agreements.[15] But different states follow different models, and the current model agreements may also differ from previously concluded IIAs. This section will discuss the provisions that many IIAs have in common but will also highlight some key differences.

The provisions on expropriation in IIAs tend to emphasize that their protection is not limited to formal transfers of ownership. Article 1110 of NAFTA, for example, states that "[n]o Party may directly or indirectly nationalize or expropriate an investment of an investor of another Party in its territory or take a measure tantamount to nationalization or expropriation of such an investment" unless certain conditions are satisfied, including compensation. Such language has sometimes been interpreted broadly. One tribunal stated:

> expropriation under NAFTA includes not only open, deliberate, and acknowledged takings of property, such as outright seizure or formal or obligatory transfer of title in favour of the host States, but also covert or incidental interference with the use of property which has the effect of depriving the owner, in whole or in significant part, of the use or reasonably-to-be-expected economic benefit of property even if not necessarily to the obvious benefit of the host State.

Metalclad Corp. v. Mexico, ICSID Case No. ARB(AF)/97/1, Award, ¶ 103 (2000). In its more recent IIAs, the United States has tried to limit the concept of indirect expropriation to exclude legitimate regulatory activity. An annex to the current U.S. Model BIT provides: "Except in rare circumstances, non-discriminatory regulatory actions by a Party that are designed and applied to protect legitimate public welfare objectives, such as public health, safety, and the environment, do not

---

agreements or trade promotion agreements that include investment protections with Australia; Canada and Mexico (NAFTA); Chile; Colombia; Costa Rica, Dominican Republic, El Salvador, Guatemala, Honduras, and Nicaragua (CAFTA-DR); Korea; Morocco; Oman, Peru, and Singapore. See https://ustr.gov/trade-agreements/free-trade-agreements.

[15] The United States revised its Model BIT in 2012. See https://www.state.gov/documents/organization/188371.pdf.

constitute indirect expropriations." U.S. Model Bilateral Investment Treaty, Annex B(4)(b) (2012).

Most IIAs also address the standard of compensation required for expropriations, typically adopting a standard of full compensation equivalent to the Hull formula of "prompt, adequate, and effective" compensation. Article 1110 of NAFTA, for example, requires that compensation "shall be paid without delay" (prompt), "shall be equivalent to the fair market value of the expropriated investment immediately before the expropriation took place" (adequate), and shall be "fully realizable" and "freely transferable" (effective). The difficulty usually lies in determining the fair market value of the investment. If the investment is a going concern—that is, an enterprise that has been generating income and would reasonably have been expected to continue doing so—then discounted cash flow (DCF) is "the standard economic approach to measuring the fair market value." Occidental Petroleum Corp. v. Ecuador, ICSID Case No. ARB/06/11, Award, ¶ 708 (2012). DCF means cash receipts less cash expenditures realistically expected in each future year, discounted to present value by a factor reflecting the time value of money, expected inflation, and the risk associated with investments of the particular kind. Tribunals have found DCF inappropriate, however, when there is no record of profits on which the analysis may be based. See, e.g., Metalclad Corp. v. Mexico, ICSID Case No. ARB(AF)/97/1, Award, ¶ 121 (2000). In such cases, alternatives include liquidation value (the amount for which the assets of an enterprise could be sold in liquidation to a willing buyer less any liabilities) and book value (the difference between the assets and the liabilities as recorded on an enterprise's financial statements).

In addition to protection against expropriation, IIAs set forth various standards of treatment for foreign investment. Most IIAs provide for both "national treatment" and "most-favored-nation treatment." National treatment means treatment no less favorable than the treatment given to the host state's own nationals in like circumstances. See, e.g., NAFTA art. 1102. Most-favored-nation treatment means treatment no less favorable than the treatment given to nationals of third states in like circumstances. See, e.g., NAFTA art. 1103. These standards are sometimes called "contingent" because the treatment required depends on the treatment given to others. The key issue in applying such contingent standards is finding the proper comparator—that is, determining when a national of the host state or of a third state is in like circumstances with the foreign investor. With respect to most-favored-nation treatment, the question has also arisen whether the standard applies only to the substantive protections of agreements with third states (e.g., the protection against expropriation) or also to procedural provisions (e.g., the right to bring an arbitral claim without first resorting to the courts of the host state). That question is discussed further below. See infra p. 481.

Most IIAs also set forth "non-contingent" standards of treatment that apply irrespective of how others are treated. These include "fair and equitable treatment" and "full protection and security." The United States has tied these standards to the minimum standard of treatment for foreign investors under customary international law. For example, Article 1105(1) of NAFTA provides: "Each Party shall accord to investments of investors of another Party treatment in accordance with international law, including fair and equitable treatment and full protection and security." The current U.S. Model BIT expressly states that fair and equitable treatment and full protection and security "do not require treatment in addition to or beyond that which is required by [customary international law]." U.S. Model BIT art. 5(2). Other IIAs do not tie these standards to customary international law. See, e.g., Netherlands Model Investment Agreement art. 9(1) ("Each Contracting Party shall ensure fair and equitable treatment of the investments of investors of the other Contracting Party. In addition, each Contracting Party shall accord to such investments full physical security and protection."). But tying fair and equitable treatment and full protection and security to customary international law does not prevent the evolution of these standards. One tribunal interpreting NAFTA Article 1105(1) observed that "like all customary international law, the international minimum standard has evolved and can evolve" and that today this standard "is shaped by the conclusion of more than two thousand bilateral investment treaties." Mondev International Ltd. v. United States, ICSID Case No. ARB(AF)/99/2, Award, ¶¶ 124, 125 (2002).

Over the past twenty years, fair and equitable treatment has emerged as one of the most important and most litigated issues under IIAs. A leading treatise states that "the fair and equitable standard gives modern expression to a *general principle of due process* in its application to the treatment of investors" and that it "encapsulates the minimum requirements of the rule of law." McLachlan, Shore & Weiniger, International Investment Arbitration: Substantive Principles 272 (2d ed. 2017). Sometimes a breach of fair and equitable treatment takes the form of a denial of justice by the courts of the host state. See, e.g., Dan Cake (Portugal) S.A. v. Hungary, ICSID Case No. ARB/12/9, Decision on Jurisdiction and Liability, ¶ 145 (2015) (court's denial of a hearing with creditors constituted violation of fair and equitable treatment). Sometimes a breach of fair and equitable treatment results from a fundamental change in the governing legal regime. See, e.g., Perenco Ecuador Ltd. v. Ecuador, ICSID Case No. ARB/08/6, Decision on Remaining Issues of Jurisdiction and on Liability, ¶¶ 590–607 (2014) (increasing government participation in production-sharing contracts to 50% was not a violation of fair and equitable treatment but increasing participation to 99% in order to force a change to service contracts was a violation). In language that has been widely quoted, one tribunal wrote:

[T]he minimum standard of treatment of fair and equitable treatment is infringed by conduct attributable to the State and harmful to the claimant if the conduct is arbitrary, grossly unfair, unjust or idiosyncratic, is discriminatory and exposes the claimant to sectional or racial prejudice, or involves a lack of due process leading to an outcome which offends judicial propriety—as might be the case with a manifest failure of natural justice in judicial proceedings or a complete lack of transparency and candour in an administrative process. In applying this standard it is relevant that the treatment is in breach of representations made by the host State which were reasonably relied on by the claimant.

Waste Management Inc. v. Mexico, ICSID Case No. ARB(AF)/00/3, Award, ¶ 98 (2004).

Fair and equitable treatment claims often arise in cases involving contracts with the host state because the contract contains representations by the state and creates legitimate expectations on the part of the investors. See Perenco Ecuador Ltd. v. Ecuador, ICSID Case No. ARB/08/6, Decision on Remaining Issues of Jurisdiction and on Liability, ¶ 561 (2014) ("In cases where a contract exists between the investor and the host State, the terms of the contract and the State's legislation in relation thereto, assume particular significance in the analysis."). In LG & E Energy Corp. v. Argentine Republic, ICSID Case No. ARB/02/1, Decision on Liability, ¶ 133 (2006), for example, foreign investors had been granted long-term licenses for the transportation and distribution of natural gas, including certain provisions for the calculation of tariffs. The arbitral tribunal found that Argentina's changes to those tariffs violated the fair and equitable treatment provision of the Argentina-United States BIT. "Having created specific expectations among investors, Argentina was bound by its obligations concerning the investment guarantees vis-à-vis public utility licensees, and in particular, the gas distribution licensees. The abrogation of these specific guarantees violates the stability and predictability underlying the standard of fair and equitable treatment." Id. at 58; see also Total S.A. v. Argentine Republic, ICSID Case No. ARB/04/1, Decision on Liability, ¶ 117 (2010) ("The expectation of the investor is undoubtedly 'legitimate', and hence subject to protection under the fair and equitable treatment clause, if the host State has explicitly assumed a specific legal obligation for the future, such as by contracts, concessions or stabilisation clauses on which the investor is therefore entitled to rely as a matter of law."); Micula v. Romania, ICSID Case No. ARB/05/20, Final Award, ¶ 667 (2013) ("where the investor has acquired rights, or where the state has acted in such a way so as to generate a legitimate expectation in the investor and that investor has relied on that expectation to make its investment, action by the state that reverses or destroys those legitimate expectations will be in breach of the fair and equitable treatment standard and thus give rise to compensation").

The other non-contingent standard, full protection and security, has led to fewer claims and is generally understood to be limited to protection from physical harm, for example the failure of the police to protect property during a riot. One tribunal explained: "the stability of the business environment and legal security are more characteristic of the standard of fair and equitable treatment, while the full protection and security standard primarily seeks to protect investment from physical harm." Suez v. Argentina, Decision on Liability ¶ 173, ICSID Case No. ARB/03/17 (2010).

Another provision, found in about 40% of IIAs, is an "umbrella clause"—that is, a clause in which the state-parties agree to observe other obligations they have entered into with respect to investments. Umbrella clauses are contained in many older U.S. BITs. See, e.g., Argentina-U.S. BIT art. II(2)(c) ("Each Party shall observe any obligation it may have entered into with regard to investments."). But similar clauses were not included in NAFTA or in the 2004 and 2012 U.S. Model BITs. A critical question is whether umbrella clauses should be interpreted to include *contractual* obligations.[16]

Arbitral tribunals have taken different positions on this point. Some tribunals have interpreted umbrella clauses not to apply to contractual obligations at all. In SGS v. Pakistan, for example, the tribunal rejected the argument that, because of an umbrella clause, "breaches of contract alleged by an investor in relation to a contract it has concluded with a State (widely considered to be a matter of municipal rather than international law) are automatically 'elevated' to the level of breaches of international treaty law." SGS Société Générale de Surveillance S.A. v. Pakistan, ICSID Case No. ARB/01/13, Decision on Jurisdiction, ¶ 166 (2003). The tribunal worried that reading the umbrella clause to cover contractual obligations would make other provisions of the BIT superfluous. "There would be no real need to demonstrate a violation of those substantive treaty standards if a simple breach of contract, or of municipal statute or regulation, by itself, would suffice to constitute a treaty violation on the part of a Contracting Party and engage the international responsibility of the Party." Id. ¶ 168. The tribunal was also concerned that a broad reading of an umbrella clause would allow an investor to avoid any dispute resolution clause in the contract itself (in SGS, an arbitration clause), because "[t]he investor would remain free to go to arbitration either under the contract or under the BIT." Id.

Other tribunals have tried to distinguish between obligations that a state might undertake as a sovereign from those that a state might undertake as a merchant, and to limit umbrella clauses to the former

---

[16] For an excellent analysis on which the following discussion draws, see McLachlan, Shore & Weiniger, International Investment Arbitration: Substantive Principles 128–140 (2d ed. 2017).

category. In the El Paso Energy case, for example, the arbitral tribunal concluded that an umbrella clause "will not extend the Treaty protection to breaches of an ordinary commercial contract entered into by the State or a State-owned entity, but will cover additional investment protections contractually agreed by the State as a sovereign—such as a stabilization clause—inserted in an investment agreement." El Paso Energy International Co. v. Argentina, ICSID Case No. ARB/03/15, Decision on Jurisdiction, ¶ 81 (2006).

A third position maintains that umbrella clauses apply to contractual obligations assumed by the state, but that such obligations continue to be subject to the law governing the contract and to the contract's dispute resolution provisions. In SGS v. Philippines, the arbitral tribunal noted:

> The term "any obligation" is capable of applying to obligations arising under national law, e.g. those arising from a contract; indeed, it would normally be under its own law that a host State would assume obligations "with regard to specific investments in its territory by investors of the other Contracting Party." Interpreting the actual text of Article X(2), it would appear to say, and to say clearly, that each Contracting Party shall observe any legal obligation it has assumed, or will in the future assume, with regard to specific investments covered by the BIT.

SGS Société Générale de Surveillance S.A. v. Republic of the Philippines, ICSID Case No. ARB/02/6, Objections to Jurisdiction, ¶ 115 (2004). But the tribunal observed that the umbrella clause did not change the law governing the contract "from the law of the Philippines to international law." Id. ¶ 126. So, although the umbrella clause "includes commitments or obligations arising under contracts entered into by the host State," "[t]he extent of the obligation is still governed by the contract, and it can only be determined by reference to the terms of the contract." The tribunal further concluded that the umbrella clause did not override the dispute resolution clause in the contract itself: "the BIT did not purport to override the exclusive jurisdiction clause in the CISS Agreement, or to give SGS an alternative route for the resolution of contractual claims which it was bound to submit to the Philippine courts under that Agreement." Id. ¶ 143.

Finally, some tribunals have read umbrella clauses "as transforming municipal law obligations into obligations directly cognizable in international law." Noble Ventures Inc. v. Romania, ICSID Case No. ARB/01/11, Award, ¶ 53 (2005). Some tribunals following this approach have held that claims based on a contract may be brought to arbitration under an IIA even if the contract itself chooses a different forum for the resolution of disputes. In SGS v. Paraguay, for example, the arbitral tribunal emphasized that a claim for breach of the umbrella clause was distinct from a claim for breach of the contract: "Even if the alleged breach of the treaty obligation depends upon a showing that a contract or other qualifying commitment has been breached, the source of the obligation cited by the claimant, and hence the source of the claim, remains the treaty itself." SGS Société Générale de Surveillance S.A. v. Paraguay, ICSID Case No. ARB/07/29, Decision on Jurisdiction, ¶ 142 (2010). Declining to hear claims under the umbrella clause because of the contract's forum selection clause, the tribunal concluded, "would place the Tribunal at risk of failing to carry out its mandate under the Treaty and the ICSID Convention." Id. ¶ 172. Whether an umbrella clause in an IIA will allow an investor to bring claims based on a state's breach of a concession contract will depend, therefore, on which approach the tribunal takes to interpreting umbrella clauses and on what the concession contract's own dispute resolution clause says.

Procedural Provisions

In addition to the substantive protections discussed above, IIAs typically create procedures that allow foreign investors to bring claims directly against host governments. These procedural provisions may differ significantly in their details. In analyzing them, a lawyer should pay particular attention to the following questions. First, to which disputes do the provisions apply? Do they cover all disputes relating to the investment or only violations of the IIA itself? Second, what are the foreign investors' options in case of a dispute? Under most IIAs the alternatives will include the domestic courts of the host state and one or more options for arbitration. Third, what effect does choosing one of these options have on the foreign investor's ability to resort to any of the others? Some IIAs contain a "fork in the road" provision that requires an investor to choose a single dispute resolution alternative at the outset. Others allow a foreign investor to try domestic courts first, requiring the investor to waive its right to resort to other dispute resolution procedures only when it files an arbitration claim under the IIA.

As an example, consider Article 8 of the Argentina-France BIT, which reads in relevant part as follows:

> 1. Any dispute relating to investments made under this Agreement between one Contracting Party and an investor of the other Contracting Party shall, as far as possible, be settled amicably between the two parties concerned.
>
> 2. If any such dispute cannot be so settled within six months of the time when the claim is made by one of the parties to the dispute, the dispute shall, at the request of the investor, be submitted:
>
> — Either to the domestic courts of the Contracting Party involved in the dispute;
>
> — Or to international arbitration under the conditions described in paragraph 3 below.

Once an investor has submitted the disputes to the courts of the Contracting Party concerned or to international arbitration, the choice of one or the other of these procedures is final.

3. Where recourse is had to international arbitration, the investor may choose to bring the dispute before one of the following arbitration bodies:

— The International Centre for Settlement of Investment Disputes (ICSID), established by the Convention on the Settlement of Investment Disputes between States and Nationals of other States opened for signature in Washington on 18 March 1965, if both States Parties to this Agreement have already acceded to the Convention. Until such time as this requirement is met, the two Contracting Parties shall agree to submit the dispute to arbitration, in accordance with the procedure of the Additional Facility of ICSID;

— An *ad hoc* arbitral tribunal established in accordance with the Arbitration Rules of the United Nations Commission on International Trade Law (UNCITRAL).

4. The ruling of the arbitral body shall be based on the provisions of this Agreement, the legislation of the Contracting Party which is a party to the dispute, including rules governing conflict of laws, the terms of any private agreements concluded on the subject of the investment, and the relevant principles of international law.

5. Arbitral decisions shall be final and binding on the parties to the dispute.

First, note that Article 8 is drafted broadly so that it applies not just to violations of the BIT itself but to "[a]ny dispute relating to investments made under this Agreement." Such a provision might allow an investor to bring claims for breach of contract against the host government even in the absence of an umbrella clause. (The effect on this possibility of a forum selection clause in the contract is considered below. See infra p. 483.) In SGS v. Philippines, the arbitral tribunal concluded that a broadly worded disputes clause gave it jurisdiction over purely contractual claims. It reasoned:

The term "disputes with respect to investments" . . . is not limited by reference to the legal classification of the claim that is made. A dispute about an alleged expropriation contrary to Article VI of the BIT would be a "dispute with respect to investments;" so too would a dispute arising from an investment contract . . . .

SGS Société Générale de Surveillance S.A. v. Republic of the Philippines, ICSID Case No. ARB/02/6, Objections to Jurisdiction, ¶ 131 (2004). The tribunal in SGS v. Pakistan reached the opposite conclusion, reasoning that "disputes with respect to investments" simply described the subject matter of the disputes and was not sufficient to show that "purely contract claims are intended to be covered." SGS Société Générale de Surveillance S.A. v. Pakistan, ICSID Case No. ARB/01/13, Decision on Jurisdiction, ¶ 161 (2003).

Second, note that Article 8 gives the foreign investor three dispute resolution alternatives: (1) "the domestic courts of the Contracting Party involved in the dispute"; (2) ICSID arbitration (if both states are parties to the ICSID Convention) or ICSID Additional Facility arbitration (if only one state is a party to the ICSID Convention); or (3) *ad hoc* arbitration under the UNCITRAL Rules. One might assume that a foreign investor would always want to avoid the domestic courts of the host state, but as discussed further below those courts may be the only ones able to reverse the host government's decision or to give the foreign investor relief other than damages. See infra pp. 482–483. With respect to the choice among arbitration alternatives, recall that ICSID arbitration has its own procedure for the review and annulment of awards, whereas arbitrations under the ICSID Additional Facility and the UNCITRAL Rules rely on the framework of the New York Convention. See supra p. 463.

Third, note that Article 8 contains a "fork in the road" provision: "Once an investor has submitted the disputes to the courts of the Contracting Party concerned or to international arbitration, the choice of one or the other of these procedures is final." This means that a foreign investor must choose at the outset where to bring its claims. It cannot challenge the host state's repudiation of a concession contract in domestic courts and then, if unsuccessful, seek damages from an arbitral tribunal under the IIA. As discussed below, this may force the investor to make some difficult choices. See infra pp. 482–485.

Of course, not all IIAs contain the same provisions on dispute resolution. Chapter 11 of NAFTA, for example, allows an investor to submit only claims for violations of Chapter 11 itself and a few provisions of Chapter 15 dealing with state enterprises. See NAFTA Arts. 1116(1), 1117(1). As one tribunal observed in the course of denying an investor's claims, "NAFTA Chapter 11 does not give jurisdiction in respect of breaches of investment contracts such as the Concession Agreement." Waste Management Inc. v. Mexico, Case No. ARB(AF)/00/3, Award, ¶ 73 (2004). Chapter 11 of NAFTA gives the foreign investor the same arbitration options as the Argentina-France BIT: ICSID arbitration (if both states are parties to the ICSID Convention), ICSID Additional Facility arbitration (if only one state is a party to the ICSID Convention), or (3) *ad hoc* arbitration under the UNCITRAL Rules. See NAFTA Art. 1120. Chapter 11 of NAFTA does not have a "fork in the road" provision. It simply requires that when the investor submits a claim to arbitration, it must "waive [the] right to initiate or continue before any administrative tribunal or court under the law of any Party, or other dispute settlement procedures, any proceedings with respect to the measure of the disputing Party that is alleged to be a breach." NAFTA Arts. 1121(1), (2). This means that an investor is free to pursue its rights in the domestic courts of the host state or any other available forum before turning to NAFTA arbitration.

Traditionally, resort to the domestic courts of the host state was not just permitted but required before filing an international claim. See Interhandel Case (Switz. v. U.S.), Preliminary Objections, 1959 I.C.J. 6, 27 (Mar. 29) ("The rule that local remedies must be exhausted before international proceedings may be instituted is a well-established rule of customary international law."). But IIAs have been interpreted to waive the rule requiring the exhaustion of local remedies by providing investors a choice of dispute resolution alternatives. See, e.g., Mytilineos Holdings SA v. Serbia and Montenegro, Partial Award on Jurisdiction, ¶¶ 197–225 (2006).

Treaty Shopping

The proliferation of IIAs has also opened up possibilities for "treaty-shopping"—that is, for an investor to seek out favorable provisions in treaties between the host state and states other than its own home state. One means of accomplishing this is to create a holding company in a third state with a favorable BIT. Aguas del Tunari v. Bolivia involved a concession contract to operate water and sewer service between Bolivia and a Bolivian subsidiary ultimately controlled by the American firm Bechtel. Although the United States subsequently concluded a BIT with Bolivia, that treaty was not in force at the time the dispute arose. Prior to the dispute, however, Bechtel had reorganized its investment so that it was held through two Dutch subsidiaries, and the claim was brought under the provisions of the Bolivia-Netherlands BIT. The tribunal held that it had jurisdiction under the Dutch BIT despite Bechtel's ultimate ownership. The tribunal noted that this reorganization occurred before the dispute and may have been done for business or tax reasons, but it also observed that "it is not uncommon in practice, and—absent a particular limitation—not illegal to locate one's operations in a jurisdiction perceived to provide a beneficial regulatory and legal environment in terms, for examples, of taxation or the substantive law of the jurisdiction, including the availability of a BIT." Aguas del Tunari, S.A. v. Republic of Bolivia, ICSID Case No. ARB/02/3, Objections to Jurisdiction, ¶ 330(d) (2005). In two claims brought against Venezuela for nationalization of oil projects, it was undisputed that the foreign companies had restructured their investments through Dutch holding companies to gain the protections of the Netherlands-Venezuela BIT. Both tribunals distinguished between pre-existing and future claims in rejecting Venezuela's argument that the investors had abused rights under the treaty. The tribunal in the Mobil case reasoned that "gaining access to ICSID arbitration through the BIT . . . was a perfectly legitimate goal as far as it concerned future disputes" but that "to restructure investments only in order to gain jurisdiction under the BIT for [pre-existing] disputes would constitute . . . 'an abusive manipulation of the system of international investment protection under the ICSID Convention and the BITs.' " Mobil Corp. v. Venezuela, ICSID Case No. ARB/07/27, Decision on Jurisdiction, ¶¶ 204–205 (2010) (quoting Phoenix Action, Ltd. v. The Czech Republic, ICSID Case No. ARB/06/5, Award, ¶ 144 (2009)); see also ConocoPhillips Petrozuata B.V. v. Venezuela, ICSID Case No. ARB/07/30, Decision on Jurisdiction and the Merits, ¶ 278 (2013).

Alternatively, assuming the BIT between the host state and the investor's home state includes a most-favored-nation provision, the investor may try to rely on this provision to claim the benefit of more favorable provisions in agreements with third states. Arbitral tribunals have generally permitted this, although controversy exists as to whether most-favored-nation clauses apply only to the substantive provisions of other BITs or also to their dispute resolution provisions. Compare Maffezini v. Kingdom of Spain, ICSID Case No. ARB/97/7, Objections to Jurisdiction, ¶ 64 (2000) (MFN clause applies to dispute resolution provisions of other treaties) and Teinver S.A. v. Argentine Republic, ICSID Case No. ARB/09/1, Decision on Jurisdiction, ¶ 186 (2012) (same), with Salini Construttori S.p.A. & Italstrade S.p.A. v. Hashemite Kingdom of Jordan, ICSID Case No. ARB/02/13, Decision on Jurisdiction, ¶ 119 (2004) (MFN clause does not apply to dispute resolution provisions of other treaties) and ICS Inspection and Control Services Ltd (United Kingdom v. Argentine Republic), PCA Case No. 2010–9, Award on Jurisdiction, ¶ 318 (2012) (same).

IIAs in Flux

Although the number of IIAs has increased dramatically since 1995, the standard model of investor-state dispute settlement has come under attack from a number of quarters. Several countries, including Bolivia, Ecuador, India, Indonesia, and South Africa have announced that they will terminate some or all of their BITs. UNCTAD has launched a "reform package" to help countries revise their IIAs. See UNCTAD's Reform Package for the International Investment Regime (2017), http://investmentpolicyhub.unctad.org/News/Report/Home/1576. And the European Union has decided to replace investor-state arbitration with an investment court system, which has already been included in its new Comprehensive Economic and Trade Agreement (CETA) with Canada.

Brazil has developed an alternative to the standard IIA model, called a Cooperation and Facilitation Investment Agreement (CFIA). Brazil published a model CFIA in 2015[17] and has signed such agreements with four African countries (Angola, Ethiopia, Malawi, and Mozambique) and five Latin American countries (Chile, Colombia, Guyana, Mexico, and

---

[17] See Brazil Model CFIA, available at http://investmentpolicyhub.unctad.org/Download/TreatyFile/4786.

Suriname). Although the details of each agreement differ, it is possible to make some general observations. First, the substantive protections of CFIAs are limited to national treatment, most-favored-nation treatment, and protection against direct expropriation. They do not include protection against indirect expropriation, fair and equitable treatment, full protection and security, or umbrella clauses. Second, and perhaps most significantly, CFIAs do not allow foreign investors to bring direct claims against host governments. Instead the agreements require each country to establish a National Focal Point, or "Ombudsman," to support investors from the other country, to receive complaints, and to try to resolve disputes. The agreements also establish Joint Committees composed of government representatives from each of the countries to supervise implementation of the agreements and to resolve disputes at an inter-country level. As a last resort, CFIAs provide for state-to-state arbitration, but only once the procedures of the Joint Committees have been exhausted.

It is difficult to predict whether other countries will follow Brazil's new model dispensing with direct investor claims, follow the EU in shifting to an investment court system, or develop additional alternatives. Perhaps the most likely outcome in the short term is the proliferation of different models, with none enjoying the same consensus that traditional IIAs did in the 1990s and 2000s. But whatever direction new IIAs take, it seems clear that existing IIAs will continue to protect foreign investment, and to provide options for dispute settlement, for some time to come.

3. CHOICES WHEN DISPUTES ARISE

When a dispute arises between a foreign investor and a host state, the investor may face choices about where to bring its claims. Possible forums may include the courts of the host state, the courts of the investor's home state, the forum designated in the contract's forum-selection clause, and the dispute resolution mechanisms provided in the relevant IIA, if any. The choice may depend in part on the nature of the investor's claims. Claims for breach of contract may typically be brought in domestic courts or before an arbitral tribunal pursuant to a contract's arbitration clause. Whether contractual claims may also be brought before an arbitral tribunal established under an IIA depends on the breadth of the IIA's disputes clause and whether the IIA contains an umbrella clause. See infra pp. 475–480. Claims for violation of an IIA may typically be brought before an arbitral tribunal established under the treaty, but may or may not be cognizable in domestic courts depending on the status of treaties in the domestic legal system. The investor's choice may also depend on what relief the investor seeks. For example, the courts of the host state may be able to order the government to reverse or modify its decision, whereas an IIA tribunal can only award damages. Finally, the investor must consider whether resorting to one forum may prevent it from subsequently trying another, for example because of a "fork in the road" provision.

When a host government breaches or repudiates a concession contract, a foreign investor will often turn first to the courts of the host state. This might seem odd in light of the potential for bias in favor of the host government. But if the foreign investor wants to continue with the contract, only the courts of the host state may be able to order the government to reverse its decision. In addition, the courts of the host state may be the only forum where the investor may bring its contractual claims, which the investor may feel are stronger than its treaty claims. Whether contractual claims may only be brought in the courts of the host state will depend, of course, on what the IIA says—for example, whether its disputes clause extends to all disputes relating to the investment and whether it contains an umbrella clause. It will also depend on whether the contract's forum selection clause requires contractual claims to be brought in domestic courts. In one widely followed decision, an ICSID annulment committee held that the effect of a forum selection clause depended on the nature of the investor's claims. See Compañia de Aguas del Aconquija S.A. & Vivendi Universal v. Argentine Republic, ICSID Case No. ARB/97/3, Decision on Annulment (2002). The committee wrote: "In a case where the essential basis of a claim brought before an international tribunal is a breach of contract, the tribunal will give effect to any valid choice of forum clause in the contract." Id. ¶ 98. But, the committee continued:

> where "the fundamental basis of the claim" is a treaty laying down an independent standard by which the conduct of the parties is to be judged, the existence of an exclusive jurisdiction clause in a contract between the claimant and the respondent state or one of its subdivisions cannot operate as a bar to the application of the treaty standard.

Id. ¶ 101. In other words, Vivendi holds that a contractual choice of forum provision will bar contractual claims from being brought under the IIA but will not preclude treaty claims.

Even when resort to the courts of the host state is a sensible decision, it may nevertheless carry substantial risks. First, if the IIA contains a "fork in the road" provision, resort to the domestic courts of the host state may preclude a subsequent arbitration under the treaty. This risk is smaller if the disputes clause is limited to breaches of the treaty, because submitting claims that are not cognizable under the treaty to domestic courts should not trigger the "fork in the road" provision. But the risk is greater when the disputes clause extends to "any dispute relating to investments" (as in the Argentina-France BIT above), because submitting claims that are cognizable under the treaty to domestic courts may trigger the "fork in the road" provision. Second, even if the IIA does not contain a "fork in the road" provision, the decision of the host state's courts on questions of domestic law may prejudice the investor's subsequent treaty claims. In Azinian v. Mexico, the foreign investors challenged Mexico's repudiation of their concession contract in Mexican courts, and those courts held that the contract was invalid because it had been induced by fraud. The investors then brought an expropriation claim under NAFTA Chapter 11, but the tribunal rejected that claim because of the Mexican courts' decision: "For if there is no complaint against a determination by a competent court that a contract governed by Mexican law was invalid under Mexican law, there is by definition no contract to be expropriated." Azinian v. Mexico, ICSID Case No. ARB(AF)/97/2, Award, ¶ 100 (1999).

Theoretically, an investor could seek to bring its claims against the host state in the domestic courts of its home state, but this is rarely done. The U.S. Foreign Sovereign Immunities Act (FSIA) contains a "commercial activities" exception that may allow contractual claims to be brought against a foreign state. 28 U.S.C. § 1605(a)(2). However, each of its three clauses requires some connection to the United States, which may be absent in the case of a concession contract performed abroad. See infra pp. 522–523. The FSIA also contains an "expropriation" exception that may allow expropriation claims to be brought against a foreign state. 28 U.S.C. § 1605(a)(3). But like the Hickenlooper Amendment to the act of state doctrine—which might also be raised against such claims—the FSIA's expropriation exception applies to claims against a foreign state only if the expropriated property or its proceeds are present in the United States. See supra pp. 78–79. In addition, with respect to contractual claims, U.S. courts will generally give effect to any forum selection clause contained in the concession contract. See supra pp. 22–32. And treaty claims would generally be precluded in U.S. courts by implementing legislation barring such claims. See, e.g., 19 U.S.C. § 3312(c) (providing that "[n]o person other than the United States . . . shall have any cause of action or defense" under NAFTA); see also supra p. 84.

Choosing arbitration under the IIA carries its own risks. Most fundamentally, it may preclude the foreign investor from going to the domestic courts of the host state, either by operation of a "fork in the road" provision, see, e.g., Argentina-France BIT Art. 8, or because the investor is required to waive its right to initiate or continue other proceedings as a precondition to filing its arbitration claim, see, e.g., NAFTA Art. 1121. An arbitral tribunal constituted under an IIA can typically only award damages, which will be most attractive when the investor has given up any hope of continuing with the concession contract. Even when damages are the only realistic remedy, an investor will have to consider whether the claims that it can bring under the IIA—which may or may not include some kinds of contractual arguments—are its strongest claims.

In Waste Management v. Mexico, for example, a Mexican subsidiary entered into a concession contract with the city of Acapulco to provide waste disposal services. The concession contract had an arbitration clause and was guaranteed by a second contract providing for dispute resolution in Mexican courts. When Acapulco failed to pay its invoices, the subsidiary tried to initiate arbitration under the concession contract and filed claims in Mexican courts under the guarantee agreement. Waste Management tried to preserve these contractual claims when it brought its NAFTA claims for breach of fair and equitable treatment and expropriation by submitting a waiver that excluded claims under Mexican law. The NAFTA tribunal dismissed these claims on the ground that the waiver was not sufficient. See Waste Management, Inc. v. Mexico, ICSID Case No. ARB(AF)/98/2, Award (2000). Waste Management discontinued its other proceedings and filed an unconditional waiver. The second NAFTA tribunal then denied the fair and equitable treatment and expropriation claims on the merits, emphasizing that NAFTA Chapter 11 does not extend to contractual claims and that the relevant contracts had chosen other forums to resolve such claims. "In the Tribunal's view, an enterprise is not expropriated just because its debts are not paid or other contractual obligations towards it are breached." Waste Management, Inc. v. Mexico, ICSID Case No. ARB(AF)/00/3, Award, ¶ 160 (2004).

QUESTIONS

(1) Why shouldn't every breach or repudiation of a contract by a state be considered a violation of customary international law? Are these same reasons relevant to the interpretation of IIAs?

(2) How do each of the following provisions in an IIA affect the protection of foreign investors under a concession contract: (a) a provision for "fair and equitable treatment"; (b) an "umbrella clause"; (c) a broadly worded disputes clause; (d) a "fork in the road" provision?

(3) What effect does a clause in a concession contract choosing the domestic courts of the host state have on the ability of the foreign investor to bring the following kinds of claims under an IIA: (a) claims for breach of contract; (b) claims for breach of an umbrella clause; (c) claims for expropriation?

(4) Assume that Texxon, Inc., a U.S. company, has entered a concession agreement with the nation of Guatador for the exploration and production of oil. Guatador and the United States have signed a Bilateral Investment Treaty identical to the U.S. Model BIT, which includes protections against expropriation and guarantees of national treatment, most-favored-nation treatment, fair and equitable treatment, and full protection and security. The disputes clause permits arbitration of claims that a host state has breached the BIT, an investment authorization, or an investment agreement. The BIT does not have a "fork in the road" provision, but does require an investor to waive all other dispute resolution proceedings. When the local community complains about the environmental effects of Texxon's operations, Guatador imposes strict new regulations that would increase Texxon's costs by 50%. When Texxon refuses to comply with the new regulations, Guatador terminates the concession agreement, also alleging that Texxon misrepresented future environmental impacts when the agreement was being negotiated. What claims might Texxon have against Guatador and where should it bring those claims? Would your answer be different if the contract contains a stabilization clause?

Additional reading: Schwebel, Whether the Breach by the State of Contract with an Alien is a Breach of International Law, in III International Law at the Time of Its Codification: Essays in Honour of Roberto Ago 401 (1987); Dolzer & Schreuer, Principles of International Investment Law (2d ed. 2012); Newcombe & Paradell, Law and Practice of Investment Treaties (2009); Salacuse, The Law of Investment Treaties (2010); McLachlan et al., International Investment Arbitration: Substantive Principles (2d ed. 2017); Schreuer et al., The ICSID Convention: A Commentary (2d ed. 2009); Shifting Paradigms in International Investment Law (Hindelang & Krajewski eds., 2016); Reconceptualizing International Investment Law from the Global South (Badin & Morosini eds., 2018).

E. POLITICAL RISK INSURANCE

It is possible to purchase insurance against political risk. The Overseas Private Investment Corporation (OPIC), a U.S. government agency, sells insurance to cover three kinds of political risk: expropriation, political violence, and currency inconvertibility.[18] OPIC policies are available only to U.S. citizens, corporations organized under U.S. law and more than 50% owned by U.S. citizens, and foreign corporations at least 95% owned by U.S. citizens, and only to insure investments in countries that have signed an investment guarantee agreement with the United States (currently more than 150 countries). In general, OPIC policies will cover up to 90% of the book value of an investment—an amount that does not take into account expected future profits and may be significantly lower than an investment's fair market value. Because OPIC is required to be self-sustaining, its premiums are relatively high—approximately 1.5% to cover all three kinds of political risk. Since 1988, political risk insurance has also been available through the Multilateral Investment Guarantee Agency (MIGA), a member of the World Bank Group. It provides coverage for the three risks covered by OPIC plus breach of contract and non-honoring financial obligations by a host government. OPIC and its counterparts in other capital-exporting countries have good records not only of paying off claims when investors' property was taken, but also of preventing expropriations from happening. A host government may well be less eager to antagonize a government agency than a private investor. Political risk insurance is also available from private insurers, such as American International

---

[18]   See generally Overseas Private Investment Corporation Act, 22 U.S.C.A. §§ 2191 et seq.

Group (AIG), Chubb Group, Lloyd's of London, and Zurich Financial Services Group.

OPIC has elaborately defined what is meant by expropriation. Consider the following provisions from one of its 2007 contracts:

Article IV—Expropriation—Scope of Coverage.

4.01 Total Expropriation.

Compensation is payable for total expropriation (§ 5.01), subject to the exclusions (§ 4.03) and limitations (§ 5.04), if an act or series of acts of the foreign governing authority satisfies all of the following requirements:

(a) the act(s) (i) constitute an outright taking of the Investor's property or (ii) have the effect of taking the Investor's insured investment in that the acts (A) prevent, unreasonably interfere with, deprive, or unduly delay effective enjoyment of the Investor's fundamental rights in the insured investment (rights are "fundamental" if without them the Investor is substantially deprived of the benefits of the investment) or (B) deny the Investor an adequate, effective forum to review the legality under applicable law of the act(s) that prevents, unreasonably interferes with, deprives, or unduly delays effective enjoyment of the Investor's fundamental rights in the insured investment; and

(b) the taking is not accompanied by prompt, adequate, and effective compensation; and

(c) the act(s) and/or the expropriatory effect thereof continues (§ 9.01.9) for six consecutive months.

* * *

4.03 Exclusions.

No compensation shall be payable if:

(a) _Provocation._ The preponderant cause of the expropriation is (i) actions, other than actions taken in the ordinary course of business, attributable to the Investor, the foreign enterprise, or the controlling equity holder of the foreign enterprise, provided such actions are in any way related to the project, or (ii) violations of Corrupt Practices Laws by the Investor, the foreign enterprise, or such controlling equity holder.

(b) _Government Relationship to the Project._ The act(s) described in § 4.01 and § 4.02 are those of the foreign governing authority exercising commercial (as distinguished from governmental) functions in relation to the project.

* * *

Article V—Expropriation—Amount of Compensation.

5.01 Total Expropriation.

For total expropriation (§ 4.01), OPIC shall pay compensation in United States dollars in the amount of the book value of the insured investment, subject to adjustments (§ 5.03) and limitations (§ 5.04).

QUESTIONS

(1) How does the definition of expropriation in OPIC's insurance policy compare to the definition in the IIAs discussed above? See supra pp. 471–472.

(2) How does the standard of compensation in OPIC's insurance policy compare to the standard in the IIAs discussed above? See supra p. 472.

Additional reading: Bekker & Ogawa, The Impact of Bilateral Investment Treaty (BIT) Proliferation on Demand for Investment Insurance: Reassessing Political Risk Insurance After the "BIT Bang," 28 ICSID Rev. 314 (2013).

F. RENEGOTIATION OF CONCESSION AGREEMENTS

The tension between the need for contractual stability on the one hand and the need to adjust to changed circumstances on the other is endemic in concession agreements.

With particular reference to natural resource agreements, the concerns of transnational corporations are accentuated by the peculiar problems of the extractive industry. In many cases, transnational corporations expend vast sums in survey work, exploration and prospecting for several years—five to 10 years, that is, the time before achieving successful production. Having regard to the size of the risk capital involved, and the conditions stipulated by their financiers, transnational corporations insist, as a matter of prudent investment, on definitive long-term guarantees as to the fiscal package from host governments even before embarking on the preliminary phases of the survey, exploration and prospecting. They maintain that such projects cannot be mounted without solid financial backing from banks and other institutions, and that such institutions will not provide financing in the absence of unequivocal guarantees from host governments in respect of the financial package for the entire duration of the agreement.

But understandable as the financial concerns of transnational corporations may be, the very nature of such long-term assurances poses acute problems for the developing country. In the nature of things, governments of developing countries are expected to determine the price of the ore or the fuel, the tax payable, the royalty and other impositions chargeable and all the elements of the fiscal regime over a 10, 15 or 30-year period even before the government has the vaguest idea of the size of the ore body or other national resource or the economic prospects of such resource. The feasibility study for the project which should properly be the basis of any fiscal regime is prepared not before but *after* the conclusion of the long-term contract. Thus, a government which is anxious to attract an investor is compelled by its weak bargaining position and the insistence of transnational corporations and their banks to conclude long-term fiscal arrangements without the benefit of all the facts essential to the determination of the components of that package—the price of ore, tax, the royalty rent consideration and other fiscal impositions. The result is that these transactions are invariably lopsided and highly advantageous to the investor. However, in time, the bargaining position changes. The feasibility report is prepared, the government has a better appreciation of the size of the ore body and the economic prospects of the undertaking. The venture turns out to be much more profitable than was vaguely anticipated, and the company is in full production, realizing a high return if not excessive profits. In these circumstances, whatever the theorists may say about *pacta sunt servanda*, the government is bound to call for a renegotiation of the agreements either on its own initiative or in response to overwhelming political pressure. . . .[19]

To this, one might add the factor of "sunk costs."

Once the investment is made, the host country no longer needs to offer benefits sufficient to attract the investment, it only has to treat the investor well enough to keep the investment. The difference between the two time periods (before and after investment) comes about because both the host and the investor know that once the firm has made its investment, it typically cannot disinvest fully. In other words, once it has invested, withdrawal would impose a cost on the firm. The host country can take advantage of this situation, and extract additional value from the firm by, for example, increasing the tax rate beyond the level that was agreed upon when the investment took place. Had the firm known that the tax rate would be higher than the agreed upon level, it may have chosen to invest elsewhere, or not to invest at all. Once the investment is made,

---

[19]   Asante, Stability of Contractual Relations in the Transnational Investment Process, 28 Int'l & Comp. L.Q. 401, 410–411 (1979).

however, it may be cheaper for the firm simply to pay the higher tax rather than to disinvest and reinvest elsewhere.[20]

Asante argues that renegotiation should "be acknowledged as an integral feature of the foreign investment process."[21] Some concession agreements include renegotiation clauses. For example, Article 38 of the 1980 Oil Concession Agreement between Abu Dhabi and Amerada Hess provided that if future arrangements between governments and companies operating in the petroleum industry in the Middle East were more favorable to governments, "then the Government and the Company shall review and discuss the changed circumstances within the petroleum industry in order to decide whether any alteration to the terms of this Agreement would be equitable to both parties." A more recent example is found in the 2006 Petroleum Agreement between Ghana and Tullow Ghana Ltd., which provides:

> 26.4 Where a Party considers that a significant change in the circumstances prevailing at the time the Agreement was entered into, has occurred affecting the economic balance of the Agreement, the Party affected hereby shall notify the other Parties in writing of the claimed change with a statement of how the claimed change has affected the relations between the Parties.
>
> 26.5 The other Parties shall indicate in writing their reaction to such representation within a period of three (3) Months of receipt of such notification and if such significant changes are established by the Parties to have occurred, the Parties shall meet to engage in negotiations and shall effect such changes in, or rectification of, these provisions as they may agree are necessary to restore the relative economic position of the Parties at the date of this Agreement.

Renegotiation clauses differ from the equilibrium clauses discussed above. See supra pp. 465–466. First, equilibrium clauses are triggered only by changes in government regulation that have an adverse effect on the foreign investor. Renegotiation clauses may be triggered by other kinds of changes that affect the economic balance of the agreement. Second, equilibrium clauses frequently provide for arbitration if the parties are unable to agree on modifications. Renegotiation clauses typically do not. They impose an obligation to negotiate in good faith, but no obligation to agree to changes.

Whether or not the contract contains a renegotiation clause, bargaining often occurs in the shadow of threats from each side. The host state may threaten to expropriate the investment entirely if the agreement cannot be renegotiated to its satisfaction. On the other side of

---

[20] Guzman, Why LDCs Sign Treaties That Hurt Them: Explaining the Popularity of Bilateral Investment Treaties, 38 Va. J. Int'l L. 639, 661–662 (1998).

[21] 28 Int'l & Comp. L.Q. at 413.

the table, the foreign investor may threaten to pull out, leaving the host state to its own devices, or to bring an arbitral claim if the investment is expropriated or unilaterally modified. Expropriation may impose substantial costs on the host state. First, the government may be less competent to run the operation than the foreign investor; production and profits may fall as a result of the investor's departure. Second, expropriation may affect the host country's reputation as a safe place to invest, discouraging future investment or raising the price of attracting it in the future. Although demands to renegotiate may also affect reputation, the impact of expropriation tends to be more severe. Third, the foreign investor may bring and perhaps win an expropriation claim against the host state.

After many years when host governments competed to offer favorable terms to attract foreign investors, renegotiation has reemerged as a subject of considerable importance. Since 2004, Bolivia, Ecuador, and Venezuela, among others, have moved to renegotiate existing agreements with foreign oil companies. For example, between 2004 and 2006, Venezuela increased the effective royalty on oil production from 1% to 33.33% and the tax on oil production from 34% to 50%. In 2007, Venezuelan President Hugo Chávez signed a decree requiring the renegotiation of projects in the Orinoco Oil Belt to give the state-owned oil company PDVSA at least a 60% stake. BP, Chevron, Statoil, and Total agreed to new terms with Venezuela, while Exxon Mobil and ConocoPhillips refused. Although the United States has no IIA with Venezuela, both Exxon Mobil and ConocoPhillips had restructured their investments through Dutch companies in 2005 and 2006, affording them the protection of the Netherlands-Venezuela BIT. Both companies filed claims against Venezuela with ICSID in the fall of 2007.

In the Mobil case, the ICSID tribunal held that it lacked jurisdiction over disputes relating to royalties and taxes that already existed at the time of the restructuring, but that it had jurisdiction over the claims for expropriation that arose after the restructuring. Mobil Corp. v. Venezuela, ICSID Case No. ARB/07/27, Decision on Jurisdiction (2010). The tribunal subsequently awarded Mobil $1.6 billion in compensation. Venezuela Holdings, B.V. v. Venezuela, ICSID Case No. ARB/07/27, Award (2014). An ICSID annulment committee subsequently reduced the compensation to $188 million, reasoning that the tribunal had failed to take proper account of a price cap on compensation applicable to one of the investments under Venezuelan law. Venezuela Holdings, B.V. v. Venezuela, ICSID Case No. ARB/07/27, Decision on Annulment (2017).

In the ConocoPhillips case, the ICSID tribunal held that it had jurisdiction under the BIT, rejected the investor's claims based on increased taxes and royalties, and upheld its claim of expropriation. ConocoPhillips Petrozuata B.V. v. Bolivarian Republic of Venezuela, ICSID Case No. ARB/07/30, Decision on Jurisdiction and the Merits (2013). The tribunal subsequently awarded $8.7 billion in damages.

ConocoPhillips Petrozuata B.V. v. Bolivarian Republic of Venezuela, ICSID Case No. ARB/07/30, Award (2019).

QUESTIONS

(1) How does the presence or absence of a BIT affect the process of renegotiation?

(2) Suppose that an investor agrees to renegotiate a concession agreement under threat of expropriation. Could the investor subsequently bring a claim for compensation claiming that its agreement to the new terms was not voluntary? How would you go about framing such an argument?

Additional reading: Kröll, The Renegotiation and Adaptation of Investment Contracts, in Arbitrating Foreign Investment Disputes: Procedural and Substantive Legal Aspects (Horn & Kröll eds., 2004); Berger, Renegotiation and Adaptation of International Investment Contracts: The Role of Contract Drafters and Arbitrators, 36 Vand. J. Transnat'l L. 1347 (2003); Kolo & Waelde, Renegotiation and Contract Adaptation in International Investment Projects, 1 J. World Investment 5 (2000).

PROBLEM 8

INTERNATIONAL DEBT INSTRUMENTS

A. INTRODUCTION

Our final problem involves the borrowing of funds by a sovereign government. Even in debt obligations between private parties, governments cast their shadow—for instance, the parties must take account of potential exchange-rate fluctuations and the possibility of currency controls that might prevent repayment. But when the borrower itself is a sovereign government, one must worry about other things that might affect enforceability, such as foreign sovereign immunity. Finally, the restructuring of debts when the borrower cannot pay is different with sovereign governments, because there is no procedure equivalent to bankruptcy that can be used to force a restructuring upon dissenting creditors.

We begin with a brief review of debt crises over the past forty years. Of course, the debt crisis that began in 1982 was not the first. In the nineteenth century, debt problems resulted in western powers taking control of public finances in Egypt and in Turkey. At the turn of the twentieth century, Germany, Great Britain, and Italy blockaded Venezuela in an attempt to collect debts owed to their nationals—an event that led to the Drago Doctrine outlawing the use of force to collect debts. World War I and the depression caused widespread repudiation and default by Russia, Germany, and others.

But the debt crisis that began with Mexico's announcement of a moratorium on payments in August 1982 was unique in various ways. The amounts owed by some of the Latin American states were enormous. By early 1985 Brazil was estimated to owe $100 billion, Mexico over $96 billion, and Argentina some $45 billion. The exposure of commercial banks, particularly in the United States, was also enormous. The nine largest banks, as a group, were owed by developing countries amounts more than twice their capital and more than 10% of their total assets. Sharp increases in the price of oil during the 1970s had created huge capital surpluses in oil-producing countries. Much of this money was deposited with commercial banks, which lent it freely to other developing nations. Many of the loans had floating rates, so borrowers' debt service costs rose dramatically in the early 1980s when the U.S. Federal Reserve Bank raised interest rates sharply to tame inflation. The worldwide recession of the early 80s also reduced demand for the exports that many developing countries were using to pay their debts.

The IMF and the United States provided emergency financing, commercial banks began to restructure their loans, and the debtor countries agreed to adjustment programs with the IMF, but the crisis persisted. The threat that the crisis posed to the banking system attracted the attention of U.S. policy makers. In 1985 Treasury Secretary James Baker proposed a plan that called for new lending and the restructuring (but not reduction) of existing debts. New lending, however, fell well short of the targets, growth failed to materialize, and the so-called "Baker Plan" was soon acknowledged as a failure. In 1989, the new Treasury Secretary Nicholas Brady announced a different plan under which lenders would forgive some of their loans in exchange for new obligations called "Brady Bonds" secured by U.S. zero-coupon bonds. The "Brady Plan" worked, and ultimately 17 countries were able to negotiate Brady deals with their creditors. The IMF imposed conditions requiring changes in economic policies. Although the commercial banks had to accept losses, they were able to exit the debt market by selling their Brady Bonds to other investors. By the mid-1990s, developing countries were again able to borrow freely on international capital markets, but such borrowing was now predominantly in the form of bonds rather than syndicated loans.

There have been a number of debt crises since the 1980s, including in Mexico in 1994, a number of Asian countries in 1997, and Russia in 1998. The two most significant, both in size and in consequence, have been Argentina's 2001 default and the Greek debt crisis that began in 2009.

In 2001, in the midst of a deep recession, Argentina defaulted on more than $100 billion of external debt. Argentina restructured some of this debt with an exchange offer in 2005 that 76% of bondholders accepted. In 2010, Argentina made another, substantively identical exchange offer that brought the level of participation in the restructuring above 90%. But some holdout bondholders refused to accept the exchange offers and sought to enforce their payment obligations in U.S. courts. In 2012, a district court held that the *pari passu* clause in Argentina's bonds prohibited the country from paying bondholders who had agreed to restructure while refusing payment to the holdouts. The court enjoined payments to the restructured bondholders, causing Argentina to default on its restructured bonds in 2014. As we shall see in Section D, this litigation led to changes in the *pari passu* clauses now included in most sovereign debt. See infra pp. 543–545. In 2016, following the election of a new president, Argentina reached agreement with most of its holdout creditors and successfully issued new bonds to finance the payment of its old obligations.

The Greek debt crisis began in 2009, when the government announced that the country's budget deficit had been significantly underreported. In fact, Greek debt at the time exceeded €300 billion, and its budget deficit was more than 12% of the country's GDP, four times the level permitted by the EU's Stability and Growth Pact. However, the crisis engulfed other countries as well—Ireland, Portugal, Spain, and Cyprus—and the precise causes of distress were complex and varied from country to country. In Portugal, for example, sovereign debt had expanded in part due to government spending on public projects and on the wages and pensions of public sector employees; in Ireland, a primary cause was state guarantees issued to the depositors and bondholders of banks that had financed a collapsing property market. In Cyprus, the crisis was triggered largely by the exposure of local banks to troubled Greek debt.

As the crisis spread, it raised fears of contagion within the Eurozone (and indeed around the globe) due to various forms of systemic risk. European states responded with a set of emergency measures including the creation of the European Financial Stability Facility and the European Financial Stabilisation Mechanism. These temporary programs were used to issue bonds, backed by the guarantees of Eurozone member states and the EU, respectively, whose proceeds helped fund bailout packages for the affected countries. In 2012, these programs were replaced by the European Stability Mechanism, a permanent program adopted through an amendment to the Treaty on the Functioning of the European Union and intended to serve as a firewall between a defaulting country and other countries and banks within the Eurozone. The Eurozone crisis has resulted in large bailouts for several countries, funded by the mechanisms described above as well as the EU and the International Monetary Fund (and accompanied by conditions including the adoption of significant austerity measures).

In 2012, Greece completed the largest debt restructuring in history, covering nearly €200 billion in government bonds. Just under 10% of these bonds had been issued under English law, with collective action clauses (CACs) that allowed modification of their terms by a supermajority vote of bondholders. Voting on these bonds was series by series, and while about 70% of the principal amount was restructured using the CACs, dissenting bondholders in series representing the remaining 30% were able to establish positions large enough to block Greece's proposed amendments. The vast majority of Greece's debt—more than 86%—had no CACs but were governed by Greek law. Taking advantage of that fact, the Greek legislature enacted the Greek Bondholder Act, which authorized the restructuring of bonds issued under Greek law with the consent of holders of two-thirds of the bonds' face value. Importantly, this voting was *not* series by series. All Greek-law bonds were aggregated for purposes of the vote, making it impossible for dissenting bondholders to establish a position large enough to block the restructuring. Although the restructuring involved a substantial "haircut"—a reduction in the principal value of the bonds of approximately 60%—the terms were made more attractive by subjecting the new debt to English law (beyond the reach of the Greek government to change again) and by issuing much of it in the form of highly-rated, short-term notes. Finally, the success of the restructuring was helped by the fact that as much as 40% of Greece's privately held debt was owned by banks and insurance companies, which were subject to pressure from European governments not to hold out.

Many things about sovereign debt have changed since 1982, but perhaps the single most important has been the shift from syndicated bank loans to bonds. This shift has changed the restructuring of sovereign debt obligations. During the 1980s banks were generally willing to negotiate with sovereign borrowers rather than go to court, both because the amounts they were owed were large enough to threaten their viability and because the number of creditors involved was small enough to reduce the collective action problem. The incentives for bondholders are different. They are more numerous, more varied, and more independent than commercial banks. As a result, they tend to have less reason to agree to a restructuring that would pay them less than full value, and more reason to litigate. Indeed, some—the so-called "vulture funds"—may even have purchased the bonds at a discount betting that they could recover full value through litigation, or at least obtain a more favorable settlement than was initially offered. We shall consider how sovereign debt instruments have responded to these new problems below in Section D. See infra pp. 534–545.

Additional reading: Scott & Gelpern, International Finance: Transactions, Policy, and Regulation ch. 18 (22d ed. 2018); Blustein, Laid Low: Inside the Crisis that Overwhelmed Europe and the IMF (2016); Rieffel, Restructuring Sovereign Debt: The Case for Ad Hoc Machinery chs. 8 & 10 (2003); The International Debt Crisis in Historical Perspective (Eichengreen & Lindert eds., 1989); Hébert & Schreger, The Costs of Sovereign Default: Evidence from Argentina, 107 Am. Econ. Rev. 3119 (2017); Zettlemeyer, Trebesch & Gulati, The Greek Debt Restructuring: An Autopsy, 28 Econ. Policy 513 (2013).

B. DRAFTING INTERNATIONAL DEBT INSTRUMENTS

Historically, sovereign states (and private firms as well) have issued debt principally through two instruments: syndicated bank loans and bonds. (Bonds with shorter maturities are also commonly referred to as "notes.") The terms of a bank loan are set forth in a loan agreement negotiated with a lead bank or banks. With a syndicated loan, the lead bank sells "participations" to other banks, allowing banks to lower their overall risk by diversifying their portfolios of borrowers. These participations may even be traded among banks on secondary markets.

Bonds, on the other hand, are securities and are sold to and traded among a broader market of investors. Sovereign bonds are often listed on an exchange such as the Luxembourg Stock Exchange. The terms of bonds follow standard patterns and are agreed with "underwriters," investment banks that buy the bonds initially but sell them on to investors within a matter of hours. Securities offered to the American public must be registered. This means the issuer must comply with two basic requirements. First, it must file a registration statement with the Securities and Exchange Commission (SEC) in which it sets forth the detailed information required by the Securities Act of 1933 and its implementing regulations. Second, it must furnish to each purchaser (after the registration statement has been declared effective by the SEC) a part of the statement known as the prospectus that, in somewhat less detail, contains the data that the purchaser supposedly needs to appraise the value of the securities. After an offering has been successfully completed, the issuer is subject to periodic reporting requirements. Schedule B to the Securities Act sets forth the minimum requirements for registration statements filed by foreign governments.

To avoid these registration requirements, issuers sometimes rely on two exemptions: Regulation S and Rule 144A. Regulation S exempts from registration offers and sales of securities made in an "offshore transaction" with no "directed selling efforts" in the United States, requirements the SEC has defined in elaborate detail. Rule 144A permits the sale and resale in the United States of unregistered securities to qualified institutional investors. Foreign governments used to rely heavily on Regulation S and Rule 144A when issuing bonds. But foreign governments that frequently issue bonds (like Mexico) have increasingly been willing to file registration statements with the SEC, allowing them broader access to U.S. capital markets.

Bonds come in various forms. Bearer bonds entitle whoever physically holds the bonds to receive principal and interest payments by presenting "coupons" attached to the bonds to the paying agent. With registered bonds, by contrast, the paying agent maintains a register of bondholders and makes payments to whoever is listed as the owner on the record date. Bonds may also be issued in either "certificated" or "book-entry" form. Holders of certificated bonds receive a form of the bonds themselves. Bonds issued in book-entry form, by contrast, are registered in the name of a company that acts as a depositary, with the bondholders owning beneficial interests.

For all their differences in structure, loan agreements and bonds face many of the same issues and contain many of the same terms, dealing with the payment of principal and interest, events of default, and the risk of taxation. Both typically include *pari passu* clauses and negative pledges, discussed below. See infra pp. 516–521. As a focus for discussion, consider the terms of the global notes issued by Mexico on January 21, 2016 in the amount of $2.25 billion. These notes reflect changes Mexico adopted for future debt issuances in 2014, including changes to the collective action clause and the *pari passu* clause, as well as a shift from a fiscal agency agreement to a trust indenture.

UNITED MEXICAN STATES

U.S. $100,000,000,000

Global Medium-Term Notes, Series A

U.S. $2,250,000,000 4.125% Global Notes due 2026

The notes will mature on January 21, 2026. Mexico will pay interest on the notes on January 21 and July 21 of each year, commencing July 21, 2016. Mexico may redeem the notes in whole or in part before maturity, at par plus the Make-Whole Amount and accrued interest, as described herein. The notes will not be entitled to the benefit of any sinking fund.

The notes will be issued under an indenture, each issuance of which constitutes a separate series under said indenture. The indenture contains provisions regarding future modifications to the terms of the notes that differ from those applicable to Mexico's outstanding public external indebtedness issued prior to November 10, 2014. Under these provisions, which are described beginning on page 6 of the accompanying prospectus dated February 3, 2016, Mexico may amend the payment provisions of the notes and other reserved matters listed in the indenture with the consent of the holders of: (1) with respect to a single series of notes, more than 75% of the aggregate principal amount of the outstanding notes of such series; (2) with respect to two or more series of notes, if certain "uniformly applicable" requirements are met, more than 75% of the aggregate principal amount of the outstanding notes of all series affected by the proposed modification, taken in the aggregate; or (3) with respect to two or more series of notes, more than 66 2/3% of the aggregate principal amount of the outstanding notes of all series affected by the proposed modification, taken in the aggregate, and more than 50% of the aggregate principal amount of the outstanding notes of each series affected by the proposed modification, taken individually.

Mexico has applied to list the notes on the Luxembourg Stock Exchange and to have the notes admitted to trading on the Euro MTF market of the Luxembourg Stock Exchange.

* * *

DESCRIPTION OF THE NOTES

Mexico will issue the notes under an amended and restated indenture, dated as of June 1, 2015, between Mexico and Deutsche Bank Trust Company Americas, as trustee. The information contained in this section and in the prospectus supplement and the prospectus summarizes some of the terms of the notes and the indenture. This summary does not contain all of the information that may be important to you as a potential investor in the notes. You should read the indenture and the form of the notes before making your investment decision. Mexico has filed or will file copies of these documents with the SEC and will also file copies of these documents at the offices of the trustee.

Aggregate Principal Amount:	U.S. $2,250,000,000
Issue Price:	99.676%, plus accrued interest, if any, from January 21, 2016
Issue Date:	January 21, 2016
Maturity Date:	January 21, 2026
Specified Currency:	U.S. dollars (U.S. $)
Authorized Denominations:	U.S. $200,000 and integral multiples of U.S. $1,000 in excess thereof
Form:	Registered; Book-Entry through the facilities of DTC, Euroclear and Clearstream, Luxembourg
Interest Rate:	4.125% per annum, accruing from January 21, 2016
Interest Payment Date:	Semi-annually on January 21 and July 21 of each year, commencing on July 21, 2016
Regular Record Date:	January 14 and July 14 of each year
Optional Redemption:	_X_ Yes ___ No

Mexico will have the right at its option, upon giving not less than 30 days' nor more than 60 days' notice, to redeem the notes, in whole or in part, at any time or from time to time prior to their maturity, at a redemption price equal to the principal amount thereof, plus the Make-Whole Amount (as defined below), plus interest accrued but not paid on the principal amount of such notes to the date of redemption. "Make-Whole Amount" means the excess of (i) the sum of the present values of each remaining scheduled payment of principal and interest on the notes to be redeemed (exclusive of interest accrued but not paid to the date of redemption), discounted to the redemption date on a semi-annual basis (assuming a 360-day year consisting of twelve 30-day months) at the Treasury Rate (as defined below) plus 30 basis points over (ii) the principal amount of the notes.

* * *

Optional Repayment:	___ Yes	_X_ No
Indexed Note:	___ Yes	_X_ No
Foreign Currency Note:	___ Yes	_X_ No

Managers:

Citigroup Global Markets Inc.

J.P. Morgan Securities LLC

Morgan Stanley & Co. LLC

Purchase Price:

99.506%, plus accrued interest, if any from January 21, 2016

Method of Payment:

Wire transfer of immediately available funds to an account designated by Mexico.

Listing:

Mexico has applied to list the notes on the Luxembourg Stock Exchange.

Trading:

Mexico has applied to have the notes admitted to trading on the Euro MTF Market of the Luxembourg Stock Exchange.

Securities Codes:

    CUSIP: 91086Q BG 2

    ISIN: US91086QBG29

    Common Code: 134892722

Trustee, Principal Paying Agent, Transfer Agent and Registrar:

Deutsche Bank Trust Company Americas

Luxembourg Listing Agent:

KBL European Private Bankers S.A.

Further Issues:

Mexico may from time to time, without the consent of holders of the notes, create and issue notes having the same terms and conditions as the notes offered pursuant to these final terms in all respects, except for the issue date, issue price and, if

| | applicable, the first payment of interest thereon; provided, however, that any such additional notes shall be issued either in a "qualified reopening" for U.S. federal income tax purposes or with no more than de minimis original issue discount for U.S. federal income tax purposes. Additional notes issued in this manner will be consolidated with, and will form a single series with, any such other outstanding notes. |

Payment of Principal and Interest:

Principal of and interest on the notes will be payable by Mexico to the Paying Agent in U.S. dollars.

Governing Law:

New York; *provided, however*, that all matters governing Mexico's authorization and execution of the indenture and the notes will be governed by and construed in accordance with the law of Mexico. Notwithstanding any authorization or any reserved matter modification, all matters related to the consent of holders and to modifications of the indenture or the notes will always be governed by and construed in accordance with the law of the State of New York.

Additional Provisions:

The notes will contain provisions regarding future modifications to their terms that differ from those applicable to Mexico's outstanding public external indebtedness issued prior to November 10, 2014. Those provisions are described beginning on page 6 of the accompanying prospectus dated February 3, 2016.

———————

The terms and conditions of the notes are set forth in an exhibit to the trust indenture between Mexico and Deutsche Bank Trust Company Americas, dated June 1, 2015, and are incorporated by reference in each series of notes issued under Mexico's Global Medium-Term Notes Program:

[FORM OF REVERSE OF DEBT SECURITIES]

TERMS AND CONDITIONS OF
THE DEBT SECURITIES

1. General. (a) This Debt Security is one of a duly authorized Series of debt securities of the UNITED MEXICAN STATES ("Mexico"), designated as its [%] [Title of Debt Securities] due _____ (each Debt of this Series a "Debt Security", and collectively, the "Debt Securities"), and issued or to be issued in one or more Series pursuant to an Amended and Restated Indenture dated as of _____, between Mexico and Deutsche Bank Trust Company Americas, as trustee (the "Trustee"), as amended from time to time (the "Indenture"). The Holders of the Debt Securities will be entitled to the benefits of, be bound by, and be deemed to have notice of, all of the provisions of the Indenture. A copy of the Indenture is on file and may be inspected at the Corporate Trust Office. All capitalized terms used in this Debt Security but not defined herein shall have the meanings assigned to them in the Indenture.

(b) The Debt Securities constitute and will constitute direct, general, unconditional and unsubordinated Public External Indebtedness (as defined below) of Mexico for which the full faith and credit of Mexico is pledged. The Debt Securities rank and will rank without any preference among themselves and equally with all other unsubordinated Public External Indebtedness of Mexico. It is understood that this provision shall not be construed so as to require Mexico to make payments under the Debt Securities ratably with payments being made under any other Public External Indebtedness.

(c) The Debt Securities are in fully registered form, without coupons, in denominations of [U.S. $2,000 and integral multiples of U.S. $1,000 in excess thereof] [other denominations as contemplated by Section 2.4 of the Indenture]. The Debt Securities may be issued in certificated form (each, a "Certificated Security" and, collectively, the "Certificated Securities"), or may be represented by one or more registered global securities (each, a "Global Security") held by or on behalf of the Depositary. Certificated Securities will be available only in the limited circumstances set forth in the Indenture. The

Debt Securities, and transfers thereof, shall be registered as provided in Section 2.6 of the Indenture. Any person in whose name a Debt Security shall be registered may (to the fullest extent permitted by applicable law) be treated at all times, by all persons and for all purposes as the absolute owner of such Debt Security regardless of any notice of ownership, theft, loss or any writing thereon.

(d) For the purposes of this paragraph and paragraphs 4 and 5 below, the following terms shall have the meanings specified below:

(i) "Public External Indebtedness" means any Public Indebtedness that is a payment obligation or contingent liability payable in any currency other than the currency of Mexico (other than any such Public Indebtedness that is originally issued or incurred within Mexico). For this purpose, settlement of original issuance by delivery of Public Indebtedness (or the instruments evidencing such Public Indebtedness) within Mexico shall be deemed to be original issuance within Mexico; and

(ii) "Public Indebtedness" means any payment obligation, including any contingent liability, of any person arising from bonds, debentures, Debt Securities or other securities that (A) are, or were intended at the time of issuance to be, quoted, listed or traded on any securities exchange or other securities market (including, without limiting the generality of the foregoing, securities eligible for resale pursuant to Rule 144A under the Securities Act, as amended (or any successor law or regulation of similar effect)) and (B) have an original maturity of more than one year or are combined with a commitment so that the original maturity of one year or less may be extended at the option of Mexico to a period in excess of one year.

2. Payments. (a) Mexico covenants and agrees that it will duly and punctually pay or cause to be paid the principal of, and premium, if any, and interest (including Additional Amounts (as defined below)) on, the Debt Securities and any other payments to be made by Mexico under the Debt Securities and the Indenture, at the place or places, at the respective times and in the manner provided in the Debt Securities and the Indenture. Principal of the Debt Securities will be payable against surrender of such Debt Securities at the Corporate Trust Office of the Trustee in New York City or, subject to applicable laws and regulations, at the office outside of the United States of a paying agent, by [U.S. dollar] [Other Currency] check drawn on, or by transfer to a [U.S. dollar] [Other Currency] account maintained by the Holder with, a bank located in [New York

City] [Other Location]. [If the Debt Security is to bear interest prior to maturity, insert: Payment of interest or principal (including Additional Amounts) on the Debt Securities will be made to the persons in whose name such Debt Securities are registered at the close of business on the relevant Record Date, whether or not such day is a Business Day (as defined below), notwithstanding the cancellation of such Debt Securities upon any transfer or exchange thereof subsequent to the Record Date and prior to such Interest Payment Date; provided that if and to the extent Mexico shall default in the payment of the interest due on such Interest Payment Date, such defaulted interest shall be paid to the persons in whose names such Debt Securities are registered as of a subsequent record date established by Mexico by notice, as provided in paragraph 11 of these Terms, by or on behalf of Mexico to the Holders of the Debt Securities not less than 15 days preceding such subsequent record date, such record date to be not less than 10 days preceding the date of payment of such defaulted interest. Notwithstanding the immediately preceding sentence, in the case where such interest or principal (including Additional Amounts) is not punctually paid or duly provided for, the Trustee shall have the right to fix such subsequent record date, and, if fixed by the Trustee, such subsequent record date shall supersede any such subsequent record date fixed by Mexico. . . .

* * *

3. Additional Amounts. (a) All payments by Mexico in respect of the Debt Securities shall be made without withholding or deduction for or on account of any present or future taxes, duties, assessments or other governmental charges of whatever nature imposed or levied by or on behalf of Mexico, or any political subdivision or taxing authority or agency therein or thereof having the power to tax (collectively, "Relevant Tax"), unless the withholding or deduction of such Relevant Tax is required by law. In that event, Mexico shall pay such additional amounts ("Additional Amounts") as may be necessary to ensure that the amounts received by the Holders after such withholding or deduction shall equal the respective amounts of principal and interest that would have been receivable in respect of the Debt Securities in the absence of such withholding or deduction; provided, however, that no such Additional Amounts shall be payable in respect of any Relevant Tax:

(i) imposed by reason of a Holder or beneficial owner of a Debt Security having some present or former connection with Mexico other than merely being a Holder or beneficial owner of the Debt Security or receiving payments of any nature on the Debt Security or enforcing its rights in respect of the Debt Security;

(ii) imposed by reason of the failure of a Holder or beneficial owner of a Debt Security, or any other person through which the Holder or beneficial owner holds a Debt Security, to comply with any certification, identification or other reporting requirement concerning the nationality, residence, identity or connection with Mexico of such Holder or beneficial owner or other person, if compliance with the requirement is a precondition to exemption from all or any portion of such withholding or deduction; or

(iii) imposed by reason of a Holder or beneficial owner of a Debt Security, or any other person through which the Holder or beneficial owner holds a Debt Security, having presented the Debt Security for payment (where such presentation is required) more than 30 days after the Relevant Date (as defined below), except to the extent that the Holder or beneficial owner or such other person would have been entitled to Additional Amounts on presenting the Debt Security for payment on any date during such 30-day period.

As used in this paragraph 3(a), "Relevant Date" in respect of any Debt Security means the date on which payment in respect thereof first becomes due or, if the full amount of the money payable has not been received by the Trustee on or prior to such due date, the date on which notice is duly given to the Holders in the manner described in paragraph 11 below that such monies have been so received and are available for payment. Any reference to "principal" and/or "interest" hereunder or in the Indenture shall be deemed to include any Additional Amounts which may be payable hereunder.

(b) Mexico will pay any present or future stamp, court or documentary taxes or any excise or property taxes, charges or similar levies which arise in Mexico or any political subdivision thereof or taxing authority thereof or therein in respect of the creation, issue, execution, initial delivery or registration of the Debt Securities or any other document or instrument referred to therein. Mexico will also indemnify the Holders from and against any stamp, court or documentary taxes or any excise or property taxes, charges or similar levies resulting from, or required to be paid by any of them in any jurisdiction in connection with, the enforcement of the obligations of Mexico under the Debt Securities or any other document or instrument referred to therein following the occurrence of any Event of Default (as defined below).

4.   Negative Pledge Covenant of Mexico. So long as any Debt Security shall remain Outstanding, or any amount payable by Mexico under the Indenture shall remain unpaid, Mexico agrees that Mexico will not create, incur, assume or suffer to exist any Security Interest (as defined below) in the whole or any part of its present or future revenues or assets to secure Public External Indebtedness of Mexico, unless the Debt Security is secured equally and ratably with such Public External Indebtedness; provided, however, that Mexico may create or permit to subsist:

(i)   Security Interests created prior to December 3, 1993;

(ii)   Security Interests securing Public External Indebtedness incurred in connection with a Project Financing (as defined below), provided that the Security Interest is solely in assets or revenues of the project for which the Project Financing was incurred;

(iii) Security Interests securing Public External Indebtedness which (A) is issued by Mexico in exchange for debt of Mexican public sector bodies (other than Mexico) and (B) is in an aggregate principal amount outstanding (with debt denominated in currencies other than U.S. dollars expressed in U.S. dollars based on rates of exchange prevailing at the date such debt was incurred) that does not exceed U.S. $29 billion; and

(iv) Security Interests securing Public External Indebtedness incurred or assumed by Mexico to finance or refinance the acquisition of the assets in which such Security Interest has been created or permitted to subsist.

For the purposes of this paragraph 4, the following terms shall have the meanings specified below:

"Project Financing" means any financing of all or part of the costs of the acquisition, construction or development of any project if the person or persons providing such financing (A) expressly agree to limit their recourse to the project financed and the revenues derived from such project as the principal source of repayment for the moneys advanced and (B) have been provided with a feasibility study prepared by competent independent experts on the basis of which it was reasonable to conclude that such project would generate sufficient foreign currency income to service substantially all Public External Indebtedness incurred in connection with such project.

"Security Interest" means any lien, pledge, mortgage, encumbrance or other preferential right granted to any person or entity over Mexico's revenues or assets.

5.   Events of Default; Acceleration. If one or more of the following events ("Events of Default") shall have occurred and be continuing (whatever the reason for such Event of Default and whether it shall be voluntary or involuntary or be effected by operation of law or pursuant to any judgment, decree or order of any court or any order, rule or regulation of any administrative or governmental body):

(a)   default in the payment of principal, premium, if any, or interest on any of the Debt Securities as and when the same shall become due and payable, whether at maturity, by declaration or otherwise, and continuance of such default for 30 days; or

(b)   failure on the part of Mexico to observe or perform any of the covenants or agreements provided herein or in the Indenture (in each case, other than those referred to in (a) above) for a period of 30 days after the date on which written notice shall have been given to Mexico by the Trustee or the Holders of at least 25% in aggregate principal amount of the Debt Securities then Outstanding; or

(c)   Mexico shall fail to make any payment of principal or interest in respect of Public External Indebtedness of Mexico when due and such failure shall result in the acceleration of an aggregate principal amount of not less than U.S.$10,000,000 (or its equivalent in other currencies) of such Public External Indebtedness, and such acceleration shall not have been rescinded or annulled; or

(d)   Mexico shall fail to make any payment in respect of Public External Indebtedness of Mexico in an aggregate principal amount in excess of U.S. $10,000,000 (or its equivalent in other currencies) for a period of 30 days after the date on which Mexico receives written notice from the Trustee or the Holders of at least 25% in aggregate principal amount of the Debt Securities then Outstanding; or

(e)   the declaration by Mexico of a moratorium with respect to the payment of principal of or interest on Public External Indebtedness of Mexico;

then in each and every such case, upon notice in writing by the Holders (the "Demanding Holders") (acting individually or together) of not less than 25% of the aggregate Outstanding principal amount of the Debt Securities to Mexico, with a copy to the Trustee, of any such Event of Default and its continuance, the Demanding Holders may declare the principal amount of all the Debt Securities due and payable immediately, and the same shall become and shall be due and payable upon the date that such written notice is received by or on behalf of Mexico, unless prior to such date all Events of Default in respect of all the Debt Securities shall have been cured; provided that, if at any time after the principal of the Debt Securities shall have been so declared due and payable, and before the sale of any property pursuant to any judgment or decree for the payment of monies due which shall have been obtained or entered in connection with the Debt Securities, Mexico shall pay or shall deposit (or cause to be paid or deposited) with the Trustee a sum sufficient to pay all matured installments of interest and principal upon all the Debt Securities which shall have become due otherwise than solely by acceleration (with interest on overdue installments of interest, to the extent permitted by law, and on such principal of each Debt Security at the rate of interest specified herein, to the date of such payment of interest or principal) and such amount as shall be sufficient to cover reasonable compensation to the Demanding Holders, the Trustee and each predecessor Trustee, their respective agents, attorneys and counsel, and all other documented expenses and liabilities reasonably incurred, and all advances made for documented expenses and legal fees, reasonably incurred by the Demanding Holders, the Trustee and each predecessor Trustee, and if any and all Events of Default hereunder, other than the nonpayment of the principal of the Debt Securities which shall have become due solely by acceleration, shall have been cured, waived or otherwise remedied as provided herein, then, and in every such case, the Holders of more than 50% in aggregate principal amount of the Debt Securities then Outstanding, by written notice to Mexico and to the Trustee, may, on behalf of all of the Holders, waive all defaults and rescind and annul such declaration and its consequences, but no such waiver or rescission and annulment shall extend to or shall affect any subsequent default, or shall impair any right consequent thereon. Actions by Holders pursuant to this paragraph 5 need not be taken at a meeting pursuant to paragraph 6 hereof. Actions by the Trustee and the Holders pursuant to this paragraph 5 are subject to Article Four of the Indenture.

* * *

9.   Paying Agents; Transfer Agents; Registrar. Mexico has initially appointed the paying agents, transfer agents and registrar listed at the foot of this Debt Security. Mexico may at any time appoint additional or other paying agents, transfer agents and registrars and terminate the appointment of those or any paying agents, transfer agents and registrar, provided that while the Debt Securities are Outstanding, Mexico will maintain in The City of New York (i) a paying agent, (ii) an office or agency where the Debt Securities may be presented for

exchange, transfer and registration of transfer as provided in the Indenture and (iii) a registrar. In addition, if and for so long as the Debt Securities are listed on the Luxembourg Stock Exchange and the rules of such Exchange so require, Mexico will maintain a paying agent and transfer agent in Luxembourg. Notice of any such termination or appointment and of any change in the office through which any paying agent, transfer agent or registrar will act will be promptly given in the manner described in paragraph 11 hereof.

10. Enforcement. Except as provided in Section 4.6 [eds.: this should read "Section 4.7"] of the Indenture, no Holder of any Debt Securities of any Series shall have any right by virtue of or by availing itself of any provision of the Indenture or of the Debt Securities of such Series to institute any suit, action or proceeding in equity or at law upon or under or with respect to the Indenture or of the Debt Securities, or for any other remedy hereunder or under the Debt Securities, unless (a) such Holder previously shall have given to the Trustee written notice of default and of the continuance thereof with respect to such Series of Debt Securities, (b) the Holders of not less than 25% in aggregate principal amount Outstanding of Debt Securities of such Series shall have made specific written request to the Trustee to institute such action, suit or proceeding in its own name as Trustee hereunder and shall have provided to the Trustee such reasonable indemnity or other security as it may require against the costs, expenses and liabilities to be incurred therein or thereby and (c) the Trustee for 60 days after its receipt of such notice, request and provision of indemnity or other security shall have failed to institute any such action, suit or proceeding and no direction inconsistent with such written request shall have been given to the Trustee pursuant to Section 4.9 of the Indenture; it being understood and intended, and being expressly covenanted by every Holder of Debt Securities of a Series with every other Holder of Debt Securities of such Series and the Trustee, that no one or more Holders shall have any right in any manner whatever by virtue or by availing itself of any provision of the Indenture or of the Debt Securities to affect, disturb or prejudice the rights of any other Holder of Debt Securities of such Series or to obtain priority over or preference to any other such Holder, or to enforce any right under the Indenture or under the Debt Securities of such Series, except in the manner herein provided and for the equal, ratable and common benefit of all Holders of Debt Securities of such Series. For the protection and enforcement of this paragraph, each and every Holder and the Trustee shall be entitled to such relief as can be given either at law or in equity.

11. Notices. Mexico will mail any notices to the Holders of the Debt Securities at their registered addresses as reflected in the books and records of the Trustee. Mexico will consider any mailed notice to have been given five Business Days after it has been sent. Mexico will also publish notices to the Holders (a) in a leading newspaper having general circulation in New York City and London (which is expected to be The Wall Street Journal and the Financial Times, respectively) and (b) if and so long as the Debt Securities are listed on the Euro MTF market of the Luxembourg Stock Exchange and the rules of the exchange so require, in a leading newspaper having general circulation in Luxembourg (which is expected to be d'Wort - Luxemburger Wort für Wahrheit und Recht) and on the website of the Luxembourg Stock Exchange at http://www.bourse.lu. If publication in a leading newspaper in Luxembourg is not practicable, Mexico will publish such notices in a leading English language daily newspaper with general circulation in Europe. Mexico will consider any published notice to be given on the date of its first publication.

12. Further Issues of Debt Securities. Mexico may from time to time, without the consent of Holders of the Debt Securities, create and issue additional Debt Securities having the same Terms as the Debt Securities in all respects, except for issue date, issue price and the first payment of interest thereon; provided, however, that any such additional Debt Securities shall be issued either in a "qualified reopening" for U.S. federal income tax purposes or with no more than de minimis original issue discount for U.S. federal income tax purposes. Additional Debt Securities issued in this manner will be consolidated with and will form a single Series with the previously Outstanding Debt Securities.

13. Prescription. To the extent permitted by law, claims against Mexico for the payment of principal of, or interest or other amounts due on, the Debt Securities (including Additional Amounts) will become void unless made within five years of the date on which that payment first became due.

14. Authentication. This Debt Security shall not become valid or obligatory until the certificate of authentication hereon shall have been duly signed by the Trustee or its agent.

15. Governing Law. (a) This Debt Security will be governed by and construed in accordance with the laws of [the State of New York]; provided, however, that all matters governing Mexico's authorization and execution of the Indenture and the Debt Securities shall in all cases be governed by and construed in accordance with the laws of Mexico.

(b) Each of the parties hereto hereby irrevocably submits to the jurisdiction of any state or federal court sitting in the Borough of Manhattan, The City of New York in any action or proceeding arising out of or based on the Indenture [or the Debt Securities]. Mexico will appoint the Consul General of Mexico acting through his or her offices at 27 East 39th Street, New York, New York, 10016, and his or her successors, as its authorized agent (the "Authorized Agent") upon whom process may be served in any action arising out of or based on the Indenture [or the Debt Securities], which may be instituted in any such court as provided in the Indenture. Mexico hereby waives irrevocably, to the extent permitted by law, any immunity from the jurisdiction of such court (including sovereign immunity under the U.S. Foreign Sovereign Immunities Act of 1976 and immunity from pre-judgment attachment, post-judgment attachment and execution), except that under Article 4 of the Federal Code of Civil Procedure of Mexico attachment prior to judgment or attachment in aid of execution may not be ordered by Mexican courts against property of Mexico, and any objections to the laying of venue in any such courts in respect of any such action to which it might otherwise be entitled in any actions arising out of or based on the Indenture or the Debt Securities of any Series which may be instituted as provided in the Indenture in any state or federal court in the Borough of Manhattan, The City of New York. In addition, each of the parties hereby waives any rights to which it may be entitled on account of place of residence or domicile outside of such jurisdiction. Such appointment shall be irrevocable until all amounts in respect of the principal of (and premium, if any) and any interest due and to become due on or in respect of all the Debt Securities have been provided to the Trustee pursuant to the terms hereof or paid or returned to Mexico in accordance with the Indenture, except that, if for any reason, the Consul General of Mexico ceases to be able to act as Authorized Agent or no longer has an address in the Borough of Manhattan, The City of New York, Mexico will appoint another person (which may be the Trustee) in the Borough of Manhattan, The City of New York, selected in its discretion, as such Authorized Agent, a copy of which acceptance it shall provide to the Trustee. Mexico will take any and all action, including the filing of any and all documents and instruments, that may be necessary to continue such appointment or appointments pursuant to Section 9.7 of the Indenture in full force and effect as aforesaid. Service of process upon the Authorized Agent at the address indicated above, or at such other address in the Borough of Manhattan, The City of New York by notice given by the Authorized Agent to each party hereto, shall be deemed, in every respect, effective service of process upon Mexico.

(c)   A final non-appealable judgment in any such action or proceeding shall be conclusive and may be enforced in other jurisdictions by a suit upon such judgment or in any other manner provided by law.

(d)   Notwithstanding the provisions of this paragraph 15, any action against Mexico arising out of or based on the Debt Securities of any Series may also be instituted as provided in the Indenture in any competent court in Mexico.

(e)   Notwithstanding anything else in this paragraph 15 to the contrary, neither such appointment nor such submission to jurisdiction or such waiver of sovereign immunity shall be interpreted to include actions brought under the United States securities laws or any state securities laws.

(f)   Nothing in this paragraph 15 shall affect the right of the Trustee or (in connection with legal actions or proceedings by any Holder as permitted by the Indenture and this Debt Security) any Holder to serve legal process in any other manner permitted by law, or affect the right of the Trustee or any such Holder to bring any action or proceeding against Mexico or its property in the courts of other jurisdictions.

* * *

20. Modifications. (a) Any Modification to the Debt Securities or the Indenture insofar as it affects the Debt Securities shall be made in accordance with Article Ten and Article Eleven of the Indenture.

(b)   Any Modification pursuant to this paragraph 20 will be conclusive and binding on all Holders of the Debt Securities and on all future Holders of the Debt Securities whether or not notation of such Modification is made upon the Debt Securities. Any instrument given by or on behalf of any Holder of a Debt Security in connection with any consent to or approval of any such Modification will be conclusive and binding on all subsequent Holders of that Debt Security.

(c)   For purposes of this Debt Security, [specific definitions, if any, to be added].

_____

As noted in paragraph 20 of the terms and conditions, the provisions for modification of the notes are found in the trust indenture. Those provisions read as follows:

ARTICLE ELEVEN
MODIFICATIONS

SECTION 11.1. Modifications Not Requiring the Consent of Holders. Mexico and the Trustee may, without the vote or consent of any Holder of Debt Securities of any Series, agree to a Modification of Debt Securities of such Series or to this Indenture as it relates to that Series for the purpose of:

i.   adding to Mexico's covenants for the benefit of the Holders;

ii.   surrendering any right or power conferred upon Mexico with respect to Debt Securities of that Series;

iii.   securing the Debt Securities of that Series;

iv.   curing any ambiguity or curing, correcting or supplementing any defective provision in the Debt Securities of that Series or the Indenture;

v.   amending the Debt Securities of that Series or this Indenture in any manner which Mexico and the Trustee may determine and which does not materially adversely affect the interests of any Holders of Debt Securities of that Series; or

vi.   correcting, in the opinion of the Trustee, a manifest error of a formal, minor or technical nature.

Any such technical Modification shall be binding on all Holders of Debt Securities of that Series intended to be affected by the Modification and, unless the Trustee otherwise requires, any such technical Modification shall be notified by the Trustee to such Holders of Debt Securities as soon as practicable thereafter.

SECTION 11.2. Single Series Non-Reserved Matter Modifications. Single Series Non-Reserved Matter Modifications proposed by Mexico that are not technical Modifications covered by Section 11.1 may be approved by Holders of Debt Securities (by vote at a meeting of Holders of Debt Securities or by a written action), and future compliance therewith may be waived, with the written consent of Mexico and the affirmative vote (if approved at a meeting of Holders of the Debt Securities) or consent (if approved by a written action) of Holders of more than 50% of the aggregate principal amount of the Outstanding Debt Securities of that Series.

SECTION 11.3. Reserved Matter Modification Methods.[1] Reserved Matter Modifications proposed by Mexico may be

---

[1] The trust indenture defines "Reserved Matter Modification" to mean any modification that would:

approved by Holders of the Debt Securities (by vote at a Holder of the Debt Securities' meeting or by a written action) in one of three ways (each, a "Modification Method"):

    i.   for a Single Series Modification, by the Holders of the Debt Securities of the Series subject to the proposed Modification,

    ii.   for a proposed Cross-Series Modifications with Single Aggregated Voting, by the Holders of two or more Series of Debt Securities whose votes or written consents will be aggregated for the purpose of determining whether the approval threshold has been met, and

    iii.   for a proposed Cross-Series Modifications with Two-Tier Voting, by the Holders of two or more Series of Debt Securities whose votes or written consents (x) taken together, must meet an aggregated approval threshold and (y) taken separately for each Series of Debt Securities covered by that proposed Cross-Series Modification, must meet a separate approval threshold.

Mexico shall have the discretion to select a Modification Method for a proposed Reserved Matter Modification and to designate which Series of Debt Securities will be included in the aggregated voting for a proposed Cross-Series Modification; *provided, however*, that once Mexico selects a Modification Method and designates the Series of Debt Securities that will be subject to a proposed Cross-Series Modification, those elections will be final for purposes of that vote or consent solicitation.

---

i.   change the date on which any amount is payable on the Debt Securities;

ii.   reduce the principal amount (other than in accordance with the express terms of the Debt Securities and this Indenture) of the Debt Securities;

iii.   reduce the interest rate on the Debt Securities;

iv.   change the method used to calculate any amount payable on the Debt Securities (other than in accordance with the express terms of the Debt Securities and this Indenture);

v.   change the currency or place of payment of any amount payable on the Debt Securities;

vi.   modify Mexico's obligation to make any payments on the Debt Securities (including any redemption price therefor);

vii.   change the identity of the obligor under the Debt Securities;

viii.   change the definition of "Outstanding" or the percentage of affirmative votes or written consents, as the case may be, required for the taking of any action pursuant to Section 11.4, Section 11.5 and Section 11.6;

ix.   change the definition of "Uniformly Applicable" or "Reserved Matter Modification";

x.   authorize the Trustee, on behalf of all Holders of the Debt Securities, to exchange or substitute all the Debt Securities for, or convert all the Debt Securities into, other obligations or securities of Mexico or any other Person; or

xi.   change the legal ranking, governing law, submission to jurisdiction or waiver of immunities provisions of the Terms of the Debt Securities.

Mexico may simultaneously propose two or more Cross-Series Modifications, each affecting different Series of Debt Securities, or one or more Cross-Series Modifications together with one or more Single Series Reserved Matter Modifications.

SECTION 11.4. Single Series Reserved Matter Modifications. Any Single Series Reserved Matter Modification may be made, and future compliance therewith may be waived, with the written consent of Mexico and the affirmative vote or consent of Holders of more than 75% of the aggregate principal amount of the Outstanding Debt Securities of that Series.

SECTION 11.5. Cross-Series Modifications with Single Aggregated Voting. Any Cross-Series Modification with Single Aggregated Voting may be made, and future compliance therewith may be waived, with the written consent of Mexico and the affirmative vote or consent of Holders of more than 75% of the aggregate principal amount of the Outstanding Debt Securities of all the Series affected by the proposed Modification (taken in the aggregate).

SECTION 11.6. Cross-Series Modifications with Two-Tier Voting. Any Cross-Series Modification with Two-Tier Voting may be made, and future compliance therewith may be waived, with the written consent of Mexico and:

i.   the affirmative vote or consent of Holders of more than 66 2/3% of the aggregate principal amount of the Outstanding Debt Securities of *all* the Series affected by that proposed Modification (taken in the aggregate), and

ii.   the affirmative vote or consent of Holders of more than 50% of the aggregate principal amount of the Outstanding Debt Securities of *each* Series affected by that proposed Modification (taken individually).

It is understood that a Cross-Series Modification constituting or including a Reserved Matter Modification that it is *not* Uniformly Applicable to the terms and conditions of the affected Debt Securities must be effected pursuant to this Section 11.6; a Cross-Series Modification that is Uniformly Applicable may be effected pursuant to Section 11.5 or Section 11.6, at Mexico's option.

* * *

SECTION 11.8. Binding Effect. Any Modification consented to or approved by the Holders of Debt Securities pursuant to this Article Eleven will be conclusive and binding on all Holders of the relevant Series of Debt Securities or all Holders of all Series of Debt Securities affected by a Cross-Series Modification, as the case may be, whether or not they have given such consent, and on all future Holders of those Debt Securities whether or not notation of such Modification is made upon the Debt Securities. Any instrument given by or on behalf of any Holder of a Debt Security in connection with any consent to or approval of any such Modification will be conclusive and binding on all subsequent Holders of that Debt Security.

* * *

COMMENT ON TERMS AND CONDITIONS

At the heart of any debt instrument are the clauses providing when, where, and in what currency the funds are to be advanced to the debtor and then the terms on which the debtor is to repay what it owes. Mexico borrowed U.S. dollars and would therefore be required under Paragraph 2(a) of the terms and conditions to make payments of principal and interest in U.S. dollars, a choice that requires Mexico to bear the risks of currency fluctuations. For many years, most sovereign borrowers were simply unable to borrow internationally in their own currencies. A number of developing countries have now issued global bonds in their local currencies, however, having found that investors are willing to assume the risk of currency fluctuations in exchange for higher interest rates.

Next, there is the rate of interest, which may be either a fixed or a floating rate. In the case of Mexico's notes, the interest rate is fixed at 4.125% over the ten-year term of the notes. With a fixed-rate obligation, it becomes important to limit the options for early repayment and redemption. If creditors have the option of demanding early repayment (other than in the case of a default) and interest rates rise, the borrower may be forced to refinance at a higher rate. Conversely, if the borrower has the option of redeeming the debt early and rates fall, creditors may be forced to refinance at a lower rate. Mexico's notes deny borrowers the right to demand early repayment, but they give Mexico the option to redeem the notes early by paying a "make-whole amount" that represents the net present value of its future payments. See supra pp. 499–500.

With a floating rate obligation, the interest rate is calculated based on an underlying rate plus a "margin." The margin may be either: (1) a fixed spread expressed in basis points (hundredths of a percentage point), e.g., 90 basis points, that is added to the underlying rate; or (2) a spread multiplier expressed as a percentage, e.g., 150%, by which the underlying rate is multiplied. The margin gives the lender a measure of profit and takes into account the riskiness of the particular borrower. Historically, the underlying rate most often used was the London Interbank Offered Rate (LIBOR), the rate at which major banks estimated that they could borrow funds on the London market. In 2012, however, it came to light that certain banks had submitted false rates to benefit the positions of derivative traders and to maintain their reputations for being able to borrow during the financial crisis. Efforts to rehabilitate LIBOR failed, and in 2018 the UK Financial Conduct Authority announced that LIBOR would be discontinued in 2021. Countries have been developing new rates to take its place in financial contracts, like the Standard Overnight Financing Rate (SOFR) published by the Federal Reserve Bank of New York. The problem remains of what to do for sovereign debt obligations and other financial contracts that used LIBOR and mature after the rate will be discontinued. It also remains to be seen which underlying rates governments will choose when they issue new floating-rate obligations.

There may, of course, be legal limits on the amount of interest that may be charged, resembling U.S. usury laws. There may also be rules providing that it is unlawful to charge the borrower a higher rate of interest after a default. In the Islamic world, the Koran's prohibition on interest means that debt obligations using interest rates are frowned upon even when they are not prohibited. This has given rise to a growing industry in Islamic finance, with instruments like *sukuk* that resemble bonds but are structured to pay rents or profits rather than interest.

Paragraph 1(b) contains a *pari passu* clause promising that the notes will rank equally with all other unsecured and unsubordinated public external indebtedness. When the borrower is a private firm, such clauses serve to prevent the creation of senior claims that would have priority in bankruptcy. Because sovereign debtors cannot go into bankruptcy, the presence of such clauses in their debt obligations is something of a mystery. In NML Capital, Ltd. v. Republic of Argentina, 699 F.3d 246 (2012), the Second Circuit Court of Appeals held that a *pari passu* clause in a bond issued by Argentina prohibited that country from paying creditors who had agreed to restructure Argentina's debts unless it also paid holdout creditors who had refused to restructure. As discussed below, this decision threatened the ability of sovereign debtors to engage in debt restructuring during periods of financial difficulty. See infra pp. 543–545. Paragraph 1(b) of Mexico's notes responds to this decision by making explicit that the *pari passu* clause addresses only ranking and not payment: "It is understood that this provision shall not be construed so as to require Mexico to make payments under the Debt Securities ratably with payments being made under any other Public External Indebtedness."

Paragraph 3 of the terms and conditions is known as an "additional amounts" or "tax gross-up" clause. It is a response to the possibility that the borrower's country might tax the flow of interest payments. Of course, in our case, Mexico itself is the borrower, but additional amounts provisions are routine in sovereign debt obligations as well as those of private borrowers. The function of such a provision is to shift the risk of taxation by the borrower's home country to the borrower. It provides that if the borrower is required by law to withhold or deduct taxes, it will pay additional amounts to make up the difference. There are several important limitations, however, on Mexico's obligations under paragraph

3(a). First, it applies only to taxes imposed by Mexico and its subdivisions and not to taxes on interest that might be levied by the noteholder's home jurisdiction. Second, it does not apply to taxes that might be owed on the basis of some connection with Mexico other than simply being a noteholder—for example, if a particular noteholder created a permanent establishment in Mexico that subjected it to Mexican income tax.

Paragraph 4 is the "negative pledge," which prohibits the borrower from creating security interests—defined broadly to include "any lien, pledge, mortgage, encumbrance or other preferential right"—over any of Mexico's revenues or assets unless the notes are similarly secured. The purpose of the clause is to make sure that the borrower's assets remain available to satisfy the claims of unsecured creditors like the noteholders. As with most negative pledges, this one contains exceptions (often called "permitted liens"). Permitted liens commonly include: security interests that were in existence prior to the date of the loan or the issuance of the bonds (see, e.g., para. 4(i)); security interests in newly purchased assets, because they do not affect the position of unsecured creditors (see, e.g., para. 4(iv)); security interests in project finance transactions, because they should generate sufficient income to pay back the project finance loans and so should have no negative impact on creditors (see, e.g., para. 4(ii)); and other security interests up to some maximum amount (see, e.g., para. 4(iii)).

The default provisions in paragraph 5 entitle noteholders to "accelerate" payment—that is, to declare that the notes are immediately due and payable. Observe, however, that a single, small noteholder may not accelerate the notes even if an event of default occurs. That right may be exercised only by holders of at least 25% of the aggregate principal amount outstanding. Moreover, if the event of default is subsequently cured, the acceleration may be rescinded by holders of a majority of the aggregate principal amount. These limitations, which have been found in loan agreements and bonds for some time, represent an early attempt to deal with some of the collective action problems further discussed below. See infra pp. 536–545.

The events of default in paragraph 5 include, most obviously, the failure to make principal or interest payments under the notes (with a grace period) and the failure to comply with other terms of the notes or of the trust indenture (for example, the negative pledge). They also include the sovereign equivalent of bankruptcy—the declaration of a moratorium on the payment of external debt. Less immediately obvious is the point of paragraphs 5(c) and 5(d), which make the failure to pay debts *other than* the notes an event of default. Such provisions are generically known as "cross-default" clauses and come in two basic types. The true "cross-default" clause makes it an event of default if creditors under any other indebtedness are *entitled* to accelerate, even if those creditors do not actually accelerate. The "cross-acceleration" clause, by contrast, makes it an event of default only if creditors under another indebtedness actually accelerate. The purpose of such provisions is to give a lender the right to seek repayment from a troubled borrower as soon as any other lender is able to seek repayment. Such a right may be important because a borrower might otherwise be inclined to negotiate first with other lenders who pose a more immediate threat, and because in some jurisdictions (like New York) the order in which a borrower's assets are attached determines the order in which judgments are paid.

Although noteholders holding at least 25% of the aggregate principal amount outstanding may accelerate payment in case of a default under paragraph 5, paragraph 10 limits the right of noteholders to bring suit against Mexico for the accelerated amounts. Noteholders may do so only if holders of at least 25% have made a written request to the trustee to bring suit, holders have provided a reasonable indemnity to the trustee for its costs in bringing suit, and the trustee has failed to bring suit within 60 days. Paragraph 10 also provides that any suit must be brought "for the equal, ratable and common benefit of all Holders of Debt Securities of such Series," limiting the ability of noteholders to pursue their individual interests through litigation. Individual noteholders do have the right, however, to seek payments of principal and interest that are past due *other than* accelerated amounts, a right preserved in Section 4.7 of the trust indenture. The provisions on enforcement found in paragraph 10 of the terms and conditions and in Article 4 of the trust indenture represent another aspect of Mexico's attempt to address the collective action problem in debt restructuring discussed below. See infra pp. 536–545.

Paragraph 15 addresses the governing law and choice of forum. Paragraph 15(a) chooses New York law to govern the notes, except with respect to Mexico's authority to issue them, which is governed by Mexican law. When foreign governments issue debt governed by a law other than their own, they generally choose New York or English law. Since the mid-1990s, however, the number of sovereign debt issuances governed by local law has grown substantially. Some countries, like the United States and many European nations, always or almost always issue debt subject to their own laws. In 2012, Greece took advantage of the fact that most of its debt was governed by Greek law by introducing a collective action clause into existing debt obligations that allowed those obligations to be restructured. See supra pp. 495–496.

Paragraph 15(b) is a forum-selection clause choosing state or federal courts located in the Borough of Manhattan, City of New York. As we shall see in Section C, because Mexico is a foreign state, it is entitled to certain immunities from suit, attachment, and execution under the U.S. Foreign Sovereign Immunities Act of 1976. Paragraph 15(b) waives Mexico's immunity from suit to enforce the notes, as well as its immunity from pre-judgment attachment, post-judgment attachment, and execution. But paragraph 15(e) exempts from Mexico's consent to jurisdiction and waivers of immunity any actions brought under federal or state securities laws, such as actions for securities fraud.

Paragraph 20 indicates that the notes may be modified under the terms of the trust indenture and that such modifications will bind all noteholders. The procedure for modification depends on the kind of modification sought. Under Section 11.1 of the trust indenture, modifications that benefit the noteholders or do not materially affect their interests may be made without the noteholders' consent. The trustee serves to protect the interests of noteholders in this situation by determining when their interests are materially adversely affected. Under Section 11.2, modifications to "non-reserved matters" may be made for a single series of notes with the approval of holders of 50% of the aggregate principal amount outstanding of that series. Non-reserved matters are relatively unimportant terms that do not affect payment, ranking of creditors, governing law, jurisdiction, or the waiver of immunities.

The key provisions of Article 11, however, are those permitting the modification of "reserved matters," including the principal, interest, and maturity of the notes. It is these terms that a government typically wants to change in a debt restructuring. Sections 11.3–11.6 give Mexico three options that may be combined in various ways:

- Under Section 11.4, a reserved matter may be modified for a single series of notes with the approval of holders of 75% of the aggregate principal amount outstanding of that series.

- Under Section 11.5, a reserved matter may be modified for more than one series of notes with the approval of holders of 75% of the aggregate principal amount outstanding for all series affected. For example, if Mexico wanted to modify a reserved matter in ten different series, each with $1 billion in principal outstanding, it could make the modification to each of the series if holders of $7.5 billion approved, even if the holders of one or two of the series unanimously disapproved.

- Under Section 11.6, a reserved matter may be modified for more than one series of notes with the approval of the holders of two-thirds of the aggregate principal amount outstanding for all series affected, so long as holders of 50% of the aggregate principal amount outstanding in each series affected also approve. For example, if Mexico wanted to modify a reserved matter in ten different series, each with $1 billion in principal outstanding, it could make the modification to each of the series if holders of $6.67 billion approved, so long as holders of at least $500 million in each series also approved.

These provisions are typically known as "collective action clauses" because they are designed to prevent holdout creditors from blocking modifications favored by a supermajority. Mexico's provisions reflect a conscious effort to improve collective action clauses initiated by the U.S. Treasury Department in 2013, published by the International Capital Market Association in 2014, and revised again in 2015. Section D on restructuring sovereign debt will consider collective action clauses in greater detail. See infra pp. 542–545.

Finally, it is worth noting some terms that are not found in these notes. First, there is no limitation on the use of the funds (although Mexico stated in its prospectus that it would use these proceeds to redeem other debt). Second, apart from the negative pledge, there are almost no covenants restricting the behavior of the borrower. Such limitations are commonly found in debt obligations of private borrowers, but are often resisted by governments as an infringement on their sovereignty. Extensive covenants are found in project finance loans, however, even when the borrower is a government. In a project finance transaction, the lenders agree to look for repayment only to the revenues and assets of the project and not to any other revenues and assets of the borrower. Because repayment depends on the success of the project, lenders insist upon exercising a much greater degree of control than is the case with most other lending arrangements.

QUESTIONS

(1) What advantages might accrue to a government from being able to borrow funds in its own currency?

(2) From the borrower's point of view, what are the advantages and disadvantages of a floating interest rate? Consider that question also from the lender's perspective.

(3) Consider paragraphs 5(c) and (d) of Mexico's notes. Should they be properly characterized as "cross-default" provisions, "cross-acceleration" provisions, or something in between?

(4) Paragraph 15 provides that the notes will be governed primarily by New York law. In Problem 7, we saw that concession agreements between foreign investors and governments are almost never governed by the law of the foreign investor's home state. See supra pp. 463–464. What explains the difference here?

Additional reading: Buchheit, How to Negotiate Eurocurrency Loan Agreements (2d ed. 2000); Díaz de León, Mexico's Adoption of New Standards in International Sovereign Debt Contracts, 11 Capital Markets L. Rev. 12 (2016).

C. ENFORCEABILITY OF INTERNATIONAL DEBT INSTRUMENTS

Paragraph 1(b) of the Mexican notes' terms and conditions states that Mexico has pledged its "full faith and credit" for the repayment of the notes. Yet we have seen that sovereign debtors frequently default on their debt obligations. If a country cannot or will not pay, can its obligation be enforced in a court of law?

1. FOREIGN SOVEREIGN IMMUNITY

Historically, governments were considered immune from suit in the courts of another state. During the twentieth century, a number of countries moved from an absolute to a restrictive theory of immunity. Under the restrictive theory, foreign states continue to enjoy immunity from claims arising out of its governmental activities (*de jure imperii*) but are not immune from claims arising out of its non-governmental activities (*de jure gestionis*), particularly its commercial activities. The United States adopted the restrictive theory of foreign sovereign immunity in 1952, and it was codified in the Foreign Sovereign Immunities Act of 1976 (FSIA).

Section 1330 of Title 28 of the United States Code gives the district courts personal and subject-matter jurisdiction over claims against a foreign state from which it is not entitled to immunity. "Foreign state" is defined to include political subdivisions as well as any "agency or instrumentality" of a foreign state. This latter phrase includes corporations "a majority of whose shares or other ownership interest is owned by a foreign state or political subdivision thereof." 28 U.S.C.A. § 1603(b)(2). The Supreme Court has held that the FSIA is the sole basis for obtaining jurisdiction over a foreign state. See Argentine Republic v. Amerada Hess Shipping Corp., 488 U.S. 428, 109 S.Ct. 683, 102 L.Ed.2d 818 (1989).

Under 28 U.S.C.A. § 1604, foreign states are immune from the jurisdiction of both state and federal courts except as provided in §§ 1605–1607. Section 1605 sets forth the most important exceptions to immunity from suit.

§ 1605. General exceptions to the jurisdictional immunity of a foreign state

(a) A foreign state shall not be immune from the jurisdiction of courts of the United States or of the States in any case—

(1) in which the foreign state has waived its immunity either explicitly or by implication, notwithstanding any withdrawal of the waiver which the foreign state may purport to effect except in accordance with the terms of the waiver;

(2) in which the action is based upon a commercial activity carried on in the United States by the foreign state; or upon an

act performed in the United States in connection with a commercial activity of the foreign state elsewhere; or upon an act outside the territory of the United States in connection with a commercial activity of the foreign state elsewhere and that act causes a direct effect in the United States;

(3) in which rights in property taken in violation of international law are in issue and that property or any property exchanged for such property is present in the United States in connection with a commercial activity carried on in the United States by the foreign state; or that property or any property exchanged for such property is owned or operated by an agency or instrumentality of the foreign state and that agency or instrumentality is engaged in a commercial activity in the United States;

* * *

(6) in which the action is brought, either to enforce an agreement made by the foreign state with or for the benefit of a private party to submit to arbitration all or any differences which have arisen or which may arise between the parties with respect to a defined legal relationship, whether contractual or not, concerning a subject matter capable of settlement by arbitration under the laws of the United States, or to confirm an award made pursuant to such an agreement to arbitrate, if (A) the arbitration takes place or is intended to take place in the United States, (B) the agreement or award is or may be governed by a treaty or other international agreement in force for the United States calling for the recognition and enforcement of arbitral awards, (C) the underlying claim, save for the agreement to arbitrate, could have been brought in a United States court under this section or section 1607, or (D) paragraph (1) of this subsection is otherwise applicable; . . .

Whether bondholders could bring suit under § 1605(a)(2)'s commercial activities exception was the question at issue in the decision that follows.

Republic of Argentina v. Weltover, Inc.

Supreme Court of the United States, 1992
504 U.S. 607, 112 S.Ct. 2160, 119 L.Ed.2d 394

[To resolve a foreign exchange crisis of 1981–82, Argentina issued obligations called "Bonods" that provided for the payment of principal and interest in United States dollars in London, Frankfurt, Zurich, or New York, at the election of the creditor. When Argentina ran into difficulties again in 1986, it unilaterally extended the time of payment on the Bonods and offered creditors the right to exchange their Bonods for other securities. Plaintiffs refused the offer and sued. Justice Scalia delivered the opinion for a unanimous Court.]

* * *

II

The Foreign Sovereign Immunities Act of 1976 (FSIA), 28 U.S.C. § 1602 *et seq.*, establishes a comprehensive framework for determining whether a court in this country, state or federal, may exercise jurisdiction over a foreign state. Under the Act, a "foreign state *shall* be immune from the jurisdiction of the courts of the United States and of the States" unless one of several statutorily defined exceptions applies. § 1604 (emphasis added). The FSIA thus provides the "sole basis" for obtaining jurisdiction over a foreign sovereign in the United States. *See Argentine Republic v. Amerada Hess Shipping Corp.*, 488 U.S. 428, 434–439, 109 S. Ct. 683, 688–690, 102 L. Ed. 2d 818 (1989). The most significant of the FSIA's exceptions—and the one at issue in this case—is the "commercial" exception of § 1605(a)(2), which provides that a foreign state is not immune from suit in any case

> in which the action is based upon a commercial activity carried on in the United States by the foreign state; or upon an act performed in the United States in connection with a commercial activity of the foreign state elsewhere; or upon an act outside the territory of the United States in connection with a commercial activity of the foreign state elsewhere and that act causes a direct effect in the United States. § 1605(a)(2).

In the proceedings below, respondents relied only on the third clause of § 1605(a)(2) to establish jurisdiction, 941 F.2d, at 149, and our analysis is therefore limited to considering whether this lawsuit is (1) "based . . . upon an act outside the territory of the United States"; (2) that was taken "in connection with a commercial activity" of Argentina outside this country; and (3) that "cause[d] a direct effect in the United States."[2] The complaint in this case alleges only one cause of action on behalf of each of the respondents, viz., a breach-of-contract claim based on Argentina's attempt to refinance the Bonods rather than to pay them according to their terms. The fact that the cause of action is in compliance with the first of the three requirements—that it is "based upon an act outside the territory of the United States" (presumably Argentina's unilateral extension)—is uncontested. The dispute pertains to whether the unilateral refinancing of the Bonods was taken "in connection with a commercial activity" of Argentina, and whether it had a "direct effect in the United States." We address these issues in turn.

---

[2] It is undisputed that both the Republic of Argentina and Banco Central are "foreign states" within the meaning of the FSIA. *See* 28 U.S.C. § 1603(a), (b) ("[F]oreign state" includes certain "agenc[ies] or instrumentalit[ies] of a foreign state").

A

Respondents and their amicus, the United States, contend that Argentina's issuance of, and continued liability under, the Bonods constitute a "commercial activity" and that the extension of the payment schedules was taken "in connection with" that activity. The latter point is obvious enough, and Argentina does not contest it; the key question is whether the activity is "commercial" under the FSIA.

The FSIA defines "commercial activity" to mean:

> [E]ither a regular course of commercial conduct or a particular commercial transaction or act. The commercial character of an activity shall be determined by reference to the nature of the course of conduct or particular transaction or act, rather than by reference to its purpose. 28 U.S.C. § 1603(d).

This definition, however, leaves the critical term "commercial" largely undefined: The first sentence simply establishes that the commercial nature of an activity does *not* depend upon whether it is a single act or a regular course of conduct; and the second sentence merely specifies what element of the conduct determines commerciality (*i.e.*, nature rather than purpose), but still without saying what "commercial" means. Fortunately, however, the FSIA was not written on a clean slate. As we have noted, *see Verlinden B.V. v. Central Bank of Nigeria*, 461 U.S. 480, 486–489, 103 S. Ct. 1962, 1967–1969, 76 L. Ed. 2d 81 (1983), the Act (and the commercial exception in particular) largely codifies the so-called "restrictive" theory of foreign sovereign immunity first endorsed by the State Department in 1952. The meaning of "commercial" is the meaning generally attached to that term under the restrictive theory at the time the statute was enacted. . . .

This Court did not have occasion to discuss the scope or validity of the restrictive theory of sovereign immunity until our 1976 decision in *Alfred Dunhill of London, Inc. v. Republic of Cuba*, 425 U.S. 682, 96 S. Ct. 1854, 49 L. Ed. 2d 301. Although the Court there was evenly divided on the question whether the "commercial" exception that applied in the foreign-sovereign-immunity context also limited the availability of an act-of-state defense, . . . there was little disagreement over the general scope of the exception. The plurality noted that, after the State Department endorsed the restrictive theory of foreign sovereign immunity in 1952, the lower courts consistently held that foreign sovereigns were not immune from the jurisdiction of American courts in cases "arising out of purely commercial transactions," *id.*, at 703, 96 S. Ct., at 1865–1866. . . . The plurality stated that the restrictive theory of foreign sovereign immunity would not bar a suit based upon a foreign state's participation in the marketplace in the manner of a private citizen or corporation. 425 U.S., at 698–705, 96 S. Ct., at 1863–1866. A foreign state engaging in "commercial" activities "do[es] not exercise powers peculiar to sovereigns"; rather, it "exercise[s] only those powers that can also be exercised by private citizens." *Id.*, at 704, 96 S. Ct., at 1866. The dissenters did not disagree with this general description. *See id.*, at 725, 96 S. Ct., at 1875–1876. Given that the FSIA was enacted less than six months after our decision in *Alfred Dunhill* was announced, we think the plurality's contemporaneous description of the then-prevailing restrictive theory of sovereign immunity is of significant assistance in construing the scope of the Act.

In accord with that description, we conclude that when a foreign government acts, not as regulator of a market, but in the manner of a private player within it, the foreign sovereign's actions are "commercial" within the meaning of the FSIA. Moreover, because the Act provides that the commercial character of an act is to be determined by reference to its "nature" rather than its "purpose," 28 U.S.C. § 1603(d), the question is not whether the foreign government is acting with a profit motive or instead with the aim of fulfilling uniquely sovereign objectives. Rather, the issue is whether the particular actions that the foreign state performs (whatever the motive behind them) are the *type* of actions by which a private party engages in "trade and traffic or commerce," Black's Law Dictionary 270 (6th ed. 1990). . . . Thus, a foreign government's issuance of regulations limiting foreign currency exchange is a sovereign activity, because such authoritative control of commerce cannot be exercised by a private party; whereas a contract to buy army boots or even bullets is a "commercial" activity, because private companies can similarly use sales contracts to acquire goods. . . .

The commercial character of the Bonods is confirmed by the fact that they are in almost all respects garden-variety debt instruments: They may be held by private parties; they are negotiable and may be traded on the international market (except in Argentina); and they promise a future stream of cash income. We recognize that, prior to the enactment of the FSIA, there was authority suggesting that the issuance of public debt instruments did not constitute a commercial activity. *Victory Transport*, 336 F.2d, at 360 (dicta). There is, however, nothing distinctive about the state's assumption of debt (other than perhaps its purpose) that would cause it always to be classified as *jure imperii*, and in this regard it is significant that *Victory Transport* expressed confusion as to whether the "nature" or the "purpose" of a transaction was controlling in determining commerciality, *id.*, at 359–360. Because the FSIA has now clearly established that the "nature" governs, we perceive no basis for concluding that the issuance of debt should be treated as categorically different from other activities of foreign states.

* * *

B

The remaining question is whether Argentina's unilateral rescheduling of the Bonods had a "direct effect" in the United States, 28 U.S.C. § 1605(a)(2). In addressing this issue, the Court of Appeals rejected the suggestion in the legislative history of the FSIA that an effect is not "direct" unless it is both "substantial" and "foreseeable." 941 F.2d, at 152. . . . Of course the generally applicable principle *de minimis non curat lex* ensures that jurisdiction may not be predicated on purely trivial effects in the United States. But we reject the suggestion that § 1605(a)(2) contains any unexpressed requirement of "substantiality" or "foreseeability." As the Court of Appeals recognized, an effect is "direct" if it follows "as an immediate consequence of the defendant's . . . activity." 941 F.2d, at 152.

The Court of Appeals concluded that the rescheduling of the maturity dates obviously had a "direct effect" on respondents. It further concluded that that effect was sufficiently "in the United States" for purposes of the FSIA, in part because "Congress would have wanted an American court to entertain this action" in order to preserve New York City's status as "a preeminent commercial center." *Id.*, at 153. The question, however, is not what Congress "would have wanted" but what Congress enacted in the FSIA. Although we are happy to endorse the Second Circuit's recognition of "New York's status as a world financial leader," the effect of Argentina's rescheduling in diminishing that status (assuming it is not too speculative to be considered an effect at all) is too remote and attenuated to satisfy the "direct effect" requirement of the FSIA. *Ibid.*

We nonetheless have little difficulty concluding that Argentina's unilateral rescheduling of the maturity dates on the Bonods had a "direct effect" in the United States. Respondents had designated their accounts in New York as the place of payment, and Argentina made some interest payments into those accounts before announcing that it was rescheduling the payments. Because New York was thus the place of performance for Argentina's ultimate contractual obligations, the rescheduling of those obligations necessarily had a "direct effect" in the United States: Money that was supposed to have been delivered to a New York bank for deposit was not forthcoming. We reject Argentina's suggestion that the "direct effect" requirement cannot be satisfied where the plaintiffs are all foreign corporations with no other connections to the United States. We expressly stated in *Verlinden* that the FSIA permits "a foreign plaintiff to sue a foreign sovereign in the courts of the United States, provided the substantive requirements of the Act are satisfied," 461 U.S., at 489, 103 S. Ct., at 1969.

* * *

We conclude that Argentina's issuance of the Bonods was a "commercial activity" under the FSIA; that its rescheduling of the maturity dates on those instruments was taken in connection with that commercial activity and had a "direct effect" in the United States; and that the District Court therefore properly asserted jurisdiction, under the FSIA, over the breach-of-contract claim based on that rescheduling. Accordingly, the judgment of the Court of Appeals is

Affirmed.

2. ACT OF STATE DOCTRINE

If the court has jurisdiction, the next question is whether the defendant can raise any defense on the merits. Sovereign debtors raised a number of defenses in litigation arising from the debt crisis of the 1980s. In Libra Bank Ltd. v. Banco Nacional de Costa Rica, 570 F.Supp. 870 (S.D.N.Y.1983), Costa Rica had imposed exchange controls preventing its state-owned banks from repaying their loans. One of these banks argued that non-enforcement of its loans was consistent with U.S. policy as reflected in Article VIII(2)(b) of the Bretton Woods Agreement, which provides: "Exchange contracts which involve the currency of any member and which are contrary to the exchange control regulations of that member maintained or imposed consistently with this Agreement shall be unenforceable in the territories of any member." The district court rejected this defense, reasoning (1) that "exchange contracts" were contracts for the exchange of one currency for another and thus did not include bank loans, and (2) that even if the loans were considered exchange contracts, the defendant had not shown that Costa Rica's exchange controls had been imposed consistently with the Bretton Woods Agreement.

In parallel litigation, other Costa Rican banks raised the act of state doctrine as a defense. As we saw in Chapter III, the Supreme Court held in Sabbatino that U.S. courts would not question the validity of foreign acts of state fully performed within another country's territory. See supra pp. 70–78. The Second Circuit initially affirmed the District Court's dismissal of the suit. It did not reach the act-of-state question, but reasoned that Costa Rica's exchange controls were consistent with U.S. policy and should therefore be recognized as a matter of comity. Upon rehearing, the United States filed an *amicus* brief, and the Court of Appeals reversed its earlier decision in an opinion by Judge Meskill.

Allied Bank International v. Banco Credito Agricola

U.S. Court of Appeals for the Second Circuit, 1985
757 F.2d 516

* * *

II

In our previous decision, we affirmed the district court's dismissal. We did not address the question of whether the act of state doctrine applied because we determined that the actions of the Costa Rican government which precipitated the default of the Costa Rican banks were fully consistent with the law and policy of the United States. We therefore concluded that principles of comity compelled us to recognize as valid the Costa Rican directives.

Our interpretation of United States policy, however, arose primarily from our belief that the legislative and executive branches of our government fully supported Costa Rica's actions and all of the economic ramifications. On rehearing, the Executive Branch of the United States joined this litigation as *amicus curiae* and respectfully disputed our reasoning. The Justice Department brief gave the following explanation of our government's support for the debt resolution procedure that operates through the auspices of the International Monetary Fund (IMF). Guided by the IMF, this long established approach encourages the cooperative adjustment of international debt problems. The entire strategy is grounded in the understanding that, while parties may agree to renegotiate conditions of payment, the underlying obligations to pay nevertheless remain valid and enforceable. Costa Rica's attempted unilateral restructuring of private obligations, the United States contends, was inconsistent with this system of international cooperation and negotiation and thus inconsistent with United States policy.

The United States government further explains that its position on private international debt is not inconsistent with either its own willingness to restructure Costa Rica's intergovernmental obligations or with continued United States aid to the economically distressed Central American country. Our previous conclusion that the Costa Rican decrees were consistent with United States policy was premised on these two circumstances.

In light of the government's elucidation of its position, we believe that our earlier interpretation of United States policy was wrong. Nevertheless, if, as Judge Griesa held, the act of state doctrine applies, it precludes judicial examination of the Costa Rican decrees. Thus we must first consider that question.

III

The act of state doctrine operates to confer presumptive validity on certain acts of foreign sovereigns by rendering non-justiciable claims that challenge such acts. The judicially created doctrine is not jurisdictional; it is "a rule of decision under which an act meeting the definition . . . is binding on the court." Restatement (Revised) of Foreign Relations Law § 428 comment c (Tent. Draft No. 4, 1983); *Empresa Cubana Exportadora de Azucar y Sus Derivados v. Lamborn & Co.,* 652 F.2d 231, 239 (2d Cir.1981). The applicability of the doctrine is purely a matter of federal law. *Banco Nacional de Cuba v. Sabbatino,* 376 U.S. 398, 427, 84 S. Ct. 923, 939, 11 L. Ed. 2d 804 (1964).

* * *

The Supreme Court has been quite careful to avoid the creation of "an inflexible and all-encompassing rule" to govern the application of the doctrine; "the less important the implications of an issue are for our foreign relations, the weaker the justification for exclusivity in the political branches." *Sabbatino,* 376 U.S. at 428, 84 S. Ct. at 940. The doctrine demands a case-by-case analysis of the extent to which in the context of a particular dispute separation of powers concerns are implicated. . . .

This analysis must always be tempered by common sense. *See Tabacalera Severiano Jorge, S.A. v. Standard Cigar Co.,* 392 F.2d 706, 715 (5th Cir.), *cert. denied,* 393 U.S. 924, 89 S. Ct. 255, 21 L. Ed. 2d 260 (1968). The doctrine does not necessarily "preclude judicial resolution of all commercial consequences" that result from acts of foreign sovereigns performed within their own borders. *Arango v. Guzman Travel Advisors Corp.,* 621 F.2d 1371, 1380–81 (5th Cir.1980). But, obviously, where the taking is wholly accomplished within the foreign sovereign's territory, "it would be an affront to such foreign government for courts of the United States to hold that such act was a nullity." *Tabacalera,* 392 F.2d at 715. Furthermore, under such circumstances, the court's decision would almost surely be disregarded within the borders of the foreign state.

The extraterritorial limitation, as inevitable conjunct of the foreign policy concerns underlying the doctrine, dictates that our decision herein depends on the situs of the property at the time of the purported taking. The property, of course, is Allied's right to receive repayment from the Costa Rican banks in accordance with the agreements. The act of state doctrine is applicable to this dispute only if, when the decrees were promulgated, the situs of the debts was in Costa Rica. Because we conclude that the situs of the property was in the United States, the doctrine is not applicable.

As the Fifth Circuit explained *Tabacalera,* the concept of the situs of a debt for act of state purposes differs from the ordinary concept. It depends in large part on whether the purported taking can be said to have "come to complete fruition within the dominion of the [foreign] government." *Tabacalera,* 392 F.2d at 715–16. In this case, Costa Rica could not wholly extinguish the Costa Rican banks' obligation to timely pay United States dollars to Allied in New York. Thus the situs of the debt was not Costa Rica.

The same result obtains under ordinary situs analysis. The Costa Rican banks conceded jurisdiction in New York and they agreed to pay the debt in New York City in United States dollars. Allied, the designated syndicate agent, is located in the United States, specifically in New York; some of the negotiations between the parties took place in the United States. The United States has an interest in maintaining New York's status as one of the foremost commercial centers in the world. Further, New York is the international clearing center for United States dollars. In addition to other international activities, United States banks lend billions of dollars to foreign debtors each year. The United States has an interest in ensuring that creditors entitled to payment in the United States in United States dollars under contracts subject to the jurisdiction of United States courts may assume that, except under the most extraordinary circumstances, their rights will be determined in accordance with recognized principles of contract law.

In contrast, while Costa Rica has a legitimate concern in overseeing the debt situation of state-owned banks and in maintaining a stable economy, its interest in the contracts at issue is essentially limited to the extent to which it can unilaterally alter the payment terms. Costa Rica's potential jurisdiction over the debt is not sufficient to locate the debt there for the purposes of act of state doctrine analysis. *Cf. United Bank Ltd. v. Cosmic International, Inc.*, 542 F.2d 868, 874 (2d Cir.1976).

Thus, under either analysis, our result is the same: the situs of the debt was in the United States, not in Costa Rica. Consequently, this was not "a taking of property within its own territory by [Costa Rica]." *Sabbatino,* 376 U.S. at 428, 84 S. Ct. at 940. The act of state doctrine is, therefore, inapplicable.

IV

Acts of foreign governments purporting to have extraterritorial effect—and consequently, by definition, falling outside the scope of the act of state doctrine—should be recognized by the courts only if they are consistent with the law and policy of the United States. *United States v. Belmont*, 301 U.S. 324, 332–33, 57 S. Ct. 758, 761–62, 81 L. Ed. 1134 (1937); *Banco Nacional de Cuba v. Chemical Bank*, 658 F.2d at 908–09; *Republic of Iraq*, 353 F.2d at 51. Thus, we have come full circle to reassess whether we should give effect to the Costa Rican directives. We now conclude that we should not.

The Costa Rican government's unilateral attempt to repudiate private, commercial obligations is inconsistent with the orderly resolution of international debt problems. It is similarly contrary to the interests of the United States, a major source of private international credit. The government has procedures for resolving intergovernmental financial difficulties. *See, e.g.,* Foreign Assistance Act of 1961, Pub. L. No. 87–195, 75 Stat. 424 (1961) (codified as amended in scattered sections of 22 U.S.C.). With respect to private debt, support for the IMF resolution strategy is consistent with both the policy aims and best interests of the United States.

Recognition of the Costa Rican directives in this context would also be counter to principles of contract law. Appellees explicitly agreed that their obligation to pay would not be excused in the event that Central Bank failed to provide the necessary United States dollars for payment. This, of course, was the precise cause of the default. If we were to give effect to the directives, our decision would vitiate an express provision of the contracts between the parties.[3]

---

[3]   Each agreement specifically provided:

    7. Events of Default:

    If any of the following events of default should occur and is not remedied within a period of 30 days as of the date of occurrence, the Agent Bank may, by a written notice

The Costa Rican directives are inconsistent with the law and policy of the United States. We refuse, therefore, to hold that the directives excuse the obligations of the Costa Rican banks. The appellees' inability to pay United States dollars relates only to the potential enforceability of the judgment; it does not determine whether judgment should enter. . . .

* * *

3. ENFORCING JUDGMENTS

Even if a court has jurisdiction and enters a judgment for the bondholders on the merits, those bondholders may still have to enforce that judgment against the debtor's assets either in the United States or elsewhere. The FSIA provides separately for the immunity of a foreign state's assets in 28 U.S.C.A. §§ 1609–1611. These provisions are Byzantine in their complexity, but a few salient points are worth keeping in mind.

First, § 1610 distinguishes between the property of a foreign state and its political subdivisions on the one hand and the property of an agency or instrumentality of a foreign state on the other. If the judgment is against a foreign state, only its property "used for a commercial activity in the United States" is subject to attachment or execution, and then only if the foreign state has waived its immunity from attachment or execution, or the property was used for the commercial activity on which the claim was based, etc. 28 U.S.C.A. § 1610(a). If the judgment is against an agency or instrumentality engaged in commercial activity in the United States on the other hand, *all* of its property is generally subject to attachment or execution.

Second, § 1611 contains a special rule for the assets of central banks. Notwithstanding the provisions of § 1610, the property of a central bank or monetary authority "held for its own account" is immune from attachment or execution "unless such bank or authority, or its parent foreign government, has explicitly waived its immunity from attachment in aid of execution, or from execution." 28 U.S.C.A. § 1611(b)(1).

Third, these provisions distinguish between prejudgment and post-judgment attachment. The provisions quoted above relate solely to post-judgment attachment. Under § 1610(d), prejudgment attachment is only permitted if property is "used for a commercial activity in the United States" and the foreign state has "explicitly waived its immunity from attachment prior to judgment." 28 U.S.C.A. § 1610(d). Moreover, § 1611's

---

to the Borrower declare the promissory notes to be due and payable. In such an event, they shall be considered to be due without presentment, demand, protest or any other notice to the Borrower, all of which are expressly waived by this agreement:

7.1 Any payment of principal or interest under this transaction shall not have been paid on its maturity date. If the Borrower shall not effect any payment of principal or interest on the promissory notes at maturity, due solely to the omission or refusal by the Central Bank of Costa Rica to provide the necessary U.S. Dollars, such an event shall not be considered to be an event of default which would justify the demandability of the obligation, during a period of 10 days after such maturity date.

special rule for central bank assets refers only to waivers "from attachment in aid of execution, or from execution," suggesting that a waiver of the immunity of such assets from prejudgment attachment will not be effective even if it is explicit. In the absence of a rule allowing prejudgment attachment, debtors generally have ample time to move their assets beyond the reach of creditors.

Creditors have occasionally been successful in attaching assets outside the United States to enforce a U.S. judgment. In the best-known case, Elliott Associates purchased Peruvian debt at a discount and brought suit rather than participate in a restructuring. After prevailing in Elliott Associates LP v. Banco de La Nacion, 194 F.3d 363 (2d Cir.1999), it obtained a judgment of $55.7 million against Peru. Based on the *pari passu* clauses in the debt, see supra p. 517, it was able to convince a Belgian court to attach payments about to be made to creditors who had accepted the restructuring, forcing Peru to settle.[4] Such cases are unusual, however, and may be harder to maintain under the revised *pari passu* clauses that many governments have now adopted. See supra p. 517; infra pp. 544–545. Sovereign borrowers are also adept at keeping their assets in places where they will be immune from attachment.[5]

QUESTIONS

(1) In both Weltover and Allied Bank, the fact that payments were to be made in New York proved significant in overcoming the debtors' defenses. Should an investor be reluctant to purchase bonds that provide for payment only in the issuer's country? How about in a third country but not in the United States?

(2) After Weltover, is it necessary any longer to include a waiver of immunity in a bond or loan agreement?

(3) Consider Mexico's waiver of immunity and consent to jurisdiction. See supra pp. 511–512. For what sorts of disputes does it submit to the jurisdiction of New York courts? For what sorts does it not? Why might it have drawn such a distinction?

Additional reading: Schumacher, Trebesch & Enderlein, Sovereign Defaults in Court, CESifo Working Paper No. 6931 (2018); Fisch & Gentile, Vultures or Vanguards?: The Role of Litigation in Sovereign Debt Restructuring, 53 Emory L.J. 1043 (2004); Delaume, The Foreign Sovereign Immunities Act and Public Debt Litigation: Some Fifteen Years Later, 88 Am. J. Int'l L. 257 (1994).

---

[4] See Gulati & Klee, Sovereign Piracy, 56 Bus. Law. 645 (2001).

[5] The Bank of International Settlements in Switzerland, for example, advertises that the immunities it enjoys under Swiss law will protect deposits of central bank assets from attachment. See www.bis.org/banking/bisbank.htm.

D. RESTRUCTURING SOVEREIGN DEBT

As we have already noted, sovereign borrowers have sometimes been unable or unwilling to repay their debts as promised and have sought to restructure them in various ways. Restructuring may be in the best interests of both the debtor and its creditors. A restructuring package that restores confidence in the debtor can lower interest rates and increase the growth prospects of the economy. This in turn can increase the debtor's ability to provide for its people and to service its debts. This section describes some of the key players in sovereign debt restructurings and then considers the principal barrier to such restructurings—the so-called "collective action problem."

1. KEY PLAYERS

Sovereign debt restructurings have involved a number of institutions of varying levels of formality.

The Paris Club

The Paris Club is the forum through which creditor countries negotiate to restructure their bilateral loans to debtor countries. There are currently 22 permanent members of the Paris Club—mostly developed countries like France, Germany, Japan, the United Kingdom, and the United States—with other creditor countries invited to participate on a case-by-case basis. The Paris Club began in 1956 and is now housed in the French Treasury, which serves as its Secretariat. While each Paris Club negotiation is different, the institution has developed a set of rules and principles to guide it. For example, the Paris Club requires "conditionality"—that is, it requires the debtor country to agree to an appropriate program of economic reforms with the IMF, a topic discussed further below. Importantly, the Paris Club also insists on "comparability of treatment," specifically that a sovereign debtor may not offer its private creditors more favorable terms than those agreed to by the Paris Club. (The Club has, however, allowed debtor nations to give preferential treatment to international financial institutions like the IMF and the World Bank.) Because Paris Club deals are generally concluded more quickly than agreements with private creditors, the principle of comparability has allowed the Paris Club to set the baseline terms for many debt restructurings.[6]

The London Club

The London Club is a forum for the restructuring of commercial bank loans (although most negotiations actually occur in New York). It began in the 1970s and was instrumental in resolving the debt crisis of the 1980s. Unlike the Paris Club, the London Club has no Secretariat and no formal procedures. Its typical practice has been to organize a Bank Advisory Committee of the 12 to 15 banks with the largest exposure to

---

[6]   See www.clubdeparis.org.

negotiate an agreement in principle with the sovereign debtor. Banks with less exposure, who might have been tempted not to cooperate in a restructuring, were threatened with the loss of their relationships with other banks and often went along. The shift from commercial bank lending to bonds in the 1990s has changed the ways in which debts to private creditors are restructured. Today, such restructurings typically occur through exchange offers developed by the debtor countries (sometimes with input from a committee of bondholders). Bondholders are offered the opportunity to exchange their existing bonds for new bonds that may differ in maturity, principal amount, interest rate or some combination of the three. The exchange offer will often give bondholders a menu of new bonds with different characteristics from which to choose. Although bondholders cannot be pressured to participate in restructurings in the same ways as banks, new techniques have developed to reduce the number of holdout creditors. See infra pp. 541–545.

The International Monetary Fund

The IMF is an international organization of 189 countries. It was founded in 1945 to oversee the Bretton Woods system of fixed exchange rates. After that system collapsed in 1971, the IMF evolved into a provider of economic advice and a manager of economic crises, particularly with respect to the developing world. In the context of sovereign debt restructurings since 1982, the IMF has played a number of important roles. First, it has served as an "honest broker" among lenders encouraging restructuring and arranging new lending from private and official sources. Second, it has itself extended credit to countries in financial crisis, a role that expanded as banks withdrew from sovereign lending in the 1990s. During the 1980s, the IMF had a policy of not lending into arrears—that is, it would not makes its own funds available until the debtor had reached an agreement with private creditors to restructure its existing debts and obtain new funding. Moreover, when the Fund did lend, it generally limited the amount to no more than the debtor country's IMF quota. The IMF changed its policy in 1989 to permit lending into arrears if restructuring negotiations had begun and had a reasonable likelihood of success and again in 1999 to permit such lending so long as the debtor was making "good faith efforts" to reach an agreement with creditors. Beginning with Mexico's crisis in 1994, the Fund also began to provide credit in amounts well above the debtor's IMF quota. Lending to Greece in 2010 was more than thirty times its quota. As a condition of extending credit, however, the IMF has required debtor countries to adopt reforms of their domestic economies, a policy known as "conditionality." This has led to a third important role for the IMF—providing a seal of approval for the economic policies of developing countries. This role extends beyond countries in crisis. Increasingly other members of the IMF have entered into IMF programs without drawing on its funds in order to signal their economic good health to the international community.

The IMF's current roles have been criticized in a number of respects, and two seem particularly worth mentioning here. First, it is argued that the possibility of a bailout from the Fund creates a "moral hazard" for both debtors and creditors. The phrase "moral hazard" generally describes a situation in which people are encouraged to engage in risky behavior because they are protected from its consequences. In the context of sovereign debt, a country that expects to be rescued by the Fund may have less incentive to adopt prudent economic policies. Similarly, if creditors expect that the IMF will cushion the impact of a sovereign default, they may take greater financial risks. Thus, paradoxically, the IMF's efforts to manage financial crises may create conditions that make them more likely to occur. Second, some have criticized the economic reforms required under the IMF's policy of "conditionality." These reforms—often referred to as the "Washington Consensus"—have included reduced public spending, liberalization of trade and foreign investment, deregulation, and privatization. Some have argued that reduced public spending has had too harsh an impact on the people of developing nations, particularly the poor, while others have argued that liberalization of foreign investment has made developing countries more exposed to international financial crises.

Regional Institutions

European institutions played a leading role in addressing the sovereign debt crisis affecting multiple countries within the Eurozone. First, the European Commission and the European Central Bank, together with the IMF, formed the so-called Troika that generated the economic and fiscal plan linked to the provision of financial assistance to struggling Eurozone countries. (The austerity programs imposed under that plan generated significant criticism along the lines discussed above.) Second, the crisis resulted in the creation of the European Stability Mechanism, a permanent agency charged with providing financial assistance to Eurozone states where necessary and improving structural stability within the Eurozone's banking sector.

2. THE COLLECTIVE ACTION PROBLEM

Although debt restructuring may benefit all of the parties involved, it may be difficult to reach agreement because of a so-called "collective action problem." Creditors who might otherwise be willing to reach an agreement with the debtor—which generally means accepting a significant reduction in the amount of principal owed—may hesitate to do so because of fear that other creditors will hold out and seek full payment. As an illustration of this dynamic, consider the following case.

Pravin Banker Associates, Ltd.
v. Banco Popular del Peru

U.S. Court of Appeals for the Second Circuit, 1997
109 F.3d 850

■ CALABRESI, CIRCUIT JUDGE:

* * *

I.   Background

Banco Popular, a state-owned bank since 1970, provided loans and credit to public and private companies and individuals in Peru. In order to do so, it borrowed funds from many foreign financial institutions. This action concerns the small part of Peru's foreign debt that was borrowed by Banco Popular from Mellon Bank, N.A. of Pittsburgh, PA ("Mellon") and later sold to Pravin.

Following Mexico and a number of other Latin American countries, Peru announced in March 1983 that it had insufficient foreign exchange reserves to service its foreign debt, and that it was unable to get credit to do so. After its announcement, Peru negotiated with its creditors a series of agreements that stated terms for the settlement of various categories of Peruvian debt. Two of these, the Mellon Letter Agreements, attempted to resolve more than $14 million owed as a result of over thirty separate short-term working capital loans that Mellon had made to Banco Popular. The agreements, signed by Mellon Bank and Banco Popular, extended the due dates on these loans for 360 days. In exchange, the government of Peru itself guaranteed the loans.

In 1984, a round of negotiations intended to provide a longer-term solution to Peru's liquidity crisis failed, and Peru imposed new restrictions on the payment of foreign exchange in order to prevent the depletion of its external reserves. As a result, Banco Popular stopped making the principal payments on the Mellon debt that were required by the Letter Agreements, and from 1984 until 1992, only paid interest. This put Banco Popular in default on the loans. In 1989, many of Peru's commercial lenders, including Mellon, filed lawsuits to preserve their legal claims because they worried that, if they did not do so, the statute of limitations would expire on the outstanding debts.

In 1990, after Alberto Fujimori was elected President of Peru, Peru's economic policies changed dramatically. President Fujimori began a major reform of the Peruvian economy and in doing so attempted to comply with International Monetary Fund ("IMF") policies. Following these changes, the Bank Advisory Committee, a committee of Peru's creditors headed by Citibank, N.A., signed an agreement with Peru to stay all pending lawsuits in order to promote negotiations to resolve the entire problem of the unpaid foreign debts. The stay was conditioned on Peru's continued efforts to maintain fiscally sound economic policies, and on none of the individual lawsuits being permitted to go forward alone.

Mellon participated in these meetings and agreed to a stay of its own lawsuit on analogous terms. Since then, Peru has made significant strides in restructuring its economy, reducing inflation, and decreasing the government deficit.

* * *

The appellee, Pravin, acquired, at a discount in the secondary market for sovereign debt, $9 million (face value) of Banco Popular's debt to Mellon in 1990. Pravin resold most of this debt almost immediately, but continues to hold $1,425,000. Peru and Banco Popular were notified of the assignment from Mellon to Pravin, and Banco Popular, thereafter, made interest payments directly to Pravin.

* * *

Pravin refused to join either the Peruvian liquidation proceedings or the Brady Plan negotiations. Instead, Pravin brought this suit against Banco Popular, and its guarantor, Peru, for non-payment of the debt. The defendants cross-moved to dismiss, stay, or deny Pravin's motion for summary judgment arguing that allowing the action to go forward would reawaken all of the other lawsuits that the Bank Advisory Committee had succeeded in having stayed. It would, Peru contends, result in a creditor stampede to find and attach Peruvian assets, and such a stampede would, in turn, disrupt Peru's structural reform efforts.

The district court granted a six-month stay to allow the orderly completion of Banco Popular's Peruvian liquidation proceedings. *See Pravin Banker Assocs., Ltd. v. Banco Popular del Peru*, 165 B.R. 379 (S.D.N.Y.1994) ("*Pravin I*"). After the six-month stay elapsed, Pravin renewed its motion for summary judgment and Banco Popular and Peru renewed their cross-motions for a stay or for dismissal of the complaint. . . .

* * *

The court . . . denied the motion of Banco Popular and Peru to dismiss or stay the action, and granted Pravin's motion for summary judgment, thereby allowing enforcement of the debt. *See Pravin Banker Assocs. Ltd. v. Banco Popular del Peru*, 895 F.Supp. 660 (S.D.N.Y.1995) ("*Pravin III*"). On January 19, 1996, it entered judgment for Pravin in the amount of $2,161,539.78, plus pre-judgment simple interest accrued from October 26, 1995 through the date of judgment, plus post-judgment interest calculated pursuant to 28 U.S.C. § 1961. *See Pravin Banker Assocs. Ltd. v. Banco Popular del Peru*, 912 F.Supp. 77 (S.D.N.Y.1996) ("*Pravin IV*").

* * *

II. Discussion

A. International Comity

International comity is "the recognition which one nation allows within its territory to the legislative, executive or judicial acts of another nation." *Hilton v. Guyot*, 159 U.S. 113, 164, 16 S.Ct. 139, 143, 40 L.Ed. 95 (1895). Under the principles of international comity, United States courts ordinarily refuse to review acts of foreign governments and defer to proceedings taking place in foreign countries, allowing those acts and proceedings to have extraterritorial effect in the United States. *See, e.g., Cunard Steamship Co. v. Salen Reefer Servs. AB*, 773 F.2d 452, 456–60 (2d Cir.1985); *Somportex Ltd. v. Philadelphia Chewing Gum Corp.*, 453 F.2d 435, 440–44 (3d Cir.1971).

Although courts in this country have long recognized the principles of international comity and have advocated them in order to promote cooperation and reciprocity with foreign lands, comity remains a rule of "practice, convenience, and expediency" rather than of law. *Somportex Ltd.*, 453 F.2d at 440; see also id. ("Although more than mere courtesy and accommodation, comity does not achieve the force of an imperative or obligation."); *Cunard S.S. Co.*, 773 F.2d at 457 (quoting *Somportex*). And courts will not extend comity to foreign proceedings when doing so would be contrary to the policies or prejudicial to the interests of the United States. *See Allied Bank Int'l v. Banco Credito Agricola de Cartago*, 757 F.2d 516, 522 (2d Cir.1985); *Somportex Ltd.*, 453 F.2d at 440. "No nation is under unremitting obligation to enforce foreign interests which are fundamentally prejudicial to those of the domestic forum. Thus, from the earliest times, authorities have recognized that the obligation of comity expires when the strong public policies of the forum are vitiated by the foreign act." *Laker Airways Ltd. v. Sabena, Belgian World Airlines*, 731 F.2d 909, 937 (D.C.Cir.1984).

Peru's efforts to negotiate a settlement of its unpaid debt to foreign creditors are acts by a foreign government that have extraterritorial effect in the United States. Because Peru contends that this suit, and the district court's grant of summary judgment, is inconsistent with and disruptive to those efforts, the grant of summary judgment must be evaluated in the light of principles of international comity. *See Allied Bank Int'l*, 757 F.2d at 522 (considering the application of international comity to Costa Rica's efforts to renegotiate its foreign debt).

As the district court recognized, however, extending comity to Peru's debt negotiations is only appropriate if it is consistent with United States government policy. The district court in *Pravin I* and *Pravin III* correctly identified two substantial aspects of United States policy that are implicated by this suit. First, the United States encourages participation in, and advocates the success of, IMF foreign debt resolution procedures under the Brady Plan. *See* Brief for the United States as *amicus curiae*, at 6–7, *CIBC Bank and Trust Co. (Cayman) v. Banco Central do Brasil*, 886 F.Supp. 1105 (S.D.N.Y.1995) (No. 94 Civ. 4733) [A 362–63]; Brief for the United States as *amicus curiae*, at 9–10, *Allied Bank Int'l v. Banco Credito Agricola de Cartago*, 757 F.2d 516 (2d Cir.1985) (No. 83–7714) [hereinafter *U.S. Allied Bank Brief*] [A 314–15]; International Debt Management Act of 1988, 22 U.S.C. §§ 5321–33. Second, the United States has a strong interest in ensuring the enforceability of valid debts under the principles of contract law, and in particular, the continuing enforceability of foreign debts owed to United States lenders. *See Allied Bank Int'l*, 757 F.2d at 521–22; *Weltover Inc. v. Republic of Argentina*, 941 F.2d 145, 153 (2d Cir.1991), *aff'd*, 504 U.S. 607, 112 S.Ct. 2160, 119 L.Ed.2d 394 (1992). This second interest limits the first so that, although the United States advocates negotiations to effect debt reduction and continued lending to defaulting foreign sovereigns, it maintains that creditor participation in such negotiations should be on a strictly voluntary basis. It also requires that debts remain enforceable throughout the negotiations. *See Allied Bank Int'l*, 757 F.2d at 519; *U.S. Allied Bank Brief* at 12, 15–16 (labeling the IMF framework "an essentially voluntary and cooperative process"); *National Union Fire Ins. Co. v. People's Republic of Congo*, 729 F.Supp. 936, 944 n. 5 (S.D.N.Y.1989) (quoting Secretary of the Treasury Nicholas F. Brady, Address to the Brookings Institution and the Bretton Woods Committee (Mar. 10, 1989)).

In *Pravin I*, the district court found that a six-month stay to allow the completion of the on-going liquidation proceedings for Banco Popular would not significantly harm United States interests, and the court therefore granted the stay. In *Pravin III*, however, the court found that an indefinite stay to allow Peru to complete its efforts to renegotiate its foreign debt would prejudice United States interests, and it refused to grant one, instead granting summary judgment in favor of Pravin. We agree with the court's conclusion in both instances.

The six-month stay in *Pravin I* allowed Banco Popular's liquidation proceedings to be concluded. As such it followed the federal courts' long-standing recognition of foreign bankruptcy proceedings, *see, e.g.*, *Drexel Burnham Lambert Group, Inc. v. Galadari*, 777 F.2d 877, 880 (2d Cir.1985), and did not threaten the long-term enforceability of the debt. To deny summary judgment in *Pravin III*, however, would have had a very different effect. It would first have denied Pravin its right to enforce the underlying debt—despite clear United States policy that it be able to do so—by making Pravin's rights conditional on the completion of a process which had no obvious (and reasonably proximate) termination date. Second, it would have converted what the United States intended to be voluntary and open-ended negotiations between Peru and its creditors into the equivalent of a judicially-enforced bankruptcy proceeding, for it would, in effect, have prohibited the exercise of legal rights outside of the negotiations. *See U.S. Allied Bank Brief* at 11–12. Under the circumstances, the district court correctly ruled that summary judgment was appropriate.

In the case of private debtors, national bankruptcy laws are used to solve the collective action problem. In Pravin, the original debtor Banco Popular went into liquidation in Peru. As the Second Circuit noted, U.S. courts have long cooperated with foreign bankruptcy proceedings. In 1978, Congress expressly authorized such cooperation through § 304 of the Bankruptcy Code. In 2005, § 304 was superseded by Chapter 15 of the Code, which largely adopts the UNCITRAL Model Law on Cross-Border Insolvency. Under Chapter 15, a representative appointed by the court in a foreign bankruptcy proceeding may petition for recognition of the foreign proceeding, which results in an automatic stay with respect to the debtor's property in the United States. The foreign representative may also seek other relief including the turnover of assets for distribution in the foreign proceeding.

National bankruptcy laws do not apply, however, to sovereign debtors like Peru. In the early 2000s, there was a proposal to establish a Sovereign Debt Restructuring Mechanism (SDRM) modeled on domestic bankruptcy courts. See Krueger, A New Approach to Sovereign Debt Restructuring (IMF 2002). The United States opposed the SDRM, and efforts shifted instead to redesigning contractual terms to address collective action problems.

The collective action problems surrounding sovereign debt restructuring were exacerbated by a shift that took place during the 1990s in the form of sovereign debt, from syndicated bank loans to bonds. In comparison to commercial banks, bondholders are more numerous, more diverse in their interests and goals, and less susceptible to arm-twisting. In addition, bonds are easily traded in the secondary market, and a practice emerged under which private equity funds would purchase the debt of distressed sovereign debtors at significant discounts with the sole aim of suing for repayment of the full principal. The incentive of these so-called "vulture funds" was to hold out from, not participate in, any proposed debt restructuring. These characteristics led some observers to speculate that sovereign issuers would find it impossible to restructure their debts successfully in the event of impending default.

This speculation proved to be mistaken. Since the mid-1990s, a number of sovereign debtors have been able to restructure their bonds through exchange offers, pursuant to which the holders of existing bonds agreed to tender them in exchange for newly issued bonds with different (and less favorable) payment terms. Governments were able to make creative use of the terms in existing bonds, to include collective action clauses in new bonds, and to reject interpretations of contractual terms that threatened to give holdout creditors greater leverage.

Initially, sovereign debtors encouraged creditors to participate in exchange offers through the use of so-called "exit consents."[7] These were built into the terms of the exchange offer, and provided as a condition of exchange that the tendering bondholders would vote to amend the terms of the existing bonds, leaving any non-tendering bondholders with instruments of drastically reduced value. Exit consents were particularly useful in situations where governing law required the unanimous consent of bondholders to change the payment terms of a bond, but permitted the amendment of non-payment terms by holders of either a simple or a two-thirds majority of the bonds. Such amendments could, for example, insert a call option that the issuer could subsequently use to redeem outstanding bonds, or remove protective covenants such as cross-default provisions or negative pledges. In 2000, Ecuador took advantage of this possibility with an exchange offer under which bondholders tendering their old bonds agreed to vote for such amendments to the bonds they were leaving. This made the old bonds less attractive to remaining bondholders, pressuring them to tender their bonds as well. Ultimately 97% of bondholders participated in Ecuador's exchange offer.

Exit consents have received a mixed reaction from courts. One English court has held that exit consents may not be used to coerce other bondholders. See Assenagon Asset Management S.A. v. Irish Bank Resolution Corporation Ltd., [2012] EWHC 2090. The U.S. Court of Appeals for the Second Circuit, on the other hand, has upheld the use of exit consents, at least in the context of corporate bonds. See Marblegate Asset Management, LLC v. Education Management Finance Corp., 846 F.3d 1 (2d Cir. 2017). As a practical matter, exit consents are less likely to play a prominent role in future sovereign debt restructurings, both because newer bonds have increased the majority required to modify non-payment terms and because collective action clauses in newer bonds offer a more straightforward way of modifying the payment terms.

A collective action clause (CAC) allows a supermajority of bondholders to change the payment terms of the original bonds and bind all bondholders to those terms. Bonds governed by English law have contained CACs since the nineteenth century; bonds governed by New York law, however, generally required unanimous consent to amend the payment terms. Mexico issued the first New York-law bonds with a CAC in 2003, and since that time most foreign-law bonds issued by emerging-market sovereigns have included some version of a CAC.

The first generation of CACs permitted modifications only within a single series of bonds (like Section 11.4 of Mexico's trust indenture above, see supra p. 515). While these CACs mitigated the collective action problem among bondholders within a single series of bonds, they did nothing to solve the collective action problem that exists across different series. In the context of a restructuring, the holders of bonds with a CAC

---

[7]   See Buchheit & Gulati, Exit Consents in Sovereign Bond Exchanges, 48 UCLA L. Rev. 59 (2000).

might be reluctant to modify their payment terms because they could not be certain that the holders of other bonds would be willing to do the same.

A second generation of CACs permitted the aggregation of multiple series of bonds, requiring approval by holders of a supermajority of the principal amount outstanding for all the bonds being aggregated and approval by holders of a simple majority or a lower supermajority of the principal amount outstanding for each of the series (like Section 11.6 of Mexico's trust indenture above, see supra p. 515). These CACs came to be known as "two-limb aggregation clauses," referring to the two sets of approvals that are required. Uruguay issued the first bonds with this kind of clause in 2003. Since 2013, all Eurozone countries have been required to include two-limb aggregation clauses in their government securities.

Greece's debt restructuring in 2012 demonstrated the limits of single-series CACs and the promise of aggregation clauses. As noted in the introduction to this Problem, see supra pp. 495–496, dissenting bondholders in several of the English-law bonds with single-series CACs were able to establish positions large enough to block restructuring. Dissenting bondholders in the Greek-law bonds, on the other hand, were not able to do so because all of those bonds were aggregated for purposes of the vote. Greece's experience would establish a precedent for a third generation of CACs that require approval by holders of a supermajority of the principal amount outstanding for all the bonds being aggregated but no separate approval by the holders of bonds in each series (like Section 11.5 of Mexico's trust indenture above, see supra p. 515). These CACs would come to be known as "single-limb aggregation clauses."

In the meantime, bondholder litigation against Argentina demonstrated the need to revise another standard term—the *pari passu* clause. As noted in the introduction to this Problem, see supra p. 494, Argentina defaulted on its existing debt obligations in 2001. It successfully restructured much of its debt with two exchange offers in 2005 and 2010, but some bondholders refused the offers. They sued for breach of contract and sought to enjoin payments to the restructured bondholders as violations of the *pari passu* clause. The clause in Argentina's bonds read as follows:

> [T]he Securities will constitute ... direct, unconditional, unsecured and unsubordinated obligations of the Republic [of Argentina] and shall at all times rank *pari passu* without any preference among themselves. The payment obligations of the Republic under the Securities shall at all times rank at least equally with all its other present and future unsecured and unsubordinated External Indebtedness. . . .

In 2012, the district court enjoined payment of the restructured bondholders and the U.S. Court of Appeals for the Second Circuit affirmed. NML Capital, Ltd. v. Republic of Argentina, 699 F.3d 246 (2d Cir.2012). The Second Circuit noted that the second sentence of

Argentina's clause (not found in all *pari passu* clauses) referred specifically to "payment obligations" and that Argentina had effectively ranked its payment obligations to the holdout bondholders below those to the restructured bondholders—by paying the restructured bondholders but not the holdouts for six years, by declaring in its prospectuses that it would not pay the holdouts, and by enacting a "Lock Law" prohibiting any payment of the holdouts. The Second Circuit did not go so far as to hold that *any* nonpayment of holdouts coupled with payment of restructured bondholders would violate a *pari passu* clause, but it concluded that Argentina's conduct in this case did violate the clause. Id. at 264 n. 16.

Against the background of these events, the U.S. Treasury Department convened a group of issuers, investors, and experts in 2013 to discuss changes to some of the standard terms in sovereign debt obligations. For *pari passu* clauses, the group agreed to support model language that would disavow the Second Circuit's ratable payment interpretation. For collective action clauses, the group supported a "single-limb" aggregation option (like Section 11.6 of Mexico's trust indenture above, see supra p. 515) that would permit modifications with the approval of a supermajority of holders of the principal amount outstanding for all bonds being aggregated, without an additional requirement of the approval from holders in each series. This was essentially the aggregation mechanism that Greece had imposed on the holders of bonds governed by Greek law in 2012. But because single-limb aggregation would not necessarily be appropriate in all situations, it became one of a menu of options, along with single-series collective action clauses and two-limb aggregation clauses.

In 2014, the International Capital Market Association published standard *pari passu* and collective action clauses based on the consensus of this group. In 2015, these were revised to provide separate standard terms for bonds governed by English law and bonds governed by New York law.[8] The New York-law *pari passu* clause provides:

> The Bonds constitute and will constitute direct, general, unconditional and unsubordinated External Indebtedness of the Issuer for which the full faith and credit of the Issuer is pledged. The Bonds rank and will rank without any preference among themselves and equally with all other unsubordinated External Indebtedness of the Issuer. It is understood that this provision shall not be construed so as to require the Issuer to make payments under the Bonds ratably with payments being made under any other External Indebtedness.

The New York-law CAC is substantively identical to Article Eleven of Mexico's trust indenture quoted above. See supra pp. 513–516.

---

[8]   See ICMA New York and English Law Standard CACs, Pari Passu, and Creditor Engagement Provisions (May 2015).

According to the IMF, nearly 85% of new bond issuances between October 2014 and September 2017 included modified *pari passu* clauses, while more than 87% of bond issuances included enhanced CACs. In addition, 42% of new bonds governed by New York law used trust indentures rather than fiscal agency agreements. None of these changes appear to have had any effect on the pricing of bonds with the new terms. And the outstanding stock of sovereign debt without these new terms remains large. As of 2017, almost 75% of outstanding sovereign debt lacked enhanced CACs, and approximately 30% of the debt without such terms will not mature until after 2027.[9]

QUESTIONS

(1) Under the common-law doctrine of champerty, it was once illegal to buy debt for the sole purpose of litigating it; however, that doctrine has been rejected in the United States and elsewhere. Is there anything wrong with buying debt at a discount and then bringing suit for the full amount?

(2) Since the new CACs and *pari passu* clauses both reduce the rights of bondholders, why has the introduction of these terms had no effect on bond pricing? Are there ways in which the ability to restructure debt might benefit not just issuers but bondholders as well?

(3) Are the changes in contractual terms discussed above a sufficient solution to the collective action problem? Would a bankruptcy system for sovereigns be better?

Additional reading: On debt restructuring generally, see Guzman, Ocampo & Stiglitz, Too Little, Too Late: The Quest to Resolve Sovereign Debt Crises (2016); Lienau, Rethinking Sovereign Debt: Politics, Reputation, and Legitimacy in Modern Finance (2014); Rieffel, Restructuring Sovereign Debt: The Case for Ad Hoc Machinery (2003). On the players in debt restructuring, see Rieffel, supra, chs. 3, 5 & 6; Stiglitz, Globalization and Its Discontents (2002); Gelpern, Building a Better Seating Chart for Sovereign Restructurings, 53 Emory L.J. 1115 (2004). With respect to collective action problems, see Buchheit & Gulati, Sovereign Bonds and the Collective Will, 51 Emory L.J. 1317 (2002); Lipson, Bankers' Dilemmas: Private Cooperation in Rescheduling Sovereign Debts, in Cooperation Under Anarchy 200 (Oye ed., 1986). On collective action clauses, see Gelpern, Heller & Setser, Count the Limbs: Designing Robust Aggregation Clauses in Sovereign Bonds, in Guzman, Ocampo and Stiglitz, supra; Gelpern & Gulati, The Wonder-Clause, 41 J. Comp. Econ. 367 (2013); Choi & Gulati, Innovation in Boilerplate Contracts: An Empirical Examination of Sovereign Bonds, 53 Emory L.J. 929 (2004).

---

[9] See Third Progress Report on Inclusion of Enhanced Contractual Provisions in International Sovereign Bond Contracts (IMF Dec. 2017).

ANNEX

Convention between the United States and the Federal Republic of Germany for the avoidance of double taxation and the prevention of fiscal evasion with respect to taxes on income and capital and to certain other taxes, signed at Bonn, 29 August 1989, as amended by the Protocol signed at Berlin, 1 June 2006

The United States of America and the Federal Republic of Germany,

Desiring to conclude a new Convention for the avoidance of double taxation and the prevention of fiscal evasion with respect to taxes on income and capital and to certain other taxes,

Have agreed as follows:

Article 1

General Scope

1. This Convention shall apply to persons who are residents of one or both of the Contracting States, except as otherwise provided in this Convention.

2. This Convention shall not restrict in any manner any exclusion, exemption, deduction, credit, or other allowance now or hereafter accorded:

(*a*) by the laws of either Contracting State; or

(*b*) by any other agreement to which the Contracting States are party.

3. (*a*) Notwithstanding the provisions of subparagraph (*b*) of paragraph 2:

(*aa*) the Contracting States agree that any question arising as to the interpretation or application of the Convention and, in particular, whether a taxation measure is within the scope of the Convention, shall be determined exclusively in accordance with the provisions of Article 25 (Mutual Agreement Procedure) of the Convention; and

(*bb*) the provisions of any other agreement shall not apply to a taxation measure unless the competent authorities agree that the measure is not within the scope of Article 24 (Nondiscrimination) of this Convention.

(*b*) For the purposes of this paragraph, a "measure" is a law, regulation, rule, procedure, decision, administrative action, or any similar provision or action.

4. (*a*) Except to the extent provided in paragraph 5, this Convention shall not affect the taxation by the United States of its residents (as determined under Article 4 (Residence)) and its citizens.

(*b*) Notwithstanding the other provisions of this Convention, a former citizen or long-term resident of the United States may, for the period of ten years following the loss of such status, be taxed in accordance with the laws of the United States.

5.   The provisions of paragraph 4 shall not affect the benefits conferred by the United States:

(*a*) under paragraph 2 of Article 9 (Associated Enterprises), paragraph 6 of Article 13 (Gains), paragraphs 3, 4 and 5 of Article 18 (Pensions, Annuities, Alimony, Child Support, and Social Security), paragraph 1 and 5 of Article 18A (Pension Plans), paragraph 3 of Article 19 (Government Service), and under Articles 23 (Relief from Double Taxation), 24 (Nondiscrimination), and 25 (Mutual Agreement Procedure); and

(*b*) under paragraph 2 of Article 18A (Pension Plans), subparagraph b) of paragraph 1 of Article 19 (Government Service), and under Articles 20 (Visiting Professors and Teachers; Students and Trainees) and 30 (Members of Diplomatic Missions and Consular Posts), upon individuals who are neither citizens of, nor have immigrant status in, the United States.

6.   Nothing in the Convention shall be construed to prevent the Federal Republic of Germany from imposing its taxes on amounts included in the income of a resident of the Federal Republic of Germany according to part 4, 5, and 7 of the German "Aussensteuergesetz". Where such imposition of tax gives rise to double taxation, the competent authorities shall consult for the elimination of such double taxation according to paragraph 3 of Article 25 (Mutual Agreement Procedure).

7.   In the case of an item of income, profit or gain derived by or through a person that is fiscally transparent under the laws of either Contracting State, such item shall be considered to be derived by a resident of a State to the extent that the item is treated for the purposes of the taxation law of such State as the income, profit or gain of a resident.

Article 2

Taxes Covered

1.   The existing taxes to which this Convention shall apply are:

(*a*) In the United States:

(*aa*) the federal income taxes imposed by the Internal Revenue Code (but excluding the accumulated earnings tax, the personal holding company tax, and social security taxes); and

(*bb*) the excise tax imposed on insurance premiums paid to foreign insurers

(hereinafter referred to as "United States tax").

This Convention shall, however, apply to the excise tax imposed on insurance premiums paid to foreign insurers only to the extent that the risks covered by such premiums are not reinsured with a person not entitled to the benefits of this or any other convention that provides exemption from such tax.

(b) In the Federal Republic of Germany:

(aa) the income tax (Einkommensteuer);

(bb) the corporation tax (Koerperschaftsteuer);

(cc) the trade tax (Gewerbesteuer); and

(dd) the capital tax (Vermoegensteuer)

(hereinafter referred to as "German Tax").

2. This Convention shall apply also to any identical or substantially similar taxes that are imposed after the date of signature of this Convention in addition to, or in place of, the existing taxes. The competent authorities of the Contracting States shall notify each other of any significant changes that have been made in their taxation laws.

Article 3

General Definitions

1. For the purposes of this Convention, unless the context otherwise requires:

(a) the terms "a Contracting State" and "the other Contracting State" mean the United States or the Federal Republic of Germany as the context requires;

(b) the term "United States", when used in a geographical sense, means the United States of America, but does not include Puerto Rico, the Virgin Islands, Guam, or any other possession or territory of the United States of America;

(c) the term "Federal Republic of Germany", when used in a geographical sense, means the area in which the tax law of the Federal Republic of Germany is in force;

(d) the term "person" includes but is not limited to an individual and a company;

(e) the term "company" means any body corporate or any entity that is treated as a body corporate for tax purposes;

(f) the terms "enterprise of a Contracting State" and "enterprise of the other Contracting State" mean respectively an enterprise carried on by a resident of a Contracting State and an enterprise carried on by a resident of the other Contracting State;

(g) the term "international traffic" means any transport by a ship or aircraft, except when the ship or aircraft is operated solely between places in one of the Contracting States;

(h) the term "national" means:

(*aa*) in respect of the United States, United States citizens and any legal person, partnership or association deriving its status as such from the law in force in the United States; and

(*bb*) in respect of the Federal Republic of Germany, any German within the meaning of paragraph 1 of Article 116 of the Basic Law of the Federal Republic of Germany and any legal person, partnership, or association deriving its status as such from the law in force in the Federal Republic of Germany; and

(*i*)   the term "competent authority" means:

(*aa*) in the United States, the Secretary of the Treasury or his delegate; and

(*bb*) in the Federal Republic of Germany, the Federal Minister of Finance or his delegate.

2.   As regards the application of this Convention by a Contracting State any term not defined therein shall, unless the context otherwise requires or the competent authorities agree to a common meaning pursuant to the provisions of Article 25 (Mutual Agreement Procedure), have the meaning that it has under the law of that State concerning the taxes to which this Convention applies.

Article 4

Residence

1.   For the purposes of this Convention, the term "resident of a Contracting State" means any person who, under the laws of that State, is liable to tax therein by reason of his domicile, residence, place of management, place of incorporation, or any other criterion of a similar nature, and also includes that State and any political subdivision or local authority thereof. The term, however, does not include any person who is liable to tax in that State in respect only of income from sources in that State or of profits attributable to a permanent establishment in that State or capital situated therein.

2.   Where by reason of the provisions of paragraph 1 an individual is a resident of both Contracting States, then his status shall be determined as follows:

(*a*)   he shall be deemed to be a resident of the State in which he has a permanent home available to him; if he has a permanent home available to him in both States, he shall be deemed to be a resident of the State with which his personal and economic relations are closer (center of vital interests);

(*b*)   if the State in which he has his center of vital interests cannot be determined, or if he has not a permanent home available to him in either State, he shall be deemed to be a resident of the State in which he has an habitual abode;

(c) if he has an habitual abode in both States or in neither of them, he shall be deemed to be a resident of the State of which he is a national; and

(d) if he is a national of both States or of neither of them, the competent authorities of the Contracting States shall settle the question by mutual agreement.

3.   Where by reason of the provision of paragraph 1 a person other than an individual is a resident of both Contracting States, then the competent authorities of the Contracting States shall seek to determine through consultation the Contracting State of which the person shall be deemed to be a resident for the purposes of this Convention, and, if they are unable so to determine, such person shall not be considered to be a resident of either Contracting State for purposes of enjoying benefits under this Convention.

Article 5

Permanent Establishment

1.   For the purposes of this Convention, the term "permanent establishment" means a fixed place of business through which the business of an enterprise is wholly or partly carried on.

2.   The term "permanent establishment" includes especially:

(a)   a place of management;

(b)   a branch;

(c)   an office;

(d)   a factory;

(e)   a workshop; and

(f)   a mine, an oil or gas well, a quarry, or any other place of extraction of natural resources.

3.   A building site or a construction, assembly or installation project constitutes a permanent establishment only if it lasts more than twelve months.

4.   Notwithstanding the foregoing provisions of this Article, the term "permanent establishment" shall be deemed not to include:

(a)   the use of facilities solely for the purpose of storage, display, or delivery of goods or merchandise belonging to the enterprise;

(b)   the maintenance of a stock of goods or merchandise belonging to the enterprise solely for the purpose of storage, display, or delivery;

(c)   the maintenance of a stock of goods or merchandise belonging to the enterprise solely for the purpose of processing by another enterprise;

(d)   the maintenance of a fixed place of business solely for the purpose of purchasing goods or merchandise, or of collecting information, for the enterprise;

(*e*) the maintenance of a fixed place of business solely for the purpose of advertising, or the supply of information, or scientific activities, or of similar activities that have a preparatory or auxiliary character for the enterprise; or

(*f*) the maintenance of a fixed place of business solely for any combination of activities mentioned in subparagraphs (*a*) to (*e*), provided that the overall activity of the fixed place of business resulting from this combination is of a preparatory or auxiliary character.

5.   Notwithstanding the provisions of paragraphs 1 and 2, where a person (other than an agent of an independent status to whom paragraph 6 applies) is acting on behalf of an enterprise and has, and habitually exercises, in a Contracting State an authority to conclude contracts in the name of the enterprise, that enterprise shall be deemed to have a permanent establishment in that State in respect of any activities which that person undertakes for the enterprise, unless the activities of such person are limited to those mentioned in paragraph 4 that, if exercised through a fixed place of business, would not make this fixed place of business a permanent establishment under the provisions of that paragraph.

6.   An enterprise shall not be deemed to have a permanent establishment in a Contracting State merely because it carries on business in that State through a broker, general commission agent, or any other agent of an independent status, provided that such persons are acting in the ordinary course of their business.

7.   The fact that a company that is a resident of a Contracting State controls or is controlled by a company that is a resident of the other Contracting State, or that carries on business in that other State (whether through a permanent establishment or otherwise), shall not of itself constitute either company a permanent establishment of the other.

Article 6

Income From Immovable (Real) Property

1.   Income derived by a resident of a Contracting State from immovable (real) property (including income from agriculture or forestry) situated in the other Contracting State may be taxed in that other State.

2.   The term "immovable property" shall have the meaning that it has under the law of the Contracting State in which the property in question is situated. The term shall in any case include property accessory to immovable property; livestock and equipment used in agriculture and forestry; rights to which the provisions of general law respecting landed property apply; usufruct of immovable property; and rights to variable or fixed payments as confederation for the working of, or the right to work, mineral deposits, sources, and other natural resources. Ships and aircraft shall not be regarded as immovable property.

3. The provisions of paragraph 1 shall apply to income derived from the direct use, letting, or use in any other form of immovable property.

4. The provisions of paragraphs 1 and 3 shall also apply to the income from immovable property of an enterprise and to income from immovable property used for the performance of independent personal services.

Article 7

Business Profits

1. The business profits of an enterprise of a Contracting State shall be taxable only in that State unless the enterprise carries on business in the other Contracting State through a permanent establishment situated therein. If the enterprise carries on business as aforesaid, the business profits of the enterprise may be taxed in the other State but only so much of them as is attributable to that permanent establishment.

2. Subject to the provisions of paragraph 3, where an enterprise of a Contracting State carries on business in the other Contracting State through a permanent establishment situated therein, there shall in each Contracting State be attributed to that permanent establishment the business profits that it might be expected to make if it were a distinct and independent enterprise engaged in the same or similar activities under the same or similar conditions.

3. In determining the business profits of a permanent establishment, there shall be allowed as deductions expenses that are incurred for the purposes of the permanent establishment, including executive and general administrative expenses so incurred, whether in the State in which the permanent establishment is situated or elsewhere.

4. No business profits shall be attributed to a permanent establishment by reason of the mere purchase by that permanent establishment of goods or merchandise for the enterprise.

5. For the purposes of this Convention, the business profits to be attributed to the permanent establishment shall include only the profits derived from the assets or activities of the permanent establishment.

6. Where business profits include items of income that are dealt with separately in other Articles of this Convention, then the provisions of those Articles shall not be affected by the provisions of this Article.

7. For the purposes of this Convention the term "business profits" includes income derived from the rental of tangible personal property and the rental or licensing of cinematographic films or works on film, tape, or other means of reproduction for use in radio or television broadcasting and income from the performance of professional services and of other activities of an independent character.

Article 8

Shipping and Air Transport

1.   Profits of an enterprise of a Contracting State from the operation of ships or aircraft in international traffic shall be taxable only in that State.

2.   Profits of an enterprise of a Contracting State from the use or rental of containers (including trailers, barges, and related equipment for the transport of containers) used in international traffic shall be taxable only in that State.

3.   The provisions of paragraphs 1 and 2 shall also apply to profits from the participation in a pool, a joint business, or an international operating agency.

Article 9

Associated Enterprises

1.   Where

(*a*) an enterprise of a Contracting State participates directly or indirectly in the management, control, or capital of an enterprise of the other Contracting State or

(*b*) the same persons participate directly or indirectly in the management, control, or capital of an enterprise of a Contracting State and an enterprise of the other Contracting State,

and in either case conditions are made or imposed between the two enterprises in their commercial or financial relations that differ from those that would be made between independent enterprises, than any profits which would, but for those conditions, have accrued to one of the enterprises, but, by reason for those conditions have not so accrued, may be included in the profits of that enterprise and taxed accordingly.

2.   Where a Contracting State includes in the profits of an enterprise of that State, and taxes accordingly, profits on which an enterprise of the other Contracting State has been charged to tax in that other State, and that other Contracting State agrees that profits so included are profits that would have accrued to the enterprise of the first-mentioned State if the conditions made between the two enterprises had been those that would have been made between independent enterprises, then that other State shall make an appropriate adjustment to the amount of the tax charged therein on those profits. In determining such adjustment, due regard shall be paid to the other provisions of this Convention and the competent authorities of the Contracting States shall if necessary consult each other.

Article 10

Dividends

1.   Dividends paid by a company that is a resident of a Contracting State to a resident of the other Contracting State may be taxed in that other State.

2.   However, such dividends may also be taxed in the Contracting State of which the company paying the dividends is a resident and according to the laws of that State, but if the dividends are derived and beneficially owned by a resident of the other Contracting State, the tax so charged shall not exceed:

(*a*) 5 percent of the gross amount of the dividends if the beneficial owner is a company that owns directly at least 10 percent of the voting stock of the company paying the dividends;

(*b*) 15 percent of the gross amount of the dividends in all other cases.

This paragraph shall not affect the taxation of the company in respect of the profits out of which the dividends are paid.

3.   Notwithstanding the provisions of paragraph 2, such dividends shall not be taxed in the Contracting State of which the company paying the dividends is a resident if the beneficial owner is:

(*a*)   a company that is a resident of the other Contracting State that has owned directly shares representing 80 percent or more of the voting power in the company paying the dividends for a 12-month period ending on the date entitlement to the dividend is determined and:

(*aa*) satisfies the conditions of clause (*aa*) or (*bb*) of subparagraph (*c*) of paragraph 2 of Article 28 (Limitation on Benefits);

(*bb*) satisfies the conditions of clauses (*aa*) and (*bb*) of subparagraph (*f*) of paragraph 2 of Article 28, provided that the company satisfies the conditions described in paragraph 4 of Article 28 with respect to the dividends;

(*cc*) is entitled to benefits with respect to the dividends under paragraph 3 of Article 28; or

(*dd*) has received a determination pursuant to paragraph 7 of Article 28 with respect to this paragraph; or

(*b*)   a pension fund that is a resident of the other Contracting State, provided that such dividends are not derived from the carrying on of a business, directly or indirectly, by such pension fund.

4.   Subparagraph (*a*) of paragraph 2 and subparagraph (*a*) of paragraph 3 shall not apply in the case of dividends paid by a United States person that is a U.S. Regulated Investment Company (RIC), a United States person that is a U.S. Real Estate Investment Trust (REIT) or a German Investment Fund or a German Investmentaktiengesellschaft (collectively referred to as

Investmentvermögen). In the case of dividends paid by a RIC or an Investmentvermögen, subparagraph (*b*) of paragraph 2 and subparagraph (*b*) of paragraph 3 shall apply. In the case of dividends paid by a REIT subparagraph (*b*) of paragraph 2 shall apply only if:

(*a*) the beneficial owner of the dividends is an individual holding an interest of not more than 10 percent in the REIT;

(*b*) the dividends are paid with respect to a class of stock that is publicly traded and the beneficial owner of the dividends is a person holding an interest of not more than 5 percent of any class of the REIT's stock; or

(*c*) the beneficial owner of the dividends is a person holding an interest of not more than 10 percent in the REIT and the REIT is diversified.

For purposes of this paragraph a REIT shall be diversified if no single interest in real property exceeds 10 percent of its total interests in real property. For the purposes of this paragraph foreclosure property shall not be an interest in real property. Where a REIT holds an interest in a partnership, it shall be treated as owning directly a proportion of the partnership's interests in real property corresponding to its interest in the partnership.

5.   The term "dividends" as used in this Article means income from shares, "jouissance" shares or "jouissance" rights, founders' shares, or other rights (not being debt-claims) participating in profits, as well as other income from other rights that is subjected to the same taxation treatment as income from shares by the laws of the Contracting State of which the company making the distribution is a resident. The term "dividends" also includes in the Federal Republic of Germany income under a sleeping partnership (Stille Gesellschaft), a participating loan (partiarisches Darlehen), or "Gewinnobligation", as well as distributions on certificates of a German Investmentvermögen.

6.   Notwithstanding the first sentence of paragraph 2 of this Article, paragraph 3 of this Article and paragraph 1 of Article 11 (Interest), income from arrangements carrying the right to participate in profits (including in the Federal Republic of Germany income under a sleeping partnership (Stille Gesellschaft), a participating loan (partiarisches Darlehen), or "Gewinnobligation", or "jouissance" shares or "jouissance" rights and in the United States contingent interest of a type that would not qualify as portfolio interest) that is deductible in determining the profits of the payor may be taxed in the Contracting State in which it arises according to the laws of that State.

7.   The provisions of paragraphs 2 and 3 shall not apply if the beneficial owner of the dividends, being a resident of a Contracting State, carries on business in the other Contracting State, of which the company paying the dividends is a resident, through a permanent establishment situated therein, and the holding in respect of which the dividends are

paid forms part of the business property of such permanent establishment. In such case, the provisions of Article 7 (Business Profits) shall apply.

8. A Contracting State may not impose any tax on dividends paid by a company which is a resident of the other Contracting State, except insofar as such dividends are paid to a resident of the first-mentioned State or insofar as the holding in respect of which the dividends are paid forms part of the business property of a permanent establishment situated in that State, nor may it impose tax on a company's undistributed profits except as provided in paragraph 9 of this Article, even if the dividends paid or the undistributed profits consist wholly or partly of profits or income arising in that State.

9. A company that is a resident of a Contracting State and that has a permanent establishment in the other Contracting State, or that is subject to tax on a net basis in that other Contracting State on items of income that may be taxed in that other State under Article 6 (Income from Immovable (Real) Property) or under paragraph 1 of Article 13 (Gains), may be subject in that other Contracting State to a tax in addition to the tax allowable under the other provisions of this Convention. Such tax, however, may be imposed only on:

(a) the portion of the business profits of the company attributable to the permanent establishment, and

(b) the portion of the income referred to in the preceding sentence that is subject to tax under Article 6 or paragraph 1 of Article 13, that represents the "dividend equivalent amount" of those profits and income; the term "dividend equivalent amount" shall, for the purposes of this subparagraph,

(aa) in the case of the United States, have the meaning that it has under the law of the United States as it may be amended from time to time without changing the general principle thereof; and

(bb) in the case of the Federal Republic of Germany, be that portion of the income described in subparagraph (a) that is comparable to the amount that would be distributed as a dividend by a locally incorporated subsidiary.

10. The tax referred to in subparagraphs (a) and (b) of paragraph 9 of this Article shall not be imposed at a rate exceeding the rate specified in subparagraph (a) of paragraph 2. In any case, it shall not be imposed on a company that:

(a) satisfies the conditions of clause (aa) or (bb) of subparagraph (c) of paragraph 2 of Article 28 (Limitation on Benefits);

(b) satisfies the conditions of clauses (aa) and (bb) of subparagraph (f) of paragraph 2 of Article 28, provided that the company satisfies the conditions described in paragraph 4 of that Article with respect to an item of income, profit or gain described in paragraph 9 of this Article;

(*c*) is entitled under paragraph 3 of Article 28 to benefits with respect to an item of income, profit or gain described in paragraph 9 of this Article; or

(*d*) has received a determination pursuant to paragraph 7 of Article 28 with respect to this paragraph.

11. The term "pension fund" as used in this Article means any person that:

(*a*) is established under the laws of a Contracting State;

(*b*) is established and maintained in that Contracting State primarily to administer or provide pensions or other similar remuneration, including social security payments, disability pensions and widow's pensions or to earn income for the benefit of one or more of such persons; and

(*c*) is either,

(*aa*) in the case of the United States, exempt from tax in the United States with respect to the activities described in subparagraph (*b*) of this paragraph, or

(*bb*) in the case of the Federal Republic of Germany, a plan the contributions to which are eligible for preferential treatment under the Income Tax Act.

Article 11

Interest

1.   Interest derived and beneficially owned by a resident of a Contracting State shall be taxable only in that State.

2.   The term "interest" as used in this Article means income from debt claims of every kind, whether or not secured by mortgage, and, in particular, income from government securities and income from bonds or debentures, including premiums and prizes attaching to such securities, bonds or debentures, as well as all other income that is treated as income from money lent by the taxation law of the Contracting State in which the income arises. Penalty charges for late payment shall not be regarded as interest for the purpose of this Convention. However, the term "interest" does not include income dealt with in Article 10 (Dividends).

3.   The provisions of paragraph 1 shall not apply if the beneficial owner of the interest, being a resident of a Contracting State, carries on business in the other Contracting State through a permanent establishment situated therein, and the debt claim in respect of which the interest is paid forms part of the business property of such permanent establishment. In such a case the provisions of Article 7 (Business Profits) shall apply.

4.   Where, by reason of a special relationship between the payor and the beneficial owner or between owner or between both of them and some other person, the amount of the interest, having regard to the debt

claim for which it is paid, exceeds the amount that would have been agreed upon by the payor and the beneficial owner in the absence of such relationship, the provisions of this Article shall apply only to the last-mentioned amount. In such a case the excess part of the payments shall remain taxable according to the laws of each Contracting State, due regard being had to the other provisions of the Convention.

5. Where a company that is a resident of a Contracting State derives profits or income from the other Contracting State, then that other State may not impose any tax on interest paid by the company except insofar as such interest is paid by a permanent establishment of such company located in that other State, or out of income described in subparagraph (b) of paragraph 9 of Article 10 (Dividends), so insofar as such interest in paid to a resident of that other State, or insofar as the debt claim underlying such interest payment forms part of the business property of a permanent establishment situated in that other State.

6. Notwithstanding the provisions of paragraph 1, interest that is an excess inclusion with respect to a residual interest in a U.S. real estate mortgage investment conduit may be taxed by the United States in accordance with its domestic law.

Article 12
Royalties

1. Royalties derived and beneficially owned by a resident of a Contracting State shall be taxable only in that State.

2. The term "royalties" as used in this Article means payments of any kind received as a consideration for the use of, or the right to use, any copyright of a literary, artistic, or scientific work (but not including cinematographic films, or works on film, tape, or other means of reproduction for use in radio or television broadcasting); for the use of, or the right to use, any patent, trademark, design or model, plan, secret formula or process, or other like right or property; or for information concerning industrial, commercial, or scientific experience. The term "royalties" also includes gains derived from the alienation of any such right or property that are contingent on the productivity, use, or further alienation thereof.

3. The provisions of paragraph 1 shall not apply if the beneficial owner of the royalties, being a resident of a Contracting State, carries on business in the other Contracting State through a permanent establishment situated therein and the right or property in respect of which the royalties are paid forms part of the business property of such permanent establishment or fixed base. In such a case the provisions of Article 7 (Business Profits) shall apply.

4. Where, by reason of a special relationship between the payor and the beneficial owner or between both of them and some other person, the amount of the royalties, having regard to the use, right, or information for which they are paid, exceeds the amount that would have

been agreed upon by the payor and the beneficial owner in the absence of such relationship, the provisions of this Article shall apply only to the last-mentioned amount. In such a case the excess part of the payments shall remain taxable according to the laws of each Contracting State, due regard being had to the other provisions of this Convention.

Article 13

Gains

1.   Gains derived by a resident of a Contracting State from the alienation of immovable property referred to in Article 6 (Income from Immovable (Real) Property) and situated in the other Contracting State may be taxed in that other State.

2.   For the purposes of this Article, the term "immovable property situated in the other Contracting State" shall include

(*a*) immovable property referred to in Article 6 (Income from Immovable (Real) Property); and

(*b*) shares or comparable interests in a company that is, or is treated as, a resident of that other Contracting State, the assets of which company consist or consisted wholly or principally of immovable property situated in such other Contracting State, and an interest in a partnership, trust, or estate, to the extent that its assets consist of immovable property situated in the other Contracting State.

3.   Gains from the alienation of movable property forming part of the business property of a permanent establishment that an enterprise of a Contracting State has in the other Contracting State, including such gains from the alienation of such a permanent establishment (alone or with the whole enterprise), may be taxed in that other State.

4.   Gains from the alienation of ships, aircraft, or containers operated in international traffic or movable property pertaining to the operation of such ships, aircraft, or containers shall be taxable only in the Contracting State in which the profits of the enterprise deriving such income are taxable according to Article 8 (Shipping and Air Transport).

5.   Gains from the alienation of any property other than that referred to in the preceding paragraphs shall be taxable only in the Contracting State of which the alienator is a resident.

6.   Where an individual who, upon ceasing to be a resident of one of the Contracting States, is treated under the taxation law of that State as having alienated property and is taxed in that State by reason thereof, the individual may elect to be treated for purposes of taxation in the other Contracting State as if the individual had, immediately before ceasing to be a resident of the first-mentioned State, alienated and reacquired the property for an amount equal to its fair market value at that time.

Article 14

[Deleted by 2006 Protocol]

Article 15

Dependent Personal Services

1.   Subject to the provisions of Articles 16 (Directors' fees), 17 (Artistes and Athletes), 18 (Pensions, Annuities, Alimony, Child Support and Social Security), 19 (Government Service), and 20 (Visiting Professors and Teachers; Students and Trainees), salaries, wages, and other similar remuneration derived by a resident of a Contracting State in respect of an employment shall be taxable only in that State, unless the employment is exercised in the other Contracting State. If the employment is so exercised, such remuneration as is derived therefrom may be taxed in that other State.

2.   Notwithstanding the provisions of paragraph 1, remuneration derived by a resident of a Contracting State in respect of an employment exercised in the other Contracting State shall be taxable only in the first-mentioned State if:

(*a*)   the recipient is present in the other State for a period or periods not exceeding in the aggregate 183 days in the calendar year concerned; and

(*b*)   the remuneration is paid by, or on behalf of, an employer who is not a resident of the other State; and

(*c*)   the remuneration is not borne by a permanent establishment that the employer has in the other State.

3.   Notwithstanding the foregoing provisions of this Article, remuneration derived by a resident of a Contracting State in respect of an employment as a member of the regular complement of a ship or aircraft operated in international traffic may be taxed only in that State.

Article 16

Directors' Fees

Directors' fees and other similar payments derived by a resident of a Contracting State for services rendered in the other Contracting State in his capacity as a member of the board of directors of a company that is a resident of the other Contracting State may be taxed in that other Contracting State.

Article 17

Artistes and Athletes

1.   Notwithstanding the provisions of Articles 7 (Business Profits) and 15 (Dependent Personal Services), income derived by a resident of a Contracting State as an entertainer (such as a theater, motion picture, radio or television artiste, or a musician), or as an athlete, from his personal activities as such exercised in the other Contracting State may be taxed in that other State, except where the amount of the gross

receipts derived by such entertainer or athlete, including expenses reimbursed to him or borne on his behalf, from such activities does not exceed $20,000 (twenty thousand United States dollars) or its equivalent in Euro for the calendar year concerned.

2.   Where income in respect of activities exercised by an entertainer or an athlete in his capacity as such accrues not to the entertainer or athlete but to another person, that income of that other person may, notwithstanding the provisions of Articles 7 (Business Profits), be taxed in the Contracting State in which the activities of the entertainer or athlete are exercised, unless it is established that neither the entertainer or athlete nor persons related thereto participate directly or indirectly in the profits of that other person in any manner, including the accrual or receipt of deferred remuneration, bonuses, fees, dividends, partnership income, or other income or distributions.

3.   The provisions of paragraphs 1 and 2 shall not apply to income derived from activities performed in a Contracting State by entertainers or athletes if the visit to that State is substantially supported, directly or indirectly, by public funds of the other Contracting State or a political subdivision or a local authority thereof. In such a case the income shall be taxable only in the Contracting State of which the entertainer or athlete is a resident.

Article 18

Pensions, Annuities, Alimony, Child
Support, and Social Security

1.   Subject to the provisions of Article 19 (Government Service), pensions and other similar remuneration derived and beneficially owned by a resident of a Contracting State in consideration of past employment shall be taxable only in that State.

2.   Subject to the provisions of Article 19 (Government Service; Social Security), annuities derived and beneficially owned by a resident of a Contracting State shall be taxable only in that State. The term "annuities" as used in this paragraph means a stated sum paid periodically at stated times during a specified number of years, under an obligation to make the payments in return for adequate and full consideration (other than services rendered).

3.   Alimony paid by a resident of a Contracting State and deductible therein to a resident of the other Contracting State shall be taxable only in that other State. The term "alimony" as used in this Article means periodic payments (made pursuant to a written separation agreement or a decree of divorce, separate maintenance, or compulsory support) that are taxable to the recipient under the laws of the State of which he is a resident.

4.   Nondeductible alimony, and periodic payments for the support of a minor child (made pursuant to a written separation agreement or a decree of divorce, separate maintenance, or compulsory support) paid by

a resident of a Contracting State to a resident of the other Contracting State shall be taxable only in the first-mentioned State.

5. Social security benefits paid under the social security legislation of a Contracting State and other public pensions (not dealt with in Article 19 (Government Service)) paid by a Contracting State to a resident of the other Contracting State shall be taxable only in that other Contracting State. In applying the preceding sentence, that other Contracting State shall treat such benefit or pension as though it were a social security benefit paid under the social security legislation of that other Contracting State.

Article 18A

Pension Plans

1. Where an individual who is a resident of a Contracting State is a member or beneficiary of, or participant in, a pension plan established in the other Contracting State, income earned by the pension plan may be taxed as income of that individual only when, and, to the extent that, it is paid to, or for the benefit of, that individual from the pension plan (and not transferred to another pension plan in that other Contracting State).

2. Where an individual who is a beneficiary of, or participant in, a pension plan established in a Contracting State exercises an employment or self-employment in the other Contracting State:

(*a*) contributions paid by or on behalf of that individual to the pension plan during the period or attributable to the period that he exercises an employment or self-employment in the other State shall be deductible (or excludable) in computing his taxable income in that other State; and

(*b*) any benefits accrued under the pension plan, or contributions made to the pension plan by or on behalf of the individual's employer, during that period shall not be treated as part of the employee's taxable income; any such contributions shall be allowed as a deduction in computing the business profits of his employer in that other State.

The relief available under this paragraph shall not exceed the relief that would be allowed by the other State to residents of that State for contributions to, or benefits accrued under, a pension plan or plans established in that State. The competent authorities of the Contracting States shall determine the relief available under this paragraph pursuant to the preceding sentence.

3. The provisions of paragraph 2 shall not apply unless:

(*a*) contributions by or on behalf of the individual, or by or on behalf of the individual's employer were made before the individual began to exercise an employment or self-employment in the other State; and (*b*)   the pension plan is accepted by the competent authority of that State as generally corresponding to a pension plan recognized as such for tax purposes by that State.

4.   The term "pension plan" means an arrangement established in a Contracting State which is operated principally to administer or provide pension or retirement benefits or to earn income for the benefit of one or more such arrangements.

5.   (*a*) Where a citizen of the United States who is a resident of the Federal Republic of Germany exercises an employment in the Federal Republic of Germany the income from which is taxable in the Federal Republic of Germany and is borne by an employer who is a resident of the Federal Republic of Germany or by a permanent establishment situated in the Federal Republic of Germany, and the individual is a beneficiary of, or participant in, a pension plan established in the Federal Republic of Germany,

(*aa*) contributions paid by or on behalf of that individual to the pension plan during the period or attributable to the period that he exercises the employment in the Federal Republic of Germany, and that are attributable to the employment, shall be deductible (or excludable) in computing his taxable income in the United States; and

(*bb*) any benefits accrued under the pension plan, or contributions made to the pension plan by or on behalf of the individual's employer, during that period or attributable to that period, and that are attributable to the employment, shall not be treated as part of the employee's taxable income in computing his taxable income in the United States. This paragraph shall apply only to the extent that the contributions or benefits qualify for tax relief in the Federal Republic of Germany.

(*b*)   The relief available under this paragraph shall not exceed the relief that would be allowed by the United States to its residents for contributions to, or benefits accrued under, a generally corresponding pension plan established in the United States.

(*c*)   For purposes of determining an individual's eligibility to participate in and receive tax benefits with respect to a pension plan established in the United States, contributions made to, or benefits accrued under, a pension plan established in the Federal Republic of Germany shall be treated as contributions or benefits under a generally corresponding pension plan established in the United States to the extent relief is available to the individual under this paragraph.

(*d*)   This paragraph shall not apply unless the competent authority of the United States has agreed that the pension plan generally corresponds to a pension plan established in the United States.

Article 19

Government Service

1. Notwithstanding the provisions of Articles 15 (Dependent Personal Services), 16 (Directors' Fees), and 17 (Artistes and Athletes):

(*a*) salaries, wages and other similar remuneration, other than a pension, paid by a Contracting State or a political subdivision, local authority or an instrumentality thereof to an individual in respect of services rendered to that Contracting State or a political subdivision, local authority or an instrumentality thereof shall, subject to the provisions of subparagraph b), be taxable only in that State;

(*b*) such remuneration, however, shall be taxable only in the other Contracting State if the services are rendered in that State and the individual is a resident of that State who:

(*aa*) is a national of that State; or

(*bb*) did not become a resident of that State solely for the purpose of rendering the services.

2. (*a*) Notwithstanding the provisions of paragraph 1, pensions and other similar remuneration paid by, or out of funds created by, a Contracting State or a political subdivision, local authority or an instrumentality thereof to an individual in respect of services rendered to that State or subdivision, authority or instrumentality shall be taxable only in that State.

(*b*) However, such pensions and other remuneration shall be taxable only in the other Contracting State if the individual is a

(*aa*) resident of, and a national of, that State; or

(*bb*) the pension is not subject to tax in the Contracting State for which the services were performed because the services were performed entirely in the other Contracting State.

3. Pensions, annuities, and other amounts paid by one of the Contracting States or by a juridical person organized under the public laws of that State as compensation for an injury or damage sustained as a result of hostilities or political persecution shall be exempt from tax by the other State.

4. The provisions of Articles 15 (Dependent Personal Services), 16 (Directors' Fees), 17 (Artistes and Athletes), and 18 (Pensions, Annuities, Alimony, Child Support, and Social Security) shall apply to salaries, wages and other similar remuneration, and to pensions, in respect of services rendered in connection with a business carried on by a Contracting State or by a political subdivision, local authority or an instrumentality thereof.

5. In this Article, the term "instrumentality" means any agent or entity created or organized by a Contracting State, one of its states or a political subdivision or local authority thereof in order to carry out

functions of a governmental nature which is specified and agreed to in letters exchanged between the competent authorities of the Contracting States.

Article 20

Visiting Professors and Teachers; Students and Trainees

1.   Remuneration that a professor or teacher who is a resident of a Contracting State and who is temporarily present in the other Contracting State for the primary purpose of carrying out advanced study or research or for teaching at an accredited university or other recognized educational institution, or an institution engaged in research for the public benefit, receives for such work shall be taxable only in the first-mentioned Contracting State for a period not exceeding two years from the date of his arrival. This Article shall not apply to income from research if such research is undertaken not in the public interest but primarily for the private benefit of a specific person or persons. The benefits provided in this paragraph shall not be granted to an individual who, during the immediately preceding period, enjoyed the benefits of paragraph 2, 3, or 4.

2.   Payments other than compensation for personal services that a student or business apprentice (including Volontaere and Praktikanten in the Federal Republic of Germany) who is or was immediately before visiting a Contracting State a resident of the other Contracting State and who is present in the first-mentioned State for the purpose of his fulltime education or training receives for the purpose of his maintenance, education, or training shall not be taxed in that State, provided that such payments arise from sources, or are remitted from, outside that State.

3.   Payments other than compensation for personal services that a person who is or was immediately before visiting a Contracting State a resident of the other Contracting State receives as a grant, allowance, or award from a non-profit religious, charitable, scientific, literary, or educational private organization or a comparable public institution shall not be taxed in the first-mentioned State.

4.   A student or business apprentice within the meaning of paragraph 2, or a recipient of a grant, allowance, or award within the meaning of paragraph 3, who is present in a Contracting State for a period not exceeding four years shall not be taxed in that State on any income from dependent personal services that is not in excess of $9,000 (nine thousand United States dollars) or its equivalent in Euro per taxable year, provided that such services are performed for the purpose of supplementing funds available otherwise for maintenance, education, or training.

5.   A resident of one of the Contracting States who is an employee of an enterprise of such State or of an organization or institution described in paragraph 3, and who is temporarily present in the other Contracting State for a period not exceeding one year solely to acquire

technical, professional, or business experience from any person other than such enterprise, organization, or institution, shall be exempt from tax by that other State on compensation remitted from outside that other State for services wherever performed paid by such enterprise, organization or institution if such compensation does not exceed $10,000 (ten thousand United States dollars) or its equivalent in Euro.

Article 21

Other Income

1. Items of income of a resident of a Contracting State, wherever arising, not dealt with in the foregoing Articles of this Convention shall be taxable only in that State.

2. The provisions of paragraph 1 shall not apply to income, other than income from Immovable Property as defined in paragraph 2 of Article 6 (Income from Immovable (Real) Property), if the recipient of such income, being a resident of a Contracting State, carries on business in the other Contracting State through a permanent establishment situated therein, and the right or property in respect of which the income if paid forms part of the business property of the permanent establishment.

Article 22

Capital

1. Capital represented by immovable property referred to in Article 6 (Income from Immovable (Real) Property), owned by a resident of a Contracting State, and situated in the other Contracting State may be taxed in that other State.

2. Capital represented by movable property, forming part of the business property of a permanent establishment that an enterprise of a Contracting State has in the other Contracting State, may be taxed in that other State.

3. Capital represented by ships, aircraft, or containers operated in international traffic and by movable property pertaining to the operation of such ships, aircraft, or containers shall be taxable only in the Contracting State in which the profits of the enterprise owning such capital are taxable according to Article 8 (Shipping and Air Transport).

4. All other elements of capital of a resident of a Contracting State shall be taxable only in that State.

Article 23

Relief from Double Taxation

1. In accordance with the provisions and subject to the limitations of the law of the United States (as it may be amended from time to time without changing the general principle hereof), the United States shall allow to a resident or citizen of the United States as a credit against the United States tax on income:

(*a*) the income tax paid or accrued to the Federal Republic of Germany by or on behalf of such resident or citizen; and

(*b*) in the case of a United States company owning at least 10 percent of the voting stock of a company that is a resident of the Federal Republic of Germany and from which the United States company receives dividends, the income tax paid or accrued to the Federal Republic of Germany by or on behalf of the payer with respect to the profits out of which the dividends are paid.

For the purposes of this paragraph, the taxes referred to in subparagraph b) of paragraph 1 of Article 2 (Taxes Covered) and paragraph 2 of Article 2, other than the capital tax (Vermögensteuer), shall be considered income taxes.

2.   For the purposes of applying paragraph 1 of this Article, an item of gross income, as determined under the laws of the United States, derived by a resident of the United States that, under this Convention, may be taxed in the Federal Republic of Germany shall be deemed to be income from sources in the Federal Republic of Germany.

3.   Where a resident of the Federal Republic of Germany derives income or owns capital which, in accordance with the provisions of this Convention, may be taxed in the United States or is exempt from United States tax under paragraph 3 of Article 10 (Dividends), tax shall be determined as follows:

(*a*) Except as provided in subparagraph (*b*), the income or capital shall be excluded from the basis upon which German tax is imposed. The Federal Republic of Germany, however, retains the right to take into account in the determination of its rate of tax items of income and capital excluded under the provisions of this Convention. In the case of income from dividends the foregoing provisions shall apply only to such income from distributions of profits on corporate rights subject to corporate income tax under United States law as are paid to a company (not including partnerships) being a resident of the Federal Republic of Germany by a company being a resident of the United States at least 10 percent of the voting shares of which is owned directly by the German company. The exclusion provided by the first sentence of this subparagraph shall not apply to dividends paid by a U.S. Regulated Investment Company (RIC) or a U.S. Real Estate Investment Trust (REIT) and distributions that are deductible for United States tax purposes by the company distributing them. For the purposes of taxes on capital there shall also be excluded from the basis upon which German tax is imposed any shareholding the dividends of which, if paid, would be excluded, according to the two immediately foregoing sentences, from the basis upon which German tax is imposed.

(*b*) There shall be allowed as a credit against German tax on income, subject to the provisions of German tax law regarding credit for foreign tax, the United States tax paid in accordance with the law of the

United States and with the provisions of this Convention on the following items of income:

(*aa*) income from dividends within the meaning of Article 10 (Dividends) to which subparagraph a) does not apply;

(*bb*) gains to which Article 13 (Gains) applies provided such gains are taxable in the United States by reason only of subparagraph (*b*) of paragraph 2 of Article 13;

(*cc*) income to which Article 16 (Directors' Fees) applies;

(*dd*) income to which Article 17 (Artistes and Athletes) applies;

(*ee*) income which would, but for Article 28 (Limitation on Benefits), remain exempt from United States tax under this Convention.

For the purposes of this paragraph, income, profit or gain derived by a resident of the Federal Republic of Germany that, under this Convention, may be taxed in the United States shall be deemed to be income from sources within the United States.

4.   (*a*) Notwithstanding subparagraph (*a*) of paragraph 3, double taxation shall be avoided by a credit as provided for in subparagraph (*b*) of paragraph 3, if income or capital would be subject to double taxation due to the placement of such income or capital under different provisions of the Convention and this conflict cannot be settled by a procedure pursuant to Article 25 (Mutual Agreement Procedure).

(*b*) The provisions of subparagraph (*a*) of paragraph 3 shall not apply to income or capital where the United States applies the provisions of the Convention to exempt such income or capital from tax, or applies paragraphs 2 or 3 of Article 10 (Dividends) to such income, or may under the provisions of the Convention tax such income or capital but is prevented from doing so under its laws.

(*c*) The provisions of subparagraph (*b*) and not the provisions of subparagraph (*a*) of paragraph 3 shall apply to items of income or capital of which the Federal Republic of Germany has, after due consultation, notified the United States through diplomatic channels. In such a case, the provisions of subparagraph (*b*) shall apply for any taxable year following the year of such notification.

5.   Where a United States citizen is a resident of the Federal Republic of Germany:

(*a*) With respect to items of income not excluded from the basis of German tax under paragraph 3 that are exempt from United States tax or that are subject to a reduced rate of United States tax when derived by a resident of the Federal Republic of Germany who is not a United States citizen, the Federal Republic of Germany shall allow as a credit against German tax, subject to the provisions of German tax law regarding credit for foreign tax, only the tax paid, if any, that the United States may impose under the provisions of this Convention, other than taxes that may be imposed solely by reason of citizenship under paragraph 4 of Article 1 (General Scope);

(*b*)   For purposes of computing United States tax, the United States shall allow as a credit against United States tax the income tax paid to the Federal Republic of Germany after the credit referred to in subparagraph (*a*); the credit so allowed shall not reduce that portion of the United States tax that is creditable against the German tax in accordance with subparagraph (*a*); and

(*c*)   For the exclusive purpose of relieving double taxation in the United States under subparagraph (*b*), items of income referred to in subparagraph (*a*) shall be deemed to arise in the Federal Republic of Germany to the extent necessary to avoid double taxation of such income under subparagraph (*b*).

Article 24

Nondiscrimination

1.   Nationals of a Contracting State shall not be subjected in the other Contracting State to any taxation or any requirement connected therewith that is other or more burdensome than the taxation and connected requirements to which nationals of that other State in the same circumstances are or may be subjected. Notwithstanding the provisions of Article 1, this provision shall also apply to persons who are not residents of one or both of the Contracting States.

2.   The taxation on a permanent establishment that an enterprise of a Contracting State has in the other Contracting State shall not be less favorably levied in that other State than the taxation levied on enterprises of that other State carrying on the same activities. This provision shall not be construed as obliging a Contracting State to grant to residents of the other Contracting State any personal allowances, reliefs, and reductions for taxation purposes on account of civil status or family responsibilities that it grants to its own residents.

3.   Except where the provisions of paragraph 1 of Article 9 (Associated Enterprises), paragraph 4 of Article 11 (Interest), or paragraph 4 of Article 12 (Royalties) apply, interest, royalties, and other disbursements paid by an enterprise of a Contracting State to a resident of the other Contracting State shall, for purposes of determining the taxable profits for such enterprise, be deductible under the same conditions as if they had been paid to a resident of the first-mentioned State. Similarly, any debts of an enterprise of a Contracting State to a resident of the other Contracting State shall, for purposes of determining the taxable capital of such enterprise, be deductible under the same conditions as if they had been contracted to a resident of the first-mentioned State.

4.   Enterprises of a Contracting State, the capital of which is wholly or partly owned or controlled, directly or indirectly, by one or more residents of the other Contracting State, shall be subjected in the first-

mentioned State to any taxation or any requirement connected therewith that is other or more burdensome than the taxation and connected requirements to which other similar enterprises for the first-mentioned State are or may be subjected.

5.   Nothing in this Article shall prevent a Contracting State from imposing the tax described in paragraph 8 of Article 10 (Dividends).

6.   The provisions of this Article shall, notwithstanding the provisions of Article 2 (Taxes Covered), apply to taxes of every kind and description imposed by a Contracting State or a political subdivision or local authority thereof.

Article 25

Mutual Agreement Procedure

1.   Where a person considers that the actions of one or both of the Contracting States result or will result for him in taxation not in accordance with the provisions of this Convention, he may, irrespective of the remedies provided by the domestic law of those States, present his case to the competent authority of the Contracting State of which he is a resident or, if his case comes under paragraph 1 of Article 24 (Nondiscrimination), to that of the Contracting State of which he is a national. The case must be presented within four years from the notification of the assessment giving rise to the double taxation or to taxation not in accordance with the provisions of this Convention.

2.   The competent authority shall endeavor, if the objection appears to it to be justified and if it is not itself able to arrive at a satisfactory solution, to resolve the case by mutual agreement with the competent authority of the other Contracting State, with a view to the avoidance of taxation which is not in accordance with this Convention. Any agreement reached shall be implemented notwithstanding any time limits or other procedural limitations in the domestic law of the Contracting States.

3.   The competent authorities of the Contracting States shall endeavor to resolve by mutual agreement any difficulties or doubts arising as to the interpretation or application of this Convention. In particular the competent authorities of the Contracting States may agree

(*a*) to the same attribution of income, deductions, credits, or allowances of an enterprise of a Contracting State to its permanent establishment situated in the other Contracting States;

(*b*) to the same allocation of income, deductions, credits, or allowances between associated enterprises and other persons in accordance with the principles of Article 9 (Associated Enterprises);

(*c*) to the settlement of conflicting application of this Convention, including conflicts regarding

(*aa*) the characterization of particular items of income;

(*bb*) the characterization of persons;

(*cc*) the application of source rules with respect to particular items of income, and

(*dd*) the treatment of income that is assimilated to income from shares by the taxation law of the State of source and that is treated as a different class of income in the other State;

(*d*) to a common meaning of a term;

(*e*) to the application of the procedural provisions of domestic law including those regarding penalties, fines, and interest, in a manner consistent with the purposes of this Convention; and

(*f*) to increase the amounts referred to in Articles 17 (Artistes and Athletes) and 20 (Visiting Professors and Teachers; Students and Trainees) to reflect economic or monetary developments.

They may also consult together for the elimination of double taxation in cases not provided for in this Convention.

4. The competent authorities of the Contracting States may communicate with each other directly for purposes of reaching an agreement in the sense of the preceding paragraphs. Where the procedure relates to a particular case, the persons concerned shall be permitted to present their views to the competent authorities of either or both of the Contracting States. When it seems advisable in order to reach agreement to have an oral exchange of opinions, such exchange may take place through a Commission consisting of representatives of the competent authorities of the Contracting States.

5. Where, pursuant to a mutual agreement procedure under this Article, the competent authorities have endeavored but are unable to reach a complete agreement in a case, the case shall be resolved through arbitration conducted in the manner prescribed by, and subject to, the requirements of paragraph 6 and any rules or procedures agreed upon by the Contracting States, if:

(*a*) tax returns have been filed with at least one of the Contracting States with respect to the taxable years at issue in the case;

(*b*) the case

(*aa*) is a case that

(*A*) involves the application of one or more Articles that the Contracting States have agreed shall be the subject of arbitration, and

(*B*) is not a particular case that the competent authorities agree, before the date on which arbitration proceedings would otherwise have begun, is not suitable for determination by arbitration, or

(*bb*) is a particular case that the competent authorities agree is suitable for determination by arbitration; and

(*c*) all concerned persons agree according to the provisions of subparagraph (*d*) of paragraph 6.

6. For the purposes of paragraph 5 and this paragraph, the following rules and definitions shall apply:

(*a*) The term "concerned person" means the presenter of a case to a competent authority for consideration under this Article and all other persons, if any, whose tax liability to either Contracting State may be directly affected by a mutual agreement arising from that consideration;

(*b*) The "commencement date" for a case is the earliest date on which the information necessary to undertake substantive consideration for a mutual agreement has been received by both competent authorities;

(*c*) Arbitration proceedings in a case shall begin on the later of:

(*aa*) Two years after the commencement date of that case, unless both competent authorities have previously agreed to a different date, and

(*bb*) The earliest date upon which the agreement required by subparagraph d) has been received by both competent authorities;

(*d*) The concerned person(s), and their authorized representatives or agents, must agree prior to the beginning of arbitration proceedings not to disclose to any other person any information received during the course of the arbitration proceeding from either Contracting State or the arbitration board, other than the determination of such board;

(*e*) Unless any concerned person does not accept the determination of an arbitration board, the determination shall constitute a resolution by mutual agreement under this Article and shall be binding on both Contracting States with respect to that case; and

(*f*) For purposes of an arbitration proceeding under paragraph 5 and this paragraph, the members of the arbitration board and their staffs shall be considered "persons or authorities" to whom information may be disclosed under Article 26 (Exchange of Information and Administrative Assistance) of the Convention.

Article 26

Exchange of Information and Administrative Assistance

1. The competent authorities of the Contracting States shall exchange such information as is necessary for carrying out the provisions of this Convention and of the domestic law of the Contracting States concerning taxes covered by this Convention insofar as the taxation thereunder is not contrary to this Convention. The exchange of information is not restricted by Article 1 (Personal scope). Any information received by a Contracting State shall be treated as secret in the same manner as information obtained under the domestic laws of that State and shall be disclosed only to persons or authorities (including courts and administrative bodies) involved in the assessment, collection, or administration of, the enforcement or prosecution in respect of, or the determination of appeals in relations to the taxes covered by this Convention. Such persons or authorities shall use the information only

for such purposes. They may disclose the information in public court proceedings or in judicial decisions, unless the competent authority of the Contracting State supplying the information raises an objection.

2.   In no case shall the provisions of paragraph 1 be construed to impose on a Contracting State the obligation:

(*a*) to carry out administrative measures at variance with the laws and administrative practice of that or of the other Contracting State;

(*b*) to supply information that is not obtainable under the laws or in the normal course of the administration of that or of the other Contracting States;

(*c*) to supply information that would disclose any trade, business, industrial, commercial, or professional secret or trade process, or information, the disclosure of which would be contrary to public policy.

3.   If information is requested by a Contracting State in accordance with this Article, the other Contracting State shall obtain the information to which the request relates in the same manner and to the same extent as if the tax of the first-mentioned States were the tax of that other State and were being imposed by that other State. If specifically requested by the competent authority of a Contracting State, the competent authority of the other Contracting State shall, if possible, provide information under this Article in the form of deposition of witnesses and authenticated copies of unedited original documents (including books, papers, statements, records, accounts, and writings), to the same extent such depositions and documents can be obtained under the laws and administrative practices of that other State with respect to its own taxes.

4.   Each of the Contracting States shall endeavor to collect on behalf of the other Contracting State such amounts of tax as may be necessary to ensure that relief granted by this Convention from taxation imposed by that other State does not inure to the benefit of persons not entitled thereto.

5.   Paragraph 4 shall not impose upon either of the Contracting States the obligation to carry out administrative measures that are of a different nature from those used in the collection of its own taxes, or that would be contrary to its sovereignty, security, or public policy.

6.   The Contracting States may, through diplomatic channels, exchange notes under which they may, subject to the provisions of this Article, exchange information for the purposes of taxes imposed by a Contracting State not referred to in Article 2 (Taxes Covered).

Article 27

Exempt Organizations

1.   Notwithstanding the provisions of Article 28 (Limitation on Benefits), a German company or organization operated exclusively for religious, charitable, scientific, educational, or public purposes shall be

exempt from tax by the United States in respect of items of income, if and to the extent that

(a)   such company or organization is exempt from tax in the Federal Republic of Germany, and

(b)   such company or organization would be exempt from tax in the United States in respect of such items of income if it were organized, and carried on all its activities, in the United States.

2.   Notwithstanding the provisions of Article 28 (Limitation on Benefits), a United States company or organization operated exclusively for religious, charitable, scientific, educational, or public purposes shall be exempt from tax by the Federal Republic of Germany in respect of items of income, if and to the extent that

(a)   such company or organization is exempt from tax in the United States, and

(b)   such company or organization would be exempt from tax in the Federal Republic of Germany in respect of such items of income if it were a Germany company or organization and carried on all its activities in the Federal Republic of Germany.

Article 28

Limitation on Benefits

1.   Except as otherwise provided in this Article, a resident of one of the Contracting States that derives income from the other Contracting State shall be entitled, in that other Contracting State, to all the benefits of this Convention otherwise accorded to residents of a Contracting State only if such resident is a "qualified person" as defined in paragraph 2 of this Article and satisfies any other conditions specified in the Convention for the obtaining of such benefits.

2.   A resident of one of the Contracting States is a qualified person for a taxable year only if such resident is either:

(a)   an individual;

(b)   a Contracting State, political subdivision or local authority thereof;

(c)   a company, if

(aa) its principal class of shares (and any disproportionate class of shares) is regularly traded on one or more recognized stock exchanges, and either

(A)   its principal class of shares is primarily traded on a recognized stock exchange located in the Contracting State of which the company is a resident; or

(B)   the company's primary place of management and control is in the Contracting State of which it is a resident; or (*bb*) shares representing at least 50 percent of the aggregate voting power and value (and at least 50 percent of any disproportionate class of shares) of the company are owned directly or indirectly by five or fewer companies entitled to benefits under clause (*aa*) of this subparagraph, provided that, in the case of indirect ownership, each intermediate owner is a resident of either Contracting State;

(*d*) an entity organized under the laws of one of the Contracting States and established and maintained in that Contracting State exclusively for a religious, charitable, educational, scientific, or other similar purpose;

(*e*) an entity organized under the laws of one of the Contracting States and established and maintained in that Contracting State to provide, pursuant to a plan, pensions or other similar benefits to employed and self-employed persons, provided that:

(*aa*) more than 50 percent of the entity's beneficiaries, members or participants are individuals resident in either Contracting State; or

(*bb*) the organization sponsoring such person is entitled to the benefits of the Convention pursuant to this paragraph;

(*f*)   a person other than an individual, if:

(*aa*) on at least half the days of the taxable year at least 50 percent of each class of shares or other beneficial interests in the person is owned, directly or indirectly, by residents of that Contracting State that are entitled to the benefits of this Convention under subparagraph (*a*), subparagraph (*b*), clause (*aa*) of subparagraph (*c*), subparagraph (*d*) or subparagraph (*e*) of this paragraph, provided that, in the case of indirect ownership, each intermediate owner is a resident of that Contracting State; and

(*bb*) less than 50 percent of the person's gross income for the taxable year is paid or accrued, directly or indirectly, to persons who are not residents of either Contracting State entitled to the benefits of this Convention under subparagraph (*a*), subparagraph (*b*), clause (*aa*) of subparagraph (*c*), subparagraph (*d*) or subparagraph (*e*) of this paragraph in the form of payments that are deductible for purposes of the taxes covered by this Convention in the person's State of residence.

3.   Notwithstanding that a company that is a resident of a Contracting State may not be a qualified person, it shall be entitled to all the benefits of this Convention otherwise accorded to residents of a Contracting State with respect to an item of income if it satisfies any other specified conditions for the obtaining of such benefits and:

(*a*)   shares representing at least 95 percent of the aggregate voting power and value (and at least 50 percent of any disproportionate class of shares) of the company are owned, directly or indirectly, by seven or fewer persons who are equivalent beneficiaries; and

(b) less than 50 percent of the company's gross income for the taxable year in which the item of income arises is paid or accrued, directly or indirectly, to persons who are not equivalent beneficiaries, in the form of payments that are deductible for the purposes of the taxes covered by this Convention in the Contracting State of which the company is a resident.

4.   (a) Notwithstanding that a resident of a Contracting State may not be a qualified person, it shall be entitled to all the benefits of this Convention otherwise accorded to residents of a Contracting State with respect to an item of income derived from the other Contracting State, if the resident is engaged in the active conduct of a trade or business in the first-mentioned Contracting State (other than the activities of making or managing investments for the resident's own account, unless these activities are banking, insurance or securities dealing carried on by a bank, insurance company or registered securities dealer), the income derived from the other Contracting State is derived in connection with, or is incidental to, that trade or business and that resident satisfies any other specified conditions for the obtaining of such benefits.

(b) If a resident of one of the Contracting States or any of its associated enterprises carries on a trade or business activity in the other Contracting State which gives rise to an item of income, subparagraph (a) of this paragraph shall apply to such item only if the trade or business activity in the first-mentioned Contracting State is substantial in relation to the trade or business activity in the other Contracting State.

(c) In determining whether a person is engaged in the active conduct of a trade or business in a Contracting State under subparagraph (a) of this paragraph, activities conducted by persons connected to such person shall be deemed to be conducted by such person. A person shall be connected to another if one possesses at least 50 percent of the beneficial interest in the other (or, in the case of a company, shares representing at least 50 percent of the aggregate voting power and value of the company or of the beneficial equity interest in the company) or another person possesses, directly or indirectly, at least 50 percent of the beneficial interest (or, in the case of a company, shares representing at least 50 percent of the aggregate voting power and value of the company or of the beneficial equity interest in the company) in each person. In any case, a person shall be considered to be connected to another if, on the basis of all the facts and circumstances, one has control of the other or both are under the control of the same person or persons.

5.   Notwithstanding the preceding provisions of this Article, where an enterprise of a Contracting State derives income from the other Contracting State, and that income is attributable to a permanent establishment which that enterprise has in a third jurisdiction, the tax benefits that would otherwise apply under the other provisions of the Convention will not apply to that income if the combined tax that is actually paid with respect to such income in the first-mentioned

Contracting State and in the third jurisdiction is less than 60 percent of the tax that would have been payable in the first-mentioned State if the income were earned in that Contracting State by the enterprise and were not attributable to the permanent establishment in the third jurisdiction. Any dividends, interest or royalties to which the provisions of this paragraph apply shall be subject to tax at a rate that shall not exceed 15 percent of the gross amount thereof. Any other income to which the provisions of this paragraph apply will be subject to tax under the provisions of the domestic law of the other Contracting State, notwithstanding any other provision of the Convention. The provisions of this paragraph shall not apply if:

(a) in the case of royalties, the royalties are received as compensation for the use of, or the right to use, intangible property produced or developed by the permanent establishment itself; or

(b) in the case of any other income, the income derived from the other Contracting State is derived in connection with, or is incidental to, the active conduct of a trade or business carried on by the permanent establishment in the third jurisdiction (other than the business of making, managing or simply holding investments for the person's own account, unless these activities are banking or securities activities carried on by a bank or registered securities dealer).

6. Notwithstanding the preceding provisions of this Article, a German Investment Fund or German Investmentaktiengesellschaft (collectively referred to as Investmentvermögen) may only be granted the benefits of this Convention if at least 90 percent of the shares or other beneficial interests in the German Investmentvermögen are owned, directly or indirectly, by residents of the Federal Republic of Germany that are entitled to the benefits of this Convention under subparagraph (a), subparagraph (b), clause (aa) of subparagraph (c), subparagraph (d) or subparagraph (e) of paragraph 2 of this Article or by persons that are equivalent beneficiaries with respect to the income derived by the German Investmentvermögen for which benefits are being claimed. For the purposes of this paragraph, beneficiaries of entities that are subject to numbers 3 and 5 of paragraph 1 of section 1 of the German Corporate Tax Act shall be treated as indirectly owning shares of a German Investmentvermögen. Foundations referred to in number 5 of paragraph 1 of section 1 of the German Corporate Tax Act, other than those referred to in subparagraph (d) of paragraph 2 of this Article, shall not be taken into account in determining whether a German Investmentvermögen meets the 90 percent minimum ownership threshold.

7. A person resident of one of the Contracting States, who is not entitled to some or all of the benefits of this Convention because of the foregoing paragraphs, may, nevertheless, be granted benefits of this Convention if the competent authority of the Contracting State in which the income in question arises so determines. In making such determination, the competent authority shall take into account as its

guidelines whether the establishment, acquisition or maintenance of such person or the conduct of its operations has or had as one of its principal purposes the obtaining of benefits under this Convention. The competent authority of the Contracting State in which the income arises will consult with the competent authority of the other Contracting State before denying the benefits of the Convention under this paragraph.

8. For the purposes of this Article the following rules and definitions shall apply:

(a) the term "recognized stock exchange" means:

(aa) the NASDAQ System and any stock exchange registered with the U.S. Securities and Exchange Commission as a national securities exchange under the U.S. Securities Exchange Act of 1934;

(bb) any German stock exchange on which registered dealings in shares take place;

(cc) any other stock exchange which the competent authorities agree to recognize for the purposes of this Article;

(b)(aa) the term "principal class of shares" means the ordinary or common shares of the company, provided that such class of shares represents the majority of the voting power and value of the company. If no single class of ordinary or common shares represents the majority of the aggregate voting power and value of the company, the "principal class of shares" is that class or those classes that in the aggregate represent a majority of the aggregate voting power and value of the company;

(bb) the term "shares" shall include depository receipts thereof or trust certificates thereof;

(c) the term "disproportionate class of shares" means any class of shares of a company resident in one of the Contracting States that entitles the shareholder to disproportionately higher participation, through dividends, redemption payments or otherwise, in the earnings generated in the other Contracting State by particular assets or activities of the company;

(d) the company's primary place of management and control will be in the Contracting State of which it is a resident only if executive officers and senior management employees exercise day-to-day responsibility for more of the strategic, financial and operational policy decision making for the company (including its direct and indirect subsidiaries) in that Contracting State than in any other state and the staffs conduct more of the day-to-day activities necessary for preparing and making those decisions in that Contracting State than in any other state.

(e) an equivalent beneficiary is a resident of a member state of the European Union or of a European Economic Area state or of a party to the North American Free Trade Agreement but only if that resident:

(aa)(A) would be entitled to all the benefits of a comprehensive convention for the avoidance of double taxation between any member state of the European Union or a European Economic Area state or any party to the North American Free Trade Agreement and the State from which the benefits of this Convention are claimed under provisions analogous to subparagraph (*a*), subparagraph (*b*), clause (*aa*) of subparagraph (*c*), subparagraph (*d*) or subparagraph (*e*) of paragraph 2 of this Article provided that if such convention does not contain a comprehensive limitation on benefits article, the person would be a qualified person under subparagraph (*a*), subparagraph (*b*), clause (*aa*) of subparagraph (*c*), subparagraph (*d*) or subparagraph (*e*) of paragraph 2 of this Article if such person were a resident of one of the States under Article 4 (Resident) of this Convention; and

(*B*) with respect to insurance premiums and to income referred to in Article 10 (Dividends), 11 (Interest) or 12 (Royalties) of this Convention, would be entitled under such convention to a rate of tax with respect to the particular class of income for which benefits are being claimed under this Convention that is at least as low as the rate applicable under this Convention; or

(*bb*) is a resident of a Contracting State that is a qualified person by reason of subparagraph (*a*), subparagraph (*b*), clause (*aa*) of subparagraph (*c*), subparagraph (*d*) or subparagraph (*e*) of paragraph 2 of this Article.

For the purposes of applying paragraph 3 of Article 10 (Dividends) in order to determine whether a person, owning shares, directly or indirectly, in the company claiming the benefits of this Convention, is an equivalent beneficiary, such person shall be deemed to hold the same voting power in the company paying the dividend as the company claiming the benefits holds in such company;

(*f*) with respect to dividends, interest or royalties arising in the Federal Republic of Germany and beneficially owned by a company that is a resident of the United States, a company that is a resident of a member state of the European Union will be treated as satisfying the requirements of clause (*aa*)(*B*) of subparagraph (*e*) for purposes of determining whether such United States resident is entitled to benefits under this paragraph if a payment of dividends, interest or royalties arising in the Federal Republic of Germany and paid directly to such resident of a member state of the European Union would have been exempt from tax pursuant to any directive of the European Union, notwithstanding that the income tax convention between the Federal Republic of Germany and that other member state of the European Union would provide for a higher rate of tax with respect to such payment than the rate of tax applicable to such United States company under Article 10 (Dividends), 11 (Interest), or 12 (Royalties) of this Convention.

Article 29

Refund of Withholding Tax

1.   If in one of the Contracting States the taxes on dividends, interest, royalties, or other items of income are levied by withholding at source, then the right to apply the withholding of tax at the rate provided for under the domestic law of that State is not affected by the provisions of this Convention.

2.   The tax so withheld at source shall be refunded on application to the extent that its levying is limited by this Convention.

3.   The period for application for a refund is four years from the end of the calendar year in which the dividends, interest, royalties, or other items of income have been received.

4.   The Contracting State in which the income arises may require an administrative certification by the Contracting State of which the taxpayer is a resident, with respect to the fulfillment of the conditions for the unlimited tax liability in that State.

5.   The competent authorities of the Contracting States shall implement the foregoing provisions by mutual agreement pursuant to Article 25 (Mutual agreement procedure).

6.   The competent authorities of the Contracting States may establish by mutual agreement other procedures for the implementation of tax reductions provided under this Convention.

Article 30

Members of Diplomatic Missions and Consular Posts

1.   Nothing in this Convention shall affect the fiscal privileges of diplomatic agents or consular officers under the general rules of international law or under the provisions of special agreements.

2.   To the extent that, due to such privileges, income or capital is not taxed in the receiving States, the sending State shall have the right to tax such income or capital.

3.   Notwithstanding the provisions of Article 4 (Residence), an individual who is a member of a diplomatic mission or a consular post of a Contracting State that is situated in the other Contracting State or in a third State shall be deemed for the purposes of this Convention to be a resident of the sending State if;

(a) in accordance with international law he is not liable to tax in the receiving State in respect of income from sources outside that State or on capital situated outside that State, and

(b) he is liable in the sending State to the same obligations in relation to tax on his total income or on capital as are residents of that State.

4.   This Convention shall not apply to international organizations, or organs or officials thereof, or to persons who are members of a

diplomatic mission, consular post, or permanent mission of a third State, being represented in a Contracting State and not liable in either Contracting State to the same obligations in respect of taxes on income or on capital as are residents.

* * *

DONE in duplicate at Bonn this 29th day of August 1989 in the English and German languages, both texts being equally authentic.

INDEX

References are to Pages